Terry Fox

Elemental Gestures

Ausstellung und Katalog sind eine
Kooperation / The exhibition
and catalogue are a cooperation
of the following institutions:

Akademie der Künste, Berlin
BAM – Musée des Beaux-Arts, Mons
Von der Heydt-Museum, Wuppertal
Kunstmuseum Bern

Hg. von / edited by
Arnold Dreyblatt
und / and
Angela Lammert

im Auftrag der /
on behalf of the
Akademie der Künste

VERLAG **KETTLER**

SLIDE (on the Inn)

Sunday, Nov 20 1-4 o'clock

Ravens, fish jumping in the Inn, bells of Innsbruck, cold
clear day with constantly changing wind, 2 facing empty chairs
on the slope (of the slide) the wooden snow slide into the
river. protecting the domestic flame, maintaining the flame
(heat) the rythm of the water, the rythm of the wind, the
rythm of the flame, the rythm of the bells, the rythm of the
clock, the rythm of the awakening (ressurection) plant, maintaining the movement of the domestic flame towards the fish.
the fish consumes and is consumed by the flame. bound by the
candle, freed by the flame. the plant rises, the wax falls.
hands into house, slide into mountain, wind into storm, river
into rythm, plant into rythm, flame into rythm, match after
match after match ....

performance sponsered by "forum für aktuelle kunst" with
the collaboration of galerie krinzinger, innsbruck.

Terry Fox, *Slide on the River Inn*, 1977, poster, © Galerie Krinzinger

Inhalt / **Contents**

Ludwig Forum für Internationale Kunst,
    Videoarchiv, Aachen / Video Archive, Aix-la-Chapelle

LIMA, Amsterdam

Akademie der Künste, Berlin, Wulf-Herzogenrath-Archiv

Ursula Block – Broken Music Archive

Sammlung Block, Berlin

Sammlung Marzona

Klaus vom Bruch, Berlin

Staatliche Museen zu Berlin, Kupferstichkabinett;
    Nationalgalerie, Sammlung Marzona; Nationalgalerie,
    2013 Schenkung Wolfram und / and Martina Gärtner

Kunstmuseum Bern

Dany Keller Galerie, Eichelhardt

Hélène und / and Paul Panhuysen, Het Apollohuis Eindhoven

Museum Folkwang, Essen

Barbara Klemm, Frankfurt am Main

Sammlung Oehmen

Estate of Terry Fox, Köln / Cologne

Museum Ludwig, Köln / Cologne

Getty Research Institute, Los Angeles

De Vleeshal, Middelburg

Galerie Löhrl, Mönchengladbach

Ross Family Collection

Electronic Arts Intermix (EAI), New York

Capp Street Project Archive
    California College of the Arts, Oakland

Paule Anglim Gallery, San Francisco

Berkeley Art Museum and
    Pacific Film Archive (BAM/PFA), Berkeley

Marilyn Bogerd, San Francisco

Hubertus Butin, Berlin

Marion Gray, San Francisco

San Francisco Museum of Modern Art,
    Gift of Joy E. Feinberg, Berkeley

De Saisset Museum, Santa Clara University, Santa Clara

Galerie Krinzinger, Wien / Vienna

Privatsammlung, Wien / Hattorf am Harz /
    private collection, Vienna / Hattorf am Harz

mumok Museum moderner Kunst, Wien / Vienna

Von der Heydt-Museum, Wuppertal

sowie Privatsammlungen, die namentlich nicht genannt
werden möchten. / as well as private collections, where
the lenders prefer to remain anonymous.

Einführung

Introduction

Terry Fox sei kein Videokünstler, schreibt David Ross in seinem Essay. Genauso wenig kann seine Arbeit auf Konzept- oder Klangkunst reduziert werden. Auch Bezeichnungen wie Body-Art, Fluxus oder Performance treffen das Flüchtige, doch gleichzeitig Haptisch-Materielle und Humorvolle seiner genre- und medienübergreifenden Arbeiten nicht in Gänze. Seine temporären Interventionen verbinden körperlich-existentielle Rituale und überraschende Leichtigkeit. Die Aufladung von Räumen mit Energie ermöglicht für ihn die gemeinsame Erfahrung mit dem Publikum. Er ist zu einer Legende geworden und gilt als „artists' artist". Das war der Hintergrund für den Vorschlag, im Rahmen einer Ausstellungsreihe der Akademie der Künste, die sich Phänomene jenseits des Kanons widmen wollte, ein Terry-Fox-Projekt zu realisieren.

Aus der Faszination für das Werk dieses Grenzgängers entwickelte sich die Fragestellung, die den Kern einer gegenwärtigen Diskussion trifft: Wie ist es möglich, temporäre künstlerische Interventionen in Ausstellungen sichtbar zu machen? Der amerikanisch-europäische Künstler Terry Fox (1943–2008) thematisierte als einer der Ersten dieses gleichermaßen für Künstler, Kuratoren, Kritiker und Theoretiker zentrale Problem. Obwohl er in Opposition zum Begriff der Performance von *Situationen* sprach und die technologische Beschränktheit der Aufzeichnungsformen von Ereignissen problematisierte, verwandte er zeit seines Lebens die klassischen Dokumentationsmedien und agierte im Ausstellungskontext mit Relikten seiner Aktionen. Insofern ist die Arbeitsweise von Terry Fox modellhaft für das Verhältnis von Archiv und Reenactment – wenngleich sein Kosmos nichts mit dem zu tun hat, was heute darunter verstanden wird. Fox' Bezeichnungen für seinen Umgang mit selbst entwickelten Ausdrucksformen wie „(re/de) construction" oder „remixing" grenzen seine Auffassung von der gegenwärtigen Reenactment-Welle ab.

Es ist Ziel des Projekts, erstmals die Verschränkung der performativen und politisch brisanten Arbeiten von Terry Fox, die er in den USA geschaffen hat und die neben denen von Vito Acconci und Dennis Oppenheim zu den bedeutendsten Äußerungen ihrer Generation gehören, mit seiner Vorreiterrolle für die sich entwickelnde Klangkunstszene in Europa in den Fokus zu nehmen. Das führte zu der Entscheidung, die frühen – zum großen Teil heute völlig unbekannten – Videoarbeiten von Terry Fox zeitgenössisch zu präsentieren und für drei ausgewählte Klangarbeiten separate Räume einzurichten.

Introduction

"Terry Fox is not a video artist," wrote David Ross in his essay. Nor is his work reducible to conceptual or sound art. Descriptions such as body art, Fluxus, or performance are also inadequate to describe the elusive, yet tactually material and humorous nature of his cross-genre and transmedia works. His temporary interventions combined physically existential rituals and a surprising lightness. The energizing of spaces made the shared experience possible for him. Unknown to a broader public, he is, however, a legend among aficionados, and deserving of the term "an artists' artist." That was the background for the proposal to put together a Terry Fox project within the context of the Akademie der Künste's exhibition series on phenomena beyond the canon.

From a fascination for this boundary-crossing artist a question touching on a key aspect of a current discussion evolved: How can temporary artistic interventions be presented in an exhibition setting? The American-European artist Terry Fox (1943–2008) was one of the first to address this central problem confronting curators, critics and theoreticians alike. Although he spoke of *situations* in contrast to performance and discussed the technological limitations of the means available for recording events, he employed classical documentary media throughout his life and operated in exhibition contexts with the relics of his art actions. In this respect Terry Fox's approach is exemplary of the relationship between archive and reenactment – although his cosmos had nothing to do with present-day conceptions. Fox's designations for his handling of self-developed forms of expression, such as "(re/de) construction" or "remixing," sets his concept apart from the prevailing wave of reenactment.

The project aims to focus for the first time on the intertwining of Terry Fox's performative and politically explosive works – which he produced in the United States and were, alongside works by Vito Acconci and Dennis Oppenheim, among the most important statements of their generation – with his pioneering role in the European sound art scene. This objective led to the decision to contemporarily present Terry Fox's early, currently mostly unknown video works and to set up separate areas for three selected sound works.

The exhibition and catalogue are not structured chronologically, concentrating instead on the way in which the artist played out his themes in various media. The exhibition is thus divided into four merging, associative *Denkräume*, or thinking spaces, handling the main themes of Fox's work:

Ausstellung und Katalog sind nicht chronologisch strukturiert, sondern zeigen, auf welche Art und Weise der Künstler seine Themen in allen Medien durchspielte. Folglich ist die Ausstellung in vier ineinander übergehende assoziative Denkräume zu zentralen Themen seines Werkes gegliedert:

1. Situations / Körperliche Zustände
2. Elements / Material
3. Mapping / Labyrinth
4. Sound as Sculpture / Raum als Instrument

Diese Denkräume gehen von Video- und Klangmaterial sowie von fotografischen Dokumentationen exemplarischer Aktionen aus und machen Fox' prozessuale Arbeitsweise sinnlich nacherlebbar. Den Videos und frühen Fotografie-Serien werden Objekte, Zeichnungen, Klangzonen und Texte zugeordnet, um sein Gefühl für Materialität und die Fragilität der Sinne zu vermitteln. Im Kapitel „Elements / Material" wird zwischen zwei Aspekten unterschieden: der Demonstration von Phänomenen (ob es sich um physikalische Vorgänge handelt oder um die visuelle Auswirkung von Klangwellen) und „Codes and Signs / Chiffren und Zeichen" (das Spiel mit der Verrätselung in den Textarbeiten). Im Zentrum eines der drei Klangräume stehen Materialien für die Arbeit *Berlin Wall Scored for Sound*, die Terry Fox 1980/81 während seines DAAD-Aufenthaltes in Berlin realisierte.

Wir verstehen das Vorhaben als ein Recherche- und Ausstellungsprojekt. Marita Loosen-Fox hat uns durch ihre großzügige und kundige Unterstützung nicht nur die Schätze des Nachlasses zugänglich gemacht, sie hat durch ihre detaillierte Sachkenntnis wesentlich zum Gelingen des Vorhabens beigetragen. Die digitale Erfassung und Aufarbeitung des Archivs ist derzeit im Gange und wird noch manche Überraschung zutage fördern. Der sensationelle Fund bisher unveröffentlichter oder selten gezeigten Video- und Fotomaterials der frühen Jahre ermöglicht eine Neubewertung von Terry Fox, der so unterschiedliche Künstler wie Bill Viola, Jochen Gerz, Paul McCarthy und Robert Frank in seinen Bann zieht. Auch Hans Haacke und Daniel Spoerri haben sich für ihn eingesetzt. Ein Novum in der Ausstellung ist die Einbeziehung bisher nicht publizierter Werknotizen und Skizzen aus dem Nachlass. Sie werfen ein neues Licht auf den frühen Umgang mit der Videotechnik und auf die Dematerialisierung performativer und konzeptueller Kunst und hinterfragen auch heute noch bestehende Klischees der Kunstgeschichtsschreibung. Es gilt, für eine jüngere Generation die präzise Vorbereitung von Performances in Erinnerung zu rufen.

Für den Katalog konnten internationale Experten gewonnen werden, deren Texte unbekannte Materialien ergänzen. Er umfasst drei Teile:

1. Situations / Körperliche Zustände
2. Elements / Material
3. Mapping / Labyrinth
4. Sound as Sculpture / Raum als Instrument

These thinking spaces present video and sound material as well as photographic documentation of typical art actions and allow visitors to experience of Fox's process-oriented working methods. Objects, drawings, sound zones and texts are joined with the videos and earlier photographic series to convey a sense of his feel for materiality and the fragility of the senses. In the section "Elements / Material" two aspects are distinguished from one another: the demonstration of phenomena (whether it has to do with physical processes or with the visual effect of sound waves) from "Codes and Signs / Chiffren und Zeichen" (the playing with mystification in the text-based works). The focus of one of the three sound rooms is on materials for the work *Berlin Wall Scored for Sound*, which Terry Fox performed in 1981–82 during his stay in Berlin in the context of a DAAD scholarship (German Academic Exchange Service).

We understand the venture as a research and exhibition project. Through her generous and knowledgeable support, Marita Loosen-Fox not only made the estate's resources accessible, but also significantly contributed to the success of this undertaking through her detailed expertise. The digitizing and processing of the archive is currently in progress and is likely to unearth more surprises. The sensational discovery of previously unpublished or seldom shown videos and photographs from the early years allows a reevaluation of Terry Fox, who fascinated quite different artists, such as Bill Viola, Jochen Gerz, Paul McCarthy, and Robert Frank. Hans Haacke and Daniel Spoerri were also among his champions. A novelty in the exhibition is the inclusion of previously unpublished work notes and sketches from Fox's estate. They shed new light on the early approach to video technology and on the dematerialization of performative and conceptual art, as well as questioning some of art history's lingering clichés. The aim is to recall for a younger generation the precise preparation of performances.

International experts, whose texts enhance the little-known materials, were engaged to write for the catalogue. It is divided into three parts:

— *Essays* examining the artistic and political context of Fox's work,
— *an illustrated section related to the subsections of the exhibition,* which are introduced with texts and artist statements, and

— *Essays,* die den künstlerischen und politischen Kontext von Fox' Arbeit beleuchten,
— den *Bildteil zu den Kapiteln der Ausstellung,* die mit Texten und Künstlerstatements eingeführt werden,
— die *Dokumentation,* die überwiegend unveröffentlichte Texte von Terry Fox sowie eigens für diesen Katalog verfasste Statements von Weggefährten und Interviews umfasst.

In dem sich anschließenden Verzeichnis der ausgestellten Arbeiten wird zwischen Performance (nicht-öffentlich, öffentlich oder Variation und Transformation von Grundritualen), Video-Aufzeichnung und Video als künstlerischer Arbeit differenziert und die Zusammenarbeit mit Fotografinnen und Fotografen dokumentiert.

Die visuelle Argumentation soll Fox' Affinität zur Verwandlung von Materialien Ausdruck verleihen. Obwohl die Künstlerstatements als Teil seiner Arbeit verstanden werden müssen, verstellen sie zum Teil den Blick auf sein Interesse am Experiment mit den Medien – ob es sich um radikale Ausschnitte, das Spiel mit der Unschärfe in Fotografie und Video oder um die Freude an der Körnigkeit des von ihm so geliebten Materials wie Mehl und dem Effekt von Licht und Schatten in allen seinen Transformationen handelt.

Das sowohl inhaltlich als auch in seinen Produktions- und Präsentationsformen prototypische Recherche- und Ausstellungsprojekt knüpft an Erkenntnisse der Akademie-Projekte „John Cage" (2011/12), „Iannis Xenakis – Kontrolle und Zufall" (2011) und „Schwindel der Wirklichkeit" (2014) an. Das mit unterschiedlichen Institutionen entwickelte Programm legt vor allem Wert auf das Zeitgenössische des Themas und fragt danach, was die Arbeit von Terry Fox für eine jüngere Generation reizvoll macht. Der Titel „Elemental Gestures", der sich auf die zeitgenössische Rezeption der Straßenaktionen von Terry Fox aus den 1970er Jahren bezieht und die Anfänge seiner lebenslangen Suche nach einer Neudefinition der Skulptur verdeutlicht, beschreibt seinen Glauben an eine kathartische Wirkung von Kunst, die in ihrem utopischen Gehalt neu zu diskutieren ist. Fox blieb zeit seines Lebens anarchisch und politisch radikal. Wie heute ersonnen, hört sich sein 1979 formulierter Vorschlag an, die einzige Möglichkeit, politische Kunst zu machen, sei der Boykott oder der Streik, zum Beispiel wenn niemand zur nächsten Biennale ginge.

Arnold Dreyblatt
Mitglied der Akademie der Künste

Angela Lammert
Leiterin interdisziplinäre Sonderprojekte

— *documentation,* which consists mainly of unpublished texts by Terry Fox, as well as statements written specially for this catalogue by fellow artists and associates and from interviews.

The subsequent index of the exhibited works differentiates between performance (non-public, public, and the variation and transformation of basic rituals); the relationship between live video art actions and video recordings as the sum of different art actions; video as artistic work; and photography as documentation and as instrument of co-authorship.

The visual argumentation is intended to express Fox's affinity to the transformation of materials. Although artist statements have to be understood as part of his work, they sometimes obstruct his clear interest in experimenting with media – whether it involved radical cropping; playing with out-of-focus imagery in photography and video; the pleasure in the graininess of materials he loved so much, such as flour; or the effect of light and shadow in all of his transformations.

The research and exhibition project, with its prototypical content and forms of production and presentation, draws on the insights of the Akademie der Künste's projects *John Cage* (2011–12), *Iannis Xenakis – Kontrolle und Zufall* (2011), and *Schwindel der Wirklichkeit / Vertigo of Reality* (2014). The program developed with various institutions attaches particular importance to the subject's contemporariness and asks what makes Terry Fox's work appealing to a younger generation. The title *Elemental Gestures* stems from the contemporary reaction to Terry Fox's street actions in the 1970s. It points out the beginnings of his life-long search for a redefinition of the concept of sculpture and describes his belief in the cathartic effect of art, which in its utopian substance is to be readdressed. Fox remained anarchistic and politically radical throughout his life. His proposition made in 1979, that the only possibility to make political art is through a boycott or a strike – if, for instance, no one went to the next Biennale – sounds quite up to date.

Arnold Dreyblatt
Member of the Akademie der Künste

Angela Lammert
Head of Interdisciplinery Projects

Translated from the German by James Bell

Dank

Wir möchten uns an erster Stelle bei Marita Loosen-Fox, Nachlassverwalterin und Gründungsmitglied der Terry Fox Association e.V., bedanken, ohne deren Sachkenntnis und großzügige Unterstützung Ausstellung und Katalog nicht hätten realisiert werden können. Ihr gilt unser ganz besonderer Dank. Man darf gespannt sein, welche Schätze sich im Zuge der Digitalisierung des Nachlasses noch finden werden. Nicht weniger herzlich danken wir all denen, die an der Ausstellung und dem gesamten Projekt „Elemental Gestures – Terry Fox" mitgewirkt haben. Viele Mitglieder und Mitarbeiter der Akademie der Künste, Berlin, und Vertreter der Kooperationspartner in Mons, Wuppertal und Bern haben beigetragen, ebenso die Leihgeber, Autoren, Künstlerfreunde und Gestalter des Kataloges.

Ohne die großzügige Unterstützung des Hauptstadtkulturfonds, der Gesellschaft der Freunde der Akademie der Künste, Berlin, und der Rudolf Augstein Stiftung Hamburg hätten wir dieses Projekt nicht durchführen können. Ihnen und all unseren Unterstützern gilt unser großer Dank.

Arnold Dreyblatt und Angela Lammert
Akademie der Künste, Berlin

Nikola Doll und Xavier Roland
BAM – Musée des Beaux-Arts, Mons

Beate Eickhoff
Von der Heydt-Museum, Wuppertal

Kathleen Bühler
Kunstmuseum Bern

Acknowledgments

First and foremost, we would like to thank Marita Loosen-Fox, the executor of the estate and a founding member of the Terry Fox Association e.V., without whose expert knowledge and generous support the exhibition and catalogue could not have been realized. We are very grateful and particularly indebted to her. It will be interesting to see what new discoveries come to light in the course of the digitalization of the estate. We would also like to sincerely thank all those who played a part in the exhibition and the entire project *Elemental Gestures – Terry Fox*. Many of the Akademie der Künste's members and staff in Berlin, and representatives of our cooperation partners in Mons, Wuppertal and Bern have contributed, as have lenders, authors, friends of the artist, and those who have shaped the catalogue.

Without the generous support of the Hauptstadtkulturfonds (Capital Cultural Fund), the Society of Friends of the Academy of Arts, Berlin, and the Rudolf-Augstein-Stiftung in Hamburg, we would not have been able to carry out this project. We wish to express our deepest thanks to them and to all of our supporters.

Arnold Dreyblatt and Angela Lammert
Akademie der Künste, Berlin

Nikola Doll and Xavier Roland
BAM – Musée des Beaux-Arts, Mons

Beate Eickhoff
Von der Heydt-Museum, Wuppertal

Kathleen Bühler
Kunstmuseum Bern

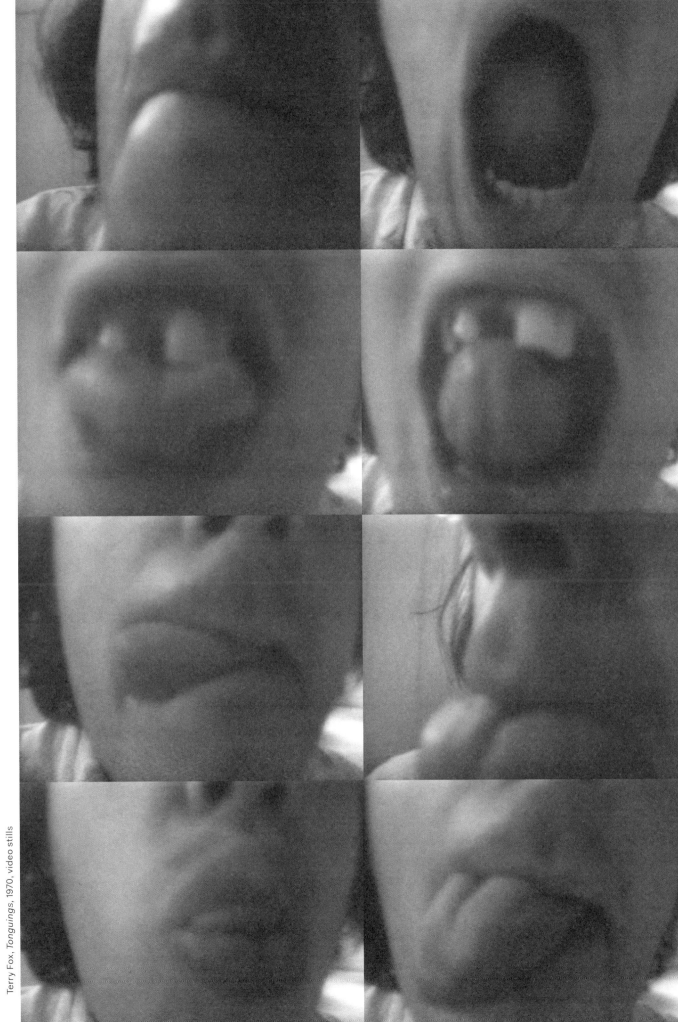

Terry Fox, *Tonguings*, 1970, video stills

Was wir machen können (Walkthrough)

What We Can Do (A Walkthrough)

Wir können uns beispielsweise das Zungenvideo ansehen. Wir können uns das Zungenvideo ansehen und bemerken, wie die Zeit vergeht. Während wir uns das Zungenvideo ansehen, wird uns vielleicht der Gedanke an eines der Löffelexperimentevideos kommen, wir werden möglicherweise an Streichholzexperimente denken oder zumindest an Wasserschalenexperimente der *Children's Tapes*, die wir bisher hier nur als Stills wahrgenommen haben. Haarscharf montiert und doch sehr eigenartig. Als würde das Material permanent einer Dokumentationsvorstellung widersprechen wollen, als würden die Darstellungsverhältnisse sich kommentieren. Wir werden also Verbindungen herstellen, auch zu dem Labyrinthgedanken, der hier so oft mitschwingt. Ein Motiv, das einfach so auftauchen kann und jede Menge mitmeint, wie man leichthin sagt (wo?). Spätestens jetzt werden wir uns fragen können, was eine *Situation* ist, und warum Terry Fox diesen Begriff lieber mochte als Performance. Vielleicht, weil er mehr den Raum mit einschließt oder vielleicht weil er die Personen, die wir normalerweise als „das Publikum" bezeichnen, zu Beteiligten macht? Aber wo ist uns das Labyrinthmotiv noch einmal zuerst aufgefallen? Im Klang oder im Raum? War es einfach nur ein Labyrinth oder war bereits etwas mit ihm geschehen? Mit Labyrinthen geschieht immer etwas, würde Terry Fox vielleicht sagen (stelle ich mir jedenfalls vor), das heißt Labyrinthe geben einfach etwas her, genauso wie ein Eckzahn, der in einem Apfel steckengeblieben ist, oder ein Krankenhausaufenthalt, der in einen Gesundheitsaufenthalt mündet, der wieder zu einem Krankenhausaufenthalt wird. Auch Napalm auf Jasmin gibt etwas her, so als Situation, vor allem zu Beginn der 1970er Jahre. Vor allem in San Francisco. Berkeley? Berkeley! Aber ist es etwas Vergleichbares wie ein Hubschraubergedanke in Berlin zu Beginn der 1980er? Der Versuch für eine Ausstellung im Künstlerhaus Bethanien Hubschrauber zu organisieren, die die Berliner Mauer akustisch übersetzen könnten? Schwer zu sagen, (ich habe keine Ahnung).

Heute wissen wir jedenfalls: Man kann durch Medien durchgehen und an kein Ende kommen. Man muss von Übersetzungsverhältnissen ausgehen, die immer etwas übriglassen. Nur was? Haben wir es wirklich aus den Augen verloren, wie es immer über die sogenannten heutigen Generationen heißt?

We can, for instance, watch the tongue video. We can watch the tongue video and notice how time passes. While we're watching the tongue video, perhaps one of the spoon experiment videos will come to mind; we might think about experiments with matches or at least about the ones with bowls of water in *Children's Tapes*, which until now we've only experienced as stills. Precisely assembled and yet quite strange, it's as if the material is constantly seeking to contradict the idea of documentation, as if its commenting on representation itself. We will, therefore, establish connections, including those related to the idea of labyrinth that so often resonates here. A motif that can just simply pop up, and imply so much – which is said so lightly (where?). Now, at the latest, we must ask ourselves what a *situation* is, and why Terry Fox liked this term more than performance. Perhaps because it better included the space or perhaps because it made participants of the people we normally refer to as "the audience." But where did we first notice the motif of labyrinth? In sound, or in space? Was it merely a labyrinth, or had something already happened to it? Something always happens with labyrinths – as Terry Fox might have said (at least I imagine he might have); that is, they are simply good for something; just like an eyetooth that gets stuck in an apple, or a hospital stay leading to a health or spa treatment that again becomes a hospital stay. Even napalm on jasmine is good for something – as a situation – particularly in the early 1970s. Particularly in San Francisco. Berkeley? Berkeley! But is it comparable to the idea with a helicopter in Berlin at the beginning of the 1980s? To the attempt to locate helicopters for an exhibition at the Künstlerhaus Bethanien that could translate the Berlin Wall into acoustics? Hard to say (I have no idea).

Today, in any case, we know that media can be walked through and yet no end is reached. The assumption is that what constitutes translation always leaves something out. Now what? Have we really lost sight of it – as is always claimed to be the case with "today's generation." At least we now know (while still watching the tongue video) that a slowly greasesmeared camera lens tells of things other than just itself. Letters of the alphabet have more than one orientation. And sounds can also be sculptural! Of course? Of course! By now, we have some idea of all this, too, but may have already

Heute wissen wir jedenfalls (während wir uns noch immer das Zungenvideo ansehen): Ein langsam verschmiertes Kameraobjektiv erzählt nicht nur von sich. Buchstaben haben nicht nur eine Richtung! Und: Klänge können auch skulptural sein! Natürlich? Natürlich! Auch davon haben wir bereits eine Ahnung, aber dass sie auch in Kellerräumen stattfinden, auf der Straße, vor Baustellen, haben wir vielleicht schon wieder vergessen! Mit zwei blinden Musikern, die scheinbar daher organisiert sind, wie es nachher heißt. Dass es Aufzeichnungen und Vorzeichnungen, Vorbereitungen für ein gewisses Geschehen gibt, einen Plan, eine Orientierungssuche, eine Anordnung. Dass wir einer permanenten Forschung beiwohnen, bliebe noch hinzuzufügen, aber das macht vielleicht am Ende niemand (oder doch? Auch das Gespräch zwischen diesen Anordnungen und Durchführungen wiederherzustellen?). Und wie viel Zeit haben wir, es zu erfahren? Aber es ist eben nicht einfach, nur mal so blind zu sein und Straßenmusiker und vor einer Baustelle zu spielen, es ist nicht einfach, Räume zu benutzen, dass sie hochenergetische Instrumente unserer Wahrnehmungen werden. Und dennoch könnten wir immer noch auf die Straße gehen und glauben, dass auf ihr etwas passiert, auch heute noch, etwas, das sich der Warenform entzieht und gewissermaßen unerwartet ist. Das Zungenvideo geht einstweilen weiter und wirft uns auf seine sehr reduzierte Anordnung zurück. Vielleicht bemerken wir erst jetzt, wie wir die ganze Zeit dabei sind, aus einem gewissen Konzept der Sichtbarkeit herauszukommen, aus der Vorstellung einer Künstlerbiografie, eines Themenkomplexes, eines festgefahrenen Verhältnisses zwischen Material und Gestaltung. Elementare Gesten, so hat Terry Fox es genannt. Was wir davon sehen, wird immer zeitgleich sein: Video und Performance, Skulptur und Klang, Komposition und Material, und das erzeugt seinen eigenen Realismus. Am Schluss bleibt jedenfalls die gestreckte Zunge übrig. (Nein die Zunge wird langsam wieder eingepackt und das Kinn vorgestreckt.) Wir können das jetzt deuten oder weitergehen.

Kathrin Röggla
Vizepräsidentin der Akademie der Künste, Berlin

forgotten that they also take place in cellars, on the street, or before construction sites. With two blind musicians, who were somehow engaged – as was said afterwards. There are recordings and preliminary drawings, preparations for a specific event, a plan, a search for orientation, and directions. It's important to add that we are part of a permanent investigation, but in the end nobody really does this (or do they? Should we also reconstruct the conversation between these instructions and how they are carried out?). And how much time do we have to experience this? But it is certainly not easy to be blind and a street musician, and to play in front of a building site, nor is it easy to use spaces in a way that transforms them into high-energy instruments of our perceptions. Yet, we could still go out in the street and believe that something was happening there, even today, something that is somewhat unexpected, which goes beyond the commodity form. Meanwhile the tongue video continues and carries us back to its much reduced form. Perhaps we first notice now how we have been continuously moving away from a certain concept of the visible and from the idea of an artist biography, of a thematic range of topics, of an entrenched relationship between material and form. "Elemental gestures" was what Terry Fox called it. What we see of them will always be simultaneous: video and performance, sculpture and sound, composition and material. And that produces its own realism. In the end, what remains is a tongue sticking out (no, the tongue is slowly retracted and the chin thrust forward). We can now interpret that or just continue.

Kathrin Röggla
Vice President of the Akademie der Künste, Berlin

Translated from the German by James Bell

I

CHILDRENS TAPES LOOP ONE

1. spoon , fork, toothpick and pen.   2:25

   from original 2

2 ② candle draws water, lighting the wet candle,   3:40
        relighting the candle

   from original 2

3 *a* ③ *fork resting on cards*   3:00
        from 4

   vertical candle drip ·   2:
   ④ from original 2

4. forked candle lit from both ends over water   10:35
   ⑤

        from original 2

   from 4 fork resting on the candle

   cloth draws water to the table   8:15
   ⑥   from original 1

Terry Fox, Loose leaf collection for *Children's Tapes*, notes with stills from video, c. 1974

Foreword

Das BAM (Musée des Beaux-Arts in Mons) in Belgien wird im Anschluss an die Ausstellung, die Terry Fox in der Akademie der Künste in Berlin gewidmet wird, die emblematischen Werke dieses amerikanisch-europäischen Künstlers zeigen. Terry Fox war eine zentrale Figur innerhalb der Performancekunst der 1970er Jahre, der weder geografische noch künstlerische Grenzen kannte. Er lebte mehrere Jahre in Liège und hat der europäischen Performance- und Klangkunst entscheidende Impulse gegeben. Fox arbeitete mit den richtungsweisenden Künstlern der Zeit zusammen, dazu zählten Joseph Beuys, Vito Acconci oder Dennis Oppenheim.

In der Ausstellung im BAM werden wir eine Verbindung mit einem anderen bedeutsamen Vertreter der internationalen Kunstszene herstellen: Bill Viola. Tatsächlich haben beide zusammengearbeitet und ihre Ideen und wegweisenden künstlerischen Ansätze miteinander konfrontiert.

Nikola Doll, Kuratorin der Ausstellung in Mons, stellt die beiden Pioniere der Videokunst einander gegenüber. So wie Bill Viola dieses Medium als künstlerischen Ausdruck nutzte, verwendete Terry Fox es, um seine Performances zu dokumentieren. Zugleich lotete er das Medium Video als Ausgangspunkt für Neuschöpfungen in seinen vielfältigen Möglichkeiten spielerisch aus.

Die Herausforderung dieser Gegenüberstellung besteht darin, gewohnte Wahrnehmungsformen in Ausstellungen hinter sich zu lassen, um zur ursprünglichen schöpferischen Energie der Performances und des Videos zurückzufinden, die bei beiden Künstlern vorherrschte. Denn beide gehörten zu den Initiatoren künstlerischer Tendenzen, die in enger Verbindung mit der sinnlichen, körperlichen Wahrnehmung stehen. Darüber hinaus veranschaulichen sowohl die Werke als auch die Ausstellung die frühesten Verknüpfungen zwischen der Kunst und den neuen Bildtechnologien – eines der Leitthemen von Mons, der Europäischen Kulturhauptstadt 2015. Schließlich sind wir besonders glücklich, mit der Ausstellung eine internationale Kooperation realisieren zu können, die Mons und das BAM nunmehr als anerkannten Partner der großen europäischen Museumsinstitutionen bestätigt.

Elio Di Rupo
Staatsminister
Oberbürgermeister der Stadt Mons

Aus dem Französischen übersetzt von Nikolaus G. Schneider

The BAM (Musée des Beaux-Arts) in Mons, Belgium will show emblematic works of the American-European artist Terry Fox (1943–2008) following the retrospective of his work at the Akademie der Künste in Berlin.

Terry Fox was a central figure in 1970s performance art who knew neither geographic nor artistic borders. He lived several years in Liège and was a strong catalyst for European performance and sound art. Fox worked with seminal artists of his day, including Joseph Beuys, Vito Acconci and Dennis Oppenheim.

In the exhibition at BAM we will draw a connection between Terry Fox and another extremely important representative of the international art scene: Bill Viola. The two worked together and were thus confronted with each other's ideas and groundbreaking artistic approaches.

Nikola Doll, curator of the Mons exhibition, contrasts the two pioneers of video art. Bill Viola employed the medium of video as artistic expression, while Terry Fox used it to document his performances and as a starting point for new creations based on his playful exploration of the medium's diverse possibilities.

The scenographic challenge of this comparison involves casting off modes of perception commonly associated with exhibitions, to find our way back to the original creative energy of performance and video that prevailed in the works of these two artists. For both were among the initiators of artistic tendencies closely linked to a sensual, physical awareness. The works and exhibition illuminate the earliest connections between art and new image technologies – one of the key themes at Mons, the 2015 European Capital of Culture.

In conclusion, we are especially pleased that the exhibition has served to bring about an international cooperation, confirming Mons and the BAM as recognized partners of major European art institutions and museums.

Elio Di Rupo
Minister of State
Mayor of the City of Mons

Translated from the German by James Bell

Foreword

Das Von der Heydt-Museum ist die einzige Station der Ausstellung „Elemental Gestures – Terry Fox" in Nordrhein-Westfalen, und sie zeigt erneut die zentrale Bedeutung unserer Region für die jüngste Kunstgeschichte. Künstlerisch zunächst vor allem in Kalifornien beheimatet, war Fox mit der Kunstszene in Nordrhein-Westfalen besonders eng verbunden. So arbeitete er mit Künstlern wie Joseph Beuys und Ute Klophaus zusammen, die beide hierzulande eine wichtige Rolle spielten. Seine letzten Lebensjahre verbrachte er in Köln, wo sich heute neben seinem Nachlass auch das Büro der Terry Fox Association e.V. befindet.

Schon länger hatte Beate Eickhoff, Kuratorin am Von der Heydt-Museum, die Idee, diesen Schatz zu sichten und auf die Möglichkeiten seiner musealen Präsentation hin zu überprüfen. Nur die Zusammenarbeit mit weiteren Institutionen kann aber ein so umfangreiches Forschungsprojekt erfolgreich werden lassen. Deshalb sind wir für Initiative und Engagement der Akademie der Künste dankbar. Unser besonderer Dank gilt überdies der Kunststiftung Nordrhein-Westfalen und der Stadtsparkasse Wuppertal, die die Realisierung der Ausstellung in unserem Haus großzügig unterstützt haben.

Das Von der Heydt-Museum Wuppertal ist der geeignete Ort für eine Präsentation des Amerikaners Terry Fox im Rheinland, da er hier bereits in früheren Gruppenausstellungen zu sehen war und sich zudem eines seiner bekanntesten Werke, *Ovum Anguinum* (1990), in der Von der Heydt-Sammlung befindet. Darüber hinaus wird nun auch die Klangkunst eines Künstlers, der eher dem Bereich bildende Kunst zuzuordnen ist, in Wuppertal viel Resonanz erfahren. Denn die freie Musikszene hat in Wuppertal eine lange, ruhmreiche Geschichte und kann auf legendäre Musikgrößen wie Peter Kowald und Peter Brötzmann verweisen. Indem wir den Klangkünstler Terry Fox in Erinnerung rufen, wird die Geschichte der Musikperformance, die Wurzeln auch in unserem Museum hat, um einen ganz wesentlichen Aspekt bereichert.

Gerhard Finckh
Direktor des Von der Heydt-Museums Wuppertal

The Von der Heydt-Museum is the sole venue in North Rhine-Westphalia of the exhibition *Elemental Gestures – Terry Fox.* It again shows the key role our region has played in recent art history. An artist who began working in California, Terry Fox later became closely connected to the art scene in North Rhine-Westphalia. For example, he collaborated with artists such as Joseph Beuys and Ute Klophaus, both of whom played significant roles in art. Fox spent the last years of his life in Cologne, where next to his Estate one now finds the office of the Terry Fox Association e.V..

For a long time Beate Eickhoff, curator at the Von der Heydt-Museum, considered how to approach and delve deeper into this treasure trove of materials to determine how it might be presented in a museum setting. Such an extensive research project can only succeed in cooperation with other institutions. We are therefore grateful for the initiative and commitment of the Akademie der Künste. We are therefore grateful for the initiative and commitment of the Akademie der Künste. Our special thanks also go to the Kulturstiftung Nordrhein-Westfalen and to the Stadtsparkasse Wuppertal, whose generous support has made it possible for us to realize this exhibition at our museum.

The Von der Heydt-Museum in Wuppertal is a fitting place for a presentation of the American Terry Fox in the Rhineland, because he participated in early local group exhibitions, and one of his best-known works, *Ovum Anguinum* (1990) is part of the Von der Heydt-Museum's collection. In addition, the sound art of an artist generally associated with the visual arts will have particular resonance, because the general music scene in Wuppertal has a long and illustrious history that includes legendary music greats, such as Peter Kowald and Peter Brötzmann. Our retrospective including Terry Fox's sound art will add a very significant aspect to the history of music performance, which also has a tradition at our museum.

Gerhard Finckh
Director of the Von der Heydt-Musem, Wuppertal

Translated from the German by James Bell

Foreword

Terry Fox' Name ist nicht Teil des Kanons. Nur Insidern ist er ein Begriff. Seine Werke unterlaufen die Kunsterwartungen des Publikums. In Sammlungen ist er nur ganz selten vertreten. Er hat eingelöst, was Guillaume Apollinaire 1916 als neue Problemstellung der Kunst beschrieben und womit sich Picasso seither zeit seines Lebens beschäftigt hatte, ohne wirklich je ans Ziel gelangen zu können, – mit der Skulptur „aus Nichts, aus Leere". Terry Fox hat wirkliche Skulpturen aus „Nichts" realisiert, konzentrierte er sich doch in vielen seiner Aktionen und Performances auf die immateriellen Dimensionen von Klang und Sprache, um gleichzeitig sein Gefühl für die Materiäliät und die Fragilität der Sinne erfahrbar zu machen. Zur Verdeutlichung seiner Absichten schuf er aus alltäglichsten Materialien wie Staub, Klaviersaiten, Brettern, Spiegeln, Sardinenbüchsen Bühnen und Sockel, auf denen sich das Unsichtbare ereignet. Terry Fox ist seit den 1960er Jahren eine der konsequentesten und radikalsten Künstlerpersönlichkeiten der Fluxus-Bewegung, der Body-Art, Konzept- und Performance-Kunst, ohne sich als ihr Vertreter zu fühlen. Mit der Vergänglichkeit verebbender Klänge und Worte verwies er auf die existentiellen Grundfragen – auf Ekstase und Sex, Wahnsinn und Krankheit, Geburt und Tod. Es ist ein Glück, dass in Bern Elka Spoerri und Jean Hubert Martin früh seine Bedeutung erkannten und ihn Jürgen Glaesemer und Gerhard Johann Lischka zu Performances einluden. Von diesen gibt es leider keine Aufzeichnungen, doch hatte man im Kunstmuseum Bern systematisch seine Werke zu sammeln begonnen. Aus diesen Gründen übernehmen wir mit Freude die Ausstellung, die die Akademie der Künste Terry Fox in Berlin ausrichtet. – Ich danke unserer Gegenwartskunstkuratorin Kathleen Bühler, die einen wichtigen Beitrag zum Katalog verfasst hat und die Ausstellung in Bern kuratieren wird.

Matthias Frehner
Direktor des Kunstmuseums Bern

Terry Fox's name is not part of the canon. He is only known to insiders. His works frustrate the public's expectations of art. Only rarely is he represented in collections. He has addressed that which Guillaume Apollinaire described in 1916 as art's new problem and which occupied Picasso throughout his life – without the latter ever truly achieving his goal: to make a sculpture "out of nothing, out of emptiness." Terry Fox created real sculptures out of "nothing" but concentrated in many of his art actions and performances on the immaterial dimensions of sound and language in order to make his awareness of materiality and of the fragility of the senses simultaneously experiencable. To illustrate his intentions, he used the most everyday items, such as dust, piano strings, boards, mirrors, and sardine cans, to create stages and pedestals on which the invisible took place. As of the 1960s, Terry Fox was one of the most rigorous and radical artist personalities of the Fluxus movement, of body art, conceptual art, and performance art, without ever having seen himself as being associated with these movements. With the temporality of sounds and words ebbing into the past, he referred to the fundamental questions of existence – to ecstasy and sex, insanity and illness, and birth and death.

It is fortunate that Elka Spoerri and Jean Hubert Martin, both in Bern, recognized Fox's importance early on and that Jürgen Glaesemer and Gerhard Johann Lischka invited him to performances. Unfortunately there are no recordings of these, but the Kunstmuseum Bern had begun to systematically collect his work. We are therefore quite pleased to show the exhibition on Terry Fox that the Akademie der Künste in Berlin has organized. I would like to sincerely thank our curator of contemporary art, Kathleen Bühler, who made an important contribution to the catalogue and will curate the exhibition in Bern.

Matthias Frehner
Director of the Kunstmuseum Bern

Translated from the German by James Bell

Terry Fox, *A.A.*, 1971–72, art book

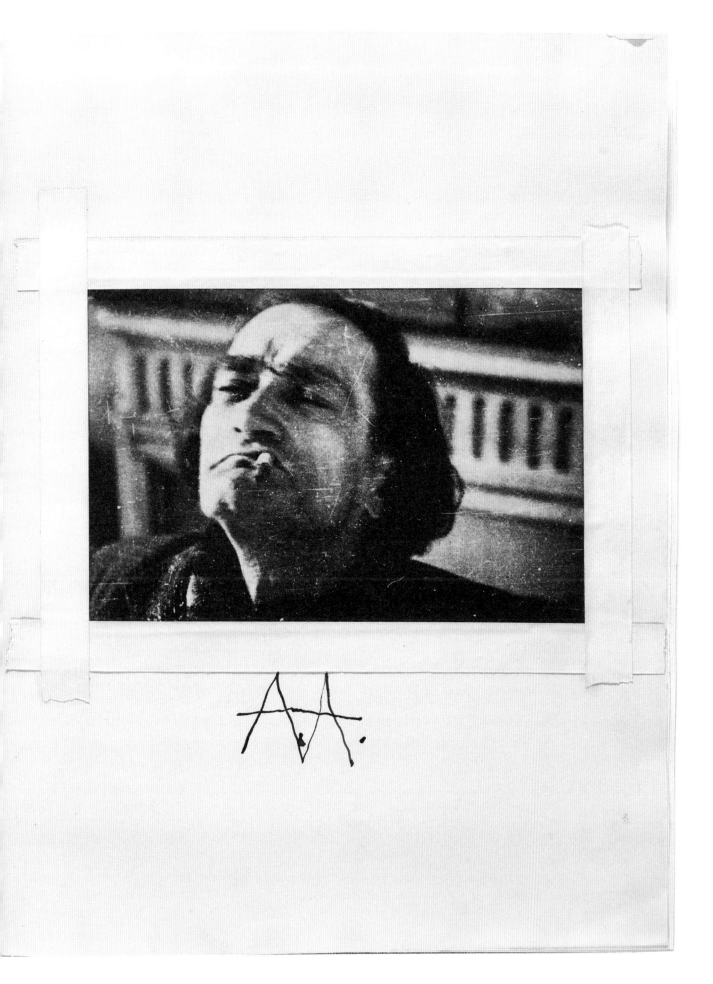

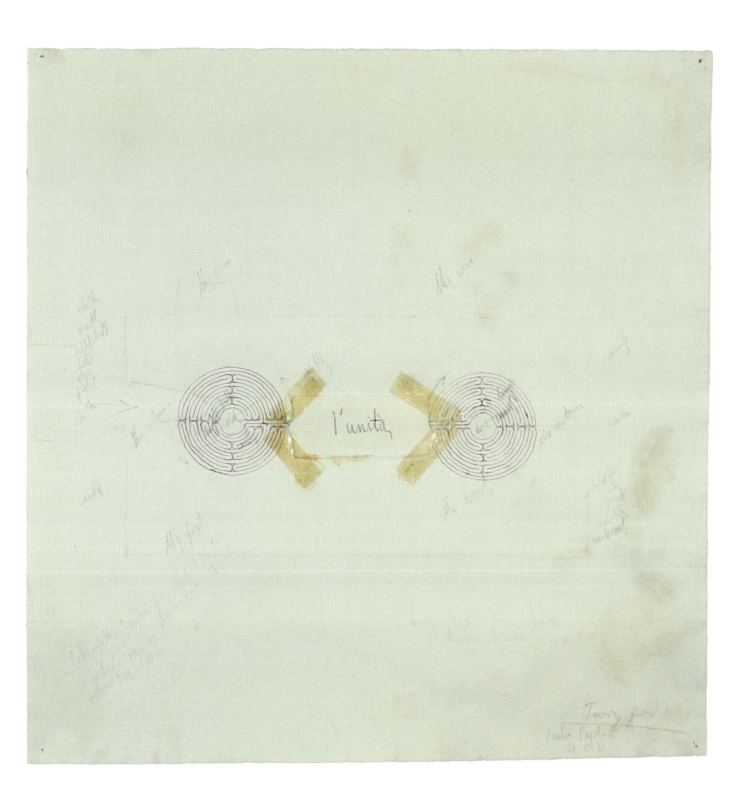

18   Terry Fox: *L'Unita*, 1972

Eine „materiale Gemeinsamkeit
der Dinge"[1]

Arnold Dreyblatt

A "Material Community of Things"[1]

An Leben und Werk von Terry Fox zeigt sich, wie schwierig es ist, den Lebenslauf eines Künstlers von seinem Werk getrennt zu betrachten. Terrys künstlerische Arbeit stammt aus einer Zeit, in der man vom Einfluss der Kunst echte persönliche und soziale Veränderungen erwartete. Seine Arbeit ist nicht „Anti-Kunst", sondern sie ist eher eine Bestandsaufnahme des Wesentlichen durch einen Dialog, der sich in gleichem Maße an die Außenwelt, die Situation und den Betrachter richtet wie an die Innenwelt, das Bewusstsein und die Wahrnehmung – im Grunde genommen an Geburt und Tod. Terrys Arbeit eröffnet einen hermetischen und häufig verschlüsselten Dialog, der sich sehr einfacher und elementarer Materialien bedient. Dennoch spricht er uns unmittelbar an, entweder durch ein gemeinsames Erlebnis oder dadurch, dass er die Zerbrechlichkeit des Lebens würdigt – die verschlungenen Pfade und Grenzen des Bewusstseins. Terry vertraute auf die kommunikative Kraft der Unmittelbarkeit, der einfachen Handlung, der Resonanz sowie der Sprache und des Zeichens, und zwar nicht nur bei der Interaktion mit einem Publikum, sondern auch als individuelle Übung für sich selbst.

Diese Doppelfunktion von künstlerischer Praxis war bei ihm bereits in frühen Jahren festgelegt: Sie bestand aus extrem persönlichen Erkundungen einerseits und dem zuschauenden Publikum andererseits. Terry sagte zu seiner performativen Praxis: „Was ich mache, bedeutet etwas für mich, und etwas anderes für die Person, die zuschaut."[2] „Nur die Leute können den Raum, die Skulptur verstehen, die gesehen haben, wie sie entstanden ist. Ich agierte nicht für die Leute. Ich arbeitete mit den Gegenständen und das Publikum konnte sehen, was geschah."[3] Diese Dichotomie zwischen der Empfindung/Beobachtung und der Wahrnehmung eines Einzelnen oder als Gruppe war bei seinen ersten körperzentrierten Langzeitperformances am stärksten ausgeprägt. Terry vertraute auf die Spannung zwischen sich als Performer oder aktiv Handelndem und den Anwesenden, die ihm als sein Publikum zuschauten. Bei der Vorbereitung dieser Ausstellung wurde immer deutlicher, dass diese kommunikative

The life and work of Terry Fox exemplifies the difficulty of separating an artist's biography from the body of work. Terry's work originated in a period in which one believed in the power of art to effect genuine personal and social transformation. His work was not "anti-art," but rather an identification through essential communication, directed as much towards the external, the environment and the viewer, as towards the internal, consciousness and awareness – essentially, to birth and death itself.

Terry's work speaks to us in a hermetic and often coded dialogue, performed with the most basic and fundamental materials, yet we are addressed directly, either through a shared performed experience, or through his well-earned recognition of the fragility of life – the twisted paths and the limits of memory. Terry had confidence in the communicative power of immediacy, of simple actions, of resonance, and of language and sign, not only in interaction with a public, but as a personal practice for himself.

A sense of this dual function of artistic practice was defined early on in his own biography: consisting of extremely personal research on the one hand, and the observing public on the other. Terry pointed this out in relation to performance practice: "What I make is something for me and something else for the person who watches."[2] The "only people who would be able to understand that space, that sculpture, would be the ones who'd seen it being created. I wasn't performing for the people: I was working with objects and the audience could see what was happening."[3] This dichotomy between perception / observation and individual and group experience was at its most acute in his long duration, early body performances. Terry was confident in the connective tension between him, as performer or initiator, and those present as his observing public. In the course of preparing this exhibition, I have come to understand the ways in which this communicative potential infuses all of Terry's work. Themes from distant periods and with contrasting materials and mediums interact, suggesting a network of possibilities that has made the planning process especially compelling.

Spannung das Werk von Terry vielfach durchdringt. Themen aus verschiedenen Schaffensphasen mit ganz unterschiedlichen Materialien und Medien reagieren miteinander und deuten Vernetzungen von Möglichkeiten an, was sich im Planungsprozess als besonders herausfordernd erwies. Text und Symbolzeichen sind in Terrys Kunst gleichbedeutend. Der Text dient als visuelles, akustisches und skulpturales Feld wie ein Schleier oder eine Chiffre. Wir müssen ihn durchdringen und entschlüsseln, um hinter seinen Sinn zu kommen, und er lädt uns ein, poetische Zusammenhänge zu entdecken. Arrangements mit Objekten bilden eine Art symbolische Grammatik, einmal stellen sie fertige Aussagen dar, ein anderes Mal überlagern sich Andeutungen, deren Schlichtheit trügerisch ist. In ihrer manchmal schonungslosen Ehrlichkeit ist Terrys Sprache persönlich und universell zugleich. Und genau wie seine Rezeption verbirgt auch das Werk ebenso viel, wie es offenlegt.

Terry sammelte Bücher über Geheimzeichen. Als er in Neapel lebte, wurde seine Wohnung immer wieder aufgebrochen. Auf Anraten eines Nachbarn hängte er das Symbolzeichen für den „bösen Blick" an seine Tür. Danach wurde nie wieder eingebrochen. Dann gab es in den USA die ersten Performances mit Wanderarbeitern und Obdachlosen. Terry schuf eine Werkgruppe mit 52 *Hobo Signs* [↗**191**] 4, Zeichen, die auf dem Weg als Nachrichten oder Markierungen für Nachfolgende hinterlassen werden.

1969 bat Terry zwei blinde Straßenmusiker in San Francisco, an einer Baugrube auf der Straße zu singen, und verschickte Einladungen zu dieser Straßenaktion, die er *Public Theater #3: What Do Blind Men Dream?* [↗**119**] nannte. Die blinde Musikerin, von der Terry später als der „schönen Dame" sprach, erklärte ihm, dass der Körper sich selbst in einen „schlechten Wirt" für eine Erkrankung verwandeln müsse, um sie loszuwerden. Seine Krankheit begleitete ihn unablässig, und sein Körper war ein Archiv von Operationsnarben und Eingriffen, aber auch eine Landschaft, ein Weg. Seine „Elemental Gestures" bleiben nach wie vor Rezepte für aufgenommene oder Live-Transformationen: Dieser Körper könnte unser Körper sein, das Blut unser Blut, die Handlungen unsere Rituale. Die „Reenactments" durch das Labyrinth könnten unsere Spuren sein. Im Labyrinth begegnen wir uns selbst. Hermann Kern vermutet in seinem hervorragenden historischen Buch über Labyrinthe (in dem auch Terrys Werk erwähnt ist)5, dass das Labyrinth in der Antike ursprünglich eine Tanzbewegung war, die von den Tänzern nach den Zeichnungen auf der „Tanzfläche" nachvollzogen wurde, während sie für die „Außenstehenden" unverständlich blieb.6 Als weitgehender Autodidakt mit einer knapp ausgefallenen akademischen Kunstausbildung hatte Terry ein gespaltenes

Text and sign are correlative in Terry's work; the text is a visual, acoustic and sculptural field which functions as a veil, a cypher. We must dig and uncode in order to arrive at meaning, and he gives us an invitation to discover poetic correspondences. Arrangements of objects create a kind of symbolic grammar, in some cases forming phrases of representation, in others an overlapping of allusions which deceive us in their simplicity. Savagely honest at times, Terry's vocabulary is at once personal and universal. And just like its reception, his work conceals as much as it reveals.

Terry collected books on secret signs. When he lived in Naples, his apartment was continuously broken into. A neighbor suggested that he put the sign for the "evil eye" on his door, after which his home was never broken into again. There were early performances in the US involving hobos and bums. He created a serial work containing fifty-two *Hobo Signs* [↗**191**] 4, representing the images they left behind as messages or marks for others who would follow in their footsteps.

In 1969, Terry asked two blind musicians in San Francisco to sing on the street before an open pit and mailed invitations for this street event, titled *Public Theater #3: What Do Blind Men Dream?* [↗**119**] One of the blind musicians, who Terry later referred to as a "beautiful lady," explained to him that the body should make itself a "bad host" for an illness in order to be rid of it. Illness had always been his companion, his body an archive of incisions and interventions, but also a landscape, a path. His "Elemental Gestures," remain prescriptions for live and recorded transformation: this body could be our body, the blood our blood, the actions our rituals. The reenactments of paths through the labyrinth could be our traces. In the labyrinth we meet ourselves. Hermann Kern, who wrote one of the most important historical books on the labyrinth (in which Terry's work is noted),5 presumes that in ancient times the labyrinth was originally a dance movement, which was only understood by the dancers through the markings on the "dance floor," but incomprehensible to those on the "outside."6

Having had little formal education in the arts, Terry was mostly self-educated and he maintained a complex relationship to the artistic community. He matured as an artist in a world of galleries and exhibitions, where his work was often bought and sold – yet he longed for distance from the commercial urban centers. He gravitated to Europe again and again, most often to Italy, where he had lived in his youth. His decision to move to Liège, Belgium from Florence in the 1980s reflected a desire to have the best of both worlds: a site near the cultural centers of Northern Europe and the chance to remain invisible in a marginal working-class city (with a large Italian population) and most importantly, to be left alone.

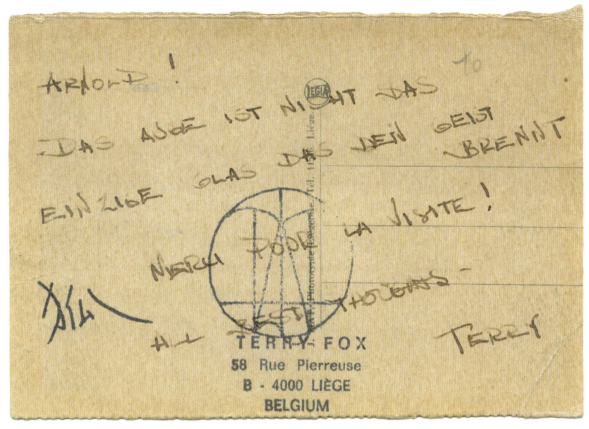

ARNOLD !

DAS AUGE IST NICHT DAS

EINZIGE GLAS DAS DEN GEIST BRENNT

MERCI POUR LA VISITE !

ALL BEST THOUGHTS –

TERRY

TERRY FOX
58 Rue Pierreuse
B - 4000 LIÈGE
BELGIUM

Terry Fox, Postcard to Arnold Dreyblatt, 1987

Verhältnis zur Künstlerszene. Er reüssierte als Künstler in der Welt der Galerie- und Museumsausstellungen, wo seine Werke häufig angekauft und verkauft wurden, – dennoch hielt er sich der Agora fern. Es zog ihn immer wieder nach Europa, meistens nach Italien, wo er in jungen Jahren gelebt hatte. Seine Entscheidung, in den 1980er Jahren von Florenz nach Lüttich in Belgien zu ziehen, spiegelt seinen Wunsch, die Vorteile beider Welten zu nutzen: sich in der Nähe der Kulturzentren Nordeuropas zu positionieren und sich in dieser Arbeiterstadt (mit einem hohen Anteil italienischer Einwohner) unsichtbar machen zu können, und vor allem, in Ruhe gelassen zu werden.

Ich wohnte nebenan und besuchte ihn oft am späten Vormittag auf einen Espresso. Terry kombinierte Fundobjekte, die er von den zahlreichen Flohmärkten in dieser Stadt mit ihren vielen Arbeitslosen mitbrachte. Die Gegenstände arrangierte er als Bilderrätsel, als Pseudo-Reliquien oder als optische Puzzles. Ich sah sie in einer Küchenecke oder in seiner Bibliothek – aber sie waren stets verschwunden, wenn ich am nächsten Tag wiederkam. Fragte ich ihn, wo die Arbeiten geblieben seien, die ich nicht mehr entdecken konnte, antwortete er nicht oder war verstimmt. Einmal ließ ich nicht locker, bis er sagte: „Ach so, ja, das – ich habe es nur für mich selbst gemacht."

I lived next door, and I often visited in the late morning for an espresso. Terry would create ensembles of found objects, collected from the abundant flea markets in a city filled with the unemployed. The items would be arranged as in a rebus, as pseudo-relics, or as optical puzzles. I would notice them in the corners of the kitchen, or in his library – yet they had always disappeared when I visited the following day. I would prod him about the whereabouts of a no longer visible work, only to be answered with indifference and annoyance. I once pushed him a bit harder, and he answered, "Oh, yes, that one – I made that only for myself."

His house on the Rue Pierreuse was a "Museum of Curiosities": an ascending tower of mind-states, each floor revealing the next rung, recalling the stages of the labyrinth. When I visited, Terry would devilishly unveil an item from his collection of unique artifacts, much like a medieval monk might show his special relics, including exceptional books, found and rare items.

Terry especially prized his books by Antonin Artaud, to whom he dedicated an artist's book: *A.A.*[7] In *The Theater and Its Double*, Artaud wrote, "the need to act directly and profoundly upon the sensibility through the organs invites research, from the point of view of sound, into qualities and

Sein Haus in der Rue Pierreuse war ein „Museum der Kuriositäten": ein Turm, in dem jede Etage zu einer weiteren Bewusstseinsstufe führte, wie der Einstieg in ein Labyrinth. Wenn ich zu Besuch war, zeigte Terry mir verschmitzt wie ein mittelalterlicher Mönch, der seine speziellen Reliquien hervorholt, Stücke aus seiner Sammlung einzigartiger Gegenstände, darunter außergewöhnliche Bücher, Fundstücke oder Raritäten.

Ganz besonders schätzte Terry seine Bücher von Antonin Artaud, dem er ein Künstlerbuch widmete: A.A.[7] In *Das Theater und sein Double* schrieb Artaud: „[...] die Notwendigkeit, durch die Organe direkt und tiefgreifend auf das Empfinden einzuwirken, legt nahe, die Klangeigenschaften und Schwingungen völlig neuer Klänge zu erforschen, Eigenschaften, welche die bekannten Musikinstrumente nicht besitzen und die eine Rekonstruktion antiker und vergessener Instrumente oder die Erfindung neuer erfordern. Abgesehen vom musikalischen Bereich müssen Instrumente und Geräte erforscht werden, welche auf Basis spezieller Zusammensetzungen oder anderer Metalllegierungen eine neue Klangbreite und einen Tonumfang erreichen können, der unerträglich durchdringende Töne oder Lärm erzeugt."[8]

David Ross schreibt in seinem Aufsatz „Wenn es jemals so etwas wie einen Videokünstler gab, dann war es nicht Terry Fox"[9], und ich würde hinzufügen, dass er auch kein Klangkünstler war, obwohl er, lange bevor die „Klangkunst" sich als künstlerische Praxis klar definierte, wusste, dass das Hörbare nicht nur eine Begleiterscheinung des sichtbaren Bereichs ist, sondern ein Medium für sich. Terry hörte mit den Videoarbeiten auf, da er von institutioneller Produktion unabhängig bleiben wollte, aber er arbeitete bis zu seinem Tod im Jahr 2008 weiterhin intensiv mit Klang. Seine Klanginstallationen und Performances sind legendär und grundlegend, doch sie sind als Teile in einem zusammenhängenden Ganzen zu sehen. Er schätzte den Klang als Medium, weil dieser unbelastet durch Sprache oder Geschichte direkt übertragen und empfangen werden kann und rein intuitiv erfassbar ist. Er stimmte seine Wahrnehmung auf die Resonanzwellen im Raum und die Erzeugung von physikalischen Schwingungen in Materialien ein. Terry liebte die oszillierenden Überlagerungen harmonischer Obertöne, die er durch quer im Raum aufgespannte Stahldrähte erzeugte: ein Phänomen, das er entdeckte und benutzte, um den Raum als Skulptur in verschiedene Schwingungszonen aufzuteilen. Einmal ließ er ein Flugzeug über einer Performance kreisen und die Motorengeräusche harmonisch mit seinem in einer Vertiefung gespielten selbstentworfenen Saiteninstrument klingen.

Marilyn Bogerd, Mitbegründerin des Site, eines alternativen Kunstraums in San Francisco, machte mich um 1980 auf

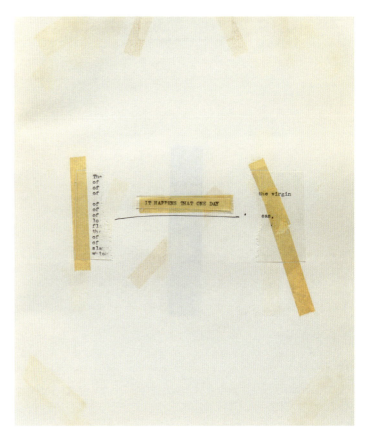

Terry Fox, *A.A.*, 1971–72, art book

vibrations of absolutely new sounds, qualities which present-day musical instruments do not possess and which require the revival of ancient and forgotten instruments or the invention of new ones. Research is also required, apart from music, into instruments and appliances which, based upon special combinations or new alloys of metal, can attain a new range and compass, producing sounds or noises that are unbearably piercing."[8]

David Ross writes in this volume that, "If there ever was such a thing as a video artist, it wasn't Terry Fox,"[9] and I would add that he was also not a sound artist, yet had understood the audible as not merely an accompaniment to the visual field, but as a medium in itself – long before "sound art" had clearly been defined as an artistic practice. Terry abandoned working in video to maintain his independence from institutional production, yet he continued to work intensively with sound until his death in 2008. His sound installations and performances are legendary and essential, yet remain a component to a coherent whole. He treasured sound as a medium for direct transmission and reception, unhindered by the baggage of language and history, functioning as purely visceral experience. He was attuned to the perception of resonating waves in space, and to initiating vibration in physical materials. Terry reveled

Terrys Werk und unser gemeinsames Interesse für Langzeit-performances mit Klangsaiten aufmerksam. Sie stellte mir Terrys Zwillingsbruder Larry Fox in New York vor. Terry hatte mit Pinsel und Farbe angefangen zu arbeiten, Larry mit dem Fotoapparat. Wir besuchten ihn in der Bowery Street und sahen ein 8-mm-Amateurvideo aus ihrer Kindheit, in dem Terry und Larry beim Schwimmen in einem radioaktiven See bei Seattle zu sehen waren. Ich habe Terry erst einige Jahre später persönlich kennengelernt.

Terry, der seine Bilder und Performances als „Skulpturen" bezeichnete, wird vielleicht Walter Benjamins Gedanken über die „Sprache der Dinge" im Sinn gehabt haben, „[...] daß die Sprache der Plastik oder Malerei etwa in gewissen Arten von Dingsprachen fundiert sei, daß in ihnen eine Übersetzung der Sprache der Dinge in eine unendlich viel höhere Sprache [...] vorliegt. Es handelt sich hier um namenlose, unakustische Sprachen, um Sprachen aus dem Material; dabei ist an die materiale Gemeinsamkeit der Dinge in ihrer Mitteilung zu denken."[10] Ich kann mir vorstellen, dass Terry uns zusieht und leise lacht, während wir versuchen, den „Dingen" gerecht zu werden, die er zurückgelassen hat. Dass diese „Dinge" im aktiven „Dialog" bleiben, ist einer einzigartigen Sprachform der Kunst zu verdanken, in der Klang schweigen und Gegenstände sprechen können.

Aus dem Englischen übersetzt von Anne Pitz

1 Walter Benjamin, Über Sprache überhaupt und über die Sprache des Menschen. In: Ders.: *Gesammelte Schriften*. Hg. v. Rolf Tiedemann und Hermann Schweppenhäuser, Band II.1: Aufsätze, Essays, Vorträge, Frankfurt am Main 1991, S. 156, fortan Benjamin 1991
2 Terry Fox, zitiert nach Achille Bonito Oliva, Interview mit Terry Fox. In: *Domus*, 521, April 1973, wiederabgedruckt in: Eva Schmidt (Hg.), *Terry Fox. Ocular Language. 30 Jahre Reden und Schreiben über Kunst. 30 Years of Speaking and Writing about Art*. Gesellschaft für Aktuelle Kunst Bremen, Köln 2000, S. 56, fortan Schmidt 2000
3 Terry Fox, zitiert nach Willoughby Sharp, Interview mit Terry Fox. In: *Avalanche*, Winter 1971, wiederabgedruckt in: Schmidt 2000, vgl. Anm. 2, S. 36
4 *Terry Fox. Hobo Signs*. Ausst.-Kat. Kunstraum München, München 1985
5 Hermann Kern, *Labyrinthe. Erscheinungsformen und Deutungen. 5000 Jahre Gegenwart eines Urbilds*. München 1999
6 Jürgen vom Scheidt, im Gespräch mit Hermann Kern, Bayrischer Rundfunk, 27. Mai 1993, http://www.hyperwriting.de/loader.php?pid=563, zuletzt am 1.7.2015
7 Terry Fox, *A.A.*, 1971–72, Sammlung des San Francisco Museum of Modern Art
8 Antonin Artaud, *The Theater and Its Double*, übersetzt ins Englische von M. C. Richards, New York 1958. Übersetzung hier von Anne Pitz
9 David A. Ross, Terry Fox – Kein Videokünstler, in diesem Buch S. 39
10 Benjamin 1991, vgl. Anm. 1, S. 156

in the sympathetic oscillation of harmonic overtones generated by the transverse excitation of steel wires in architectural spaces – a phenomena that he discovered and developed – sculpturally dissecting a space into a vibratory suspension. For a performance, he once arranged for an airplane to circle overhead, its single engine resonating sympathetically in tune with a homemade string instrument being performed in a pit below it.

Marilyn Bogerd, cofounder of Site, an alternative art space in San Francisco, about 1980 introduced me to Terry's work and noted our corresponding interests in durational performances on vibrating strings. She introduced me to Terry's fraternal twin, Larry Fox, in New York. Terry began working with brush and paint, Larry with a photo camera. We visited him on the Bowery and watched 8mm home movies from their childhood showing young Terry and Larry swimming in a radioactive lake near Seattle. I would not meet Terry in person until some years later.

Terry, who referred to his drawings and performances as sculpture, might have had Walter Benjamin's "Language of Things" in mind: "the language of sculpture or painting is founded on certain kinds of thing languages, that in them we find a translation of the language of things into an infinitely higher language [...]" and that " we are concerned here with [...] languages issuing from matter; here we should recall the material community of things in their communication."[10] I can sense Terry watching us, gently laughing, as we attempt to do justice to the "things" he left behind. That these "things" remain in active "conversation" makes use of a unique dialect of the arts, where sound is silent and objects speak.

1 Walter Benjamin, "On Language as Such and on the Language of Man," Walter Benjamin, *Reflections*, trans. by Edmund Jephcott, New York: Harcourt Brace Jovanovich, 1978, p. 314, hereafter: Benjamin 1978
2 Terry Fox, interviewed by Achille Bonito Oliva, *Domus*, 521, April 1973, p. 45, reprinted in: Eva Schmidt (ed.), *Terry Fox. Ocular Language. 30 Jahre Reden und Schreiben über Kunst. 30 Years of Speaking and Writing about Art*. Gesellschaft für Aktuelle Kunst Bremen, Cologne, 2000, p. 57, hereafter: Schmidt 2000
3 Terry Fox, interviewed by Willoughby Sharp, *Avalanche*, Winter 1971, pp. 70-81, reprinted in Schmidt 2000 (cf. note 2), p. 37
4 Terry Fox, *Hobo Signs*, exhibition catalogue, Kunstraum München, Munich, 1985
5 Hermann Kern, *Labyrinthe. Erscheinungsformen und Deutungen. 5000 Jahre Gegenwart eines Urbilds*, Munich, 1999
6 Jürgen vom Scheidt, interview with Hermann Kern, Bayrischer Rundfunk, May 27, 1993, http://www.hyperwriting.de/loader.php?pid=563, (last accessed on July 1, 2015)
7 Terry Fox, *A.A.*, 1971–72, collection of the San Francisco Museum of Modern Art
8 Antonin Artaud, *The Theater and Its Double*, trans. by M. C. Richards, New York, 1958, p. 95
9 David A. Ross, "Terry Fox: Not a Video Artist," in this volume p. 39
10 Benjamin 1978 (cf. note 1), p. 314

Constance Lewallen

Terry Fox – Performance in San Francisco

In den 1960er Jahren kam die Performance als neues Genre der Kunst auf. Wie andere neue Kunstformen damals, zum Beispiel Video und Installation, die als Teilaspekte oder Nebenprodukte aus der Konzeptkunst hervorgingen, wurde sie, im Geist der politischen Radikalität jener Zeit, als Ablehnung der zunehmenden Kommerzialisierung in der Kunstwelt verstanden – als ein Weg, die Trennung von Künstler und Publikum, Kunst und Alltag abzuschaffen und dem Kunstobjekt weniger Gewicht beizumessen als dem Schaffensprozess. Terry Fox war einer der vielen jungen Künstler, die sich von der klassischen Malerei und Bildhauerei abwandten und neue Formen suchten, die das revolutionäre Denken jener Zeit besser umsetzen konnten.

In der Hauptphase der Performance-Aktivitäten zwischen 1967 und 1980 konkurrierte die San-Francisco-Bay-Area mit New York. Dort war in den ersten Jahren der Künstler Tom Marioni ihr Initiator. Von 1968 bis 1971 arbeitete er als Kurator am Richmond Art Center und war anschließend Direktor des Ausstellungsraums Museum of Conceptual Art (MOCA), den er im März 1970 in der 86 Third Street im Stadtteil South of Market von San Francisco gründete. Zwei Jahre später zog das MOCA um die Ecke in der 75 Market Street ein, wo es zwölf Jahre lang betrieben wurde. Fox und Marioni lernten sich 1969 in der Vanderwort Gallery in San Francisco bei einer Ausstellung kennen, an der sie beide beteiligt waren. Bald darauf lud Marioni Fox in die von ihm kuratierte Ausstellung „The Return of Abstract Expressionism" im Richmond Art Center ein; 1974 bot er ihm an, den Ausstellungsraum des MOCA mit zu nutzen. Das tat Fox, bis er 1978 aus San Francisco wegzog. Fox war ein Hauptakteur der überwiegend temporären Aktionen im MOCA. (Marioni zog den in Europa verwendeten Begriff der Aktion dem der Performance vor, um die begriffliche Nähe zum Schauspiel zu vermeiden.)

Der in Seattle, Washington, geborene Terry Fox war 1963 nach einem Italienaufenthalt nach San Francisco gezogen. Damals malte er einige Jahre lang mit schwarzer Farbe auf Glas, wodurch ein Spiegeleffekt erzeugt wurde. Was diese Arbeiten, die sehr wenige Menschen zu sehen bekamen,

Performance emerged as a new genre in contemporary art at the end of the 1960s. Alongside other new forms, such as video and installation, which developed contemporaneously as aspects or offshoots of conceptual art and concurrent with the radical politics of the time, it was conceived as oppositional to the increasing commercialism of art – a way to break down boundaries between artist and audience, art and life, and to de-emphasize the art object in favor of the process of creation. Terry Fox was one of many young artists who abandoned traditional painting or sculpture to explore other forms more consistent with the revolutionary spirit of the time.

The San Francisco Bay Area rivaled New York for performance activity in the seminal period between 1967 and 1980. In the early years, artist Tom Marioni was its prime catalyst, as curator at the Richmond Art Center, across the bay from San Francisco, from 1968 to 1971, and continuing as director of the Museum of Conceptual Art (MOCA), which he founded in March 1970, at 86 Third Street in San Francisco's South of Market district. Two years later, MOCA relocated across the street to 75 Market Street where it operated for the next twelve years. Fox and Marioni met in 1969 at the Vanderwort Gallery in San Francisco, where they were both included in an exhibition. Subsequently, Marioni invited Fox to be in a show he curated in Richmond titled *The Return of Abstract Expressionism*; in 1974, he invited him to share the MOCA space, which Fox did until he left the area in 1978. Fox was a major participant in MOCA's activities, of which most were ephemeral actions. (Marioni preferred the term action, used by Europeans, to performance, to avoid the theatrical connotation.)

A native of Seattle, Washington, Fox moved to San Francisco in 1963 after a sojourn in Italy. At the time, and for the next several years, he made black-on-glass paintings, creating a mirror effect. What is interesting about these works, which very few people saw, is that they demonstrate Fox's early attempt to involve the spectator in his work. After his return to Europe in 1967, he soon found himself in Paris, where students were in the streets protesting against the rigid and antiquated French educational system. Being there was a

bemerkenswert macht, ist, dass sie Fox' frühe Versuche zeigen, den Betrachter in seine Arbeit einzubeziehen. 1967 reiste er wieder nach Europa und landete bald in Paris, wo die Studenten auf die Straßen gingen und gegen das rigide und antiquierte französische Bildungssystem demonstrierten. Was er hier sah, veränderte sein Leben: Fox hatte die Macht der direkten Konfrontation erkannt. Er gab die Malerei auf und begann, die später von ihm als *Public Theater* bezeichneten Aktionen durchzuführen. Diese waren teilweise inspiriert von Antonin Artauds radikalem, kathartischen „Theater der Grausamkeit", das Mythos und Ritual hervorhob und versuchte, die Wand zwischen Schauspieler und Publikum niederzureißen. Fox beschrieb seine Veranstaltungen als „Theater ohne Schauspieler, ohne Manuskript, ohne Plot, ohne Bühne und ohne Regisseur"[1]. Er verstand sie als lebende Readymades, das heißt er bezeichnete vorgefundene Situationen als Kunst, ähnlich wie Marcel Duchamp, der gewöhnliche Alltagsgegenstände, zum Beispiel ein Abtropfgestell für Flaschen, zu Kunst machte. Wieder zurück in der San-Francisco-Bay-Area schickte Fox seinen Freunden Postkarten mit der Einladung, sich an einem bestimmten Tag zu einer

life-changing experience for Fox: having learned the power of direct confrontation, he ceased painting and began to stage what he later termed *Public Theater*, in part inspired by French poet and playwright Antonin Artaud's radical, cathartic "Theater of Cruelty," which emphasized myth and ritual and attempted to break the wall between actor and audience. Fox described his events as "theater with no actors, no script, no plot, no stage, and no director."[1] He thought of them as living readymades, that is, existing situations framed as art in much the same way as Marcel Duchamp designated ordinary items, such a bottle-drying rack, as art. Once back in the Bay Area, Fox sent postcards to friends inviting them to a Woolworth store counter at a particular day and time to witness an especially dramatic salesman's pitch. He titled this event *Buying and Selling*. A few months later, in *What Do Blind Men Dream?* [↗**119**], which he called a "dislocation,"[2] he asked street musicians, a blind female singer accordionist and her boyfriend, to perform in a location other than their usual at a specific day and time. Again Fox sent out and posted announcements but, not having gone himself, never knew how many people actually turned up.

Terry Fox, *Wall Push*, 1970, photo: Barry Klinger

bestimmten Uhrzeit an einem Ladentisch von Woolworth einzufinden und ein besonders spannendes Verkaufsgespräch mitzuerleben. Er nannte diese Veranstaltung *Buying and Selling*. Einige Monate später inszenierte er mit *What Do Blind Men Dream?* [↗**119**] eine „Dislokation"[2]. Hierfür bat er eine blinde, singende Akkordeonspielerin mit ihrem Freund, die Straßenmusikanten waren, an einem anderen Ort und zu einer anderen Tageszeit als gewohnt aufzutreten. Wieder verschickte Fox schriftliche Ankündigungen per Post, doch da er selbst nicht hinging, erfuhr er nie, wie viele Leute tatsächlich kamen.

Nach diesen ersten öffentlichen Veranstaltungen machte Fox eine Kehrtwende und arbeitete einige Jahre an ganz privaten Aktionen wie *Wall Push* (1970) [↗**25**], bei der er seinen Körper in einer Gasse an eine Ziegelmauer presste. Fox sagte dazu: „Es war so etwas wie ein Dialog mit der Wand, ein Austausch von Energie mit ihr. Ich presste acht oder neun Minuten lang, bis ich vor Erschöpfung nicht mehr konnte."[3] Bei dieser Aktion gab es kein Publikum; sie ist nur durch ein Schwarzweißfoto überliefert. Ähnlich führte er 1970 auch *Opening My Hand as Slowly as Possible* in seinem Studio und *Pushing into a Corner* [↗**253**] in der Reese Palley Gallery in der Maiden Lane, San Francisco, ohne Publikum auf. Zu letzterer sagte Fox im Interview, dass eine Ecke das Gegenteil einer Wand sei. Er habe sich bemüht, seinen Körper so weit wie möglich in die Ecke zu drücken, habe aber am Ende das Gleichgewicht verloren.[4]

Diese und ähnliche Aktionen kreisen um die Themen Energieaustausch, Materialerkundung und Abtasten der eigenen körperlichen Grenzen. Etwa zur gleichen Zeit unternahmen einige seiner Künstlerkollegen vergleichbare Studien: Chris Burden (1946–2015) war noch Student an der University of California, Irvine, als er sich in einen Metallspind zwängte und fünf Tage lang nur Wasser zu sich nahm, Bruce Nauman zeichnete ein 60-minütiges Video auf, in dem er rückwärts gegen eine Mauer fällt[5], und Vito Acconci zwang sich in *Hand and Mouth* [↗**27**] immer wieder die Faust in den eigenen Mund, bis er würgte.

Für die Interpretation von Fox' Arbeiten ist es erwähnenswert, dass er im Alter von 17 Jahren am Hodgkin-Lymphom erkrankte, einem bösartigen Tumor des Lymphsystems, was viele seiner frühen Performances und Installationen prägte. Seinem Künstlerkollegen Barney Bailey zufolge bewahrte sich Fox trotz seines Gesundheitszustands, der wiederholte Krankenhausaufenthalte und eine viermonatige Quarantäne im Krankenhaus der University of California erforderte, seinen Humor. Er war „besonders vom Ironischen angezogen, das er als Brücke in eine andere Welt nutzte, und wenn er dort war, machte er sich diese zu eigen"[6].

Following these first very public events, Fox did an about-face and for the next few years engaged in a series of intensely personal actions, such as *Wall Push*, 1970 [↗**25**] in which he pressed his body against a brick wall in an alley. As Fox described it, "it was like having a dialogue with the wall, exchanging energy with it. I pushed as hard as I could for about eight or nine minutes, until I was too tired to push anymore."[3] No one witnessed this action; we know it only through a black-and-white photograph. Similarly, in 1970 he performed *Opening My Hand as Slowly as Possible* in his studio, and *Pushing into a Corner* [↗**253**], without an audience, at the Reese Palley Gallery on Maiden Lane in San Francisco. Speaking of the latter, Fox noted that the corner is the opposite of a wall. He tried with difficulty to push as much of his body as possible into the corner, but finally lost his balance.[4]

These and similar actions were about energy exchange, the exploration of matter, and testing the limits of his body. Around the same time several of his peers were undertaking related explorations: Chris Burden (1946–2015), while still a graduate student at the University of California, Irvine, wedged himself into a metal locker for five days, consuming only water; Bruce Nauman videotaped falling backwards against a wall for a full sixty minutes;[5] and Vito Acconci, in *Hand and Mouth* [↗**27**], forced his fist into his mouth again and again until he gagged.

In interpreting Fox's work, however, it is important to know that, from the age of seventeen, he suffered from Hodgkin's disease, a type of lymphoma, and this informed much of his early performance and installation work. According to fellow artist Barney Bailey, despite his condition, which required repeated hospitalizations including four months in isolation at the University of California Medical Center, Fox retained a sense of humor. He was "especially drawn to the ironic, which he would use as a bridge to another world and, once there, make it his own."[6]

It was Nauman who led Fox to regard his body as a sculptural material. Nauman admits to "using my body as a piece of material and manipulating it"[7] in fiberglass sculptures as early as the mid-1960s. He had been a graduate student at the University of California, Davis, about two hours northeast of San Francisco, from 1964 to 1966 and subsequently taught part-time at the San Francisco Art Institute before moving to Pasadena, California, at the end of the decade. Despite their proximity, none of the artists in the MOCA circle knew Nauman personally – he was leaving the area just as they were getting started – but many of them, including Fox, saw and were struck by Nauman's 1969–70 exhibition at the Reese Palley Gallery that featured a number of his body-related films and videos. *Art Make-Up* (1967–68) especially impressed Fox; in it Nauman

Es war Bruce Nauman, der Fox darauf brachte, seinen Körper als bildnerisches Material zu betrachten. Nauman berichtet, schon Mitte der 1960er Jahre für Glasfaserplastiken „den eigenen Körper als Werkmaterial benutzt und bearbeitet zu haben"[7]. Er hatte nach seinem Studium von 1964 bis 1966 an der University of California, Davis, die zwei Stunden nordöstlich von San Francisco lag, in Teilzeit am San Francisco Art Institute unterrichtet, bevor er gegen Ende des Jahrzehnts nach Pasadena, Kalifornien, umzog. Trotz der räumlichen Nähe kannte keiner der Künstler des MOCA-Kreises Nauman persönlich – und so verließ er die Region, als die anderen gerade erst anfingen. Aber viele von ihnen, auch Terry Fox, sahen Naumans Ausstellung 1969/70 in der Reese Palley Gallery, die eine Reihe seiner körperbezogenen Filme und Videos zeigte, und waren tief beeindruckt. *Art Make-Up* (1967/68) imponierte Fox besonders. In dem Film bearbeitete Nauman sein Gesicht und seinen Torso wie eine Leinwand, die er nach und nach weiß, rosa, grün und schließlich schwarz bemalte. Wie Fox hatte Nauman mit Malerei angefangen, aber das Medium nach einigen Monaten im Hauptstudium aufgegeben – man könnte sagen, dass *Art Make-Up* seine Abkehr von der traditionellen Malerei repräsentiert.

Der New Yorker Künstler Vito Acconci und der in Südkalifornien lebende Chris Burden, zwei häufige Gäste im MOCA, machten ebenfalls körperzentrierte Performances. In *Trademarks* (1970) [↗**27**] beispielsweise biss sich Acconci in die Haut. Burden gab eine Reihe durchaus gefährlicher Körperperformances, darunter die berüchtigte *Shoot* (1971) [↗**29**], in der sein Freund eine Kugel durch Burdens Arm schoss. Bei allen Gemeinsamkeiten von Fox mit Nauman, Acconci und Burden sind Fox' Performances eher meditativ und persönlich, fördern häufig einen tranceähnlichen Zustand, wohingegen die von Nauman kühl und distanziert wirken und die von Burden spannungsgeladen bis angsteinflößend. Solche Arbeiten wurden durch Berichte der Zeitschrift *Avalanche* bekannt, dem Hausblatt der internationalen Konzeptkunst. Ihr Herausgeber Willoughby Sharp organisierte eine Videoschau für das MOCA – die erste in den USA – mit dem Titel „Body Works", die Tom Marioni in Breen's Bar im Erdgeschoss des MOCA-Gebäudes in der 75 Market Street vorführte. Neben Marioni und Fox enthielt das Sammelvideo Nauman, Burden, Acconci, Dennis Oppenheim, William Wegman und Keith Sonnier. Fox verehrte diese Künstler – er bot Acconci und Oppenheim an, bei seiner Ausstellung 1971 in der Reese Palley Gallery, New York, mitzumachen. Doch die eigentlichen Impulse für seine künstlerische Entwicklung bezog er nach eigener Einschätzung von Fluxus. Fluxus war für ihn vor allem eine europäische, ur-konzeptuelle Bewegung, die die Herstellung vermarktungsfähiger Objekte ablehnte. Fluxus-Mitglieder

Vito Acconci, *Hand and Mouth*, 1970,
photo: Kathy Dillen, courtesy Vito Acconci

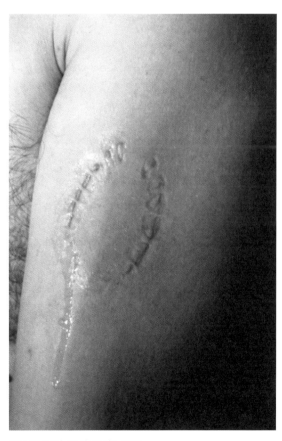

Vito Acconci, *Trademarks*, 1970,
photo: Bill Beckley, courtesy Vito Acconci

wie George Brecht und Yoko Ono hatten tatsächlich seit den späten 1950er Jahren kurze, körperorientierte Performances aufgeführt. Und aus der Zeitschrift *Dé-collage* von Wolf Vostell erfuhr Fox von Joseph Beuys (1921–1986), der den größten Einfluss auf ihn haben sollte.

Damals war Beuys noch nicht in den Vereinigten Staaten aufgetreten, aber in Künstlerkreisen durch ein Interview mit dem *Avalanche*-Herausgeber Sharp in der Dezember-Ausgabe der Zeitschrift *Artforum* von 1969 bekannt geworden. (Sharp porträtierte Beuys 1970 in der ersten Ausgabe von *Avalanche*.) Fox jedoch kannte Beuys und auch italienische Künstler der Arte Povera von seinen Reisen nach Europa, und dieses Wissen gab er seinen Freunden in San Francisco weiter. Obwohl er sich bei aller Bewunderung für Joseph Beuys nie in der Rolle des Predigers sah, lag es doch vor allem an Fox, dass die Arbeiten der jungen Konzeptkünstler in San Francisco mehr Gemeinsamkeiten mit ihren europäischen Pendants hatten als mit denen in New York, dessen Künstler, mit Ausnahme von Acconci und weniger anderer, eher auf der Grundlage von Systemen und linguistischen Strukturen arbeiteten. Paul Kos etwa, der zum MOCA-Kreis gehörte, verwendete gewöhnliche Alltagsmaterialien, wie es Beuys und die italienischen Vorbilder taten.[8] Und Marioni übernahm seine Idee der Sozialen Plastik von Beuys, der 1970 im Oakland Museum ein „soziales Kunstwerk" vorgestellt hatte, bei dem er eine Gruppe von Freunden ins Museum einlud, das an diesem Tag geschlossen hatte. Nachdem sie dort Bier getrunken und sich „gut unterhalten" hatten, ließen sie zur Dokumentation ihrer Aktion die Abfälle liegen.[9]

Wie Fox hatte Beuys schweres körperliches Leid durchlebt – in seinem Fall war es keine Krankheit, sondern ein Flugzeugabsturz im Zweiten Weltkrieg auf der Krim, wo er Bordschütze bei der Luftwaffe war. Beuys' Bericht zufolge war er kurz vor dem Erfrieren, als ihn nomadisierende Tataren aus dem Schnee holten und in ihr Dorf mitnahmen, wo sie ihn in Schichten aus tierischem Fett und Filzdecken hüllten und wärmten. Man muss nichts von den erlittenen Qualen wissen, um einen Zugang zur Kunst der beiden Künstler zu finden, nichtsdestotrotz bilden sie die Grundlage für vieles von dem, was sie später schaffen sollten. In beiden Fällen kommen bestimmte Materialien in ihren Arbeiten vor, die mit ihren jeweiligen traumatischen Erfahrungen zusammenhängen: bei Fox das Blut, die Schläuche und Verbände, bei Beuys der immer wieder verwendete Filz und das Fett. Fox stellte fest, dass er mit Beuys das Interesse an Energie und Regeneration teilte.[10] Dies wird bei *Levitation* (1970) [↗**31**] deutlich sichtbar, einer der aufwendigsten frühen Performances von Fox im Richmond Art Center.[11] Er beschrieb sie so: „Ich wollte mit meiner Arbeit einen Raum schaffen, der für eine Levitation geeignet war.

treats his face and torso as a canvas, painting them sequentially white, pink, green, and finally black. Like Fox, Nauman had begun as a painter but a few months into his graduate studies had abandoned the medium – one could say that *Art Make-Up* represented his rejection of traditional painting.

New York artist Acconci and Southern California–based Burden, frequent visitors to MOCA, were also doing body-centered performances. In *Trademarks*, 1970 [↗**27**] for example, Acconci bit his own skin. Burden did a series of potentially dangerous body performances, including the notorious *Shoot*, 1971 [↗**29**] in which his friend put a bullet through Burden's arm. Although Fox had many commonalities with Nauman, Acconci, and Burden, his performances tended to be meditative and personal, often inducing a trancelike state, while Nauman's were cool and detached, Acconci's often confrontational, and Burden's tense or even frightening. Works like these were being disseminated through reportage in *Avalanche* magazine, which served as the house organ for international conceptual art. Willoughby Sharp, its editor, organized a video show for MOCA – the first in the US – titled *Body Works*, which Marioni showed at Breen's Bar located on the ground floor of the MOCA building at 75 Market Street. In addition to Marioni and Fox, the compilation tape included Nauman, Burden, Acconci, Dennis Oppenheim, William Wegman, and Keith Sonnier.

Fox admired these artists – he invited Acconci and Oppenheim to participate in an exhibition he had at Reese Palley's New York gallery in 1972 – but he cites Fluxus as the real catalyst for his artistic development. Fluxus was a mostly European, proto-conceptual movement that rejected marketable object making. Indeed, Fluxus members such as George Brecht and Yoko Ono had been enacting short, body-oriented performances since the late 1950s. And it was through Fluxus artist Wolf Vostell's magazine *Dé-collage* that Fox first learned of German artist Joseph Beuys (1921–1986), who became his strongest influence.

At the time Beuys hadn't yet been seen in the United States, but artists there were becoming aware of him through an interview in the December 1969 issue of *Artforum* magazine by *Avalanche* editor Sharp. (Sharp would also feature Beuys in the first issue of *Avalanche* in 1970.) Fox, however, knew of Beuys and also the Italian Arte Povera artists from his trips to Europe, and he brought back that information to his friends in San Francisco. While Fox, in his admiration for Beuys, never assumed the role of preacher, it was largely because of Fox that the young San Francisco conceptual artist made work that had more in common with their European counterparts than those in New York who, with the exception of Acconci and a few others, tended to base their work on systems and

Zuerst bedeckte ich den 18 × 9 Meter großen Fußboden mit weißem Papier und klebte auch weißes Papier an die Wände. Der Fußboden war vorher dunkel und wurde jetzt so leuchtend weiß, dass es flimmerte und in den Augen schmerzte, wenn man jemanden am anderen Ende anschaute. Es war ein so federnder Raum, dass jeder, der in ihm war, schon schwebte. Dann breitete ich anderthalb Tonnen Erde, die unterhalb des Highways in der Nähe der Army Street entnommen waren, auf einer quadratischen Fläche aus, 3,5 × 3,5 Meter groß. Die Form wurde mit vier Mammutbaumplanken – jeweils das Doppelte meiner Körperlänge – hergestellt, ich benutzte meinen Körper als eine Maßeinheit für die meisten Teile dieser Arbeit. Die Erde wurde bei dem Highway entnommen wegen der Idee der Explosion. Als der Highway gebaut wurde, wurde die Erde zusammengepresst. Jetzt kann man sich vorstellen, wie sie sich ausdehnt und aufgeht, wenn man sie befreit. Natürlich ist das physikalisch unmöglich. Aber mir genügte die reine Vorstellung davon. Ich versuchte ja auch aufzusteigen. Vorher fastete ich, um mich zu entleeren. […] Mit meinem Blut zog ich in der Mitte einen Kreis. Der Durchmesser entsprach meiner Körperlänge. Nach mittelalterlicher Vorstellung wird auf diese Weise ein magischer Ort erzeugt. Dann legte ich mich auf den Rücken in die Mitte des Kreises und hielt vier durchsichtige Plastikschläuche fest, die mit Blut, Urin, Milch und Wasser gefüllt waren. Sie repräsentierten die elementaren Flüssigkeiten, die ich aus meinem Körper austrieb. Ich lag sechs Stunden lang da mit den Schläuchen in meiner Hand und versuchte zu schweben.[12] Die Türen waren verschlossen. Niemand sah mich. Ich bewegte keinen Muskel. Ich schloss meine Augen nicht. Ich versuchte, die Blickrichtung nicht zu ändern. […] Ich versuchte, mir vorzustellen, den Boden zu verlassen, bis ich begriff, dass ich mir vorstellen musste, mich in die Luft zu erheben. Das änderte für mich alles, es funktionierte. Ich schwebte. Nach vier Stunden konnte ich keinen einzigen Teil meines Körpers mehr fühlen, noch nicht einmal meine sich ausdehnende und zusammenziehende Brust. […] Ich glaubte, anderswo zu sein. […] das Gefühl, außerhalb meines Körpers zu sein, hielt für zwei Stunden an."[13]

Nachdem Fox gegangen war, konnten Besucher den Raum betreten, wenn sie Marionis Werkbeschreibung vor dem Eingang zur Ausstellung gelesen hatten. Marioni schrieb: „In der Welt des Okkulten nimmt die Seele die Gestalt von Rauch oder Gas an und entweicht den Körperöffnungen, wenn sie den Körper verlässt."[14] (Auf dem Foto von Fox auf der Ankündigung der Ausstellung kommt Rauch aus seinem Mund. [↗110, 111]) Terry Fox war überzeugt davon, dass der Raum die Kraft und Essenz des Erlebten speicherte. Er war zwar nicht im herkömmlichen Sinn religiös, doch seine Aktionen

linguistic structures. Paul Kos, for example, who was in the MOCA circle, was inspired to use ordinary, everyday materials the way that Beuys and the Italians did.[8] And Marioni derived his idea of social sculpture from Beuys, initiating his first "social artwork" at the Oakland Museum in 1970 when he invited a group of friends to join him at the museum on a closed day. After they drank beer and "had a good time," they left the debris behind as a record of the act.[9]

Like Fox, Beuys had undergone severe physical hardship – in his case not an illness but a plane crash in Crimea during World War II when he was a gunner for the Luftwaffe. By his own account, Beuys was nearly frozen in the snow when he was rescued by a group of nomadic Tartars who took him to their village and warmed him with felt blankets over layers of animal fat. It was not necessary to know their personal ordeals to access the two artists' art, but these conditions underpin much of what they subsequently created. In both cases, certain materials related to their respective traumatic experiences appear in their work: for Fox, blood, tubes, and bandages; for Beuys, the repeated use of felt and fat. Fox noted that he shared with Beuys an interest in energy and regeneration,[10] which can be seen clearly in one of Fox's most elaborate early performances, *Levitation*, 1970 [↗**31**] at the Richmond Art Center.[11] Fox described it this way: "I wanted to create a space that was conducive to levitation. The first thing I did was to cover the sixty-by-thirty-foot floor with white paper and to tape white paper to the walls. The floor had been dark, but it became such a brilliant white that if you were at one end of it, it glared; it hurt your eyes to look at someone standing at the other end. It was such a buoyant space that anyone in it was already walking on

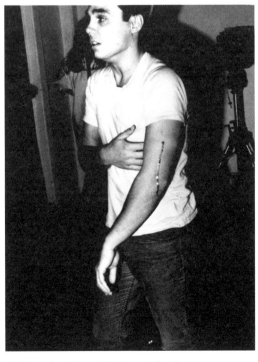

Chris Burden, *Shoot*, 1971, photo: Alfred Lutjeans

sprachen oft Spirituelles an. Vito Acconci legte es so aus: „Er wollte ein nicht-religiöser religiöser Mensch sein."[15] Acconci erinnert sich, dass Fox Beuys „verehrte"[16], dessen Vorliebe für ritualisierte Handlungen mit einfachen Gegenständen und Materialien er teilte. Bevor er Beuys 1970 in der Düsseldorfer Akademie aufsuchte, wo dieser unterrichtete, korrespondierte Fox mit ihm per Post. Die beiden Künstler verabredeten, gemeinsam eine Performance zu machen, bei der sie – gleichzeitig, aber jeder für sich – in einem kleinen Kohlenkeller unter der Akademie vor einem Publikum von etwa 30 Personen auftreten würden. Joseph Beuys für seinen Teil sah seine Performance als Requiem für ein gestorbenes Haustier, eine Maus. In seinem üblichen Anzug aus Filz und mit schwarzem Hut bekleidet, ließ er die Maus auf einer Tonbandspule kreisen. Daraufhin nahm er die Maus in die Hand, während er eine Cherimoyafrucht aß und die Kerne einzeln in eine kleine silberne Schale spuckte, was einen hellen Klang erzeugte. Terry Fox benutzte eine Kerze, einen Fensterrahmen mit vier Scheiben, zwei Rohre, ein langes und ein kurzes, Brandpaste, die an Napalm erinnerte, und eine tief abgehängte Glühlampe. Er formte mit der Paste ein Kreuz auf dem Boden und zündete es an. Dann schlug er die Rohre klingend auf den Boden und an das Fenster, wo er das Glas nach akustisch toten Stellen absuchte, bevor er die Glasscheiben mit den Rohren einschlug. Darauf nahm er die Kerze, stellte sie in der Raummitte auf den Boden und versuchte, ihre Flamme mit den Schallwellen der Rohre zu krümmen.

Das nachgeahmte Napalm bezog Fox in dieser Performance mit dem Titel *Isolation Unit* [↗**77–81**] auf die toxische Brandwaffe Napalm B, die von den US-amerikanischen Truppen in dem noch immer wütenden Vietnamkrieg breit eingesetzt wurde. Die erste Demonstration gegen den Einsatz von Napalm hatte bereits 1966 auf dem Berkeley-Campus stattgefunden, der rasch zum Ort der Antikriegsbewegung wurde. *Isolation Unit* war nicht das erste Mal, dass Fox seinen Protest gegen den Krieg ausdrückte. Im gleichen Jahr hatte Fox am Eröffnungsempfang einer Gruppenausstellung im University Art Museum von Berkeley nichtsahnende Wartende in Angst und Schrecken versetzt, als er in der Nähe des Eingangs ein rechteckiges Feld in einem Beet mit chinesischem Jasmin in Brand gesetzt hatte. Das Museum hatte Fox die Aktion zwar genehmigt, aber den Mitarbeitern war nicht bewusst, wie großflächig sie sein würde, sagte er.[17] In dieser Aktion mit dem Titel *Defoliation* (1970) [↗**32, 102, 103**] thematisierte Fox eindeutig die Gräuel, die sowohl das Land als auch die Bevölkerung Vietnams erlitten. Später sagte er: „Als die Leute am nächsten Tag kamen, um Mittag zu essen, gab es nur ein ausgebranntes Beet. Ich meine, es war genau das, was man

air. Then I laid down on a ton and a half of dirt, taken from under a freeway on Army Street, in an 11 ½ foot square. The mold was made with four redwood planks, each twice my body height – I used my body as a unit of measure for most of the elements in the piece. The dirt was taken from the freeway because of the idea of explosion. When the freeway was built, the earth was compressed, held down. You can conceive of it expanding when you release it, rising, becoming buoyant. Of course, it's physically impossible. But for me the mere suggestion was enough. I was trying to rise, too. I fasted to empty myself. […] I drew a circle in the middle of the dirt with my own blood. Its diameter was my height. According to the medieval notion, that creates a magic space. Then I lay on my back in the middle of the circle, holding four clear polyurethane tubes filled with blood, urine, milk, and water. They represented the elemental fluids that I was expelling from my body. I lay there for six hours with the tubes in my hands, trying to levitate.[12] The doors were locked. Nobody saw me. I didn't move a muscle. I didn't close my eyes. I tried not to change my focal point. […] I was trying to think about leaving the ground until I realized I should be thinking about entering the air. For me, that changed everything, made it work, I mean, I levitated. After the fourth hour, I couldn't feel any part of my body, not even my chest expanding and contracting […] the feeling of being out of my body persisted for about two hours."[13]

After Fox left, people could enter the space once they had read Marioni's description posted at the entrance to the gallery. Marioni wrote, "In the world of the occult, when the spirit leaves the body, it takes the form of smoke or gas and leaves through the openings in the body."[14] (The announcement of the show has a photograph of Fox's head with smoke coming from his mouth. [↗**110, 111**]) Fox believed that the space retained the powerful essence of what had occurred. Although Fox was not religious in the conventional sense, his actions often evoked the spiritual. As Vito Acconci put it, "He wanted to be a non-religious religious person."[15]

Acconci remembers that Fox "idolized"[16] Beuys, with whom he shared a penchant for ritualistic actions involving simple objects and materials. Before seeking Beuys out in 1970 at the Kunstakademie Düsseldorf where Beuys was teaching, Fox communicated with him by mail. The two artists agreed to perform together – working simultaneously though independently – in a small coalstorage room in the basement of the school before an audience of around thirty. For his part, Beuys viewed his performance as a requiem for a pet mouse that had died. Wearing his customary felt suit and black hat, he gave the mouse a ride on a tape recorder reel. He then held the mouse in his hand while eating a cherimoya fruit and spitting out the seeds one at a time into a small silver bowl, which

Terry Fox, *Levitation*, Richmond Art Center, 1970, photo: Jerry Wainright

in Vietnam machte. Niemand von ihnen regte sich auf, weil auf Vietnam Napalm abgeworfen wurde, aber wenn einige Blumen verbrannt werden, neben denen sie gerne sitzen …"[18] Bonnie Sherk, eine der wenigen weiblichen Künstlerinnen im MOCA-Kreis, hat diese Aktion als ebenso schrecklich wie eindrucksvoll in Erinnerung. Es war ihre erste Begegnung mit Fox.[19] Auch Howard Fried, der ebenfalls ein prägendes Mitglied der MOCA-Gruppe werden sollte, lernte Fox an diesem Abend kennen.

Doch *Defoliation* war Fox' einzige direkt politische Aktion. Sonst drückten sich seine politischen Ansichten genau wie seine anfällige Gesundheit in seinen Performances jener Jahre viel eher auf poetische Weise aus, wie bei *Pisces* und *Turgescent Sex* (beide 1971). Grundsätzlich war Fox überzeugt, dass eine direkte politische Stellungnahme im Bereich der Kunst nichts bewirkt. 1992 sagte er bei einer Podiumsdiskussion während seiner Ausstellung im Moore College of Art

created a ringing sound. Fox used a candle, a four-paned window, two pipes, one long and one short, fuel gel (resembling napalm), and a low-hanging light bulb. He made the shape of a cross on the floor with the fuel gel setting it on fire, and played the pipes by striking the floor and then the window as he searched for acoustic dead spots in the glass before shattering the glass panes with the pipe. He then took the candle, placed it in the middle of the floor, and attempted to bend its flame with the sound waves from the pipe.

Fox's simulation of napalm in this performance, titled *Isolation Unit* [↗**77–81**], was a reference to napalm B, a toxic incendiary device used widely by American troops in the still-raging Vietnam War. In fact, the first demonstrations against the use of napalm had taken place in 1966 on the Berkeley campus, which soon became the locus of the antiwar movement. Nor was *Isolation Unit* the first time Fox expressed his anger at the war. Earlier that same year, at the opening reception of

and Design in Philadelphia, es sei Unsinn, in der Kunstwelt politisch zu handeln, „weil man offene Türen einrennt"[20]. Auch andere zeitgenössische Künstler thematisierten ihre politischen Meinungen indirekt. Chris Burden beispielsweise sagte, *Shoot* sei eine Reaktion darauf gewesen, dass unbewaffnete Studenten, die 1970 in der Kent State University gegen den Krieg demonstrierten, von der Nationalgarde ermordet worden waren, aber er stellte dieses Ereignis bei seiner Performance nicht in den Vordergrund. Ähnlich stellte Nauman fest: „Ich glaube, ich kenne keine gute Kunst oder nur sehr, sehr wenig gute Kunst, die irgendeine unmittelbare politische oder gesellschaftliche Auswirkung im Kulturellen hat [...]. Kunst ist politisch, weil sie die Grenzen dessen, was akzeptiert wird oder nicht akzeptiert wird, abklopft."[21]

Pisces war Fox' Beitrag zu der Ausstellung „Fish, Fox, Kos"[22] [↗104–107] im de Saisset Museum in Santa Clara. Fox fing *Pisces* im MOCA als nicht-öffentliche Aktion an. Ähnlich wie Beuys, der bei *Isolation Unit* eine tote Maus in der Hand wiegte und 1974 mit einem Kojoten drei Tage in einem Ausstellungraum lebte[23], benutzte Fox gelegentlich Tiere stellvertretend für Menschen. Er kaufte in San Franciscos China Town zwei lebende Seebarsche, setzte sich im Schneidersitz auf den Fußboden und befestigte den einen Fisch mit einer gespannten Schnur an seiner Zunge, den anderen an seinem Penis. So konnte er jede Erschütterung der beiden nach Luft schnappenden Fische wahrnehmen, bis sie starben. Danach lag er ruhend im de Young unter einem weißen Tuch, das horizontal im Raum aufgespannt war. Neben ihm lagen zwei eingeschaltete Stablampen und die beiden toten Fische, die nun mit Schnüren an seinem Haar und seinen Zähnen befestigt waren. Eine 1000-Watt-Lampe hing über dem Tuch. Fox blieb so liegen, bis die beiden Stablampen allmählich schwächer wurden und ausgingen. Der Gedanke an den Tod war ihm in dieser Phase angesichts der täglichen Nachrichten von Opfern auf beiden Seiten des Vietnamkriegs und der eigenen Gefährdung aufgrund seiner labilen Gesundheit allgegenwärtig.

Bei einer anderen nicht-öffentlichen Aktion, *Turgescent Sex* [↗76], packte Fox einen Fisch fest mit einer verknoteten Kordel ein und wickelte ihn dann sorgfältig wieder aus, wobei er Knoten für Knoten auflöste. Wieder dachte Fox über Tod und Krieg nach, insbesondere über die Opfer des Massakers von Mỹ Lai.[24] In einem Interview von 1979 beschrieb er seine Enttäuschung: „Was kann man tun? Man kann gegen den Krieg nichts tun, man kann auf die Straße gehen und sich erschießen lassen, man kann protestieren und Petitionen unterschreiben. Aber nichts hilft. [...] Der Fisch stellte die Vietnamesen dar, aber auch mich. [...] Mit verbundenen Augen löste ich einen Knoten, legte das eine Ende des Seils

a group exhibition at Berkeley's University Art Museum, Fox shocked unsuspecting attendees by burning a rectangular area in a bed of Chinese jasmine plants near the gallery entrance. Although the museum authorized Fox's action, he said they didn't know how extensive it would be.[17] In this act, titled *Defoliation*, 1970, [↗**32, 102, 103**], Fox was clearly alluding to the atrocities being visited upon both the land and the people of Vietnam. He later wrote, "So, then, the next day, when these people came to have their lunch there, it was just a burned out plot, you know. I mean it was the same thing they were doing in Vietnam, but you burn some flowers that they like to sit near."[18] Bonnie Sherk, one of the only female artists in the MOCA circle, remembers the action as both horrifying and powerful; it was her first encounter with Fox.[19] Howard Fried, who also became an integral part of the MOCA group, met Fox for the first time that evening as well.

Still, *Defoliation* was Fox's only overt political action. More commonly in his performances of the time, such as *Pisces* and *Turgescent Sex*, both 1971, political sentiment as well as his fragile health was expressed poetically. In general, Fox believed

Terry Fox, *Defoliation*, University Art Museum, Berkeley, 1970, photo: Barry Klinger

auf die linke Seite, das andere zur rechten, und dann löste ich die andere Hälfte des Knotens; wenn ich die Enden verwechselt hätte, hätte ich einen neuen Knoten erzeugt – das war wie das ganze System, der ganze Krieg war so komplex und es war so schwer, sich – wie nennst du es? –[herauszuziehen]. Genau das tat ich mit dieser Arbeit, ständig versuchte ich, die eine Hälfte von der anderen getrennt zu halten, damit schließlich der Fisch von seinen Fesseln befreit war. Und dann nahm ich die Fesseln, machte ein Nest daraus, legte den in die Augenbinde eingewickelten Fisch hinein und blies Rauch darüber, es war einfach wie eine Erlösung von Schuld. Es war so persönlich für mich, weil es ein Labyrinth von Umständen war, man weiß, dass es einen Weg hinaus geben muss, egal wie schwer es ist, man kann es schaffen. Es spielt keine Rolle, ob es 400 fest verschnürte Knoten sind – man muss einfach sehr langsam arbeiten, eins nach dem anderen."25

Es mag ein Zufall sein, dass Fox auf ein Labyrinth anspielte, jedenfalls beschäftigte er sich wenig später – fast wie ein Besessener – mit dem Labyrinth der Kathedrale von Chartres, in der er eine Metapher für seine eigene Existenz sah. Von 1972 bis 1978 beziehen sich viele seiner Arbeiten darauf, einige davon sind Klangarbeiten: *The Labyrinth Scored for the Purrs of 11 Different Cats* (1973) [↗238, 239] – jede Katze steht für einen der elf konzentrischen Ringe im Labyrinth; ein Pendel, das an einer Klaviersaite von der Decke hängt und von Hand mit Schwung angestoßen um ein Glas mit Wasser kreist, bis es schließlich sanft klingend das Glas streift; und eine andere Arbeit mit einem Pendel, bei der ein Warnton erzeugt wird. Das Labyrinth selbst war ein performativer Raum für diejenigen Besucher, die bereit waren, dem 55 m langen Pfad bis zur Mitte auf Händen und Füßen zu folgen. Es symbolisierte den beschwerlichen Weg in den Himmel.

Die Arbeit, die am deutlichsten mit Fox' gesundheitlicher Verfassung zusammenhing, war die Installation *Hospital* von 1971 in der Reese Palley Gallery. Vier Monate vor der Eröffnung war er nach der Entfernung seines durch die Bestrahlungen zerstörten Brustbeins im Krankenhaus in Quarantäne gewesen [↗114]. Die Einladungskarte zeigte eine Fotografie von Fox im Krankenhaus mit einem Infusionsschlauch, der auf seine Rippen geklebt war, und ein Zitat von Artaud: „Diese Sünde bestand in einer Versuchung, die mich überkam, den Odem meines Herzens durch einen Schlauch über Innen- und Außenhaut zu leiten." *Hospital* sollte die „Furcht, Beklemmung und Langweile" erzeugen, die er selbst erfahren hatte.26 Er verteilte Gegenstände auf die Ausstellungsräume, die aber miteinander verknüpft waren: roter Stoff auf dem Fußboden, an Blut erinnernd, daneben eine Schüssel mit Wasser und Seife; eine Wärmelampe; eine Tafel mit zum Teil weggewischten Behandlungsgebühren; zwei Kassettenrekorder, auf dem

that direct political commentary in art was ineffectual. In a panel discussion during his 1992 exhibition at the Moore College of Art and Design in Philadelphia he said that to do something political in the art world is pointless, "since you are simply preaching to the converted."20 Other artists of the time also addressed their political views obliquely. Burden, for example, said *Shoot* was a response to the 1970 killing of unarmed student war protestors at Kent State University by the National Guard, but he did not foreground that event at the time of the performance. Likewise, Nauman observed, "I don't think I know any good art, very, very little good art that has any direct political or social impact on culture [...] art is political in the sense that it pokes at the edges of what's accepted or what's acceptable."21

Pisces was Fox's contribution to the exhibition "Fish, Fox, Kos"22 [↗104–107] at the de Saisset Museum in Santa Clara. Fox began *Pisces* at MOCA as a private action. Like Beuys, who had cradled a dead mouse in *Isolation Unit* and in 1974 famously lived with a wild coyote for three days in a gallery,23 Fox at times used animals as human surrogates. Having purchased two live sea bass in San Francisco's Chinatown, Fox sat cross-legged on the floor with one fish attached to his tongue by a taut cord, the other to his penis, so he could experience every vibration of the two fish as they struggled to breath before expiring. Later, at the de Young, he lay sleeping under a white cloth stretched horizontally across the gallery. He had placed beside him two illuminated flashlights and the two dead fish, now attached with strings to his hair and teeth. A thousand-watt light bulb was suspended above the cloth. Fox remained in this position until the two flashlights grew progressively dimmer and burned out. Death was never far from his mind during this period, what with the daily reports of casualties on both sides of the war in Vietnam and the very real possibility of death from his own precarious health.

In another private action, *Turgescent Sex* [↗76], Fox wrapped a fish tightly in knotted cord and then released it by painstakingly untying the rope, knot by knot. Fox was again thinking about death and the war, specifically the victims of the Mỹ Lai massacre.24 He expressed his frustration in a 1979 interview: "What can you do? You can't do anything about the war, you could go out in the street and get shot, or you could protest and sign a petition, but nothing was working. [...] The fish represented the Vietnamese and also represented me. [...] Blindfolded, I untied one knot and put this side of the rope to the left, this side to the right, and then untied the other half of the knot; if I got the strands mixed up the whole thing formed another knot and – it was like the whole system, the whole war was like that – it was so complex and hard to – what do you call it, extradite yourself – [...] Extricate. And that's what I did

einen war Fox' Atmen zu hören, auf dem anderen sein Gesang von Nadeln, die in seinen Körper eindringen; zwei mit Brotteig umhüllte Pfosten, Kabel, getrocknete Weißbrotstücke, mehrere strukturierte Schwarzweißzeichnungen sowie eine angelehnte Krankentrage.[27] Er erklärte: „Die Wasserschüssel und die Seife sind Ritual, die Krankentrage ist Klaustrophobie [...] die Zeichnungen zeigen die Brotoberfläche, das ist meine Wunde [...] die Kabel – der arterielle Blutkreislauf [...]."[28]

Im Jahr 1973 organisierte die Kuratorin des University Art Museums, Brenda Richardson, die Einzelausstellung „Yield" [↗55, 56, 142–153], in der Fox den Ausstellungsraum mit einem Nesselvorhang abtrennte und seine Aktionen wie in Trance durchführte. Wieder ließ Fox einfache, natürliche Materialien und Objekte zusammenwirken: Mehl, Wasser, einen Spiegel und eine Emaille-Schüssel. Die Aktionen konnten von den Besuchern als Schatten beobachtet werden oder vom Außenbalkon aus direkt durch die Fenster. Über drei Tage machte Fox Brot, blies Rauch, gestaltete mit Mehl ein Bild von einem Brustkorb. Obwohl seine Krankheit inzwischen geheilt worden war, beschäftigte ihn das Thema seiner bisher anfälligen Gesundheit weiter.

Die Berkeley-Ausstellung stellt einen Wendepunkt in der Performancekunst von Fox dar. Bis dahin hatte er sich wenig für sein Publikum interessiert und sich bewusst nicht um die Zuschauer gekümmert, um sich auf seine eigenen Handlungen zu konzentrieren. Seine Einstellung war: „ich bin in meine Arbeit involviert, so sehr ich kann. Ich versuche, alles zu geben. Und wenn ich das tue, dann ist es das, wofür ich verantwortlich bin. Das Publikum ist dafür verantwortlich, was es davon hat."[29] Doch in seiner nächsten Folge von Performances fand er einen Weg, mit dem Publikum durch Klang intuitiv und direkt zu kommunizieren, über Sprach- und Kulturgrenzen hinweg, bis hin zur Veränderung von Bewusstseinszuständen.

Auch wenn Fox sich bis dahin in den öffentlichen und nichtöffentlichen Performances vor allem mit seinem Körper und dem Zusammenwirken von Material und Energie auseinandergesetzt hatte, spielte Klang, insbesondere Perkussion, dabei oft eine Rolle. Unter anderem symbolisierte Klang für ihn den Herzschlag – und zwar den seines eigenen Herzens. Tom Marioni gab diesem neuen Interessengebiet ein Forum. Eine von Marionis ersten Veranstaltungen im MOCA hieß „Sound Sculpture As", und sie widmete sich 1970 wahrscheinlich als seine erste ausschließlich der Klangkunst. An diesem Abend entwickelten neun Künstler aufeinanderfolgende Stücke, in denen Klang das Hauptmedium war. Fox erzeugte perkussive Klänge durch Schläge und Bewegungen mit einer Metallschale, die mit Wasser gefüllt war, und kratzte später mit einer Schaufel am Fußboden. Für *Halation*, seinen

with this piece, always trying to keep the one half separate from the other, so that finally the fish could get removed from its bonds. And then taking the bonds and making a nest out of them and putting it in the nest, and then blowing smoke over it – it was like – it was just like a release, a release from guilt. And it was also personal for me, because it was a labyrinth of circumstances, you know that there must be a way to get out of it, no matter how hard it is, you really can do it – it doesn't matter if there are four hundred knots and they're tied real tight – you just have to go real slowly, one at a time."[25]

It might be coincidental that Fox alluded to a labyrinth, but very soon after, he became engaged – one could even say obsessed – with the labyrinth at Chartres Cathedral, which he saw as a metaphor for his own being. From 1972 to 1978 he made many works related to it, several of which included sound: *The Labyrinth Scored for the Purrs of 11 Different Cats* [↗238, 239] (each cat representing one of the eleven concentric rings in the labyrinth); a pendulum suspended by piano wire from the ceiling, manually swung around a glass of water, and finally gently hitting the glass; and another pendulum work that produced a warning sound. The labyrinth itself was a performative space designed for worshippers to follow the 180-foot path on their hands and knees until they reached the center, symbolizing the difficult path to heaven.

The culmination of Fox's works connected to his health was his 1971 installation *Hospital*, at the Reese Palley Gallery. Four months before the show he had been in isolation in the hospital following the removal of his sternum, which successive radiation treatments had destroyed [↗114]. On the announcement card was a photograph of Fox in the hospital with a tube penetrating his bandaged ribs and a quote by Artaud: "This sin consisted of a temptation visited on me to pass the breath of my heart through a tube to both sides of the surface." *Hospital* was designed to evoke the "fear, anxiety, and boredom" he experienced.[26] He filled the gallery with dispersed but related elements: red cloth, evoking blood, on the floor next to a bowl of water and soap; a heat lamp; a blackboard with hospital charges partially erased; two tape recorders, one with Fox's breathing, the other his chanting about the needles entering parts of his body; two poles wrapped in bread; wires; dried slices of white bread; several textured black-and-white drawings; and a leaning stretcher.[27] He explained, "The water bowl and the soap are ritual, the stretcher is claustrophobia [...] the drawings show the surface of the bread which is my wound [...] the wires = the arterial system [...]."[28]

In 1973 University Art Museum curator Brenda Richardson organized Fox's solo exhibition, titled *Yield* [↗55, 56, 142–153], in which he performed trancelike actions in a gallery sealed off by a muslin curtain. As usual, Fox interacted with

Klangbeitrag zu der Gruppenausstellung „South of the Slot" im Jahr 1974, schlug er mit einem Violinbogen an die Kanten einer Aluminiumschale und einer eisernen parabolischen Scheibe, was tiefe, nachklingende Töne erzeugte. Wie auch in anderen Arbeiten verwendete er Kerzen als Zeittaktung. Klang war für Fox stets skulptural und ortspezifisch. Nach *Halation* konzentrierte er sich vor allem auf die Geräusche, die durch das Schlagen, Zupfen oder Streichen von Klaviersaiten entstehen, die er an verschiedenen Objekten und Wänden befestigte und manchmal über größere Abstände spannte. Seine erste Klaviersaite verdankte er Barney Bailey, mit dem er das Atelier in der 16 Rose Street teilte.[30] Als er damit zu experimentieren begann, entdeckte Fox, dass der Klang nicht aus der Saite selbst kam, sondern aus dem, woran sie jeweils befestigt war.[31] „Es hat etwas mit Raum zu tun, [...] die Architektur des Raumes mithilfe von Klang verändern", stellte er fest.[32] Bei *Timbre* (1976), einer der ersten Aktionen mit Klaviersaiten, schlug Fox zur Antwort auf den Lärm einer vorbeifliegenden einmotorigen Cessna mit einem Stock die Klaviersaiten eines selbstgebauten Instruments. Die viereinhalbstündige Performance fand im Freilichttheater auf dem Gipfel des Mount Tamalpais in Marin County, nördlich von San Francisco, statt. „Die Saiten waren" bei diesem ungewöhnlichen Stück, so Fox, „über einen zwei Meter langen Holzkasten mit einer Metallschüssel als verschiebbarem Steg gespannt. Jedesmal, wenn das Flugzeug das Gebiet um die Performance überflog, änderte es die Geschwindigkeit, was wiederum die Tonhöhe des Propellergeräusches veränderte. Sobald sich das Flugzeug näherte, stimmte ich mein Instrument auf die neue Tonhöhe des Flugzeugs, indem ich den Steg verschob. Ich spielte dann in dieser Tonhöhe weiter, bis das Flugzeug erneut vorbeiflog. Um den Klang des Instruments zu verstärken, füllte ich den Souffleurkasten bis in Kniehöhe mit Wasser."[33] Obwohl Fox immer behauptete, John Cage habe ihn nicht beeinflusst[34], performte er wie Cage oft über einen längeren Zeitraum, einmal 22 Stunden, und machte noch weiter, als die meisten Zuhörer schon gegangen waren. Al Wong, sein Künstlerkollege und enger Freund, sagte rückblickend, dass er der Einzige war, der bis zum Ende von *Timbre* geblieben sei.[35]

Nach *Timbre* kamen viele weitere Arbeiten mit Klaviersaiten: *552 Steps Through 11 Pairs of Strings* (1976) wurde im Atelier von Fox performt; *Culvert* (1977) fand in einem Tunnel in Missoula, Montana, statt. In vielen weiteren erkundete er die akustische Beschaffenheit der jeweiligen Umgebung. Nachdem er die San-Francisco-Bay-Area verlassen hatte, setzte er die Performances mit Klaviersaiten in New York und später in Europa fort, wo er bis zu seinem Tod 2008 lebte. Er war der erste Künstler, der die akustischen Einsatzmöglichkeiten

simple, elemental materials and props: flour, water, a mirror, and an enamel bowl. These actions were perceived by the visitor as shadows but could also be seen directly through the windows on the exterior balcony. Over a three-day period, Fox made bread, blew smoke, created an image of a rib cage with flour. Although by then his illness had been cured, he continued to allude to his previously precarious health.

The Berkeley exhibition marked a turning point in Fox's performance work. Until then he showed little interest in his audience, deliberately trying not to pay attention to spectators so that he could concentrate on his own actions. His attitude was, "I'm involved in the work the most that I can be involved in it; I try and give everything to it. And if I do that, then that's all that I am responsible for, you know? They're responsible for what they get out of it."[29] However, in his next series of performances he found a way to communicate directly with an audience through sound, which could be understood across languages and cultures, viscerally and emotionally, to the point of creating altered states of consciousness.

Even though Fox had focused primarily on his body and the interaction of matter and energy in his public and private performances up to this time, sound, particularly percussive sound, had often played a role. Among other things, sound symbolized the beating of the heart – his heart. Marioni provided a forum for this new area of interest. One of his first shows at MOCA was *Sound Sculpture As*, 1970, believed to be the first devoted solely to sound. During this one-night event, nine artists created sequential works in which sound was the primary medium. Fox made percussive sound by striking and moving a metal bowl filled with water and later scraped the floor with a shovel. For *Halation*, Fox's contribution to a 1974 group exhibition, *South of the Slot*, he made sounds by striking the edges of an aluminum bowl and an iron parabolic disc with a violin bow, producing deep, resonant sounds. As was his custom, he used candles as a timing element.

Sound for Fox was always sculptural and site specific. Subsequent to *Halation*, he concentrated primarily on the sounds made by striking, plucking, or bowing piano wire, which he attached to various objects and walls, sometimes stretched over very long distances. He credited Barney Bailey, fellow occupant of the studios at 16 Rose Street, with giving him his first piano wire.[30] As he began to experiment with it, Fox discovered that the sound came not from the wire itself but from whatever the wire was attached to.[31] "It has to do with space, changing the architecture of space with sound," he said.[32] In one of the earliest piano wire actions, *Timbre*, 1976, Fox beat with a stick a homemade piano wire instrument in response to the noise of a Cessna single-engine airplane flying above. The four-and-a-half-hour performance took place in an

von Klaviersaiten in Performances und Installationen umfänglich erforschte, doch er hörte damit auf, als andere Kollegen Klaviersaiten in ihre Performances übernahmen und vermarkteten.

Was denken Künstler seiner Generation über Fox? Bonnie Sherk findet seine Arbeiten kraftvoll, poetisch, aufregend und visuell wie konzeptuell herausragend. Sie empfindet eine besondere Verbundenheit mit ihm, weil beide, wie sie sagt, sowohl mit dem Herzen als auch dem Verstand arbeiteten.[36] Al Wong hatte früh erkannt, dass Fox ein großer Künstler war. Er erinnert sich an ein kleines Skizzenbuch von Fox im Atelier in der Rose Street mit Zeichnungen, die er für Tuschezeichnungen hielt. In Wirklichkeit hatte Fox das Buch über die Feuertreppe gehängt, wo Regen, Ruß und Wind Spuren auf den Seiten hinterlassen hatten. Einmal habe Fox ein brachliegendes Grundstück in der Nähe des MOCA betreten und Wong gebeten, ihm beim Anheben eines weggeworfenen metallenen Bürotischs zu helfen. Fox habe Klaviersaiten um ein Tischbein gebunden und das andere Ende an ein Gitter auf der Straße, dann habe er mit einem Essstäbchen auf der Saite gespielt. Wong bezeichnet dies als typisch für die intelligente und unkonventionelle Herangehensweise von Fox an alles, was er machte.[37] Für die Konzeptkünstler in der San-Francisco-Bay-Area waren Alltag und Kunst kaum zu trennen. Das traf in besonderer Weise auf Fox zu. Manchmal konnten selbst Fox' Künstlerfreunde nicht unterscheiden, was Kunst und was eventuell nur Atelierabfälle waren. Bailey erzählt von einem Besuch im Atelier von Fox: „Es war normal, dass alle möglichen Dinge in den Ateliers herumlagen und meistens fragte ich nicht nach, weil ich dachte, dass das zum Arbeitsprozess gehört und man später sehen würde, was es war. Einmal interessierte mich ein alter Holztisch. Vielleicht war es ein Zeichentisch, denn die Oberseite war schräg, soweit ich mich erinnere. Das Holz war auf der Oberseite mit etwas beschichtet, das sehr wässrigem Brotmehl glich und beim Trocknen zu einem schönen Muster geworden war. In der Mitte des Tischs lag etwas, das aussah wie zwei klotzige, backsteinartige Formen, die aus Wachs gewesen sein könnten. Sie lagen im rechten Winkel zueinander wie ein T und darauf lag ein ausgehöhltes Brot, um das eine Schnur gewickelt war. Mich erinnerte dieser Gegenstand auf dem T an eine Mumie. Es war eine gute Gelegenheit, ein Foto zu machen, da ich angefangen hatte, selbst zu entwickeln und dies ein gutes Testfoto sein würde. Ich machte es und habe das Foto noch heute. Ich hebe es auf, weil es mich an den Tag erinnert und daran, dass man sich beim Zuschauen im Arbeitsprozess immer wie kurz vor einer Entdeckung, einer Überraschung, fühlte. Ich habe Terry nie gefragt, was es mit dieser Arbeit auf sich hatte, ob etwas daraus geworden ist oder nicht."[38]

amphitheater atop Mount Tamalpais in Marin County, north of San Francisco. As Fox described this unusual piece, "The wires stretched over a 2-meter-long wooden box with a metal bowl and sliding bridge. Each time the airplane made a pass over the performance area it changed speed, which changed its propeller pitch. As the airplane approached, I returned my instrument to the new pitch of the airplane by moving the sliding bridge under the strings. I continued playing the same pitch until the next passing. To amplify the sound of my instrument, I filled the prompter's box to knee height with water."[33] Although Fox always said that John Cage was not an influence,[34] like Cage, he often performed over an extended period, once for twenty-two hours, continuing even after most of the audience had left. Al Wong, fellow artist and close friend, remembers that he was the only person who stayed to the very end of *Timbre*.[35]

Timbre was followed by many other piano wire works: *552 Steps Through 11 Pairs of Strings*, 1976, performed in Fox's studio; *Culvert*, 1977, performed in a tunnel in Missoula, Montana; and others in which he explored the acoustic nature of each environment. He continued piano wire performances once he left the Bay Area, first for New York and then for Europe, where he remained until his death in 2008. He had been the first artist to fully explore the sonic possibilities of piano wire in performances and installations, but he stopped once others began to adopt and commercialize piano wire performance.

What did Fox's peers think of him? Bonnie Sherk found his work to be powerful, poetic, exciting, as well as visually and conceptually stunning. She felt a special kinship with him, believing they both were working with the heart and the mind.[36] Al Wong recognized at the time that Fox was a great artist. He remembers seeing a small sketchbook in Fox's Rose Street studio that contained what looked like ink drawings. Actually, Fox had laid the book on the fire escape, and the rain and soot created the marks as the wind turned the pages. Another time, in an empty lot near MOCA, Fox went down below street level and asked Wong to help him lift up a discarded metal office desk. Fox tied one of its legs to piano wire and the other end to a grate on the street and struck the wire with a chopstick. To Wong this typified Fox's brilliant and unconventional approach to everything he did.[37] Characteristically, Bay Area conceptual artist made little distinction between their life and their art. This was certainly true of Fox. Sometimes even fellow artists were unable to distinguish between Fox's art and what might just be studio detritus. Bailey recalls being in Fox's studio one day: "It was common to see all sorts of things lying around artist studios, and I often did not ask about something, thinking it was in progress and time would tell what it was. In this case it was an old wood table. Maybe a draftsman's

Howard Fried erinnert sich, dass Fox an die Energie glaubte, mit der er bestimmte Gegenstände aufgeladen hatte, und dass er, wenn er mit ihnen hantierte, sein Publikum verzaubern konnte.[39] Der Künstler und emeritierte Professor der University of California, Berkeley, Jim Melchert erinnert sich, dass die Ausstellung von Fox 1973 im University Art Museum ihn sehr beeindruckte. Man habe Fox' Eigensinnigkeit schon an seinem Look erkannt, der sich mit den runden Brillengläsern und langen Haaren von allen anderen unterschied.[40] John Woodall, der zur selben Zeit in San Francisco Performance machte, verwendet das deutsche Wort „Handlung" im Sinne von Aktion oder Drama, um Fox' Arbeit zu beschreiben, und erklärt weiter: „Das Konzept ist natürlich maßgeblich, aber die eigentliche Sache ist die Tat – für ihn und für sein Publikum gleichermaßen äußerst emotional, herausfordernd und widersprüchlich. Ich bin seit je ein Bewunderer."[41] Fox machte weiter mit Performance, als die meisten seiner Generation – Acconci, Burden, Oppenheim, Sherk und andere – damit abgeschlossen hatten. In Europa sah er viele Möglichkeiten, seine Vorstellungen von Performance umzusetzen. Er war entsetzt über die Entwicklung der Performance zu einer Art Theaterbetrieb, vor allem in den USA, da er weiterhin von ihrem experimentellen Charakter überzeugt war. „Du musst bereit sein zu scheitern", betonte er 1991 im Gespräch.[42] „Performance ist medialisiert worden", meinte er, „[...] sodass man heute ebenso gut eine Schallplatte anhören oder einen Film ansehen kann."[43] Obwohl er Dutzende von Ausstellungen gemacht hatte, international aufgetreten war und sogar in jenen frühen Jahren an so wichtigen Ausstellungen wie der documenta 5 (1972), der São-Paulo-Biennale (1975) und der Whitney Biennial (1995) beteiligt war und ihm zahlreiche Artikel und Kataloge gewidmet wurden, blieb Fox immer eine Art Underground-Künstler. Er ist zwar in Europa bekannter als in den USA, aber ihm ging es nie um Berühmtheit. Er war sogar entschieden dagegen: „Ich will keinen Ruhm. Mein ganzes Leben lang habe ich versucht, meine Person so gut wie möglich aus allem herauszuhalten."[44]

Aus dem Englischen übersetzt von Anne Pitz

table, as I recall the top was at a slant. The wood top was resurfaced with what might have been very wet bread flour that had dried with a beautiful texture. In the middle of the table were what appeared to be two crude brick-shaped forms of what might have been wax, one positioned perpendicular to the other to form a T shape. On top of the T's spine was a hollow bread form coiled with string, an object that looked like or suggested a mummy laid out on the T. It was a great opportunity to shoot a photo as I was just starting printing my own, and this would be a good test shot. I did, and I still have the photo. I keep it just because it reminds me of the day and how seeing something in the making feels like you're on the edge of some discovery, some adventure. I never did ask Terry about that work and whether or not it developed into something."[38]

Howard Fried recalls that Fox believed in the power invested in certain objects, and that he could cast a spell on his audience when he interacted with those.[39] Jim Melchert, artist and professor emeritus at the University of California, Berkeley, recalls that Fox's 1973 exhibition at the University Art Museum made a very strong impression on him. He also notes that one sensed Fox's eccentricity, saying Fox even looked different from everyone else, with his round glasses and long hair.[40] John Woodall, who was doing performance in San Francisco at the same time, used the German word *Handlung*, meaning action or drama, to describe Fox's work, and went on to explain that "yes, concept is significant, but the act is the thing – intensely emotional, challenging, conflicting, for him as well as his audience. I have long been an admirer."[41]

Fox continued to perform long after most of his peers – Acconci, Burden, Oppenheim, Sherk, et al. – had ceased doing so. In Europe, he found many opportunities to perform on his own terms. He was dismayed at what performance had developed into, especially in the United States, that is, a kind of theater, a business, while he continued to believe in its experimental nature. "You should be willing to fail," he asserted in a 1991 interview.[42] "Performance has been media-ized," he believed, "[...] so that now it's not any different from listening to a record or watching a film."[43] Although he had dozens of exhibitions, performed widely, and even in those early years was included in such important exhibitions as documenta 5 (1972), the 1995 Whitney Biennial, and São Paulo Biennial (1975), and has been the subject of numerous articles and catalogues, Fox has remained something of an underground artist. Although better known in Europe than in the United States, he never sought fame. In fact he was very clear about not wanting it: "I don't want a big reputation. My whole life I've tried to stay as marginal as possible."[44]

1 Terry Fox im Gespräch mit der Verfasserin, San Francisco, 3.12.1991, fortan Fox/Lewallen 1991

2 Ebd.

3 Terry Fox, zitiert nach: Eva Schmidt (Hg.), *Terry Fox. Ocular Language. 30 Jahre Reden und Schreiben über Kunst. 30 Years of Speaking and Writing about Art.* Gesellschaft für Aktuelle Kunst Bremen, Köln 2000, S. 24, fortan Schmidt 2000 (Ich wollte, dass meine Stimmung ihr Aussehen beeinflusst. Interview mit Willoughby Sharp, zuerst in: *Avalanche*, Winter 1971, S. 70–81)

4 Ebd., S. 26

5 Bruce Nauman, *Bouncing in a Corner, No. 1*, 1968, Videoband, schwarzweiß, Klang, 60 Min.

6 Barney Bailey, E-Mail an die Verfasserin, 2.6.2015, fortan Bailey 2015

7 Bruce Nauman, zitiert nach Willoughby Sharp, Nauman Interview. In: *Arts Magazine*, (March 1970); nachgedruckt in: Janet Kraynak (Hg.), *Please Pay Attention Please: Bruce Nauman's Words*. Cambridge, MA 2002, S. 122, fortan Kraynak 2002

8 Paul Kos im Telefongespräch mit der Verfasserin, 8.6.2015

9 Tom Marioni, *Beer, Art and Philosophy*. San Francisco 2003, S. 93. Marionis Aktion hatte den Titel *The Act of Drinking Beer with Friends Is the Highest Form of Art*.

10 Terry Fox, vgl. Schmidt 2000, vgl. Anm. 3, S. 58 (Interview von Achille Bonito, zuerst in: *Domus*, Neapel, Italien, April 1973, S. 45)

11 Marioni verlor kurz nach dieser Veranstaltung seine Anstellung als Kurator. Die Verwaltung machte ihn für die entstandene Brandgefährdung verantwortlich.

12 Bruce Nauman versuchte ebenfalls in einer Aktion von 1966 zu schweben, bei der sein Körper zwischen zwei Stühlen balancierte. Die Aktion dokumentierte er mit einem doppelt belichteten Foto.

13 Schmidt 2000, vgl. Anm. 3, S. 14

14 Suzanne Foley (Hg.), *Space/Time/Sound: Conceptual Art in the San Francisco Bay Area, the 1970s.* San Francisco Museum of Modern Art, San Francisco 1981, S. 60f.

15 Vito Acconci, E-Mail an die Verfasserin, 3.6.2015

16 Ebd.

17 Terry Fox, vgl. Schmidt 2000, vgl. Anm. 3, S. 82 (Es ist der Versuch einer neuen Kommunikation: Interview von Robin White, zuerst in: *View*, Oakland, CA 1979, S. 11)

18 Ebd.

19 Bonnie Sherk im Telefongespräch mit der Verfasserin, 6.6.2015, fortan Sherk 2015

20 Fox Überblicksausstellung „Articulations" wurde vom 2. November bis zum 18. Dezember 1992 gezeigt.

21 Bruce Nauman, zitiert nach: Michele de Angelus, An Interview with Bruce Nauman, May 27 and 30, 1980. In: Kraynak 2002, vgl. Anm. 7, S. 285

22 Während er als Kurator am Richmond Art Center arbeitete, trug Marioni das Pseudonym Alan Fish, um seine künstlerischen Aktivitäten von seiner Arbeit als Kurator zu trennen.

23 Beuys' Stück *I Like America and America Likes Me* fand 1974 in der Galerie René Block in New York statt.

24 Bericht in Carl E Loeffler (Hg.), *Performance Anthology: A Source Book for a Decade of California Performance Art.* San Francisco 1980, S. 37

25 Schmidt 2000, vgl. Anm. 17, S. 82, 84

26 Cecile N. McCann, Hospital as Environment. In: *Artweek*, San Francisco, 2 (13.9.1971), Nr. 19, S. 1

27 Ebd.

28 Terry Fox, zitiert nach: Peter Plagens, Terry Fox: The Impartial Nightmare. In: *Artforum*, New York, Februar 1972, S. 76f.

29 Schmidt 2000, vgl. Anm. 17, S. 86, 88

30 Fox/Lewallen 1991, vgl. Anm. 1

31 Terry Fox, Vorlesung am San Francisco Art Institute, 15. April 1987, Mitschrift, San Francisco Art Institute Library

32 Schmidt 2000, vgl. Anm. 17, S. 92

33 Terry Fox, zitiert nach: Bernd Schulz (Hg.), *works with sound.* Saarbrücken 1998, S. 66

34 Fox/Lewallen 1991, vgl. Anm. 1

35 Al Wong im Telefongespräch mit der Verfasserin, 5.6.2015, fortan Wong 2015

36 Sherk 2015, vgl. Anm. 19

37 Wong 2015, vgl. Anm. 35

38 Bailey 2015, vgl. Anm. 6

39 Howard Fried im Telefongespräch mit der Verfasserin, 5.6.2015

40 Jim Melchert im Telefongespräch mit der Verfasserin, 6.6.2015

41 John Woodall, E-Mail an die Verfasserin, 7.6.2015

42 Fox/Lewallen 1991, vgl. Anm. 1

43 Schmidt 2000, vgl. Anm. 17, S. 15

44 Fox/Lewallen 1991, vgl. Anm. 1

1 Terry Fox, interview with the author, December 3, 1991, San Francisco, hereafter Fox/Lewallen 1991,

2 Ibid.

3 Terry Fox in Willoughby Sharp, "Terry Fox: I Wanted to Have My Mood Affect Their Looks" (interview), *Avalanche* (Winter 1971), pp. 70–81, hereafter Fox/Sharp 1971.

4 Ibid., p. 75.

5 Bruce Nauman, *Bouncing in a Corner, No. 1*, 1968, videotape, black and white, sound, 60 min.

6 Barney Bailey, email message to the author, June 2, 2015, hereafter Bailey 2015.

7 Bruce Nauman in Willoughby Sharp, "Nauman Interview," *Arts Magazine*, March 1970; reprinted in Janet Kraynak (ed.), *Please Pay Attention Please: Bruce Nauman's Words*, Cambridge, MA, 2002, p. 122.

8 Paul Kos, telephone conversation with the author, June 8, 2015.

9 Tom Marioni, *Beer, Art and Philosophy*, San Francisco, 2003, p. 93. Marioni's action was titled *The Act of Drinking Beer with Friends is the Highest Form of Art.*

10 Terry Fox in Achille Bonita Oliva, "Terry Fox" (interview), *Domus* (Naples, Italy), April 1973, p. 45.

11 Marioni lost his job as curator shortly after this event, the administration claiming it had constituted a fire hazard.

12 Bruce Nauman also attempted to levitate, in 1966, balancing his body between two chairs, an action that he documented in a double exposure photograph.

13 Fox/Sharp 1971, cf. note 3, p. 71.

14 Suzanne Foley (ed.), *Space/Time/Sound: Conceptual Art in the San Francisco Bay Area, the 1970s*, San Francisco Museum of Modern Art, San Francisco, 1981, pp. 60–61.

15 Vito Acconci, email message to the author, June 3, 2015.

16 Ibid.

17 Terry Fox, interview by Robin White, *View* (Oakland, CA, 1979), p. 11, hereafter Fox/White 1979.

18 Ibid.

19 Bonnie Sherk, telephone conversation with the author, June 6, 2015, hereafter Sherk 2015.

20 Fox's survey exhibition *Articulations* took place November 2 – December 18, 1992.

21 Bruce Nauman in Michele de Angelus, "An Interview with Bruce Nauman, May 27 and 30, 1980," Janet Kraynak (ed.), *Please Pay Attention Please: Bruce Nauman's Words*, Cambridge, MA, 2002, p. 285.

22 While a curator at the Richmond Art Center, Marioni adopted the pseudonym Alan Fish to distinguish his art activities from those as a curator.

23 Beuys's piece, *I Like America and America Likes Me*, took place in 1974 at the Rene Block Gallery in New York.

24 Statement in Carl E Loeffler (ed.), *Performance Anthology: A Source Book for a Decade of California Performance Art*, San Francisco, 1980, p. 37.

25 Fox/White, cf. note 17, p. 11.

26 Cecile N. McCann, "Hospital as Environment," *Artweek*, San Francisco, 2 (September 13, 1971) no. 19, p. 1.

27 Ibid.

28 Terry Fox, quoted in Peter Plagens, "Terry Fox: The Impartial Nightmare," *Artforum* (New York), February 1972, pp. 76–77.

29 Fox/White, cf. note 17, p. 14.

30 Fox/Lewallen 1991, cf. note 1.

31 Terry Fox, lecture at the San Francisco Art Institute, April 15, 1987, transcript, San Francisco Art Institute Library.

32 Fox/White, cf. note 17, p. 18.

33 Terry Fox, Bernd Schulz (ed.), *works with sound*, Saarbrücken, 1998, p. 66.

34 Fox/Lewallen 1991, cf. note 1.

35 Al Wong, telephone conversation with the author, June 5, 2015, hereafter Wong 2015.

36 Sherk 2015, cf. note 19.

37 Wong 2015, cf. note 35.

38 Bailey 2015, cf. note 6.

39 Howard Fried, telephone conversation with the author, June 5, 2015.

40 Jim Melchert, telephone conversation with the author, June 6, 2015.

41 John Woodall, email message to the author, June 7, 2015.

42 Fox/Lewallen 1991, cf. note 1.

43 Fox/White, cf. note 17, p. 15.

44 Fox/Lewallen 1991, cf. note 1.

Terry Fox – Kein Videokünstler   David A. Ross

Terry Fox – Not a Video Artist

Wenn es jemals so etwas wie einen Videokünstler gab, dann war es nicht Terry Fox. Nicht dass Fox an Künstlervideos desinteressiert gewesen wäre, im Gegenteil. Und es ist auch keineswegs so, dass Fox sich nicht mit den ideologischen Wurzeln der Technologie der Videokunst identifiziert hätte, denn das tat er voll und ganz. In ihrer ersten Phase stand die Videokunst in einem direkten Bezug zu denjenigen, die nach alternativen Formen des Widerstands, und, durch den Widerstand, der Opposition gegen die herrschende Kultur suchten. Tatsächlich gab es nur wenige Künstler, die ähnlich beunruhigt darüber waren, wie die Kunstwelt zu einer Teilmenge des Kunstmarkts geworden war. Und Video war ganz deutlich keine Funktion des Kunstmarkts. Fox war nicht einfach bloß ein weiterer reflexhafter Kunstwelt-Marxist, sprich, er lehnte nicht einfach nur die Idee ab, dass Künstler ihren Lebensunterhalt verdienen, indem sie ihre Werke im Kontext des Spätkapitalismus verkaufen. Doch die rasante Kommerzialisierung der amerikanischen Kunstszene war ihm zunehmend suspekt, und er äußerte offen seine Abscheu davor, wie Bildhauer aus rein ästhetischem Macho-Gebaren gewaltige Formate und Berge von Material verwendeten. Ich erinnere mich noch, wie unverhohlen er sich über Werke von Künstlern empörte, die er lange bewundert hatte, etwa Walter de Marias *Broken Kilometer* (1979) oder Richard Serras Stahlskulpturen im industriellen Maßstab. Fox empfand solche Skulpturen als eine Beleidigung gegenüber einer Welt, die von den Armen und Machtlosen bevölkert ist, und bemühte sich, Kunst zu machen, die nicht an einem solchen demonstrativen Konsum teilhatte.

Fox war ein Konzeptkünstler, der seine Werke auf ihre materielle und formale Kernaussage reduzieren wollte. Und das auf das absolut Wesentliche beschränkte, billige, schwarzweiße, verbrauchergerechte Video war hierfür zu diesem Zeitpunkt das richtige Medium, denn tragbares Video war noch kein industriell gefertigtes Produktionswerkzeug. Es war ein Produktionsmittel für das, was man als *Volksfernsehen* bezeichnen könnte. Das, was die Arbeit mit dieser Art Videoproduktionssystem implizierte, war inhärent alternativ und mit dem Aufstieg dessen verbunden, was man heute unter

If there ever was such a thing as a video artist, it wasn't Terry Fox. It's not that Fox was uninterested in artists' video, for he surely was. And it's not that Fox didn't deeply identify with the ideological roots of video art's technology – he most certainly did. In its first phase, video art was directly related to those seeking alternate ways of resisting (and by resisting, opposing) the dominant culture. In fact, there were few artists as deeply concerned by the manner in which the art world had become a subset of the art market than Terry Fox. And video was so clearly not a function of the art market. Fox wasn't just another art world knee-jerk Marxist – that is to say, he wasn't simply opposed to the idea of artists making a living by selling their work within the framework of Late Capitalism. But he was increasingly suspicious of the rapid commercialization of the American art scene, and openly disgusted by the way sculptors used massive scale and mountains of material simply for the sake of aesthetic machismo. I recall how openly upset he was by works by artists he had long-admired – like Walter de Maria's *Broken Kilometer* or the industrial-scale steel sculptures by Richard Serra. Fox felt that kind of sculpture was an insult to a world populated by the poor and the powerless, and sought to make art that did not partake of such obvious conspicuous consumption.

Fox was a conceptual artist who wanted to pare down his work to its material and formal essence. And bare-bone, cheap, black-and-white, consumer-grade video was the right medium for the moment, because portable video was not an industrial-level production tool. It was the means of production for what might be termed *people's television*. The implication of working with this kind of video production system was inherently alternative, and was linked to the rise of what is now known as a DIY (do-it-yourself) aesthetic. Publications, like *Radical Software*, and documentary video collectives, like the New York-based Videofreex or the San Francisco-based Video Free America, made it clear that individuals could challenge the hegemony of the broadcast television industry – at least in theory.

Although Fox was not part of the underground community's documentary video scene flourishing in San Francisco,

der Bezeichnung DIY (Do-it-yourself)-Ästhetik kennt. Zeitschriften wie *Radical Software* und Dokumentarvideokollektive wie Videofreex in New York oder Video Free America in San Francisco machten deutlich, dass der Einzelne, zumindest theoretisch, die Vorherrschaft der Fernsehindustrie herausfordern konnte.

Obwohl Fox nicht Teil der im Untergrund agierenden Gemeinschaft der Dokumentarvideoszene war, die in San Francisco florierte, wie andere, die in den späten 1960er und frühen 1970er Jahren in der Bay Area arbeiteten, sah er im Video ein geeignetes Medium für die Ausweitung performativer Aktionen. Und da er sich weniger für Kunst als Idee denn für Kunst als reine Erfahrung interessierte, schien ihm Video eine perfekte Möglichkeit, Aktionen aufzuzeichnen und mit anderen zu teilen, allerdings nicht als Teil einer gängigen, oder gar avantgardistischen, narrativen Strategie.

Nochmals: Fox hatte nichts gegen Ideen und definitiv nichts gegen Intellektualität, doch er suchte nach Kunst, die vor oder unterhalb der Sprache funktionierte, aber auf eine nicht-hierarchische Weise. Fox ging es nicht um ontologische Fragen, er suchte vielmehr nach etwas, das tatsächlich unsichtbar war. Seine performativen Arbeiten strebten nach dem Epischen und waren rigoros nicht-narrativ. Und obwohl Fox sich für den Körper als Subjekt und Objekt interessierte, mied er alles gängig Autobiografische oder Selbstporträthafte.

like others working in the Bay Area during the late 1960's and early 1970's, Fox saw video as an appropriate medium for the extension of performative actions. And since he was less interested in art as idea, than in art as pure experience, video seemed a perfect way of recording and sharing actions, yet not as part of a some standard (or even avant-garde) narrative strategy.

Again, Fox was not anti-idea, and clearly was not an anti-intellectual, but he was looking for art that would function before or below language, but in a non-hierarchical manner. Fox was not concerned with ontological issues, but rather he was searching for something that was actually invisible. His performative work aspired to the epic and was rigorously non-narrative. And though Fox was interested in the body as subject and object, he eschewed the stuff of standard autobiography or self-portraiture. As such, his video work was self-conscious, but not overtly so. It functioned in an abstract fashion, as an exploration of alternative notions of self and the *idea* of consciousness.

Generally speaking, Bay Area artists working in the early 1970's used video not for it's intrinsic formal capacities (i.e. the way the Fluxus artist Nam June Paik explored video as a way of provoking a response to popular media culture, or the way the performance artist Joan Jonas investigated its function as a different sort of mirror). One group of San

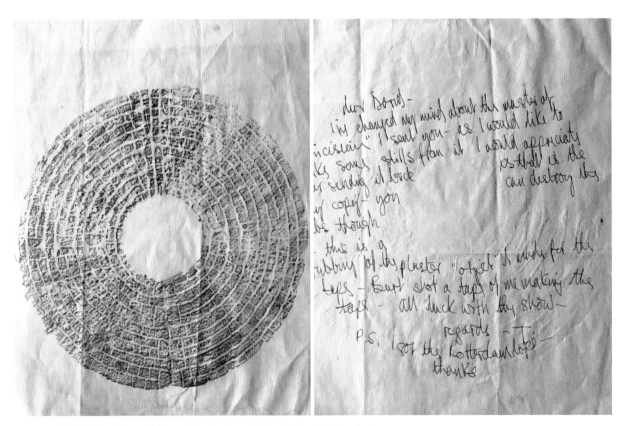

Terry Fox, Untitled (graphite rubbings of the plaster model for *Incision*), 1977, recto / verso

Insofern waren seine Videoarbeiten sich ihrer selbst bewusst, jedoch nicht auf unverhohlene Weise. Sie funktionierten in einer abstrakten Manier, als Erkundung alternativer Vorstellungen des Selbst und der *Idee* des Bewusstseins. Allgemein gesagt benutzten in den frühen 1970er Jahren tätige Künstler aus der Bay Area Video nicht wegen der diesem Medium innewohnenden formalen Fähigkeiten (das heißt so wie der Fluxuskünstler Nam June Paik Video als eine Möglichkeit erkundete, eine Reaktion auf die populäre Medienkultur zu provozieren, oder so wie die Performancekünstlerin Joan Jonas die Funktion von Video als eine andere Art Spiegel untersuchte). Eine Gruppe von Künstlern aus San Francisco wie etwa Stephen Beck untersuchte Video als Instrument zur Herstellung abstrakten Fernsehens. In der psychedelischen Kultur der Bay Area fand man rasch Gefallen daran. Andere Künstler aus San Francisco wie Paul Kos oder Howard Fried verwendeten Video einfach, um nicht-öffentliche Performances zu dokumentieren. Kos interessierte sich dafür, wie Sprache und Handeln miteinander in Konflikt geraten konnten, während Fried Video primär zur Erkundung komplexer psychologischer Perspektiven einsetzte. Fox' erstes Video, *Turgescent Sex* (1970) [↗**76**], zeigt den Künstler einfach mit verbundenen Augen und beim rituellen Zusammenbinden und Einwickeln eines Fischs. Das Werk, das wie eine buddhistische Zeremonie wirkt, tatsächlich aber eine Handlung ist, die mit der langen und schmerzhaften Genesung des Künstlers von einem Hodgkin-Lymphom zusammenhängt, hat ein langsames Tempo, und sein stummes, körniges Schwarzweißbild macht es zu einem idealen Format für eine private Meditation über die eigene Sterblichkeit. Allerdings sollte das Werk nicht als ein Mantra oder irgendeine Meditationshilfe für den Betrachter fungieren, sondern als ziemlich direkte Aufzeichnung einer Aktion, die nicht theatralisch in Szene gesetzt, sondern vielmehr als Zurschaustellung eines privaten Rituals gedacht war. Fox ging es nicht um irgendetwas, das mit Video an sich zu tun hatte, sondern vielmehr darum, einen Raum unterhalb der Sprache zu finden, in dem er Verbindung zu den unsichtbaren Energiequellen aufnehmen konnte, zu jener Schönheit der Welt, die jenseits des Sehvermögens liegt.

Seine ein Jahrzehnt während Besessenheit von dem Labyrinth, das in den Boden der großen gotischen Kathedrale in Chartres eingelassen ist, ist ein weiteres Beispiel für Fox anhaltende Auseinandersetzung mit dem Unsichtbaren und dem Unsagbaren. Das Labyrinth war kein bloßes Ziermotiv, sondern stellte eine Analogie zum Kreuz dar, so dass man sich, indem man die scheinbar verwickelten Wendungen des Labyrinths abschritt, vermittels einer direkten Handlung des Körpers dreimal auf die Gestalt des Kreuzes einließ. So wie

Francisco artists, such as Stephen Beck, explored video as a tool for making electronic abstract television. It quickly found favor in the Bay Area's psychedelic culture. Other San Francisco artists like Paul Kos or Howard Fried simply used video to document private performances. Kos was interested in the way language and action could be in conflict, while Fried was primarily using video to explore complex psychological perspectives.

Fox's first video, *Turgescent Sex* (1970) [↗**76**], simply presents the artist blindfolded and engaged in a ritualistic binding and wrapping of a fish. Seeming like some Buddhist ceremony, but in fact an action relating to his long and painful recovery from Hodgkin's Lymphoma, the work has a slow pace and its silent, grainy black-and-white image makes it an ideal format for a private meditation on one's mortality. The work was not intended to function as a mantra or any kind of viewer's meditation-aid, but rather as a very straightforward recording of an action that was not posed theatrically, but intended instead as the exposure of a private ritual. What interested Fox was not anything that had to do with video per se, but rather with finding a sub-linguistic space in which he could connect to the invisible sources of energy – the beauty of the world that lies beyond vision.

His decade-long obsession with the labyrinth embedded into the floor of the great French Gothic cathedral in Chartres is another example of Fox's ongoing concern with the invisible and the ineffable. More than a simple decorative motif, the labyrinth represented a physical analogue to the cross, and as such, if one walked the labyrinth's seemingly convoluted turns, one would have engaged three times – through direct action of the body – with the form of the cross. Like Buddhist prayer wheels, which allow illiterate Buddhist peasants to experience prayer through direct touch, the labyrinth allowed illiterate French Christian peasants to experience the cross in a physical, ecstatic fashion. Fox was interested in this idea of a direct physical, spiritual experience.

Fox made models and drawings of the Chartres labyrinth [↗**40**], and was excited by the idea that those who successfully walked its turns had experienced the cross three times.

Accordingly, in his most hermetic video, *Two Turns* (1975) [↗**42, 210, 211**], Fox focuses a portable video camera at his own feet as he walked out of the 16 Rose Street studio building where he lived and worked while in San Francisco, and literally mapped the turns of the Chartres labyrinth onto a walk through his neighborhood. We see and hear no one. There is no cultural ambience. No architectural features of the blocks surrounding his studio are visible, only the sight and sounds of his own feet as he re-inscribed the labyrinth onto the streets of San Francisco.

buddhistische Gebetsmühlen, die es des Lesens und Schreibens unkundigen buddhistischen Bauern erlauben, das Beten durch unmittelbare Berührung zu erleben, erlaubte es das Labyrinth, ungebildeten französischen christlichen Bauern das Kreuz auf eine körperliche, ekstatische Weise zu erleben. Fox interessierte sich für diese Idee einer direkten physischen, spirituellen Erfahrung.

Fox machte Modelle und Zeichnungen des Labyrinths von Chartres [↗**40**] und war begeistert von der Idee, dass diejenigen, die dessen Wendungen erfolgreich abschritten, das Kreuz dreimal erlebt hatten. Dementsprechend richtet er in seinem hermetischsten Video *Two Turns* (1975) [↗**42, 210, 211**] eine tragbare Videokamera auf seine eigenen Füße, während er aus dem Ateliergebäude in der Rose Street 16 lief, wo er während seiner Zeit in San Francisco lebte und arbeitete, und die Wendungen des Labyrinths von Chartres buchstäblich auf einen Gang durch sein Viertel übertrug. Wir sehen und hören niemanden. Es gibt keine kulturelle Umgebung. Man sieht keine architektonischen Merkmale der Häuserblöcke in der Umgebung seines Ateliers, sondern man nimmt lediglich das Bild und den Klang seiner Füße wahr, während er gewissermaßen das Labyrinth den Straßen von San Francisco neu einschreibt.

Bei diesem Werk ging es weder einfach um seinen Körper, noch war es eine Reaktion auf die Idee der *dérive*, der situationistischen Idee der psycho-geografischen Neu-Kartierung der Stadt auf der Grundlage der Verbindung zum reinen Begehren. Es war ein Akt des Zeichnens und Erinnerns, der Auseinandersetzung mit einem der Religiosität entkleideten Gefühl der Transzendenz. Man kann diese Arbeit mit Vito Acconcis Arbeit *Following* (1971) vergleichen, bei der Acconci seine Aktivität aus seinem Studio heraus verlagerte und in eine direkte Beziehung zur Stadt trat. Nur dass es für Fox nicht um die Verknüpfung seiner Aktion mit dem Leben zufälliger Fremder ging, sondern darum, wie sich eine einfache Handlung mit transzendenter Bedeutung erfüllen ließ.

Mit Fox' bekanntester Einkanal-Videoarbeit, *Children's Tapes* (1974) [↗**12, 61, 138**], reagierte der Künstler auf die Einladung, ein Werk zu einer Ausstellung von West Coast-Videos im Everson Museum beizusteuern. Dank der bemerkenswerten kuratorischen Arbeit Brenda Richardsons, die damals als Chefkuratorin am Berkeley Art Museum fungierte (das man früher unter der Bezeichnung University Art Museum, Berkeley, kannte), war mir Terry Fox und sein Werk sehr deutlich bewusst geworden, und ich hatte sowohl *Turgescent Sex* als auch *Two Turns* in meinem laufenden Videokunst-Ausstellungsprogramm im Everson Museum gezeigt. Nachdem ich Fox (zusammen mit Howard Fried, Paul Kos, Judith Barry, Tom Marioni, George Bolling und anderen) 1972 bei einem

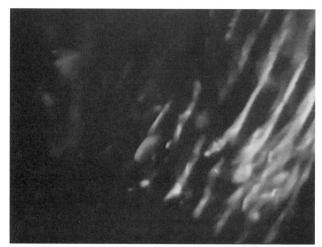

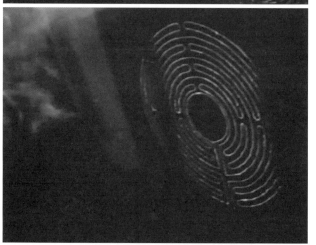
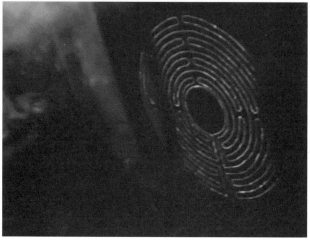

Terry Fox, *Two Turns*, 1975, video stills

Besuch in San Francisco kennengelernt hatte, wollte ich ihn mit einer neuen Videoarbeit beauftragen. Fox reagierte, indem er ein bemerkenswertes, vordergründig zur Freude seines eigenen Sohnes Foxy entstandenes Werk schuf. *Children's Tapes* präsentiert eine Reihe von Tischexperimenten, die alle auf der geduldigen Beobachtung einfacher naturwissenschaftlicher Prinzipien beruhen.

Doch das Werk verlangt, oder benötigt zumindest, mehr als bloße Geduld. Mit seinem „eisigen", sprich extrem langsamen Tempo ist es nichts Geringeres als eine Apparatur, die zum stillen Meditieren ermutigt, auch wenn sie den Betrachter auf häufig dramatische Weise vereinnahmt. Es handelte sich hier schwerlich um eine kommerzielle Wissenschaftssendung für das Kinderfernsehen, wie das in den 1950er Jahren klassisch bekannte amerikanische Programm *Watch Mr. Wizard*, oder auch ein pädagogisches Fernsehprogramm wie das angesehene nicht-kommerzielle Kinderprogramm der *Sesamstraße*. Bei Fox' *Children's Tapes* ging es vielmehr um sorgfältige Beobachtung und geduldiges Schauen (wenn auch mit einer Art kindlichem Staunen). Ja, im Grunde war dieses Werk gar nicht wie Fernsehen, sondern eher so, als würde man „wissenschaftliche" DIY-Experimente mit den Augen eines besonders begabten Kindes sehen.

Man kann Fox' später zur Aufführung gelangte Klangarbeiten, vor allem diejenigen, bei denen Klaviersaiten ertönten, die er in verlassenen, aufgegebenen Gebäuden durch große offene Räume gespannt hatte, als eine Ausweitung seiner indirekten Erkundung von Materialien sowie der Art und Weise begreifen, wie sie in einem performativen Kontext eingesetzt werden können. Das war der Kern seiner künstlerischen Praxis. Das Offenlegen von, sozialen und metaphysischen, Formen im Alltagsleben bildete den Schwerpunkt seines Lebenswerks und eine Zeitlang spielte Video eine entscheidende Rolle bei diesem Bemühen. Diese Werke konnten auf Video dokumentiert werden, aber es gab keine Möglichkeit, die wesentliche Eigenschaft des Klanges innerhalb dieses Raums durch Video zu übermitteln und, offen gesagt, empfand Fox Video schon bald zu sehr als eine elitäre globale Kunstform, so dass er aufhörte, dieses Medium zu benutzen.

Viele Videokünstler, die in den frühen 1970er Jahren arbeiteten, waren daran interessiert, Videomodelle für eine Art Fernsehen zu produzieren, das sich dem vorherrschenden kommerziellen Einsatz des Mediums widersetzte. Obwohl Fox sehr politisch und geradeheraus war, verfolgte er mit seinem Werk nicht diese Intention. Von seiner frühesten Auseinandersetzung mit dem Medium an verwendete er es lediglich zur Erweiterung eines skulpturalen oder performativen Konzepts.

The work was not simply about his body, nor was it a response to the notion of the *dérive* – the Situationist notion of the psycho-geographic remapping of the city based on the connection to pure desire. It was an act of drawing and remembering, of engaging a sense of transcendence stripped of religiosity. It is comparable to Vito Acconci's 1971 work *Following,* in which Acconci transferred his activity out of his studio and into a direct relationship with the city. Only for Fox, it was not about linking his action to the lives of random strangers, but rather about the ways in which a simple action could be imbued with transcendent meaning.

Fox's most well known single-channel video work, *Children's Tapes* (1974) [↗**12, 61, 138**], was a response to an invitation to submit a work to an exhibition of West Coast video at the Everson Museum. I had become acutely aware of Fox and his work through the remarkable curatorial work of Brenda Richardson, the head curator at that time of the Berkeley Art Museum (formerly known as the University Art Museum, Berkeley), and had been screening both *Turgescent Sex* and *Two Turns* in my ongoing Everson Museum video art exhibition program. Having met Fox (along with Howard Fried, Paul Kos, Judith Barry, Tom Marioni, George Bolling, and others in a 1972 visit to San Francisco), I wanted to commission him to create a new video work. Fox responded by producing a remarkable series of works ostensibly made for the delight of his own son Foxy. *Children's Tapes* take the form of a series of tabletop science experiments, all based on patient observation of simple scientific principles.

However watching the work demands (or at least requires) more than simple patience. In its "glacial" pacing, it is nothing less than a device to encourage quiet meditation – albeit engaging in ways that are often quite dramatic. This was hardly a commercial children's television science production, like the 1950's classic American program known as *Watch Mr. Wizard*, or even like an educational television program, such as *Sesame Street*, a well-respected, non-commercial children's program. Fox's *Children's Tapes* were about close observation and patient looking (albeit with a child-like sense of wonder). In fact, it was not like television at all; instead watching them seemed as if you were experiencing DIY "scientific" experiments through the eyes of a particularly gifted child.

Fox's subsequent performed sound works – especially those involving the voicing of piano wire strung across vast open spaces in derelict abandoned buildings – can be seen as an extension of his indirect exploration of materials, and the ways in which they can be employed within a performative context. This was the core of Fox's practice. Revealing forms (both social and metaphysical) in everyday life was the focus of his life's work, and for a time, video served a central role in that

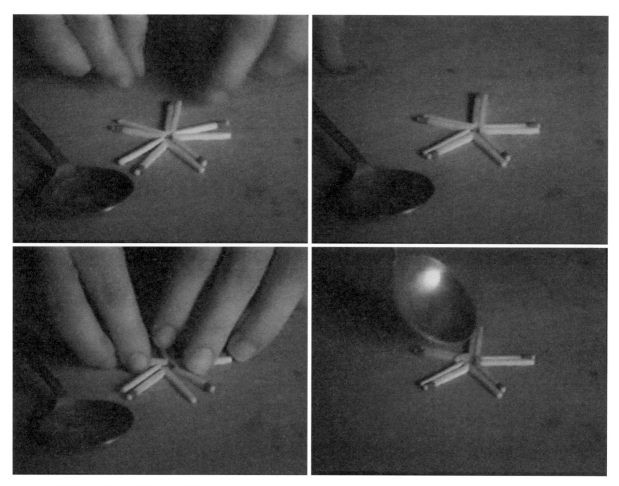

Terry Fox, *Children's Tapes*, 1974, video stills

Und obwohl ich anfangs sehr bestrebt war, so viele ernsthafte Künstler wie möglich in die im Entstehen begriffene amerikanische Videoszene einzubeziehen, folgten in Wahrheit schon in der Frühzeit von Video viele Künstler John Baldessaris Prophezeiung, dass diesem Medium keine größere oder geringere Bedeutung als dem Bleistift zukommen würde. Terry Fox begriff dies früher als die meisten, und als eine Folge hieraus stehen seine Videoarbeiten weiterhin in völligem Einklang mit seinem tieferen Bemühen um eine Kunst, die seinen Wunsch zum Ausdruck bringt, Momente reiner Transzendenz zu finden und mit anderen zu teilen.

Aus dem Englischen übersetzt von Nikolaus G. Schneider

pursuit. These works could be documented on video, but there was no way to transmit the essential quality of sound within that space through video, and frankly, Fox soon felt video to be too much of an elite art world feature, so he brought an end to his use of the medium.

Many video artists working in the early 1970's were interested in producing video models for a kind of television that would oppose the dominant commercial use of the medium. Though Fox was quite political and outspoken, his work was not intended in that fashion. From his earliest engagement with the medium, he used it only to extend a sculptural or performative concept.

And though in my early zeal to include as many serious artists as possible into the developing American video scene, in truth, many artists during video's early days were already following John Baldessari's prediction that video would eventually be seen as nothing more or less than a pencil. Terry Fox understood that earlier than most, and as a result, his video work remains fully consistent with his deeper concerns for an art that expressed his desire to find and share moments of pure transcendence.

Terry Fox –
Ein „Handlungsreisender"
in Europa

Lisa Steib

Terry Fox –
A World Traveler
in Europe

Viele Jahre lang war Terry Fox ein Weltenbummler: „Ich bin nicht die Art von Person, die sich an einem Ort dauerhaft niederlässt. Ich mag es, herumzuziehen. Und ich mag die Erfahrung von verschiedenen Kulturen und Sprachen. Daher bekomme ich meine Inspiration."[1] Er bewegte sich dabei lieber an den Rändern der Kunst als in ihren Zentren. Terry Fox' künstlerische Entwicklung begann in den Vereinigten Staaten und wurde vor allem in den 1970er Jahren durch den Austausch mit Künstlern und Kuratoren in und um San Francisco geprägt. Doch auch die Erfahrungen, die er seit den 1960er Jahren in Europa sammeln konnte, waren prägend. Im Zentrum stand für Terry Fox nicht das strategische Streben danach, Teil einer Szene, Gruppe oder Strömung zu werden, sondern die aufmerksame Beobachtung von scheinbar Nebensächlichem. Das Spazierengehen, das Belauschen der Klänge des Alltags und das Lesen gehörten zu seinen Arbeitsmethoden.

Während Magazine wie *Avalanche* und *Interfunktionen* in den 1970er Jahren den transatlantischen Austausch im Printformat beförderten, setzte Terry Fox diesen Trend ganz praktisch in die Tat um: durch intensives Reisen. So brachte er einerseits Erfahrungen aus Europa nach Kalifornien und genoss andererseits die Offenheit des Kunstsystems europäischer Prägung. Die Aktion *Isolation Unit,* die 1970 im Keller der Düsseldorfer Kunstakademie in eher spontaner Kooperation mit Joseph Beuys stattfand, wird häufig zitiert. Bisher weniger bekannt ist, dass Terry Fox 1971 im Museum of Conceptual Art (MOCA), einem alternativen Raum für Kunst in San Francisco, eine Aktion von Tomas Schmit zur (Wieder-) Aufführung brachte: *Zyklus (by Tomas Schmit)* [↗**46**].[2] Obwohl Terry Fox in den 1960er und 1970er Jahren in San Francisco lebte, hielt er sich häufig in Europa auf. Teils blieb er mehrere Wochen oder Monate, im Fall von Rom, Paris und Berlin (1981/1982) jeweils für ein Jahr. In den 1980er Jahren, als die Malerei boomte, lebte er zudem in Neapel und Florenz. In den 1990er Jahren führte ihn sein Lebensweg vom belgischen Liège aus schließlich nach Köln. Bei einigen seiner

For many years, Terry Fox was a globetrotter, preferring to move on the margins of art rather than at its centers. As he once remarked: "I am not the kind of person who wants to settle down permanently in one place. I like to move around, and I like the experience of different cultures and languages. That's where I get the sources of my inspiration."[1] The roots of his artistic development were in the United States, influenced particularly by his exchanges with artists and curators in and around San Francisco in the 1970s , yet his experiences on his travels in Europe from the 1960s also proved to be formative. In all this, though, Terry Fox was never motivated by some strategic plan to become part of a scene, group or movement. Instead, he devoted his attention to carefully observing the seemingly peripheral, applying methods which included walking, listening to the sound of daily life, and reading.

While an international exchange in print was being fostered in the 1970s by magazines such as *Avalanche* and *Interfunktionen*, Terry Fox had essentially put this trend into practice by traveling intensively across Europe. In this way, for example, he not only brought his experience of Europe to California, but also enjoyed the openness of the European art world. In this context, *Isolation Unit* – Fox's more or less spontaneous performance with Joseph Beuys in the basement of the Kunstakademie Düsseldorf in 1970 – is often cited, yet his presentation at the alternative art space of San Francisco's Museum of Conceptual Art the following year of *Zyklus (by Tomas Schmit)* [↗**46**], a (re)enactment of Tomas Schmit's performance, remains far less well known.[2]

Although Terry Fox was primarily based in San Francisco in the 1960s and 1970s, he often visited Europe. He stayed for several weeks or months and, in the case of Rome, Paris and Berlin, even lived in each city for a year (Berlin, 1981-82). In the 1980s, when painting again experienced a boom, he also lived in Naples and Florence. Finally, in the following decade, the path of his life took him from Liège in Belgium to Cologne. In some cases, the cities where he stayed briefly conjure up immediate associations: Kassel = *documenta*

Stationen folgt die Assoziation prompt: Kassel = documenta (1972, 1977 und 1987), Venedig = Biennale (1984). Terry Fox' Videobänder, die in den Niederlanden und Italien entstanden sind, warten hingegen noch darauf, Beachtung zu finden, wie die Aktion vor einer Videokamera *Lunedi* (1975, Kamera: Bill Viola, produziert von Art/tapes/22) [↗**124, 139**]. Terry Fox' *Situationen* mit Klaviersaiten fanden in Europa unter anderem in einem Stall und in Kirchen statt, doch durchaus auch in musealen Räumen. Wichtig waren der Bezug zur Architektur und die Klangqualitäten des jeweiligen Raumes, den Terry Fox mit wenigen Mitteln in eine Skulptur verwandelte.

1961 reiste Terry Fox erstmals nach Europa. Nach seinem High-School-Abschluss in Seattle, Washington, arbeitete er ein Jahr lang und wagte mit seinen Ersparnissen den Aufbruch nach Rom. Der Grund lag in der Malerei, mit der er als Teenager in der Natur und durch das Kopieren von Abbildungen bekannter Werke der europäischen Kunstgeschichte begonnen hatte. Ein Buch über Michelangelo ließ ihn vermuten, dass Rom nach wie vor der Nabel der Welt der Kunst sei: „Weil Michelangelo dort lebte. dumm, nicht? Naiv. […] Ich war achtzehn, als ich wegging. Ich nahm einen Zug nach New York, nahm ein Schiff, die ‚Leonardo da Vinci' – nach Neapel, dann einen Zug nach Rom und blieb ein Jahr lang. So fing alles an. Weg von Issaquah und in Rom sein."[3] Was sich liest wie ein Künstlermythos, kam anders als geplant. Einen Monat nach Terry Fox' Ankunft wurde die Akademie bestreikt und geschlossen. Statt als Kunststudent lebte er als „freier Maler" in Rom – und blieb Autodidakt.[4] Zum Kunstmarkt wahrte Terry Fox stets eine gewisse Distanz, was sich schon im Oktober 1967 ankündigte: Radikal und endgültig verabschiedete er sich vom Medium der Malerei.

(1972, 1977 and 1987) and Venice = *Biennale* (1984). In contrast, Terry Fox's video works dating from his time in the Netherlands and Italy are still waiting to attract interest, as is his video performance *Lunedi* (1975, camera: Bill Viola, produced by the studio Art/tapes/22) [↗**124, 139**]. Terry Fox performed his *situations* with piano wire in Europe in locations as varied as a stable and a church, but also in museum spaces. In each particular venue, he carefully considered how sound related to the specific architectural surround and acoustics of the space which he then transformed into a sculpture using only minimal means.

In 1961, Terry Fox visited Europe for the first time. After finishing high school in Seattle, Washington, he worked for a year. With his savings and inspired by his love of painting, he then ventured off and moved to Rome. As a teenager, he had started painting scenes from the countryside around him and copying canonical works in European art history from prints. After reading a book on Michelangelo, Fox's choice of Rome as a destination crystalized, sure that the city was still the hub of the art world: "Because that's where Michelangelo lived. Stupid, huh? Naive. […] I was eighteen when I got out. Took a train to New York, took a ship – the *Leonardo da Vinci* – to Naples, a train to Rome, and I stayed there for a year. And that was the beginning of everything. Being away from Issaquah, and living in Rome."[3] Although this reads like the myth of the artist as a young man, it all turned out rather differently. Just one month after he arrived, the art academy in Rome was hit by a strike and closed. Instead of becoming an art student, he now lived in the city as a freelance painter – and remained self-taught.[4] He always maintained a certain distance to the art market, a stance heralded early on in his

Tomas Schmitt, *# 1 zyklus* für *wassereimer (oder flaschen)*, MOCA, San Francisco, 1962

In der Galerie von Rudolf Zwirner in Köln, so die (Kunst-)Geschichte des Künstlers, habe er seine zuvor aus Paris antransportierten Bilder deponiert, ohne Wissen des Galeristen und auf Nimmerwiedersehen: *Art Deposit*.

1967 hielt sich Terry Fox einige Monate lang in Amsterdam auf. Er interessierte sich in dieser Zeit für Fluxus, die ZERO-Künstler und Wolf Vostells *dé-coll/age. Bulletin aktueller Ideen* (1962–1969). In Interviews werden in späteren Jahren die Künstler Dick Higgins, Emmett Williams und Benjamin Patterson als teils freundschaftliche Einflüsse genannt. Terry Fox las zeitlebens viel: Von Antonin Artaud über Paul Klee bis zu Roland Barthes weckte vieles, was Literaten, Künstler und Philosophen zu schreiben wussten, seine Neugier. In einigen Werken bezog er sich explizit auf Arthur Rimbaud, Raymond Roussel und John Cage. Einzelne Publikationen und sprachliche Fundstücke konnten Eingang in seine Textobjekte finden. Der gewitzte Einsatz von Textfragmenten und das Spiel mit der meist englischen Sprache stellen den Nicht-Muttersprachler angesichts der Werke in europäischen Museen vor Rätsel und zugleich vor sprachliche Herausforderungen.

All seine Werke, ob Aktion oder Objekt, fielen für Terry Fox unter den Begriff Skulptur. So war für ihn eine Performance eine Form von Bildhauerei vor den Augen des Publikums. In seiner Argumentation grenzte er sich von der üblichen Historie der Aktionskunst mit ihren Vorläufern in der europäischen Kunstgeschichte ab. Er sah in Futurismus, Dadaismus und Surrealismus vielmehr Erweiterungen der Bildhauerei: „Meine Kunst ist gewissermaßen eine Fortführung dieser Tradition, indem ich das Bewusstsein der Zuschauer öffnete und sie zwang, Verbindungen zu machen, die normalerweise in der Kunst nicht gemacht werden."[5]

Im Dezember 1967 bewies Terry Fox erstmals, dass die Verbindung von Kunst und Alltag keine Utopie sein muss. Als ihm in Amsterdam mit dem Rauswurf aus seiner Wohnung gedroht wurde, entwickelte er die Idee für ein Vorhaben in den (noch) eigenen vier Wänden: Er schlug ein Loch in die Wand zwischen seiner Wohnung und dem Hausflur und versteckte darin, hinter einem Möbelstück, zehn saure Heringe: *Fish Vault* (Sarphatikade, Amsterdam). In einem Interview mit Willoughby Sharp erinnerte er sich an dieses Vorhaben, das noch darauf wartet, in den Kanon der Aktionskunst aufgenommen zu werden.[6] *Fish Vault* zeigt, wie schwierig und zugleich leicht es sein kann, eine Aktion langfristig zu bewahren: Teils genügt die Anekdote. Die Sprache ist neben Fotografien, Video- oder Audioaufnahmen ein wichtiges Medium der Dokumentation. Dem Interview[7] und dem (Künstler-)Archiv[8] kommen damit prominente Rollen in der Bewahrung des Werkes zu. Für Terry Fox beginnt das eigene Gesamtwerk im Rückblick erst im Moment der Abkehr von

career by his decision in October 1967 to break radically and definitively with the medium of painting. To seal this break, he designed and performed his *Art Deposit* action. In Fox's later (art historical) account, he describes how he took all his paintings brought from Paris and left them in Rudolf Zwirner's Cologne gallery without telling Zwirner and in the full knowledge that he would never see them again.

In 1967, Terry Fox stayed in Amsterdam for a few months and became interested in Fluxus, the Zero artists and Wolf Vostell's art journal *dé-coll/age. Bulletin aktueller Ideen* (1962–69). In later interviews, he cited artists such as Dick Higgins, Emmett Williams and Benjamin Patterson as influences, some of whom were his friends. Throughout his life, Terry Fox read extensively. Many writers, artists and philosophers, from Antonin Artaud to Paul Klee or Roland Barthes, awakened his interest and curiosity, while in some of his works he explicitly referenced Arthur Rimbaud, Raymond Roussel and John Cage. He also integrated individual publications and linguistic finds into his text-objects. His witty and clever use of text fragments and his language games, usually in English, present non-English speaking viewers of his works in European museums with enigmatic conundrums and linguistic challenges.

Terry Fox considered all his works, whether performances, actions or objects, to be sculpture; in his view, performance was rather like sculpting a work in front of an audience. In taking this position, he drew a line between his work and the mainstream history of performance art as developing from its predecessors in European art. Instead, in his view, Futurism, Dada and Surrealism had expanded the concept of sculpture: "My art is in a way a continuation of this tradition of redefining sculpture by opening up the mind of the spectators, forcing them to make connections they would normally not do in art."[5] In December 1967, Terry Fox showed for the first time in his oeuvre that the link between art and everyday life did not have to remain utopian. When threatened with eviction from his Amsterdam apartment, he developed his project *Fish Vault* as an action in (what was still) his own home (Sarphatikade, Amsterdam). After breaking open the wall between his apartment and the hallway, he hid ten pickled herrings in the hole behind a piece of furniture. In an interview with Willoughby Sharp, he later recalled this piece, which is still waiting to become part of the canon of performance art.[6] *Fish Vault* illustrates just how difficult and, at the same time, how easy it can be for a performance to stand the test of time. In some cases, just an anecdote alone may be sufficient. Although photography, and video and audio recordings are important means of documentation, so too is language. Consequently, the interview[7] and the (artist's) archive[8] play a prominent

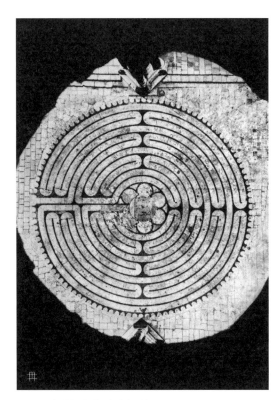

Postcard of the Labyrinth in Chartres

role in preserving a work. In retrospect, Terry Fox felt that his entire oeuvre started when he turned his back on painting. The wave of student protests in Paris in 1968 had a lasting impact on his art. The anarchic mood and energy in the city inspired him to produce his first sculptures. These were created, he recalled, from his enjoyment in opening the water hydrants and watching the water stream across the streets – a point at which there is no gap between art and life.[9]

Terry Fox was not drawn to joining groups of artists, but preferred engaging in debates and exchanges with individual fellow artists. In the late 1960s, for instance, he created his *Dust Exchange* sculpture with William T. Wiley, an action conducted by mail between Europe and the United States. For a series of street situations (*Public Theater*), Fox also cooperated with Wolf Vostell who was to stage a performance at Cologne's main station while Fox worked at the same time with dancers in Anna Halprin's studio in San Francisco (*Simultaneous Theater,* June 30 / July 1, 1969). For the individual manifestations of his *Public Theater* series, Terry Fox put up posters on walls and sent out invitations asking people to be at a particular place at a particular time. For example, one poster told everyone to come to the London Billingsgate fish market at a certain time, promising "PLENTYOFFISH."

Fox recalled that he also sent Joseph Beuys an announcement of each of his public theater pieces. While publications have often cited the link between the renowned artist Beuys and Terry Fox, they rarely deal with Fox's cooperation with other artists in Europe such as Marino Vismara, Henning Christiansen and Bjørn Nørgaard, Paul Panhuysen, Claudine Denis, Yunko Wada or Rolf Julius. In his work with other artists, Fox particularly valued their integrity and the feeling of strong bond between them. His most intensive collaboration may well have been his joint performances with Georg Decristel, an Austrian Jew's harp player and poet. Just as in Terry Fox's case, Decristel's work also escapes the accepted categories of art.[10] Fox gave some of his performances without a live audience, only in front of a camera or video camera. In 1971 in Mönchengladbach, Germany, after already working with photographers such as Larry Fox (his twin brother) and Barry Klinger, Terry Fox created *Hefe* (for Ute Klophaus) [↗82–87] with and for the photographer Ute Klophaus, producing a unique photo series.

In 1972, Terry Fox made a momentous discovery. On a trip from Paris to Chartres, he visited its famous cathedral. When he saw the labyrinth floor mosaic [↗48] in Chartres Cathedral, he experienced an epiphany: the labyrinth's eleven concentric circles seemed to echo a series of severe illnesses he had suffered for eleven years. This epiphany was to inspire an entire series of works over the following years. In 1971, when Harald Szeemann wrote the following euphoric

der Malerei. Die Studentenproteste 1968 in Paris wirkten sich nachhaltig auf seine Kunst aus. Die anarchistische Stimmung und Energie um ihn herum regten ihn zu ersten Skulpturen an: Terry Fox fand Gefallen daran, Wasserhydranten zu öffnen und dem Wasser dabei zuzusehen, wie es über die Straßen lief.[9] Kunst und Leben sind in diesem Moment nicht zu unterscheiden.

Terry Fox tendierte nicht dazu, sich Künstlergruppen anzuschließen, er suchte vielmehr den Austausch mit einzelnen Kollegen. So führte er Ende der 1960er Jahre mit William T. Wiley einen postalischen *Dust Exchange* zwischen Europa und den Vereinigten Staaten durch. Für eine Serie von Straßensituationen (*Public Theater*) kam es zu einer Kooperation mit Wolf Vostell, der eine Aktion am Kölner Hauptbahnhof durchgeführt haben soll, während Terry Fox parallel mit Tänzern im Atelier von Anna Halprin in San Francisco zusammenarbeitete (*Simultaneous Theater,* 30. Juni / 1. Juli 1969). Zu den einzelnen *manifestations* der *Public-Theater*-Serie verteilte Terry Fox Plakate vor Ort und verschickte Einladungen, die beispielsweise dazu aufriefen, zu einer bestimmten Uhrzeit auf einem Londoner Fischmarkt, dem Billingsgate Market, zu erscheinen. Das Plakat versprach: „PLENTYOFFISH".

Auch Joseph Beuys soll jedes Mal eine Einladung zum *Public Theater* bekommen haben. Während der berühmte Kollege im Zusammenhang mit Terry Fox häufig genannt wird, wurden die Kooperationen mit anderen in Europa beheimateten

Künstlern wie Marino Vismara, Henning Christiansen und Bjørn Nørgaard, Paul Panhuysen, Claudine Denis, Yunko Wada oder Rolf Julius in Publikationen bisher weniger beachtet. Freundschaftliche Verbundenheit und die Integrität der Kooperationspartner schätzte Terry Fox besonders. Die wohl intensivste Zusammenarbeit in gemeinsamen Aktionen fand mit Georg Decristel statt, einem österreichischen Maultrommelspieler und Poeten, dessen Werk sich gängigen Kategorien auf ähnliche Weise entzieht wie das von Terry Fox.[10] In einigen Fällen fanden die Aktionen ohne Publikum vor der Foto- oder Videokamera statt. Nachdem Terry Fox bereits mit Fotografen wie Larry Fox (seinem Zwillingsbruder) und Barry Klinger zusammengearbeitet hatte, entstand 1971 in Mönchengladbach eine einmalige Fotoserie mit der und für die Fotografin Ute Klophaus: *Hefe* (for Ute Klophaus) [↗82–87]. 1972 machte Terry Fox eine folgenschwere Entdeckung. Von Paris aus unternahm er einen Ausflug nach Chartres. Das labyrinthische Bodenmosaik [↗48] der dortigen Kathedrale wurde für ihn zu einer Art „Offenbarung". Elf Jahre lang war sein Leben von Phasen schwerer Krankheit geprägt, die er in diesem Labyrinth zu erkennen glaubte. Eine ganze Werkserie entstand in den folgenden Jahren. Als Harald Szeemann 1971 euphorisch die folgenden Zeilen an Carol Lindsley (Reese Palley Gallery, San Francisco) schrieb, ahnte Terry Fox also

lines to Carol Lindsley (Reese Palley Gallery, San Francisco), Terry Fox was not yet aware that his performance for the exhibition would relate to the labyrinth: "Many thanks again for the guided tour through the Bay Area. It was one of the richest evenings during our trip: in one night four artists for documenta 5. This is to confirm the *documenta* will officially invite for participation Terry Fox, Howard Fried, John C. Fernie and Jim Melchert."[11]

Ultimately, Terry Fox's action was as minimalistic as it was sustained. Six hours a day over three days, he played the tambura, an Indian drone instrument, which he claimed filled the space with a "continuous circular sound"[12] (*Action for a Tower Room* [↗**49**]). He did not particularly like *documenta* itself: "Very negative exhibition [...] Wiley and Oldenburg are two pluses here [...] The art of the insane was pure exaltation and was the only thing in the entire exhibition that really moved me. I am really sick of modern art, in fact I don't like much of anything done since the decline of painting and sculpture in the 1300's, with a few exceptions [...]."[13]

In his *situations*, Terry Fox pursued the goal of direct communication which, in some cases, was only perceivable through the physical senses. In his fascinating performance in the Santa Felicitá Church in Florence, for instance, he played the lowest note of the organ as one unbroken note. The audience

Terry Fox, *Action for a Tower Room*, *documenta 5*, Kassel, 1972, photo: James Pennuto

noch nicht, dass sich sein Ausstellungsbeitrag auf das Laby-rinth beziehen würde: „Many thanks again for the guided tour through the Bay Area. It was one of the richest evenings during our trip: in one night four artists for documenta 5. This is to confirm the documenta will officially invite for partici-pation Terry Fox, Howard Fried, John C. Fernie and Jim Melchert."[11]

Terry Fox' Aktion war schließlich so reduziert wie ausdau-ernd: Drei Tage lang spielte er je sechs Stunden auf einem indischen Instrument, einer Tambura, die den Raum mit einem „continuous circular sound"[12] gefüllt haben soll (*Action for a Tower Room* [↗**49**]). Die documenta selbst kam bei Terry Fox nicht gut an: „Very negative exhibition ... Wiley and Oldenburg are two pluses here ... The art of the insane was pure exaltation and was the only thing in the entire exhibition that really moved me. I am really sick of modern art, in fact I don't like much of anything done since the decline of pain-ting and sculpture in the 1300's, with a few exceptions [...]."[13] Mit seinen *Situationen* verfolgte Terry Fox das Ziel einer direkten, teils nur körperlich wahrnehmbaren Kommuni-kation. So spielte er in der Kirche Santa Felicitá in Florenz bezaubernd einfach ohne Unterbrechung den tiefsten Ton der Orgel. Allein über die Schwingungen, die sich durch die Holzbänke auf die Anwesenden übertrugen, ließ sich der Klang wahrnehmen (*Tronci,* 1986). Doch konnten Aktionen auch in den 1980er Jahren unbemerkt, ohne Ankündigung und ohne geladenes Publikum stattfinden: *Segreto* (das „Ge-heimnis" oder „Rätsel"), ereignete sich im Umkreis der Piazza del Duomo ebenfalls 1986 in Florenz. Auf einem Balkon spielte der Künstler von Zeit zu Zeit auf einer singenden Säge, für sich und für andere.

Terry Fox hat sich in Europa mit seinen Skulpturen vor allem in das Gedächtnis Einzelner eingeprägt. Für ihn selbst war eine der eindrücklichsten Erfahrungen *vor einem Publikum* zu spielen, das aus den Bewohnern eines kleinen italienischen Bergdorfes namens Gallignano bestand. Die Zuhörer betei-ligten sich im Anschluss an die Aktion in der Dorfkirche rege an der Klangerzeugung. An diesem Ort fand Terry Fox höchste Aufmerksamkeit für die Klänge seiner Klaviersaiten und wohl das, wonach er mit seiner Kunst suchte: „Heute, dreißig Jahre später, arbeite ich immer noch mit dem Aspekt der Neudefi-nition von Skulptur, aber in einer äußerst persönlichen Weise. Ich möchte eher ein sympathetisches Ohr oder Auge erreichen als ein breites Publikum."[14]

Terry Fox, *Bird of Prey*, 1981

could perceive the sound through their own bodies, simply from the sound waves resonating in the wooden pews (*Tronci*, 1986). Yet even in the 1980s, Terry Fox could still stage actions almost unnoticed, without announcing them and without an invited audience, just as he did with *Segreto* ("Secret" or "Mystery") also performed in Florence in 1986, this time near the Piazza del Duomo. From time to time, he appeared unannounced on a balcony and played a musical saw, for himself and for others.

In Europe, Terry Fox's sculptures left their mark above all on the memory of individuals. For him, one of his most impressive experiences was a performance playing piano wire in front of an audience from a small Italian hilltop village called Gallignano. At the end of the action in the village church, his listeners also enthusiastically participated in generating the sounds. It was at this location that the sound of Terry Fox's piano wires received the most positive form of attention, and he may well have found exactly what he was searching for through his art: "So after 30 years I'm still working on the aspect of redefinition of sculpture, but in an extremely personal way. What I like is trying to find a sympathetic ear or eye more than trying to reach a broad audience."[14]

Translated from the German by Andrew Boreham

1 „Vom Boden zur Decke und von Wand zu Wand / From Floor to Ceiling and Wall to Wall". Interview Johannes Lothar Schröder / Terry Fox (1999). In: Eva Schmidt (Hg.), *Terry Fox. Ocular Language. 30 Jahre Reden und Schreiben über Kunst. 30 Years of Speaking and Writing about Art.* Gesellschaft für Aktuelle Kunst Bremen, Köln 2000, fortan Schmidt 2000, S. 192–209, hier S. 202

2 Vgl. die Liste der „Actions" in: Brenda Richardson (Hg.), *Terry Fox.* Ausst.-Kat. University Art Museum, Berkeley, Berkeley 1973, fortan Richardson 1973, unpag.

3 „Die Grenzen erforschen / Exploring the Limits". Interview René van Peer / Terry Fox (engl. Erstveröffentlichung 1993), zit. nach Schmidt 2000, vgl. Anm. 1, S. 156–183, hier S. 156–158

4 1961 besuchte Terry Fox Kurse an der Cornish School of Allied Arts, Seattle. Anders als Willoughby Sharp es in seinem Katalogtext 1970 darstellte, „studierte" er jedoch lediglich acht Tage lang an der Accademia di Belle Arti in Rom. In Interviews äußerte Terry Fox sich später durchaus kritisch über das „System Kunsthochschule", was ihn nicht davon abhielt, Lehraufträge anzunehmen, Vorträge vor Studenten zu halten oder eine Aktion vor Bremer Kunsthochschul-publikum durchzuführen. Vgl. Michael Glasmeier, Rede zur Eröffnung der Ausstellung „Terry Fox – LOCUS SOLUS", Heinrich-Vogeler-Museum / Barkenhoff, Worpswede, 13. August 2011, http://www.recalling-terryfox.de/o_text.php (Terry Fox Association), zuletzt am 29.7.2015

5 Schmidt 2000, vgl. Anm. 1, S. 200

6 Vgl. Terry Fox. „I Wanted to Have my Mood Affect their Looks." Interview Willoughby Sharp / Terry Fox. In: *Avalanche,* Winter 1971, S. 70–81, hier S. 72

7 Für die aufschlussreichen Gespräche über Terry Fox danke ich v. a. Vito Acconci, Ronald Feldman, Howard Fried, Michael Glasmeier, Paul Kos, Constance M. Lewallen, Carol Lindsley, Dietmar Löhrl, Tom Marioni, Ron Meyers, Brenda Richardson, David A. Ross, Alan Scarritt, Bernd Schulz, Andreas Schröder, William T. Wiley und Al Wong.

8 Ein besonderer Dank gilt Marita Loosen-Fox für ihre gastfreundliche wie kritische Begleitung der Erforschung von Archiv und Werk von Terry Fox seit 2009.

9 Siehe dazu Willoughby Sharp, Terry Fox. In: *Terry Fox. Exhibition.* Reese Palley Gallery, San Francisco 1970, unpag.

10 „Despite substantial evidence to the contrary, critics have consistently categorized Fox as a ‚body artist' (or as a ‚process artist' or ‚conceptual artist'), when in fact his work stands outside any of these possible classifications", bemerkte Brenda Richardson bereits 1973. In: Richardson 1973, vgl. Anm. 2, unpag. (Fußnote 3).

11 Harald Szeemann an Carol Lindsley, 16. Dezember 1971, zit. nach Tanya Zimbardo, Receipt of Delivery: Reese Palley / San Francisco, 29. September 2012, http://openspace.sfmoma.org/2012/09/receipt-of-delivery15/ (*SFMOMA OPEN SPACE),* zuletzt am 31.7.2015. Ich danke Tanya Zimbardo, Assistant Curator of Media Arts, San Francisco Museum of Modern Art, für ihre Unterstützung bei der Recherche zu Terry Fox.

12 Bernd Schulz (Hg.), *Terry Fox. works with sound. Arbeiten mit Klang.* Ausst.-Kat. Stadtgalerie Saarbrücken 1999, S. 62

13 Terry Fox an Carol Lindsley und Brenda Richardson (1972), zit. nach Richardson 1973, vgl. Anm. 2, unpag.

14 Schmidt 2000, vgl. Anm. 1, S. 200

1 "Vom Boden zur Decke und von Wand zu Wand / From Floor to Ceiling and Wall to Wall," interview between Johannes Lothar Schröder / Terry Fox (1999), Eva Schmidt (ed.), *Terry Fox. Ocular Language. 30 Jahre Reden und Schreiben über Kunst. 30 Years of Speaking and Writing about Art.* Gesellschaft für Aktuelle Kunst Bremen, Cologne, 2000, hereafter Schmidt 2000, pp. 192–209, here, p. 203

2 Cf. the list of "actions" *Terry Fox,* exh. cat., University Art Museum, Berkeley, Brenda Richardson (ed.), Berkeley, 1973, hereafter Richardson 1973, unpaginated

3 "Die Grenzen erforschen / Exploring the Limits," interview between René van Peer / Terry Fox (first published in English in 1993), quoted in Schmidt 2000, cf. note 1, pp. 156–183, here pp. 157–159

4 In 1961, Terry Fox attended courses at the Cornish School of Allied Arts, Seattle. However, in contrast to Willoughby Sharp's description in his exhibition catalogue text in 1970, Fox only "studied" for eight days at Accademia di Belle Arti in Rome. In later interviews, Terry Fox was certainly critical of the "art academy system," though this did not stop him from accepting positions as an adjunct professor, giving lectures to students or performing an action in front of an audience from Bremen's art school. Cf. Michael Glasmeier, "Rede zur Eröffnung der Ausstellung *Terry Fox – LOCUS SOLUS*," Heinrich-Vogeler-Museum / Barkenhoff, Worpswede, August 13, 2011, http://www.recalling-terryfox.de/o_text.php (Terry Fox Association), last accessed on July 29, 2015

5 Schmidt 2000, cf. note 1, p. 200

6 Cf. "Terry Fox. ‚I Wanted to Have My Mood Affect Their Looks,'" interview between Willoughby Sharp / Terry Fox, *Avalanche,* Winter 1971, pp. 70–81, here p. 72

7 For the interesting and informative conversations about Terry Fox, I would like to thank, among others, Vito Acconci, Ronald Feldman, Howard Fried, Michael Glasmeier, Paul Kos, Constance M. Lewallen, Carol Lindsley, Dietmar Löhrl, Tom Marioni, Ron Meyers, Brenda Richardson, David A. Ross, Alan Scarritt, Bernd Schulz, Andreas Schröder, William T. Wiley and Al Wong.

8 I would especially like to thank Marita Loosen-Fox for her hospitality and influential support in my research into the archive and work of Terry Fox since 2009.

9 Cf. Willoughby Sharp, Terry Fox, *Terry Fox. Exhibition,* Reese Palley Gallery, San Francisco, 1970, unpaginated

10 As early as 1973, Brenda Richardson noted: "Despite substantial evidence to the contrary, critics have consistently categorized Fox as a 'body artist' (or as a 'process artist' or 'conceptual artist'), when in fact his work stands outside any of these possible classifications." Richardson 1973, cf. note 2, unpaginated (note 3)

11 Harald Szeemann to Carol Lindsley, December 16, 1971, cited in Tanya Zimbardo, "Receipt of Delivery," Reese Palley / San Francisco, September 29, 2012, http://openspace.sfmoma.org/2012/09/receipt-of-delivery15/ (*SFMOMA OPEN SPACE),* last accessed on July 31, 2015. I would like to thank Tanya Zimbardo, Assistant Curator of Media Arts, San Francisco Museum of Modern Art, for her support in my research on Terry Fox.

12 *Terry Fox. works with sound. Arbeiten mit Klang,* exh. cat., Bernd Schulz (ed.) Stadtgalerie Saarbrücken 1999, p. 62

13 Terry Fox to Carol Lindsley and Brenda Richardson (1972), quoted in Richardson 1973, cf. note 2, unpaginated

14 Schmidt 2000, cf. note 1, p. 200

Terry Fox, *The Beginning of the "Dream of the Eyetooth in the Labyrinth,"* 1975

Angela Lammert

Skulpturale Notation
des Temporären
in Video, Fotografie
und Zeichnung

Sculptural Notation of the Ephemeral in Video, Photography and Drawing

„Wer hat eigentlich überhaupt gesehen, wie Joseph Beuys dem toten Hasen die Bilder erklärt? Braucht man die Photos dazu? Ist es nicht die ‚Software', die reine Erinnerung, an ein Ereignis, die sich in unser Gehirn eingrassiert?"[1] Diese Fragen liest man unter dem Titel „Das Recht, fliegen zu können" 1987 kurz nach dem Tod von Beuys im Katalog der documenta 8. Terry Fox ging anlässlich dieser Kasseler Großausstellung in eine Tiefgarage und erzeugte Sound mit Klaviersaiten, die an zwei einander gegenüberstehenden Autos befestigt waren. Mit den Autohupen wurde in ohrenbetäubender Lautstärke gemorst. Die Polizei kam drei Mal und beendete schließlich das Event.[2] Von dieser Performance haben sich ein Video und einige Fotografien erhalten, paradoxerweise von der Autorin des brillanten Katalogtextes aufgenommen.

Terry Fox gilt jenseits seiner Berühmtheit in der sich seit den 1980er Jahren in Europa entwickelnden Klangkunst als eine Schlüsselfigur der US-amerikanischen Konzept- und Performancekunst und als Vertreter der Body-Art- und Videoszene der 1970er Jahre.[3] Dennoch war er eher ein „artists' artist", der weitgehend in Isolation von der marktorientierten Kunstszene arbeitete und sich deren Kategorien entzog. Bekannt wurde er vor allem durch Aktionen, die wenige sahen oder niemand sah. Legendär waren seine Arbeiten mit dem über zwanzig Jahre älteren und von ihm bewunderten Joseph Beuys (1970), mit seinen Künstlerfreunden und Generationsgefährten Vito Acconci und Dennis Oppenheim (1971) oder die Performance für das Video Lunedi (1975) [↗124, 139], bei dem der jüngere Bill Viola als Kameramann assistierte. In allen diesen Arbeiten spielte der Klang eine konstituierende Rolle, der für Terry Fox, im Gegensatz zur Struktur von Musik, als nonverbale und universale Kommunikation fungierte. Zu den erfolgreichsten eigenen Arbeiten, die in den ersten Videoausstellungen schon Anfang der 1970er Jahre weltweit gezeigt wurden, gehörten Children's Tapes (1974) [↗12, 61, 138] und Turgescent Sex (1971) [↗76] – beides Videoperformances ohne Publikum. Seine vielleicht politischste Arbeit, das Abbrennen von Jasminpflanzen mit Brandpaste, deren

"Who really saw how Joseph Beuys explained pictures to a dead hare? Do we actually need the photographs? Isn't it the 'software,' the sheer memory, of an event that pervades our brains?"[1] In 1987, shortly after Beuys' death, these questions appeared in an essay entitled "Das Recht, fliegen zu können" (The Right to Be Able to Fly) in the documenta 8 catalogue. As his contribution to this major exhibition in Kassel, Germany, Terry Fox presented a work in an underground parking garage, sounding piano wires stretched between two facing cars. Car horns played a Morse code score at a deafening volume. The police were called to the performance three times, and finally stopped it entirely.[2] A video and a few photos of the performance have survived, paradoxically taken by Elizabeth Jappe, the author of the brilliant documenta catalogue essay.

Quite aside from his renowned role in sound art as it developed in Europe from the 1980s, Terry Fox is regarded as a key figure in US conceptual and performance art, and as one of the artists working with body and video art in the 1970s.[3] Nonetheless, he was far more an "artists' artist," largely working away from the market-driven art scene and refusing to fit in with its categories. His reputation was primarily based on performances that often few, if anyone, had seen. Fox's works with Joseph Beuys (1970), over twenty years older and someone he much admired, or with Vito Acconci and Dennis Oppenheim (1971), both friends and of the same generation of artists, or his performance for the Lunedi (1975) [↗124, 139] video with a younger Bill Viola assisting as camera operator are legendary. In all these works, sound played a constituent role. In contrast to the structure of music, Terry Fox regarded sound as a universal, nonverbal form of communication. Some of his most successful video works were also performed without an audience. In the early 1970s, his Children's Tapes (1974) [↗12, 61, 138] and Turgescent Sex (1971) [↗76] were both shown around the word in the first video exhibitions. In what is probably his most political work performed for the opening night of a group exhibition at the height of the Vietnam War, Fox used fuel gel, which had an effect that seemed like

Wirkung an Napalm denken ließ, anlässlich einer Ausstellungseröffnung auf dem Höhepunkt des Vietnamkrieges, schockierte die kleine Gruppe von Besuchern, die eine kurzweilige Performance erwartet hatten – eine Frau weinte 20 Minuten lang. Bekannt wurde *Defoliation* (1970) [↗**32, 102, 103**], wie er diese Aktion nannte, vor allem durch Fox' Interviews in Zeitschriften und die Erinnerung der damals Anwesenden.[4] Legendär ist auch die dreitägige Klangperformance *Suono Interno* (1979) [↗**123, 284**] in der ehemaligen Kirche von Santa Lucia in Bologna[5], zu der Publikum keinen Zutritt hatte und die nur durch den aus einem kleinen Loch austretenden Klang sowie eine Kreidemarkierung neben dem Guckloch, durch das man ins Innere sehen konnte, wahrnehmbar war.[6] Die Ausstrahlung seiner Person, die Übertragung der Energie auf den Raum, seine enigmatischen und verrätselten Rituale, vor allem auch seine politisch anarchische Kraft und seine meditativen Gesten sind von Künstlerfreunden und Zeitgenossen immer wieder beschrieben worden. Gleichzeitig haben zahlreiche Fotografien und Videotapes seiner Aktionen einen ästhetischen Eigenwert. Darum wäre die eingangs zitierte Frage heute zu erweitern: Ist der Gebrauch von Fotografie, Video und Zeichnung nur einer der Aufzeichnung oder Vorbereitung von Performances? Ist die Notation des Temporären nur Dokumentation? Was bleibt von den Performances, wenn sich niemand mehr persönlich an sie erinnern kann und die Künstler nicht mehr leben?

Dokumentation – Künstlerische Arbeit

Die präzis geschwungenen und zum Teil doppelt gezogenen Linien einer Zeichnung aus seinen Werknotizen zur Vorbereitung der ersten musealen Einzelausstellung des damals dreißigjährigen Terry Fox in Berkeley (1973)[7] faszinieren durch die Eleganz ihrer fast ornamentalen Form. Der klare Federstrich verbindet die schneckenförmigen Ausbuchtungen mit drei aus unterschiedlichen Perspektiven gefassten Schalen für die Performance. Auf einem anderen wahrscheinlich früheren Blatt dieser Werknotizen ist die geplante Raumstruktur von Fox verbal in einer Liste zusammengefasst. [↗**55, 56**] Die untereinander mit Schreibmaschine getippten Notizen enden wie in einem Gedicht immer wieder mit dem Wort „labyrinth" und offenbaren in der an den Rand des Blattes gerückten und mit Anmerkungen versehenen Zeichnung die Nähe des für ihn so wichtigen Themas zum eigenen Körper. Ausgehend von seiner Entdeckung des Bodenlabyrinths in der Kathedrale von Chartres 1972 wurde das Labyrinth zu *der* Metapher seiner Arbeit. Die elf konzentrischen Kreise schienen Terry Fox, eine Entsprechung zu seinen elf

napalm, to burn a section of jasmine flowers, shocking a small audience of onlookers who had expected something more entertaining. One woman cried for twenty minutes. Terry Fox's performance, which he titled *Defoliation* (1970) [↗**32, 102, 103**], became well known later, above all through Fox's interviews in journals and the recollections of those present at the time.[4] *Suono Interno* (1979) [↗**123, 284**], his three-day performance in the former Santa Lucia church in Bologna, also gained legendary status.[5] Since the general public were not allowed inside the church, the performance itself was only perceptible from the sound permeating outside through a small hole in a door, or by peering through a small peephole in the door marked in chalk with an arrow.[6] Contemporaries and artist friends have left many descriptions of Terry Fox's charismatic personality, his infusion of vitality into a performance space, his obscure and enigmatic rituals, and especially his politically anarchic energy and meditative gestures.

At the same time, many photos and videos of his performances have their own aesthetic value. For this reason, today the question quoted at the start of this essay could be expanded to ask: Is photography, video and drawing just one way of recording or preparing performances? Is the notation of the ephemeral only documentation? What remains from performances if no one personally remembers them and the artists are no longer alive?

Documentation – "Art Piece"

When he was thirty years old and preparing his first solo exhibition in a museum space, scheduled to be held in Berkeley, Terry Fox sketched this drawing in his work notes (1973).[7] The elegance of the near-ornamental form of these precisely curved lines, some of them doubled, still instills profound fascination. Clear strokes of the pen link the shell-like bulges with three bowls used for the performance, each depicted here from different perspectives. On another sheet from his work notes, probably composed earlier, Fox has verbalized the planned spatial structure and typed it as a list [↗**55, 56**]. Many of the series of typed phrases set in sequence end with the word "labyrinth," rather like the refrain of a poem, and reveal in the drawing with its annotations on the edge of the page the affinity of the subject so central to him – that of his own body. After he saw the labyrinth on the floor of Chartres Cathedral in 1972, this shape became a metaphor for his work. For Terry Fox, the labyrinth's eleven concentric rings appeared to echo his eleven stays in a hospital;[8] in his later sculpture *Vortex* (1992), the eleven steel struts seem to echo the shape of a / his rib cage. In this typed list, though, aside from the minor handwritten addition above, Fox makes no mention of

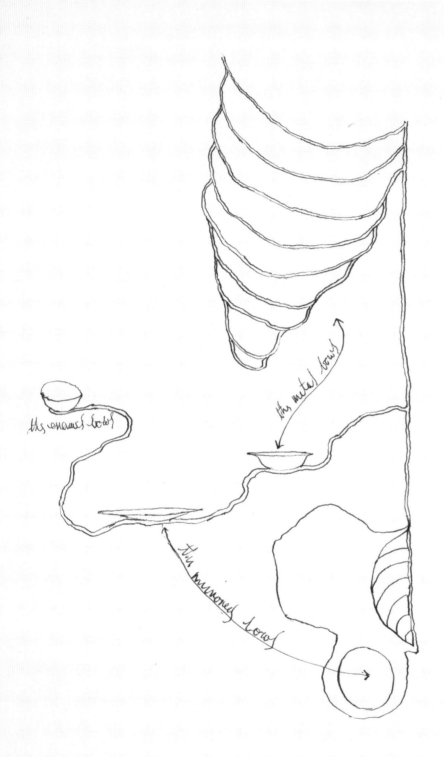

Terry Fox, Sketch for *Yield*, "Berkeley Drawings," notebook, 1973

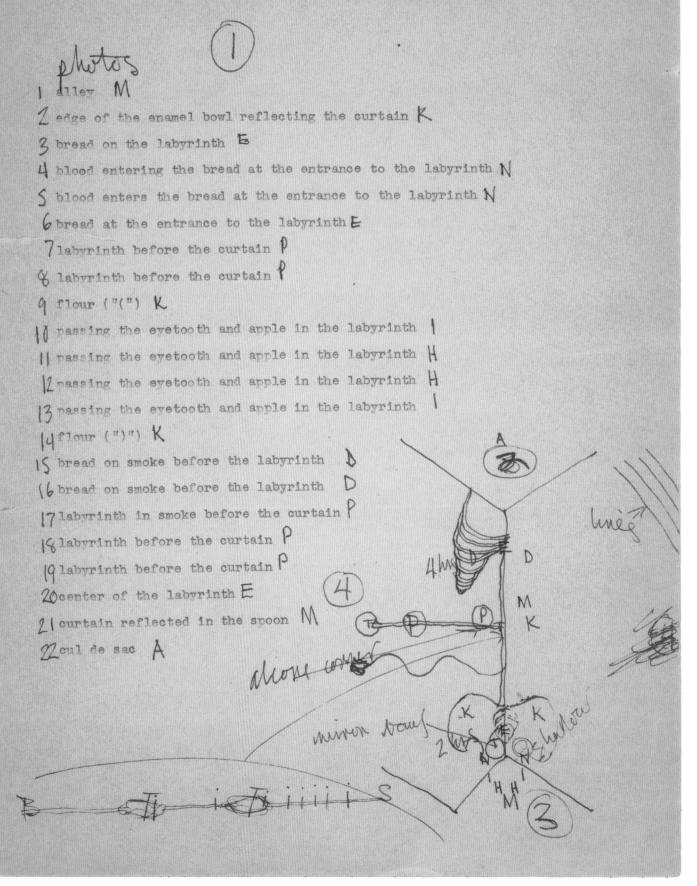

photos ①

1 alley M
2 edge of the enamel bowl reflecting the curtain K
3 bread on the labyrinth E
4 blood entering the bread at the entrance to the labyrinth N
5 blood enters the bread at the entrance to the labyrinth N
6 bread at the entrance to the labyrinth E
7 labyrinth before the curtain P
8 labyrinth before the curtain P
9 flour ("(") K
10 passing the eyetooth and apple in the labyrinth I
11 passing the eyetooth and apple in the labyrinth H
12 passing the eyetooth and apple in the labyrinth H
13 passing the eyetooth and apple in the labyrinth I
14 flour (")") K
15 bread on smoke before the labyrinth D
16 bread on smoke before the labyrinth D
17 labyrinth in smoke before the curtain P
18 labyrinth before the curtain P
19 labyrinth before the curtain P
20 center of the labyrinth E
21 curtain reflected in the spoon M
22 cul de sac A

Krankenhausaufenthalten zu sein.[8] Man vermeint, die Formen der später realisierten Skulptur *Vortex* (1992), die Rippenbögen eines/seines Brustkorbs, wahrzunehmen. Die Begriffe Fotografie, Video oder Performance tauchen im getippten Text von Fox nicht auf, vernachlässigt man einen kleinen handschriftlichen Eintrag. Der abschließenden Skizze für den Ausstellungsaufbau, in der der Performanceraum den linken oberen Teil der Zeichnung einnimmt, sind ausführliche Erläuterungen des Künstlers beigefügt. Die elegante Linien-Zeichnung erscheint jetzt wie ein Zoom aus dem Ausstellungsgrundriss.

Fox beschreibt, wie er ein Modell des Labyrinths von Chartres in seinem Atelier herstellte und kleine, von ihm angefertigte Objekte hineinlegte und fotografierte – unter anderem einen durch seine Krankheit in einem Apfel verlorenen Eckzahn. Er verwandte dafür eine Technik, die bewusst fotografische Unschärfen erzeugte, indem er vor das Objektiv eine Vergrößerungslinse setzte. Es ist sogar von neuen „fotografischen Techniken" die Rede, um die Fotografien „abstrakt und vieldeutiger (mit mannigfachen Interpretationen)" zu machen[9]. Ähnlich verfuhr er bei der Herstellung seines Videos *Incision* (1973). Diese Fotografien wurden stark vergrößert (*blow ups*), was deren ästhetischen Effekt noch verstärkte. Er platzierte ein Bord mit denjenigen Objekten innerhalb des Ausstellungsraums, die Gegenstand von Fotografien und Video waren.[10] Im Video sieht man, wie Fox mit medienspezifischen Eigenarten spielte. Die Kamera dreht sich beziehungsweise der Kameraschwenk erfolgt konzentrisch – dem Weg des Labyrinths folgend –, so dass die Rundungen und Gitterstrukturen, von denen man jeweils einen winzigen, stark vergrößerten Ausschnitt sieht, sich zu bewegen scheinen. [↗**204**] Der Prozess eines *mappings* wird visualisiert, was auch die Katalogbemerkung von Brenda Richardson zu den vergrößerten Fotografien belegt: „Blöcke auf dem Labyrinth errichten. Der Mittelpunkt des Labyrinths. Fadenspule im Labyrinth."[11]

Diese Fotografien und Videos sind keine Dokumentationen von Ausstellung oder Performance, sondern entfalten sich als Elemente einer skulpturalen und prozessualen Arbeitsweise. Terry Fox ist kein Fotograf oder Videokünstler im engeren Sinne und auch kein Klangkünstler. Dennoch würde es zu kurz greifen, von Dokumentation zu sprechen. Schon Willoughby Sharp hob 1970 im Zusammenhang mit den *Amsterdam*-Fotografien (1968) von Fox hervor, dass „diese Fotografien wie ein skulpturales Surrogat wirken"[12]. Nicht für alle Videotapes trifft zu, dass es sich um eine künstlerische Arbeit handelt, auch nicht für diejenigen, an denen Terry Fox als Kameramann oder Produzent beteiligt war. Jedoch scheint es aufschlussreich zu sein, die jeweilige konkrete Funktion seiner Mitarbeit zu befragen.

photography, video or performance. In his final drawing of the exhibition design, Fox has set the performance space in the left upper section and added detailed comments. From the perspective of this sketch, his elegant line drawing appears to be an enlarged element from his exhibition floor plan.

Fox described how he made a model of the Chartres' labyrinth in his studio, set a series of objects into it and photographed them. The objects included an apple imbedded with one of his eye teeth, lost when biting into it during his illness. Fox set a magnifying glass in front of the lens to deliberately create a blurred photographic image of the objects, an approach even described as a new "photographic technique" designed "to make [... the photographs ...] more abstract and more ambiguous (with multiple interpretations)."[9] He adopted a similar approach in his *Incision* video (1973). The *blow ups*, as he titled these photographs, were enlarged, intensifying their aesthetic effect. He set a board with the photographic and video objects inside the exhibition space.[10] The video illustrates how Fox played with media-specific qualities. The camera turns or pans in a concentric circle, following the path of the labyrinth, yet since it only ever shows a small section that is strongly enlarged, the curves and lattice structure appear to take on an independent movement. [↗**204**] This process is the visualization of a "mapping," a view also supported by the catalogue notes by Brenda Richardson on the *blow ups*: "Building blocks on the labyrinth. The center of the labyrinth. Spool of thread in the labyrinth."[11]

Rather than these photographs and videos documenting an exhibition or performance, they are expressions of elements in a sculptural and process-oriented method. In the strict sense of the word, Terry Fox is neither photographer, nor video artist, nor even a sound artist. Nonetheless, to classify this documentation would be doing the images an injustice. As early as 1970 when discussing Terry Fox's *Amsterdam* photographs (1968), Willoughby Sharp pointed out that "these photographs act as surrogate sculpture."[12] Although not all his videotapes can be said to be "art pieces" – not even those where he was involved as camera operator or producer – it nonetheless seems fruitful to consider the particular function of his cooperation in each individual case.

Such a differentiated approach is also relevant for the photos of his performances taken by others. In the exhibition catalogue at the time, the *blow ups* and stills from his *Incision* videotape appeared with photographs taken by his twin brother Larry Fox and by Ute Klophaus, a photographer who worked with Beuys. The photos by Klophaus come from Terry Fox's performance *Hefe* (1971) [↗**83–87**], which he dedicated to her and titled with the German word for yeast. In their cropped style and focus on the materiality of the

Terry Fox, Installation sketch for the exhibition *Hospital* at Reese Palley Gallery, San Francisco, 1971

Eine solche Differenzierung trifft auch auf die Fotografien seiner Performances zu, die nicht von ihm selbst stammen. Im damaligen Ausstellungskatalog erschienen die vergrößerten Fotografien und Stills aus dem Videotape *Incision* neben Fotografien seines Zwillingsbruders Larry Fox und der mit Beuys zusammenarbeitenden Fotografin Ute Klophaus. Letztere entstanden zu einer Performance, die Terry Fox *Hefe* (1971) [↗**83–87**] nannte und die er der Fotografin widmete. Sie ähneln im Ausschnitthaften und in der Konzentration auf die Materialität der Oberflächen den Fotografien, die Larry Fox zur Performance *Yield* (1973) schuf.[13] Die für die Fotografin so typischen gerissenen Ränder stärken diesen Eindruck. Das Ungewöhnliche an einer Ausstellung in institutionellem Rahmen war, dass eine der beiden Galerien ausschließlich Fox' Performance *Yield* vorbehalten blieb, ausgestattet mit einem „eigens gestalteten ,stage set'"[14]. *Yield* fand an drei aufeinanderfolgenden Tagen statt. Das Publikum konnte nicht in den Performanceraum hineingehen, das Ganze aber durch die gezackte Fensterfront von außen verfolgen. Nur Larry Fox war es gestattet, mit der Kamera hautnah dabei zu

photographic surface, these images are similar to Larry Fox's photos of the performance *Yield* (1973), an impression only intensified by the torn edges so characteristic of Klophaus' work.[13] The unusual aspect of this exhibition given in an institutional setting was that one of the two galleries retained the exclusive rights to Fox's *Yield* performance, which was equipped with a "specially-designed 'stage set.'"[14]

Yield took place on three consecutive days. The audience was not allowed into the performance space itself, and could watch the action solely from outside through a zigzag wall of windows. Only Larry Fox was allowed inside the performance space with his camera to photograph everything. Evidently the photos were later displayed close to the area where the performance took place.[15] [↗**142–149**] Since Larry Fox took fragmentary images and focused on blurred, cropped elements, many of these photographs can no longer be related to a concrete situation or object. The frame is filled with fragmentary traces of the curved lines of flour. The salivary water dripping from the mouth to form these arched shapes stands out brightly, in just the same white as the

sein und zu fotografieren. Diese Fotografien wurden offenbar später in der Nähe des Performanceraums ausgestellt.[15] [↗**142–149**] Larry Fox operierte dabei mit fragmentarischen und unscharfen Partien, die bisweilen das Konkrete nicht mehr erahnen lassen. Fragmente der gekurvten Mehlspuren nehmen das Bildformat ein; der diese Bögen bildende und aus dem Mund tropfende Speichel blitzt in demselben Weiß auf wie das lichthelle Mehl; der Körper von Terry Fox ist fast nie in Gänze aufgenommen, eher sind es einzelne Partien wie Knie, Hände oder ein angeschnittenes Gesicht.

In einer Projektbeschreibung der Ausstellung, die wahrscheinlich von Brenda Richardson stammt, ist dementsprechend zu lesen: „Neben diesem Abschnitt, der jenen Werken gewidmet ist, die fotografische Kunstwerke von Fox sind, wird die Ausstellung auch Fotografien enthalten, die die Dokumentation der Performancearbeit des Künstlers in der ganzen Welt repräsentieren (einige dieser Abzüge stammen von Fox und einige von anderen Fotografen). In den vergangenen Jahren, ist es eine anerkannte Tatsache geworden, dass die fotografische und Videodokumentation von Performancearbeiten den Status von Kunstgegenständen annehmen; solche fotografischen Materialien werden jetzt in Museen und Galerien in der ganzen Welt als Kunstwerke ausgestellt (und verkauft). Es werden auch von Fox hergestellte Videotapes ausgestellt; letztere [sind] eine fotografische Kunstform, die Fox mit großem Erfolg weiterentwickelt hat."[16] Die besondere Eigenart dieser Fotografien und Videos als Dokumentationen von Performances ist hier gerade in ihrem Status als „Kunstwerke" begründet.

Authentizität – Präzision

Allgemein gilt der Aufschwung der Performance in den 1970er Jahren als Ausdruck eines Bedürfnisses nach Unmittelbarkeit und als Authentizitätsprobe: Performance als intermediäre, grenzüberschreitende Arbeitsmethode, bei der das Video erstmals als ernstzunehmendes Medium akzeptiert wurde.[17] Das Video suggerierte Präsenz und Gegenwärtigkeit und versprach die Dokumentation in Realzeit. Es blieb aber immer Ergebnis gestalterischer Kontrolle. Die Indexikalität ist keine Eigenschaft des Mediums.
Wie präzise Terry Fox nicht nur seine Ausstellungen auf die jeweiligen Räume hin konzipierte und die oftmals damit im Zusammenhang stehenden Performances vorbereitete, wie sehr er um die exakten Spielregeln für das Authentische und Unvorhergesehene rang, das zeigen die Werknotizen zu seinen berühmten *Children's Tapes*.[18] [↗**12, 61, 138**] Sie offenbaren nicht nur ein genaues Timing und den Rhythmus für die einzelnen Aufnahmen bei der Umwandlung eines

light-colored flour. Rather than Terry Fox's body being shown completely, it is only ever seen as individual elements, such as knees, hands or a cropped face.

In line with this approach, a project description of the exhibition, probably written by Brenda Richardson, notes: "In addition to this section devoted to those pieces which are photographic artworks by Fox, the show will also include photographs representing the documentation of the artist's performance pieces all over the world (some of these prints are by Fox and some by other photographers). In the past few years it has become accepted fact that photographic and video documentation of performance pieces assume the status of art objects; such photographic material is now exhibited (and sold) as artwork in museums and galleries through the world.

Terry Fox, Installation view of his exhibition at University Art Museum, Berkeley, 1973

Installation view of *Hospital* at Reese Palley Gallery, San Francisco, 1971

der 34 Tapes in einen etwas kürzeren Loop (wieder als eine Art Liste mit der Schreibmaschine notiert und zum Teil mit kleinen Stills aus dem Originalband auf einem Blatt zusammengebracht), sondern auch sein visuelles Denken. Terry Fox kommentierte seine Zeichnung zweier Kerzen lakonisch: „Kegel in eine Halbkugel verwandelt." Es sind Überlegungen jenseits der surrealen, humorvollen physikalischen Transformation einfacher Gegenstände, wie eben einer Kerze, eines Löffels, einer Gabel oder von Streichhölzern, die sich durch Wasser unerwartet in einen Stern verwandeln. Man könnte diese zeichnerischen Überlegungen als formalen Findungsprozess verstehen, für den ich an anderer Stelle den Begriff *Notation* eingeführt habe.[19] Sie fließen bei *Children's Tapes* in minimierte Formen, vergleichbar seiner Arbeitsweise und seinem Spiel mit reduzierten Materialien und elementaren Gesten.

So tauchen Kreis und Quadrat in allen Medien immer wieder auf – angefangen von seinen Performances der frühen 1970er Jahre bis hin zu seinen letzten Zeichnungen, den sogenannten *Shadow Drawings* (2006) [↗**218–221**]. Sie verweisen auf weitere grundlegende Elemente, die mit dem Prozessualen verbunden sind: Licht und Schatten. Der Schatten auf dem Vorhang der Performance *Yield* spielt eine ebensolche Rolle wie in den Werknotizen zu *Children's Tapes*. Dort können wir lesen: „The shadow passes", „moon face in the bowl" oder „candle draws water, lighting the wet candle, relighting the candle". Daneben stehen Konstruktionszeichnungen, die Mechanismen des Prozesses sichtbar machen und dafür unterschiedliche Perspektiven auf einem Blatt vereinen. Das war für Terry Fox kein unübliches Verfahren und konnte auch nach der Entstehung des Videotapes wieder auftauchen. [↗**257**] So schrieb und zeichnete er zum Beispiel im Zusammenhang mit dem Video *Wind, water, vuur, aarde,* das er schon 1972 in Farbe drehen konnte, Ausschnitte der Versuchsanordnung auf.[20] Er tat dies zur Vermittlung der Idee seines schon gedrehten Videos.

Children's Tapes wirkt aus heutiger Sicht wie eine Vorwegnahme des bekannten Films *Der Lauf der Dinge* (1987) von Peter Fischli und David Weiß. Die Verwendung einer extremen Nahsicht auf die dreidimensionalen Objekte – die Terry Fox nicht nur aus der herkömmlichen Blickrichtung, sondern auch aus der Vogelperspektive aufnahm – scheint mit der minimalistischen Skulptur zu korrespondieren. Ihm ging es im Gegensatz zu dieser aber um die quälende Dauer, das Potential einer anhaltenden Konzentration, mit der er sich von der Kommerzialisierung des Fernsehens absetzen wollte. Diese Intensität wird durch die vollkommene Stille, in der sich die Verwandlungen vollziehen, physisch fühlbar. Man könnte von einer der ersten Notationen von Realzeit

There will also be exhibited videotapes made by Fox, the latter a photographic art form which Fox has developed with great success."[16] Here, in particular, the special quality of these photographs and videos as a record of performances is rooted in their status as an "art piece."

Authenticity – Precision

In general, the upsurge of interest in performance art in the 1970s can be read as a need for immediacy and testing the limits of authenticity. Performance offered an intermediate, transboundary and transgressive method of working, a practice where video was first accepted as a serious artistic medium.[17] Video suggested presence and contemporaneity, and held the promise of documentation in real time, yet it was always the result of artistic control. Video is never an indexical medium.

Terry Fox's working notes for his renowned *Children's Tapes* not only illustrate just how precisely he planned his exhibitions for specific spaces and prepared the performances often related to them, but also how he struggled to formulate exact rules for the authentic and unpredictable [↗**12, 61, 138**].[18] They not only reveal his meticulous timing and the rhythm of the individual shots as he transforms one of the 34 tapes into a slightly shorter loop (with notes again typed as a list and small-format stills from the original video added to some points on a sheet of paper), but also provide insights into his visual imagination. He may have added the laconic comment to his drawing of two candles "Cone transformed to a demi-sphere," but these thoughts transcend the surreal, humorous physical transformation of simple objects, such as just that candle, or a spoon or fork, or matches which, through water, unexpectedly turn into a star. Instead, these thoughts expressed in a drawing can be read as a process of formal discovery that I have described elsewhere with the term "notation."[19] They flow into the *Children's Tapes* in minimized forms, comparable to Fox's working method and playful approach to reduced materials and elemental gestures.

For example, a circle and square often appear in Terry Fox's works in a wide variety of media – from his performances in the early 1970s to *Shadow Drawings* (2006) [↗**218–221**], his last drawings. They evoke light and shadow – other fundamental elements linked to his process-oriented methods. The shadow on the curtain in *Yield* plays a similar role there as it did in his working notes on *Children's Tapes* when he wrote, "The shadow passes," "moon face in the bowl," or "candle draws, lighting the wet candle, relighting the candle." Next to the phrases, he has set design drawings illustrating the process mechanisms, combining different perspectives on

II

CHILDRENS TAPES LOOP TWO

~~12~~ ~~13.~~ ice in spoon balanced on fork   17:
(16)   from original 4

~~14~~ star matches   4:50
(17)   from original 4

~~15~~. fly caught by the bowl   3:10
(13)   from original 1

~~16~~. reflected candle sinks the spoon with wax   5:30
(18)   from original   4

~~17~~ fly caught by the spoon   1:00
~~18~~   from original 5

Terry Fox, Loose leaf collection for *Children's Tapes*, notes with stills from video, 1974

sprechen.[21] Die Aufnahmen aus seinem Atelier wurden zwischen Mitternacht und Sonnenaufgang gemacht, beleuchtet allein durch eine 1500-Watt-Glühlampe. Mit seinen eigenen Worten: „Ich fuhr mit der Kamera heran, um die Schärfe einzustellen, und dann wieder zurück."[22] Die Videotapes demonstrieren für ihn nicht nur, wie oft zu lesen ist, dass er für seinen Sohn und für die Kinder eine andere Form visueller Bildung vermitteln wollte oder dass diese Arbeit mit dem Labyrinththema verbunden sei, sondern sie kreisen auch um eine Grundmetapher seines künstlerischen Schaffens: die Demonstration von Phänomenen.

Wurde *Children's Tapes* 1974 auf zwei einander gegenüberstehenden Fernsehmonitoren[23] und 1982 im Rahmen einer Fluxus-Ausstellung auf mehreren Monitoren in der Fernsehabteilung eines Warenhauses gezeigt und gleichzeitig zur Eröffnung im Museum als großformatige Projektion mit einem Beamer[24], zählt das Videotape *Two Turns* (1975) sicherlich zu den ungewöhnlichsten Installationsformen seiner Videotapes. [↗**210–211**] Auch hier lud David Ross den Künstler zu einer Produktion ein, die er neben vier älteren Videos von Fox in Long Beach ausstellte. In einem schmalen, schwarzen Raum war das Tape auf einem Monitor zu sehen, nahe einer 1 × 1 Meter großen schwarzen Emaille-Scheibe, die heute als separates Werk gilt (*Shield*, 1975). Ein leichtes Licht hinter dieser Scheibe verband sich mit einem auf die Vidicon Tube[25] eingeätzten Bild des Labyrinths von Chartres. Das Bild des Monitors wurde von der geschwärzten Scheibe reflektiert, so dass dessen Struktur den gesamten Raum überlagerte. In der Beschreibung von Fox findet diese Installation im Raum keine Erwähnung, im Vordergrund steht die Bewegung der eigenen Person bei der Filmaufnahme, seine zwei „walks": vom Studio zur Straße und zurück und umgekehrt.[26]

Der Ausbruch aus Monitorbild und -objekt macht schon früh deutlich, warum Fox das Video als eine seiner Ausdrucksformen nicht weiterverfolgte. Neben dem Rahmen des Monitors empfand er die damals auf eine Stunde festgelegte Länge des Videobandes zunehmend als Beschränkung, und das, obwohl er Videos geeigneter fand als Fotografien, um Performances aufzuzeichnen.[27] In den 1980er Jahren, als die sogenannte Videokunst ihren Aufschwung nahm, stand Fox nicht mehr vor der Kamera. Es wurden jedoch Videodokumentationen von Künstlerfreunden realisiert, wie die von Al Wong gedrehten Aufnahmen seiner Installation *Instruments to Be Played by the Movement of the Earth* (1987) [↗**154, 155**] im Capp Street Project in San Francisco.[28]

Handelte es sich bei *Two Turns* sicherlich um eine Ausnahme, versuchte Terry Fox auch in anderen Fällen von Beginn an präzise festzulegen, in welcher Form seine Tapes gezeigt werden sollten. Die bis ins kleinste Detail gehende

one page. Such an approach was not uncommon for Terry Fox and could also reappear after the videotaping stage was finished. [↗**257**] In reference to his video *Wind, water, vuur, aarde,* which he was able to shoot in color in 1972, he describes and sketches sections of this experimental design to convey the idea of the video he had already completed.[20]

From today's perspective, *Children's Tapes* seems to anticipate Peter Fischli and David Weiss' well-known film *Der Lauf der Dinge* ("The Way Things Go," 1987). There appears to be a relationship between extreme close-ups of three-dimensional objects and minimalist sculpture. In contrast, though, to set his tapes off from the commercial nature of television, Terry Fox's images, not only taken at standard angles but also as high-angle shots, sought to address the tormenting duration of time and the potential of sustained concentration. Through the total silence of the material transformation, this intensity becomes physically perceptible. Here, one could talk of one of the first notations of real time.[21] Fox shot the videos in his studio between midnight and sunrise, only lighting the scenes with a studio light with a 1500 watt bulb. In his own words, once he had set the lighting and positions, he would "zoom all the way in to get it in focus, and then zoom it back out."[22] Many articles and interviews suggest that Fox only made these videotapes as a different kind of visual education for his son and other children, or as another way of exploring the theme of the labyrinth. However, they also revolve around a fundamental metaphor running through his entire oeuvre – the demonstration of phenomena or phenomena demonstrating themselves.

In 1974, *Children's Tapes* were shown simultaneously on two monitors facing each other.[23] As part of a Fluxus exhibition in 1982, they were then shown on several monitors in a department store's TV department and, at the same time, as a large-scale video projection at the opening event in the museum.[24] Nonetheless, his *Two Turns* (1975) must certainly be numbered among his most unusual video installations. [↗**210–211**] *Two Turns* was again the result of David Ross inviting Terry Fox to produce something new to exhibit in Long Beach together with four of his older video works. In a narrow black room, the tape was shown on a monitor next to a 1 × 1 meter black enamel disc, now regarded as a separate work (*Shield*, 1975). A low light behind this disc was merged with an image of the Chartres labyrinth which Fox had burned onto the camera's vidicon tube.[25] The image on the monitor was reflected by the blackened disc so its structure filled the entire space. Fox's description never mentions this spatial installation, but instead focuses on his movements in shooting the video – his two "walks," one from the studio to the street and back, and the other from the street to the studio and back.[26]

Vorbereitung betraf also nicht nur die Ausstellungsperformances, sondern auch die Gestaltung des Ausstellungsraums als „art piece". Das schloss die Präsentation der Videotapes und den Galerieboden ein.[29] So wurden auf Wunsch von Fox in seiner ersten großen Einzelausstellung 1973 in Berkeley die Videotapes nicht während der gesamten Ausstellungsdauer gezeigt, es gab vielmehr an bestimmten Tagen verschiedene Programme. Ähnlich war man bei David Ross' Ausstellung „St. Jude Video Invitational" 1972 in Santa Clara verfahren. Dort hatte die Direktorin Lydia Modi-Vitale 1972 den Künstler George Bolling als Videokurator eingestellt, der unabhängig von seiner Arbeit fürs Museum viele der frühen Videoperformances für Fox aufnahm.[30] Auch in Santa Clara wurden in zwei Galerien unterschiedliche Videoprogramme gezeigt.[31] Zudem scheint es üblich gewesen zu sein, Videovorführungen unter Künstlerfreunden zu veranstalten. Tom Marioni, Begründer des Museums of Conceptual Art (MOCA) und enger Freund von Terry Fox, erinnert sich daran, dass es nicht nur darum ging, sich über neue eigene Arbeiten untereinander auszutauschen, sondern auch darum, die gesamte Länge des Videotapes zu sehen.[32] Denkt man an den heutigen Konsum von Video- und Filmarbeiten im Ausstellungskontext, so okkupieren die Screenings in einer Galerie oder einem Museum nicht nur den realen Raum, sondern werden oftmals auch nur für wenige Minuten im Vorübergehen wahrgenommen.

Doch kehren wir mit unseren Überlegungen kurz zum Galerieboden zurück. Von Terry Fox' erster Einzelausstellung in der Reese Palley Gallery, San Francisco 1971, mit dem Titel „Hospital" haben sich zwei Fotografien erhalten [↗**114**]: Zum einen die Einladungskarte, auf der Fox selbst an Schläuchen im Krankenhaus zu sehen ist und auf der man folgendes Artaud-Zitat lesen kann: „Die Sünde bestand in einer Versuchung, die mich überkam, den Odem meines Herzens durch einen Schlauch über Innen- und Außenhaut zu leiten"[33], und zum anderen die Fotografie der eingerichteten Ausstellung. Die Korrespondenz zwischen den lebenserhaltenden Blutarterien und den auf dem weißen Fußboden sich schlängelnden Kabeln ist offensichtlich. Die Farbe des Bodens scheint in die Wände des Raumes überzugehen, so dass Grenzen verwischt werden und eine räumliche Orientierung schwerfällt. Die Einrichtung der an die Wand gelehnten Krankentrage oder der auf dem Fußboden liegenden Lautsprecher wirkt spontan. Wie in den Werknotizen offenkundig wird, war diese Platzierung auf das Genaueste geplant, selbst die Maße der links in der Fotografie zu sehenden Krankentrage waren festgelegt [↗**58, 59**]. Selbstverständlich gab es minimale Erweiterungen der Grundidee, wie die Verspannung der auf dem Boden liegenden Kabel in die rechte Ecke des

In this early work, Terry Fox's method of transcending the monitor image and the object already clearly indicates why he never pursued the medium of video as one of his forms of artistic expression. Even though he saw video as more suitable than photography for recording performances, he not only felt restricted by the monitor frame, but also increasingly by the fixed length of a video recording, at that time only one hour.[27] In the 1980s, when there was a major boom in what was called video art, Fox no longer used video to record his performances. However, some friends who were artists did document his works on video, such as Al Wong's video of Fox's *Instruments to Be Played by the Movement of the Earth* (1987) [↗**154, 155**] in the Capp Street Project in San Francisco.[28]

While *Two Turns* can certainly be considered an exception, Terry Fox also sought to define from the outset exactly how his video works should be shown in other locations as well. In that sense, meticulous preparation down to the smallest detail was not reserved for his exhibition performances, but was equally pertinent for the design of the exhibition space as an "art piece." This also included the presentation of the videotapes and the floor of the gallery.[29] For example, at his first major show in Berkeley in 1973, Terry Fox did not want to have the same video works shown for the entire duration of the exhibition, but asked for different works to be shown on particular days. A similar approach had also been adopted the year before at David Ross' *St. Jude Video Invitational* exhibition in Santa Clara, where different video programs were shown in two galleries.[30] In 1972, Lydia Modi-Vitale, director of the de Saisset Art Gallery and Museum at the University of Santa Clara, appointed the artist George Bolling as video curator. Independently of his work for the museum, Bolling also recorded many of the early video performances for Fox.[31] Moreover, it also seems to have been common practice among artists to show video performances to groups of friends. Tom Marioni, the founder of the Museum of Conceptual Art (MOCA) and a close friend of Terry Fox's, recalled how this practice did not just offer the chance to discuss one's own new works with others, but also provided an opportunity to watch the entire videotaped material.[32] When we consider today's consumption of video and film works in an exhibition context, the screenings in a gallery or museum not only occupy tangible space, they are often only watched for a few minutes in passing.

At this point, though, we return briefly to consider the floors of the gallery. There are two known photographs of *Hospital*, Terry Fox's first solo show, held in San Francisco's Reese Palley Gallery in 1971 [↗**114**]. The subject of one of the photos is Terry Fox himself at the hospital, shown with a tube coming out of his body. It was used as an exhibition announcement, and includes a quote from Artaud: "This sin

Galerieraumes. Aus den Rekordern strömten der Ton des eigenen Atems von Fox, Waschgeräusche sowie sein Gesang. Dieser Sound muss eine tranceartige Atmosphäre erzeugt haben.

In Erinnerung zu rufen ist, dass sich Performances in den 1970er Jahren nicht nur auf körperzentrierte Aktionsformen vor Publikum oder auf deren Partizipation[34] und die damit einhergehende Authentizität bezogen, sondern präzise Vorbereitungen der räumlichen Situation einschlossen. Die Entlarvung des gängigen „Mythos des Authentischen" lässt sich nicht erst bei den Archivierungen und Reenactments von Performances in den letzten Jahren beobachten. Dies ist schon mit der Einbeziehung des Notationsbegriffs für die Performancekunst der 1970er Jahre möglich. Aus heutiger Sicht erscheint Fox' Entscheidung, oftmals gar kein oder nur ein kleines Publikum bei seinen Performances zuzulassen, in einem gewissen Widerspruch zu seiner Utopie zu stehen, dass Performance eine andere Art von universaler Sprache sei. Dieses Paradox generiert gleichzeitig einen Teil seiner Legende.

Materialität – Skulpturale Elemente

Einem undatierten Text zur Arbeit von Terry Fox, der die Überschrift „Marioni on Terry Fox" trägt, entstammt folgender Passus: „Es ist leicht, über den Künstler zu schreiben, der immer wieder dasselbe Material verwendet. [...] Was das Werk von Terry Fox betrifft, so sind diese Gegenstände, wiewohl er manchmal in verschiedenen Werken genau dieselben Objekte verwendet, von derart verschiedenem Maßstab wie etwas, das man in einer Hand hält im Vergleich zu einem einzigen Werk, das eine ganze Galerie füllt. Der Inhalt reicht von Handlungen im buchstäblichen Sinne wie dem Kneten und Aufgehenlassen von Brotteig bis zu surrealistischen Bildern, die dadurch entstehen, dass Rauch ohne Antrieb aus seinem Mund schwebt, also insbesondere gewundene, geisthafte Formen, die sich in der Luft oder auf einem statischen Objekt auflösen. Die Materialien reichen von Objekten, die man auf der Straße finden kann wie einem Abflussrohr, bis – zu ihm selbst. Während seines Aufenthalts in Amsterdam 1969 fotografierte Fox alltägliche Dinge wie ein Seil, Schnurstücke, Pflastersteine und allgemeine Straßenabfälle. Das Thema in diesem Fall war die Materialität von Gegenständen. [...] In seinen Werken vor 1971, als sein Hauptinteresse der Kinetik des Objekts galt, waren die Elemente Wind und Wasser seine Materialien und seine Aufmerksamkeit konzentrierte sich auf die Verwandlung von Energie wie etwa Elektrizität in Hitze und von Wasser in Dampf. [...] Die Objekte in seinem Alltagsleben sind potentielle Kunstwerke. [...] Später als

consisted of a temptation visited upon me to pass the breath of my heart through a tube to both sides of the surface." [33]

The other photograph was taken of the exhibition's installation. The correspondence between the life-sustaining blood arteries and the snaking cables on the white floor is only too apparent. The color of the floor appears to continue up the walls, blurring borders and hampering spatial orientation. The easel and board leaning against the wall and the speakers on the floor seem to have been placed there spontaneously. From Terry Fox's work notes, though, it is clear that the position of these items was meticulously planned, and even the measurements of the easel on the left of the photograph were precisely determined in advance [↗**58, 59**]. Of course, there were minor enhancements to the basic idea, such as leading the cable on the ground into the right-hand corner of the gallery. Audio recorders played the sound of Terry Fox's own breathing, washing noises and his voice singing a chant – a soundscape which must have created a trance-like atmosphere.

It is worth remembering that performances in the 1970s did not only involve body-centered forms of action in front of an audience or build on audience participation and its associated exploration of authenticity, but also included a precise preparation of the spatial situation.[34] Exposing the popular "myth of the authentic" not only became an issue in the archiving and reenactments of performances over recent years; instead, by incorporating the idea of notation, it can already be seen as a potentiality in performance art in the 1970s. From today's perspective, Fox's decision to stage his performances either with no audience at all or a very sparse audience seems to partially contradict his utopian notion of performance as a kind of universal language – yet, at the same time, it is this paradox which has helped to generate his legendary status.

Materiality – Sculptural Elements

The following comes from an undated text entitled *Marioni on Terry Fox* which deals with one of Terry Fox's works: "It is easy to write about the artist who uses the same material over and over again. [...] With the work of Terry Fox, although he sometimes uses the exact same objects in different pieces, these objects are as different in scale as something one holds in one's hand to a single work that fills an entire gallery. The subject matter ranges from literal actions such as kneading and raising bread dough to surrealistic images created by smoke drifting unpropelled out of his mouth, thus in particular, serpentine, spiritlike forms dissolving into the air or onto a static object. Materials range from objects that one can pick up on a street such as a drainpipe to – himself. While in

Reaktion auf eine langwierige Krankheit verlagerte sich Fox' Hauptaugenmerk von nichtgegenständlichen Anliegen auf die eigentlichen Themen wie Schmerz, Krankheit und Tod [...]. Seine Empfindungen und sein Anliegen sind ganz und gar skulpturaler Art, insofern er Materialien auf eine direkte und aufrichtige Weise nutzt. Die Objekte in seinem Alltagsleben sind potentielle skulpturale Werke."[35]

Terry Fox war mit Tom Marioni, dem MOCA und dem Kreis des Bay Area Conceptualism sehr eng verbunden. Auch wenn der Text nicht von Marioni stammen sollte, ist er im Umkreis der Konzeptkunst anzusiedeln. Lucy Lippards 1972 in Oakland herausgegebene Publikation über die Konzeptkunst und die Dematerialisierung der Kunstobjekte hat die Kunstgeschichtsschreibung maßgeblich bestimmt. Auch im Zusammenhang mit der Videokunst wurde, wie es Bill Viola 1984 formulierte, die Formulierung „process v.s. product" in jenen Jahren zu einem Slogan.[36] Wenn in der Konzeptkunst auch eine künstlerische Idee getrennt von ihrer Ausführung gedacht werden kann[37], bedeutet das nicht, dass Ideen unabhängig von materiellen Bedingungen realisiert wurden.[38] Die Repräsentation durch Künstlertexte ist dabei *eine* Dimension. Es ist nicht verwunderlich, dass Terry Fox' eigene Statements von entscheidender Bedeutung sind und als Teil seiner Arbeit verstanden werden müssen. Bisweilen verstellen sie jedoch den Blick auf die Materialität der in den Performances eingesetzten Objekte ebenso wie auf die Videos und Fotografien. An anderer Stelle ist von „metaphorischen Instrumenten"[39] gesprochen worden, von Einsatz und Wiederverwendung spröder und komplexer Zeichen, die dinglicher wie prozessualer Natur sein können.

Das Video *Turgescent Sex* (1971) [↗76] war, Fox formulierte es selbst, „eine Performance für die Videokamera und entstand, um versendet zu werden, wie ein Brief"[40]. Das Wort wird zum Bild. Der Sound vom Verkehr vor seiner Tür und das Sonnenlicht im Flur werden zum Teil der Arbeit. George Bolling hat die Performance aufgenommen und das Video in einer handschriftlichen Notiz als „documentation of a performance" bezeichnet.[41] Der in der Performance mit einer Augenbinde agierende Fox verstand, auf dem Höhepunkt des Vietnamkrieges, das Umwickeln und Befreien des mit Seilen umfangenen Fischs als politisch intendierte Metapher für die Täter-Opfer-Problematik. Die Augenblinde erlaubte ihm einen elementareren Kontakt zum Fisch, eine andere Art, diesen zu berühren – ein geradezu vergewisserndes Berühren angesichts des Vergänglichen.

Bolling wechselte die Kameraposition und spielte mit der Aufzeichnung der räumlichen Situation bis hin zur Nahsicht und Isolierung von Details. Er erreicht damit eine Intimität, die vom Publikum bei der Performance selbst so nicht

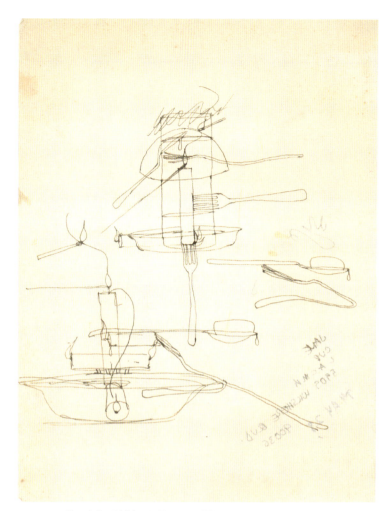

Terry Fox, Sketch for *Children's Tapes*, c. 1974

Amsterdam in 1969 Fox photographed for their sculptural qualities such common objects as rope, pieces of string, cobblestones and general street debris. The subject matter in this case was the materiality of objects. [...] In his work before 1971 when his basic interest was with the kineticism of the object, the elements of wind and water were his materials and his attention was focused upon the transformation of energies e.g. electricity into heat and water to steam. [...] The objects in his everyday life are potential works of art. [...] Later, Fox's focus changed from non-objective concerns to more literal themes dealing with pain, illness and death as a response to his prolonged illness. [...] His sensibilities and concerns are completely sculptural in that he uses materials in a direct and honest way. The objects in his everyday life are potential works of sculpture."[35]

Terry Fox had very close links to Tom Marioni, the Museum of Contemporary Art (MOCA), and conceptual artists in the San Francisco Bay Area. Even if the above text were not written by Marioni himself, it can certainly be located in those conceptual art circles. Lucy Lippard's seminal book on conceptual

erfahren werden kann.[42] Dabei sind nicht nur Fragmente des umwickelten Fischs zu erkennen, sondern auch die Stricke selbst sind durch das Kameravisier eingefangen. Gerade weil der Fisch ein vergängliches Element ist – ähnlich wie das Mehl, das sich durch Wärme von Kerzen oder Glühlampen verändert, oder die Schalen, die das Potential des Klangs enthalten, schien ein besonderes Interesse für seine Materialität zu bestehen.

Die durch Bindfäden mit seinem eigenen Körper verbundenen Fische wurden in demselben Jahr Elemente einer anderen Performance, die an zwei Orten in Fortsetzung stattfand: zunächst im MOCA in San Francisco bei Tom Marioni und dann in der Ausstellung „Fish Fox Kos" im de Saisset Museum in Santa Clara. Die Fische wurden im MOCA mit dem sitzenden Künstler an Zunge und Penis durch Bindfäden verbunden, so dass er das Vibrieren von deren Todeskampf fühlen musste. [↗68, 104–106] Das Gespür für die Materialität und Fragilität der Sinne wurde radikalisiert. In Santa Clara lag Fox unter einem aufgespannten Tuch, um nach rigider Fastenkur von den Fischen zu träumen. Auch hier war er mit den Fischen durch Bindfäden verbunden, die an seinem Körper befestigt waren.[43] Die weiße Farbe des Tuchs betonte die rohe Stofflichkeit von Fisch, Bindfaden und Körper als Material der Arbeit.

Im darauffolgenden Jahr, 1972, griff Fox in Europa den mit Seilen umwickelten Fisch und bestimmte Rituale aus dem Video *Turgescent Sex* erneut auf. Untypisch für seine sonstige Arbeitsweise führte er dafür zwei Installationen und Performances an unterschiedlichen europäischen Orten in Paris und Neapel auf.[44] In mehreren Fotografien der Performance in der Galerie Sonnabend in Paris wird sichtbar, dass Fox nicht mehr weiß gekleidet war, wie es für den filmischen Kontrast des Videos sinnvoll erschien, sondern schwarz. Der Titel der Performance *Pont* (September 1972) [↗92, 93, 121] machte die Verbindung zur Studioperformance zunächst nicht deutlich, sondern verwies eher auf das neu entdeckte Thema des Labyrinths. Eine Mehlspur war auf dem Fußboden bis in den anderen Galerieraum gezogen, wo sie in einem Mehlhaufen neben einer brennenden Kerze auslief. Der Fisch ist nicht mehr zu erkennen, nur in der Abfolge der Fotografien zu erahnen. Er ist in Mehl gehüllt. Eine andere Fotografie, in der die Struktur des schrundigen Mehls zum Bildmotiv wird, verweist darauf, dass sich das Mehl unter der Wärmeentwicklung einer Glühlampe verändert hat. Die Materialität seiner rituellen Elemente wird im Medium der Fotografie ausdrücklich betont.

In der Galerie Lucio Amelio in Neapel fand die Installation/Performance kurz darauf unter dem Titel *L'Unita* (Oktober 1972) [↗88–91] statt – der Titel der Arbeit spielt möglicherweise

art and the dematerialization of the art object, published in Oakland, California in 1972, profoundly influenced the writing of art history. Moreover, in video art as well, as Bill Viola noted in 1984, the phrase "process vs. product" became a slogan in those years.[36] Even if concept art enables an artistic idea to be imagined separately from its realization,[37] ideas still cannot be put into practice independently of the material conditions.[38] Since presentation in artists' texts is *one* dimension in this process, it is hardly surprising that Terry Fox's own statements are crucially important and need to be read as part of his work. At times, however, they obscure the view of the materiality of the objects used in the performances, just as much as the videos and photographs. In another article, they have also been described as "metaphorical instruments," as austere and complex signs, used and reused, which can be of a material as well as a process-oriented nature.[39]

In Fox's own words, the video *Turgescent Sex* (1971) [↗76] was "a performance for the video camera and was made to be sent out, like a letter."[40] The words became an image, and the sound of the traffic in front of the door and the sunlight in the hallway became part of the work. George Bolling recorded the performance, describing the video in a hand-written note as a "documentation of a performance."[41] In the performance, developed at the height of the Vietnam War, Terry Fox sits blindfolded and cross-legged on the floor tying up a fish with a rope and then freeing it again – an act he read as a politically-motivated metaphor of the perpetrator and victim. The blindfold allowed him an elemental contact to the fish, quite a different way of touching it, and nothing short of an affirmative contact in the face of the ephemeral.

Bolling changed camera positions, playing with his recording of the spatial situation, zooming in and isolating details. As a result, his video creates an intimacy that even the audience at the performance would not have experienced.[42] Not only can parts of the fish tied up in rope be identified as fragments in his shots, but the camera lens has even captured the knots in the rope. Precisely because the fish is an ephemeral object – similar to the flour transforming in the heat of candles or light bulbs or the bowls that harbor the potential of sound – its materiality seems to hold a particular interest.

In the same year, fish attached by string to Terry Fox's own body were an element in another performance presented sequentially at two locations: first at Tom Marioni's MOCA in San Francisco and then in the *Fish Fox Kos* show at the de Saisset Museum in Santa Clara. In his MOCA performance, Terry Fox was seated and the fish were connected by strings to his tongue and penis so that he would inevitably feel the vibration of their death throes – a radicalization of the

auf den Titel der Tageszeitung der italienischen Linken an. Zwei Vorhänge teilten den Ausstellungsraum der Galerie. Auf einer Fotografie ist zu erkennen, wie die kleine Gruppe des Publikums die Aktion durch die durchsichtigen Vorhänge verfolgt. Eine Zeichnung des Labyrinths – seine so folgenreiche Entdeckung während der Performance *Pont* (1972) in Paris – teilte darüber hinaus den Raum. Auf einer Großaufnahme des mit Seilen umwickelten liegenden Fisches schimmert dessen Kopf hell im Licht und verbindet sich mit dem körnigen Weiß des Mehlbetts. Die Struktur des Stofflichen erfährt eine Aufwertung. Fox beschrieb in einem Text, wie er den lebendigen Organismus des Brotlaibs mehrfach formte, danach unter einer Glühlampe aufgehen ließ, erneut durchknetete und aufgehen ließ. In einer Fotografie sieht man ihn kniend, auch hier wieder schwarz gekleidet, aber mit einer Armbinde. Dass die Armbinde rot war und für ihn die Farbe des Lebens symbolisierte, wissen wir nur aus den Selbstäußerungen des Künstlers, die Fotografien sind schwarzweiß. Sie spielen mit diesem Kontrast. Offensichtlich steigert die frontale und von schräg links oben eingenommene Perspektive der Fotokamera die dramatische Wirkung des Vorgangs. Ein Mann scheint uns von unten blind anzublicken. Seine Augenbinde und Teile seines Gesichts sind von der Textur des weißen Mehls bedeckt. Fast hilflos hängen seine Arme herab und winden die relativ starren Seile um den Fisch. Man kann geradezu von einer Inszenierung des Stofflichen sprechen.

In den 1970er Jahren waren für Fox die Fische, was für Beuys die Hasen waren, symbolisch aufgeladene Mitakteure der Performance. Lebendige Organismen sterben. Was bleibt, sind die Notationen: Videos, Fotografien, Zeichnungen, Künstlerstatements oder Erinnerungen anderer. Notationen, das sind nicht nur die Vorbereitungen und Dokumente. Notationen, das sind auch die Reste. Nicht nur bei Terry Fox versprechen skulpturale Notationen Annäherungen an eine dem Prozessualen und Ephemeren verschriebene Arbeitsweise.

Sein Interesse für die Oberfläche und Textur der Materialien kündigte sich schon in den 1967 geschaffenen *Paris*-Drawings an. Es sind Abstraktionen von Oberflächen, die er an Gebäudewänden in Paris fand. Für Brenda Richardson machten sie sein Gespür für Oberflächen sichtbar, deren Energie über das Dingliche hinausging. Die Zeichnungen „betonen Terrys Interesse an Oberfläche und Textur (wie man auch in der übrigen Ausstellung sehen kann). […] Ich würde betonen, dass es in Terrys Werk nicht um das ‚Lösen von Problemen' geht. Es gibt keine ‚richtige Antwort' auf die Frage: ‚Worum geht es da?' oder ‚Was bedeutet das?' Terry möchte jedem Betrachter die Gelegenheit geben, die visuelle Schönheit der Schau und ihres Inhalts zu erkunden und darüber

feeling for the materiality and the fragility of the senses. [↗68, 104–106] Fox then underwent a strict period of fasting before the performance in Santa Clara, where he lay under a stretched canvas sheet to dream of the fish. Here too, he was connected to the fish by a string tied to his body.[43] The white of the canvas sheet emphasized the raw physicality of the fish, string and body as the material of his work.

In Europe in 1972, the following year, Fox returned to the theme of a fish tied in rope and certain rituals from the *Turgescent Sex* video. In an approach rather different from his other works, he developed two installations and performances at different European locations in Paris and Naples.[44] As is evident in several photos of his performance at the Sonnabend Gallery in Paris, Fox no longer wore white, which ensured sufficient contrast on the video image, but was now dressed in black. Fox called his Paris performance *Pont* (September 1972) [↗92, 93, 121], though rather than clearly evoking his studio performance, this references his newly discovered theme of the labyrinth. He ran a line of flour along the floor into the second room of the gallery. There, the line ended in a heap of flour next to a lit candle. The fish is entirely coated in flour, no longer distinctly identifiable, only a presence assumed from the sequence of photographs. Another photograph focuses on how the flour changes through the warmth of the lamp, taking the structure of the fissured flour as its subject. In the medium of photography, the materiality of his ritual elements is expressly emphasized.

Shortly afterwards in Naples at the Lucio Amelio Gallery, Terry Fox presented his installation/performance *L'Unita* (October 1972) [↗88–91], whose title may well be taken from the Italian left-wing newspaper of the same name. Fox hung up two translucent curtains to divide the gallery's exhibition space, and one of the photographs shows a small group of people watching the performance through a translucent curtain. He further divided the space with a large drawing of the Chartres labyrinth – the image which was a seminal discovery during his *Pont* (1972) performance in Paris and came to have such a major influence on his work. A close-up of the fish lying tied up in the rope shows the head shining brightly in the light, merging into the grainy whiteness of a bed of flour, valorizing the structure of the material. In his comments on this work, Fox describes making bread, shaping and reshaping this living organism, then placing the bread under a heat lamp so it rose before he beat it down and kneaded it again, and again let it rise. In a photograph of the performance, he is kneeling, again dressed in black, but wearing an arm band. Since the photos of the performance are all black-and-white, we only know from Fox's own description that the arm band was red and, in his view, symbolized the color of life. The photographs

Terry Fox, *Pisces*, contact sheet of the *Fish Fox Kos* exhibition at the de Saisset Museum, Santa Clara, 1971

nachzudenken. Er versucht, eine Atmosphäre zu entwickeln, die viele verschiedene Bedeutungen für viele verschiedene Menschen hat."[45] Dieser Argumentation ist noch immer uneingeschränkt zu folgen, geht es doch bei Fox stets um das Prozessuale einer Atmosphäre. *Room Temperature* wird 1980 eine Arbeit für das Museum of Modern Art in New York heißen. Seine Wiederverwendung von einfachen Materialien betrifft nicht nur die lebendigen Mitakteure der Performances, sondern auch die statischen Objekte. Wie sehr Fox die Struktur der Einkerbungen in das *Plaster Model of a Labyrinth* interessierte, wird nicht nur in dem Video *Incision* (1973) deutlich. Im Film verwandelten sie sich in der zeitlichen Abfolge zu drehenden Fragmenten zentrischer Bögen. Die Funktion in den Performances war eine andere: Zum einen wurde die

play with this contrast. Evidently, the camera's frontal perspective angled from the top left intensifies the drama of the scene. A man seems to gaze up at us blindly from below. His blindfold and part of his face are covered by the textured surface of the white flour. His arms hang down loosely, seemingly helpless, as he winds the relatively stiff rope around the fish. Here, the performance seems nothing less than staged materiality.

In the 1970s, as symbolically-charged participants in a performance, fish played the same role for Fox as the hare for Beuys. But the living organisms die, and only the notation remains – the videos, photographs, drawings, artists' statements and the memories of others. The notations are not just preparatory material and documentation, but also the

Textur des Labyrinths als in sich ruhende Kreisform separiert und zum anderen als an einen Kopf erinnerndes Teil eines körperhaften Objektes eingesetzt. So ist auf den Fotografien seiner Ausstellung in Berkeley 1973 ein Bord zu erkennen, auf dem mehrere Elemente separat mit Kreidelinien verbunden sind. Zu ihnen gehören das *Plaster Model of a Labyrinth* (1972) und der *Eyetooth in Apple*. Motiv einer späteren Fotografie ist ein aus diesen Elementen zusammenmontiertes Objekt. Der Titel *The Beginning of the „Dream of the Eyetooth in the Labyrinth"* (1975) hat zu dem Trugschluss geführt, dass es sich um den Auftakt einer Serie gleichen Titels handele. [↗52, 59] Das Modell wird zum Teil einer 1975 in der Gallerie Schema in Florenz stattfindende Performance *Capillary Action*. Danach hat Fox das wieder separierte *Plaster Model of a Labyrinth* nach San Francisco zurückgebracht.[46] Heute befindet es sich als Kunstwerk im University Museum of Art in Berkeley. Der *Eckzahn* soll demgegenüber sein Grab in der Wand eines Hauses in Italien gefunden haben. Die jeweils sich unterscheidende räumliche Anordnung als skulpturales Element in temporären Zusammenhängen verrät die Dimension eines erweiterten Skulpturbegriffs, um den Terry Fox Zeit seines Lebens rang.

1 Elisabeth Jappe, Das Recht, fliegen zu können. Performance – Ritual und Haltung. In: *documenta 8*. Kassel 1987, S. 120, fortan Jappe 1987. Jappe war zuständig für den umfangreichen Performanceteil dieser Ausstellung und verfasste mehrere grundlegende Publikationen zur Performancekunst.

2 Terry Fox, Ricochet, 1987, Künstlerstatement. In: Bernd Schulz (Hg.), *terry fox. works with sound*. Ausst.-kat. Heidelberg 1998, S. 85, fortan Schulz 1998

3 Diese Begriffe sind ungenaue Termini, die Terry Fox früh hinterfragte. So kritisierte er die Entwicklung der Performance hin zu einer kommerziellen Veranstaltung. Verwandte er zunächst den Begriff *action*, so sprach er später von *situations*. Dennoch nahm er an mehreren Ausstellungen teil, die diesem Phänomen gewidmet waren, und gehörte zum Freundeskreis von Tom Marioni, dem Begründer des MOCA in San Francisco, mit dem er sich zwei Jahre lang ein Atelier teilte.

4 Die Fotografien geben die politische Brisanz kaum wieder. Der Versuch, Filmaufzeichnungen ausfindig zu machen – auf einer der Fotografien ist ein Mann mit einer Filmkamera zu erkennen –, scheiterte trotz meiner Kontaktaufnahme zu dem damaligen Performanceteilnehmer und Journalisten Charles Shere und seiner Vermittlung zu Peter Hobe. Siehe das Statement von Terry Fox bei Willoughby Sharp, Terry Fox: Elemental Gestures. In: *Arts* (Mai 1970), S. 48. Siehe auch: Interview mit Robert White: Es ist der Versuch einer neuen Kommunikation. In: *View*, Oakland, Vol. II, No. 3 (Juni 1979), wiederabgedruckt in: Eva Schmidt (Hg.), *Terry Fox. Ocular Language. 30 Jahre Reden und Schreiben über Kunst. 30 Years of Speaking and Writing about Art*. Gesellschaft für Aktuelle Kunst Bremen, Köln 2000

5 Interview der Verfasserin mit Wulf Herzogenrath am 27.6.2015

6 Terry Fox, Suono Interno, 1979, Künstlerstatement. In: Schulz 1998, vgl. Anm. 2, S. 75

7 Die Ausstellung gehörte zu den ersten, die Brenda Richardson für das University Art Museum in Berkeley konzipierte. *Terry Fox*. Ausst.-kat. University Art Museum, Berkeley 1973, fortan Fox 1973. Das Buch, heute eine bibliophile Kostbarkeit, das Richardson mit dem Gestalter Bruce Montgomerey herstellte, ist kein herkömmlicher Ausstellungskatalog, sondern eher „eine Reflexion des Kunstwerks, welches das Buch dokumentierte". Montgomery wollte die „Ringmappe mit Bildern und dazugehörigem Kommentar", die Brenda Richardson für jede Ausstellung anfertigte, in den Katalog transferieren. Der Katalog hat darum abgerundete Ecken. Die Abbildungen sind randfüllend platziert, die Kommentare zum Teil schräg gesetzt. Brief Brenda Richardson an Marita Loosen-Fox, 13.5.2015, Estate of Terry Fox, Köln

vestiges and residues. In Terry Fox's oeuvre, as in other artists' work as well, sculptural notations hold out the promise of accessing a working method dedicated to process and the ephemeral.

Fox's interest in surfaces and the texture of materials was already apparent in his 1967 *Paris* Drawings, created as abstraction of surfaces that he found on the walls of buildings in Paris. According to Brenda Richardson, these were a visible expression of Fox's feeling for surfaces that have an energy transcending the concretely real. The drawings "emphasize Terry's interest in surface and texture (as you can see in the rest of the exhibition as well). [...] I would emphasize that Terry's work is not about 'problem-solving': there is no 'right answer' to the question 'What is this about?' – or 'What does this mean?' Terry wants to give each viewer the opportunity to explore, to meditate, on the show's visual beauty and on its contents. He is trying to develop an atmosphere which may have many different meaning to many different people."[45] This argument is still unconditionally valid, since Fox's work was always exploring the process-oriented nature of an atmosphere – as in 1980, when he chose the title *Room Temperature* for his video installation at the Museum of Modern Art in New York.

Revisiting and reframing the simple materials in his performances was not only limited to the living participants, but also to the static objects that he used. His profound interest in the structure of indentations in the *Plaster Model of a Labyrinth* is not only evident from his video *Incision* (1973) where, through the way the video is filmed, these indentations are transformed into fragments of centric arches which turn and move. In the performances, though, the labyrinth had a different function. On the one hand, Fox focused on its texture as an independent circular form and, on the other, employed the shape as an element reminiscent of a head in a body-like object. One of the photographs of his 1973 Berkeley exhibition, for example, shows a board with several individual elements, including the *Plaster Model of a Labyrinth* (1972) and *Eyetooth in Apple*, linked by lines of chalk. A later photograph has been taken of an object assembled from these elements. Entitled *The Beginning of the "Dream of the Eyetooth in the Labyrinth"* (1975), it encouraged the erroneous belief that this was start of an eponymous series. [↗52, 59] The model was integrated into Fox's *Capillary Action* performance in the Galleria Schema in Florence in 1975. Afterwards, he took the *Plaster Model of a Labyrinth* on its own back to San Francisco, and it now belongs to the collection of the University Museum of Art in Berkeley.[46] The *Eyetooth* is said to be buried in the wall of a house in Italy. The different spatial arrangements as sculptural elements in ephemeral contexts point to an expanded concept of sculpture which preoccupied Terry Fox throughout his life.

Translated from the German by Andrew Boreham

8 Terry Fox, der schon früh an einer Krebskrankheit litt und 1972, von den Ärzten erneut aufgegeben, durch Chemotherapien überlebte, hat zeit seines Lebens um die Transformation dieser Erfahrung gerungen. Sein Glaube an die heilende Wirkung von Kunst war mit dieser existentiellen Erfahrung verbunden und ist in der Intensität seiner Arbeiten wohl zu spüren.

9 Brief Jerrold Ballein und August Manza an James R. Thomas, National Endowment for the Arts, 30.12.1974, sowie Brenda Richardson, Terry Fox Exhibition Catalogue an „all Security Staff", 5.9.1973, University Art Museum, Berkeley, Archiv

10 *Incision* entstand auf Einladung von David Ross, war aber auch in Berkeley zu sehen, vgl. *Circuit: A Video Invitational.* Ausst.-Kat. Everson Museum of Art in Syracuse, New York 1973

11 Fox 1973, vgl. Anm. 7, o. S. In dem ausgezeichneten Katalog mit Texten von David Ross, Kira Perov u. a., werden die Videoarbeiten von Terry Fox als „bahnbrechende performance-orientierte Videotape-Dokumente" verstanden (David Ross, S. 15) und als „erweitertes Medium des Konzept-/Performancekünstlers [...], das in Performances und Installationen sowie in Einkanal-Videotape-Arbeiten zum Einsatz kommt" (Kira Perov, S. 28). Das Video *Incision* findet keine weiterführende Erläuterung; vgl. Kathy Rae Huffman (Hg.), *Video: A Retrospective 1974–1984.* Long Beach Museum of Art. Long Beach, CA, 1984, fortan Huffman 1984.

12 Willoughby Sharp, *Terry Fox.* Ausst.-Kat. Reese Palley Gallery. San Francisco 1970

13 Da der Katalog zur Ausstellungseröffnung erschien, konnten die Fotografien von Larry Fox zu *Yield* (1973) nicht aufgenommen werden. Sie stellen heute jedoch die wichtigste Quelle für die Performance dar.

14 Brief, 30.12.1974, University Art Museum, Berkeley, Archiv, vgl. Anm. 9

15 „Außerdem wurde jede von Fox' Performances von seinem Zwillingsbruder Larry Fox fotografisch dokumentiert, und diese Fotos wurden am Ende der Terry-Fox-Ausstellung als eine letzte Aufzeichnung des Projekts ausgestellt." Ebd.

16 Brenda Richardson (vermutl.), Terry Fox: Project Description, University Art Museum, Berkeley, Archiv

17 Jappe 1987, vgl. Anm. 1, S. 71 und S. 116

18 *Terry Fox. Children's Videotapes.* Interview von Willoughby Sharp und Liza Bear mit Terry Fox. In: *Avalanche,* December 1974, wiederabgedruckt in: *Terry Fox – Metaphorical Instruments.* Ausst.-Kat. Museum Folkwang Essen, daadgalerie Berlin 1982, S. 50, 51, fortan Fox 1982, sowie Schmidt 2000, vgl. Anm. 4, S. 63ff.

19 Angela Lammert, *Bildung und Bildlichkeit von Notation. Von der frühen Wissenschaftsfotografie zu den Künsten des 20. Jahrhunderts.* München 2015 (im Erscheinen)

20 2003 sollte aus der Versuchsanordnung für das Video eine Installation entstehen: *Fire in the Water, Water in the Air, Air in the Earth, Earth in the Sea,* abgebildet in: *(Re/De) constructions &c. Terry Fox.* Ausst.-Kat. Kassel 2003, S. 26

21 Steve Anker, Kathy Geritz, Steve Seid (Hg.), *Radical Light. Alternative Film & Video in the San Francisco Bay Area, 1945–2000.* Berkeley, Los Angeles 2010, S. 164, fortan Anker u. a. 2010

22 Schmidt 2000, vgl. Anm. 4, S. 66

23 Ebd.

24 Gespräch der Verfasserin mit Marita Loosen-Fox am 28.4.2015. Auf den Einfall von René Block für die Fluxus-Ausstellungseröffnung „40 Jahre: Fluxus und die Folgen" im Sommer 2002 in Wiesbaden reagierte Terry Fox nicht ablehnend, sondern eher positiv überrascht. Carsten Seiffarth wies im Gespräch mit der Verfasserin am 24.6.2015 auf die geniale Installation im Warenhaus hin.

25 Bei der Vidicon Tube handelt es sich um eine mit einer Halbleiterplatte als lichtempfindlicher Schicht ausgestattete Bildröhre. *Two Turns* wurde 1975 erstmals im Long Beach Museum of Art in California gezeigt.

26 Terry Fox. In: *Anna Canepa Video Distribution.* Vertriebsbroschüre. Venice/CA 1975(?), S. 6, fortan Canepa 1975

27 In einem Interview mit Willoughby Sharp für die Zeitschrift *Avalanche,* New York, Winter 1971, S. 70–81, wiederabgedruckt in: Schmidt 2000, vgl. Anm. 4, S.10: „W.S. Man wird deine Arbeit nicht vollständig verstehen, wenn man dir nicht bei der Durchführung zusieht oder wenn man nicht ein Video davon sieht. / T.F. Genau. Fotografien sind ungeeignet, aber ein Video würde zeigen, was passiert ist. In gewisser Weise hat diese Arbeit ein begrenztes Publikum – genau wie Landschaftsarbeiten. Sehr wenige Leute haben Zugang zu den konkreten Orten dieser Kunst. Ebensowenig hat man direkten Zugang zu meiner Arbeit, wenn man nicht Zeuge einer Performance war." Siehe auch: Es ist der Versuch einer neuen Kommunikation. Interview von Robert White. In: *View,* Vol. II, No. 3, Oakland, June 1979, wieder abgedruckt in: Schmidt 2000, vgl. Anm. 4, S. 90

28 Al Wong, der zwischen den beiden „Planeten" Experimentalfilm und Videokunst changierte, sieht auch dieses Video als „art piece" an und zielt mit seiner Aufnahmetechnik ohne Schnitt auf die Dauer des Ereignisses, ein Verfahren, das er auch für die Videodokumentation einer Terry-Fox-Ausstellung in Berkeley im selben Jahr verwandte.

1 Elisabeth Jappe, *Das Recht, fliegen zu können. Performance – Ritual und Haltung, documenta 8,* Kassel 1987, p. 120, hereafter Jappe 1987. Jappe was responsible for the extensive performance section in this exhibition and wrote several seminal publications on performance art.

2 Terry Fox, *Ricochet,* 1987, "Artist's Statement," Bernd Schulz *(ed.), terry fox. works with sound,* exh. cat., Heidelberg, 1998, p. 85, hereafter Schulz 1998

3 These terms are imprecise and Terry Fox soon questioned their validity, criticizing, for example, performance developing into a commercial event. Initially, he preferred to use the term "actions," and later spoke of "situations." Nonetheless, he took part in several exhibitions devoted to these art forms and was a friend of Tom Marioni, founder of the MOCA in San Francisco, sharing a studio with him for two years.

4 The photos hardly manage to convey the politically-charged nature of the performance. In one of the photographs, a man is filming the events. Unfortunately, my attempts to locate the film material proved unsuccessful even though I managed to contact Charles Shere, a journalist and performance participant at the time, and he kindly provided a contact to Peter Hobe. See Terry Fox's statement in Willoughby Sharp, Terry Fox, "Elemental Gestures," *Arts* (May 1970), p. 48. See also the interview with Robert White, "It's an Attempt at a New Communication," *View,* Oakland, vol. II, no. 3 (June 1979), reprinted in Eva Schmidt (ed.), *Terry Fox. Ocular Language. 30 Jahre Reden und Schreiben über Kunst. 30 Years of Speaking and Writing about Art.* Gesellschaft für Aktuelle Kunst Bremen, Cologne, 2000, p. 82, hereafter Schmidt 2000

5 Wulf Herzogenrath, personal communication on June 27, 2015

6 Terry Fox, *Suono Interno,* 1979, "Artist's Statement," Schulz 1998, cf. note 2, p. 75

7 This was one of the first exhibitions that Brenda Richardson designed for the University Art Museum in Berkeley. *Terry Fox,* exh. cat., University Art Museum, Berkeley, 1973, hereafter Fox 1973. Richardson worked with designer Bruce Montgomery to produce the exhibition catalogue. Their collaboration aimed at creating "a reflection of the artwork the book documented," and generated a very different style of catalogue, now ranked as a bibliophilic gem. Since Montgomery wanted the "ring binder with images and captioned commentary," which Brenda Richardson made for every exhibition to be transferred to the catalogue, the published version has rounded edges. The images expand to fill the page margins, and some of the texts are set at an angle. Letter from Brenda Richardson to Marita Loosen-Fox, May 13, 2015, Estate of Terry Fox, Cologne

8 Terry Fox struggled with his health throughout his life. He suffered from cancer early in life; in 1972, when the doctors had again given up on his chances, he only survived due to chemotherapy. His belief in the healing power of art was strongly connected with this life-changing experience, and can be sensed in the intensity of his works.

9 Letter from Jerrold Ballein and August Manza to James R. Thomas, National Endowment for the Arts, Dec. 30, 1974, as well as Brenda Richardson, Terry Fox exhibition catalogue, to "all security staff," Sept. 5, 1973, University Art Museum, Berkeley, Archive

10 *Incision* was created at the invitation of David Ross, but was also shown in Berkeley, cf. *Circuit: A Video Invitational,* exh. cat., Everson Museum of Art in Syracuse, New York, 1973

11 Fox 1973, cf. note 7, unpaginated. In the excellent catalogue with articles by authors including David Ross and Kira Perov, Terry Fox's video works are considered to be "pioneering performance-oriented videotape documents" (David Ross, p. 15) and the "extended medium of the conceptual/performance artist [...] used in performances, and installations, as well as in single-channel videotape works" (Kira Perov, p. 28). The *Incision* video is not discussed further; cf. Kathy Rae Huffman (ed.), *Video: A Retrospective 1974–1984. Long Beach,* California, 1984, hereafter Huffman 1984.

12 Willoughby Sharp, *Terry Fox,* exh. cat., Reese Palley Gallery, San Francisco, 1970

13 Since the catalogue was published for the exhibition opening, Larry Fox's photographs of *Yield* (1973) could not be included. Today, they are the most important documentary source for this performance.

14 Letter, Dec. 30, 1974, University Art Museum, Berkeley, Archive, cf. note 9

15 "In addition, each of Fox's performances was photographically documented by his twin brother, Larry Fox, and these photos were displayed at the close of the Terry Fox exhibition as a final record of the project." Ibid.

16 Brenda Richardson (probably), Terry Fox: Project Description, University Art Museum, Berkeley, Archive

17 Jappe 1987, cf. note 1, p. 71 and p. 116

18 *Terry Fox. Children's Videotapes,* interview of Terry Fox by Willoughby Sharp and Liza Bear, *Avalanche,* December 1974, reprinted in *Terry Fox – Metaphorical Instruments,* exh. cat., Museum Folkwang Essen, daadgalerie Berlin 1982, pp. 50–51, hereafter Fox 1982, see also Schmidt 2000, cf. note 4, p. 63ff.

19 Angela Lammert, *Bildung und Bildlichkeit von Notation. Von der frühen Wissenschaftsfotografie zu den Künsten des 20. Jahrhunderts.* Munich, 2015 (in preparation)

20 In 2003, the instructions for the video were taken to create the installation *Fire in the Water, Water in the Air, Air in the Earth, Earth in the Sea,* illustrated in *(Re/De) constructions &c. Terry Fox,* exh. cat., Kassel, 2003, p. 26

21 Steve Anker, Kathy Geritz, Steve Seid (eds.), *Radical Light. Alternative Film & Video in the San Francisco Bay Area, 1945–2000.* Berkeley, Los Angeles, 2010, p. 164, hereafter Anker, et. al., 2010

22 Schmidt 2000, cf. note 4, p. 66

23 Ibid.

24 Marita Loosen-Fox, personal communication on Apr. 28, 2015. On René Block's idea of showing the video at the opening of the Fluxus exhibition in Wiesbaden in 1982 Terry Fox did not react negatively but was rather positively surprised. In a personal communication on June 24, 2015, Carsten Seiffarth mentioned the inspired installation in the department store.

25 A vidicon tube is a storage-type camera tube equipped with a semiconductor plate as a photosensitive target. *Two Turns* was first shown in 1975 at the Long Beach Museum of Art in California.

29 Gespräch der Verfasserin mit Paul Kos am 6.6.2105 und mit Barney Bailey am 7.6.2015

30 Howard Fried, der ebenfalls mit George Bolling zusammenarbeitete, bezeichnete ihn im Gespräch mit der Verfasserin am 7.6.2015 eher als „collaborator" denn als Dokumentaristen.

31 Der Film *Clutch* (1971) von Fox wurde im Programm B in der Galerie II zusammen mit Arbeiten von Douglas Davis, Video Freex, Taka Ilmura, Richard Serra, Keith Sonnier und Rainbow Video gezeigt, jeweils am Dienstag, Donnerstag und Samstag. In der Galerie I war das Programm A mit Arbeiten von John Baldessari, Lynda Benglis, George Bolling, Paul Kos, Howard Fried, Frank Gillette, Joe Glassman, Shigeko Kuboto, Nam June Paik und William Wegman zu sehen, jeweils am Montag, Freitag und Samstag. de Saissett Museum, Santa Clara, Archiv.

32 Gespräch der Verfasserin mit Tom Marioni am 5.6.2015 und mit Al Wong am 6.6.2015

33 Terry Fox hat das Zitat in der englischen Übersetzung von David Rattray dem Buch *Artaud Anthology* (hg. v. Jack Hirschmann, San Francisco 1965, S. 186) entnommen.

34 Marie-Luise Angerer, Performance und Performativität. In: Hubertus Butin (Hg.), *Begriffslexikon zur zeitgenössischen Kunst*. Köln 2014, S. 280, fortan Butin 2014. Die kluge Beobachtung der Autorin, dass das Reale immer im Medium enthalten ist und Medien wie Videokamera oder Rekorder darüber hinaus einen integralen Bestandteil von Performances bilden, stellt die Bewegung und das Prozessuale in den Mittelpunkt. Dies ist um den Begriff der Notation des Prozessualen (ich spreche hier vom Temporären) zu ergänzen. (S. 283).

35 Der mit Schreibmaschine geschriebene Text trägt den Titel „Marioni on Terry Fox" und stammt aus dem Fond Tom Marioni, den dieser an das Archiv der University Art Museums, Berkeley, gegeben hat. Marioni erklärte in einem Gespräch mit der Verfasserin am 5.6.2015 jedoch, der Text sei zwar wunderbar, aber er sei nicht der Autor, die Ausdrucksweise sei zu akademisch.

36 Bill Viola, History, 10 Years, and the Dreamtime. In: Huffman 1984, vgl. Anm. 11, S. 19. Er fasste zusammen: „In diesem Licht besteht das Hauptproblem für Künstler, die dieser Tage Video benutzen, darin, was sie nicht aufzeichnen sollen. Die Herstellung eines Videotapes wäre dann also nicht so sehr das Schaffen oder Aufbauen von etwas, sondern eher das Wegschneiden oder Weghauen von etwas anderem, bis nur noch eine spezifische Sache übrigbleibt " (S. 19–20).

37 Lucy Lippard, John Chandler, *The Dematerialization of the Art Object from 1961 to 1972*. Oakland 1972

38 Sabeth Buchmann, Conceptual Art. In: Butin 2014, vgl. Anm. 34, S. 53. Hubertus Butin wies im Sinne von Carl Andre darauf hin, dass die konzeptuelle Arbeit ihre Vermittlung eines Mediums und somit eines materiellen Zeichenträgers bedarf, sei es in bildnerischer, objekthafter oder schriftlicher Form. Hubertus Butin, „*Live in your head*". *Aspekte der Konzeptkunst der 1960er und 70er Jahre*. Unveröffentlichtes Manuskript 2015

39 Fox 1982, vgl. Anm. 18

40 Canepa 1975, vgl. Anm. 26

41 George Bolling, [Handschriftliche Notiz], de Saissett Museum, Santa Clara, Archiv. Dieser Hinweis findet sich bei der handschriftlichen Notiz zu *Clutch* (1971) nicht. Steve Seid berichtete in einem Gespräch mit der Verfasserin am 3.6.3015, dass Bolling ihm eine Kiste voller Videos für die Sammlung des Pacific Film Archive in Berkeley gab, in dem er mehrere Videotapes von Terry Fox entdeckte. Siehe auch: Conversation with Steve Seid by Tanya Zimbardo, March 17, 2015, http://www.artpractical.com/column/studio-sessions-conversation-with-steve-seid/, zuletzt am 13.7.2015

42 Steve Seid stellte überzeugend heraus, dass Fox in seinem Tape *The Rake's Progress* (1971) sein Interesse an der Spezifik des Mediums Film zeigte. Das händische Bestreichen des Kameraglases mit einer grauen Substanz, das Verwischen mit einem Tuch und die gespiegelte Reflexion erzeugten den Effekt eines vollständig sichtbaren Rahmens. In: Anker u. a. 2010, vgl. Anm. 21, S. 168

43 Terry Fox, Künstlerstatement. In: Fox 1982, vgl. Anm. 18, S. 34. Siehe auch Interview mit Achille Bonito Oliva. In: *domus* 521, April 1973, wiederabgedruckt in: Fox 1982, vgl. Anm. 18, S. 44

44 *Terry Fox. Arbeiten zum Labyrinth, 1972–1978*. Sein Text enthält Beschreibungen von *Turgescent Sex*, *Pont* und *L'Unita*. In: Ebd., S. 56

45 Brenda Richardson an Security Staff, 5.9.1973, vgl. Anm. 9

46 Fox 1982, vgl. Anm. 18, S. 62

26 Terry Fox, *Anna Canepa Video Distribution*. Venice, CA 1975 (?), p. 6, hereafter Canepa 1975

27 In an interview with Willoughby Sharp for *Avalanche*, New York, Winter 1971, pp. 70–81, reprinted in Schmidt 2000, cf. note 4, p. 11: "W.S. People won't fully understand the piece unless they watch you perform in it, or see a videotape of it. T.F. Right. Photographs are inadequate, but a videotape would show you what happened. In a sense this work has a limited audience – like earthworks. Very few people have access to the physical sites of earthworks. In the same way, people can't have a direct experience of my work unless they witness the performance." See also the interview with Robert White: "It's an Attempt at a New Communication," *View*, vol. II, no. 3, Oakland, June 1979, reprinted in Schmidt 2000, cf. note 4, p. 91

28 Al Wong, who moved between the two "planets" of experimental film and video art, also regards this video as an "art piece." In shooting this as one single take without edits, he also employs a technique he used for the video documenting a Terry Fox exhibition in Berkeley in the same year.

29 Paul Kos, personal communication on June 6, 2105 and Barney Bailey, personal communication on June 7, 2015

30 Fox's film *Clutch* (1971) was shown in Program B in Gallery II every Tuesday, Thursday and Saturday together with works by Douglas Davis, Video Freex, Taka Ilmura, Richard Serra, Keith Sonnier and Rainbow Video. Gallery I showed Program A every Monday, Friday and Saturday with works by John Baldessari, Lynda Benglis, George Bolling, Paul Kos, Howard Fried, Frank Gillette, Joe Glassman, Shigeko Kuboto, Nam June Paik and William Wegman. de Saissett Museum, Santa Clara, Archive.

31 Howard Fried, who also worked with George Bolling, called him more of a "collaborator" than a documentary filmmaker, personal communication on June 7, 2015.

32 Tom Marioni, personal communication on June 5, 2015 and Al Wong, personal communication on June 6, 2015

33 Terry Fox used an English translation of a quote from the book *Artaud Anthology* (Jack Hirshman, ed., trans. by David Rattray, San Francisco, 1965, p. 186)

34 Marie-Luise Angerer, *Performance und Performativität*, Hubertus Butin (ed.), *Begriffslexikon zur zeitgenössischen Kunst*. Cologne, 2014, p. 280, hereafter Butin 2014. The insightful remark of the article's author that the real is always contained in the medium and, moreover, media such as the video camera or recorder form an integral element of performances, underscores the centrality of movement and the process. This then needs to be supplemented by the concept of the notation of the process (in this case, I am referring to the ephemeral, p. 283).

35 The typed text is entitled "Marioni on Terry Fox" and comes from the papers which Tom Marioni donated to the archive of the University Art Museum, Berkeley. However, Marioni has stated that although the text is wonderful, he is not the author since he would not use such a scholarly style; personal communication on June 5, 2015.

36 Bill Viola, *History, 10 Years, and the Dreamtime,* Huffman 1984, cf. note 11, p. 19. He summarized: "In this light, the main problem for artists using video these days is in deciding what *not* to record. Making a videotape then might not be so much the creation or building up of something, but more like the cutting or carving away of everything else until only a specific thing remains." (pp. 19–20)

37 Lucy Lippard, John Chandler, *The Dematerialization of the Art Object from 1961 to 1972*, Oakland, 1972

38 Sabeth Buchmann, "Conceptual Art," Butin 2014, cf. note 33, p. 53. Hubertus Butin references Carl Andre to point out that the conceptual work requires a medium to be conveyed and hence a material bearer of signs, whether in sculptural, representational or written form. Hubertus Butin, "*Live in Your Head,*" *Aspekte der Konzeptkunst der 1960er und 70er Jahre*. Unpublished manuscript, 2015.

39 Fox 1982, cf. note 18

40 Canepa 1975, cf. note 26

41 George Bolling, handwritten note, de Saissett Museum, Santa Clara, archive. This reference is not included in the handwritten notes on *Clutch* (1971). Steve Seid has noted (personal communication on June 3, 2015), that he discovered several videotapes by Terry Fox in a box full of videos that Bolling gave him for the Pacific Film Archive collection in Berkeley. See also "Conversation with Steve Seid," Tanya Zimbardo, March 17, 2015, http://www.artpractical.com/column/studio-sessions-conversation-with-steve-seid/ last accessed on July 13, 2015

42 Steve Seid convincingly argues that Fox's interest in the specific nature of film as a medium is evident in his tape *The Rake's Progress* (1971). Manually brushing the camera lens with a gray substance, wiping it with a cloth and the mirror reflection create the effect of a fully visible space, Anker, et. al., 2010, cf. note 21, p. 168

43 Terry Fox, "Artist's Statement," Fox 1982, cf. note 18, p. 34. See also the interview with Achille Bonito Oliva, *domus*, 521, April 1973, reprinted in Fox 1982, cf. note 18, p. 44

44 *Terry Fox. Works from the Labyrinth, 1972–1978*. His text also contains descriptions of *Turgescent Sex*, *Pont* and *L'Unita*. Ibid., p. 61

45 Brenda Richardson to the security staff, Sept. 5, 1973, cf. note 9

46 Fox 1982, cf. note 18, p. 62

Situations

For me the most important aspect of it is treating the body as an element in its own right rather than as an initiator of some act. Instead of disregarding it in the making of sculpture, using it directly as a tool. The body is an element like any other, only a lot more flexible.

Terry Fox, *1971*

Für mich ist das Wichtigste, den Körper als ein Element für sich zu behandeln und nicht als den Initiator einer Handlung. Ihn beim Machen einer Skulptur nicht zu ignorieren, sondern ihn direkt als Werkzeug zu verwenden. Der Körper ist ein Element wie jedes andere, nur viel flexibler.

Well, it is like ... performance has changed so much. It's almost impossible to talk about performance anymore. That word means something different from what it used to. There must be a better word, we could say "situation." I make a situation. The actual situation is what's going on in the space we're in. And the situation involves everybody there, and there is a blend when everybody starts participating.

Performance hat sich ziemlich verändert. Es ist fast unmöglich, noch über Performance zu sprechen. Das Wort bedeutet etwas anderes als früher. Es muss ein besseres Wort geben, man könnte „Situation" sagen. Ich schaffe eine Situation. Die tatsächliche Situation ist das, was in dem Raum passiert, in dem wir uns befinden. Und die Situation schließt jeden mit ein und es gibt eine Vermischung, wenn jeder zu partizipieren anfängt.

Terry Fox, *1979*

Körperliche Zustände

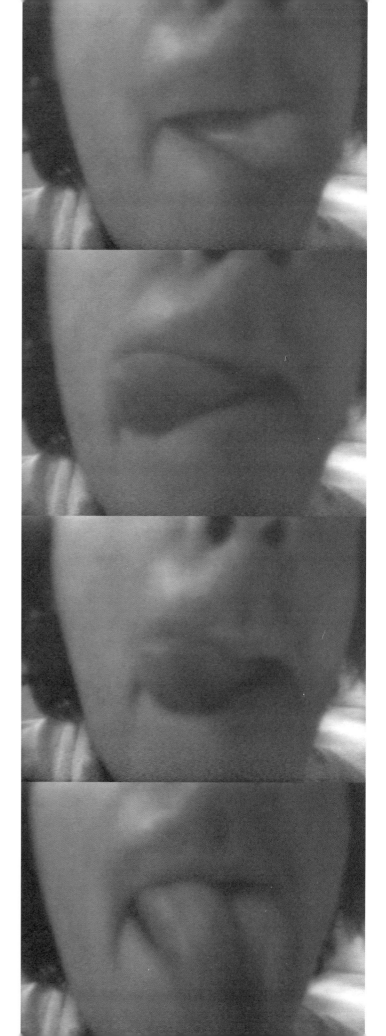

Terry Fox, *Tonguings*, 1970, video stills

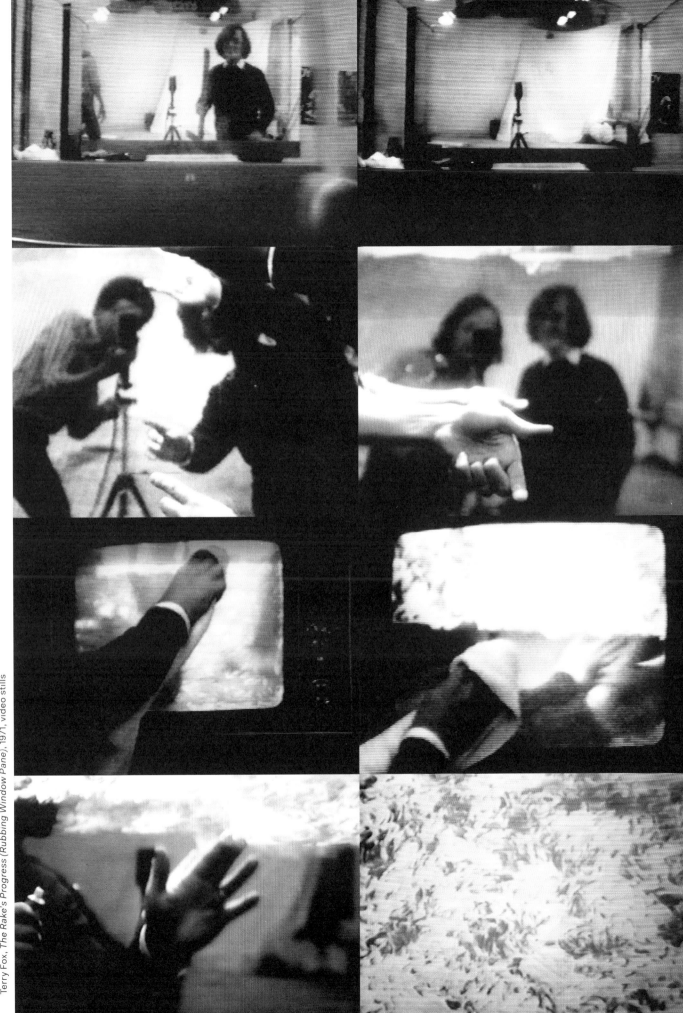

Terry Fox, *The Rake's Progress (Rubbing Window Pane)*, 1971, video stills

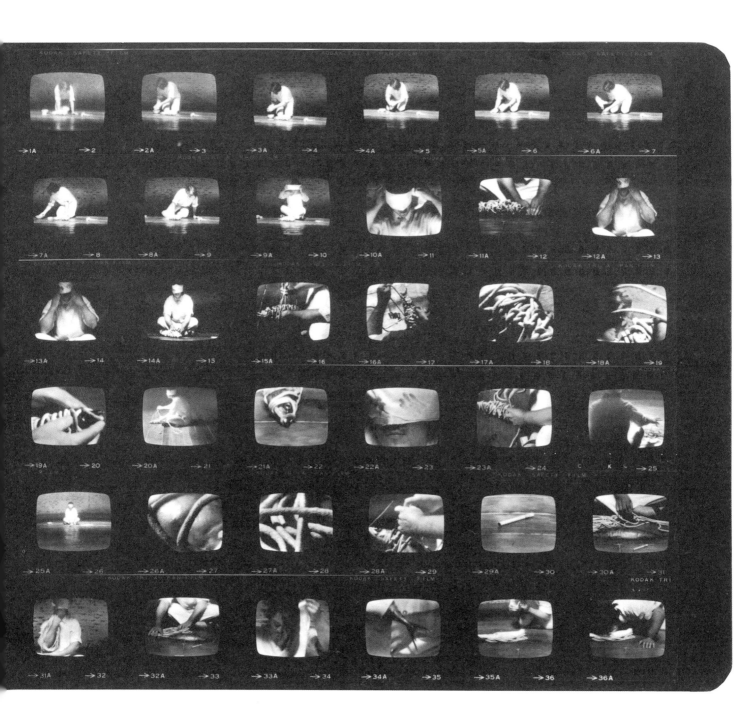

Terry Fox, *Turgescent Sex*, 1971, video stills, contact sheet

Isolation Unit, performance by Terry Fox and Joseph Beuys, 1970, photos: Ute Klophaus

Terry Fox, *Hefe* (performance for Ute Klophaus), 1971, photos: Ute Klophaus

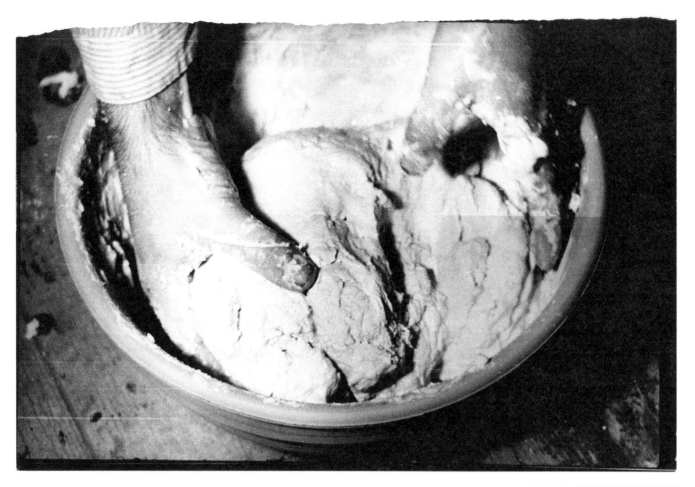

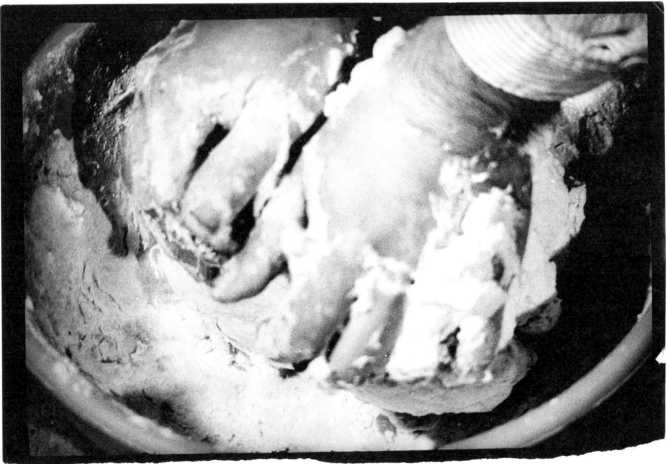

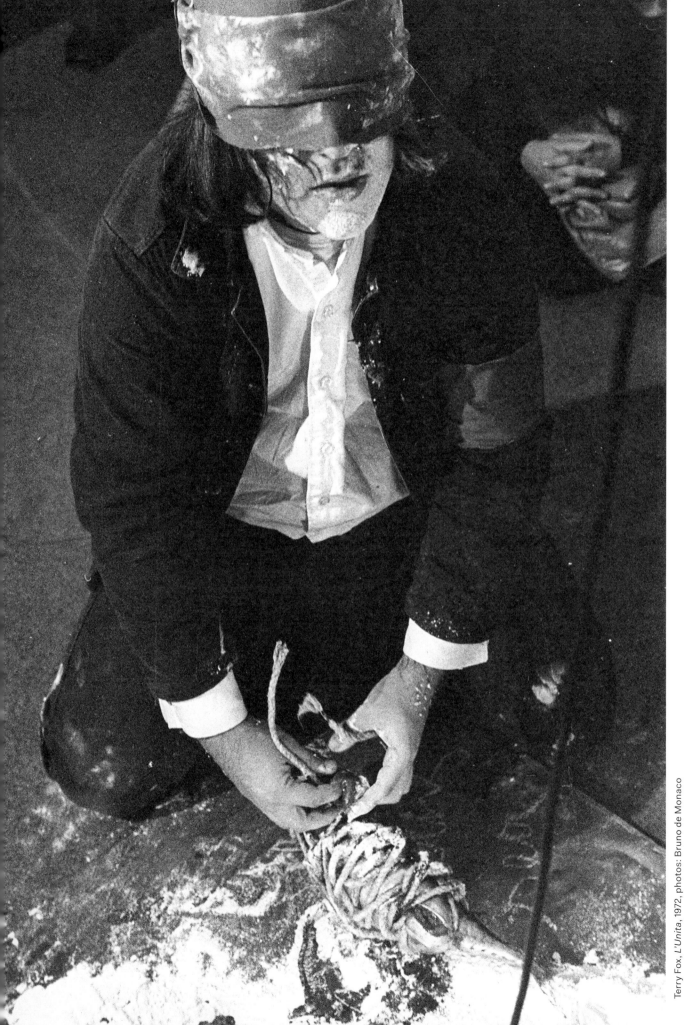

Terry Fox, *L'Unita*, 1972, photos: Bruno de Monaco

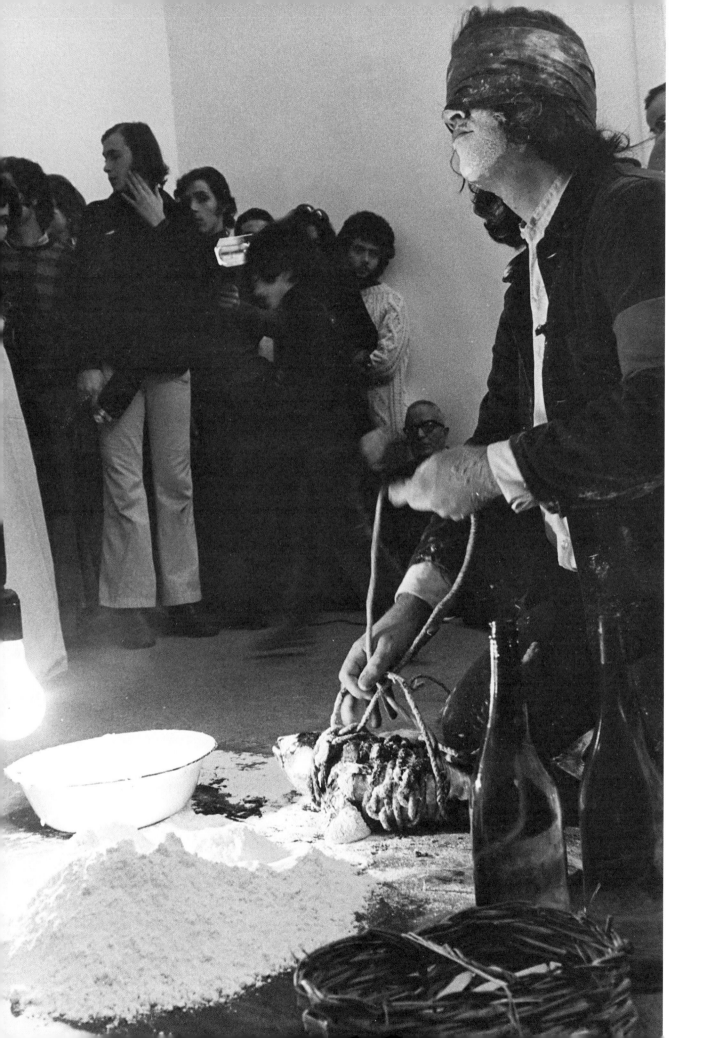

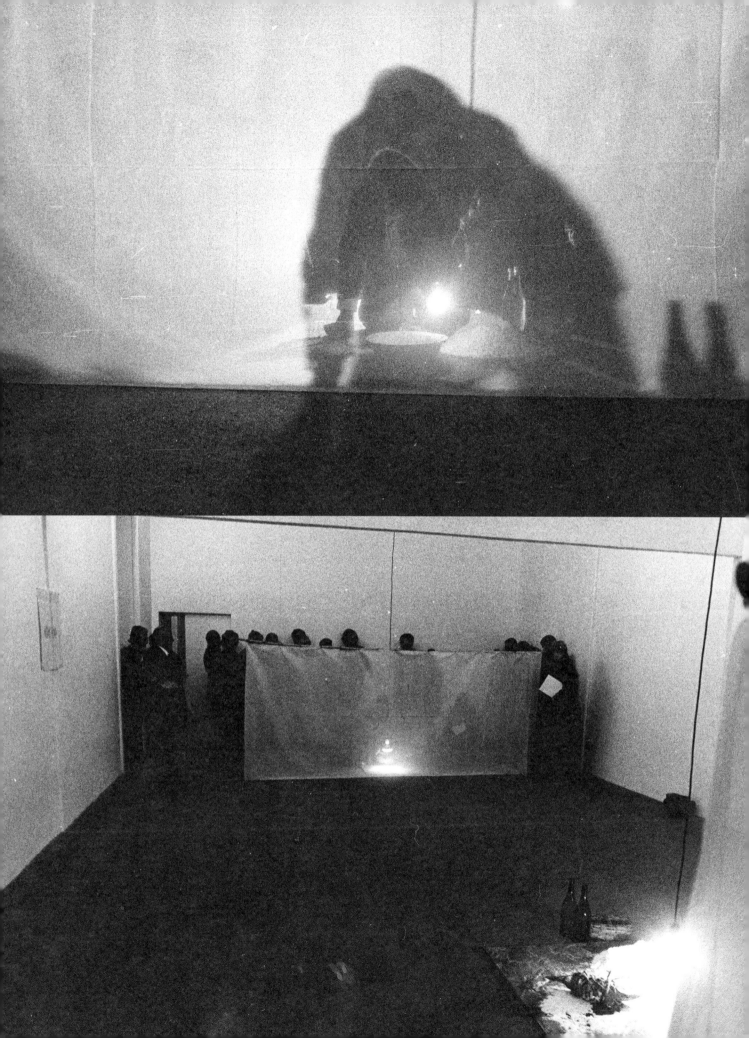

Terry Fox, *Pont*, Galerie Sonnabend, Paris, 1972, photos: Sarkis, Richard Reisman

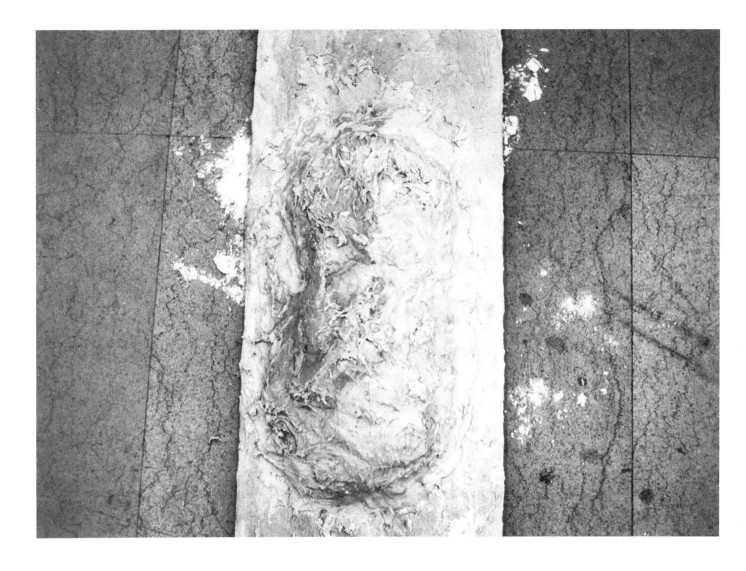

Environmental Surfaces, Three Simultaneous Situational Enclosures,
performance by Vito Acconci, Terry Fox and Dennis Oppenheim, Reese Palley Gallery,
San Francisco, 1971, photos: Peter Moore, Harry Shunk and Janos Kender

97

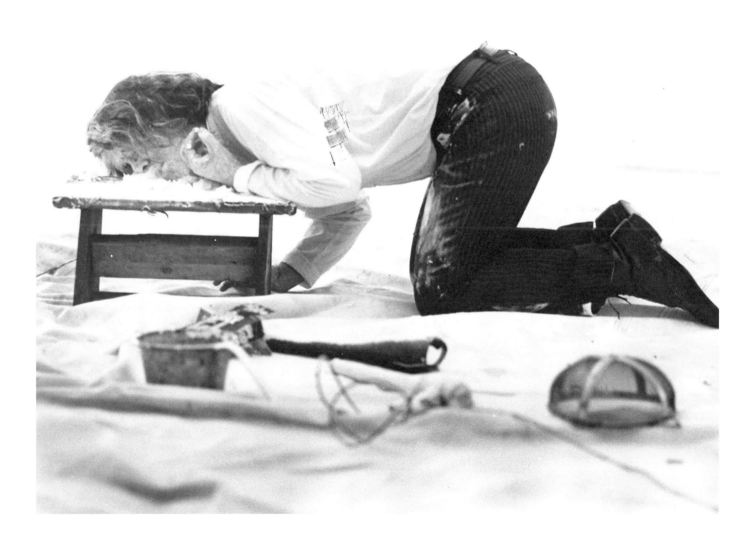

scene of the energy reversal / the passive element

Terry Fox, *Pisces*, MOCA, San Francisco (right), de Saisset Museum, Santa Clara (above), 1971, photos: Joel Glassman

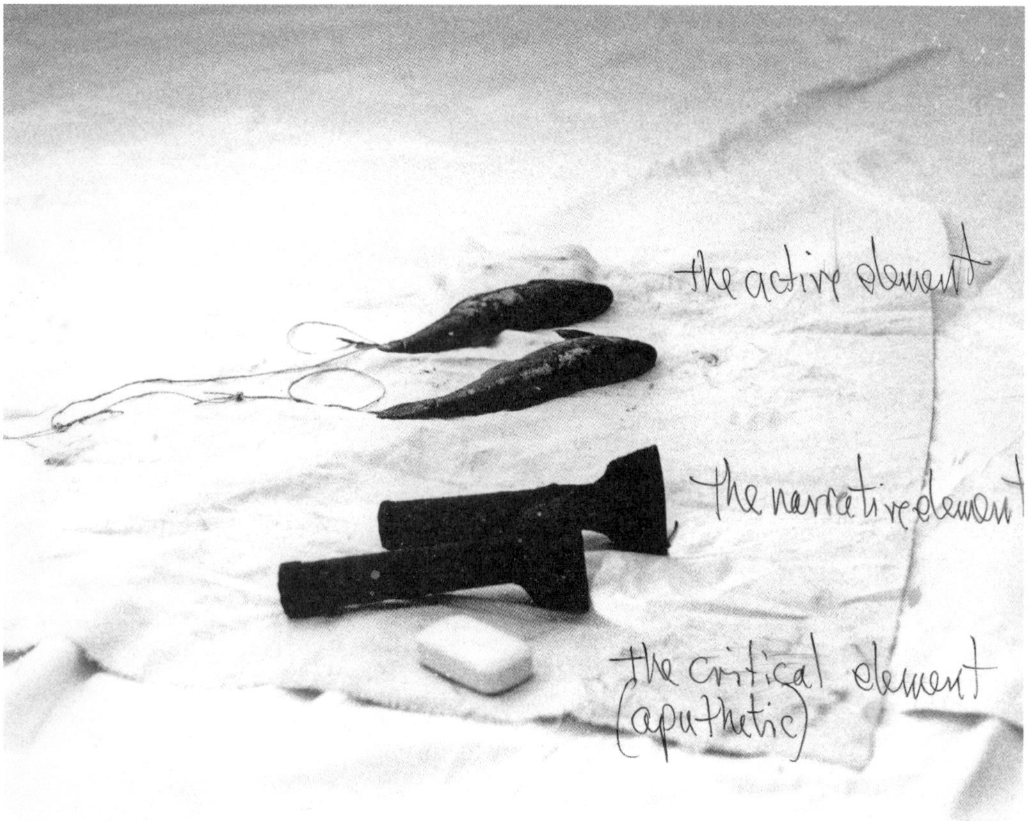
the active element
The narrative element
the critical element
(apathetic)

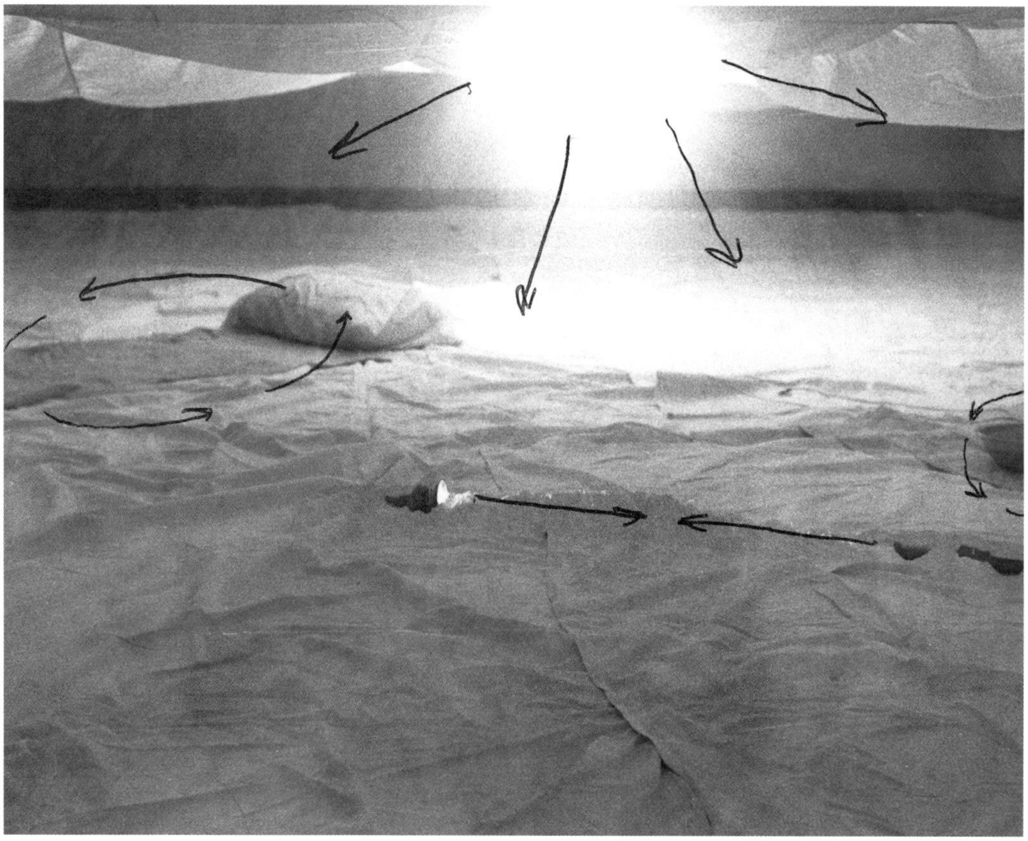

 Terry Fox, *Pisces*, de Saisset Museum, Santa Clara, 1971, photos: Joel Glassman

Terry Fox, *Virtual Volume*, 1970, photos: Barry Klinger

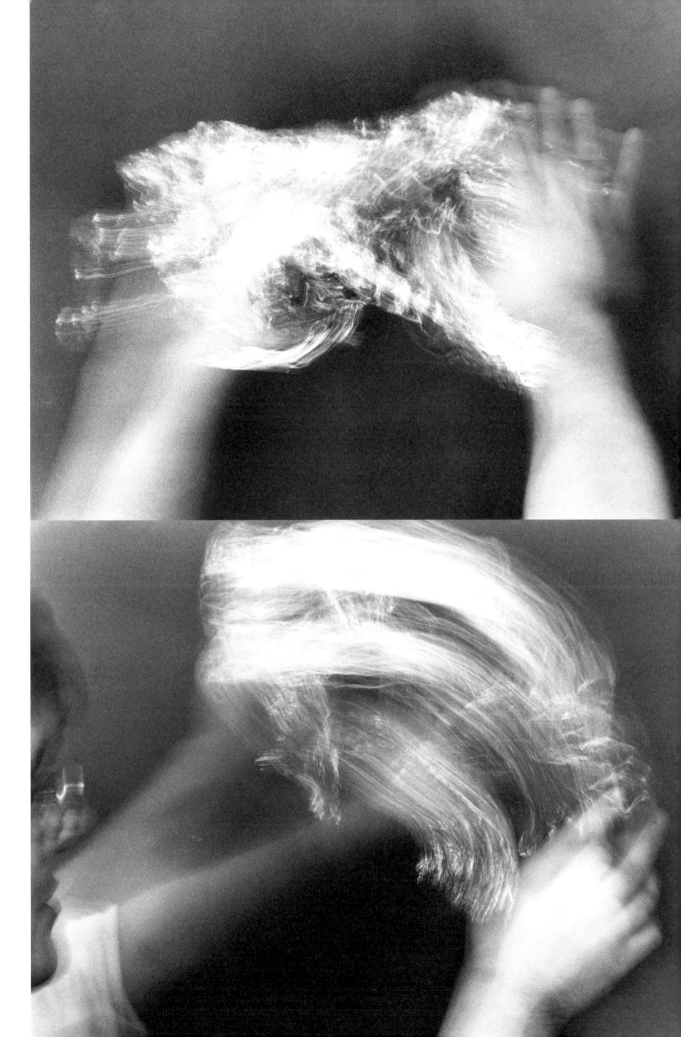

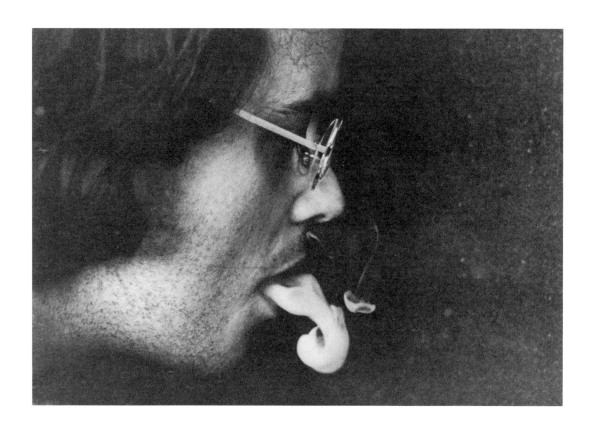

Terry Fox, *Virtual Volume (Smoke Exhalation)*, 1970, photos: Barry Klinger

Terry Fox, *Untitled (4 Match Pieces)*, 1970–71

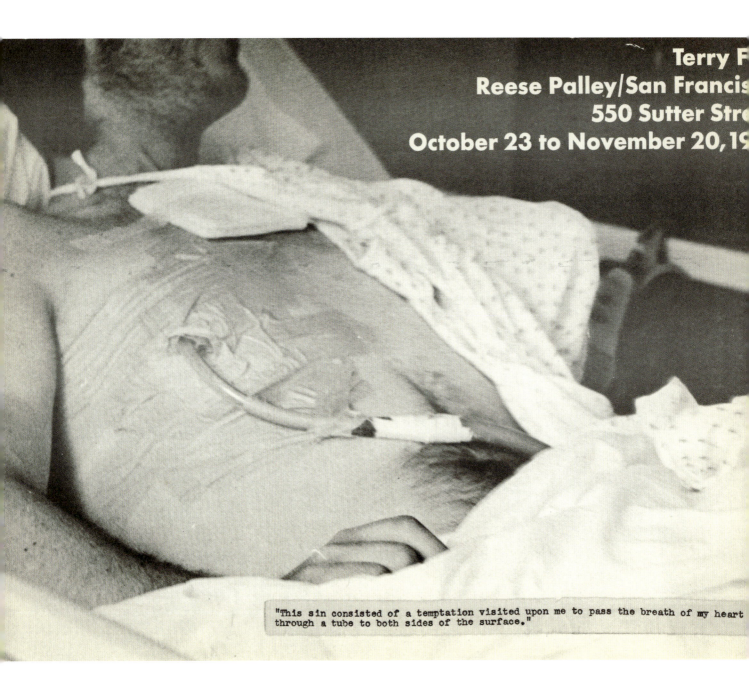

"This sin consisted of a temptation visited upon me to pass the breath of my heart through a tube to both sides of the surface."

114   Poster of the exhibition *Hospital* by Terry Fox at Reese Palley Gallery, San Francisco, 1971

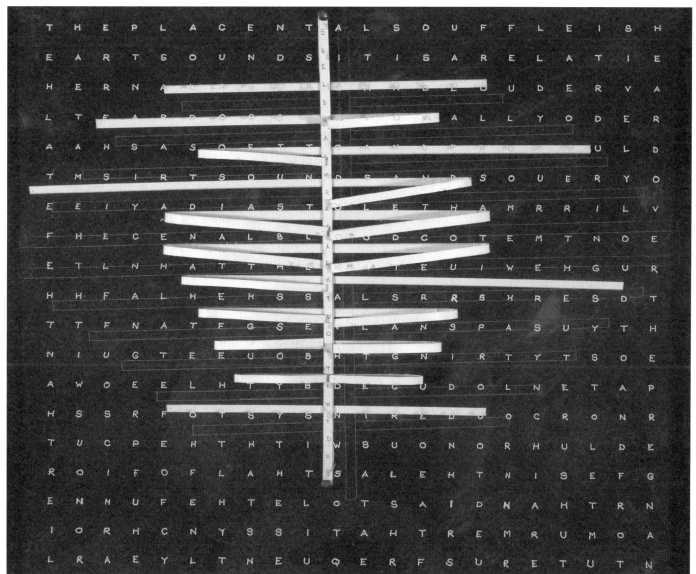

Terry Fox, *Rib Cage*, 1993

→ Terry Fox, *Hoc est corals meum*, 1972

there are no insides, no mind, no outsides or conciousness, nothing
but the body as it may be seen — a body that dosent
stop existing, even when the eye that sees it falls.
And this body is a fact.
Myself.

Terry fox

Napoli '72

Situations

Wiederholt charakterisierte Terry Fox seine Arbeiten als *Situationen*. Mit dieser begrifflichen Setzung umschrieb Fox eine spezifische Disposition von zeitlicher Struktur, Ortsbezogenheit, Handlung und Ding-Agens, die sein Werk seit seiner Rückkehr nach San Francisco 1969 bestimmte. Erstmals wählte er das Wort 1971 in einem Interview mit Willoughby Sharp anlässlich der Ausstellung „Environmental Surfaces" [↗98–101, 118] in der Reese Palley Gallery, New York. Neben Vito Acconci und Dennis Oppenheim realisierte Fox eine Performance, bei der er in einem eigens definierten Raum mit verschiedenen Dingen interagierte: mit einem Seifenstück, einer Schale mit Wasser, zwei Taschenlampen, zwei Päckchen Mehl, einer Kiste des Waschmittels Fab, einer kleinen Bank, gebogenem Draht, Zigarettenrauch sowie einem zerkratzten Spiegel, der auf einer hölzernen Garnrolle befestigt war. Seine eigenen Atemgeräusche wurden während der Performance verstärkt und von einer Tonaufnahme zuvor eingespielter Atmung kontrapunktisch begleitet.

Befragt nach seinem künstlerischen Anliegen, antwortete Fox: „Es interessiert mich, gewisse Arten von *räumlichen Situationen* zu schaffen. Ich gehe mit Objekten im Raum und mit ihren Beziehungen zueinander um und damit, wie meine Stimmung sie verändert. Die Art, wie ich eine Taschenlampe bewege, beeinflusst nicht nur die Lichtqualität, sondern auch meine Beziehung zum Licht. Zwei Taschenlampen, die auf ein Stück Seife gerichtet sind, bedeuten für mich viel mehr als der Zuschauer sich vorstellen kann. Sie schaffen eine gewisse Durchsichtigkeit, eine Modifizierung von Materialien, die ich sehr interessant finde, wie zum Beispiel die Idee von zwei Taschenlampen, die irgendwann die Seife schmelzen lassen."[1]

Die Elemente, die, Fox zufolge, seine Arbeiten auszeichnen, sind demnach Handlungen mit Objekten im Raum sowie die offene, sich jeweils im Moment des Geschehens konkretisierende Beziehung zwischen Aufführendem und Zuschauer, aus der das Werk Gestalt annimmt. Damit nimmt Fox innerhalb der seit Mitte der 1950er Jahre virulenten Tendenzen, tradierte Werkkonzeptionen und Rezeptionsmodelle zu verändern, eine entschieden eigenständige Position ein. Es geht Fox nicht allein darum, der im Kunstbetrieb dominanten Werkästhetik eine Prozessästhetik entgegenzusetzen, sondern die von der Person des Performers gesteuerte *Aktion*

Terry Fox repeatedly characterized his works as *situations*. By placing his work within this conceptual setting, he defined a specific disposition of temporal structure, site specificity, action and object agency which were a dominant feature in his works after his return to San Francisco in 1969. Fox first used the term in an interview with Willoughby Sharp in 1971 after his *Environmental Surfaces* [↗**98–101, 118**] show at the Reese Palley Gallery, New York. For this joint exhibition, including works by Vito Acconci and Dennis Oppenheim, Fox created a performance in which he interacted in a self-defined spatial environment with diverse objects: a bar of soap, a bowl of water, two flashlights, two bags of flour, a box of Fab laundry detergent, a small bench, a piece of bent wire, cigarette smoke and a scratched mirror fastened to a wooden spool. During his performance, his breathing was amplified and counterpointed by a prerecorded tape of himself breathing.

When Willoughby Sharp asked about his main artistic concerns, Fox replied: "What I am involved in is creating certain kinds of *spatial situations*. I am dealing with objects in a space and their relationships to each other, and with how my mood alters them. The way I move a flashlight is going to affect not only the quality of the light but also my relation to it. Two flashlights aimed at a bar of soap mean much more to me than anything the spectator could imagine. They create a certain translucence, a modification of materials that I find very interesting, like the idea of two flashlights eventually melting the soap."[1]

Hence, according to Fox, his works are characterized by actions with objects in space, as well as his open relationship with the audience, which takes on a concrete form at each moment of the performance and so lends the work its particular shape. In this way, Fox takes a decidedly independent position within the intensely pronounced tendencies since the mid-1950s of altering the traditional concept of an artwork and the models of its reception. However, rather than seeking to focus solely on processes and so counter the art scene's dominant view of a work conveying some aesthetically objective truth, Fox wants to add the element of shared experience to expand the "actions" in happenings and Fluxus events controlled by the performer: "The actual situation is what's going on in the space we're in. And the situation involves everybody there [....]."[2]

in Happening und Fluxus um das Element der gemeinsamen Erfahrung zu erweitern: „Die tatsächliche Situation ist das, was in dem Raum passiert, in dem wir uns befinden. Und die Situation schließt jeden mit ein [...].“[2]

Dieses Konzept eines situativen, zeitlich und räumlich gebundenen Werks kennzeichnete die Performance-Kunst der Bay Area von San Francisco, die sich im Umfeld von Tom Marioni, dem späteren Gründer des Museum of Conceptual Art in San Francisco, formierte. *Situation* bedeutete: ortsspezifische Installationen und skulpturale Handlungen, bei denen allenfalls die Spuren eines Prozesses dokumentiert waren oder das Werk nur während der Aufführungszeit existierte. In Abgrenzung zur performativen Plastik der 1960er Jahre definierte Marioni Konzeptkunst als „Idea oriented situations not directed at the production of static objects“.[3]

Zunächst setzte sich Fox in Straßenaktionen mit skulpturaler Form auseinander: „Ich machte Skulpturen, indem ich Hydranten öffnete. Ich mochte es, dem Wasser zuzuschauen, wie es die Straßen hinunterlief, ich mochte es, immer wieder den Hahn aufzudrehen und wegzulaufen.“[4] Das strömende und versiegende Wasser ist zugleich Objekt, Form und Prozess, innerhalb dessen – ausgelöst durch eine fast beiläufige Bewegung der Hand – sich die dauernde Verwandlung von Form vollzieht.

So auch bei *Dust Exchange* (1967), dem Tausch von Staubpartikeln, den Fox mit William T. Wiley betrieb. Fox sandte Staub von seinen Aufenthaltsorten in Europa an Wiley nach New Jersey, der wiederum gesammelten Staub an Fox zurückschickte. Wileys Staub platzierte Fox an den Stellen, von denen er zuvor Staub in der Pariser Metro oder im Louvre entfernt hatte. Mit der Translozierung eines Zerfallsprodukts, Staub, das sich über dauerhafte und unbewegliche Strukturen legt, griff Fox grundlegende Begriffe der Bildhauerei auf: das Verhältnis von Stabilität und Bewegung einerseits sowie von Dauerhaftigkeit und Vergänglichkeit andererseits.

Situation kann hingegen auch als eine spezifische Form von Theatralität begriffen werden, als eine Weise, sich zu bewegen oder mit Dingen zu agieren. Vorläufer seiner späteren Performances waren Straßensituationen, die sich in das alltägliche Geschehen an einem öffentlichen Ort einfügten. *What Do Blind Men Dream?* (1969) [↗**119**] fand auf der Union Street in San Francisco statt. Fox hatte eine blinde Frau gebeten, ihren Stadtteil zu verlassen und für einen Abend an einer ausgewählten Stelle Akkordeon zu spielen und zu singen. Die *Situation* entstand beim *Public Theater* aus einer Annäherung fremder Menschen, die Fox zuvor eingeladen hatte, um die Aufmerksamkeit auf einen spezifischen Ort zu lenken: „Darum geht es, und weniger um meine Beziehung zu

The idea of a work specific to a site, time and space is a distinguishing feature of the San Francisco Bay Area's performance art that developed around Tom Marioni, who later founded the Museum of Conceptual Art in San Francisco. In this context, *situational* art refers to site-specific installations and sculptural actions where, at most, the traces of a process were documented or the work itself only existed while being performed. In distinction to the performative sculptures of the 1960s, Marioni defined conceptual art as "idea-oriented situations not directed at the production of static objects."[3]

Terry Fox began to engage with sculptural form in actions on the street: "I started making sculpture by opening fire hydrants. I liked the water running down the streets: turning and running, turning and running."[4] Water as it flows and seeps away is simultaneously object, form and process, which – unleashed by an almost casual movement of the hand – produces a permanent metamorphosis of form.

Such an approach is also evident in *Dust Exchange* (1967). In this work, Terry Fox and William T. Wiley exchanged dust from Europe and New Jersey, with Fox sending Wiley dust from stops on his travels through Europe, and Wiley shipping back dust which he had collected in New Jersey. Fox then placed the dust Wiley sent at the very same spots where he had collected his dust, for example, in the Paris Metro or the Louvre. With the translocation of dust, a product of decomposition which lies on permanent and immobile structures, Fox takes up and addresses fundamental sculptural concepts – the relationship between stability and movement on the one hand, and permanence and transience on the other.

Environmental Surfaces, Three Simultaneous Situational Enclosures, performance by Vito Acconci, Terry Fox and Dennis Oppenheim, Reese Palley Gallery, San Francisco, 1971, photo: Harry Shunk and Janos Kender

Terry Fox, *What Do Blind Men Dream?*, 1969, photos: Barry Klinger

großräumigen Umgebungen oder um soziologische oder politische Fragen."⁵

Mit *Levitation* (1970) **[↗31]** präsentierte Fox eine Rauminstallation, die aus einer nicht-öffentlichen Performance hervorgegangen war. Fox hatte den Raum des Richmond Art Center vollständig mit weißem Papier ausgekleidet und auf einer Fläche von 3,5 mal 3,5 Metern Erde von einem Freeway ausgebreitet. In einem Text beschrieb er die zuvor vollzogene Handlung für die Besucher: „Mit meinem Blut zog ich in der Mitte der Erde einen Kreis. Der Durchmesser entsprach meiner Körperlänge. Nach mittelalterlicher Vorstellung wird auf diese Weise ein magischer Kreis erzeugt. Dann legte ich mich auf den Rücken in der Mitte des Kreises und hielt vier durchsichtige Plastikschläuche fest, die mit Blut, Urin, Milch und Wasser gefüllt waren. Sie repräsentieren die elementaren Flüssigkeiten, die ich aus meinem Körper ausgetrieben hatte. Ich lag sechs Stunden lang da mit den Schläuchen in meinen Händen und versuchte zu schweben."⁶

Allein die zurückgebliebenen Spuren, Plastikschläuche und der Abdruck des Körpers in der Erde, erinnerten an das vorausgegangene Ereignis. Der uniform weiße Ausstellungsraum ist dadurch als ein Handlungsraum markiert, innerhalb dessen die Relikte eine Auseinandersetzung mit dem Werk

In contrast, *situations* can also be read as a specific form of theatricality, a form of movement or actions with things. The antecedents of his later performances are street situations integrated into everyday events at public locations. For example, *What Do Blind Men Dream?* (1969) **[↗119]** took place in San Francisco's Union Street. Fox asked a blind woman to leave her own district and sing and play the accordion for one evening at a location he had chosen. This *situation* was created in *Public Theater*, encounters between strangers that Fox had invited ahead of time, as a means of drawing attention to a specific location: "That's what they are about, rather than my relationship to a large-scale environmental situation or to sociological or political questions."⁵

In *Levitation* (1970) **[↗31]** Terry Fox presented an installation from a performance he gave without an audience. He completely covered the floor and walls of the space at the Richmond Art Center with white paper, and filled a 3.5 × 3.5 m area with dirt taken from under a freeway. In a text for visitors to the installation he described his actions as follows: "I drew a circle in the middle of the dirt with my own blood. Its diameter was my height. According to the medieval notion, that creates a magic space. Then I lay on my back in the middle of the circle, holding four clear polyethylene tubes

anregen sollen. Im Unterschied zur Konzeptkunst, die versuchte, die Erfahrung von der Skulptur zu trennen, wird das Werk bei Fox nicht zu einem Konzept, einer Struktur oder Sprache „dematerialisiert"[7]. Die wechselseitige Bedingung von Physis, Zeit und Raum in der Performance und den Spuren des kreativen Prozesses stellt die Frage nach der Wirklichkeit neu. Während der Kunst der Moderne seit der Wende zum 20. Jahrhundert das Paradigma der visuellen Wahrnehmung zugrunde liegt, wird für Terry Fox die gesamthaft körperliche Wahrnehmung zum Ausgangspunkt für eine Neubestimmung von Skulptur. Skulpturale Handlungen können zunächst als Gesten verstanden werden, als eine Weise, sich zu bewegen oder mit Dingen zu agieren. Die *Situation* hingegen ist eine Erfahrung, ein Überschreiten gegebener Bedeutung und eine Annäherung an eine Realität, die rational nicht fassbar ist.

Der französische Philosoph Maurice Merleau-Ponty hat die Einheit des Körpers als lebendige, wahrnehmende und sich zur Umwelt verhaltende Größe verstanden und das „Körperschema", die bewusste und unbewusste Kenntnis des eigenen Leibes („corps propre") und seiner Performanz, als zentrale Kategorie von Wahrnehmung beschrieben.[8] Die Vorstellung, dass der Körper ein Gegenstand subjektiver Wahrnehmung ist, von dem man sich nicht entfernen kann, ist ein zentrales Moment der skulpturalen Handlungen. Fox begreift den menschlichen Körper gleichermaßen als kreatives Werkzeug und Erkenntnisinstrument. Die leiblich gebundene ästhetische Wahrnehmung wird zum Maßstab für eine Neubestimmung von Skulptur, die von allen menschlichen Organen auszugehen habe und auf diese zurückwirke.

Der eigene Körper fungierte dabei als ein Mittler, durch dessen Berührungen die Dinge miteinander verbunden, belebt und energetisch aufgeladen wurden: „But I want to have a chain of elements linked together. I'd touch something, say a rock, and light another object with the flame from my mouth. In that way I would be acted upon by one element while I was affecting another."[9]

Damit griff Fox Vorstellungen einer Verbindung von bildlichem Objekt und Aspekten der Lebendigkeit auf, die in der frühen Neuzeit abgebrochen waren und allenfalls in rituellen Zeremonien tradiert wurden. In seinen Performances verwendete er schlichte, gleichwohl symbolisch aufgeladene Gegenstände und elementare Stoffe: mit Wasser gefüllte Schalen, Seile, Kerzen, Fische, Mehl und Brot, Luft, Erde, Feuer und Wasser. Zu Beginn der 1970er Jahre war der Fisch wiederholt in Performances eingebunden, wie zum Beispiel bei *Pisces* (1971) [↗**68, 104–106**] und *Turgescent Sex* (1971) [↗**76**]. Anlass für die Studioperformance *Turgescent Sex*, die am 13. Juni 1971 im Atelier des Künstlers in der Rose Street in

filled with blood, urine, milk, and water. They represented the elemental fluids that I was expelling from my body. I lay there for six hours with the tubes in my hand trying to levitate."[6]

The performance was only evident in the traces remaining, the plastic tubes and the imprint of Fox's body in the dirt. The exhibition space's uniformly white floor and walls signal that this is a space of action, and the relics left behind are intended to encourage the viewer to engage with the work. In contrast to conceptual art, which tries to separate experience from the sculpture, the work in Fox's oeuvre is not "dematerialized" into a concept, structure or language.[7] The reciprocal conditions of physical constitution, time and space in the performance and the traces of the creative process pose the question of reality in a new way. While since the start of the 20th century, modern art has been based on the paradigm of visual perception, Terry Fox takes physical perception in its entirety as a starting point to redefine sculpture. Sculptural acts can initially be understood as gestures, as a mode of moving or acting with things. In contrast, the *situation* is an experience, transcending given meaning and approaching a reality unable to be grasped rationally.

The French philosopher Maurice Merleau-Ponty starts from the unity of the body as a living, perceiving, being-in-the-world to describe the "body image," the conscious and unconscious knowledge of one's own body (*corps propre*) and its actions, as a central category of perception.[8] The notion of the body as an object of subjective perception from which one cannot escape is a core moment of sculptural activity. In Fox's view, the human body is simultaneously a creative tool as well as an instrument of knowledge. In this sense, the aesthetic perception bound to the body becomes a touchstone for redefining sculpture as needing to be produced by and affecting all human organs.

Here, one's own body acts as an intermediary which, through touch, connects and reanimates objects, charging them with energy: "But I want to have a chain of elements linked together. I'd touch something, say a rock, and light another object with the flame from my mouth. In that way I would be acted upon by one element while I was affecting another."[9]

Fox is thus taking up an idea of connections between metaphorical objects and aspects of the nature of life which were disconnected in the early modern age and have, at most, been handed down in ritual ceremonies. In his performances, Fox employs simple yet symbolically-laden objects and artifacts as well as elementary materials: bowls filled with water, rope, candles, fish, flour and bread, air, earth, fire and water. In the early 1970s, Fox's performances often included a fish as, for example, in *Pisces* (1971) [↗**68, 104–106**] and *Turgescent Sex* (1971) [↗**76**].

San Francisco stattfand, waren Verzweiflung und Schuldgefühl angesichts des Massakers von Mỹ Lai. Von Terry Fox ist eine knappe Beschreibung überliefert: „Elements: Cloth Bandage, Cigarette, Match, Fish, Rope, Bowl of Water, Bar of Soap, Despair.

Actions: Sit crosslegged surrounded by the elements / wash hands / wash fish bound by the rope in many knots / blindfold with the bandage / mark eyes on the blindfold with the blood of the fish / release the fish from bondage / form a nest with the bindings / wrap the fish with the bandage / cover the fish with smoke."[10]

Der Performance vorausgegangen war die lange Betrachtung einer Fotografie der Opfer. Berichte über das 1968 von US-Soldaten verübte Massaker an den Bewohnern des südvietnamesischen Dorfes Mỹ Lai führten weltweit zu Protesten gegen den Vietnamkrieg. *Turgescent Sex* entstand wenige Monate nach dem Abschluss der gerichtlichen Untersuchung des Kriegsverbrechens, die mit Freisprüchen der vier angeklagten Soldaten endete.[11]

In einer zeremoniellen Handlung, der Befreiung des Fisches von seinen Fesseln und der Huldigung durch Rauch, wollte Fox ein symbolisches Opfer der Erlösung darbringen: „[...] ich sah mich als Opfer und identifizierte mich mit dem vietnamesischen Volk, und gleichzeitig betrachtete ich mich als schuldig. Der Fisch stellte die Vietnamesen dar, aber auch mich. Es gab Hunderte von Knoten, die den Fisch fesselten."[12]

Turgescent Sex, which took place on June 13, 1971 in the artist's studio on Rose Street in San Francisco, was inspired by the despair and guilt that Terry Fox felt after the Mỹ Lai massacre. A brief description of *Turgescent Sex* written by Terry Fox has survived: "Elements: Cloth Bandage, Cigarette, Match, Fish, Rope, Bowl of Water, Bar of Soap, Despair.

Actions: Sit crosslegged surrounded by the elements / wash hands / wash fish bound by the rope in many knots / blindfold with the bandage / mark eyes on the blindfold with the blood of the fish / release the fish from bondage / form a nest with the bindings / wrap the fish with the bandage / cover the fish with smoke."[10]

This performance was preceded by the prolonged viewing of a photograph of the victims. The reports of the massacre by US troops in 1968 on civilians in the South Vietnamese village of Mỹ Lai triggered global protests against the Vietnam War. *Turgescent Sex* was created just a few months after the conclusion of the legal investigation into this war crime which ended with the acquittal of the four soldiers charged.[11]

In the ceremonial act of liberating the fish from its bonds and blowing smoke over it as an act of homage, Fox wanted to offer up a symbolic sacrifice of deliverance: "[...] considering myself as a victim, and identifying with the Vietnamese people, and also considering myself as guilty. The fish represented the Vietnamese and also represented me. There were hundreds and hundreds of knots constricting this fish."[12]

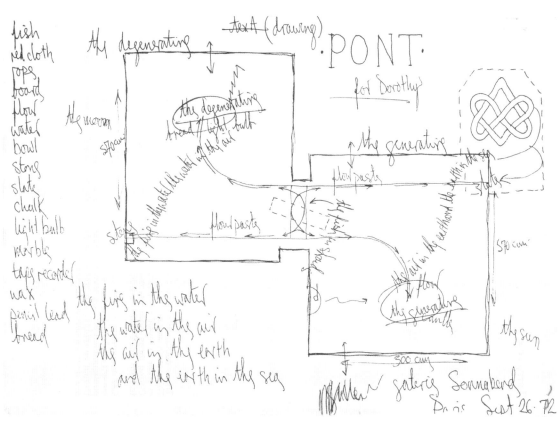

Terry Fox, Sketch of the performance *Pont*, Galerie Sonnabend, Paris, 1972

Das Lösen der Schnüre und das Waschen des Fisches griff Fox in der Performance *Pont* (1972) [↗**121**] erneut auf. Der eingeschnürte Fisch führte nicht nur eine symbolische Eigenexistenz, Handlung und Dinge waren gleichberechtigte, aufeinander bezogene produktive Kategorien. Durch die Wiederholung werden Dinge sukzessive mit neuen Bedeutungen aufgeladen und Handlungen zu Ritualen. Der Fisch fungierte jedoch auch als eine Metapher für Grenzüberschreitung. Die Idee zu einer Aktion mit einem Fisch entstand während eines Aufenthaltes in Paris. Fox hatte eine *Situation* mit Clochards vor Augen: „Clochards spielen die ganze Zeit Theater, und ich wollte ihre Art von Theater dort machen."[13] *Soluble Fish* (1970) fand unter dem Pont Neuf statt. Nach Fox' eigener Aussage inspirierten ihn der Klang der Wörter „soluble fish", die er in einer Biografie über Henry Miller gelesen hatte: „Soluble fish was the talk of Paris."[14]

Soluble Fish verweist auf André Bretons Prosatext *Poisson soluble* (1924), der dem *Ersten Surrealistischen Manifest* vorangestellt war. Für Breton fungierte *Poisson soluble*, der wasserlösliche Fisch, als eine Metapher für das automatische Schreiben. Als *der* surrealistische Schreibmodus sollte das automatische Schreiben jenseits aller ästhetischen oder ethischen Überlegungen einem Gedankenfluss ohne Kontrolle durch die Vernunft folgen. Auf diese Weise gelinge es dem Ich, sich der äußeren Wirklichkeit anzuverwandeln und aufzulösen.[15]

Die *Situation* bildet das begriffliche Zentrum von Fox' Werk: Sie umfasst die substantielle Autonomie des Materials, der Form und der Mittel, um der Kunst durch symbolische Handlungen ihren sozialen Charakter wiederzugeben. Damit grenzte sich Fox dezidiert von Happening und Fluxus ab. Fox' *Situationen* stehen vielmehr in Performance-Traditionen, die Handlung und Objekt verbinden, wie George Brechts Konzeption des Events und Joseph Beuys' rituelle Interaktionen mit ihrem wiederholten Gebrauch von Materialien, die er „Aktionen" nannte.[16]

In Brechts Konzeption des „Events" wurden Handlungen und Objekte als unbestimmte Formen aufgefasst. In der Ausstellung „Toward Events" (1959) zeigte Brecht alltägliche Dinge mit der Anleitung „To be performed". Gemeint war damit keine theatralische oder musikalische Performance, sondern dass Objekte, immer wieder in neue Zusammenhänge gebracht, um Bedeutungsschichten bereichert werden konnten.

Brechts Struktur einer neuen Ästhetik, die auf der Relativität von Zeit und Raum *(space-time-relativity)* und der Gleichwertigkeit von Material und Energie *(„matter-energy-equivalency")* aufbaute, wurde zu einer wichtigen Referenz für die *performance sculptures* der Bay-Area-Künstler und zur Grundlage

In his performance *Pont* (1972) [↗**121**], Terry Fox again worked with untying knots and washing a fish. Rather than the knotted roped fish being inscribed with an independent symbolic existence, actions and objects are treated as equal and mutually referential productive categories. Through the repetition, objects become successively charged with new meanings, and actions become rituals. In contrast, the fish also functions as a metaphor for crossing borders. Fox first had the idea of a piece involving fish while he was staying in Paris, and imagined a *situation* in a location where the clochards lived: "Clochards are doing theater all the time, and their kind of theater is what I want to do there."[13] *Soluble Fish* (1970) was performed under the Pont Neuf bridge. As Fox recalled, he took his inspiration for the piece from the sound of the words "soluble fish" that he came across in a biography of Henry Miller: "Soluble fish was the talk of Paris."[14]

Soluble Fish references André Breton's short novel *Poisson soluble* (1924), published together with the *First Surrealist Manifesto*. For Breton, the *Poisson soluble*, the soluble fish, served as a metaphor for automatic writing. Automatic writing, as the mode of Surrealist writing, was intended to facilitate the flow of thought freed from the control of reason and beyond any aesthetic or moral concerns. In this way, the ego succeeds in appropriating and dissolving external reality.[15]

The *situation* is the conceptual core of Terry Fox's oeuvre. It comprises the substantial autonomy of material and form, as well as the means to restore the social character of art through symbolic actions, and hence decisively sets Fox apart from happenings and the Fluxus movement. Instead, his *situations* can be located far more in the performance traditions which connect action and object, such as George Brecht's idea of events and Joseph Beuys' actions, those ritual interactions with a repeated use of the same material.[16]

Brecht's concept of events focuses on the indeterminate, chance-based form of actions and objects. In his *Toward Events* (1959) show, Brecht presented everyday objects with the note: "To be performed." Rather than implying some theatrical or musical performance, this was intended to point out how objects can be enriched by new levels of meaning through constantly being placed into new contexts.

The structure of Brecht's new aesthetics, based on "space-time-relativity" and "matter-energy-equivalency," became a key point of reference for the performance sculptures by Bay Area artists, and laid the foundation for conceptual sound art, fusing sculptural actions with sounds to transform space.[17]

In a number of performances, Fox employed different spaces as a resonator for just such an envisioned unity of

Terry Fox, *Suono Interno*, Chiesa Santa Lucia, Bologna, 1979, photo: Enzo Pezzi

einer konzeptuellen Klangkunst, die skulpturale Handlungen mit Klang verbindet, um Raum zu transformieren.[17]

Bei verschiedenen Performances diente Fox ein Raum als Resonanzkörper für jene angestrebte Einheit von Bewegung und Wahrnehmung. In *Suono Interno* (1979) verspannte Fox Klaviersaiten im Raum der entweihten Kirche Chiesa Santa Lucia in Bologna, ummantelte die Metallschnüre mit Kolophonium und spielte auf ihnen an drei aufeinanderfolgenden Tagen. Durch Streichen und Anschlagen der Saiten erzeugte er einen Klang, der nach draußen auf die Straße drang und die Passanten animierte, in das leere Kirchenschiff hineinzuschauen. „Suono interno", innerer Klang, war mit Kreide über das runde Loch in der Holztür geschrieben.

Durch die Ausdehnung des Klanges im Raum und seine unmittelbar physische Wirkung sollten die Architektur und ihre Wahrnehmung verändert werden: „Die Zuschauer waren da, damit sie Zeugen der Handlungen waren, die die Veränderung im Raum erzeugten. Zuschauen und dann weggehen. Ich interessierte mich für die Vorstellung, dass jemand eine Erinnerung von dem Raum hatte, eine Umgebung, die durch seine Erinnerung verändert wird."[18]

Die offene Struktur des Werks, innerhalb derer die Körper – des Künstlers wie des Betrachters – als Gegenstand der Wahrnehmung involviert sind, unterscheidet Fox' Arbeiten von Body Art und Video-Performance. Sein Konzept der *Situation* zeichnet sich also von Beginn an durch Gegenwärtigkeit und Körperlichkeit aus, wobei der zeitliche Ablauf, Ding und Handlung untrennbar miteinander verbunden sind. Oskar

movement and perception. In *Suono Interno* (1979) , Fox stretched piano wires across the interior of the deconsecrated Santa Lucia Church in Bologna, covered them in rosin and played them for set periods over three consecutive days. By stroking and pulling the metal wires, he created a sound which could be heard from the street, encouraging passersby to peer into the nave of the empty church. The words "Suono interno," internal sound, were written in chalk over a round peephole in the wooden door.

The spatial expansion of sound and its direct physical impact was intended to alter the architectural surround and its perception: "The spectators were there because I wanted them to witness the actions that brought about the change in the space. To see it and then leave. I was interested in the idea of someone having a kind of memory knowledge about a space, having an environment transformed through their memories."[18]

Fox's oeuvre can be differentiated from body art and video performance precisely by this open structure of works in which the physical bodies – the artist's just as much as the viewer's – are involved as the subject matter of perception. In his view, then, the *situation* is already characterized from the start by corporeality and contemporaneity, whereby the temporal sequence, object and action are inseparably connected. Swiss art historian Oskar Bätschmann has described the transition from the aesthetics of production and object to the aesthetics of process and reception as a shift towards "the shaping of experience."[19] In this sense, an artist becomes an "experience

Terry Fox, *Lunedi*, 1975, camera: Bill Viola, video stills

124

Bätschmann hat diese Verlagerung von einer Produktions- und Objektästhetik hin zu einer Prozess- und Rezeptionsästhetik als „Erfahrungsgestaltung" charakterisiert.[19] Der Künstler wird zum Gestalter von – eigenen und fremden – Erfahrungen, deren Bedeutungen aus dem Vollzug der Handlung entstehen. Bedeutung lässt sich demnach nicht mehr als etwas dem Werk Eingeschriebenes konzeptualisieren, vielmehr stimulieren die Kunsterfahrungen von Performances seit den 1960er Jahren eine strikte Unmittelbarkeit der Erfahrung, für die es letztlich keinen späteren Nachvollzug gibt. Das Wort *Situation* erfasst diese Radikalität. Eine spätere Annäherung an die Situation auf der Grundlage von Zitaten des Künstlers oder Beschreibungen, Fotografien oder Videofilmen bleibt also eine Illusion. Denn auch die Beschreibungen und die ihnen inhärenten Narrative sind, wie es Mieke Bal formulierte, voller „found objects", zeitlich und kulturell gebunden. Deshalb setze die Aussage des jeweils durch die eigene Gegenwart gebundenen Interpreten das Werk immer wieder aufs Neue zusammen.[20]

Diese Paradoxie kennzeichnet auch das Verhältnis von Performance und ihrer medialen Reproduktion als Fotografie oder Videotape.[21] Während Performance eine Aufführungssituation vor Anderen ist, schaffen Videos eine für Andere inszenierte Aufführungssituation. Entschieden formulierte Fox Veränderungen des Werks durch mediale Reproduktion. Video war für ihn ein Werkzeug subjektiver Dokumentation und damit ein Deutungsinstrument von Performance und ihrer Wahrnehmung.

Dies zeigt die eigens produzierte Videoperformance: *Lunedi* (1975) [↗**124, 139**] entstand für die italienische Videoproduktion Art/tapes/22 und wiederholte eine zuvor mit Tom Marioni ausgeführte Studioperformance. Im Unterschied zu den anderen Videodokumentationen dominieren bei *Lunedi* filmische Elemente. Bill Violas Kameraführung folgt der klanglichen Choreografie. Die Bild-Ton-Korrelation verstärkt die Eindringlichkeit von Fox' Gesten, der langsame, stetige Zoom steigert die sinnliche Präsenz der Handlungen und suggeriert eine stringente Dramaturgie.

An *Lunedi* zeigt sich, dass Video nicht nur ein bildlicher Verstärker sein kann, sondern den spezifischen Rhythmus von Fox' Handlungen erst erzeugt. Viola setzte gleichermaßen die interpretierende wie die erzeugende Qualität medialer Aufzeichnungsverfahren selbst ins Bild; er ließ so eine *Situation* entstehen – die sinnliche Präsenz einer physisch abwesenden Person und die metaphorische Anwesenheit des Künstlers im Bild.

shaper" who creates and shapes his or her own experiences and those of others. Since the meaning of these experiences is then produced through the performance of actions, it can no longer be conceived as something inscribed in the work. Rather, performance art since the 1960s has been informed by the strict immediacy of experience which, ultimately, is not intended to be understood in some later process of reflection.

The word *situation* denotes just this radical approach. Hence, it is illusory to expect artist's statements or descriptions, photographs or videos to provide in-depth insights into a situation after the fact. The descriptions and their inherent narratives are, as Mieke Balhas expressed it, replete with "found objects," bound both temporally and culturally. Instead, the statements by the work's interpreters, each bound in their own present, always recompose the work.[20]

This paradox also characterizes the relationship between performance and its reproduction in media such as photography or video.[21] While performance is a situation of performing actions in front of others, videos create a situation of performances staged for others. Fox uncompromisingly used medial reproduction to develop changes for works. In his view, video was a tool for subjective documentation, and thus an instrument for interpreting performances and their perception.

This is evident in his own productions of video performances. *Lunedi* (1975) [↗**124, 139**], for example, was made for the Italian video production Art/tapes/22 and repeats a studio performance given previously with Tom Marioni. Here, in contrast to other video documentation, the cinematic elements dominate. Bill Viola's camera work follows the choreography of sound. The relation between the image and sound intensifies the urgency of Fox's gestures; the slow constant zoom heightens the sensory presence of the actions and suggests a stringent dramaturgy.

Lunedi shows that video does more than merely amplify images, it actually first creates the specific rhythm of Fox's actions. By giving equal weight to the interpretative and creative qualities of media recordings, Viola allows just such a *situation* to be created – with the sensory presence of a physically absent person and the metaphorical presence of the artist in the image.

Translated from the German by Andrew Boreham

1 Willoughby Sharp, A Discussion with Terry Fox, Vito Acconci, and Dennis Oppenheim. In: *Avalanche*, New York, Nr. 3, Winter 1971, S. 86–89, S. 87, wiederabgedruckt und übersetzt in: Eva Schmidt (Hg.), *Terry Fox. Ocular Language. 30 Jahre Reden und Schreiben über Kunst. 30 Years of Speaking and Writing about Art.* Gesellschaft für Aktuelle Kunst Bremen, Köln 2000, S. 42–52, S. 44/46, fortan Schmidt 2000 [Hervorhebung der Autorin]

2 Robin White, An Interview with Terry Fox. In: *View*, Bd. 2, Nr. 3, Point Publications, Oakland, Juni 1979, wiederabgedruckt und übersetzt in: Schmidt 2000, vgl. Anm. 1, S. 70–98, S. 76

3 Tom Marioni, Introductory Statement (12. Juli 1979). In: Carl E. Loeffler, Darlene Tong (Hg.), *Performance Anthology. Source Book of California Performance Art.* San Francisco 1989 (EA 1980), S. IX. Zu Fox' und Marionis Bedeutung für die Entstehung von *sound sculpture* siehe Gascia Ouzounian: *Sound Art and Spatial Practices: Situating Sound Installation Art Since 1958.* UC San Diego Electronic Theses and Dissertations, 2008, http://escholarship.org/uc/item/4d50k2fp (zuletzt am 15.5.2015)

4 Terry Fox, Vom Boden zur Decke und von Wand zu Wand. Interview mit Johannes Lothar Schröder (1999). In: Schmidt 2000, vgl. Anm. 1, S. 192–208, S. 198

5 I Wanted to Have my Mood Affect their Looks. Interview by Willoughby Sharp. In: *Avalanche*, New York, Nr. 3, Winter 1971, S. 70–81, wiederabgedruckt und übersetzt in: Schmidt 2000, vgl. Anm. 1, S. 12

6 Ebd., S. 14

7 Lucy R. Lippard, *Six Years: Dematerialization of the Art Object from 1966 to 1972.* New York 1973

8 Maurice Merleau-Ponty, *Phénoménologie de la perception.* Paris 1945, S. 235; dt. *Phänomenologie der Wahrnehmung.* Berlin 1966

9 Tom Marioni, Terry Fox: Himself. Interview. In: *Art and Artists*, 7. Januar 1973, S. 39–41, S. 40

10 Terry Fox, Elements, Actions, and Conditions of *Turgescent Sex.* In: *Avalanche*, New York, Nr. 3, Herbst 1971, S. 7, vgl. S. 286

11 Terry Fox, Turgescent Sex. In: *Anna Canepa Video Distribution, Inc. Represents the Following Artists: Eleanor Antin, Terry Fox, Taka Iimura, Allan Kaprow, Les Levine, Dennis Oppenheim, Roger Welch.* Vertriebskatalog, New York, o. J. (1976), S. 6, vgl. S. 258

12 Robin White, An Interview with Terry Fox. In: *View*, Bd. 2, Nr. 3, Point Publications, Oakland, Juni 1979, wiederabgedruckt und übersetzt in: Schmidt 2000, vgl. Anm. 1, S. 70–98, S. 82

13 I Wanted to Have my Mood Affect their Looks. Interview by Willoughby Sharp. In: *Avalanche*, New York, Nr. 3, Winter 1971, S. 70–81, wiederabgedruckt und übersetzt in: Schmidt 2000, vgl. Anm. 1, S. 18

14 Vgl. Henry Miller, *The Colossos of Maroussi.* New York 1941, S. 141–142; dt. *Der Koloss von Maroussi.* Hamburg 1956. Miller verwendet den Begriff als Metapher für eine Unio mystica: „We have nothing to solve: it has all been solved for us. We have but to melt, to dissolve, to swim in the solution. We are soluble fish and the world is an aquarium."

15 André Breton, *Manifeste du Surréalisme.* Paris 1924, S. 36–37: „L'esprit qui plonge dans le surréalisme revit avec exaltation la meilleure part de son enfance [...]. Je suscite sur mes pas des monstres qui guettent [...] voici le ‚poisson soluble' qui m'effraye bien encore un peu. Poisson soluble, n'est-ce pas moi le poisson soluble, je suis né sous le signe des Poissons et l'homme est soluble dans sa pensée."

16 In der Literatur zu Fox findet sich wiederholt der Hinweis auf Antonin Artauds „Theater der Grausamkeit". Jedoch zielte Artaud auf eine „tobende Ordnung" ab, da es in Happening und Performance aufgehoben war, da es keines Regisseurs mehr bedurfte, der die Darsteller führte. Durch das Erlebnis, das *spectacle total,* sollten die Zuschauer in einer existentiellen Erfahrung mit ihren unbewussten Obsessionen konfrontiert werden, die über nur-ästhetische Ambitionen hinausging. Fox' Konzept einer rituell fundierten, kathartischen Kunst, das Nein zur Repräsentation ist zwar Artauds Vorstellungen verwandt. Naheliegender scheint es aber, dass Fox verschiedene Formen der Performanz mit produktiver Distanz rezipierte, so z. B. Jean Genets Ideal des rituellen Theaters, John Cages Antitheater etc. (Antonin Artaud, *Le Théâtre et son double.* Paris 1938; dt. *Das Theater und sein Double.* München 1996)

17 Gascia Ouzounian, *Sound Art and Spatial Practices: Situating Sound Installation Art Since 1958.* UC San Diego Electronic Theses and Dissertations, 2008, http://escholarship.org/uc/item/4d50k2fp, zuletzt am 15.5.2015, S. 137

18 I Wanted to Have my Mood Affect their Looks. Interview by Willoughby Sharp. In: *Avalanche*, New York, Nr. 3, Winter 1971, S. 70–81, wiederabgedruckt und übersetzt in: Schmidt 2000, vgl. Anm. 1, S. 36

19 Oskar Bätschmann, *Ausstellungskünstler. Kunst und Karriere im modernen Kunstsystem.* Köln 1997, S. 232

20 Mieke Bal, Narrative Inside Out. Louise Bourgeois' Spider as Theoretical Object. In: *Oxford Art Journal*, 22, 1999, S. 101–126

21 Herbert Molderings, Life is No Performance. In: Gregory Battock, Robert Nickas (Hg.), *The Art of Performance. A Critical Anthology.* New York 1984, S. 166–180, insbes. S. 172–173

1 Willoughby Sharp, "A Discussion with Terry Fox, Vito Acconci, and Dennis Oppenheim," *Avalanche*, no. 3, (Winter 1971), pp. 86–89, here p. 87; reprinted and translated into German in Eva Schmidt (ed.), *Terry Fox. Ocular Language. 30 Jahre Reden und Schreiben über Kunst. 30 Years of Speaking and Writing about Art.* Gesellschaft für Aktuelle Kunst Bremen, Cologne, 2000, pp. 43–53, here pp. 45; hereafter Schmidt 2000 [author's emphasis]

2 Robin White, "An Interview with Terry Fox," *View*, vol. 2, no. 3, Point Publications, Oakland, June 1979, hereafter White 1979; reprinted and translated into German in Schmidt 2000, cf. note 1, pp. 71–99, here p. 75

3 Tom Marioni, "Introductory Statement (July 12, 1979)," Carl E. Loeffler, Darlene Tong (eds.): *Performance Anthology. Source Book of California Performance Art*, San Francisco, 1989 (EA 1980), p. ix. On Fox's and Marioni's importance for the development of sound sculpture, see Gascia Ouzounian, *Sound Art and Spatial Practices: Situating Sound Installation Art Since 1958*, UC San Diego Electronic Theses and Dissertations, 2008, http://escholarship.org/uc/item/4d50k2fp (last accessed on May 15, 2015)

4 Terry Fox, "From Floor to Ceiling and Wall to Wall," in conversation with Johannes Lothar Schröder; Schmidt 2000, cf. note 1, pp. 193–209, here p. 201

5 Sharp 1971, cf. note 1, p. 87

6 Willoughby Sharp, "I Wanted to Have My Mood Affect Their Looks," interview with Terry Fox, *Avalanche*, no. 3, New York (Winter 1971), pp. 70–81; reprinted and translated into German in Schmidt 2000, cf. note 1, pp. 9–41, here p. 13

7 Lucy R. Lippard, *Six Years: Dematerialization of the Art Object from 1966 to 1972*, New York, 1973

8 Maurice Merleau-Ponty, *Phénoménologie de la perception*, Paris, 1945, p. 235

9 Tom Marioni, "Terry Fox: Himself," interview, *Art and Artists*, January 7, 1973, pp. 39–41, here p. 40

10 Terry Fox, "Elements, Actions, and Conditions of Turgescent Sex," *Avalanche*, no. 3, Fall 1971, p. 7, cf. p. 286

11 Terry Fox, "Turgescent Sex, " Anna Canepa Video Distribution, Inc. Represents the Following Artists: Eleanor Antin, Terry Fox, Taka Iimura, Allan Kaprow, Les Levine, Dennis Oppenheim, Roger Welch. Distribution catalogue, New York, no year (1976), p. 6, cf. p. 258

12 White 1979, cf. note 2; Schmidt 2000, pp. 71–99, here p. 83

13 Cf. note 6, Sharp, pp. 70–81, reprinted and translated into German in Schmidt 2000, cf. note 1, p. 17

14 Cf. Henry Miller, *The Colossos of Maroussi*, New York, 1941, pp. 141–142. Miller uses the term as a metaphor for mystical union: "We have nothing to solve: it has all been solved for us. We have but to melt, to dissolve, to swim in the solution. We are soluble fish and the world is an aquarium."

15 André Breton: *Manifeste du Surréalisme*, Paris, 1924, pp. 36–37: "L'esprit qui plonge dans le surréalisme revit avec exaltation la meilleure part de son enfance [...] Je suscite sur mes pas des monstres qui guettent [...] voici le 'poisson soluble' qui m'effraye bien encore un peu. Poisson soluble, n'est-ce pas moi le poisson soluble, je suis né sous le signe des Poissons et l'homme est soluble dans sa pensée."

16 The literature on Fox often mentions Antonin Artaud's "Theater of Cruelty." However, Artaud's attempt to "order a raging dissonance" no longer applies to happenings and performance, which do not require a director since the performer leads. Through the experience of the *spectacle total,* the audience engages in an existential experience confronted with their unconscious obsessions which extend beyond the purely aesthetic. Fox's concept of a cathartic art based in ritual and his rejection of representation approximates to Artaud's ideas. It seems more likely, though, that Fox adopts various forms of performance with productive distance such as, for example, Jean Genet's ideal of ritual theater, John Cage's anti-theater, etc. Antonin Artaud, *Le Théâtre et son double*, Paris, 1938; (*The Theatre and its Double*, Alma Classics, 2013).

17 Gascia Ouzounian, *Sound Art and Spatial Practices: Situating Sound Installation Art Since 1958*, UC San Diego Electronic Theses and Dissertations, 2008, http://escholarship.org/uc/item/4d50k2fp (last accessed on May 15, 2015), p. 137

18 Cf. note 6, Sharp, pp. 70–81, reprinted and translated into German in Schmidt 2000, cf. note 1, p. 37

19 Oskar Bätschmann, *Ausstellungskünstler. Kunst und Karriere im modernen Kunstsystem*, Cologne, 1997, p. 232

20 Mieke Bal, "Narrative Inside Out. Louise Bourgeois' Spider as Theoretical Object," *Oxford Art Journal*, 22, 1999, pp. 101–126

21 Herbert Molderings, "Life is No Performance," Gregory Battock and Robert Nickas (eds.), *The Art of Performance. A Critical Anthology,* New York, 1984, pp. 166–180, in particular pp. 172–173

Kathleen Bühler

Performative Traces:
Terry Fox in Bern

Die Verbindungen des amerikanischen Performance- und Klangkünstlers in die Schweizer Hauptstadt begannen mit seiner Freundschaft zu Elka Spoerri, die er 1972 bei der documenta 5 in Kassel kennenlernte und die ab 1975 die Adolf-Wölfli-Stiftung am Kunstmuseum Bern leitete. Bei der damaligen documenta sah Terry Fox die Werke von Adolf Wölfli zum ersten Mal und war sofort von dem Außenseiter begeistert, den er als „Künstler in Reinform" betrachtete. Für Wölfli besaß die Kunst existentielle Dringlichkeit. Außerdem betätigte er sich gleichermaßen lustvoll in Text, Bild und Musik.[1] Elka Spoerri eröffnete Terry Fox Zugang zu Wölflis Werk und erlaubte ihm freien Zutritt zum Archiv. Davon angeregt führte Fox 1980 seine Performance *A Candle for A. W.* im Kunstmuseum Bern auf.[2]

Im Jahr 1987 gastierte Terry Fox erneut mit einer Performance im Kunstmuseum Bern. Für *The Eye is Not The Only Glass That Burns The Mind* spannte er Klaviersaiten durch die Säle der Ausstellung „Die Gleichzeitigkeit des Anderen".[3] Er nutzte das Kunstmuseum als Instrument und ließ es auf neuartige Weise erklingen. Nicht nur die Architektur diente dabei zweifach als Instrument sowie Klang- und Echoraum, sondern auch die ausgestellten Werke. Die Einladung zur Klangperformance erfolgte damals durch Jürgen Glaesemer. Der Ausstellungsmacher und Klee-Spezialist führte in seiner Ausstellung eine unkonventionelle Auseinandersetzung mit der materialistischen Seite der westlichen Kultur und richtete sein Augenmerk dabei auf extreme Erfahrungen wie Ekstase, Wahnsinn, Erotik, Krankheit und Tod. In poetischen Gegenüberstellungen gesellte er Kunst von Außenseitern zu der Kunst von Paul Klee oder anderen, die durch Konfrontation mit ihrem Unterbewussten oder im Kontakt mit anderen Kulturen eine tiefreichende Begegnung mit dem „Anderen" erlebt hatten. Terry Fox befreundete sich mit dem innovativen Ausstellungsmacher, der sich mit dieser Essay-Ausstellung auch jenen schmerzhaften Ausnahmezuständen annäherte, die Fox selbst häufig in seiner Kunst behandelte. Für Glaesemer, der selbst unheilbar an AIDS erkrankt war, stellte „Die Gleichzeitigkeit des Anderen" sein kuratorisches Vermächtnis

The connection between Bern, the capital of Switzerland, and the American performance and sound artist Terry Fox was rooted in his friendship to Elka Spoerri, which began in 1972 at *documenta 5* in Kassel. Elka Spoerri was an expert on outsider artist Adolf Wölfli, a former Swiss laborer who created a massive illustrated narrative of his life while institutionalized in a mental hospital, and she became the founding curator of the Adolf Wölfli Foundation at the Kunstmuseum Bern in 1975. At *documenta 5*, which showcased a number of pieces by Adolf Wölfli, Terry Fox saw this outsider's works for the first time. He was immediately enthusiastic, regarding him as a "pure form of artist." Wölfli not only saw art as having existential urgency, but his works combine an equal delight in text, images and music.[1] Elka Spoerri provided Terry Fox access to Wölfli's work, and allowed him to visit the archive freely. In 1980, inspired by Wölfli's oeuvre, Terry Fox gave his performance *A Candle for A. W.* at the Kunstmuseum Bern.[2]

In 1987, Terry Fox was invited to give another performance at the museum which was showing the exhibition *Die Gleichzeitigkeit des Anderen* at that time. For his performance *The Eye is Not the Only Glass that Burns the Mind,* Fox stretched piano wires across the exhibition halls.[3] In this way, he used the museum as an instrument, making it resonate in a new and innovative way. Not only did the architecture doubly serve as an instrument as well as a sound and echo space, but so did the exhibited works. Fox had been invited to give his sound performance by exhibition curator Jürgen Glaesemer, a specialist on Paul Klee. In his exhibition, Glaesemer presented an unconventional critique of the materialistic side of Western culture, focusing particularly on such extreme experiences as ecstasy, madness, eroticism, illness and death. In a series of poetic juxtapositions, he combined artworks by mavericks and outsiders with those by Paul Klee or other artists who had profound encounters with the "Other" either through confronting their own subconscious mind or in the experience of other cultures. Terry Fox became friends with this innovative curator whose themes in this essay exhibition also approached those painful exceptional states which Fox often dealt with in his art. At the

dar. Ihm war Kunst der prädestinierte Ort für Ausnahmeerfahrungen, da sie für die Wahrnehmung des Anderen sensibilisiere. Mit ihren Grenzgängen, ihrer Hinwendung zu Prozessen und elementaren Gesten erforderte gerade die Kunst der 1970er und 1980er Jahre eine tolerante Haltung vom Betrachter und führte fortwährend zu Konfrontationen mit dem Unbekannten.[4]

Es erstaunt im Nachhinein nicht, dass Terry Fox an dieser Ausstellung teilnahm. Denn der häufig offene Ausgang seiner Performances oder die mehrschichtige und semantisch offene Struktur seiner Textarbeiten können durchaus als „Konfrontationen mit dem Unbekannten" gelten, ging es ihm doch um eine neuartige Kommunikation mit den Mitteln der von ihren Gattungsgrenzen befreiten Kunst. Wie Jürgen Glaesemer vertraute auch Terry Fox darauf, dass die Kunst über Mittel verfügt, welche „über entsprechende Erfahrungen dieses Anderen" Mitteilungen machen können.[5] Dafür griff Fox auf die elementare Sprache der Bilder, Klänge und Bewegungen zurück, die sich nicht zuerst in Begriffen definieren muss, sondern unmittelbar sinnliche Präsenz besitzt. Als seine eigentliche künstlerische Leistung betrachtete er die energetisch-skulpturale Transformation des Raumes durch sein Bewusstsein und durch metaphorische Handlungen, welche das Publikum in ein anderes Raum- und Zeitgefühl versetzten.[6] Seine Klangarbeit verkörpert seine Vorstellungen diesbezüglich am besten. Dabei nutzte er den Klang als eine universelle Sprache, die mühelos kulturelle Barrieren bezwingt, denn: „Er erfordert keine Intellektualisierung. Es ist nicht nötig, eine gemeinsame Sprache zu sprechen. Unwissenheit ist bedeutungslos. Der Klang zieht vorbei wie Pulsschläge in der Luft. Die Performance ist für mich ein Versuch, eine Sprache oder Kommunikationsmethode zu entdecken, die diese Barrieren überwindet wie der Klang."[7]

Als Jürgen Glaesemer 1988 starb, steckte das Kunstmuseum mitten im Akquirierungsprozess einer Textarbeit von Terry Fox, der in den 1980er und 1990er Jahren noch vier weitere Werke folgen sollten. Da sein Tätigkeitsgebiet in Bern nun Performances, Textobjekte und Objektkästen umfasste, wird im Folgenden zu untersuchen sein, auf welche Weise der Künstler seine Ansichten zur performativen und kommunikativen Austauschbeziehung mit dem Publikum auch in anderen Materialien und Medien umsetzte. Dabei vertraute Terry Fox auf die universelle Zugänglichkeit von Sinneserfahrungen, thematisierte jedoch auch deren Grenzen. Er war davon überzeugt, dass seine Kunst deshalb eine andere Art von Realitätserfahrung ermöglichte, weil sich sein Leben von der Norm unterschied und er sich stets mit Grenzen hatte auseinandersetzen müssen.[8] Das Objekt *Dal cielo del fuoco (for Joseph Beuys)* (1986) [↗**174, 175**] zumindest sprengt

time he staged *Die Gleichzeitigkeit des Anderen*, Glaesemer was incurably ill with AIDS, and this exhibition remains his curatorial legacy. For him, art was predestined to be a location of atypical experiences, since these heighten our awareness for the perception of the Other. With its crossing of borders and turn to processes and elementary gestures, the art of the 1970s and 1980s in particular requires viewers to engage with it with open minds as it constantly leads them to confront the unfamiliar.[4]

In retrospect, it is hardly surprising that Terry Fox took part in this exhibition. However, although his often open-ended performances or the multilayered and semantically open structures of his textual works could certainly be regarded as "confrontations with the unfamiliar," his primary concern was a new form of communication using the medium of art freed from its genre constraints. Like Jürgen Glaesemer, Terry Fox also believed that art had the means to communicate "about the pertinent experiences of this Other."[5] To achieve this aim, Fox drew on the elementary language of images, sounds and movements which do not first need to be defined conceptually, but have an immediate sensory presence. In Fox's view, his own artistic achievement consisted in applying his energy to transform space into sculpture through his mental states and metaphorical actions, enabling viewers to enter a different dimension of space and time.[6] His sound works employing sound as a universal language, capable of effortlessly overcoming cultural barriers, embody these ideas best of all since, as he remarked: "No intelligence is necessary. No common language need to be spoken. Illiteracy is irrelevant. Sound passes as pulses in the air. Performance is, for me, an attempt to discover a language or method of communication which bypasses these barriers as sound does."[7]

When Jürgen Glaesemer died in 1988, the Kunstmuseum Bern was in the middle of the process of acquiring one of Terry Fox's textual works. This was followed by the acquisition of four other works by Terry Fox in the 1980s and 1990s. Since the works in Bern primarily comprised performances, textual objects and object boxes, the following will consider how Terry Fox realized his views on the performative and communicative process of exchange with viewers in other material and media as well. In doing so, he relied on the universal accessibility of sensory experience, though he also addressed and explored its limits. He was convinced that his art facilitated the experience of a different kind of reality, since his life was also different from other people's and had involved a constant confrontation with limits.[8] Certainly, his *Dal cielo del fuoco (for Joseph Beuys)* from 1986 [↗**174, 175**] breaks the mold of conventional notions about textual works as it is nether printed on paper, nor does it attempt to

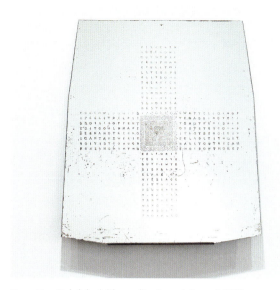

Terry Fox, *Dal cielo del fuoco (for Joseph Beuys)*, 1986

reproduce any standard paper sizes. Instead, it includes a rather uneven rectangular reflective plate with a text engraved on the reverse. This textual mirror was created as a homage to Joseph Beuys, who died in 1986. When Fox, living in Florence at that time, heard of Beuys' death by chance on Italian TV, he spontaneously decided to produce "a kind of tombstone" with the found mirror.[9] Fox's text was inspired by Beuys' performance *Ja, ja, ja, nee, nee, nee* (1968), and written in the form of the arms of a cross set around a central square.[10] Although the first sentence is taken from a postcard Beuys sent to Fox in 1970 and so represents the initial contact between the two artists, the other sentences are decontextualized fragments of presumably other letters or conversations including: YES VERY NICE FROM YOU TO TRIP[11] / YES I THANKFULLY WILL / YES I FEEL IT SO / NO THEREFORE I WONDERED / NO DONT TELL ME LESS / NO ITS A DISTANCE AWAY / YES SO IM OFTEN ASKING / YES ITS NOT FINISHED QUITE / YES COULD IT NOT BE / NO I GIVE GLADLY IT / NO I THANK YOU THE SAME / NO I DONT MORE FEEL FOR IT / YES I HAVE BUT FEW / YES I SHALL HELP AS I CAN / YES I ACCEPT YOUR ARGUMENT / NO I CANT CATCH THE TIME / NO I THINK ABOUT IT / NO I ALSO FOLLOW SOON / YES I FEEL IT DEEP / YES SO I DID OFTEN / YES IT COULD HAVE BEEN ANOTHER / NO I CANT ANSWER IT / NO IT IS TOO MUCH FIXED / NO MY MY NO.[12]

The sentences form strings of words divided into thirteen lines each with eight letters. They are read in a clockwise direction, as is the central helix. In contrast, though, the engraved square in the center is divided into 64 smaller squares matching Beuys' age when he died. Each of the smaller squares is marked

konventionelle Vorstellungen von Textarbeiten, da es weder auf Papier gedruckt wurde, noch irgendeine Papierformatnorm respektierte. Stattdessen besteht es aus einer ungleichmäßig rechteckigen Spiegelplatte mit einem Text, der auf der Rückseite eingraviert ist. Das Spiegeltextobjekt entstand als Hommage an den 1986 verstorbenen Joseph Beuys, von dessen Tod Terry Fox, der damals in Florenz lebte, per Zufall im italienischen Fernsehen erfuhr. Spontan entschied er sich, mit dem gefundenen Spiegel „eine Art Grabstein" zu fertigen.[9] Dazu schrieb Fox einen Text in Kreuzform, der um ein zentrales Quadrat herumführt und von Beuys' Performance *Ja, ja, ja, nee, nee, nee* (1968) inspiriert war.[10] Mit Ausnahme des

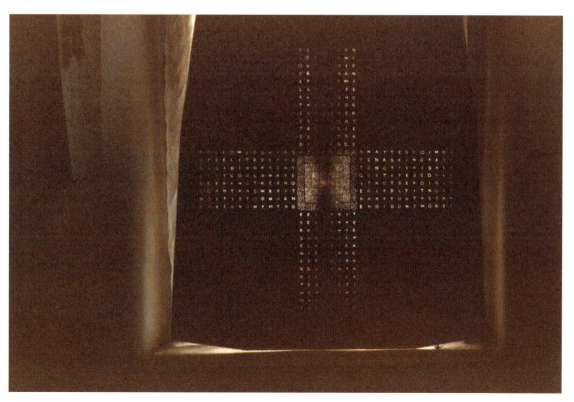

Terry Fox, *Dal cielo del fuoco (for Joseph Beuys)*, 1986

ersten Satzes, welcher einer Postkarte entstammte, die Joseph Beuys 1970 an Fox geschrieben hat und die somit den ersten Kontakt zwischen den beiden Künstlern verkörpert, sind es aus ursprünglichen Sinnzusammenhängen – vermutlich aus Briefen oder Gesprächen – herausgelöste Satzfragmente wie: YES VERY NICE FROM YOU TO TRIP[11] / YES I THANKFULLY WILL / YES I FEEL IT SO / NO THEREFORE I WONDERED / NO DONT TELL ME LESS / NO ITS A DISTANCE AWAY / YES SO IM OFTEN ASKING / YES ITS NOT FINISHED QUITE / YES COULD IT NOT BE / NO I GIVE GLADLY IT / NO I THANK YOU THE SAME / NO I DONT MORE FEEL FOR IT / YES I HAVE BUT FEW / YES I SHALL HELP AS I CAN / YES I ACCEPT YOUR ARGUMENT / NO I CANT CATCH THE TIME / NO I THINK ABOUT IT / NO I ALSO FOLLOW SOON / YES I FEEL IT DEEP / YES SO I DID OFTEN / YES IT COULD HAVE BEEN ANOTHER / NO I CANT ANSWER IT / NO IT IS TOO MUCH FIXED / NO MY MY NO.[12]

Während sich die Sätze als aneinandergereihte Wortschnur auf 13 Zeilen à 8 Zeichen aufteilen – sie werden wie die mittige Schraubenlinie im Uhrzeigersinn gelesen –, ist das gravierte Zentrum in 64 Quadrate gegliedert, welche exakt den Lebensjahren von Beuys entsprechen und mit jeweils der gleichen Anzahl Punkte wie Lebensjahre ausgefüllt sind. Im Verlaufe der spiralförmig angeordneten Felder verdichten sich also die Punkte und führen zum Schluss zur bildnerischen Auflösung. Nach Auffassung von Fox sollte das Zentrum „ein Fenster durch den Spiegel" bilden und damit Beuys' Tod versinnbildlichen.[13]

In der Gestaltung treffen zwei künstlerische Prinzipien aufeinander, die Fox schon in früheren Werken nutzte: einerseits die performative Qualität des Labyrinths und andererseits die appellative Eigenschaft des Spiegels, der den Betrachter in das Werk „hineinzieht"[14], da sein eigenes Abbild automatisch seine Aufmerksamkeit wecke, während die gedrehte Bewegung des Labyrinths diese bündele und durch das in Gedanken erfolgte Ablaufen eine meditative Konzentration aufbaue.[15] Das Spiegelobjekt Dal cielo del fuoco gibt, wie die Skizze [↗174] dazu zeigt, die Lesebewegung vor und leitet langsam in die Mitte zum „Lebenslauf" von Joseph Beuys. Die inhaltsleeren Sätze lenken die Aufmerksamkeit auf den zeitlichen Ablauf des Lesens. Quasi beiläufig wird mit der Spiegelarbeit die plastische Qualität der Sprachperformance von Joseph Beuys evoziert und dabei zum Zentrum der Arbeit geführt – der Leerstelle, die Beuys' Tod symbolisiert und vor deren Tatsache jegliche Sprache versagt.[16] Während die Person Beuys dort durch das „Fenster im Spiegel" entschwindet, rückt seine künstlerische Errungenschaft, Kunst zum sozialplastischen und performativen Prozess erweitert zu haben, umso mehr in den Mittelpunkt und wird durch das Spiegelbild

with dots, with each dot representing a year of Beuys' life. The dots in the spirally arranged fields gradually increase and become denser, leading in the end to an artistic and sculptural resolution. According to Terry Fox, the center "becomes a window through the mirror," and so symbolizes Beuys' death.[13]

This design brings together two artistic principles that Fox had already employed in earlier works: On the one hand, the performative quality of the labyrinth and, on the other, the mirror's appellative quality to draw viewers "into" the work.[14] The viewer's own image automatically awakens their interest, which is focused by the revolving movement of the labyrinth and also builds up a meditative concentration through the practice of walking around it in one's mind.[15] As the sketch of this work shows [↗174], the mirror structure of Dal cielo del fuoco prescribes just this movement of reading, guiding the viewer gradually into the center of the "course" of Joseph Beuys' own life. The empty sentences direct the viewer's attention to the passage of time that is spent reading. Almost incidentally, this mirror work evokes the plastic quality of Beuys' speech performance and, in the process, leads to the center of the work – the empty place symbolizing Beuys' death where, in the face of that fact, any attempt at language fails.[16] While Joseph Beuys as an individual vanishes there through the "window in the mirror," his artistic achievements of expanding art to social sculptural and performative processes become all the more the focus of attention and authenticated by the viewer's reflection. Not only is the viewer drawn into this form

Isolation Unit, performance by Terry Fox and Joseph Beuys, 1970, Kunstakademie Düsseldorf, photo: Ute Klophaus

des Betrachters beglaubigt. Nicht nur wird man als Betrachter in diese Reminiszenz hineingezogen, sondern es werden zugleich Terry Fox' eigene Erinnerungen an Beuys wachgerufen. Dies folgt aus der ursprünglichen Präsentationsform der Spiegelplatte in seiner Florentiner Wohnung, eingeklemmt in eine Fensteröffnung, so dass der Kreuztext als helle Erscheinung vor dunklem Grund erstrahlte[17]: „The important thing is that the wall (or sky) is seen through the mirror."[18] Damit entschlüsselt Fox den Werktitel: Der Spiegel macht den Himmel in Kreuzform sichtbar, wirft ihn als Lichtzeichen auf den Boden und erinnert dabei an das Feuer in Kreuzform, welches Terry Fox 1970 in seiner einmaligen Performance *Isolation Unit* mit Joseph Beuys auf den Boden gezeichnet hatte.[19] [↗**130**]

Die Verbindung von Fundobjekt und (manchmal) gefundenem Sprachmaterial kennzeichnet auch das nachfolgende Werk, die Wagenskulptur *Cynosure* (1990) [↗**160, 161**], deren Titel neben der wörtlichen Bedeutung „Anziehungspunkt" zudem ein weiterer Name für „Polarstern" und „Kleiner Wagen" ist.[20] Die Buchstaben führen neben- und untereinander als fortlaufendes Band über das Objekt, ihre sinngebende Gruppierung zu Begriffen offenbart sich nicht auf den ersten Blick. Nur wenn man jeden zweiten Buchstaben liest, ergeben sich auf den Holzlatten im Uhrzeigersinn die Worte: *focal point* (Brennpunkt), *centroid* (Mittelpunkt), *metacenter* (Metazentrum), *cynosure* (Anziehungspunkt). Der Text auf Mittelachse und Zugstange lautet: *magnet* (Magnet) sowie *center of attraction* (Mittelpunkt des Interesses). Es sind also lauter synonyme Begriffe für Orte oder Punkte, an denen sich Bedeutung oder Handlung bündelt. Die Wörter, die sich aus den restlichen Buchstaben bilden lassen, beziehen sich auf unterschiedliche Arten des Sehens: *short / near / dim / far / double / clear / half / dull* (kurzsichtig, nahsichtig, undurchsichtig, weitsichtig, doppelsichtig, klarsichtig, halbsichtig, schlechte Sicht). Terry Fox bringt das Begreifen, Fokussieren und Erkennen in ein schwankendes Gleichgewicht mit dem sinnlichen Erfassen. Die Wortbezüge untereinander sind ebenso fragil wie die Einzelteile des „Wagens", der lediglich aus vier aufeinandergelegten schmalen Holzlatten und zwei übereinander gekreuzten Eisenstangen auf halbierten Rädern besteht. Erst im mühsamen Abschreiten und Lesen werden die internen Bezugnahmen erschlossen. Der Betrachter muss sich auch hier körperlich engagieren, um den Text zu lesen, und erlebt ihn auf diese Weise ganzheitlich. In der Kombination der vielen Anspielungen, welche sich zugleich auf das Sehen und Erkennen im Allgemeinen beziehen, stellt sich dann die Orientierung ein, welche der „Kleine Wagen" als Himmelserscheinung gewährt. Dabei geht die partizipative Haltung des Betrachters für Terry Fox so weit, dass dieser

Terry Fox, *Cynosure*, 1990, photo: Dominique Uldry

of remembrance, but the experience also awakens Terry Fox's own recollections of Beuys – the result of the original method of showing the mirror in his apartment in Florence stuck into a window opening so that the text in the form of the cross brightly stood out against the dark support:[17] "The important thing is that the wall (or sky) is seen through the mirror."[18] In this way, Fox has decrypted the work's title. The mirror makes the sky visible in the form of a cross, casts it as a light sign onto the floor and, in doing so, recalls the fire in the shape of a cross which he himself had sketched on the ground in *Isolation Unit*, his remarkable performance with Joseph Beuys in 1970.[19] [↗**130**]

The combination of found objects with (sometimes) found language also characterizes the wagon sculpture *Cynosure* (1990) [↗**160, 161**], the next work to be discussed here. Aside from the title's literal meaning as a point of attraction, it is also another name for the Pole Star (*Cynosura*) and the constellation of Ursa Minor, known in German as the "Little Wagon" (*Kleiner Wagen*).[20] The letters, set adjacent to and below each other, form a continuous band across the object, although the viewer has to look carefully to understand how they should be grouped to decipher their meaning. The letters of the words *focal point*, *centroid*, *metacenter*, and *cynosure* are on the wooden beams, but only became apparent when every second letter is read in a clockwise direction. The text on the center axle and the connecting rod yields the words *magnet* and *center of attraction*. These are, then, all synonymous for locations or points where meaning or actions are concentrated. The words from the remaining letters all relate to different ways of seeing: *short / near / dim / far / double / clear / half / dull.*

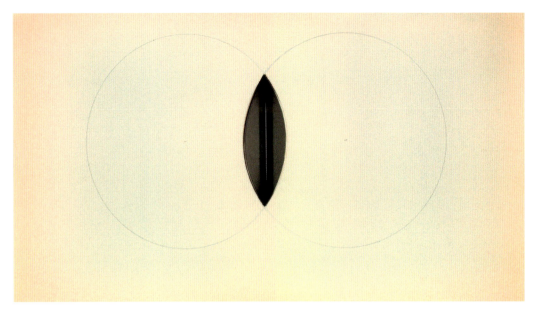

Terry Fox, *Blood*, 1997

beim Lesen eine ähnliche Erfahrung durchmachen soll wie er selbst im Moment des Textschreibens. Denn für den Künstler ist die äußere Erscheinung des Werkes nur eine Brücke, die dem Betrachter erlaubt, in die im Text beschriebene Erfahrung einzutreten.[21]

Die drei Objektkästen *Vesica*, *Salt* und *Blood* schließlich stammen aus Terry Fox' letzter Einzelausstellung 1997 in der Galerie Francesca Pia in Bern. Motto und Ausstellungstitel war „Vesica Pisces". Erneut ist der metaphorische Kontext reichhaltig und rätselhaft. Die titelgebende Fischblase bezeichnet eine perfekte geometrische Form von zwei sich überschneidenden, identischen Kreisen, deren Mittelpunkte jeweils auf der Umrisslinie des anderen liegen. Die Schnittfläche wird auch als Mandorla bezeichnet und gilt als Heilszeichen in religiösen Bildwerken. Als symbolische Form kennzeichnet die Fischblase zudem den Moment, in dem aus zwei gleichen Figuren eine dritte entsteht. Dieses schöpferische Urprinzip ist in vielen Naturphänomenen belegt: von der Teilung der befruchteten Eizelle, über Schwingungsphänomene in der Musik bis hin zu Planetenbewegungen. Terry Fox benannte als Motto der Ausstellung also den Schöpfungsprozess, der in der Verbindung von zwei Gleichwertigen etwas Drittes schafft. Robert Lawlors Untersuchung *Sacred Geometry* (1982), die eine wichtige Inspirationsquelle für den Künstler war, unterstreicht zudem die Vermittlerrolle der Fischblase, da jene sowohl an veränderlichen wie an unveränderlichen, ewigen wie ephemeren Prinzipien teilnehme.[22] Ganz konkret zeigte Terry Fox dies in der Arbeit *Blood* (1997) [↗132], einem Holzkasten, der einen breitflächig eingespannten, gebogenen Karton enthält, auf dem die Kreise mit Bleistift

Terry Fox places the acts of apprehending, focusing and understanding in a vacillating balance with sensory perception. The references of the words to each other are just as fragile as the individual elements of the "wagon," which is solely comprised of four narrow wooden beams placed one on top of the other and two crossed metal rods, all set on two semicircular wheels. Only through the laborious process of walking the length of the sculpture and reading the words are the internal references revealed. Here too, the viewer needs to become physically involved in reading the text and, in this way, experiences it holistically. The combination of the many different allusions, evoking both seeing and understanding in general, creates the right frame of mind for perceiving this "Little Wagon" as a celestial phenomenon. For Terry Fox, the viewers' participatory approach should be so intense that it allows them to undergo a similar experience in reading the words as he himself had when he wrote them. In his view, the external appearance of the work is only a bridge enabling the viewer to access the experiences described in the text.[21]

The final work of art considered here is comprised of three object boxes, *Vesica*, *Salt* and *Blood*, from Terry Fox's last solo show in 1997 at the Galerie Francesca Pia in Bern. The exhibition theme and title was *Vesica Pisces,* again offering a metaphorical context that is both rich and enigmatic. The title, which means "fish bladder" in Latin, also describes the perfect geometrical form of two identical circles intersecting so that the center point of each circle lies on the other's circumference. The almond shape created by this intersection is also known as a *mandorla*, and is regarded as a sign of salvation

eingezeichnet sind. Ihre mandelförmige Schnittfläche klebt wie eine Intarsie auf der Kastenrückwand und zeigt ein senkrecht schwebendes, mit dem Blut des Künstlers gefülltes Glasröhrchen.²³ Terry Fox verband die archaische und symbolhaltige Formensprache, welche das Entstehen von etwas Neuem versinnbildlicht, mit der eigenen Körperflüssigkeit. Er lokalisierte seinen „Lebenssaft" exakt in der Mitte zwischen Momenthaftigkeit und Ewigkeit, flüchtiger Verwandlung und unveränderlicher Konstanz.

Von gleicher, spröd-minimaler Formensprache ist *Salt* (1997). Während im oberen Teil des rechteckigen Glaskastens ein waagrechtes Kupferrohr einen Streifen abtrennt, wurde parallel dazu im unteren Teil ein Streifen mit weißen Salzkörnern aufgefüllt. Auch das lose Salz kann mit Veränderung in Verbindung gebracht werden: Eine kleine Berührung genügt und der Streifen wandelt sich. Außerdem suggeriert die fast schon alchemistische Begegnung der beiden Elemente Salz und Kupfer einen energetischen Prozess.²⁴ Eine Art entfesselte Bewegung stellt hingegen der Objektkasten *Vesica* (1997) dar. Ein kleiner Papierfetzen mit dem Wort „VESICA" klebt zentral im Bild über dem von Tusche- und Aquarellspuren zerknitterten Papier. Es scheint, als ob eine Harnblase auf dem Papier zerplatzt wäre und sich der flüssige Inhalt darüber ergossen hätte. In die gestischen Spuren hinein sind kurze handgeschriebene Textfragmente eingestreut: „Gas cloud / veiled / air drawn in and sent out / aqueous humor / liquid sound" (Gaswolke / verhüllt / Luft eingesogen und ausgestoßen / wässriger Humor / flüssiger Ton) sowie der leicht abgeänderte Titel der 1987 in Bern aufgeführten Performance *The Eye is Not the Only Glass that Burns the Mind*.²⁵ Einmal mehr weist Terry Fox nicht nur auf das sinnlich Wahrnehmbare hin, sondern auch darüber hinaus. Das Auge ist mehr als ein Glas,

in religious art. As a symbolic form, the fish bladder also represents the moment when a third figure is created from two identical figures, a primal creative principle found in many natural phenomena, from the division of the fertilized ovum to wave motion and sympathetic vibration in music or planetary movements. Here, then, Terry Fox took as his motto for the exhibition the creative process which generates something new from two identical things. Robert Lawlor's research in his book *Sacred Geometry* (1982), an important source of inspiration for Terry Fox, additionally underscores the intermediary role of the *fish bladder*, a role that can be found in concepts of change and stasis, as well as those of the eternal and ephemeral.²² Terry Fox gives this a very concrete form in his work *Blood* (1997) [↗**132**], a wooden case filled with a curved pasteboard surface that has two circles drawn on it in pencil. The almond-shaped area where the two circles intersect has been cut out and attached, rather like an inlay, to the back of the wooden case; in front of it, there is a vertically suspended test tube filled with the artist's blood.²³ Terry Fox connected this archaic and symbolically-laden formal language, which epitomizes the creation of something new, with his own bodily fluid. He localizes his "lifeblood" exactly in the center, between the ephemeral and the eternal, fleeting metamorphosis and immutable permanence.

Salt (1997) utilizes the same austerely minimal formal language. While a strip of the rectangular glass case is separated off by a horizontal copper tube in the upper section, a parallel strip is filled with white grains of salt in the lower section. The loose salt can also be associated with change, since just the slightest movement is enough to transform the line of the salt. Moreover, the meeting of the two elements of salt and copper has something almost alchemistic about it,

Terry Fox, *Salt*, 1997

nämlich Fenster („Fenster zur Welt"), Linse (das Auge fokussiert) und (blinder) Spiegel (wenn es nichts zu erkennen gibt) zugleich.[26] Dazu bemerkt Marita Loosen-Fox: „Die Sinne als Tor und Grenze zur Außenwelt sind ein durchgehendes Thema in seinem Werk, auch hier klingt immer als Grundton das mit, was nicht mehr mit den Sinnen zu erfassen ist."[27] Nachdrücklich kehrte Terry Fox damit zum Körper als dem Ausgangspunkt seiner Kunst zurück. Während seine Performances in den 1990er Jahren seltener wurden, übertrug er die performative Arbeit immer mehr dem Betrachter und überließ ihm das Lesen, Entschlüsseln und Interpretieren seiner Hinweise. Seine Objekte beziehen sich metaphorisch auf Körperzustände und Lebensstationen und bringen dem Betrachter seinen eigenen physischen Zustand zum Bewusstsein. Wie in Fox' frühen Performances verbinden die Objekte und Textassoziationen private, subjektive Erlebnisse mit universalen Erfahrungen. Indem der Körper als Blut- oder Textspur in verklausulierter Anspielung auftaucht, wird er als zentraler Zugang zur Realität bekräftigt. Darin ist immer auch die individuelle Verfassung jedes Einzelnen eingeschlossen, welche diesen Zugang prägt. Terry Fox wusste, dass dieses Bewusstsein für den körperlichen Zugang zur Welt nicht einfach vorausgesetzt werden kann, sondern meist erst in Ausnahmezuständen wie Krankheit oder Behinderung erworben und geschärft wird. Dass diesem Wissen Sprache allein nicht genügt, zeigt außerdem seine Schlussfolgerung aus dem Jahr 1998: „Viele Aussagen über den Körper sind verbal. Ich brauche den Körper, um nonverbale Dinge zu übermitteln, Dinge, die geschehen und hinterher kann man noch nicht einmal erklären, was sie bedeutet haben."[28] Die Vielschichtigkeit der Berner Objekte von Terry Fox, die sich einer einfachen Deutung entziehen, ist deshalb zentral, damit die darin enthaltenen Erfahrungen nicht leichtfertig verbalisiert und somit *ad acta* gelegt werden können, sondern sich als poetische Widerhaken ins Auge des Betrachters bohren und ihn immer wieder auf seine eigene körperliche Befindlichkeit sowie die dadurch gefärbte Realitätswahrnehmung zurückwerfen.

suggesting a dynamic process.[24] In contrast, the *Vesica* (1997) display case represents a kind of uncontrolled movement. A small strip of paper with the word "VESICA" is set in the center glued over the crumpled sheet of paper covered with traces of ink and watercolor. It seems as if a vesica, a bladder, had burst on the paper and the liquid contents spilled over it. There are short handwritten fragments of text scattered among the gestural marks: "Gas cloud / veiled / air drawn in and sent out / aqueous humor / liquid sound," as well as the slightly altered title of Terry Fox's performance *The Eye is Not the Only Glass that Burns the Mind,* shown in Bern in 1987.[25] Once again, Terry Fox not only evokes what is perceptible by the senses, but also what lies beyond. The eye is more than a glass – namely a window ("window to the world"), a lens (the eye focuses) and a (blind) mirror (when there is nothing to see), all at the same time.[26] On this point, Marita Loosen-Fox noted: "The senses as a gateway and boundary to the external world are a constant theme running throughout his work, and here too always resonate with the undertone of what the senses can no longer grasp."[27]

Terry Fox thus emphatically returned to the body as the starting point of his work. While he gave fewer performances in the 1990s, he increasingly transferred the performative work to the audiences, letting them read, decipher and interpret his hints and allusions. His objects metaphorically reference physical states and stages in life, making viewers aware of their own physical states. As in Fox's early performances, the objects and textual associations connect the private and subjective with universal experiences. Through the body appearing as vestiges of blood or as textual traces in encoded allusions, it is affirmed as a key means of access to reality – and, in this respect, always includes the particular state of each individual which influences this access as well. Terry Fox knew that this awareness of the physical access to the world cannot simply be assumed, but in most cases is usually acquired and intensified through such exceptional states as illness or disablement. Moreover, language alone is not capable of conveying this knowledge, as he pointed out in 1998 when discussing the implications this had for his work: "A lot of statements on bodies are verbal. I use the body to transmit the nonverbal things, things that happen and afterwards you couldn't even explain what they meant."[28]

The objects by Terry Fox in the Bern collection elude any simple interpretation. Their complexity is pivotal, since this prevents the experiences they contain from being casually verbalized and, in this way, simply shelved. Instead, like a lyrically baited hook, they catch and hold the eye, constantly reverberating back so that viewers reflect on their own physicality and the perception of reality colored by their physical states.

Translated from the German by Andrew Boreham

1 E-Mail von Marita Loosen-Fox an die Verfasserin, 23.5.2015

2 Leider sind keine Aufzeichnungen dazu erhalten.

3 Die Ausstellung fand vom 21. März bis 14. Juni 1987 statt.

4 Jürgen Glaesemer, Nachwort. In: ders. (Hg.), *Die Gleichzeitigkeit des Anderen. Materialien zu einer Ausstellung*. Kunstmuseum Bern 1987, S. 271

5 Ebd., S. 272

6 Vom Boden zur Decke und von Wand zu Wand. Gespräch mit Johannes Lothar Schröder. In: Eva Schmidt (Hg.), *Terry Fox. Ocular Language. 30 Jahre Reden und Schreiben über Kunst. 30 Years of Speaking and Writing about Art.* Gesellschaft für Aktuelle Kunst Bremen, Köln 2000, S. 196, fortan Schmidt 2000

7 Terry Fox, Klang. In: Schmidt 2000, vgl. Anm. 6, S. 138

8 Isolation Unit. Interview von Achille Bonito Oliva (Neapel 1972). In: Schmidt 2000, vgl. Anm. 6, S. 58

9 Notiz des Künstlers, 25.12.1988, Werkarchiv, Kunstmuseum Bern

10 Joseph Beuys führte dieses Stück am 14.12.1968 in Anwesenheit von vier Personen in der Staatlichen Kunstakademie Düsseldorf auf, nachdem seine Professorenkollegen soeben das Misstrauensmanifest gegen ihn publiziert hatten. Statt über die akademisch-politische Lage zu diskutieren, wiederholte er das Gemurmel „Ja Ja Nee Nee", das er am gleichen Tag bei einer Beerdigung stundenlang anhören musste. Die bedeutungsschwere und zugleich nichtssagende Äußerung wurde damit zum „ironischen Sinnbild der unaufhebbaren Dialektik des alltäglichen Lebens"; vgl. http://georgwassmuth.de, zuletzt am 18.5.2015.

11 Dies war die freundliche Antwort von Joseph Beuys auf das Ansinnen des ihm damals noch unbekannten Terry Fox, ihn in Düsseldorf zu besuchen; vgl. Klaus Staeck (Hg.), *Ohne die Rose tun wir's nicht. Für Joseph Beuys.* Heidelberg 1986, S. 350.

12 Undatierte fotokopierte Notiz des Künstlers, Werkarchiv, Kunstmuseum Bern

13 „The center becomes a window through the mirror – his death", Notiz des Künstlers, 25.12.1988, vgl. Anm. 9

14 Ich wollte, dass meine Stimmung ihr Aussehen beeinflusst. Interview von Willoughby Sharp. Zuerst in: *Avalanche,* Winter 1971; zit. nach: Schmidt 2000, vgl. Anm. 6, S. 18

15 Es ist der Versuch einer neuen Kommunikation. Interview von Robin White (1979). In: Schmidt 2000, vgl. Anm. 6, S. 98

16 Gemäß einer Notiz im Werkarchiv soll sich das Zentrum der Spiegelarbeit genau auf Augenhöhe befinden.

17 Als Hommage während eines Abends im Oktober 1986 im Restaurant/ Galerie La Scala in Rom ausgestellt, hing der Spiegel sogar im rechten Winkel gekippt von der Wand, so dass das Licht direkt ein Muster auf den Boden warf; siehe Notiz des Künstlers, 25.12.1988, vgl. Anm. 9.

18 Notiz des Künstlers, 25.12.1988, vgl. Anm. 9

19 *Brennpunkt 2. Düsseldorf. Die Siebziger Jahre. Entwürfe. Joseph Beuys zum 70. Geburtstag.* Kunstmuseum Düsseldorf 1991, S. 102

20 Zum ersten Mal ausgestellt wurde die Skulptur 1990 in der Galerie Löhrl in Mönchengladbach, sie kam danach in die Einzelausstellung der Galerie Francesca Pia nach Bern, wo sie der Berner Museumsleitung auffiel und angekauft wurde.

21 Vom Boden zur Decke und von Wand zu Wand (1997). In: Schmidt 2000, vgl. Anm. 6, S. 200

22 Robert Lawlor, *Sacred Geometry.* New York 1982, S. 32

23 Gemäß Notiz des Künstlers, 5.9.1997, Werkarchiv, Kunstmuseum Bern

24 Die Ausstellung zeigte insgesamt fünf Vitrinenkästen mit verschiedenen Elementen. Dazu schrieb die Kunstkritikerin Elisabeth Gerber: „Die verwendeten Gegenstände und Materialien spielen auf konkrete Erfahrungsräume an und öffnen sich durch den vom Künstler eingegrenzten Kontext gleichzeitig auf neue Bedeutungen hin. Ein beinahe alchemistischer Transformationsprozess geht hier vor sich, der in sich allerdings gesichert, nicht eindeutig festgeschrieben ist. Die Erfahrung der Brüchigkeit dieses stets neu zu leistenden Prozesses – hier auch als mögliches Scheitern der Kommunikation mitbedacht – teilt sich den Betrachtenden im Akt der Wahrnehmung unmittelbar mit und verweist damit metaphorisch auf die Verletzlichkeit des eigenen physischen und mentalen Daseins." In: *Kunst-Bulletin.* Zürich, April 1997, S. 38

25 Der Satz stammt aus dem Gedicht *The Conflagration of London, Poetically Lineated* (1667) von Simon Ford und bezieht sich auf den Brand von London im Jahr 1666. Die Flammen seien die Strafe Gottes für das politische und konfessionelle Abschwören der Bevölkerung vom König; vgl. Margery Kingsley, Interpreting Providence. In: Peter G. Platt (Hg.), *Wonders, Marvels and Monsters in Early Modern Culture*, Cranbury, London, Mississauga 1999, S. 259.

26 Dank für diese Hinweise an Ron Meyers und Marita Loosen-Fox

27 E-Mail von Marita Loosen-Fox an die Verfasserin, 16.6.2015

28 Vom Boden zur Decke und von Wand zu Wand (1997). In: Schmidt 2000, vgl. Anm. 6, S. 208

1 Personal email from Marita Loosen-Fox, May 23, 2015

2 Unfortunately, there are no recordings of the performance.

3 The exhibition took place from March 21 – June 14, 1987.

4 Jürgen Glaesemer, "Nachwort," Jürgen Glaesemer (ed.), *Die Gleichzeitigkeit des Anderen. Materialien zu einer Ausstellung*, Kunstmuseum Bern, 1987, p. 271

5 Ibid., p. 272

6 "From Floor to Ceiling and Wall to Wall," Terry Fox in conversation with Johannes Lothar Schröder; Eva Schmidt (ed.), *Terry Fox. Ocular Language. 30 Jahre Reden und Schreiben über Kunst. 30 Years of Speaking and Writing about Art.* Gesellschaft für Aktuelle Kunst Bremen, Cologne, 2000, p. 199, hereafter Schmidt 2000

7 Terry Fox, "Sound," Schmidt 2000, cf. note 6, p. 139

8 "Isolation Unit," interview by Achille Bonito Oliva (Naples, 1972); Schmidt 2000, cf. note 6, p. 59

9 Artist's note, December 25, 1988, Werkarchiv, Kunstmuseum Bern

10 Joseph Beuys performed this piece on December 14, 1968 in the presence of four people at the Staatliche Kunstakademie in Düsseldorf after faculty members at the art academy had publicly denounced him. Instead of discussing the situation at the university and in the wider political sphere, he constantly muttered "Ja Ja Nee Nee" (Yes, yes, no, no), which he had heard for hours earlier in the day at a funeral. This profoundly meaningful, yet simultaneously meaningless statement thus came to "ironically symbolize the indissoluble dialectic of everyday life," cf. http://georgwassmuth.de, last accessed on May 18, 2015.

11 At that time Joseph Beuys had not yet heard of Terry Fox. This was his friendly reply when Fox wrote to say that he was planning to visit Beuys in Düsseldorf; cf. Klaus Staeck (ed.), *Ohne die Rose tun wir's nicht. Für Joseph Beuys.* Heidelberg, 1986, p. 350

12 Undated, photocopied note by the artist, Werkarchiv, Kunstmuseum Bern

13 "The center becomes a window through the mirror – his death," artist's note, December 25, 1988, cf. note 9

14 "I Wanted to Have My Mood Affect Their Looks," interview with Willoughby Sharp, first published in *Avalanche*, (Winter 1971); cited in Schmidt 2000, cf. note 6, p. 19

15 "It's an Attempt at a New Communication," interview with Robin White (1979); Schmidt 2000, cf. note 6, p. 99

16 According to a note in the Werkarchiv (Kunstmuseum Bern), the center of the mirror is supposed to be set directly at eye level.

17 Exhibited as a homage on one evening in October 1986 in the La Scala restaurant / gallery in Rome, the mirror was even hung at a right angle to the wall so that the light directly created a pattern on the floor; see artist's note, December 25, 1988, cf. note 9

18 Artist's note, December 25, 1988, cf. note 9

19 *Brennpunkt 2. Düsseldorf. Die Siebziger Jahre. Entwürfe. Joseph Beuys zum 70. Geburtstag.* Kunstmuseum Düsseldorf, 1991, p. 102

20 The sculpture was first exhibited in 1990 at the Galerie Löhrl in Mönchengladbach, and was brought to Bern after the solo show at the Galerie Francesca Pia. There, the work attracted the attention of the staff at the Bern museum and was acquired for the collection.

21 "From Floor to Ceiling and Wall to Wall," Schmidt 2000, cf. note 6, p. 201

22 Robert Lawlor, *Sacred Geometry*, New York, 1982, p. 32

23 As stated in an artist's note from September 5, 1997, Werkarchiv, Kunstmuseum Bern

24 The exhibition showed a total of five display cases with different elements. Art critic Elisabeth Gerber wrote: "The objects and materials used here evoke concrete realms of experience and, at the same time, through the contexts circumscribed by the artist, open up to become receptive to new meanings. An almost alchemistic transformation process is taking place here which, though in itself certain, is not unequivocally determined. The experience of the fragility of this process constantly needing to be carried out anew – also considered here as a possible failure of communication – is shared by the viewer directly in the act of perception, and hence metaphorically references the vulnerability of one's own physical and mental being." *Kunst-Bulletin*, Zürich, April 1997, p. 38

25 The line comes from the poem "The Conflagration of London, Poetically Lineated" (1667) by Simon Ford. In describing the Great Fire of London in 1666, Ford portrays the flames as God's punishment for a population renouncing the political power and religious faith of the king; see Margery Kingsley, "Interpreting Providence," Peter G. Platt (ed.), *Wonders, Marvels and Monsters in Early Modern Culture*, Cranbury, London, Mississauga, 1999, p. 259

26 I would like to thank Ron Meyers and Marita Loosen-Fox for drawing my attention to this point.

27 Personal email from Marita Loosen-Fox, May 16, 2015

28 "From Floor to Ceiling and Wall to Wall," Schmidt 2000, see note 6, p. 209

Phenomena

WILLOUGHBY SHARP

So the tapes [*Children's Tapes* (1974)] are demonstrations of phenomena?

WILLOUGHBY SHARP   Die Bänder [*Children's Tapes* (1974)] sind also Demonstrationen von Phänomenen?

Elements

TERRY FOX

Phenomena and their worlds. Like all the different shapes the candle can assume, all the kinds of things you can do to it, things that happen to it. Like with the flame, you can skin the flame, take away all its color and make it invisible with a fork. There were constant variations of those objects together – the fork and the candle, or the candle and the water, or the water and the bowl [...]

1974

TERRY FOX   Phänomenen und ihren Welten. Denken wir an eine Kerze, die all die verschiedenen Formen annehmen kann, an all die Sachen, die man mit ihr anstellen kann, die mit ihr passieren können. Oder die Flamme: Man kann sie formen, ihre Farbe wegnehmen, sie mit einer Gabel unsichtbar machen. Es gibt ständig Variationen in den Zusammenstellungen der Gegenstände – die Gabel und die Kerze, oder die Kerze und das Wasser, oder das Wasser und die Schale [...]

Material

Terry Fox, *Children's Tapes*, 1974, video still

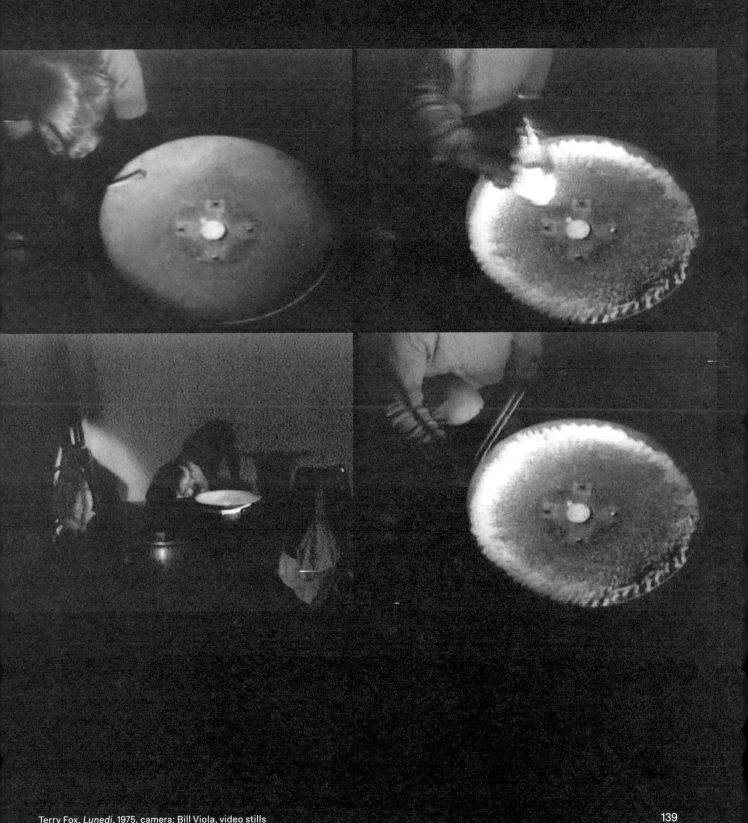

Terry Fox, *Lunedi*, 1975, camera: Bill Viola, video stills

Terry Fox, *Immersion*, 1973, photos: Thys Schouten

Terry Fox, *Yield*, 1973, photos: Larry Fox

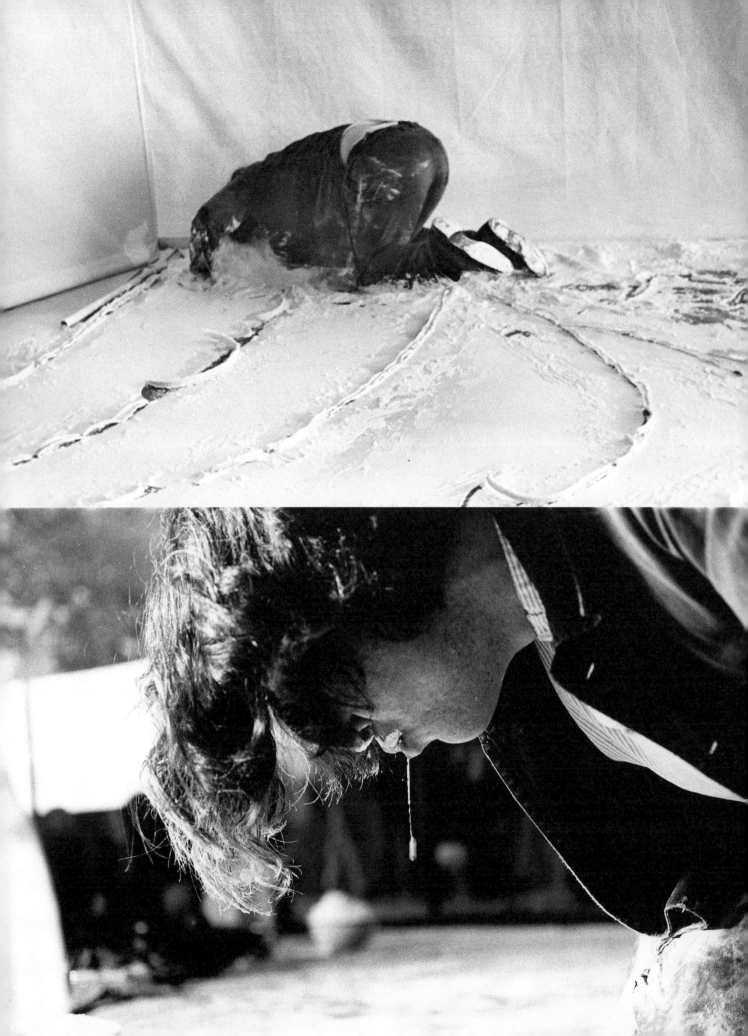

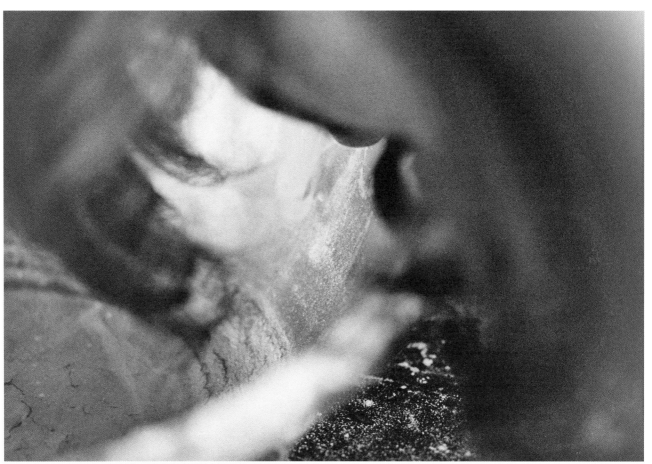

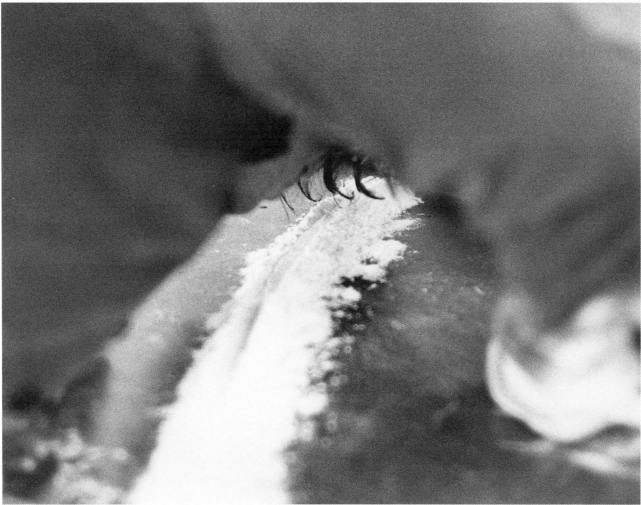

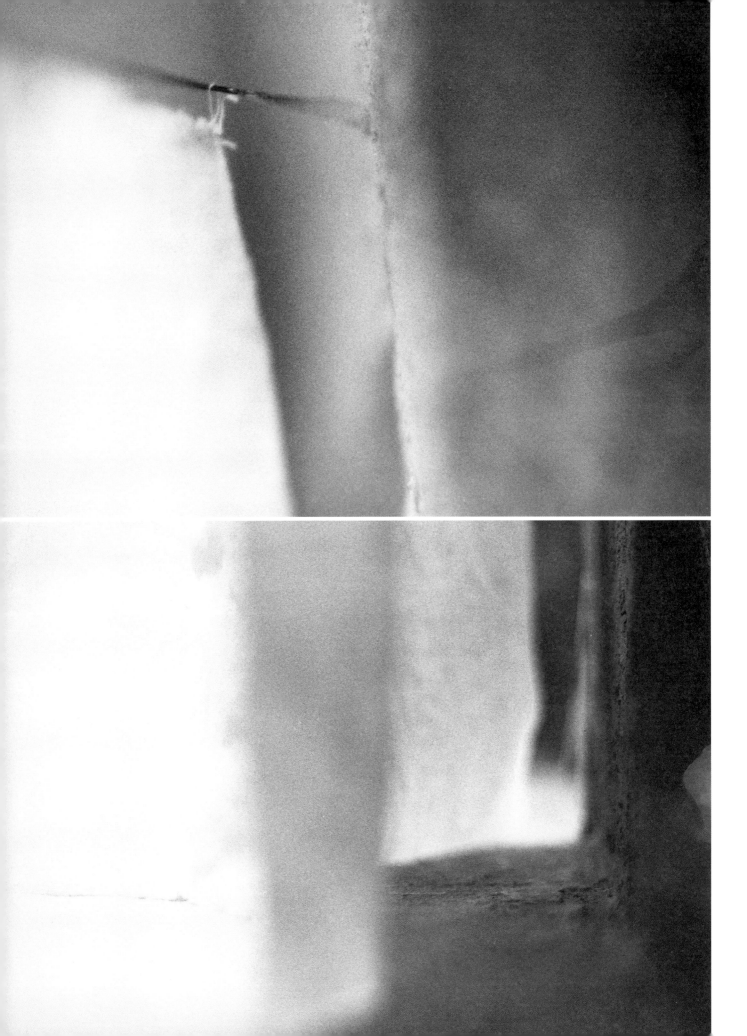

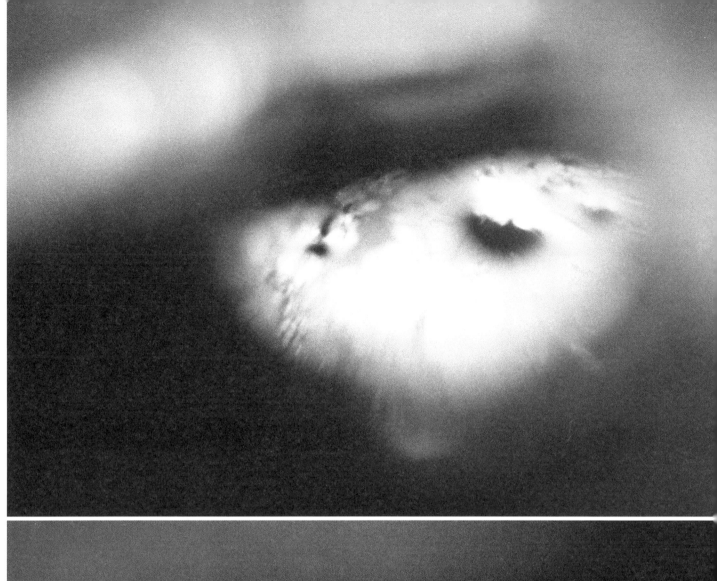

Terry Fox, *Instruments to be Played by the Movement of the Earth*, 1987, photos: Ben Blackwell

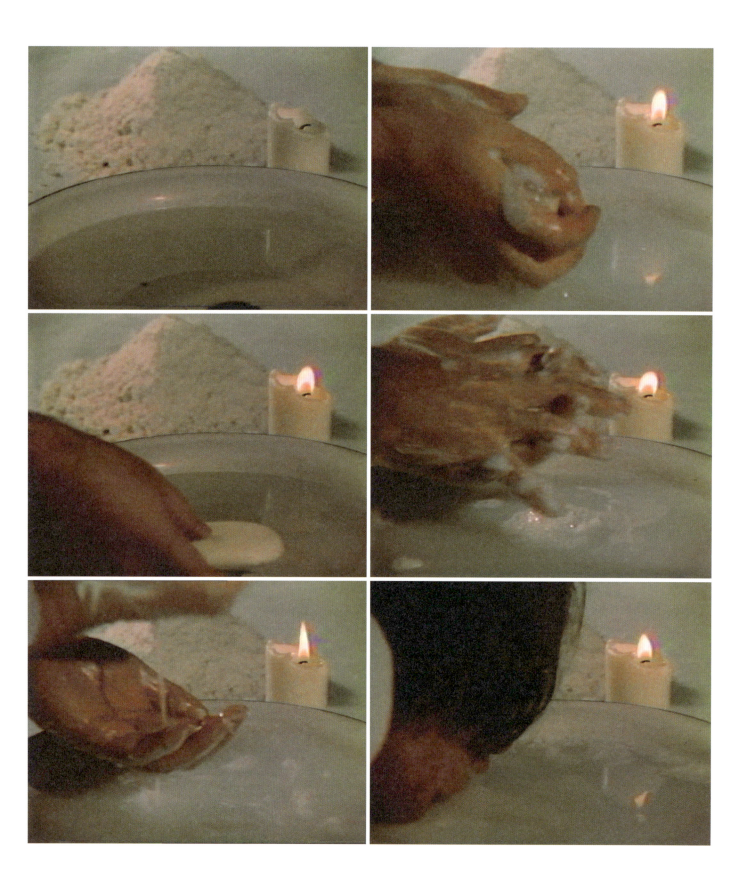

156   Terry Fox, *Wind, water, vuur, aarde*, 1972, video stills

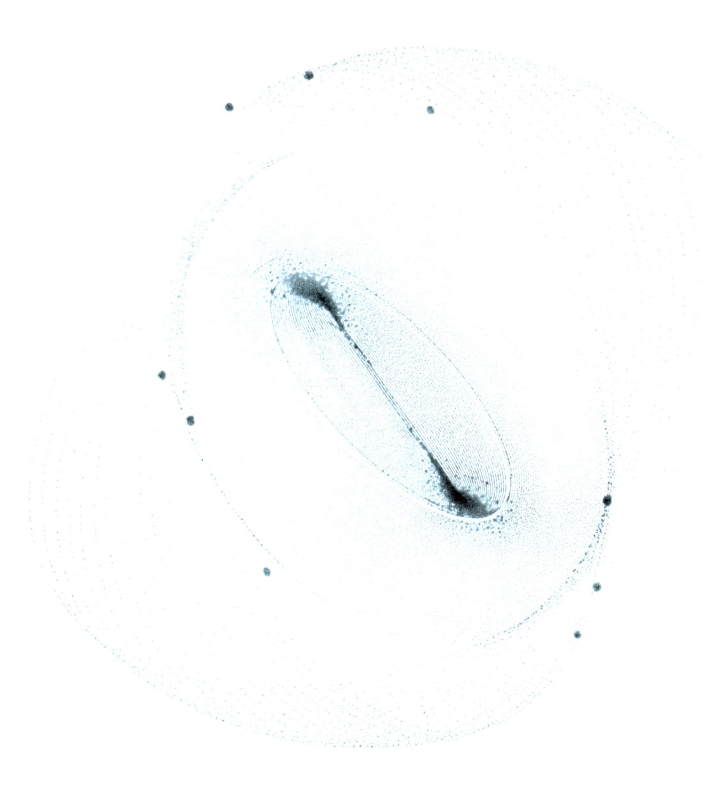

Terry Fox, *Pendulum Spit Bite*, 1977

Elements

Codes and Signs

Being forced to read it is a substitute for having the actual experience you are reading about. You get lost, you get confused, you get tired. You don't know what a certain word means. The way the letters are arranged from these signal cards is a kind of reproduction of the experience.

Zum Lesen gezwungen zu werden ist ein Ersatz für die tatsächliche Erfahrung, über die man liest. Man verliert sich, wird konfus, müde. Man weiß nicht, was ein bestimmtes Wort bedeutet. Die Art, wie die Buchstaben auf diesen Karten arrangiert sind, ist eine Art Reproduktion der Erfahrung.

Terry Fox, *1999*

Material   Chiffren und Zeichen

```
W E L L F I L L E D M A D E O F B O N E   E
S O P E N I N G D I S P L A C I N G G R   R
I N D I N G D O U B L E R O O F O F T H   H
E M O U T H R E C E I V E R D I S S O L   I
V I N G F O O D O R G A N W H I C H S E   E
P E R A T E S T H E Y E L L O W B I T T   T
E R L I Q U E D F R O M T H E B L O O D   D
F R A M E W O R K O F B O N E S T H E H   H
A N D C A L L E D F I S T W H E N I T I   I
S C L E N C H E D J O I N T O F H A N D   D
A N D A R M D O U B L E D U P S T I F E   E
E N I N G S P R E A D I N G T R A N S M   M
I T T E D B Y D I R E C T C O N T A C T   T
S P A S M O D I C E X P I R A T I O N S   S
```

TEXT ON PAPER GLUED TO WOOD
LEANING AGAINST A WALL — EACH STRIP SEPERATED BY
CA. 15 CM.

TEXT ON TAPE NAILED AT EACH END TO WOOD SLAT. 4 SLATS
BALANCED ON TOP OF 2 SEMICIRCLES OF WOOD
EVERYTHING HELD TOGETHER BY BALANCE

← 20 VERTICAL
PIECES EACH
160 × 2 × 2 cm

CYNOSURE

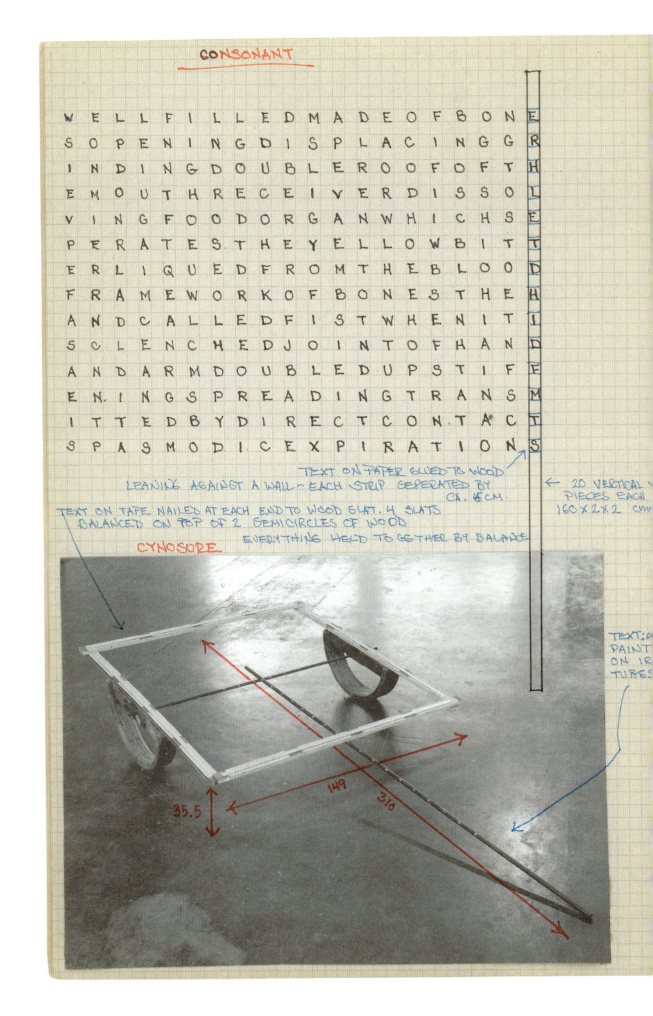

35.5

149

310

TEXT:
PAINT
ON IR
TUBES

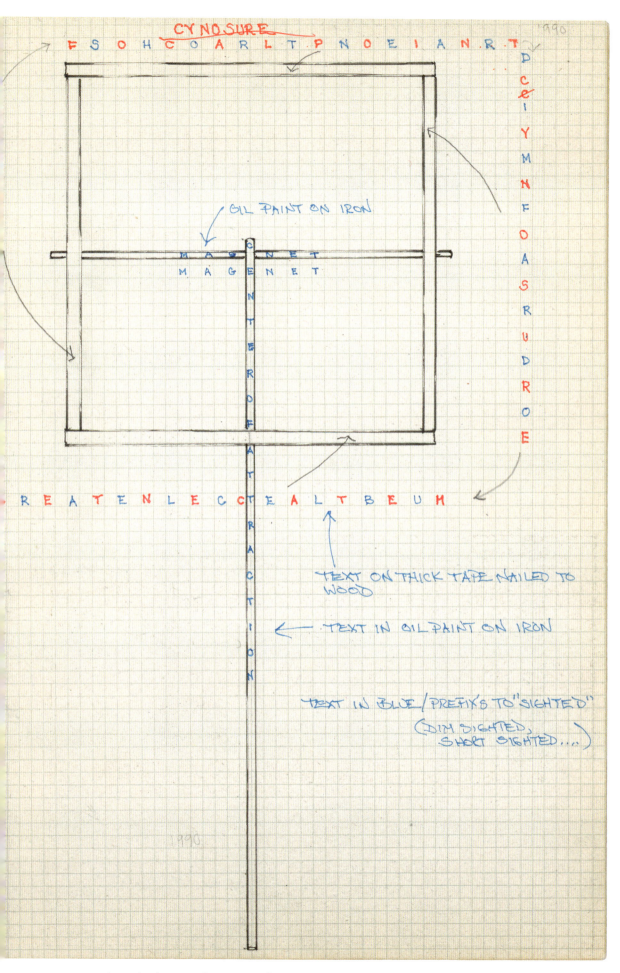

Terry Fox, From the notebook "Beuys Mirror, Bern," n.d.

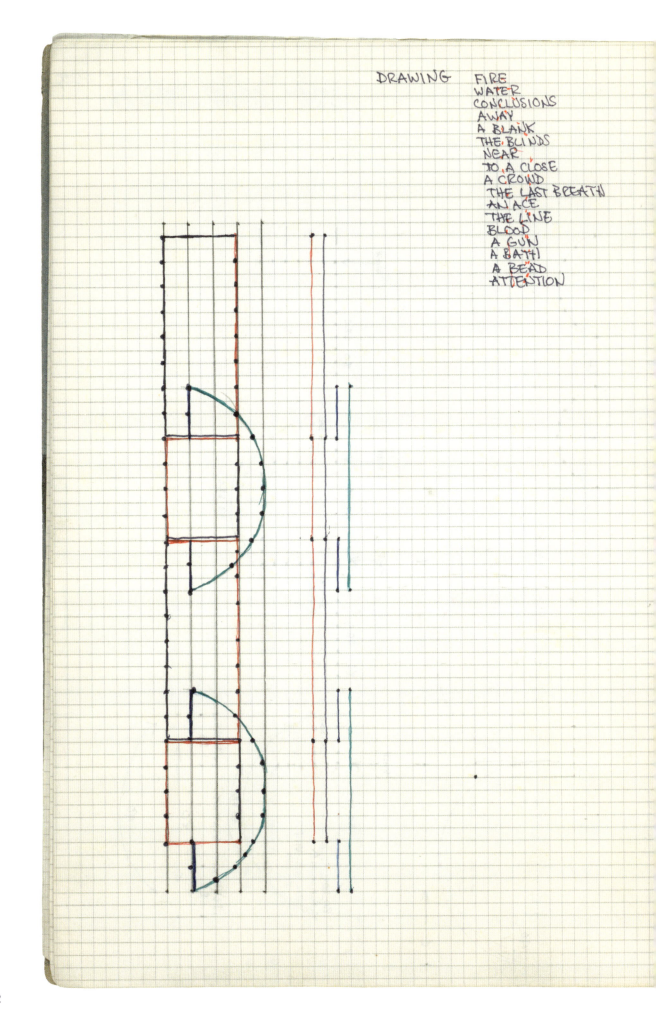

DRAWING   FIRE
WATER
CONCLUSIONS
AWAY
A BLANK
THE BLINDS
NEAR
TO A CLOSE
A CROWD
THE LAST BREATH
AN ACE
THE LINE
BLOOD
A GUN
A BATH
A BEAD
ATTENTION

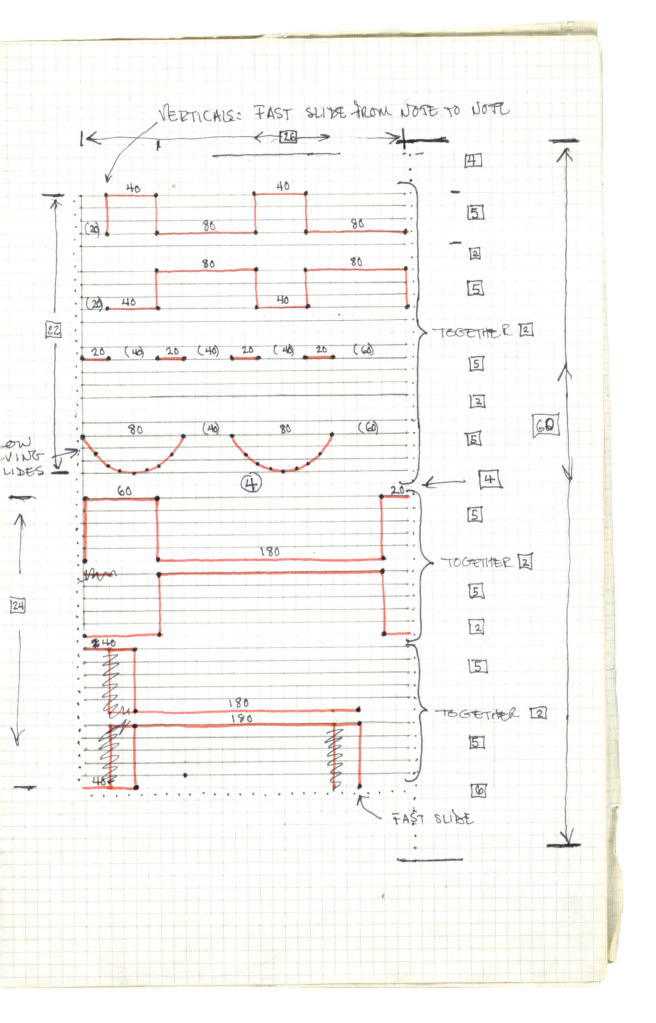

VERTICALS: FAST SLIDE FROM NOTE TO NOTE

FAST SLIDE

163

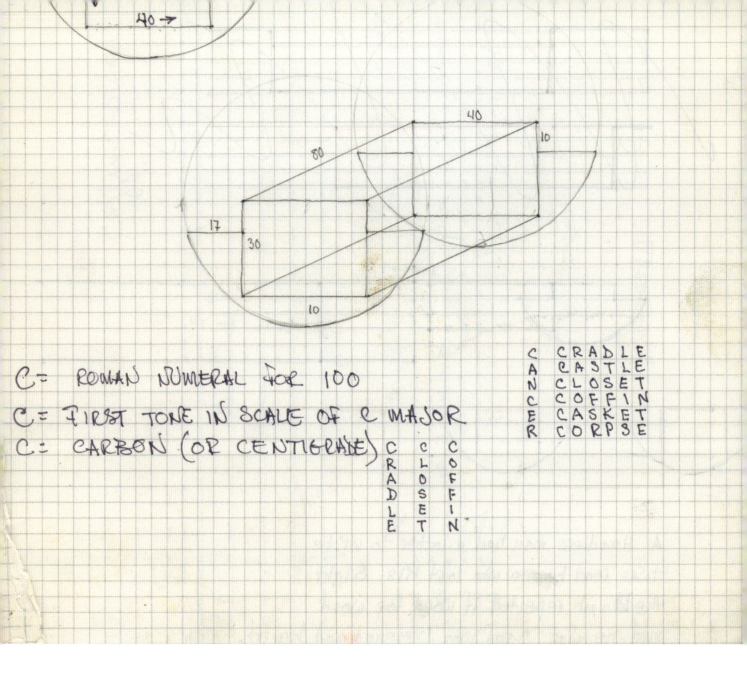

40 →

80

40

10

17

30

10

C = ROMAN NUMERAL FOR 100

C = FIRST TONE IN SCALE OF C MAJOR

C = CARBON (OR CENTIGRADE)

C R A D L E
L O S E T
O F F I N

C A N C E R

C R A D L E
C A S T L E
C L O S E T
C O F F I N
C A S K E T
C O R P S E

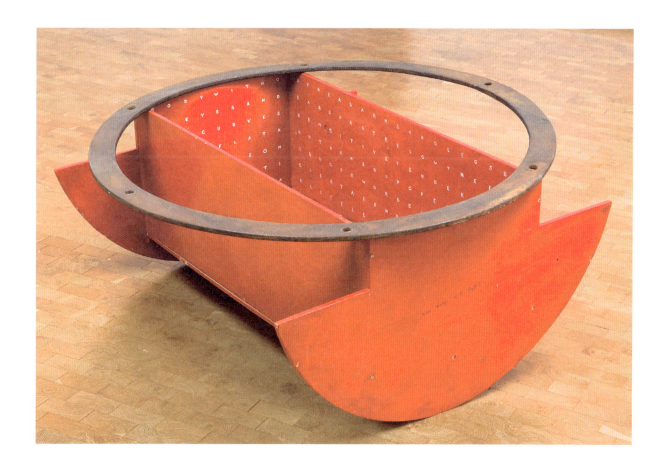

Terry Fox, *Envelope*, 1991

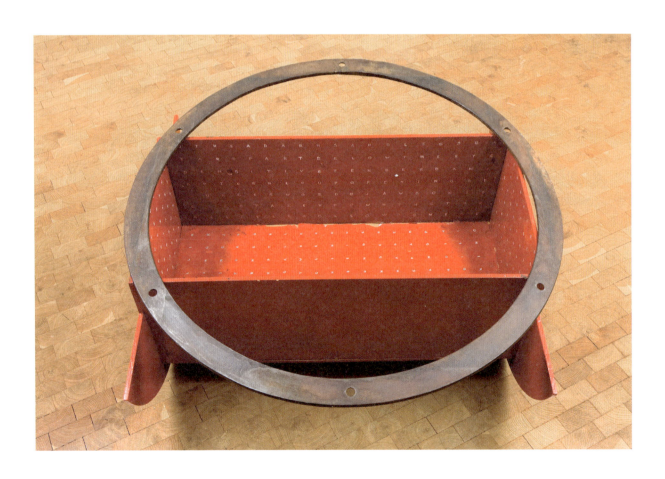

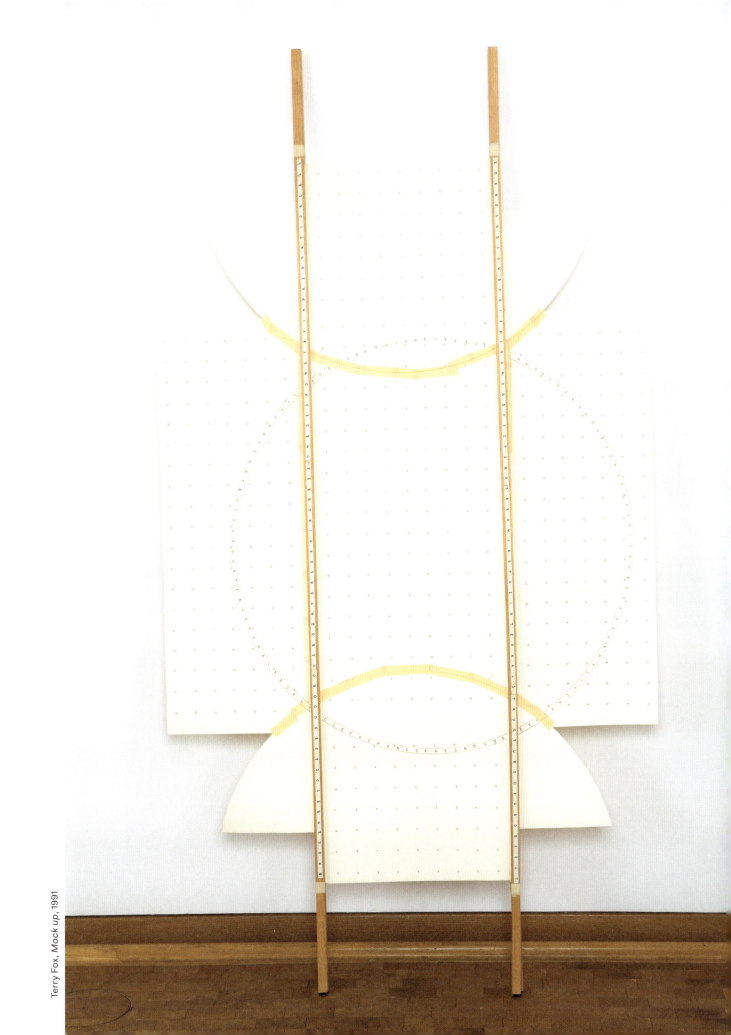

Terry Fox, *Mock up*, 1991

Terry Fox, *Ovum Anguinum*, 1990

Terry Fox, *Le décapité parlant*, 1993

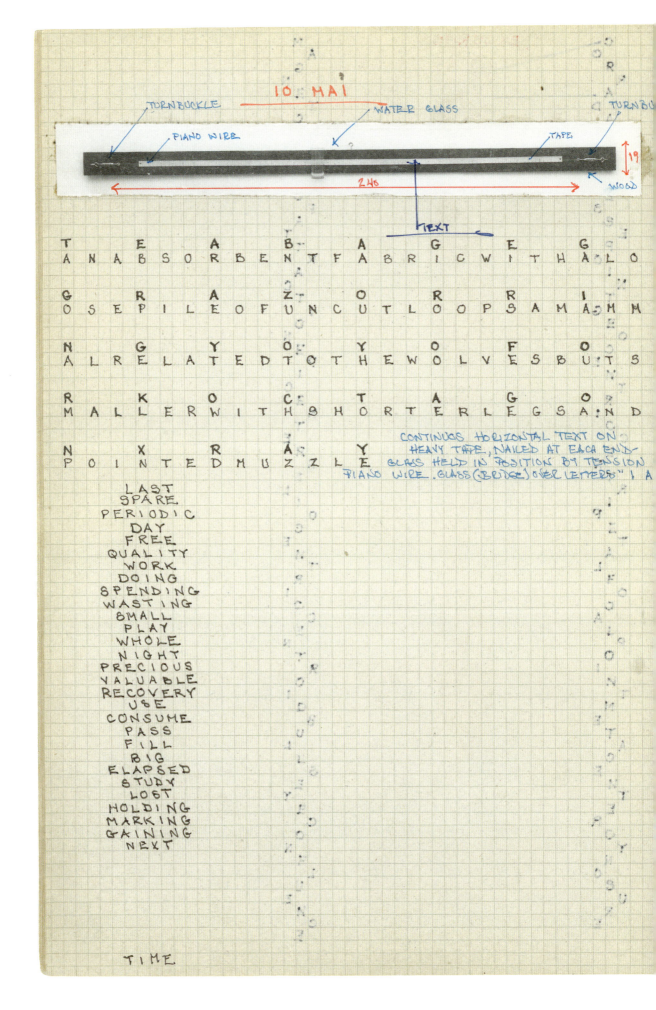

10 MAI

TURNBUCKLE   PIANO WIRE   WATER GLASS   TAPE   TURNBU...   WOOD   19   240   TEXT

T E A B A G E G
A N A B S O R B E N T F A B R I C W I T H A L O

G R A Z O R R I
O S E P I L E O F U N C U T L O O P S A M A S M M

N G Y O Y O F O
A L R E L A T E D T O T H E W O L V E S B U T S

R K O C T A G O
M A L L E R W I T H S H O R T E R L E G S A N D

N X R A Y
P O I N T E D M U Z Z L E

CONTINUOS HORIZONTAL TEXT ON
HEAVY TAPE, NAILED AT EACH END
GLASS HELD IN POSITION BY TENSION
PIANO WIRE. GLASS (BRIDGE) OVER LETTERS" I A

LAST
SPARE
PERIODIC
DAY
FREE
QUALITY
WORK
DOING
SPENDING
WASTING
SMALL
PLAY
WHOLE
NIGHT
PRECIOUS
VALUABLE
RECOVERY
USE
CONSUME
PASS
FILL
BIG
ELAPSED
STUDY
LOST
HOLDING
MARKING
GAINING
NEXT

TIME

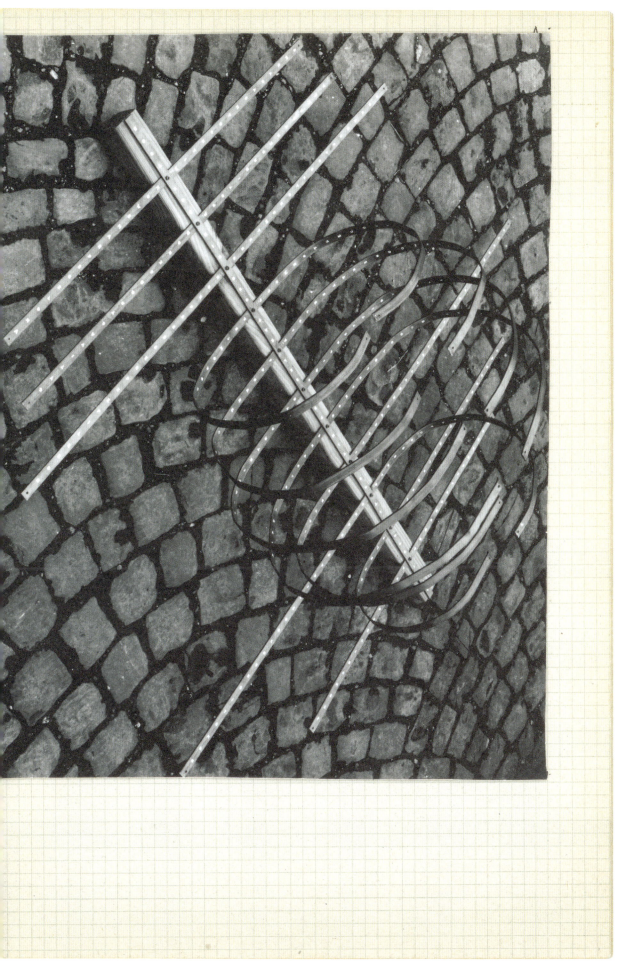

Terry Fox, From the notebook "Beuys Mirror, Bern," n.d.

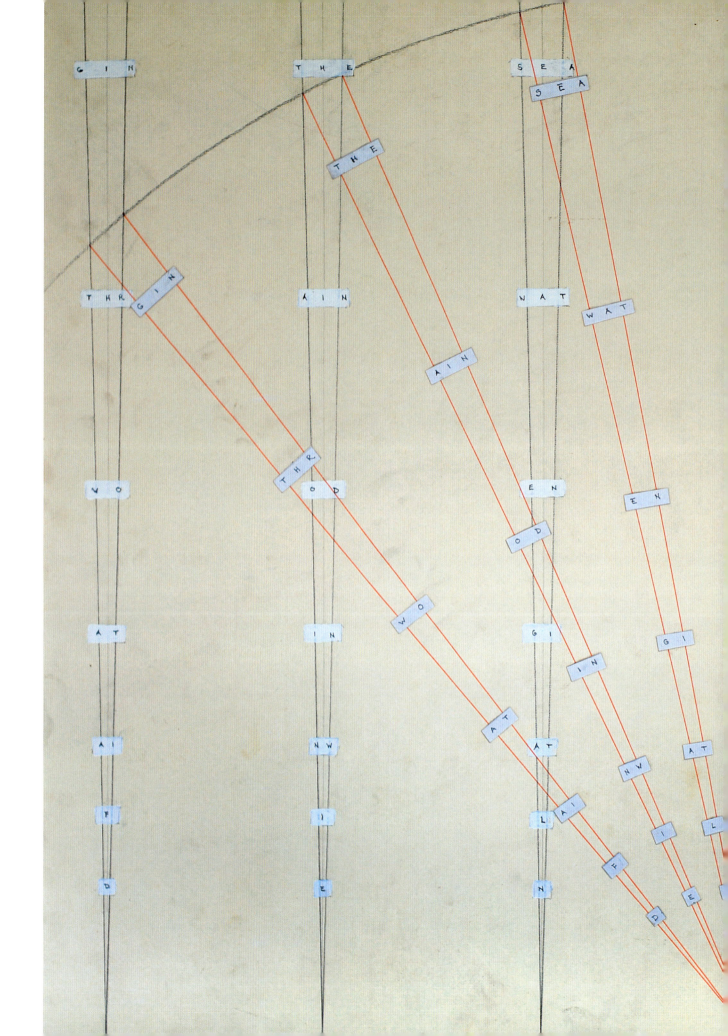

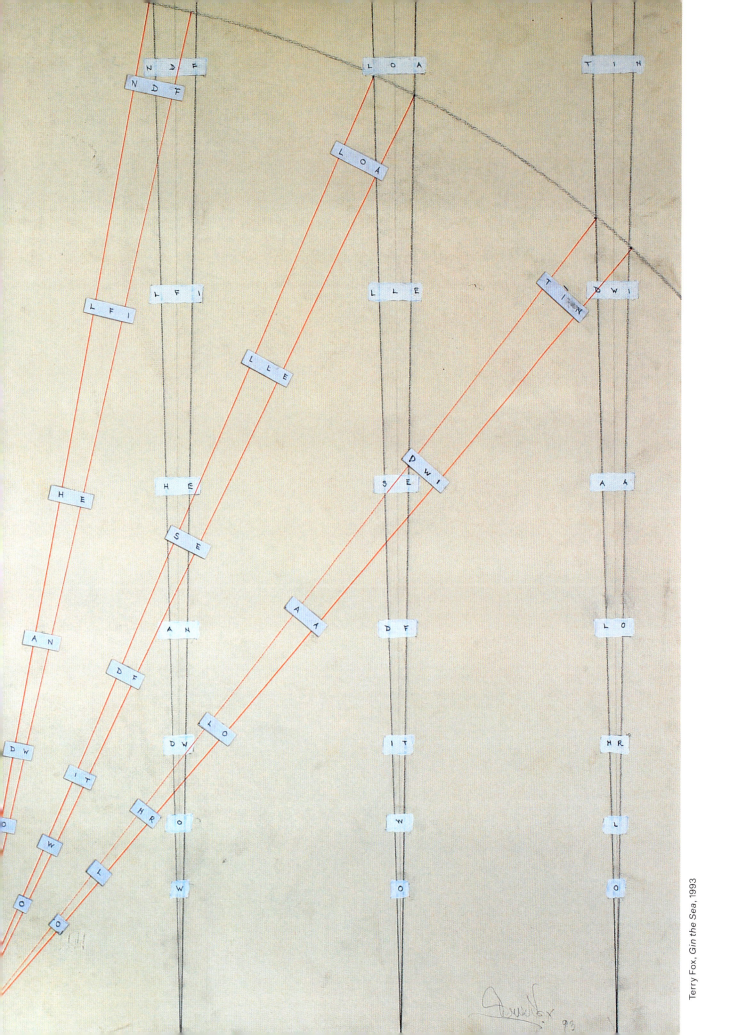

Terry Fox, *Gin the Sea*, 1993

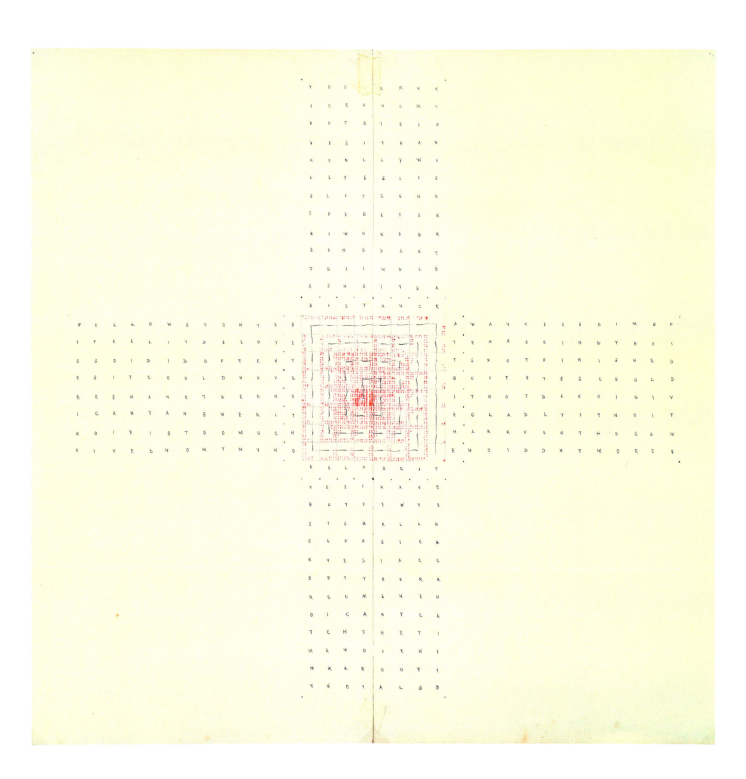

174   Terry Fox, Sketch for *Dal cielo del fuoco (for Joseph Beuys)*, n.d.

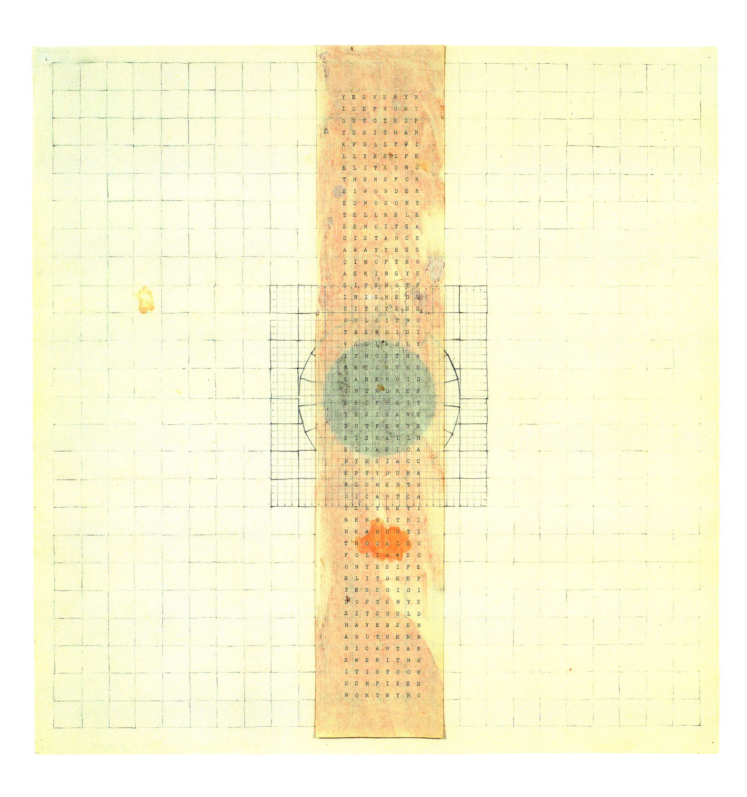

Terry Fox, *The Eye is Not the Only Glass that Burns the Mind*, 1989

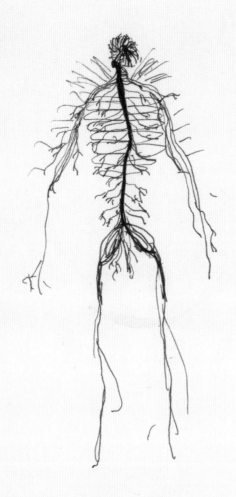

Terry Fox, *Human figure*, n.d.

Terry Fox, *Alphabet-Signet*, n.d.

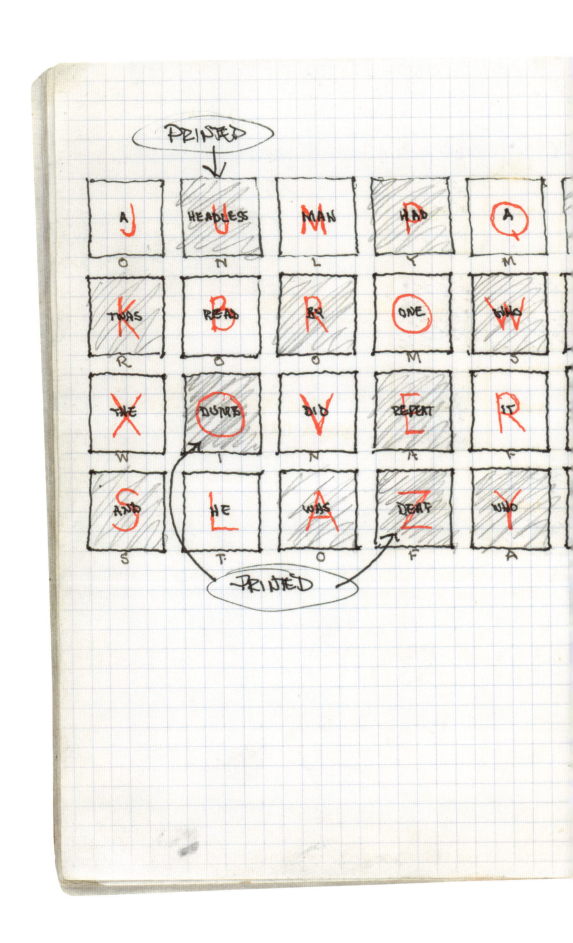

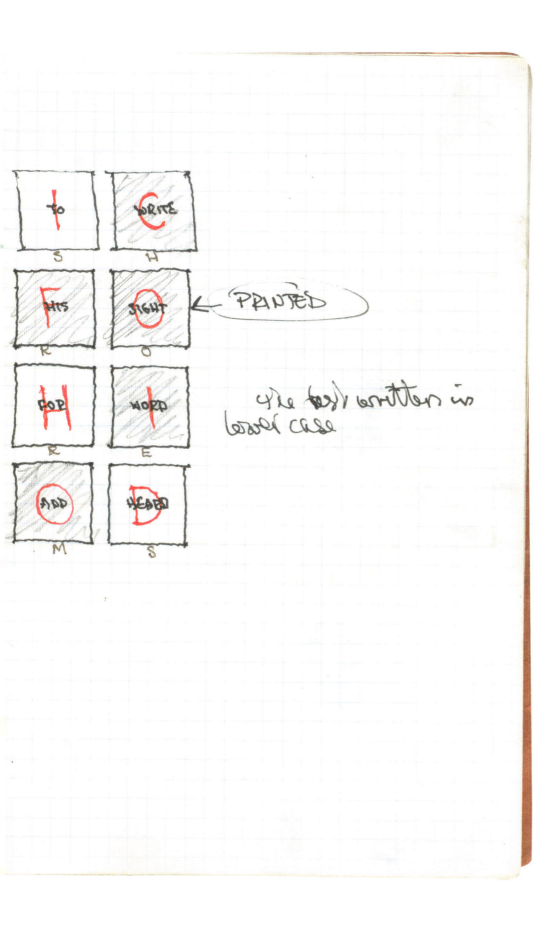

PRINTED

the text written is lower case

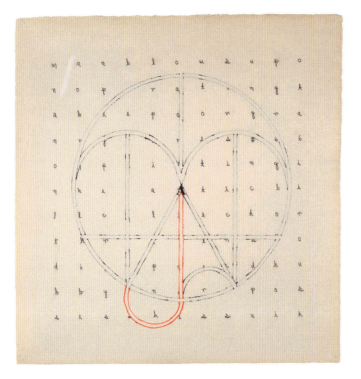
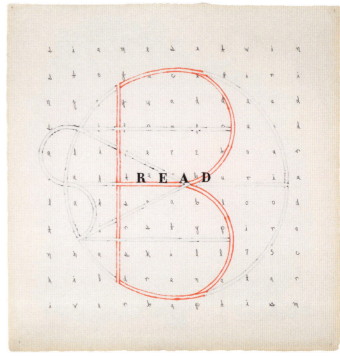
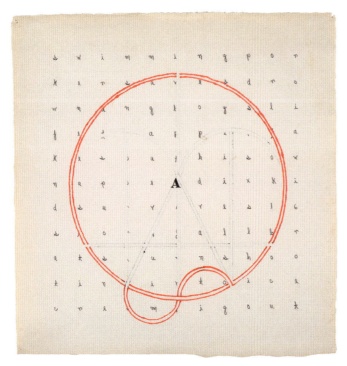
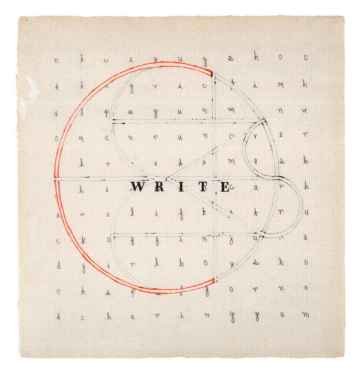

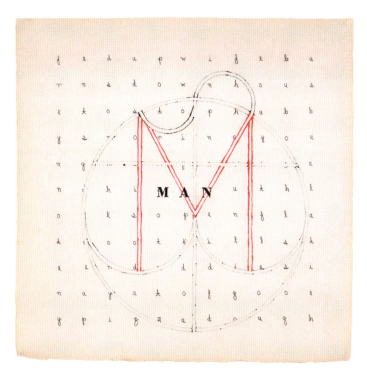

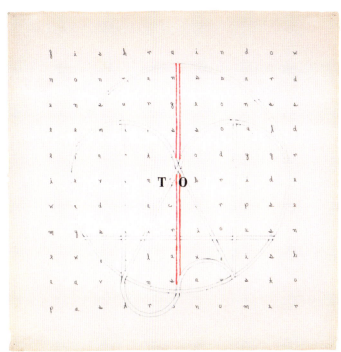

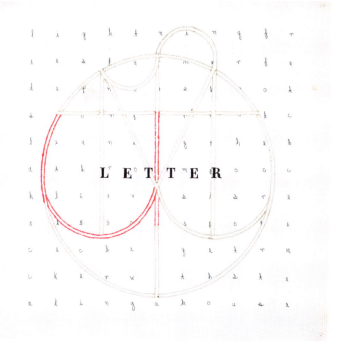

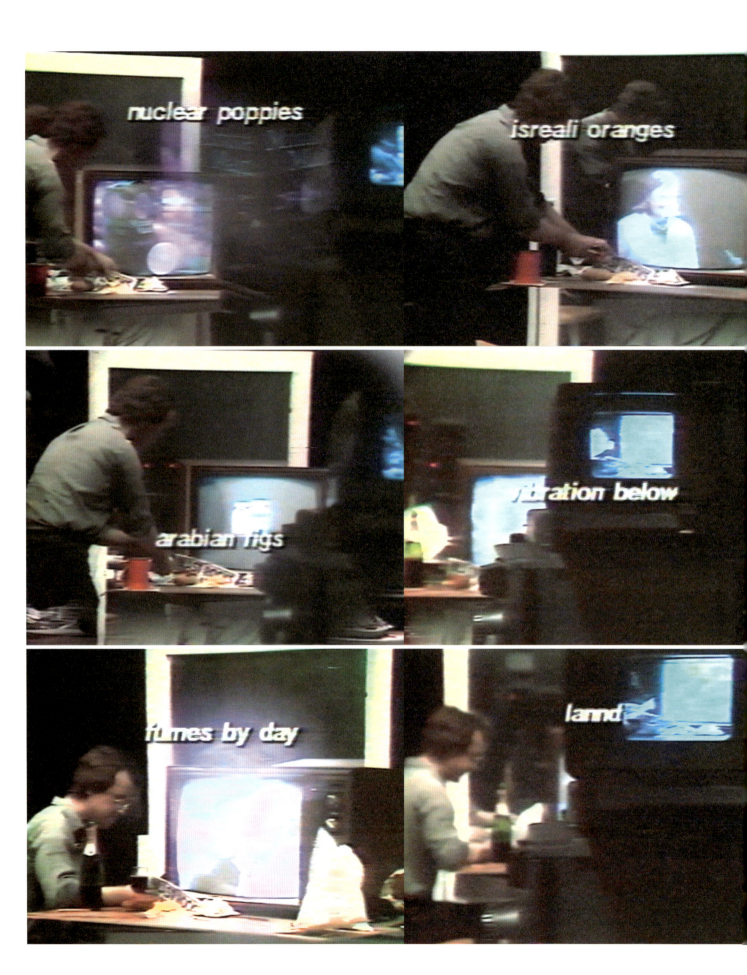

Terry Fox, *Flour Dumpling*, 1980, video stills

Terry Fox – Arbeiten mit
Schrift und Sprache

Beate Eickhoff

Terry Fox – Text and Language Works

In seinen Performances hat Terry Fox zumeist die Sprache vermieden, denn sie sollten rund um die Erde verständlich sein, ob „in New York, in Kenia oder in der Türkei"[1]. Zwar haben längere Texte in seinem Werk von Anfang an durchaus eine Rolle gespielt, insofern als er seine wortlosen Performances sehr sachlich und genau beschrieben hat, – was letztendlich eine Vergegenwärtigung heute überhaupt erst ermöglicht. Ein weiteres Beispiel für den Einsatz von Sprache ist die schriftliche Anleitung zur Visualisierung, die das Hockerobjekt *A Metaphor* (1976) [↗**213**] begleitete und in der er beschrieb, wie man sich die Lage des Mosaiklabyrinths von Chartres mittig zwischen der Kuppel der Kathedrale und einem unterirdischen Fluss vorstellen sollte. Doch erst in seinen Zeichnungen und Objekten, die seit den 1980er Jahren entstanden, wurde die Sprache zum zentralen Anliegen der künstlerischen Arbeit.

Einzelne Worte tauchen bereits einmal in seinen ganz frühen Bildwerken von 1966 auf, die allerdings nie ausgestellt wurden. Es handelte sich, laut der Beschreibung des Künstlers, um 1×1 Meter große Glasscheiben, die er einseitig mit einer dicken Schicht schwarzer Farbe besprüht hatte und in diese anschließend Linien und auch Worte einkratzte. Aufmerken lässt, wie Terry Fox sich hier die Kommunikation mit dem Betrachter vorstellte: Die Glasscheiben sollten gegen die Wand gelehnt werden, so dass jener sie kniend studieren musste. Und da Worte das sind, was jeder kennt, vermutete Fox, der Betrachter würde neugierig werden und sich dementsprechend anstrengen, die Buchstaben zwischen den eingeritzten Zeichnungen auch zu entziffern: „Ich versuchte, den Betrachter in das Werk hineinzuziehen. Eine Art, das zu tun, war, ihm seine eigene Reflexion zu geben, die ihn automatisch interessieren musste, sodass er aufmerksamer war als gewöhnlich."[2] Nicht irgendeine Wortbedeutung ist hier also das Wesentliche, sondern die Aktion des Entzifferns. Man meint, etwas entdecken zu können, so beschreibt Terry Fox weiter, aber sobald der Fokus sich verändert, verschwindet das, was man entdeckt hatte. Was von einer solchen Leseaktion bleibt, ist die Erinnerung an die Situation der Neugier und die Mühsal des Entzifferns. Um ein eindeutiges Verständnis ging es Fox – ähnlich wie bei seinen Performances – nicht.[3]

In his performances, Terry Fox usually avoided using spoken language as he wanted them to be comprehensible anywhere in the world, whether "in New York or Kenya or Turkey."[1] From his earliest works, longer texts have certainly played a part in his oeuvre with matter-of-fact, but precise descriptions of his wordless performances – and ultimately thanks to these descriptions they can be visualized today. Yet he also employed language more directly within his works as, for example, in *A Metaphor* (1976) [↗**213**], a sculpture of wood stools. Here, as a guide to viewing the work, Terry Fox included a written text suggesting how the viewer should imagine the position of the mosaic labyrinth in the center of Chartres Cathedral set between the cathedral's dome and the underground river below. Despite these examples, though, language only first became a central focus of his artistic work in his drawings and objects beginning in the 1980s.

Individual words can already be found as an element in Terry Fox's early paintings from 1966, although these works were never exhibited. As he described these paintings, he sprayed a thick layer of black color on one side of large sheets of glass measuring 1×1 meter to create a mirror effect, and then etched lines and words into the color. Here, it is striking how Terry Fox envisaged the communication with the viewer. The sheets of glass were supposed to be propped against a wall, forcing viewers to kneel down to look at them in more detail. Since some of these scratched words would be familiar to everyone, Fox assumed viewers would become curious and want to decipher the letters between the scratched patterns of lines. As he later remarked, "I was trying to get the spectator involved in the work. One way of doing this was by giving him his reflection, which would automatically interest him, enough so that he would give it a little more attention than usual."[2] In these paintings, then, it is not the meaning of a particular word which is crucial, but the act of deciphering itself. You have the feeling that something can be discovered, Terry Fox continued, but as soon as the focus shifts, whatever you discovered disappears. What remains from such an attempt to read lines and words is the memory of the curiosity and the effort involved in deciphering. Much like his performances, Terry Fox was not seeking to convey some unequivocal insight.[3]

Tatsächlich hat Terry Fox auch einmal in einer Performance, nämlich in *Left Sided Sleeper's Dream* (1981), im Grazer Opernhaus aufgeführt, mit der Sprache gearbeitet: Die Fragen „Who shall harm me?", „The missile that's shot?", „And after its crash?", „How many will fall?" wurden, begleitet von einem Paukenschlag, in ein Mikrofon gerufen, während aus einem zweiten Mikrofon das Echo schallte: „army!", „hot!", „ash!", „all!". Es sind Sätze von schockierender Prägnanz, die in der Zeit globaler Aufrüstung auf der ganzen Welt verstanden wurden. Und sie standen am Beginn einer Folge von Werken, die sich mit der politischen Brisanz von Sprache beschäftigten. In schwarzer Schreibschrift finden sich diese Fragen beispielsweise – kaum sichtbar – unter den weißen Lettern wieder, mit denen die zehn Jahre später datierte und weiter unten in diesem Text näher erläuterte Skulptur *Envelope* (1991)[4] [↗162–166] beschrieben ist.

Die Schriftarbeiten von Terry Fox, sein Spiel mit Buchstaben und Texten, in einer annähernd chronologischen Reihenfolge zu betrachten, ist insofern sinnvoll, als dieselben Sprüche, Rätselreime und Wortzusammenhänge in Zeichnungen und Objekten mehrfach wiederkehren, was wie eine sich entwickelnde Folge verstanden werden kann. So trifft man immer wieder auf das bekannte Rätsel: „A Headless man had a letter to write / 'twas read by one who lost his Sight / the Dumb repeated it word for word / and he was Deaf who listened and heard". (Ein kopfloser Mann musste einen Brief schreiben / er wurde gelesen von einem, der sein Augenlicht verloren hatte / der Stumme wiederholte ihn Wort für Wort / und der, welcher lauschte und hörte, war taub.) Die Lösung des Rätsels ist 0 oder *nothing*. 1982 schrieb Terry Fox den Satz auf die Unterseite eines Stuhles (*3 Scimmie*, Installation, Galleria Pellegrino, Bologna, 1982)[5]; er tauchte erneut beispielsweise in der Performance auf der documenta 8, 1987, auf. Während Fox damals auf Klaviersaiten spielte, die zwischen zwei Autos gespannt waren, ertönte der Spruch, als Konzert von vier Autohupen gespielt im Morsealphabet in vier verschiedenen Sprachen.[6] In der Werkfolge von Zeichnungen *Children's Drawings* (1985) [↗180–183] ist es die Wortfolge dieses Rätselreims, die die Sortierung der einzelnen Blätter bestimmt.

Die erste Reihe von auf Schrift basierenden Zeichnungen aber ist – um den chronologischen Blick beizubehalten – die Serie *Catch Phrases* [↗188, 189], entstanden 1981–1984 und untertitelt „Berlin–Neapel–Minneapolis", die verschiedenen Aufenthaltsorte seines Wanderlebens. Jede einzelne Arbeit, oder *unit*, ist mehrschichtig aufgebaut. Zunächst sind die 2 × 1 Meter messenden und damit mehr als lebensgroßen Papierstücke mit einer quadratischen Rasterung versehen. In jedes Quadrat hat Terry Fox mit Bleistift von Hand einzelne Buchstaben geschrieben, die durch die strenge Einhaltung

Terry Fox, *3 Scimmie*, Galleria Pellegrino, Bologna, 1982

Just once, in his performance *Left Sided Sleeper's Dream* (1981), presented in the Opera House in Graz, did Terry Fox explicitly work with language. Accompanied by the beating of a kettle drum, the questions "Who shall harm me?"; "The missile that's shot?"; "And after its crash?"; "How many will fall?" were shouted into one microphone with echo-like responses shouted into a second microphone: "army!"; "hot!"; "ash!"; "all!" The questions and answers are harrowingly incisive and, at a time of a global arms build up, were understood all over the world. They also mark the beginning of a series of works that address and explore the highly-charged political nature of language. These questions, for example, reappear in black cursive script – hardly visible – submerged in the white letters on Fox's sculpture *Envelope* (1991) [↗162–166].[4] This work, dated ten years later, is described in more detail below.

Setting Terry Fox's works with written language and games with letters and texts in an approximate chronological order is a valuable exercise since his drawings and objects often integrate the same phrases, riddles and combinations of words. In this way, they can be read as a developing sequence. For example, a number of works include the well-known riddle:

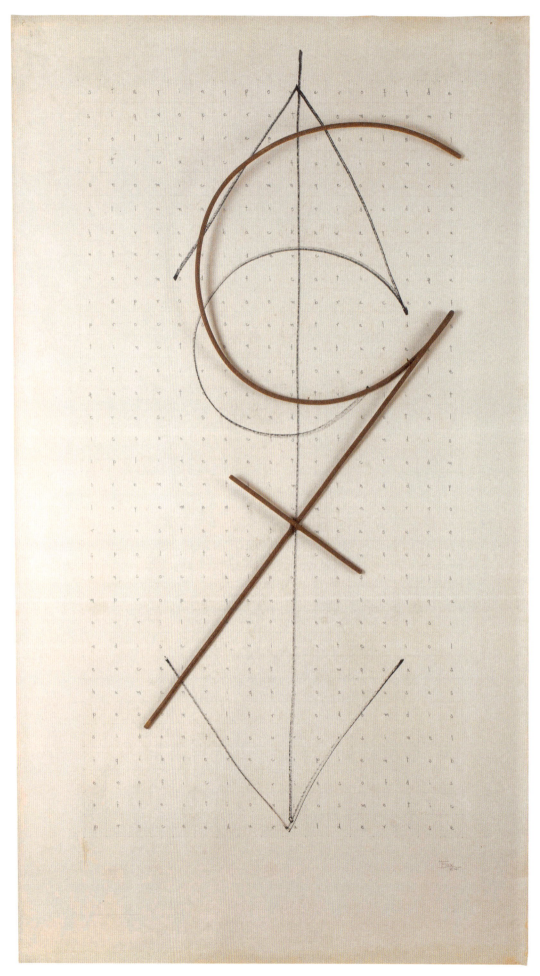

188   Terry Fox, *Catch Phrases*, 1981–84

der Felder und die großen, gleichmäßigen Abstände isoliert und vereinzelt wirken. Das Entziffern wird so erschwert, doch kann man, der normalen Leserichtung folgend und mit einiger Mühe, doch Worte ausmachen, die sich wiederum in Paare gruppieren. Diese Zwei-Wort-Ausdrücke, die *catch phrases* (Schlagworte), sind Zeitungen, zumeist aber den Radiosendungen von American Forces Network (AFN) Europe entnommen, die Fox während seiner Westberliner Zeit hörte. Es sind Wortwendungen, die besonders entsetzlich sind, weil sie – so lapidar wiederholt, wie Fox sie in undramatisch gleichmäßiger Reihung niederschrieb, – das, was sie bezeichnen, verharmlosen und beschönigen: „armed struggle, relaxation of tensions, military presence, confrontational politics, balance of terror, public disillusion, flexible response, political pressure, black program", steht dort.[7] Alles dreht sich um Krieg und gewaltsame Auseinandersetzungen, deshalb finden sich auf der Titelzeichnung auch Wortpaare, die jeweils mit „war" gebildet werden, wie etwa: „spasm war, cold war, punitive war". Man hat die Ausdrücke, die in den Medien inflationär eingesetzt werden und zu Floskeln verkommen sind, so oft gehört oder gelesen, dass sie, unhinterfragt und alltäglich geworden, ihre Brisanz längst verloren haben.

Doch Fox hat über das Buchstabennetz als zweite Schicht oder Ebene mit schwarzem Filzstift jeweils eines der Graffiti gezeichnet, die er an Hauswänden in Italien entdeckt und gesammelt hat und die eigentlich nur Eingeweihten verständlich sind. Ihren politischen Inhalt hat er sehr einleuchtend erläutert: „Einige sind Variationen des Hammer- und Sichelmotivs, der Umwandlung des Kreuzes in ein Hakenkreuz, der Zielscheibe in eine Sichel, der Sichel in eine Dollarnote."[8] Die Aggressivität dieser schnell gezeichneten Formen überträgt sich auf die Bedeutung der Wortpaare. Die gezeichneten Graffiti überdeckte er dann aber jeweils mit einem weiteren Graffito, das er aus einem Stahlstab formte. Damit ist das politische Zeichen, in dieser vordersten Ebene zum metallenen Kunstobjekt erstarrt, seiner Mitteilungsfunktion beraubt. „Dieser Raub stellt die Ausbeutung der einen Kultur durch eine begünstigtere dar"[9], schreibt er in der Publikation des Kunstraums München 1985. Schließlich verstellt das ästhetisch schöne Objekt auch den Blick auf die darunterliegenden Worte.

Wie das Alphabet 26 Buchstaben hat, so wird diese Serie aus 26 Zeichnungen (+1 Titelzeichnung) gebildet, die insofern wie ein fortlaufendes Band zu verstehen sind, als sich von einem „Blatt" zum anderen die Zeichen in Verwandlung wiederholen. Das heißt, die Filzstiftzeichnung wird im jeweils darauffolgenden Blatt von dem in Stahl geformten Graffito aufgenommen, so dass der Leser/Betrachter vom Anfang bis zum Ende geführt wird. Dennoch soll jede Zeichnung auch

Terry Fox in front of *Catch Phrases*, 1983

"A Headless man had a letter to write / 'twas read by one who lost his Sight / the Dumb repeated it word for word / and he was Deaf who listened and heard." The solution is 0 or "nothing." In 1982, Terry Fox wrote this riddle underneath an upturned wooden chair (*3 Scimmie*, installation, Galleria Pellegrino, Bologna, 1982 [↗**187**]).[5] In 1987, the same riddle also reappeared, for instance, in his performance at *documenta 8*; while Fox sounded piano wires stretched between two cars, the riddle was played in Morse code in four different languages on four battery-powered car horns.[6] In his *Children's Drawings* (1985) [↗**180–183**] series of drawings, the sequence of words in this riddle determine the sequence of the individual sheets of paper.

To return to the chronology of Terry Fox's works with language, the *Catch Phrases* [↗**188–189**] are the first set of drawings based on letters and words. The series dates from 1981–84 and is subtitled "Berlin–Naples–Minneapolis," a reference to the places where Terry Fox lived during this itinerant period of his life. Each individual drawing – or unit – is comprised of several layers. Measuring 2×1 meters, the sheets of paper, which are far larger than life-size, are covered by a

einzeln gelesen werden, und ist auch lesbar, ebenfalls von Anfang bis Ende. Der Blick wandert zwischen den entzifferten Wortpaaren zum Graffito und wieder zurück. Durch die unübliche Schreibweise ohne Wortzusammenhänge oder -abstände ist die „Leseperformance" ein langwieriger Prozess, und nur durch individuelle, sehr zeitaufwendige Anstrengung kann der Inhalt verstanden werden.

Der Klang wie auch die Performance waren für Terry Fox jeweils Mittel der Kommunikation ohne Barrieren, die sich jenseits von Vorwissen und Intellektualisierung nicht vermitteln, sondern ganz direkt – „wie Essen" – vor dem Empfänger vollziehen: „Die Aktion ist verwandeltes Leben und geschieht vor dem Empfänger."[10] Dass die Wortsprache zwar nicht allen verständlich, aber doch ein Mittel der Kommunikation ist – vor allem ein mehrdeutiges und zuweilen auch gefährliches –, welches für den Einzelnen wie für das Zusammenleben essentiell ist, erkannte er spätestens im Zusammenhang mit diesen *Catch Phrases* an: „Die Sprache zu verändern ist gefährlicher als Bomben zu legen, weil sie auch das Denken verändert", sagte Terry Fox rückblickend 1993, und: „Ich bin jetzt weg davon, ich habe es gewissermaßen aus meinem System rausbekommen, aber ich musste diese Dinge einfach zeigen."[11]

Die gefährlichen *catch phrases* findet der geduldige Leser auch in *Children's Drawings* (1985). Vom Format her gemäßigt, als eine zusammengehörige Abfolge aber ebenfalls monumental in der Erscheinung, sind die 32 quadratischen Blätter ästhetisch abermals sehr attraktiv. Wieder sind die Buchstaben über die Quadrate gleichmäßig verteilt. Neben den *catch phrases* wie „abnormal evolution", „elimination of unreliable elements", die Fox in großen Druckbuchstaben schreibt, sind in den langen, in Schreibschrift verfassten Buchstabenreihen anderer Blätter nun auch Wortfolgen auszumachen, die reißerische Schlagzeilen aus der amerikanischen Boulevardpresse aufnehmen: „man cuts his head with a chainsaw and lives" ist da zu entziffern, oder „man blown up on operating table", „fed up wife burns down house to stop hubby snoring". Darunter wird als kräftiger, die Lesbarkeit störender Durchschlag ein in seiner Komplexität erstaunlich harmonisch wirkendes Monogramm sichtbar, das Terry Fox jeweils auf die Rückseite der Blätter gezeichnet hat: Die übergeordnete Form ist der Kreis, als mittelalterlich magisches Zeichen war er schon in der Performance *Levitation* (1970) zentral; Fox hat ihn dort mit seinem Blut gezogen, im Durchmesser seiner Körperlänge. In einem der Notizbücher im Nachlass von Terry Fox ist dasselbe Monogramm zu entdecken. Es steht dort auf der einen Seite gegenüber einer wissenschaftlichen Zeichnung des menschlichen Körpers, so dass das Zeichen durchaus in Parallele zum menschlichen Körper gesehen werden

grid of small squares. Each square contains a single handwritten letter in pencil. Since the squares are set at large, even distances and Fox strictly adheres to the pattern of spaces they create, the letters seem detached and isolated, making it more difficult to read them. The letters follow a customary right-to-left direction and, with some effort, words can be deciphered. These words, all grouped in pairs, are the catch phrases of the title. Some are taken from newspapers, but they are mainly culled from radio programs on American Forces Network (AFN) Europe, which Fox listened to while he was living in West Berlin. The repetition of the phrases in the evenly spaced squares, so emotionless and plain, seems to underscore the shocking content of the things they describe, which is glossed over and downplayed in their everyday use: "armed struggle/relaxation of tensions/military presence/confrontational politics/balance of terror/public disillusion/flexible response/political pressure/black program."[7] Since all the phrases relate to war and violent conflict, the pairs of words on the title drawing also include collocations associated with war, such as "spasm war/cold war/punitive war." Heard or read so repeatedly, the inflationary presence of these phases in the media has turned them into unquestioned commonplaces which appear to have lost their highly charged meaning long ago.

Fox superimposed graffiti in black marking pen as a second level or stratum over each grid of letters. The graffiti copied signs which he had seen and collected from the walls of buildings in Italy, each sign only really comprehensible to the initiated. Terry Fox clearly elucidated their political content: "Some are variations of the sickle and hammer motif, the transformations of the cross into a swastika, the target into a sickle, the sickle into a dollar."[8] The aggressiveness of these quickly sketched forms is transferred to the meaning of the word pairs. Terry Fox then added a third level by covering each drawn graffito with a steel rod copy. In this way, the political sign becomes a metal art object in this uppermost layer, and is robbed of its function of conveying a meaning. As he wrote in 1985 in the Kunstraum München publication: "It represents the exploitation of one culture by a more advantaged one."[9] Ultimately, the steel rod copy of the sign, the aesthetically attractive object, blocks our view to the words underneath.

Just as the alphabet has 26 letters, so too Terry Fox's *Catch Phrases* comprise 26 drawings (+ 1 title drawing). In this sense, the series can be understood as one continuous band as the signs transform and repeat from one "sheet of paper" to the next; each black marking pen graffito resonates in the steel rod graffito on the next sheet in sequence, leading the reader/viewer from the start of the series to the end. Nonetheless, each sheet with its individual patterns of letters is readable in itself, and can similarly be read from start to finish.

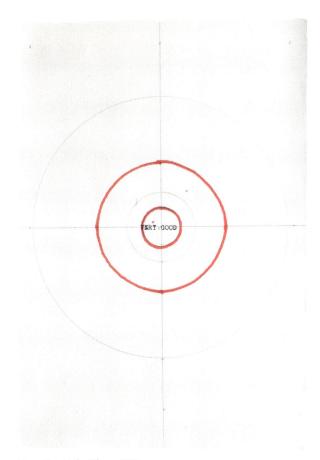

Terry Fox, *Hobo Signs*, 1985

In this process, the viewer's gaze wanders between the decoded pairs of words to the graffito and back again. The unusual writing style without contextualized words or distances makes this "reading performance" a prolonged and laborious process where the content can only be grasped through very time-consuming, individual effort.

For Terry Fox, both performance and sound offered methods of communication – "like eating" – bypassing barriers and transcending a need for preknowledge or intellectualization as a mediating power to reach the recipient immediately and directly: "The action is performed live and in front of its recipient."[10] As Terry Fox realized at the latest with his *Catch Phrase Series*, language, even if not always comprehensible, remains a medium of communication essential for individual as well as communal life – though it is, above all, an ambiguous and at times a dangerous medium. Looking back in 1993, he noted: "Changing the language is more dangerous than bombs, because it changes your thinking as well," and added: "I'm getting away from it now, I sort of got it out of my system, but I just had to show these things some way."[11]

The patient reader can also find critical catch phrases in Terry Fox's *Children's Drawings* (1985). The 32 square sheets of paper, which are very attractive aesthetically, may be in a moderately-sized format, but they also have a monumental impact when taken as a coherent sequence. Once again, the letters are evenly distributed across the squares. Aside from such catch phrases as "abnormal evolution," or "elimination of unreliable elements," which Fox has written in large capital letters, sequences of words can now also be deciphered in the long rows of letters written in longhand on other sheets of paper that incorporate sensational headlines from US tabloids: "Man Cuts His Head with a Chainsaw and Lives," "Man Blown Up on Operating Table," or "Fed Up Wife Burns Down House to Stop Hubby Snoring."

Terry Fox also drew a monogram on the reverse of all the sheets of paper. The intricate yet clear design, surprising harmonious in itself, comes through the paper so strongly that it disrupts the legibility of the text. The monogram is based on the circle, a medieval magical symbol which also played a key role in Fox's performance *Levitation* (1970). In that work, he drew a circle using his own blood to match the diameter of his height. The *Children's Drawings* monogram can also be found in a notebook among Terry Fox's unpublished papers, where it appears on a page opposite an anatomical sketch of the human body. Thus, it seems reasonable to posit parallels between the monogram and the human body. In his monogram, Terry Fox not only combines the geometrical forms of the circle, rectangle and square, but also integrates the letters of the Latin alphabet as well.

kann. In ihm vereinte Fox alle Buchstaben des lateinischen Alphabets. Gleichzeitig sind die geometrischen Formen Kreis, Quadrat, Rechteck darin enthalten.

Zu sortieren sind die 32 Zeichnungen nach den mittig in das Monogramm oder darüber eingeschriebenen Worten, die den obengenannten Rätselspruch ergeben: „A Headless man …". Zudem ist je Blatt ein Buchstabe rot hervorgehoben, und in derselben Sortierfolge des Rätselreims ergibt sich daraus der Spruch: „Jump quick brown fox over this lazy god." Es ist die Abwandlung eines englischsprachigen „Pangramms", das richtig lautet: „The quick brown fox jumps over the lazy dog", und als Blindtext verwendet werden kann, da in ihm wiederum alle 26 Buchstaben des lateinischen Alphabets enthalten sind. Terry Fox machte daraus einen Imperativ, und er ließ sich selbst, den Fox, nicht über einen faulen Hund, sondern über einen faulen Gott springen. Der Verweis auf seine Biografie ist unmissverständlich. In Kombination mit dem Rätselspruch wird Spielerisches und tiefgründig Philosophisches als Einheit gefasst, ähnlich wie in den *Children's Tapes* (1974). Zwischen sinnvoll und sinnlos ist kein Unterschied.

Im Vergleich zu den beiden bereits vorgestellten Serien von Zeichnungen ist die der 52 *Hobo Signs* (ebenfalls 1985) [↗**191**], in Originalgröße (25,3 × 17,7 cm) als Buch publiziert vom

Kunstraum München, visuell weniger komplex. Die in unterschiedlichen Radien auf den einzelnen Blättern gezogenen Kreise vermitteln den Eindruck, dass es sich hier um magisches Terrain handelt. Manche der in breiten roten Linien gezeichneten Piktogramme glaubt man deuten zu können, auch ohne die Erklärungen, die Fox mit der Schreibmaschine zusätzlich auf das Blatt getippt hat. Die abstrakten Zeichen dagegen lassen ohne Kenntnis dieser Geheimsprache keinerlei Rückschluss auf eine Bedeutung zu. Terry Fox entdeckte diese Bildsprache der Landstreicher zuerst auf Wanderungen durch Amerika und recherchierte dann auch in der Literatur. „Gauner-Zinken" wurden sie in Deutschland genannt. Sie sind nur einem kleinen Kreis Eingeweihter zugänglich, die sich darüber als Gruppe identifizieren: eine Gruppe, die jenseits der kulturell und materiell etablierten Gesellschaft wandert wie der Künstler Terry Fox selbst.

Als vierte der auf unterschiedlichen Schriftarten basierenden Serien von Zeichnungen ist *TEXTUM (Web)* **[↗193]**, entstanden 1989 für die Ausstellung mit Textarbeiten in Het Apollohuis Eindhoven[12], das wohl komplexeste, ästhetisch aber am wenigsten nach künstlerischen Maßstäben ausgerichtete Werk. 54 Seiten umfasst das Notizbuch und ist theoretisch wieder von Anfang bis Ende zu lesen. Dabei kommen verschiedene Kommunikationsweisen zueinander: Die Basis, der Schriftträger, ist ein schlichtes kariertes Papier. Die Buchstabenfolge ist diesmal mit der Schreibmaschine getippt. Wie in *Catch Phrase Series* sind Redewendungen aus den amerikanischen Nachrichten in Europa aufgeführt, dazu reißerische Überschriften aus der Boulevardzeitung *Weekly World News* wie: „Children Sucked From a Damaged Jet", „Jealous Computer Kills Top Scientist". Darüber liegen wieder italienische Graffiti-Zeichen und in den letzten Blättern des Heftes mittelalterliche Zimmermannszeichen, die zur Kennzeichnung von Holzbrettern benutzt wurden und an denen die Schreiner ablesen konnten, ob das Holz gut für Stühle, Schränke oder Kinderwiegen war.[13] Außerdem hat Fox spezielle Buchstabierweisen aufgenommen: so das Morsealphabet, umgesetzt in Balkenschrift, und die Blindenschrift von Braille, umgesetzt in rote Punkte. Das alles zu entziffern, ist eindeutig eine Überforderung, aber jeder liest daraus, was er nach seinem Vermögen kann. Schließlich erscheint auf jedem Blatt wieder das Monogramm, wie er es in *Children's Drawings* bereits benutzt hat, ein persönlicher Stempel, dessen Bedeutung offen bleibt.

Abgesehen von den beiden Folgen *Hobo Signs* und *TEXTUM (Web)*, die eher Buchcharakter haben, hat Terry Fox seine Schriftarbeiten großformatig angelegt und auch die Zeichnungen als Skulptur, als *environment* verstanden. Die Bewegung der Hand sah er als eine Art Performance.[14] Schließlich

The *Children's Drawings* series of the 32 drawings is defined by the words that are set in the center of the monogram or, are superimposed on it. These are all taken from the riddle "A Headless man [...]" mentioned earlier. In addition, a section of the monogram is highlighted in red on each sheet to form a letter. When the sheets of paper are placed in the same sequence as the words in the riddle, the highlighted letters spell out the phrase "Jump quick brown fox over this lazy god." This is Fox's version of the well-known pangram "The quick brown fox jumps over the lazy dog," which contains all 26 letters of the Latin alphabet and is commonly used to practice touch typing and for font displays. In Terry Fox's version, he transforms the phrase into an imperative where he himself – the fox – does not jump over a lazy dog, but over this lazy god. The reference to his biography is unequivocal. Combined with the riddle, the playful and profoundly philosophical are forged into a single entity, just as in his *Children's Tapes* (1974). There is no gap between the meaningful and meaningless.

In comparison to these two series of drawings, his *Hobo Signs* (also 1985) **[↗191]** are less visually complex. Kunstraum München published the series of 52 drawings in their original size (25.3 × 17.7 cm) in book form. The circles drawn with different radii on the individual sheets of paper evoke the impression of a magical terrain. Some of the pictograms sketched in thick red lines appear to suggest a meaning, even without reading the explanations Fox additionally typed onto each sheet. In contrast, the abstract signs remain opaque and indecipherable without knowing this secret language. Terry Fox came across hobo sign language on his journeys across the United States, and then also researched the literature on these pictograms. Hobo signs are only legible to a small circle of insiders who, moreover, identify themselves as a group – a group roaming outside our culturally and materially established society, much like the artist Terry Fox himself.

TEXTUM (WEB) **[↗193]**, the fourth series of sketches based on different styles of lettering, was produced in 1989 for an exhibition with text works in Het Apollohuis in Eindhoven.[12] This series may well be the most complex of these four, though aesthetically it is the furthest from mainstream artistic standards. The *TEXTUM (WEB)* notebook comprises 54 pages which could, theoretically, be read from beginning to end. The work combines diverse modes of communication. The basis is the simple graph paper, the support for the letters which, in this work, are typewritten. As in *Catch Phrases,* Fox also integrates phrases taken from American news that was broadcast in Europe, adding sensational headlines from the *Weekly World News* tabloid, such as "Children Sucked from a Damaged Jet," and "Jealous Computer Kills Top Scientist." Here too, Fox has again superimposed signs used in

Terry Fox, *Sheets of Slate* (from *TEXTUM, Web*), 1989

führte ihn sein Interesse an Sprache und Schrift als räumlichen Erlebnissen zu neuen Materialien und in die Dreidimensionalität wachsenden Formen. Fundstücke, Holzstäbe oder auch Metallringe benutzte er nun oft als Träger für seine Buchstabenkolonnen. Ein Beispiel für eine Wortskulptur ist *Ovum Anguinum* (1990) [↗**168**], das Schlangenei. Eine an die Wand gelehnte Leiter stützt einen Holzring, in dessen Mitte sich auf einer Holzstrebe die Worte: „odorless, colorless, tasteless, formless, silent" befinden. Wie bei dem Rätselreim werden auch hier alle Sinne angesprochen, zugleich wird die jeweilige Wahrnehmung verneint, eine „nihilistische Botschaft"[15]. In anderen Arbeiten wiederum ist die Leserichtung nicht wie gewohnt sich selbst entwickelnd, sondern sie nimmt Richtungen, die der Kopf nicht mitmachen kann, wenn man vor dem Objekt steht. Wenn man sich jedoch bewegt, dann gelingt es bruchstückhaft, die Zeichnung etwa (oder das Objekt) flüssig zu lesen, – und dann, so Terry Fox, „ist sie wie eine Skulptur"[16].

Im Unterschied zu den Wortpaaren, poetischen Sentenzen, Rätselsprüchen und Sprachspielen, zu denen auch die Titelgebung der Werke gehört, steht der lange, endlos erscheinende Text, der beginnt: „Body without arms and legs [...]". In den 1990er Jahren spielte dieser Text eine zentrale Rolle in Leben und Werk von Terry Fox. Handgeschrieben in Versalien

Italian graffiti. On the last pages of the notebook, he includes a medieval carpenters' mark used to classify the quality of wooden planks to let a joiner or carpenter know whether the wood was suitable for chairs, cupboards or cradles.[13] Moreover, he has worked with special forms of letters, transforming Morse code into a barcode and the Braille alphabet into red dots. Clearly, deciphering this in its entirety is overchallenging, but it also leaves viewers free to read from it what they can. Finally, each sheet of paper also includes the monogram Terry Fox had already used in his *Children's Drawings* series, although the meaning of this personal sign remains open.

Aside from *Hobo Signs* and *TEXTUM (WEB),* two works which rather resemble books, Terry Fox's works with writing and texts are all large scale. Since he viewed the movement of the hand as a kind of performance, these drawings can also be read as sculptures, as an environment.[14] His interest in language and writing systems as a spatial experience ultimately led him to new materials and forms expanding from two into three dimensions, often through using found objects, wooden rods or metal rings as the support for his columns of letters. His snake's egg work *Ovum Anguinum* (1990) [↗**168**] offers just such an example of his word sculptures. A ladder leaning against the wall holds in position an oval piece of wood with a wooden strut across its center decorated with the words

Terry Fox, *bloodline*, installation view, Fridericianum, Kassel 1996

als Fließtext ohne Wortabstände (beziehungsweise mit sehr geringen Abständen) auf kariertem Papier, erschien er 1991 erstmalig abgedruckt im Katalog der Galerie Löhrl. Dort ist er *Inventory* betitelt, und als *bloodline* hat Terry Fox ihn 1996 mit Hilfe von mehr als 7.000 Buchstabenkarten in der Pfalzgalerie Kaiserslautern über die Wände des Ausstellungsraumes fließen lassen (1997 erneut in der Gesellschaft für Aktuelle Kunst Bremen, GAK). Fox hat dort den Schritt von der Vorstellung der Schriftzeichnung als Skulptur oder eines *environment* zur realen Wortskulptur getan, wobei der Text im Unterschied zu den Serien der 1980er Jahre gegenübergestellt sein sollte.

Ein Beispiel dafür, wie er diesen Text zumindest in Auszügen zunächst in eine Skulptur fasste, ist die bereits erwähnte Arbeit *Envelope* (1991), die ähnlich vielschichtig angelegt ist wie *Catch Phrase Series*. Terry Fox liebte Mathematik, wie er einmal zugab, was auch ein Blick in seine Notizbücher offenbart. Auf kariertem Papier finden sich dort Skizzen geometrischer Formen, mehrfach etwa die Durchdringungen von Kreis und Rechteck auch bei der Notierung für eine Klangperformance. Geometrische Formen bestimmen auch die Kompositionen seiner Objekte. Bei dem Objekt *Envelope* beispielsweise bildet die Kreis und Rechteck einende Form Kopf- und Fußstück der blutrot gestrichenen Wiege. Die Halbkreisform assoziierte er zudem mit dem Buchstaben C und notierte in sein Heft die Worte „cradle, castle, closet, coffin, casket, corpse" untereinander, in der Vertikalen begleitet von dem Wort „cancer". *Envelope* ist also eine Metapher für das Sein des Menschen, von der Geburt bis zum Tod. Auch der Text „Body without arms [...]", den Fox in weißen Lettern über die Innenseiten laufen ließ, handelt vom Körper und davon, krank zu werden; die enge Verbindung zu seiner von Krankheit geprägten Biografie ist offensichtlich. Als fremd und störend empfindet man die in kleiner Handschrift hingekritzelten, von einer gleichmäßigen Schicht weißer Buchstaben verdeckten Fragen der Performance in Graz, die erst auf den zweiten Blick erkennbar werden. Fast unsichtbar sind sie, aber sie sind da und mahnen die Verletzlichkeit des Menschen an.

Die Zeichnung *Mock Up* (1991) [↗**167, 196**] hängt eng mit dem Objekt *Envelope* zusammen. Beide Werke präsentieren denselben Text. Während bei dem Objekt die Winkel sowie der aufgelegte Eisenring die Entzifferung des Textes erschweren, ist die Zeichnung eine zweidimensionale Entsprechung, denn der Text ist so angelegt, als hätte man die Wiege auseinandergeklappt. Die Buchstabenfelder stehen im Winkel zueinander, so dass, auch wenn die Zeichnung nicht räumlich ist, wir doch von der Sprache umgeben sind. Für diese räumliche Empfindung suchte Terry Fox nach Steigerung.

"odorless, colorless, tasteless, formless, silent." Here too, just as in the riddle, the words evoke all five senses even while simultaneously conveying a "nihilistic message"[15] that denies the individual acts of perception. In other works, rather than following the direction of reading customarily derived from a sequence of letters, they are arranged to take directions which the eyes of the viewer cannot follow when standing in front of the object. Only by moving can partial fragments of the words in the drawing (or the object) be made out and read. According to Terry Fox, "In the end drawing is like a statement, maybe it's obscure, but it's possible to read it. And also sculpture."[16]

In the 1990s, the long, seemingly endless text starting "Body without arms and legs [...]," played a major role in Terry Fox's life and work. This was a very different kind of text from his use of pairs of words, lyrical sentences, riddles and language games, including those in the titles of his works. Handwritten on graph paper in capital letters as a continuous text without gaps between the words (or with very slight gaps), "Body without arms and legs [...]" first appeared in a printed form in 1991 in the Galerie Löhrl catalogue under the title *Inventory*. In 1996, five years later, Fox produced his installation *bloodline* from the same text with over 7,000 letter cards covering the walls of the exhibition space in the Museum Pfalzgalerie Kaiserslautern; the installation was shown again in 1997 at the museum of the Gesellschaft für Aktuelle Kunst Bremen (GAK). Here, Fox moved from the idea of the written character as sculpture or an environment to real word sculpture, although in contrast to the series from the 1980s, the text was supposed to be displayed on facing walls.

The work *Envelope* (1991), mentioned above, provides one example of how Terry Fox initially transformed this text, or at least extracts from it, to produce a sculpture which is just as multilayered as *Catch Phrase Series*. As Terry Fox once remarked, he loved mathematics – and that love is evident from just viewing his notebooks. On the graph paper, he has sketched geometrical shapes including, for instance, multiple images of interlocking circles and rectangles, images which even appear in his notes for a sound performance. The composition of his objects is also informed by geometrical shapes. In *Envelope,* for instance, a circle and rectangle are unified to create the head and base of a cradle painted red. He also associated the semicircular shape with the letter C, jotting down in his notebook the sequence of words "cradle, castle, closet, coffin, casket, corpse" one below the other accompanied by the word "cancer" written vertically next to them: *envelope* can be read as a metaphor for the existence of the human being, from birth to death. The "Body without arms [...]" text, set in white letters across the inside of cradle, also deals with the human body and what it means to become ill. Here, the intimate

Terry Fox, *Schema Nr. 1* and *Envelope*, installation view, Museum Ludwig, Cologne, 1991

„Body without arms [...]" ist der längste Text, den Terry Fox je geschrieben hat, den er immer nur in Auszügen verwendete, der aber nach einer erneuten Krankheitserfahrung immer wichtiger für ihn wurde. Im Interview mit Johannes Lothar Schröder 1997 erläuterte er die Rauminstallation in der GAK Bremen 1997: „Ich hatte nie zuvor eine Arbeit mit Karten und mit so viel Text gemacht. Normalerweise hätte ich dem Text etwas Visuelles hinzugefügt. Aber dieser Text war zu lang. So dachte ich, die einzige Möglichkeit wäre, daraus ein Buch mit einigen Zeichnungen zu machen. Aber dafür war er zu stark und zu real für mich. Ich wollte etwas machen, was groß und stark war: vom Boden zur Decke und von Wand zu Wand."[17] Das Lesen des wandfüllenden Textes stellte wie die Zeichnungen und Objekte hohe Anforderungen an den Betrachter. Die Konzentration auf den einzelnen Buchstaben sah Fox parallel zum Tippen eines Textes mit nur einem Finger: Man sei sich „jedes Buchstabens in jedem Wort des Satzes bewusst. Es verändert die Weise des Denkens."[18] Schon ein erster Versuch, Worte zu entziffern, den Text zu verstehen, treibe einen voran, und in dem Moment, da man aufgeben möchte, gelinge es doch, ein weiteres Wort oder sogar eine Folge von Worten zu entziffern; immer zwei, drei oder auch mehr Worte ergeben

connection to Fox's own biography, influenced so greatly by his own experience of sickness and disease, is only too obvious. The textual elements also include the questions from his performance in Graz, scrawled in minuscule cursive writing and covered by an even layer of white letters. Almost invisible yet still present, only decipherable at a second glance, they seem strange and disturbing, a reminder of the vulnerability of the human body.

The *Mock Up* (1991) [↗**167, 196**] drawing is closely related to *Envelope*, and both works integrate the same text. While in the latter the iron ring and the viewer's perspective make it difficult to decipher the text, the former represents the two-dimensional equivalent of the object since the text is positioned as if the cradle had been taken apart. The fields of letters are set at an angle to each other so that even though the sketch is not three-dimensional, we are surrounded by the words – a spatial experience which Fox sought to intensify in his later works.

"Body without arms [...]" was Terry Fox's longest text. Although he only used extracts from it, the text in its entirety became increasingly central to his work after another bout with serious illness. In an interview with Johannes

zusammen einen Sinn. Doch erinnere man sich schon während des Lesens kaum mehr des Inhalts, den man zuletzt verstanden hatte, und bis zum Schluss stelle sich kein Verständnis im gewohnten Sinne ein. Die Entzifferung des monumentalen Textflusses muss sich der Betrachter tatsächlich körperlich erarbeiten, er muss sich körperlich engagieren. „Diese Partizipation", so erklärte Terry Fox in Bezug auf die Rauminstallation, „zwang den Leser in den Text hinein, er wurde Teil des Textes, er war Teil der Bildung der Skulptur."[19]

1 Die Grenzen erforschen. Interview von René van Peer, zuerst gedruckt in: Paul Panhuysen, *Interviews with Sound Artists*. Het Apollohuis, Eindhoven 1993, hier zitiert nach: Eva Schmidt (Hg.), *Terry Fox. Ocular Language. 30 Jahre Reden und Schreiben über Kunst. 30 Years of Speaking and Writing about Art*. Gesellschaft für Aktuelle Kunst Bremen, Köln 2000, S. 178, fortan Schmidt 2000
2 Ich wollte, dass meine Stimmung ihr Aussehen beeinflusst. Interview von Willoughby Sharp, zuerst gedruckt in: *Avalanche*, New York, Nr. 3, Winter 1971, S. 70–81, hier zitiert nach: Schmidt 2000, vgl. Anm. 1, S. 18
3 Ebd., S. 36
4 Ulli Seegers setzte „1984" dazu, vgl. U. Seegers, Verflüchtigungen und Verfestigungen des Seins. In: *(Re/De) constructions &c.: Terry Fox*. Kunsthalle Fridericianum, Kassel 2003, S. 14
5 Terry Fox, Statement (1982), in: Schmidt 2000, vgl. Anm. 1, S. 106–107
6 Constance Lewallen. In: *Terry Fox: Articulations (Labyrinth/TextWorks)*. Goldie Paley Gallery u.a., Philadelphia, Pennsylvania, 1992, S. 29, fortan Lewallen 1992
7 Aus Abbildungen ist dies nicht zu entziffern, deshalb sind die Ausdrücke aus Katalogtexten übernommen.
8 Terry Fox, *Catch Phrases*. Kunstraum München, 1985, o. S.
9 Ebd.
10 Terry Fox, Kommentare zu einigen Werken und Performances 1968–1981 (1981). In: Schmidt 2000, vgl. Anm. 1, S. 138
11 Die Grenzen erforschen. Interview von René van Peer. In: Schmidt 2000, vgl. Anm. 1, S. 180
12 Constance Lewallen datiert „1989", Eva Schmidt „1986"; vgl. Lewallen 1992, vgl. Anm. 6, S. 30, sowie Eva Schmidt, Textkörper, Textlabyrinthe. In: Bernd Schulz (Hg.), *Terry Fox. works with sound. Arbeiten mit Klang*. Saarbrücken 1998, S. 46
13 Lewallen 1992, vgl. Anm. 6, S. 30
14 Die Grenzen erforschen. Interview von René van Peer. In: Schmidt 2000, vgl. Anm. 1, S. 178 u. S. 180
15 Lewallen 1992, vgl. Anm. 6, S. 32
16 Die Grenzen erforschen. Interview von René van Peer. In: Schmidt 2000, vgl. Anm. 1, S. 180
17 Vom Boden zur Decke und von Wand zu Wand. Interview von Johannes Lothar Schröder. In: Schmidt 2000, vgl. Anm. 1, S. 196
18 Ebd.
19 Ebd., S. 200

Lothar Schröder in 1997, he discussed his installation from the text presented at the GAK Bremen: "I never did a work with cards and so much writing before. Normally I would have thought about something visual going with this text. But this text was too big. So the only thing I could think about doing would be to print it as a book with some drawings. But for this it was too strong and too real for me. I wanted to make something that was also big and strong: floor to ceiling and wall to wall."[17]

Much like Terry Fox's drawings and objects with text, it was no easy task for the viewer to read "Body without arms [...]" which ran, as planned, from floor to ceiling and wall to wall. For Fox, having to focus on the individual letters was similar to typing a text with one finger "where you are really conscious of every letter in every word in the sentence. It changes your way of thinking."[18] Even the initial attempt to decipher the words and understand drove you to read on, Fox commented, and just when you feel you want to give up, you manage to decipher another word or even a sequence of words; in context, two or three or more words always have meaning. Yet while you are reading, he added, you hardly remember the meaning of the part you just read and understood, and even when you finish, you do not understand the text in a normal sense. To decipher the massive flow of text required hard physical work from the viewer, a physical participation. As Terry Fox explained, "This participation forced the viewer into the text, to become part of the text, to become a part of creating the sculpture."[19]

Translated from the German by Andrew Boreham

1 "Exploring the Limits. Interview by René van Peer," first published in Paul Panhuysen, *Interviews with Sound Artists*, Het Apollohuis, Eindhoven, 1993, reprinted in Eva Schmidt (ed.), *Terry Fox. Ocular Language. 30 Jahre Reden und Schreiben über Kunst. 30 Years of Speaking and Writing about Art*. Gesellschaft für Aktuelle Kunst Bremen, Cologne, 2000, p. 181, hereafter Schmidt 2000
2 "I Wanted to Have My Mood Affect Their Looks. Interview by Willoughby Sharp," first published in *Avalanche*, New York, no. 3, Winter 1971, pp. 70–81, reprinted in Schmidt 2000, cf. note 1, p. 17
3 Ibid., p. 37
4 Ulli Seegers adds "1984" as the date, cf. U. Seegers, "The Fleetingness and Solidity of Being," http://www.recalling-terryfox.de/o_text_ulli.php# (last accessed on: July 17, 2015)
5 Terry Fox, Statement (1982), Schmidt 2000, cf. note 1, pp. 106–107
6 Constance Lewallen, *Terry Fox: Articulations (Labyrinth/Text Works)*, Goldie Paley Gallery, et al., Philadelphia, PA, 1992, p. 29, hereafter Lewallen 1992
7 Since this cannot be deciphered from illustrations, the prints from catalogue texts are included here.
8 Terry Fox, *Catch Phrases*. Kunstraum München, 1985, unpaginated
9 Ibid.
10 Terry Fox, "Comments on Some Works and Performances (1981)," Schmidt 2000, cf. note 1, pp. 139-141
11 "Exploring the Limits.," Schmidt 2000, Interview by René van Peer," Schmidt 2000, cf. note 1, p. 181
12 Constance Lewallen dates this as "1989," Eva Schmidt as "1986"; cf. Lewallen 1992, cf. note 6, p. 30 as well as Eva Schmidt "Textkörper, Textlabyrinthe," Bernd Schulz (ed.), *Terry Fox. works with sound. Arbeiten mit Klang*, Saarbrücken, 1998, p. 46
13 Lewallen 1992, cf. note 6, p. 30
14 "Exploring the Limits. Interview by René van Peer," Schmidt 2000, cf. note 1, p. 179 and p. 181
15 Lewallen 1992, cf. note 6, p. 32
16 "Exploring the Limits. Interview by René van Peer," Schmidt 2000, cf. note 1, p. 183
17 "From Floor to Ceiling and Wall to Wall, Interview by Johannes Lothar Schröder," Schmidt 2000, cf. note 1, p. 199
18 Ibid.
19 Ibid., p. 203

Mapping

I found a metaphor for my physical being, not my body, a labyrinth. I worked with the labyrinth for years. Everything I did related to the labyrinth in fact, my work was based exactly, almost scientifically, on it.

Ich entdeckte eine Metapher für mein physisches Sein, nicht meinen Körper, sondern das Labyrinth. Jahrelang arbeitete ich mit dem Labyrinth. Alles, was ich machte, setzte ich zu ihm in Beziehung. Tatsächlich war mein Werk, fast wissenschaftlich, darauf gegründet.

Terry Fox, *1979*

Works from the Labyrinth, 1972–78

1972 ging ich von San Francisco nach Europa und traf auf das große Bodenlabyrinth in der Kathedrale von Chartres. Dieses Labyrinth stellte für mich in mehrfacher Hinsicht eine Offenbarung dar. Ich hatte elf Jahre lang einen Zyklus von Gesundheit, Krankheit, Gesundheit, Krankheit und damit verbundenen Krankenhausaufenthalt, Entlassung, Kranken-hausaufenthalt, Entlassung durchgemacht. Das Labyrinth in Chartres hat elf konzentrische Kreise, die diesen elf Jahren zu entsprechen schienen. Auch die 34 Windungen, die ins Zentrum des Labyrinths führen, stimmten mit diesen Zyklen überein. Ich hatte gerade eine größere Operation durch-gestanden, die ein für alle Mal diese Zyklen beendete, und es schien, als wäre ich im Zentrum des Labyrinths angelangt. Bis zu diesem Zeitpunkt waren alle meine Energien dafür verwendet worden, dieses Zentrum zu erreichen, und ich beschloss, diesen Prozess umzukehren und meinen Weg aus dem Zentrum herauszufinden, indem ich meine gesamte künftige Arbeit auf das Labyrinth von Chartres aufbaute. [...] Einige Wochen später machte ich in der Galerie Sonnabend in Paris eine Installation, bei der ich Elemente früherer Arbei-ten verwendete. [...] [Zwei Mehlteigspuren] wurden während der Performance anlässlich der Eröffnung der Ausstellung durch eine „Brücke" miteinander verbunden, die aus einem mit Mehlteig bedeckten Brett bestand, auf dem ich zum zweiten Mal *Turgescent Sex* [↗**76**] aufführte.
In der Galerie von Lucio Amelio in Neapel machte ich einen Monat später eine andere Installation/Performance mit dieser Arbeit. Ich zeichnete das Labyrinth von Chartres spiegelverkehrt gedoppelt. Diese Zeichnung war so an der Wand befestigt, dass sie den Raum teilte, der darüber hinaus von zwei durchsichtigen Vorhängen unterteilt war. [...]
[↗**88–91**]
Nach San Francisco zurückgekehrt, fertigte ich ein kleines Gipsmodell des Labyrinths an, indem ich die 552 Schritte in eine Gipsplatte einschnitt, die ich aus dem Boden eines Eimers genommen hatte [...]. Ich machte ein Videoband *Incision* [↗**204**]. Dabei bedeckte ich die Linse einer tragbaren

In 1972, I went from San Francisco to Europe and confronted the great pavement labyrinth at Chartres Cathedral. This labyrinth was a revelation to me in many ways. I had undergone cycles of health, sickness, health, sickness, with attendant hospitalization, release, hospitalization, release, for 11 years. The labyrinth at Chartres has 11 concentric rings, which seemed to correspond to these 11 years. The 34 turns leading into the center of the labyrinth also corresponded to these cycles. I had just gone through a major operation that finished once and for all these cycles and seemed to have reached the center of the labyrinth. My energies up to this point had been involved in reaching this center and I decided to reverse this process and work my way out by basing all my future work on the labyrinth at Chartres. [...]
At the Sonnabend gallery in Paris a few weeks later, I made an installation using elements of previous work. [...]
These two tracks were connected, during the performance, at the opening of the exhibition, by a "bridge," consisting of a board covered in flour paste on which I performed, for the second time, *Turgescent Sex* [↗**76**].
One month later, at Lucio Amelio's gallery in Naples, I made another installation/performance with this work. I did a drawing of the labyrinth of Chartres doubled and reversed. This drawing was fixed to the wall, dividing the room, which was further divided by two translucent curtains. [...] [↗**88–91**]
Back in San Francisco, I made a small plaster model of the labyrinth by incising the 552 steps into a plaster disc taken from the bottom of a bucket a friend was using for casting plaster. I made a video tape (*Incision* [↗**204**]) by covering the lens of a Sony Portapak with a plastic dime store magnifying glass and following the course of the labyrinth. This 20-minute tape was accompanied by sounds produced by a homemade instrument of piano wires stretched over a metal bowl.
I also began to experiment with the actual design of the labyrinth. The most interesting discovery I made was that if the 34 turns into the center were changed into right angles of equal distance and plotted on squared paper, following the

Sony-Videokamera mit einem billigen Vergrößerungsglas und folgte dem Pfad des Labyrinths. Dieses Band hat eine Länge von 20 Minuten und wurde von Klängen begleitet, die mit einem selbst gemachten Instrument – über eine Metallschale gespannte Stahldrähte – erzeugt wurden.

Ich begann auch, mit der eigentlichen Form des Labyrinths zu experimentieren. Besonders interessant war dabei folgende Entdeckung: Wenn man die 34 Windungen zum Zentrum in rechte Winkel mit gleichem Abstand verwandelte und auf Millimeterpapier übertrug und dabei der Bewegungsrichtung des Pfades folgte, bilden die 34 Windungen (rechte Winkel) die Hälfte eines Triptychons von miteinander verbundenen Kreuzen. Wird diese Zeichnung umgekehrt und werden die beiden Zeichnungen dann miteinander verbunden, entsteht eine perfekte, schöne, endlose Windung von miteinander verbundenen Kreuzen. Ich machte Zeichnungen und kleine Objekte von diesem Phänomen.

Ich baute ein Objekt aus zwei hohen Hockern, von denen der eine mit der Sitzfläche auf dem Boden stehen blieb und der andere richtig herum auf dem ersten balancierte, Hockerbein auf Hockerbein. Von der Innenfläche des Sitzes des oberen Hockers aus war eine Schnur zum Mittelpunkt der Sitzfläche des unteren Hockers gespannt. Die Abbildung des Labyrinths auf Karton hing in der Mitte dieser vertikalen Schnur. [...]

In dieser Zeit versuchte ich auch, Klänge vom Labyrinth zu machen. Ich machte zwei Klangarbeiten, die auf seinem Weg basieren. [...] Eine [...] Klangarbeit war *The Labyrinth Scored for the Purrs of 11 Cats* [↗**238, 239**]. Für dieses Stück nahm ich von elf verschiedenen Katzen je acht Minuten kontinuierliches Schnurren auf Band auf. Diese Aufnahmen wurden dann gemischt, sodass sie dem Weg durchs Labyrinth entsprachen. Jede Katze repräsentiert einen der elf konzentrischen Kreise. Zehn Sekunden Schnurren entsprechen einem der 552 Schritte und zehn Sekunden sich überlappendes Geschnurre zweier Katzen einer der 34 Windungen. Die Aufnahme folgt genau dem Weg durch das Labyrinth und bewegt sich – so wie der Weg des Labyrinths von rechts nach links schwingt – stereofonisch zum rechten und linken Lautsprecher. Das Zentrum wird schließlich durch das gemeinsame Schnurren aller elf Katzen dargestellt. [...]

Ich machte eine Serie von 34 Tapes für Kinder, die als sehr langes Videoprojekt begann. [...] Schließlich wurden die *Children's Tapes* [↗**138**] viereinhalb Stunden lang, und so gab ich die Idee, sie zu vereinigen, auf. Es sind Bänder mit einer Länge von 50 Sekunden bis zu 17 Minuten. Sie sind alle unter Verwendung derselben Gegenstände als Mittelpunkt des Interesses entstanden: ein Löffel, eine Kerze, eine Schale, eine Gabel, Streichhölzer, Wasser usw., die immer und immer wieder in verschiedenen Formen von Interaktion manchmal

direction of movement of the path, the 34 turns (right angles) form one half of a triptych of interconnecting crosses. If this design is reversed and the two joined together, a perfect and beautiful endless loop of interconnected crosses is formed. I made drawings and small objects of this phenomenon.

I made an object consisting of two tall stools, one resting upside down on the floor and the other balanced right side up on top of it, joined feet to feet. A string was stretched from the bottom of the seat of the top stool to the center of the seat of the bottom stool. A cardboard image of the labyrinth was suspended in the center of this vertical string. [...]

I also attempted, during this time, to make sound from the labyrinth. I made two sound works based on its path. [...]

Another sound work was *The Labyrinth Scored for the Purrs of 11 Cats* [↗**238, 239**]. For this tape I recorded the continuous purring of 11 different cats. These 11 tapes were then mixed (joined) to follow the exact path of the labyrinth. Each cat represented one of the 11 concentric rings. The 552 steps into the labyrinth were changed into 10-second segments of purring for each step. The 34 turns were changed into 10 seconds of overlapping purrs as the path moved from one cat (ring) into the next. The tape follows the path of the labyrinth exactly and moves in stereo to the right or left speaker as the labyrinth path swings right or left. The center is the simultaneous purring of all 11 cats. [...]

I made a series of 34 tapes for children which began as a very long video project. The 34 video tapes were themselves to form the 34 turns in a video labyrinth which was to be one long continuous tape. The *Children's Tapes* [↗**138**] ended up being 4 ½ hours long and so the idea of uniting them was abandoned. These are tapes ranging from 50 seconds to 17 minutes. They were all made using the same objects as the focus of attention: a spoon, candle, bowl, fork, matches, water, etc., over and over in various situations of interaction, sometimes demonstrating simple mechanistic scientific principles, and other times in playful experiments and jokes.

Two Turns [↗**210, 211**] was another tape involving the labyrinth. I painted a large sheet of glass black and etched the image of the labyrinth into it. This was placed in a dark box together with my Portapak camera which was focused on it from 4 feet away. I directed the intense beam of a slide projector through the etched labyrinth directly into the lens of the camera, following the path over and over until the image of the labyrinth was burned into the vidicon tube of the camera. With the etched lens displaying this image, I made the tape, which consisted of two long walks, one by day in the sunlight and one by night in the rain. The camera was focused on my feet and both walks were return trips from the studio into the street, the first counter clockwise and the second clockwise.

einfache, mechanische, wissenschaftliche Gesetze und ein anderes Mal spielerische Experimente und Späße zeigen. Ein anderes Band, das das Labyrinth zum Gegenstand hat, war *Two Turns* [↗**210, 211**]. Ich malte eine große Glasscheibe schwarz an und ätzte das Labyrinth hinein. In einem dunklen Kasten wurde diese Scheibe zusammen mit meiner tragbaren Kamera, die aus 1,20 Meter Abstand darauf gerichtet war, aufgestellt. Durch das eingezeichnete Labyrinth hindurch richtete ich den starken Lichtstrahl eines Diaprojektors direkt in die Linse der Kamera, wobei ich dem Verlauf des Weges immer wieder folgte, bis das Bild des Labyrinths in die Vidikonröhre eingebrannt war. Mit der geätzten Linse, die nun dieses Bild zeigte, machte ich das Band. Es zeigte zwei lange Spaziergänge, einen an einem sonnigen Tag und einen in einer regnerischen Nacht. Die Kamera war dabei auf meine Füße gerichtet, und beide Wege waren Wege vom Studio auf die Straße und zurück, der eine im Uhrzeigersinn, der andere entgegen dem Uhrzeigersinn.

1977 stellte ich unter dem Titel *Metaphors for Falling* in der Künstlergalerie Site in San Francisco aus. Ich zeigte alle Objekte, die aus der Auseinandersetzung mit dem Labyrinth von Chartres entstanden waren. [...] Alle Objekte erforderten die Beteiligung der Betrachter, um sie ganz zu sehen. Kästen mussten geöffnet, Zeichnungen entrollt werden usw. [...] Ich hatte auch begonnen, mit Pendeln zu arbeiten, weil sie eine offensichtliche Beziehung zu der Bewegung und dem Rhythmus des Labyrinths haben. Eine dieser Arbeiten bestand aus einer ein Pfund schweren Bleikugel, die an einer Klaviersaite von der Decke hing, und einem halb mit Wasser gefüllten Glas, das auf dem Boden stand. Dieses Pendel sollte vom Besucher in einem schnellen, großen Bogen um das Glas herum geschwungen werden. In dem Maße, in dem sich die Umlaufbahn verringerte, bewegte sich der Ball langsamer und langsamer, bis er schließlich das Glas traf und dabei ein sanftes Klingen erzeugte. Nach dieser Berührung vollzog sich die Kreisbewegung analog zu der Bewegung der linken und rechten Kehren des Labyrinthweges. Im weiteren Verlauf berührte er den Rand des Glases in engen Kreisen im Uhrzeigersinn und dann entgegen dem Uhrzeigersinn, so wie die Kordel, an der er aufgehängt war, sich auf- oder abwickelte. [...]

Quelle: Schmidt 2000, S. 118–128, zuerst erschienen in: Terry Fox, *Linkage*. Kunstmuseum Luzern, 1982

Aus dem Englischen übersetzt von Anna H. Berger / Max Wechsler

In 1977 I staged an exhibition at [the] artists' space Site in San Francisco, entitled *Metaphors for Falling*. I showed all the objects I had made exploring the Labyrinth of Chartres. [...]

All the objects required participation in order to view them: boxes had to be opened, drawings unrolled, etc. [...]

I also had begun to work with pendulums, since they bear an obvious relationship to the movement and rhythm of the labyrinth. One such work was a one-pound lead ball suspended from the ceiling by piano wire and a glass half-filled with water resting on the floor. This pendulum was to be swung by the visitor in a wide and fast arc around the glass. As its orbit diminished the ball moved slower and slower until it finally hit the glass with a gentle ringing. After this contact the process of circling became analogous to the movement of the left and right turns of the path of the labyrinth. The ball proceeded to revolve around the glass clockwise and then counterclockwise, hugging the edge of the glass as the cord it was suspended from wound and unwound. [...]

Source: Schmidt 2000, pp. 119–131, first printed in Terry Fox, *Linkage*. Kunstmuseum Luzern, 1982

Terry Fox, Sketch for *A Triptych of Crosses* ..., n.d.

34 turns

1	left
2	right
3	left
4	left
5	left
6	right
7	left
8	right
9	right
10	left
11	right
12	left
13	left
14	right
15	left
16	right
17	left
18	right
19	left
20	right
21	left
22	right
23	right
24	left
25	right
26	left
27	left
28	right
29	left
30	right
31	right
32	right
33	left
34	right

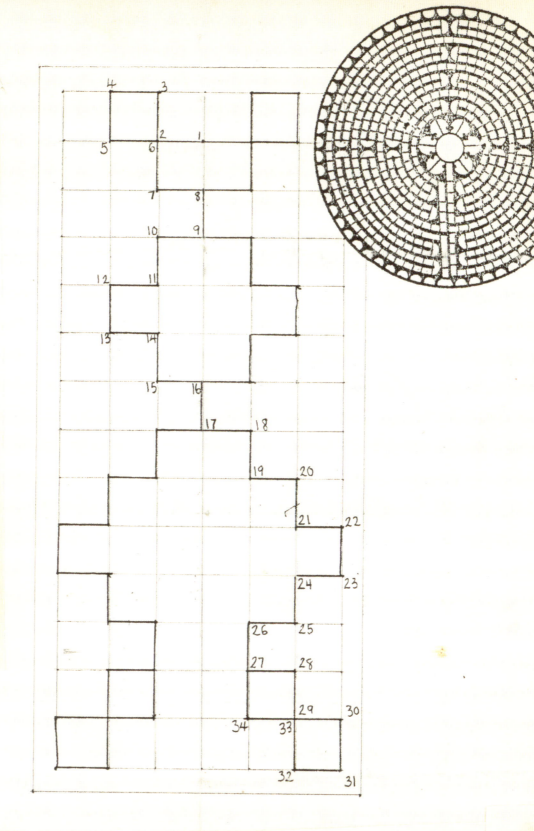

This tryptich of crosses was formed by considering the 34 turns into the labyrinth at Chartres as right angles and the distances between the turns as being equal. The turns from the center back to the starting point (35-68) are considered as being the opposite of the turns into the labyrinth (1-34). This tryptich, joined end to end, forms a loop of interconnected crosses.

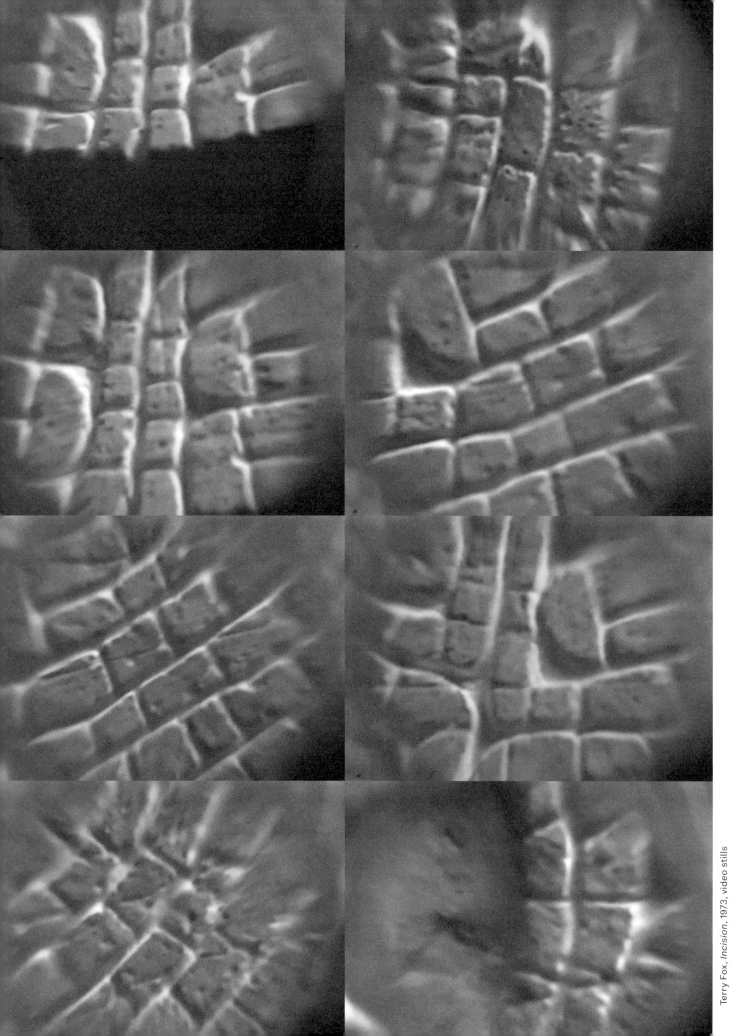

Terry Fox, *Incision*, 1973, video stills

René Block

It was during a journey to Europe in 1972 that Terry Fox spent an extended amount of time at Chartres. He discovered a mosaic on the floor of the cathedral that depicted a labyrinth with eleven concentric circles. This labyrinth would later serve as the inspiration for many of his projects, performances, and drawings. Isn't human life similar to a labyrinth, in which the wanderer – often by way of numerous detours – ultimately does always reach the final goal, a place of stillness and calm? [...] Terry Fox sees the labyrinth as a symbol of an individual finding oneself. His effort to find himself is at the root of his oeuvre as a whole. Even his early Body art performances were investigations to determine the limits of his own body and of this body in relation to time and space.

[...] Trust in yourself, you will find your way, you won't go astray. A pendulum conveys the same message in another form as it gradually nears the convex mirror below by moving continuously through constantly changing circles until it finally comes to rest at the center. The pendulum embodies calmness even in motion. [...]

Terry Fox's name is still more widely known in Europe than are his works, the inner context of which had always remained hidden. [...]

2003

Source: (*Re/De*) *constructions &c. Terry Fox*. Kassel, 2003, p. 2

Translated from the German by Allison Brown

Es war im Jahr 1972, als sich Terry Fox bei einem Besuch in Europa längere Zeit in Chartres aufhielt. Auf dem Boden der Kathedrale hatte er ein Mosaik entdeckt, das ein Labyrinth mit 11 Kreisen darstellt. Dieses Labyrinth sollte zum gedanklichen Ausgangspunkt für zahlreiche in den folgenden Jahren entstehende Objekte, Performances und Zeichnungen werden. Gleicht das menschliche Leben nicht einem Labyrinth, in dem der Wanderer – oft nach vielen Umwegen – letztendlich doch immer am Ziel, dem Ort der Stille ankommen wird? [...] Für Terry Fox ist das Labyrinth ein Symbol der Selbstfindung des Menschen. Das Bestreben, sich selbst zu finden, kennzeichnet sein gesamtes Werk. Schon die frühen Body-Art-Performances waren Untersuchungen, die Grenzen des eigenen Körpers und die dieses Körpers in Beziehung zu Raum und Zeit zu definieren.

[...] Traue Dich, Du wirst Deinen Weg finden, Du gehst nicht verloren. Eine Botschaft, die in anderer Form auch das Pendel verkündet, wenn es sich in jeweils anderen Kreisen dem konvexen Bodenspiegel unaufhaltsam nähert, bis es über dessen Zentrum ruht. Das Pendel verkörpert eine Ruhe auch in der Bewegung. [...]

Immer noch ist der Name Terry Fox in Europa bekannter als sein Werk, dessen innerer Zusammenhang immer im Verborgenen blieb. [...]

2003

Quelle: (*Re/De*) *constructions &c. Terry Fox*. Kassel *2003,* S. 2

Terry Fox, *Holes and Entrances*, 1979, video stills

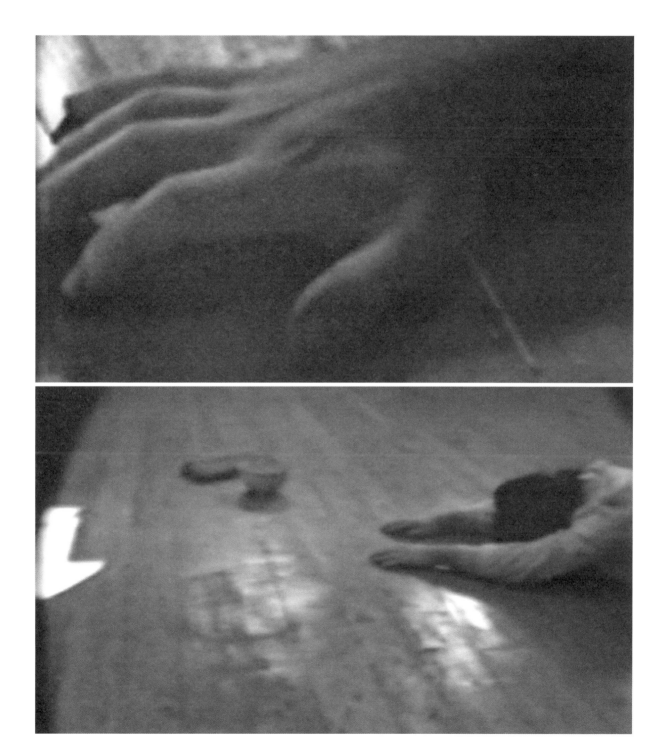

Terry Fox, *Clutch*, 1971, video stills

Terry Fox, *Two Turns*, 1975, video stills

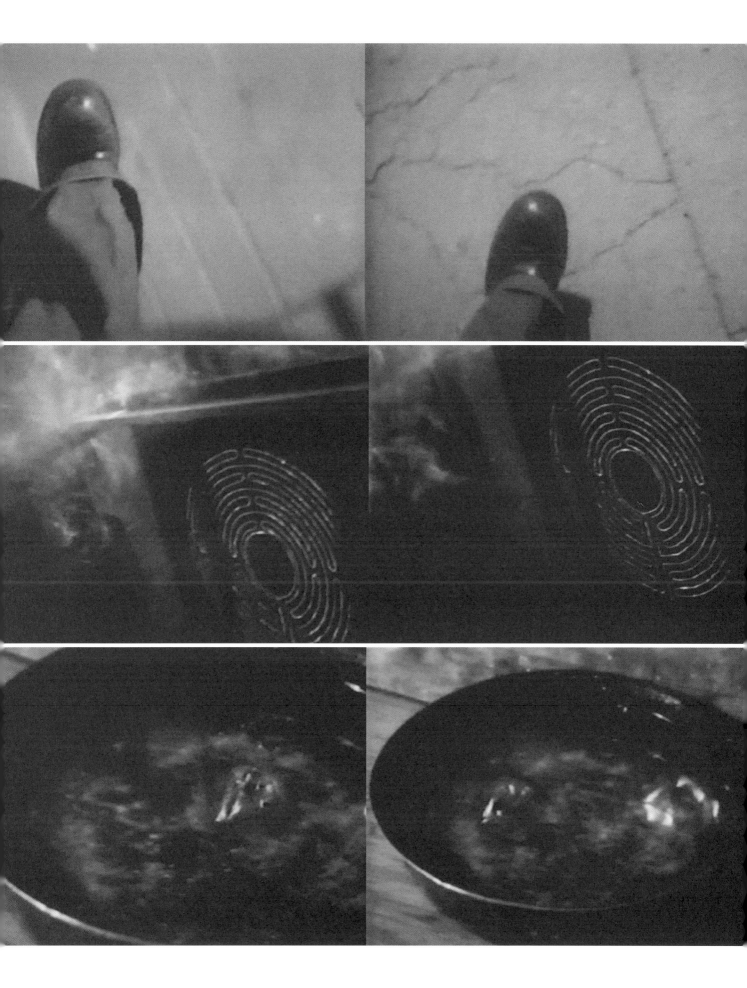

Terry Fox, *A Metaphor*, 1976

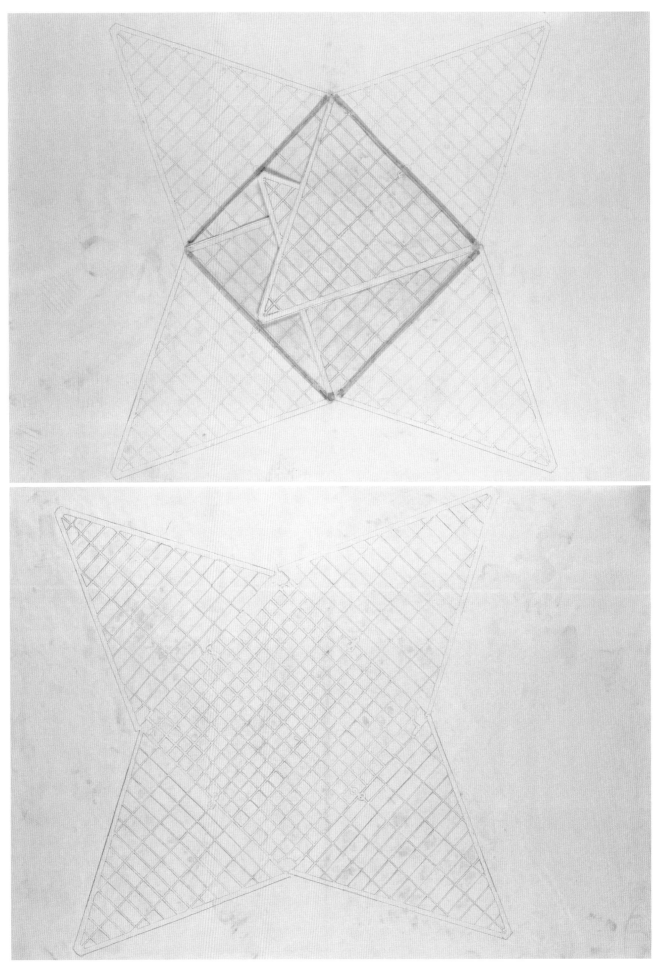

214   Terry Fox, Sketch for *Transference*, 1979

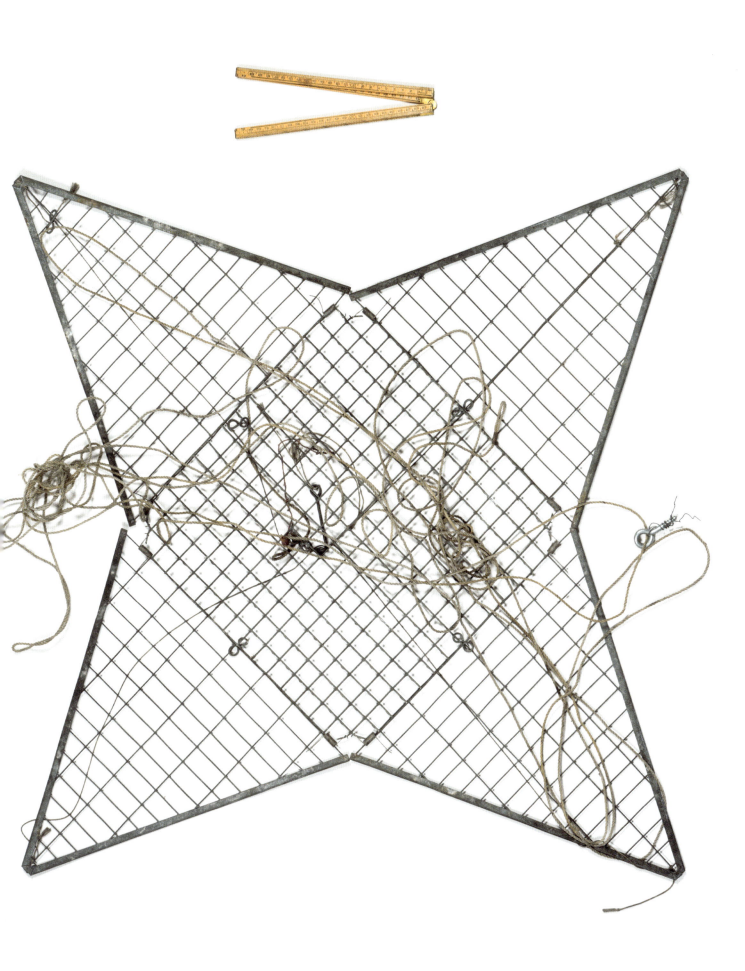

Terry Fox, *Transference*, 1979

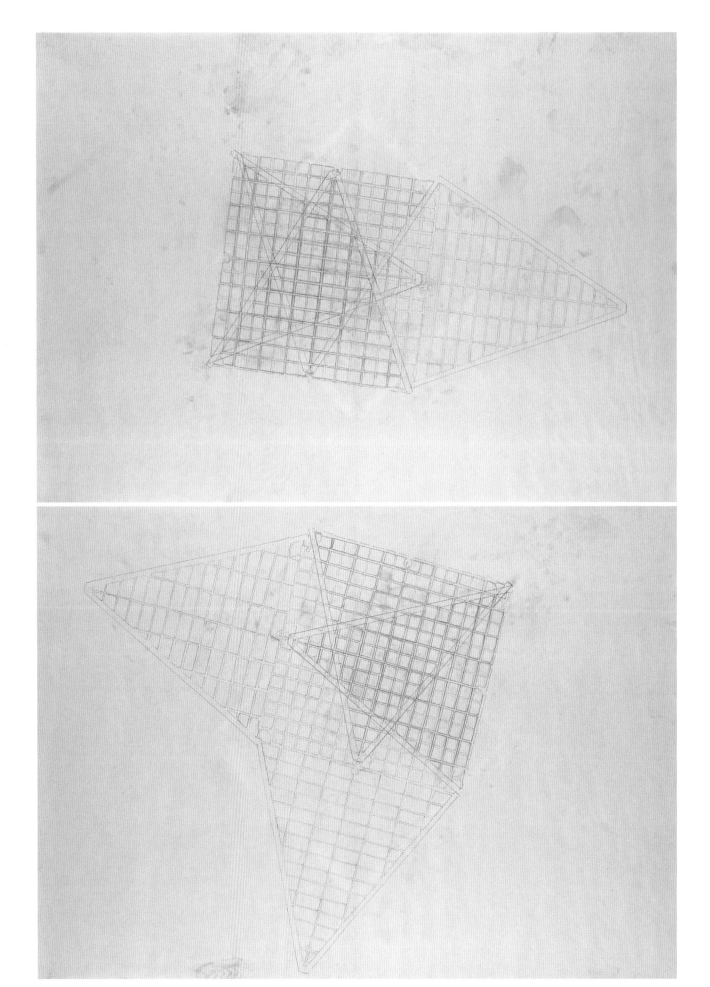

Terry Fox, Sketch for *Transference*, 1979

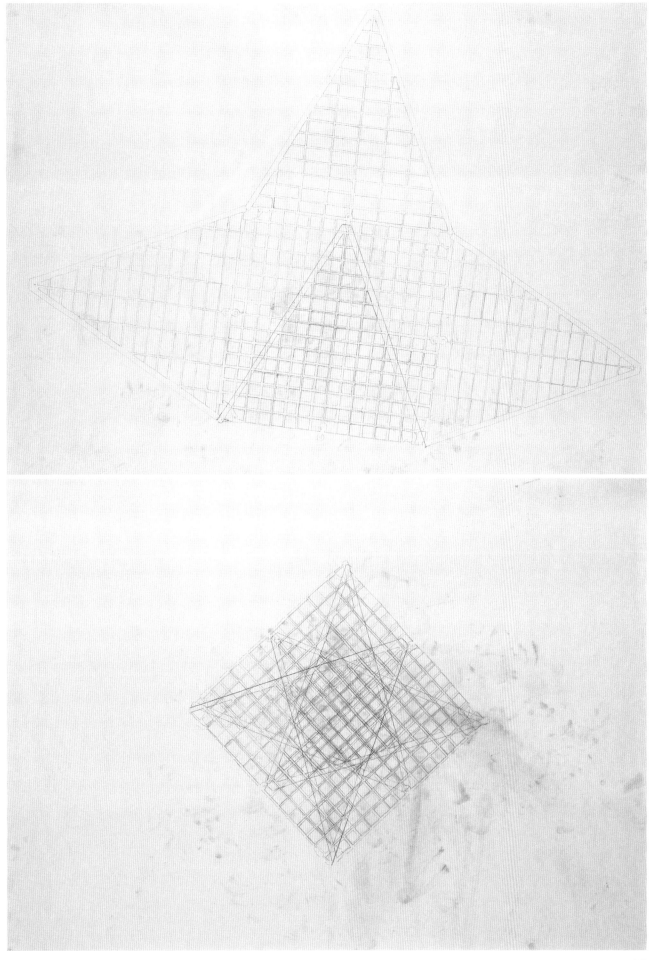

→ Terry Fox, Shadow Drawings: Balanced, Vaporous, Deserted, Temporal, Thinning, Fugitive, Extended, 2006

TEMPORAL

P. Fox   2005

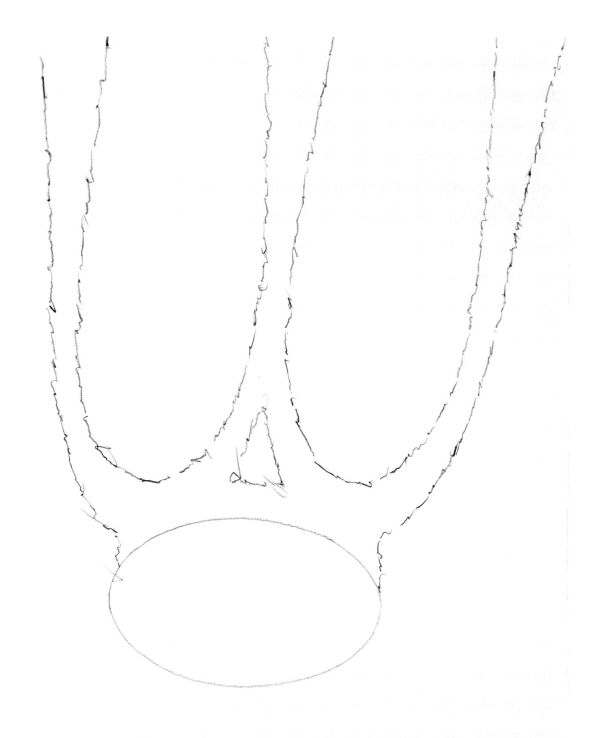

BALANCED

2005

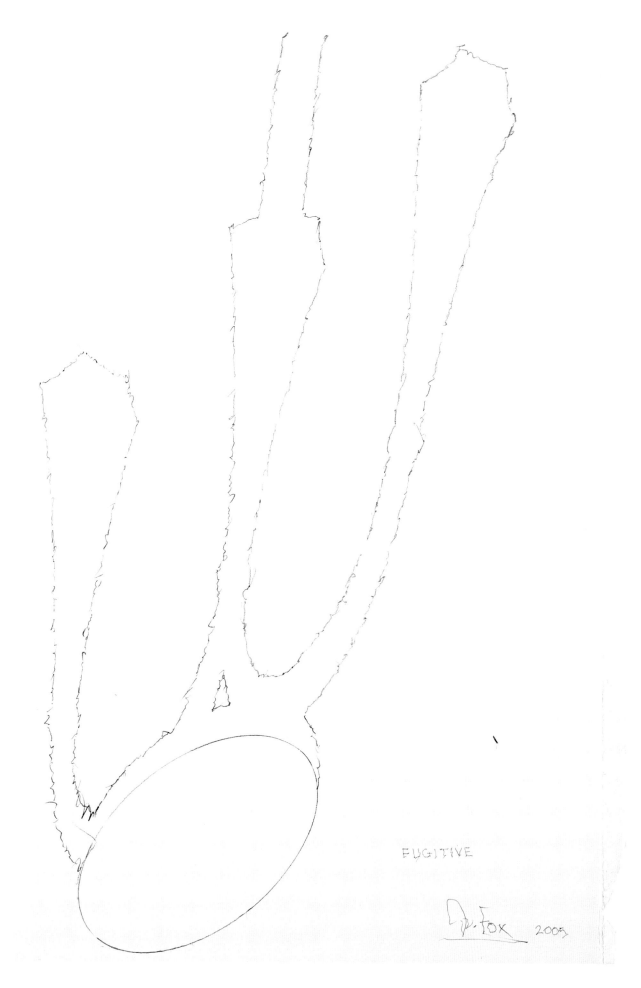

FUGITIVE

D. Fox   2005

Sound as Sculpture

Raum

Performance [...] yes, it's like singing it.
[...] Yes – I mean, sound just occurs – you get it,
and you can't close it unless you're deaf;
you don't have to think about it, you don't
even have to be conscious that it's actually
happening to you. But it's working on you.
I do performance with sound,
and it's more sculptural
than musical; it has to do with
space, filling the space or
changing the space, changing
the architecture of the space
with sound. [...] Sound can
be really deep [...] a good way
to communicate.

Terry Fox, *1979*

Performance [...] Ja, es ist wie ein Singen. [...]
Ja, ich glaube, Klang geschieht einfach,
man kann ihn nicht ausschließen, wenn man
nicht taub ist, man braucht nicht darüber
nachzudenken, man braucht sich nicht bewusst
zu sein, dass er tatsächlich da ist. Aber er
wirkt auf einen. Ich mache Performances
mit Klang, eher skulptural als musikalisch; es
hat etwas mit Raum zu tun, den Raum füllen
oder ihn verändern, die Architektur des Raumes
mit Hilfe von Klang verändern. [...] Klang
kann wirklich tief sein, [...] wirklich eine gute
Art zu kommunizieren.

als Instrument

Bernd Schulz

[...] Since the 1970s, Terry Fox has been increasingly concerned with investigating the unknown and seldom-observed energetic aspects of materials, whereby sound gains a central significance. The latter ties him to John Cage, who made permeable the boundaries between everyday perception and the artistic perception of sound. However, Terry Fox is not concerned with inventing new musical forms, but in finding sounds that make energies palpable and that connect the listener and his physical surroundings. In this, he stands closer to Buckminster Fuller (whom Cage also occasionally invoked), who, starting from the discoveries of physics, always pointed out that, in reality, no solid bodies actually exist, but merely various states of vibration, and that all bodies stand in a field of constant transformation.

Terry Fox relies on overtone-rich material sounds that are difficult to locate and that set whole rooms in resonance. But his performances go beyond the mere production of a musical atmosphere. Perception is always connected with the experience of a presence conveying a feeling that time stands still, often with an extreme dilation of time. In his inventive search for materials to produce sound, Terry Fox discovered as early as the 1970s that the vibrations of meter-long, strung piano wires call up sounds particularly suited to spatialization. He used these strung piano wires in various contexts on the most varied sites; and many who have experienced them see the performances thus created as among the most impressive and lasting in memory. [...]

1998

Source: Bernd Schulz, "Foreword," idem. (ed.), *Terry Fox. Works with Sound. Arbeiten mit Klang.* Heidelberg, 1999, pp. 8–9

Translated from the German by Mitch Cohen

[...] Seit den 70er Jahren geht es Terry Fox mehr und mehr um die Erforschung der unbekannten und wenig beachteten Energieaspekte von Stoffen und Materialien, wobei der Klang eine zentrale Bedeutung gewinnt. Letzteres verbindet ihn mit John Cage, der die Grenzen zwischen Alltagswahrnehmung und künstlerischer Klangwahrnehmung durchlässig gemacht hat. Allerdings geht es Terry Fox nicht um die Erfindung neuer musikalischer Formen, sondern um das Finden von Klängen, welche Energien spürbar werden lassen, die Hörer und physikalische Umwelt miteinander verbinden. Damit steht er eher Buckminster Fuller nah (auf den sich allerdings auch Cage gelegentlich bezieht), der, ausgehend von Erkenntnissen der Physik, immer darauf hinwies, daß es eigentlich keine Festkörper gibt, sondern unterschiedliche Schwingungszustände, und daß alle Körper sich in einem Feld ständiger Transformation befinden.

Terry Fox setzt auf obertonreiche Materialklänge, die schwer zu orten sind und ganze Räume in Resonanz versetzen. Seine Performances gehen allerdings über das bloße Erzeugen einer musikalischen Atmosphäre hinaus. Die Wahrnehmung ist immer verbunden mit dem Erlebnis einer Präsenz, die bei oft extremer Zeitdehnung ein Gefühl der stehenden Zeit vermittelt. Auf seiner erfinderischen Suche nach Materialien zur Klangerzeugung entdeckte Terry Fox bereits in den siebziger Jahren, daß die Schwingungen von meterlangen, gespannten Klaviersaiten Klänge hervorrufen, die sich besonders zur Verräumlichung eignen. Er hat diese gespannten Klaviersaiten in unterschiedlichen Kontexten an den unterschiedlichsten Orten verwendet, und die dabei zustande gekommenen Performances zählen für viele, die sie erlebt haben, zu den eindrucksvollsten, die nachhaltig in Erinnerung bleiben. [...]

1998

Quelle: Bernd Schulz, Vorwort. In: ders. (Hg.), *Terry Fox. Works with Sound. Arbeiten mit Klang.* Heidelberg 1999, S. 8–9

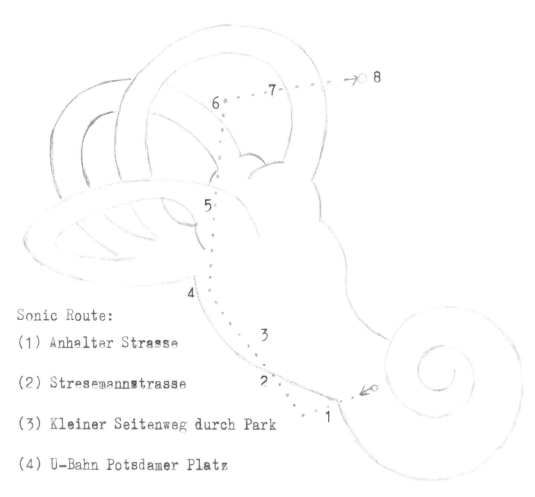

Sonic Route:

(1) Anhalter Strasse

(2) Stresemannstrasse

(3) Kleiner Seitenweg durch Park

(4) U-Bahn Potsdamer Platz

(5) Holocaust Mahnmal

(6) Brandenburger Tor

(7) Unter den Linden

(8) Ehemalige Polnische Botschaft

226   Terry Fox, *Radiation*, Museum Folkwang Essen, 1979

Terry Fox   Sound

Sound is a means of communication, a universal language. It enters the healthy ear without the impediments of language or prejudice. It is perceived by every culture in the same way: via the auditory canal. It enters the ear without consent of the listener. It vibrates the eardrum. It requires no intellectualization. No intelligence is necessary. No common language need be spoken. Illiteracy is irrelevant. Sound passes as pulses in the air.

Performance is, for me, an attempt to discover a language or method of communication which bypasses these barriers as sound does. The most important aspect of performance is the elimination of media or a mediating force or condition. The action is performed live and in front of its receiver. It exists only on these terms and in this context and no other: like eating. My work with the labyrinth led increasingly to the almost limitless sculptural possibilities of sound. [...]

c. 1980

Source: Zdenek Felix (ed.), *Terry Fox. Metaphorical Instruments*. Essen, 1982, p. 72

Klang

Der Klang ist ein Mittel der Kommunikation, eine universelle Sprache. Er dringt in das gesunde Ohr ohne Hindernisse der Sprache oder Vorurteile ein. Er wird von jeder Kultur auf demselben Wege wahrgenommen: über den Gehörgang. Er dringt ohne Einverständnis des Hörers in das Ohr ein. Er lässt das Trommelfell schwingen. Er erfordert keine Intellektualisierung. Es ist nicht nötig, eine gemeinsame Sprache zu sprechen. Unwissenheit ist bedeutungslos. Der Klang zieht vorüber wie Pulsschläge in der Luft.

Die Performance ist für mich ein Versuch, eine Sprache oder eine Kommunikationsmethode zu entdecken, die diese Barrieren überwindet wie der Klang. Der bedeutendste Aspekt der Performance liegt in der Ausschaltung von Vermittlungen oder einer vermittelnden Kraft oder Bedingung. Die Aktion ist verwandeltes Leben und geschieht vor dem Empfänger. Sie existiert nur unter diesen Bedingungen und in diesem und keinem anderen Kontext: wie Essen. Meine Arbeit mit dem Labyrinth führte immer deutlicher zu den fast grenzenlosen, skulpturalen Möglichkeiten des Klanges. [...]

ca. 1980

Quelle: Zdenek Felix (Hg.), *Terry Fox. Metaphorical Instruments*. Essen 1982, S. 69

Aus dem Englischen übersetzt von Anna H. Berger, Max Wechsler

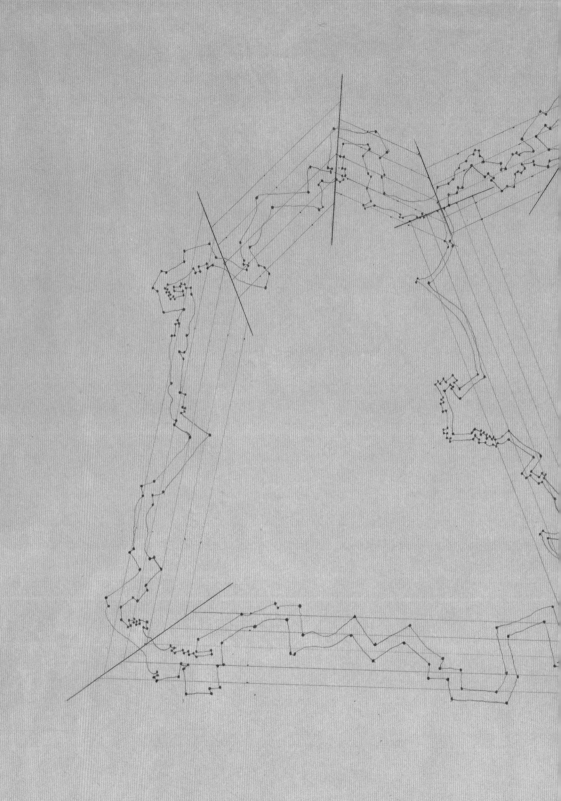

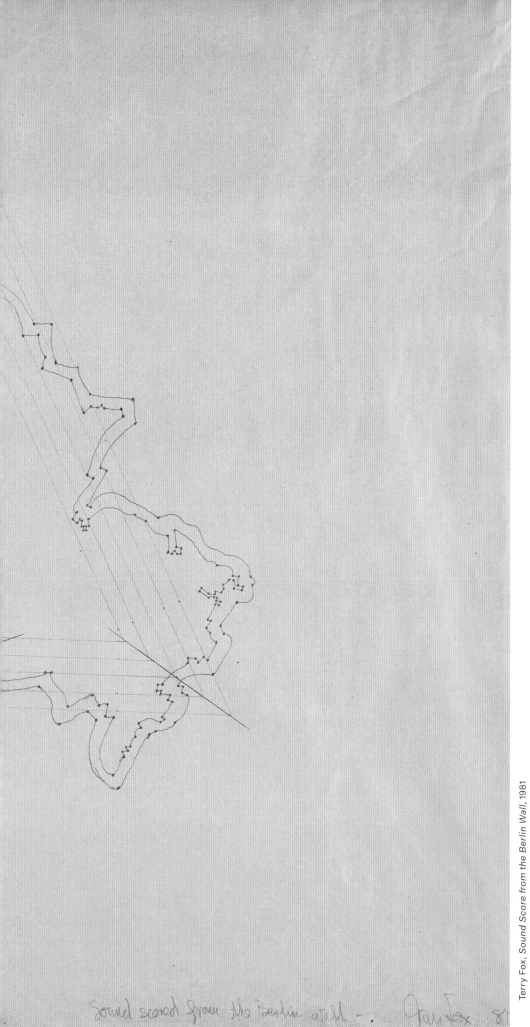

Sound scored from the Berlin wall -. Terry Fox. 8[...]

Terry Fox, Sketch for *Berlin Wall Scored for Sound*, c. 1981–82

figure from the Berlin wall

Berlin 81

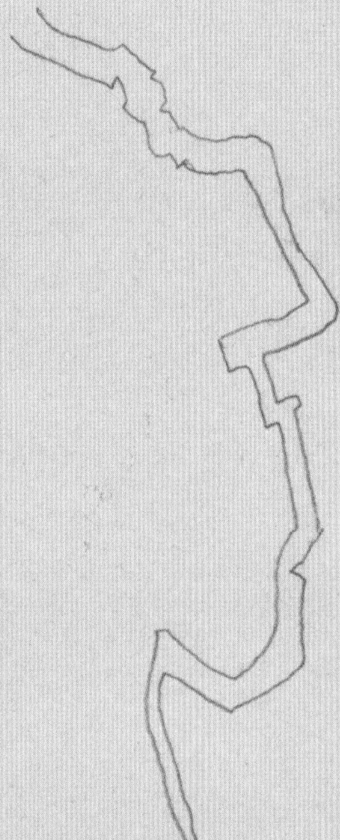

Günter

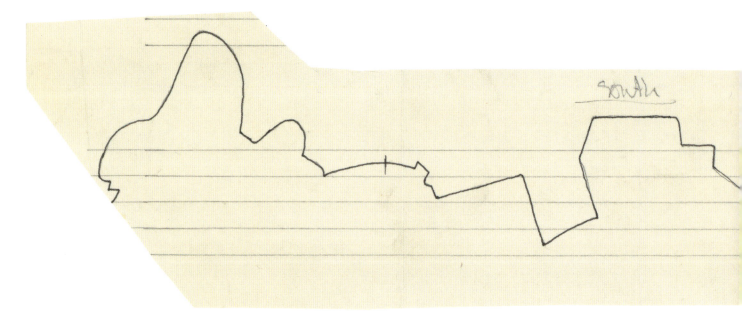

south

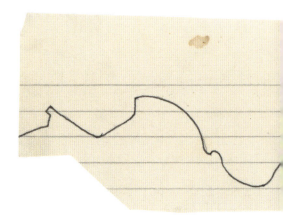

232   Terry Fox, Sketches for *Berlin Wall Scored for Sound*, *Berlin Wall transferred to lines*, c. 1981–82

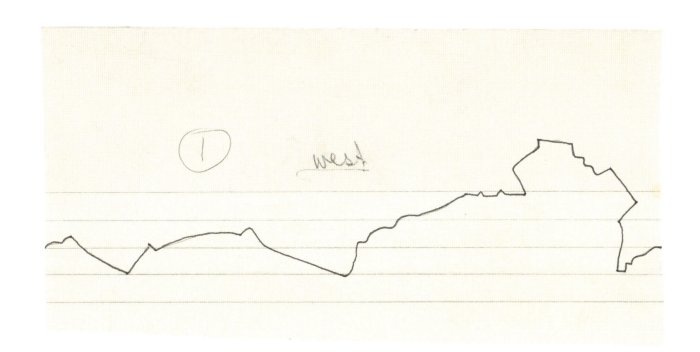

west

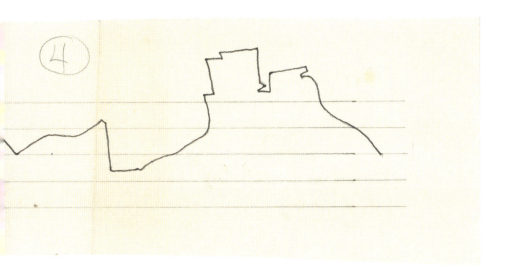

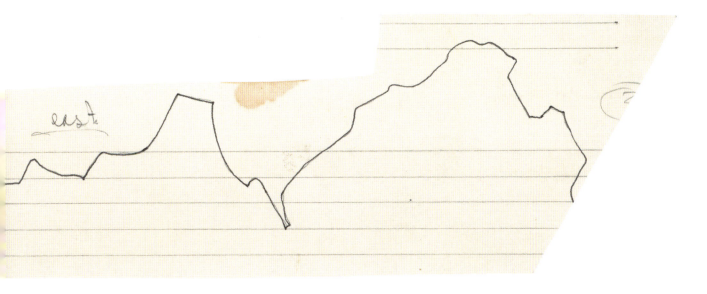

east

Aku 11 cats for the labyrin

1. TOM SUCKING SADIE. S.F.
2. PATTY — N.Y.
3. BOOGALOO S.F.
4. MIRIAM N.Y.
5. PUFFIN S.F.
6. HERA — N.Y.
7. FERGUSEN N.Y.
8. ERNEST S.F.
9. SAMANTHA S.F.
10. SPOT — N.Y.
11. ARTHUR N.Y.

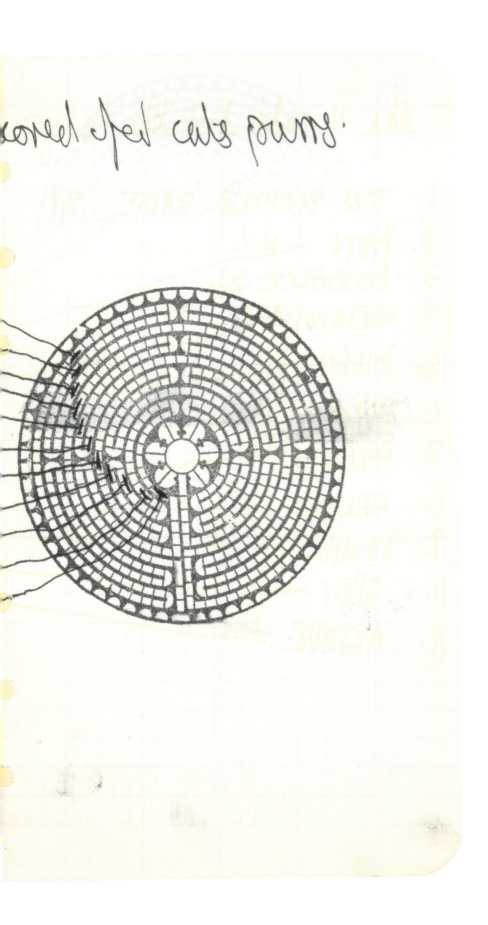

Terry Fox, Untitled, 1979, photos: Roland Fischer

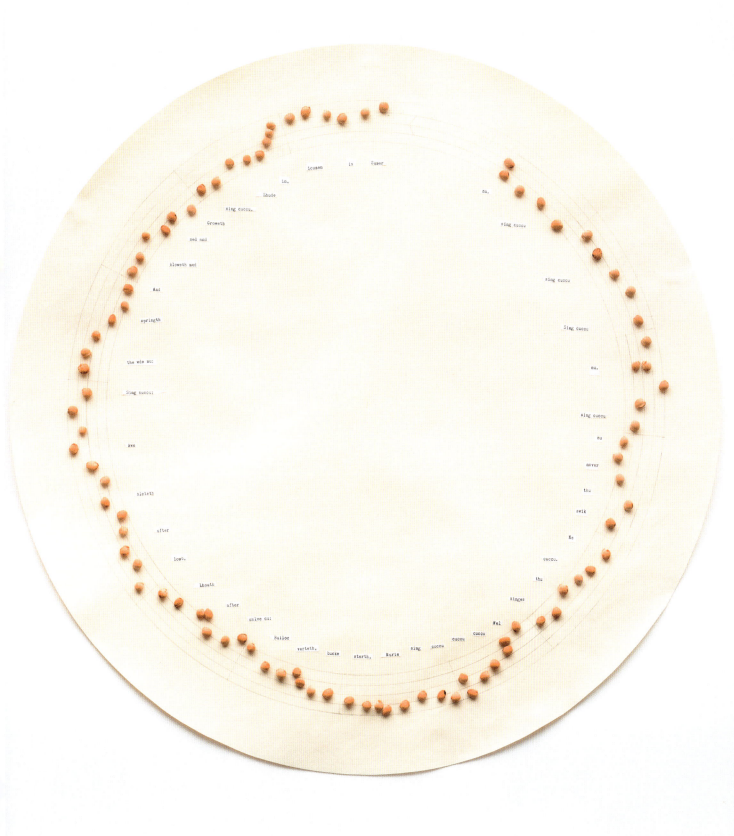

Terry Fox, *Sumer is icumen in*, 2002

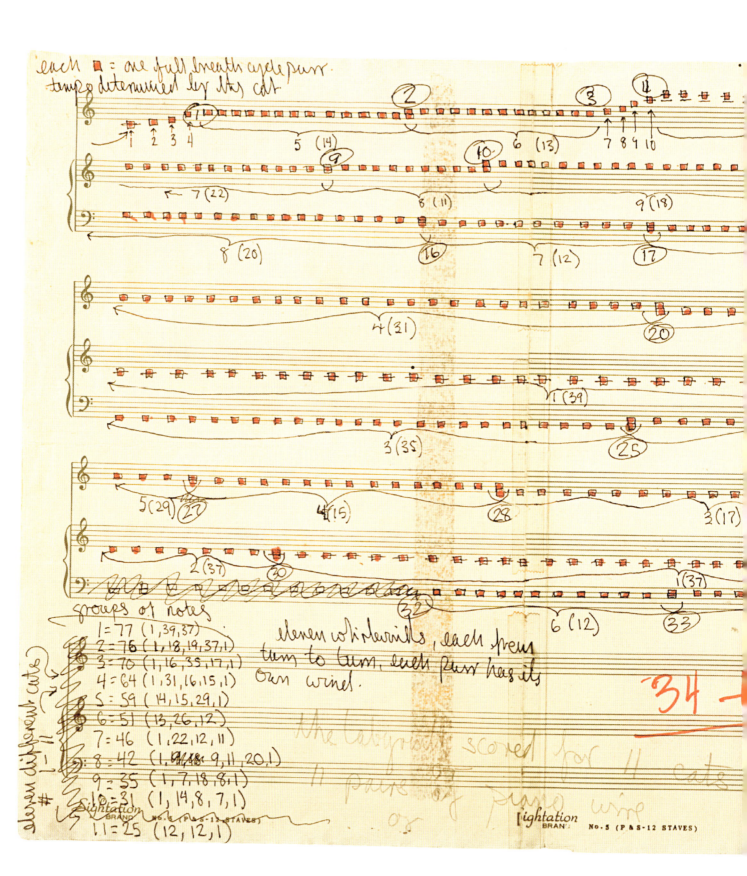

238   Terry Fox, *The Labyrinth Scored for the Purrs of 11 Different Cats*, 1973

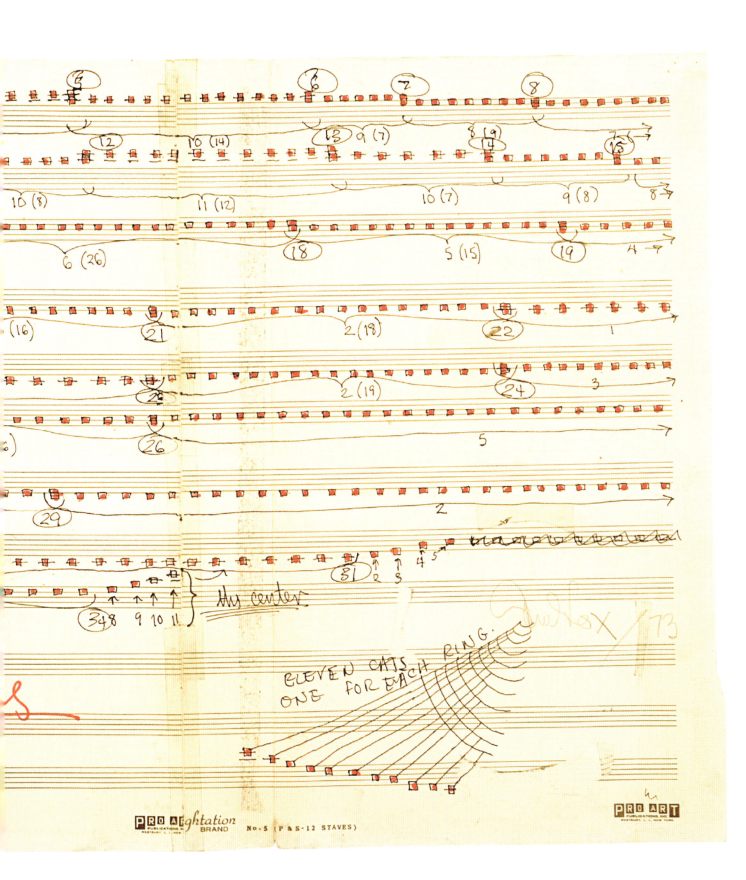

240   Terry Fox, Untitled, c. 1967

Sculpture is always being opened up –
new elements are added. [...] So after
30 years I'm still working on the
aspect of redefinition of sculpture but
in an extremely personal way. What I like
is trying to find a sympathetic ear or
eye more than trying to reach a broad
audience. [...] So the process of making
a sculpture includes the thinking and
acting on the viewer's
part in order to complete
the piece.

Terry Fox, *1999*

The documentation brings together previously unpublished archival documents from the estate of Terry Fox, Cologne, the Berkeley Art Museum and Pacific Film Archive (BAM/PFA), the de Saisset Museum at Santa Clara University, the archives of the Akademie der Künste, Berlin, the Wulf-Herzogenrath-Archiv, as well as statements and interviews written especially for this publication by artist friends and contemporaries of Terry Fox, who I was able to consult in the USA. They have been enhanced by texts from art magazines, such as *Avalanche, Arts Magazine* and *View.*

Angela Lammert

Documents Statements

Eight times I saw the repetition of a single rock, which cast two shadows on the ground; I twice saw the same animal head holding its own likeness in its jaws and devouring it; I saw, dominating the village a sort of huge phallic tooth with three stones at its summit and four holes on its outer face; and I saw, according to their principle, all these forms pass little by little into reality.

Terry Fox, *A.A.*, 1971–72, art book

Eva Schmidt
About Artists' Statements

What happened in detail? How does this relate to that? What were the reasons for this or that? The artist responds by explaining what happened, with all information provided initially being of the same order: the ways he handles his materials, the structural sequence of its presentation, anecdotes on the side, audience reactions, existential experiences, views on art and performance in general. This lack of hierarchy in one's perspective is something only an artist can afford. All reviews and interpretations that follow destroy this parity of values, distilling form and structure from it. Related to the artist's narrative in the interviews is a series of brief commentaries. These two types of discourse, where the narrator is explicitly present, make up most of this book.

One reason that the artist's narrative and commentary are so important is due to the well-known fact that performance does not easily lend itself to a museum-like setting. It happens once, and the memory of it – in addition to being recorded by photography or video – can be entered into the archive which will become increasingly important in the part of the museum specializing in art forms developed since the 1960s.

In this book narrative is accompanied by writing: the speaker has withdrawn from what has been written. The riddle, the condensed, manifest-like statement are plan and poetry. Of particular note here is the extensive text *Blood Line*, which describes an undirected process of perception which foregoes conventional syntax and punctuation. It is not clear who is speaking and from what perspective, there seems to be no subject at all. The text tends to list items one after another, accepting their lack of context. It is like a number of works based on the exploration of concepts, signs and pictograms. The series *Catch Phrases*, which Fox describes in this book, is another example for this: text material is further processed in drawings, installations and sculptural forms. Individual letters lose their conventional arrangement on the book's page. The left-right orientation and the linearity of lines set one below each other are abandoned in favor of a labyrinth complexity. This largely three-dimensional use of letters and text can only be suggested here and is discussed in several interviews.

Source: Eva Schmidt (ed.), *Terry Fox. Ocular Language. 30 Jahre Reden und Schreiben über Kunst. 30 Years of Speaking and Writing about Art.* Gesellschaft für Aktuelle Kunst Bremen, Cologne, 2000, pp. vi–vii, hereafter Schmidt 2000

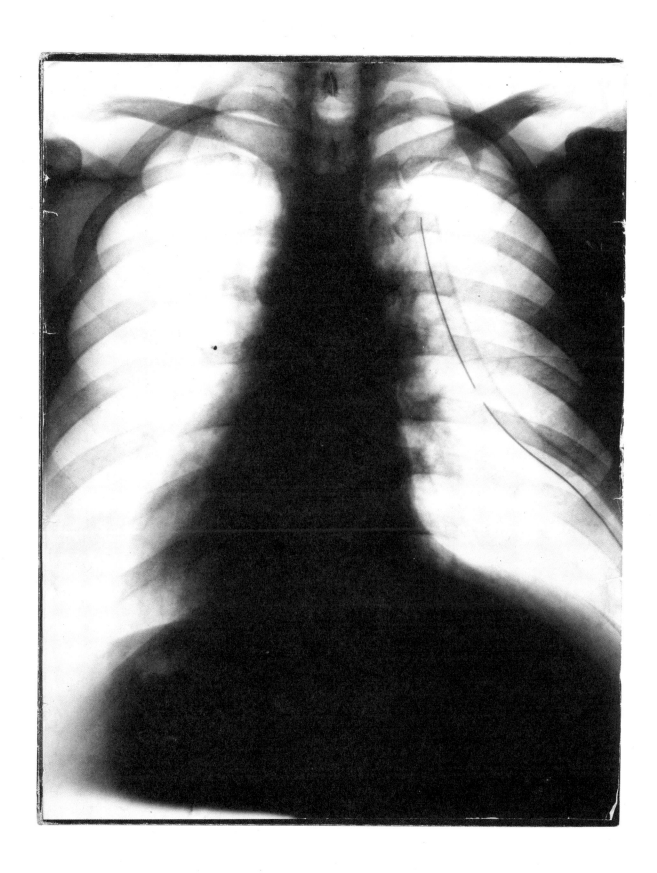

Terry Fox, *A.A.*, 1971–72, art book

Elemental Gestures: Terry Fox

I held a nine-by-twelve-foot polyethylene sheet out to the wind. When it started billowing I released it into the air. It moved vertically down the beach like a flame.

This was my first political work. I wanted to destroy the flowers in a very calculating way. By burning a perfect rectangle right in the middle, it would look as though someone had destroyed them on purpose. The flowers were Chinese jasmin planted five years ago which were to bloom in two years. It was also a theatrical piece. Everyone likes to watch fires. It was making a beautiful roaring sound. But at a certain point people realized what was going on—the landscape was being violated; flowers were being burnt. Suddenly everyone was quiet. One woman cried for twenty minutes.

I attached a polyethylene sheet to a freely rotating pivot so that the material responded to changes in the wind direction. The sheet swung in a 360° arc. These photographs show segments from one complete turn in front of a stationary camera.

The photo captions are quotes from an interview with the artist.

Photographs Courtesy of Museum of Conceptual Art, San Francisco.

246

Terry Fox, *Free Flying Polyethylene Sheet, Golden Gate Park Beach, August 1969.*

Terry Fox, *Defoliation Piece, University Art Museum, Berkeley, March 1970.*

Terry Fox, *Air Pivot, Pine Street, San Francisco, June 1969.*

otographs by BARRY KLINGER

by WILLOUGHBY SHARP

Several days before the March 16th opening of **The Eighties** exhibition at the University Art Museum in Berkeley, Terry Fox poured a small amount of gunpowder into a glass ashtray at the Mediterranian Café on Telegraph Avenue and lit it. The explosion which gave him a third-degree burn on his right hand could almost have been one of his works, whose use of violent physical and chemical changes often involves a significant element of danger. Fortunately, this accident did not prevent Fox from executing **Defoliation Piece,** a large rectangular burn-off of a bed of rare Chinese jasmin directly in front of the museum. After seeing the exhibit three times, I thought this sculptural project was the most prophetic statement in a pioneering exhibition containing new work by many of the major Bay Area artists. The inspiration for much of Fox's work stems from direct perception and a heightened awareness of ordinary events. His interest in working with water originated from a specific incident in March 1968. One overcast day, while walking up a hilly street in the Algerian section of Paris, a stream of water ran past him "like a slowly flowing liquid mirror." This experience stimulated a series of sculptural experiments with water, both in indoor and outdoor situations. The early water works included a box filled with crude black oil and water, warmed by a heating coil and thus made to interchange invisibly; a wooden plank with five water-filled concave hollows in which ripples were created by a small oscillating fan; deep tractor tracks filled with water; and two plastic sheets sprinkled with tiny droplets which exploited the reflective powers of water. These works, as well as those involving air currents illustrated on this page, display an overriding concern with the dynamics of natural processes and with elemental energy in a primitive state.

Fox's expressed attitude to objects is quite unambiguous: "All my life I've regarded objects with fear . . . but everything, a cigarette, a rock, has always been beautiful to me if I just look at it." This belief may partly account for Fox's often unorthodox selection of artistic materials. Another factor cited by Fox is the decisive role

49

played in his career by his active participation in the May 1968 Paris revolution. He draws a close aesthetic parallel between the swaying cobblestone structures he had once built and his throwing of cobblestones at the the French police: both were seen as kinetic systems, but in the latter the artist himself provided the motive force. As a result of this revelation, Fox's work shed its last traces of studio sculpture and approximated more closely real life events. His first sculptural act upon returning to America was to open fire hydrants in New York and San Francisco streets. This work foreshadowed his Public Theater, including an event on Fillmore and McAllister Street—a particularly hazardous intersection to which people were invited to gather—and **What Do Blind Men Dream?** The most recent works have moved from the theatricality of street events, in which aspects of social existence are presented, to art initiated by a human gesture. **Liquid Smoke** and **Impacted Lead** involve simple physical acts: throwing and pulling, which result in physical changes: a liquid becomes gaseous; a solid becomes fragmented. In both these works, Fox sees the aesthetic experience as occuring **after** he has performed an elemental gesture But in another respect the theatricality of the work remains since the artist is an agent, although he tries "to impose as little of his own will as possible" on the situation.

Fox's basic concern is with the interaction of matter and energy in different forms; he has little interest in exploring formal problems, and his choice of artistic media—fluid, amorphous, or non-material—precludes a tight control over the final configuration of his pieces: "I am only conscious of how the piece looks when I see the photographs." Fox works in close collaboration with a friend, the photographer Barry Klinger; the series of photographs reproduced here (none of which is complete) form unique works in their own right. The photograph no longer merely serves the utilitarian function of providing factual information, although it does provide aesthetic information. It is not a "souvenir" of the work; in several important ways, these photographs act as surrogate sculpture.

4. Terry Fox, *Liquid Smoke*, Third Street, San Francisco, April 1970.

5. Terry Fox, *A Sketch for Impacted Lead*, San Francisco, April 1970.

6. Terry Fox, *What Do Blind Men Dream?* 20001 Union Street, San Francisco, April 1969.

7. Terry Fox, *Push Piece*, Minna Street, San Francisco, April 1970.

throwing liquid smoke against the wall was really an anarchistic gesture, like throwing a Molotov cocktail. But it wasn't really that at all. As soon as the glass vial exploded

on the cement, it became an aesthetic event. Exposed to the air, the liquid began to smoke until it had completely evaporated. It was so extraordinary and so unrelated to any

previous ideas you had about that material that it became art. You would never think of a cement wall smoking, and to see it happening was stunning.

wanted to do a work with lead using physical forces, and I thought of bullets. When a bullet is fired through the barrel of a rifle, it spins at an incredible rate, moving

forward faster than the speed of sound. On impact, the lead changes its shape, just from the pure force of that energy. Hopefully the way I'm going to execute this piece at the

Reese Palley Gallery is to fire the bullets close together in a straight horizontal line. Then they might form a small, fragile bar of lead.

is was the second in a series of Public Theater ents. I discovered a beautiful blind lady d asked her to sing on a San Francisco eet corner near a gigantic open pit, from

5:30 p.m. until dark. Announcements were sent out and a lot of people came. We made a recording of the work that I still have.

hen we were moving Tom out of his studio, oticed a brick wall in an alley. I went over d started feeling it. Then I started pushing.

When I did that, I realized what that wall was, what material strength it had. I don't think I could say what that meant to me right now.

51

Video Interview with Jeanette Willison

TERRY FOX

Well, I was a painter for about 10 years and I was dissatisfied with painting, because it was impossible to get people to look at my paintings and I never got any feedback and I couldn't put ... I really couldn't express myself very well in painting. And I started out to be a painter just because that was ..., to be an artist you were a painter or a sculptor.

JEANETTE WILLISON

There was sort of a stereotype idea at that point. What kind of painting?

T.F.   Well, I did figurative painting, and then just before I stopped painting, which was in '67 ..., the last year I was doing paintings that were all black, painted on glass. That had really highly, ... like shiny, reflective surfaces that you had to get up really close, like ... the viewer had to get down on their hands and knees and go up to them and follow all the little lines. Otherwise it was just a mirror and stuff. But those paintings, the idea behind them was really to engage the viewer and trying to get them to spend some time with my work.
And I started doing work with real kinds of ephemeral materials and stuff, things with fire and with sheets of plastic, and bowls of water, like shallow ditches dug with water in them that reflected clouds and things like that.

J.W.   So, it was not a lasting art that you were doing, it was for the feeling of the moment?

T.F.   I was trying to figure out a way to make my art much more direct, like on a much more direct, one-to-one basis with people. You know like ..., the final resolution was to do performances. I started doing performances in 1970. That solved sort of the same dilemma I had with my paintings. If I did a performance it was an hour-long or three hours-long, or something. I had the people there, right then and they experienced, they experienced what I was putting out. I could put everything out right then to them. Rather than presenting an object for their contemplation which they're not gonna give it, they're usually not gonna contemplate it. What the people are putting out goes together with what I am putting out to make the whole performance. Together with the objects and all the other aspects of it.

Like performance art enables you to make your art anywhere: like in the street or in somebody's house, or like Bluxome Street, or a gallery or anyplace. You don't need any money to do it. You don't need any materials. You could do a piece with nothing.
The reason I do performances is to put out as much energy as I can, almost to save it up and put it out in an hour or two, and try and communicate that energy. All the physical aspects of what's going on, the candle and the sound and everything are like tools. In other performances, other objects, they are all like tools that help put this energy out and get it going. Like in performance, there are a lot of objects and lots of objects are created during performance. But usually those objects have had an incredible amount of concentration put on them and they reflect that.

[Film clip: *Children's Tapes*, 1974]
[Interview continues:]

T.F.   It's like people go to art school and learn how to make art objects and they get a degree that says they are a master at making those objects and they're taught to make those objects up to a point where it looks right and they can graduate and everything. I'm not saying everybody, but so many people just go on making those things, thinking that's art or something, that that's art. That if they make something that looks like art, that is art.
Or the same way like the public thinks, the general public thinks that ..., if they own a painting, they own a work of art. Or that painting is the art. The artist is the person who makes the art, but it isn't that way at all. I mean, the art is what's communicated by the painting, not the painting itself. Performance just sort of skips that, that commodity section of the communication there. And just does it directly. Like performance art, I mean nobody expects, who does performances, to reach a whole of a lot of people. Performance art is just done for the people who are there. Sometimes it's only two people.

[ends without sound, breaks off]

1975

Source: Private Collection

① THE EASEL: THE "LEGS" SHOULD HAVE THE NAILED SIDE FACING IN TOWARDS THE WALL. THE TWO BLACKBOARDS SHOULD BE SEPERATED FROM EACH OTHER BY A THUMBS WIDTH. THEY SHOULD BE BOLTED TO THE LEGS WITH ONE BOLT LIKE IN THE DRAWING. THE BOLTS SHOULD BE AS SMALL AS POSSIBLE BUT STRONG ENOUGH TO SUPPORT THE BOARDS. THE LEGS SHOULD LEAN IN AS INDICATED IN THE DRAWING. THE BLACKBOARD SHOULD BE BOLTED DIRECTLY TO THE LEGS. THE WHOLE THING SHOULD BE LEANED AGAINST THE WALL (IN THE CENTER OF THE CLEAN WALL) AND PROPPED AS VERTICALLY AS IS SAFE.

② THE FREE STANDING CHALKBOARD AND THE BREADED POLE SHOULD BE LEANED AGAINST THE WALL OPPOSITE THE EASEL, LIKE IN THE DRAWING.

③ YOU SHOULD HAVE AN EXTENSION CORD (THE ROUND BLACK KIND) CAPABLE OF ACCOMADATING BOTH RECORDERS AT ONE END AND STREACHING ACCROSS THE FLOOR TO THE STREACHER. (25')?

④ STREACHER PROPPED AS SHOWN

⑤ DRAWINGS HUNG AS SHOWN

⑥ THE LIGHT FIXTURES SHOULD BE MADE AS UNOBTRUSIVE AS POSSIBLE / REMOVE THE BLACK SHIELDS, USE THE SMALL FIXTURES AND PAINT WHITE WHERE NEEDED.

⑦ DONT MOP THE FLOOR (AT LEAST IT SHOULDN'T SHINE)

THESE THINGS WILL ALL BE RE-ADJUSTED WHEN I GET THERE BUT ITS GOING TO TAKE A GOOD COUPLE OF DAYS SO IF YOU COULD HAVE THE ABOVE THINGS ALL SET UP BY THE 20ᵗʰ THAT WOULD BE GREAT.

(diagram of easel with labels: BOLT, THUMBS WIDTH, 3½', 1', 6', 4½')

Dear Willoughby,

Just a short note to keep in touch. Im working towards a show here at the new Palley Gallery which will then go to New York and then I think to Paris. It involves a lot of props that I have been making for performances as well as some new objects to be acted upon and some tapes, magnetic cartridge tape loops and of course some performances with all this material. It will be a "substantial" show for me and its interesting because Ive never done anything like this before.

I got a nice letter from Beuys, he sounds quite bogged down in political consideration in regards to the Academy and seemed a little worried. He says he will have over 400 students this semester and they want some radical changed in the schools structure which he supports naturally.

I also got a letter from Gunter Brus who would like to do something together in Berlin, so I will do that when I go to Europe. He is the most interesting of that group for me.

I just got out of a 3 week hospital stay and am all fired and inspired and in a great creative state. Ill be sending you some new photos that may interest you in a couple of weeks. My brother Larry is doing all of my photos now

well lots of love and good feelings to you and Liza
I miss you both,
Love,

Terry Fox

Terry Fox, *Hospital*, exhibition at Reese Palley Gallery, San Francisco, 1971: Note for Barney Bailey (top),
Letter to Willoughby Sharp (bottom), source: Estate of Terry Fox, Cologne

Terry Fox

"...I wanted to hav

What have you been working on since they closed your show at the Richmond Art Center last month?

I've just taken studio space in the Reese Palley warehouse and I've been there almost every day trying out some of the elements I'm going to use in my Düsseldorf piece—flares, chalk, fire. Someone from U.C. Hospital told me about microwave transmitters and I now have access to one. If you hold a live wire connected to it in one hand, and a light bulb in the other, the light bulb will light up: your body conducts the electrical current. At first I was going to do that in Düsseldorf, but I decided it was too literal. I don't want to be merely a transmitter of energy. I want to transform it. Now I'm thinking of blowing a flame out of my mouth and lighting something with it. . . .

Blowing alcohol out of your mouth and lighting it.

Yes. But I want to have a chain of elements linked together. I'd touch something, say a rock, and light another object with the flame from my mouth. In that way I would be acted upon by one element while I was affecting another.

You prepare a piece for quite a long time before you do it, don't you. When will you do this one?

In late November. At the moment I'm not rehearsing a specific performance, I'm exploring ways of combining elements, discovering their potential.

How does your body function in that kind of heterogeneous situation?

The body is exactly one element among others, one of the links in the chain.

So you reduce it to the status of the other elements.

No. I raise the other elements to the status of the body.

That's an important distinction. People won't fully understand the piece unless they watch you perform in it, or see a videotape of it.

Right. Photographs are inadequate, but a videotape would show you what happened. In a sense this work has a limited audience—like earthworks. Very few people have access to the physical sites of earthworks. In the same way, people can't have a direct experience of my work unless they witness the performance.

It seems that in some cases there has been a fairly direct transition from earth art to body works: Oppenheim has said that as he worked alone on the land, he gradually became more involved with his own body, to the point where the environment canceled itself out.

My concern for the body has grown out of real experiences too. So many operations have been performed on me, I've been the object of action so many times that I became material. I was a piece of meat that people were acting upon. That's what you are.

How many times have you been cut open? Only twice, but I've had a lot of tests. There's one test that I've had frequently where I lie motionless on a table for about six hours, with tubes inserted into my feet. Two giant injectors pump a blue fluid into my lymph system for about an hour. It's an Xray test called a lymphangiogram. After the dye has spread they remove the tubes. Then they pass an Xray television camera up and down your body. You lie there and watch the Xray of your whole body in action on the monitor. Every time the camera reached my neck I'd swallow hard and watch the saliva move down my throat. My entire existence was reduced to normal bodily functions.

Seeing your body in that way must have been strange.

It was. I was outside myself, looking at my hulk. My mind was working well and my eyes watching the monitor were completely separate from the body lying motionless.

Do you have a new sense of time, o your own impermanence as a result of these experiences?

I'm more aware of it, more lucid than I was before. It makes you feel whole. I feel like being conscious of where I am, not crashing through a room just using things right and left.

You became less inclined to impose your will on other physical objects in the environment?

Yeah, to impose my will, but not in the empty-headed way people ususally do. They walk into a room, sit down, and are just the same as they were in a different room. My performances now, and my involvement with the body in art comes from this awareness of particular places. That's what they are about, rather than my relationship to a large-scale environmental situation or to sociological or political questions.

What did you show at Richmond?

I made one piece. I wanted to creat a space that was conducive to levitation. The first thing I did was to cover the sixty by thirt foot floor with white paper and to tape white paper on the walls. The floor had been dark, but it became such a brilliant white that if you were at one end of it, it glared, it hurt your eyes to look at someone standing at the other end. It was such a buoyant space that anyone it was already walking on air. Then I laid dowr a ton and a half of dirt, taken from under a freeway on Army Street, in an eleven and a ha foot square. The mold was made with four redwood planks each twice my body height—I used my body as a unit of measure for most of the elements in the piece. The dirt was taken from the freeway because of the idea of explosion. When the freeway was built, the earth was compressed, held down. You can conceive of it expanding when you release it rising, becoming buoyant. Of course, it's

70

y mood affect their looks."

hysically impossible. But for me the mere
iggestion was enough. I was trying to rise too.
fasted to empty myself.

How long for?
Just a
ay. I drew a circle in the middle of the dirt
ith my own blood. Its diameter was my
eight. According to the medieval notion, that
reates a magic space. Then I lay on my back in
e middle of the circle, holding four clear
olyethylene tubes filled with blood, urine,
ilk, and water. They represented the
emental fluids that I was expelling from my
ody. I lay there for six hours with the tubes in
y hand trying to levitate. The doors were
cked. Nobody saw me. I didn't move a
uscle. I didn't close my eyes. I tried not to
ange my focal point.

What were you staring
?

Nothing. I was trying to think about leaving
e ground, until I realized I should be thinking
out entering the air. For me that changed
erything, made it work. I mean, I levitated.
fter the fourth hour I couldn't feel any part
my body, not even my chest expanding and
ntracting. My legs and arms were probably
leep. I felt I was somewhere else. I'd gone, I'd
ft my body. Then something weird happened.
fly started buzzing around, and I thought I
as the fly. That hallucination didn't last very
ng, but the feeling of being out of my body
ersisted for about two hours.

The spectators
me into the room after you had finished the
ece. How could they understand what took
ace?

There was an imprint of my body in the
rth. And Tom Marioni wrote a two page
scription. For the spectators this was
finitely my strongest piece, because everyone
10 saw it felt something. I hadn't expected
at at all. At the opening there were never
ore than six people in the space at a time: I
ink they sensed the energy in there.
storically the remains of that piece can be
compared to Yves Klein's white room. A void.
You read the notice before you entered, so you
knew that a person had lain there for six hours
trying to levitate. Then you walked into this
brilliant, serial space, which emphasised the
physicality of the earth, the blood, the urine.
Most of the audience didn't even go in, they
walked around and stood on the outskirts. It
was terrifying and depressing. I consider that
my strongest piece of sculpture because the
whole room was energized. You didn't have to
trip over the piece, you felt it the minute you
walked in.

Who decided to close the
exhibition?

The head of the Department of
Recreation. There were comments throughout
the installation. The janitor would come in and
say, boy, you've done it this time. During the
performance I asked Tom to lock the doors
from the outside—he had the only key—and not
to disturb me on any account. I'd been there
about five minutes when Salvato said there was
a health hazard in the bathroom (the lightbulb
was out) and forced Tom to go in to get a
ladder. Just hassle. Salvato saw the piece a few
days later. He claims the aroma from the earth
was so powerful you couldn't . . . Anyway, he
made the health inspector, the fire chief, and
the police chief come to see if they could find a
reason for closing the show. They all came at
once. The health inspector said, well, there's no
way of determining the dirt didn't come from a
sewer. The fire chief gave a really brilliant
demonstration. He ripped a section of the paper
from the floor, held it up in front of the others
and lit it. So that made it highly flammable. I
guess that was the final reason for closing the
show: it was a fire hazard.

It's something of a
scandal.

Oh yeah, sure. The show was taken
down because it posed a threat. If that was art,
then their structure was going to start falling
apart piece by piece. I didn't think of it in that
way, but Larry Bell brought his class to the

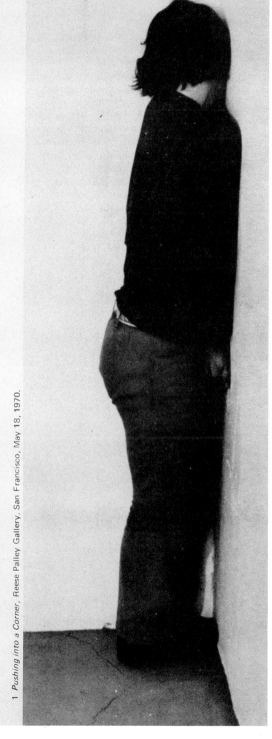

1 *Pushing into a Corner*, Reese Palley Gallery, San Francisco, May 18, 1970.

show and that's how he explained it. Those elements were just too shabby to be accepted as art—that's why the show was closed. Which makes it pure censorship. Have you planned what you'll do in Paris?

Not specifically, but I know what I'm going to work with—fish. I even have the title of the piece—*Soluble Fish*. I read it at Tom's place in the introduction to a biography of Henry Miller. He was listing the things that were "in the air" in Paris in the Twenties, like Josephine Baker, the dancer. It all made sense except one sentence: "*Soluble Fish* was the talk of Paris." That sentence leapt out. It was completely absurd. There was no explanation for it at all. *Soluble Fish* was in

2 & 3 *Opening my hand as slowly as possible,* Reese Palley, San Francisco, May 18, 1970.

quotes. I wanted to do a piece with fish anyway, so I decided to call it that. Why did you choose the Pont Neuf?

Because I want to do it on the river and I really like the Pont Neuf—that's where the clochards sleep. Clochards are doing theatre all the time, and their kind of theatre is what I want to do there. You mean, get close to their life style.

Yes . . . only with fish. I'm going to use a lot of fish and put something in a few of them to make them expand. Howard Fried suggested milk. I'm also working on the word *soluble*—I'm sure it doesn't mean what it says in the dictionary. A girl at the City of Paris department store translated it into French for me without batting an eyelid. It's probably a food dish. Once,

Marsha and I went to a free fish dinner for thousand people in a big hangar at Les Ha Anyone could go, even the clochards. It w jammed, you couldn't move. People were passing plates of fish over your head, and whole floor was about two inches deep in Everybody was dropping fish down their throats and sliding on the floor. It was unbelievable. Are you going to use live or fish under the Pont Neuf?

I'd like to have I thought about trying to catch the fish m I'd use it to represent the life style of the clochards who sleep down there. I mean, are similar. They're both cold and wet. A eye is always open, staring. They are the strangest creatures. They are extreme case isolated kind of existence—a creature that

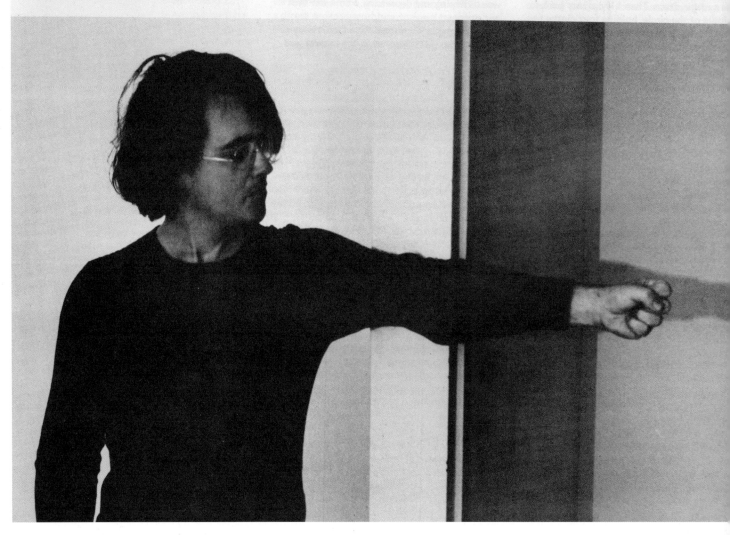

nly into its own environment. It's absurd to
tch a fish and put him in the market. A
eature like that, in the market! Beautiful
olors and scales, cold, can't breathe in the air.
hat's why I presented the Billingsgate Market
London as a *Public Theatre*.

Oh, how did you
that?

I made a poster, Billingsgate Market
a public theatre, with a date and time. It was
e market's most crowded day, Saturday, at
on. I had it put up on the walls all over
ondon.

Did people go to look at it?

I don't
ow, I was here. Marsha went.

What about
me of the other early pieces?

In 1966 I was

making black mirror paintings. They were done
on three foot square sheets of clear glass,
sprayed on one side with a solid coat of black
paint which produced a mirror on the other.
Fine marks or words were etched into the black
paint. They were meant to be shown propped
against the wall, with the shiny side out. The
scratches were almost invisible, so when you
saw the piece, you thought you understood it
but in fact you didn't. I was trying to get the
spectator involved in the work. One way of
doing this was by giving him his reflection,
which would automatically interest him,
enough so that he would give it a little more
attention than usual. But in order to see the
scratches—some were colored with a fine blue
spray—you had to get down on your hands and
knees and really scrutinize the surface. You
might detect a line or two, but it would

disappear if you changed your field of focus
even slightly. If you put your eye very close to
it and got the right lighting, you could follow
the line all over the surface. The minute you
stepped back you couldn't see it. Those
paintings were never exhibited.

What was your
very first piece of sculpture?

The first sculpture
I ever did was *Dust Exchange* with William
Wiley in 1967. I made nine or ten transfers
while I was in Europe. Once I exchanged dust
from a shelf in the American Express paperback
library with dust on an Egyptian tomb in the
Louvre. Another time I sent a big piece of dust
from a friend's barge to Wiley in New Jersey,
and replaced it with dust he sent me from a
girl's studio. Then I shipped Wiley a package of
dust from a Paris metro, and put Wiley's dust in

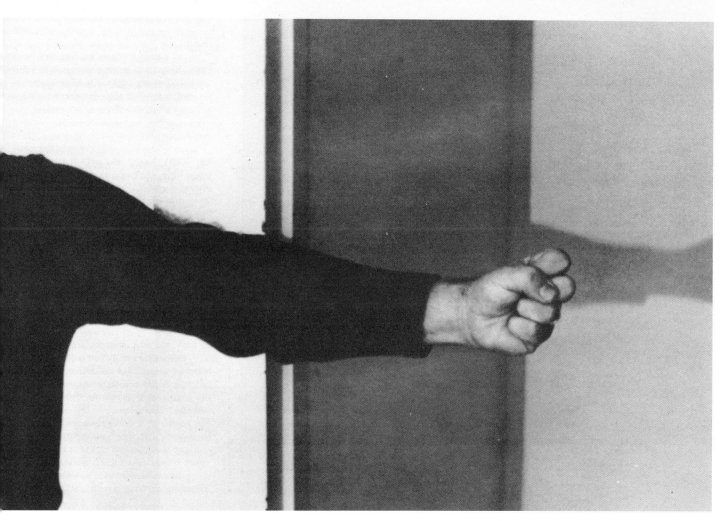

WILLOUGHBY SHARP   People won't fully understand the piece unless they watch you perform in it, or see a videotape of it.

TERRY FOX   Right. Photographs are inadequate, but a videotape would show you what happened. In a sense this work has a limited audience – like earthworks. Very few people have access to the physical sites of earthworks. In the same way, people can't have a direct experience of my work unless they witness the performance.

1971

Source: "...I Wanted to Have My Mood Affect Their Looks. Interview by Willoughby Sharp," *Avalanche*, New York, Winter 1971, pp. 70–81, reprinted in Schmidt 2000, p. 11

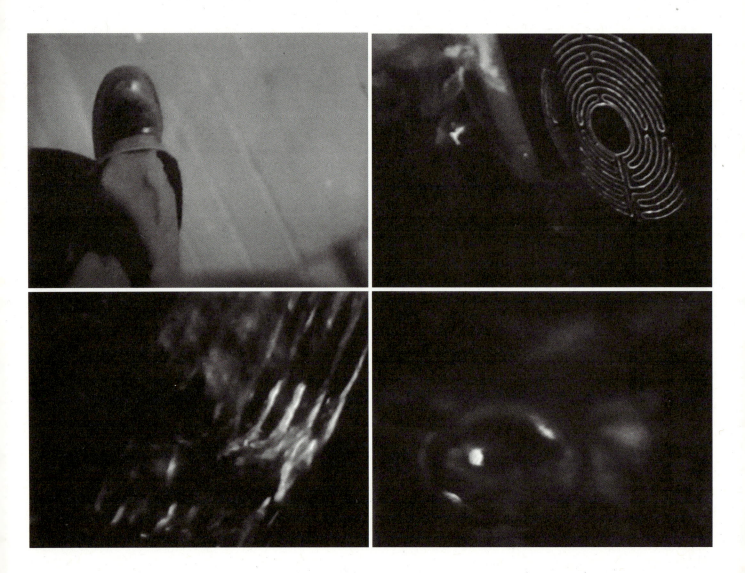

Dear Lydia: Paris Sept 19

Sorry not to have written - but I've been very busy what
with all and am a lousy letter writer anyhow. Kassel was a
horrible experience - FUCK THE GERMANS! (all except Beuys
and one or two others - When I got there I did a four day
performance and when we got ready to leave they refused to
give me so much as a penny of the final $800 owed to me -
so finally Beuys offered me the money and now they owe
the $800 to him and this way he will be able to collect.
    Now we are back in Paris where I will open the season for
Sonnabend on the 26 September. Then I get to open another
season for the modern art agency in Naples where Beuys,
Merz, George + Gilbert, etc. show - Both are real honors and
I feel great about it.
    This is supposed to be a sort of business letter - We
have very little money here - we cook ourselves on a camping
stove, etc, and live on the welfare checks from San
Francisco - well I don't want to do a sob story.
    I made a tape in Rotterdam that is the best thing
I've ever done - It's a 25 minute, one inch, Sony
system color tape. The color is totally unbelievable, like
one long, continuous color slide - except the color is
perfect - I used all whites - white flour, white candle,
white enamel bowl, smoke, flame, hands + face are
the only other tones - but it is gorgeous!! It is a fixed
pretty close camera position like this:

white flour
black rim
water
white black smoke

    It begins with the scene set up
the way I drew it here except the
candle is not lit. A spoken
text in flemish ~~the wa~~
"The fire in the water, the water is
the air, the air in the earth and the earth in the sea" then
my hand comes in, lights the candle, then ~~fills the bowl~~ I smoke
a cigarette and fill the bowl with smoke like fog on the water, then
wash my hands and fill the bowl with lather, then smoke, then
take the flour, dip it in the water and make a paste ridge around
the bowl, erasing the black rim, then smoke on the candle.
The the scene looks exactly like some sort of far out

Terry Fox
Yield, University Art Museum, 1973

I am sending 8 photographs from my latest work, at the University Art Museum, Berkeley. This was a two-month exhibition (September 4–October 21) that involved two rooms. I enclose a drawing of the floor plan of this space, with my actions indicated. This exhibition and the actions were based on my investigations into the labyrinth at Chartres. I made a model of the large space in my studio and photographed small objects in it through a magnifying glass, including an eyetooth and an apple, a plaster model of the labyrinth at Chartres, a tube of bread and a vial of blood. These photographs were blown up to 2 by 3 feet and 22 of them were placed close together completely around the smaller room (B). A blackboard with a drawing of the curtain in the larger room was placed on its back in the small room and the objects used in the photographs were on this blackboard (A) corresponding to the actions to follow in the large room. This is the first room the visitor saw and served to slow him down and place his emotional state and critical facilities at the service of the larger room, in that the actions to occur there were very slow and trancelike and analogous to the labyrinth. The visitor left this room and walked through four 50-foot tubes of blood, urine, milk and water (C) to the large room. Here I had constructed a 12-foot high curtain out of translucent muslin (D); this curtain was 40-feet long and completely covered this room, which had a solid wall of windows (G). The curtain was in the shape of a body and had a cul-de-sac at one end and a passage, through glass doors (E), to the balcony outside (F) where the viewer could watch the action in the sealed space (H) which he could not enter. It was in this hermetically sealed space that I made my actions together with my twin brother, Larry Fox, who photographed everything.

The action took 3 days: 4 hours the first, 2 hours the second and 3 hours the final day. They were continuous and each action began where the previous one left off. The first was done in the daytime and the next two were done at sunset into darkness with the aid of a spotlight.

On the first day I created a ribcage of lines of flour laid on the floor and then a trough made with my fingers, then I filled this trough with water transferred from a metal bowl through my mouth, drop by drop. This method was used to make all paste lines. Then the excess flour was blown away.

The second day I made a line (vertebrae) from the ribcage to the pelvis. Here I had an 8-foot square mirror on the floor. I made the pelvis by laying flour on the mirror, which reflected this image on the curtain. I added a mirrored bowl for the socket of the pelvis and blew smoke in it.

The third day I made a line out from the sternum to the metal bowl (1) which contained dried flour, and blew smoke. I continued this line to the mirrored bowl, which had formed a penicillin mold, and blew smoke. I continued this line to the enamel bowl at the window. Here I made a loaf of bread and laid a spoon against the bowl. I caused the bread to rise by holding a heating bowl above it. The bread rose and caused the spoon to rise.

1973

Source: http://www.artperformance.org/article-yield-terry-fox-1973-115448140.html

Terry Fox, *Yield*, University Art Museum, Berkeley, 1973, photo: Larry Fox

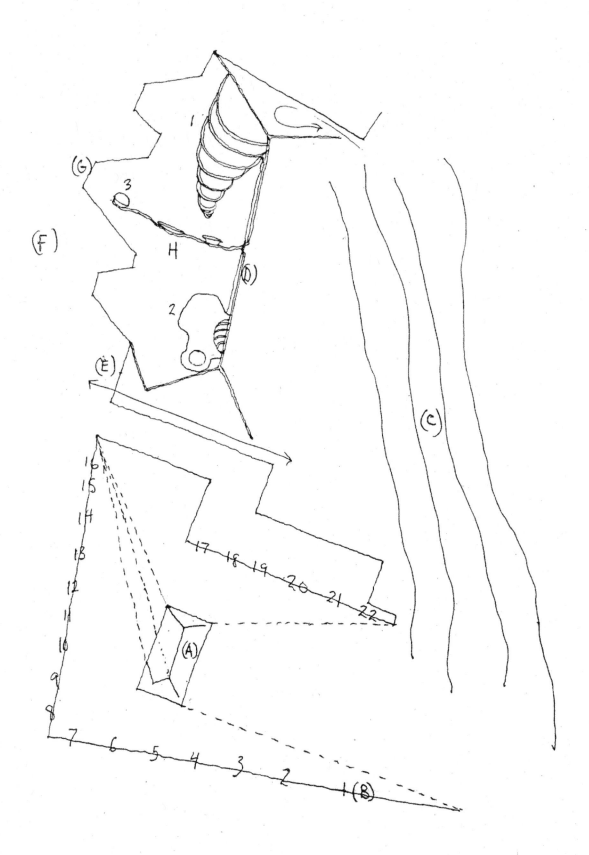

　　　Terry Fox, *Yield*, installation scene for the exhibition, University Art Museum, Berkeley, 1973, source: see p. 258

On June 1st, 1973, I filled a one liter glass bottle with
blood. The cork was well driven in and the neck and cork sealed
with many layers of friction tape. At the same time I partially
filled an eight foot iron pipe with blood, having carved wooden
plugs for each end. These plugs were driven into the pipe and
then sealed with duct tape. Since my intention had been to make
an object with a movable center of balance, the pipe was not
quite filled so that blood would rush from one end to the other
when the pipe was tilted or suspended by the middle.

On June 7th I suspended the pipe from the ceiling of my
studio with cord so that it hung horizontally five feet from
the floor. This was done by tying the cord at two points on the
pipe in an inverted Y and fastening the other end to the rafters.
The pipe was given to slowly twirling around and around, twisting
and untwisting the cord.

On June 9th Dorothy and I came home late at night after having
been away since morning. The odor coming from the studio as we
climbed the stairs was putrid and almost overwhelming. One end of
the pipe had begun to leak and as it twirled it dripped and formed
a perfect circle, eight feet in diameter, of caked, dry blood. I
sealed the leaking end of the pipe with over half a roll of
friction tape and stored the pipe on the studio floor.

On July 3rd, I discovered a pool of blood six inches across
had formed beneath the offending end of the pipe. This time I
used an entire roll of white adhesive tape to repair the leak, but
after a few minutes the blood began to ooze once more. I added
some layers of duct tape and it stopped the leak. I then took
the bottle of blood out on the roof in order to open it and fill
a small glass vial with blood. I was working the cork out of the
bottle when it shot out of my hand like a champagne cork and the
bottle became filled with an acrid yellow smoke, thick and dense.
It was nauseating but eventually passed out of the bottle and I
filled the vial and resealed the bottle.

On July 4th we awoke to find another horrendous pool of blood
under the pipe. This time Dorothy completely sealed the leak in
plaster medical bandage, many many layers thick.

In September the iron pipe was sewn into the bottom hem of a
curtain constructed for my show at the Berkeley Museum. The
bottle of blood was placed behind the curtain in a private area.
When the fire inspectors came the next morning to examine the
curtain, they lifted the hem and knocked over the bottle of blood
which exploded as it hit the concrete floor splattering blood
over a large area of the curtain and floor inside. The entire
Museum was filled with the smell of blood.

At the conclusion of the exhibition the pipe was removed from
the hem and it was found that it had been leaking, staining th e
curtain. Since It had apparently stopped leaking I brought the
pipe home and placed it on my studio roof. Since I took it back
indooors in September 1975 it has not leaked and the blood still
flows within it even though no anti-coagulent was ever added.

TERRY FOX . . . .

CANDLE CHASES WATER DOWN THE BOWL

CLOTH DRAWS WATER TO THE SPOON

FLY CAUGHT BY THE BOWL   **CLOTH DRAWS WATER TO THE TABLE**

FACE IN THE BOWL

FORKED CANDLE OVER THE BOWL

Terry Fox's *Children's Videotapes* were shown for the first time at the Everson Museum, Syracuse, from May 25 to June 25, and he spent a few weeks in New York after the opening. Willoughby Sharp and Liza Bear talked to him on May 29 and June 5.

LB: How did you get into making videotapes for children?

TF: Well, what happened was that I had been doing things and showing them to my son Foxy, and he really got into them, he liked watching them and he liked doing them. . . .

LB: What kinds of things?

TF: I was setting up situations, using the same objects over and over, a candle, a fork, a spoon, and a bowl of water and a piece of cloth. Like putting the candle in water and then putting the bottle over it: the candle devours all the oxygen and draws the water up and the flame goes out. And trying to light the candle again when it's wet . . . I did them late at night by myself a lot, inventing new situations with the same objects. And after a few months I'd done so many that I thought it would be a good idea to make a program for children out of them. I'd been wanting to make tapes for children for a couple of years, because I'd thought about Foxy and what his input is. I borrowed a Sony Port-a-Pak and did them all in a week and a half.

WS: How old is Foxy?

TF: Five. He goes to kindergarten and his input is just rotten, as far as TV goes. We don't have a TV but he stays with me three days a week and sometimes he can con the girl downstairs out of her TV.

WS: Oh, he'll go down and ask?

TF: (laughs) Yeah. He loves to watch it. But it's horrifying. Everything he watches is bad for him.

WS: How does it corrupt his vision?

TF: Well, it homogenizes him. It takes away his ability to have an actual dialogue with something rather than having passive responses. Although he can talk real well, as well as I can, his drawings tell me a lot more. You can see exactly what his mood is, what he's feeling. But even those are starting to get stylized and he's only in kindergarten.

WS: So did you make the tapes for him, in a sense?

TF: Yeah, for him and his class. There's video equipment everywhere now, every school or poverty group has it, even Foxy's kindergarten. But nobody does anything for children. Everybody does something for money. And it's not only the kids' money that they're stealing, it's everything else as well. My tapes are meant to give them something else to focus on, something that they don't know about and that isn't exploiting them, that doesn't have a consumer message. And maybe the tapes would make them want to try out some of the things that are shown.

WS: There seems to be a lot of drama in them, because something actually happens, there is tension in them.

TF: Well, the tension helps the kids to watch it. They are so used to watching the 15-second cut and stuff that looks great although the content is zero or negative that it's really hard to get them to watch something that long. Or to get studio technicians to put up with it. I showed two of those on KQED in San Francisco, the one of the fly and the bowl which I made at home, and then another one that I did in the studio in color, and those technicians were just terrible. They were going crazy having to leave the camera still for three minutes.

WS: Why did you choose those objects?

TF: Because they're objects I'm familiar with. I really get off on certain situations and objects that have their own substance and reality. But it's not so much an interest in those particular objects that the tapes convey, it's more an attitude. . . .

LB: I liked watching what was happening, though.

TF: Well, amazing things are happening. That's why I shot them really close up, to focus in on all the minute events. But besides that, there's a kind of attitude that's communicated by the tapes.

LB: What attitude?

.......CHILDREN'S VIDEOTAPES

TF: An attitude of contemplation . . . of wonderment, of relating to something real . . . without having to take sides.

LB: Right, there's no make-believe involved, no stylization. There's no assumption that a child's vision is different from an adult's.

TF: Well, the child's vision is more a vision that the adult has inflicted on him. A child is basically just a small person. The idea that things have to be scaled down to appeal to kids is a form of repression, to keep the kids down. When anyone does anything for kids, they go into this phony artificial childlike world of make-believe. But I don't think kids really want that until it's too late. Then they want it because that's all they usually get, that's the limit of their world . . . But I didn't feel I had to reduce my art to make those tapes.

WS: What's your attitude toward video?

TF: Well, I don't see it as a religion or anything. It's a tool.

WS: But that's perhaps because you're doing work in a lot of different media and you don't have your own video equipment.

TF: Oh yeah, definitely. If I had a video camera who knows what would happen. I can't wait to get one. For one thing, I think I would get a lot looser in the camera work. When I made these tapes, I'd never used video equipment before so I was really tight with it.

WS: How did you set up the shot?

TF: Well, all the tapes were made in my studio in San Francisco in March this year, between midnight and sunrise. I had the objects on a big table, a 4 by 8 foot door on sawhorses, in the positions I wanted them in, and the camera was on a tripod three and a half feet away. There was a studio portrait light with a 1500 watt bulb. Then I would figure out what kind of lighting was needed for whatever was happening, and zoom all the way in to get it in focus, and then zoom it back out. Then I'd take the objects off the table, put little crumbs down to mark their positions, turn the camera on and put the objects down so you could see how the situation was set up . . . And while I was doing that I would zoom all the way in, so the tapes were shot either all the way out or all the way in.

WS: You didn't think there had to be an explicative narrative at any point?

TF: No, there didn't need to be a narrative.

WS: So the tapes are demonstrations of phenomena.

TF: Phenomena and their worlds. Like all the different shapes the candle can assume, all the kinds of things you can do to it, things that happen to it. Like with the flame, you can skin the flame, take away all its color and make it invisible with a fork. There were constant variations on those objects together—the fork and the candle, or the candle and the water, or the water and the bowl. . . .

WS: Your show at the Everson Museum consisted just of these tapes?

TF: Yeah. The reason for showing them there was that it's a community museum and they were able to organize field trips to the museum for all the school kids in Syracuse. I edited what I'd shot, which was about two and a half hours of tape, down to two one hour tapes.

WS: And they were shown on two monitors simultaneously?

TF: Yeah. With two monitors all the objects are in use at once, like the candle and fork are on one monitor while the spoon and bowl are on the other. The pieces are all different lengths, the shortest one is a minute and the longest seventeen.

WS: How did the kids react when you showed them in San Francisco?

TF: Well, I showed them to a kindergarten class and they liked them, and I showed them to the Marioni boys and they wanted to see a couple of them again. They weren't really completed until the Everson show.

WS: Would you ever show them in a gallery situation?

TF: No.

WS: And they're not made to sell, particularly? You're not filling a market for your art work with these tapes.

TF: No. In my whole life, I've sold four drawings and traded a sculpture for a set of false teeth, when I showed at Lucio Amelio's. (Laughter).

WS: That's pretty remarkable, isn't it? That you've sold so little. You've shown in a lot of the important galleries in New York and Europe.

TF: Well, I haven't had anything for sale. I showed with Sonnabend in Paris, there was nothing for sale. With Lucio too. That's not why I show, why I make art.□

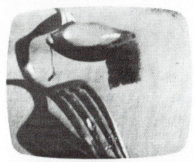 

ICE UPSETS THE SPOON

REFLECTED CANDLE SINKS THE SPOON

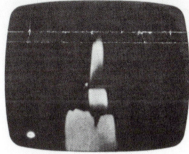 

SKINNING THE FLAME   **WATER DROPS FROM THE SPOON**

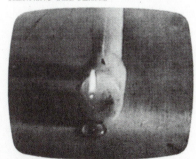 

ONE CANDLE LIGHTS ANOTHER

FORKED CANDLE LIT FROM BOTH ENDS

Avalanche, New York, December 1974

Terry Fox
About the Videos

1 *Turgescent Sex:* This is a performance for the video camera and was made to be sent out, like a letter. In this tape, I wash my hands/wash the fish bound by the rope in many knots/blindfold myself with the bandage/release the fish from bandage/cover the nest with smoke. The sound is the flow of traffic outside my door, the light is the sunlight on my floor. Unedited, taped in my studio in San Francisco by George Bolling on a Sony Portapak in 1971.

Black and white, 40 min.

2 *Clutch:* Is a tape about disengagement. I am lying on my studio floor face down, eyes closed. My fingertips are at the edge of the patch of sunlight from my skylight. I follow its progress across the floor by feeling its warmth with my fingers, until it slips out of reach. The sound is the phonograph needle stuck in the groove until it finally wears through and rejects itself. George Bolling on a Sony Portapak in 1971.

Black and white, 50 min.

3 *Children's Tapes: A Selection:* Contains eleven of the 34 tapes I made for children. These tapes involve five elements (a spoon, fork, candle, bowl and water) in constantly changing states of interaction. These tapes were conceived as part of my translation of the 34 turns in the labyrinth at Chartres. Unedited, the sound is the natural sounds of the actions, the light is a 1000 watt spot, taped and performed by me in my studio in San Francisco on a Sony Portapak in 1974.

Black and white, 30 min.

4 *Two Turns:* It was made after burning the image of the labyrinth at Chartres into the vidicon tube of my Portapak camera. *Two Turns* is two walks. The first walk is from my studio to the street and back to my studio where sunbeams are streaming through a glass painting of the labyrinth used to burn the vidicon tube. The circuit of the labyrinth is made visible by smoke curling through sun rays. The second walk is at night, in the rain, out to the street and back again. The camera comes to rest at a bowl on the floor of my studio, collecting raindrops from leaking rafters and transforming them into concentric rings. Hand-held camera, natural light and sound. 1975

Black and white, 42 min.

5 *Timbre:* A tape on a five-hour performance given on March 13, 1976, on Mount Tamalpais in Northern California, for two instruments: a Cessna 170, single engine airplane, and a homemade instrument made from piano wires tuned to the drone through the woods, to the site of the performance, and the beginning minutes of the performance itself. 1976

Black and white, 30 min.

1976

Source: *Anna Canepa Video Distributions Inc. Represents the Following Artists: Eleanor Antin, Terry Fox, Taka Iimura, Allan Kaprow, Les Levine, Dennis Oppenheim, Roger Welch*. Distribution catalogue, New York, 1976, pp. 6–7

Terry Fox, *Timbre*, 1976, photos: Tom Marioni

40a 42

Herzogenrath, Archiv Fox, Sign 122

I HOPE YOU GOT TO SEE MY LABYRINTH SHOW AT DE APPEL, IT SHOWS MY CONCERNS WITH THE LABYRINTH BETTER THAN I COULD DESCRIBE THEM!

Dear M.B.,

I'm terribly sorry about getting this to you so late, I had a great deal to do as soon as I got back to San Francisco but now I am clear and so here is the material.

I am sending you the desiegn taken from a book which I used to make my rubber stamp of the labyrinth as I think the printed image will be more presice for the stone cutter to work from or for a blow up. I am very quikly sending you this and tomorrow I will send you more information for the press and so forth.

I think we agreed on the size and type of stone and so you may beging cutting immediatly. I hope it is still possible to find the sensitive man with the metal rod to locate the exact spot for the stone in the PODIO. I would also like, if it is possible, to have a hollow under the stone so that it will be RESONANT when when struck or knocked with the knuckles. This may be done as follows, but you may know of a better way.

OVER

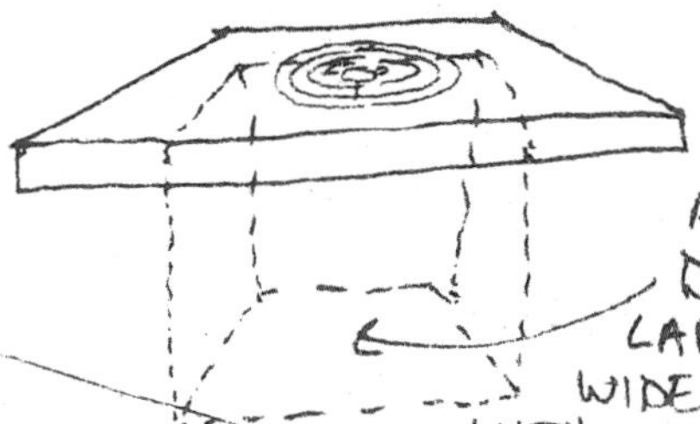

A HOLLOW EMPTY SPACE DIRECTLY BELOW THE LABYRINTH SIGN, BUT NOT AS WIDE AS THE STONE, PERHAPS WITH STONE WALLS + FLOOR OR ANOTHER ARRANGEMENT YOU MAY BE ABLE TO CONCIEVE, THE OBJECT IS TO HAVE THE STONE WITH THE LABYRINTH ON IT TO BE RESONENT, BY HAVING A EMPTY SPACE UNDER IT. I'M VERY EXCITED ABOUT THIS PROJECT + HAVE TOLD A GREAT MANY PEOPLE ABOUT IT!!

I hope all is well in Middleberg and with you family and I want to thank you again for you freindship and hospitality. It is fine being back in San Francisco but I look very much forward to returning to Europe in the Spring. If there is any kind of material you may need from me, please write and I will send it at once.

best greeting and love,

Terry Fox

16 rose street
san francisco 94102

BEST GREETING ALSO TO AD
PLEASE GIVE HIM THIS ADRESS IN GRAZ:
(CAN'T FIND THE ADRESS – I'LL SEND IT TO HIM

Terry Fox, Letter to Marinus Boezem, c. 1978, source: Akademie der Künste, Wulf-Herzogenrath-Archiv, no. 122

Terry Fox

"The impetus might have been similar in Dada, but it has nothing to do with this art form. Performance art has to do with the day in which it originated, the 70's. . . . It really is an attempt at synthesizing communication. It's an attempt at a new communication."

View

Interview by Robin White at Crown Point Press, Oakland, California, 1979.

TERRY FOX   I am still interested in making tapes – I've got a real long project that I want to do on tape, but video is similar to painting, it's the same kind of restrictions. So you're going to do a performance and use a tape and the longest tape you could get is an hour. So your performance turns out to be an hour long. And that's really stupid, you know. You have all these equipment restrictions. You have a given technology and you are seeing what you can do with it. But you can't do anything that the tape recorder can't do.

1979

Source: "It's an Attempt at a New Communication. Interview by Robin White," *View*, vol. II, no. 3, Point Publications, Oakland, June 1979, reprinted in Schmidt 2000, p. 91

Terry Fox, *Erossore*, 1978, photos: Larry Fox

Interview by M. A. Greenstein
with Terry Fox

M. A. GREENSTEIN

Artaud said, "Theater is an opportunity to fill physical space." John Cage said, "Theater takes place all the time and art simply facilitates persuading one this is the case." The Otis catalogue essay alludes to the influence of both Artaud and Cage upon your own work, and the work in the Otis exhibition does seem to build on them.

TERRY FOX

Yes, it does. Artaud was definitely a big influence for me in the late 1960s and early 1970s, but not John Cage. When I began, I was more interested in theater, and at that time it came directly from this experience of living in Paris and seeing the theater in the street. And changing then from painting to theater. When I came back to San Francisco, I tried to make theater in the street, and it was [Jerzy] Grotowski that I actually started reading.

[...]

M.A.G. The Otis catalogue mentions that you were interested in his "theatre of cruelty," and yet I thought to myself, there's the other part of Fox's work that seems closer to Artaud's idea of the non-literal or ritual theater, that is, theater that has nothing to do with cruelty per se.

T.F. Actually, I wasn't interested in every aspect of Artaud's, I was interested in the transformational quality that theater has. As you said, it's the idea of transforming a space through action, even if the space is the body, to transform the body through action. Or as Artaud writes, to turn the body inside-out in a space – what kind of effect that has on the physical space and the body both.

[...]

T.F. The Labyrinth at Chartres was built in 1290, and I think it really is a form of theater. One of the things that attracted me to it is that it's an object but it's not an object really. And it needs to be acted on. It's actually a kind of stage with the move- ment directions embedded in the floor and you follow them. So what is it? It's not an object, it's not a sculpture. It's a metaphor. But it's also like a score, a score for movement. What happens when you do this movement, what kind of transformation takes place? You go through the process of moving and I think it's a transformational process. I think it's very important to go through that before you continue on to whatever you are going to do in the cathedral. I stopped doing a particular kind of performance in '72. And when I stopped, it occurred together with finding the labyrinth. And finding this it was a cross-over, because it

is a kind of score. It's a stage, with all of the movement directions. And I started moving inside that labyrinth and it changed my work – the work got more and more hermetic, and less and less public. But I still, even now, have a strong idea about doing something live in front of people. It just changed to sound.

[...]

M.A.G. I think it makes sense that you would choose acoustic sound, given your interest in Artaud and transformation. Acoustic sound is, after all, so space dependent.

T.F. Yes. Like now, these piano wires – the piano wires don't make the sound. The walls of the space make the sound. When it's being played, it not only transforms the physical space, but also the space itself is creating the sound. So the space becomes an instrument.

[...]

M.A.G. And yet we don't think of objects transforming themselves, do we?

T.F. No, no, that's good. It's true. But also, like this [he points to *Vortex* on the floor nearby]: Is it an instrument or a sculpture? Basically it's a steel sculpture. But it's also an instrument. And other people can play it. Anybody can play it.

[...]

M.A.G. So what are we talking about?

T.F. For me, there's a criterion, it can work or it doesn't work. But I don't know what it means when it works. I can think of some times when it was really incredible, because I never know what the results are going to be. But for me, when it works, I get opened up by the experience. Opened up to listening. That relates to Cage in a way. And when that happens to other people, it's a form of communication, and it's important for me that it's communication, that it's not just entertainment – it really *is* communication. It's about realizing what's making the sound. How is the sound being produced? And how are you perceiving the sound? Why does it sound like that? What's happening? Why are you interested in listening to it or not listening to it? People can walk everywhere and they can also play after or before.

[...]

1994

Source: *Artweek*, February 17, 1994, vol. 25, no. 4, p. 15

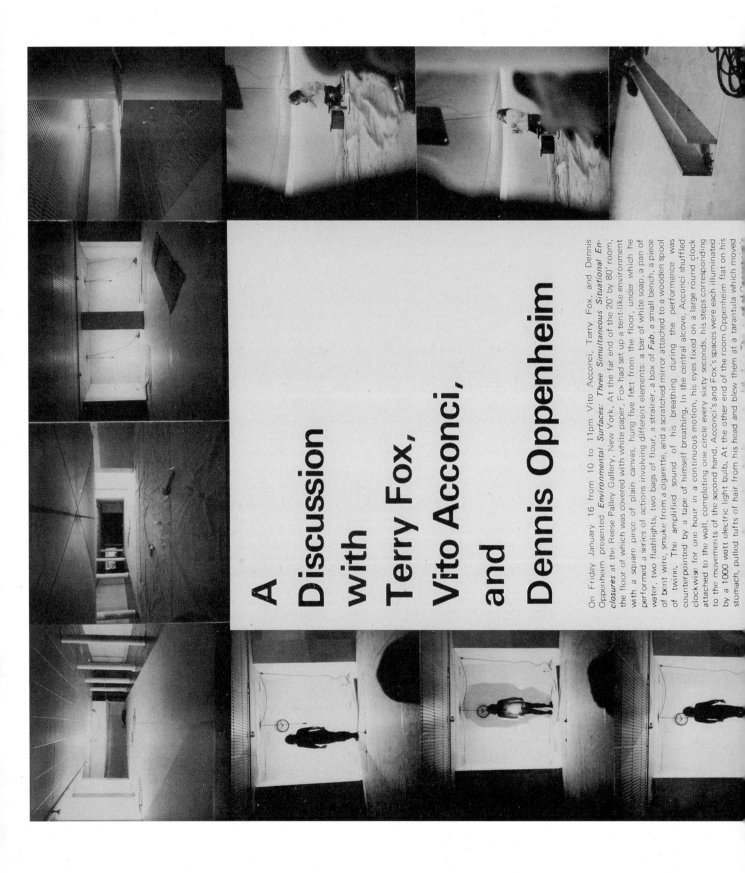

A Discussion with Terry Fox, Vito Acconci, and Dennis Oppenheim

On Friday January 16 from 10 to 11pm Vito Acconci, Terry Fox, and Dennis Oppenheim presented *Environmental Surfaces: Three Simultaneous Situational Enclosures* at the Reese Palley Gallery, New York. At the far end of the 20' by 80' room, Fox had set up a tent-like environment the floor of which was covered with white paper, hung five feet from the floor, under which he performed a series of actions involving different elements: a bar of white soap, a pan of water, two flashlights, two bags of flour, a strainer, a box of *Fab*, a small bench, a piece of bent wire, smoke from a cigarette, and a scratched mirror attached to a wooden spool of twine. The amplified sound of his breathing during the performance was counterpointed by a tape of himself breathing. In the central alcove, Acconci shuffled clockwise for one hour in a continuous motion, his eyes fixed on a large round clock attached to the wall, completing one circle every sixty seconds, his steps corresponding to the movements of the second hand. Acconci's and Fox's spaces were each illuminated by a 1000 watt electric light bulb. At the other end of the room Oppenheim flat on his stomach, pulled tufts of hair from his head and blew them at a tarantula which moved

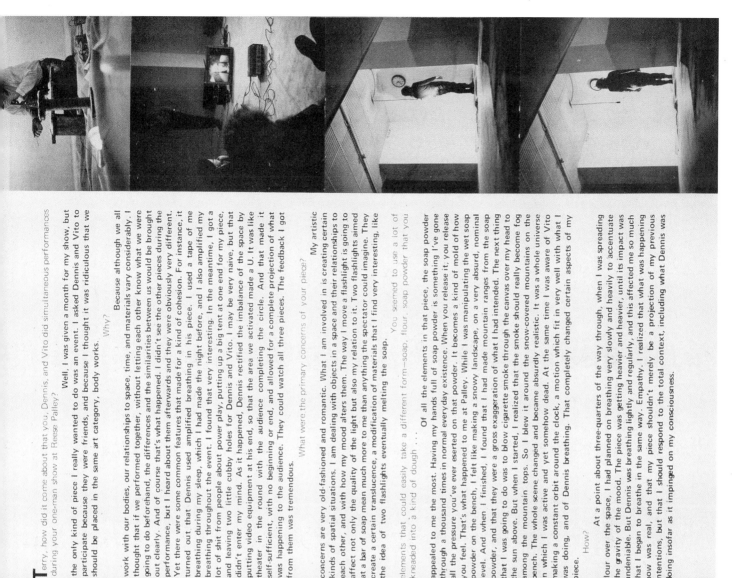

T erry, how did it come about that you, Dennis, and Vito did simultaneous performances during your one-man show at Reese Palley?

Well, I was given a month for my show, but the only kind of piece I really wanted to do was an event. I asked Dennis and Vito to participate because they were friends, and because I thought it was ridiculous that we should be placed in the same art category, body works.

Why?

Because although we all work with our bodies, our relationships to space, time, and materials vary considerably. I thought that if we performed together, without letting each other know what we were going to do beforehand, the differences and the similarities between us would be brought out clearly. And of course that's what happened. I didn't see the other pieces during the performance, but I heard about them afterwards and they were obviously very different. Yet there were some common features that made for a kind of cohesion. For instance, it turned out that Dennis used amplified breathing in his piece. I used a tape of me breathing during my sleep, which I had made the night before, and I also amplified my breathing throughout the event. I found that very interesting. In the meantime, I got a lot of shit from people about power play, putting up a big tent at one end for my piece, and leaving two little cubby holes for Dennis and Vito. I may be very naive, but that didn't enter my mind. As it happened, Dennis rectified the imbalance of the space by putting video equipment at his end, so that the area we activated made a U. It was like theater in the round with the audience completing the circle. And that made it self-sufficient, with no beginning or end, and allowed for a complete projection of what was happening to the audience. They could watch all three pieces. The feedback I got from them was tremendous.

What were the primary concerns of your piece?

My artistic concerns are very old-fashioned and romantic. What I am involved in is creating certain kinds of spatial situations. I am dealing with objects in a space and their relationships to each other, and with how my mood alters them. The way I move a flashlight is going to affect not only the quality of the light but also my relation to it. Two flashlights aimed at a bar of soap mean much more to me than anything the spectator could imagine. They create a certain translucence, a modification of materials that I find very interesting, like the idea of two flashlights eventually melting the soap.

You seemed to use a lot of elements that could easily take a different form—soap, flour, soap powder that you kneaded into a kind of dough . . .

Of all the elements in that piece, the soap powder appealed to me the most. Having my hands full of soap powder is something I've gone through a thousand times in normal everyday existence. When you release it, you release all the pressure you've ever exerted on that powder. It becomes a kind of mold of how you feel. That's what happened to me at Palley. While I was manipulating the wet soap powder on the bench, I felt like making a snowy landscape, on a very absurd, nominal level. And when I finished, I found that I had made mountain ranges from the soap powder, and that they were a gross exaggeration of what I had intended. The next thing that I was going to do was to blow cigarette smoke through the canvas over my head to the sun above. But when I started, I realized that the smoke should really become fog among the mountain tops. So I blew it around the snow-covered mountains on the bench. The whole scene changed and became absurdly realistic. It was a whole universe in which I was active and yet somehow dead. At the same time I was aware of Vito making a constant orbit around the clock, a motion which fit in very well with what I was doing, and of Dennis breathing. That completely changed certain aspects of my piece.

How?

At a point about three-quarters of the way through, when I was spreading flour over the space, I had planned on breathing very slowly and heavily to accentuate the gravity of the mood. The piece was getting heavier and heavier, until its impact was undeniable. But Dennis was breathing lightly and regularly, and this affected me so much that I began to breathe in the same way. Empathy. I realized that what was happening now was real, and that my piece shouldn't merely be a projection of my previous intentions, but that I should respond to the total context, including what Dennis was doing insofar as it impinged on my consciousness.

What do you mean?

Both Dennis and Vito had a very definite relationship to their spaces. The structure of their pieces involved a basic repetition which made for a certain overall cohesiveness. But my piece consisted of a series of discontinuous acts, so it changed every few minutes. When I became aware of Dennis breathing, I felt that I should work with them and make everything harmonize in terms of sound quality and mood, so that the audience could respond to the whole situation. It wasn't a conscious decision, it was just a strong impulse I had at that moment.

Dennis, could you describe how your piece was set up?

First, of all, my piece had very little to do with the specific locale. During the four days prior to the event, I had wondered whether to take the hour for the performance in segments and go through a series of attempts, feedbacks, and results, or just to do it and let it be as unstructured as possible. Basically, the piece is about control of material at a distance and its objectification once it has been separated from its source. It grew out of an earlier work, *Extended Armor*, in which I was pulling hair from my head and blowing it through a channel into a receptacle that tried to suck it up. This was a way of extending material from one point to another. I was also interested that my own hair, once removed from my scalp, could be objectified, treated as a separate object, and still controlled. In the Palley piece I used it to block a certain activity, namely the approach of an animal . . .

Why did you choose a tarantula?

I used the spider as an aggressor, an ongoing force which could be persuaded or dissuaded from going in a particular direction. It could be enticed or repelled. The tarantula was selected because it just made sense—it wasn't too big or too small; it was hairy; it was relatively slow.

How much research did you do for this piece?

Not a hell of a lot. In the earlier version which I've already mentioned, I made use of the antidote to venom: I was interested in the fact that a certain substance could result in the expulsion of another. So the soundtrack for the piece was an account of what to do if you are poisoned. But I never found out whether a tarantula bite is actually poisonous, so at Palley I decided not to use that soundtrack.

What role did your breathing play?

Well, the breathing provided the impetus for and regulated the activity within the channel. I was slowly pulling hair out, putting it in front of my mouth, and breathing. Every time I let out a breath, the hair moved further and further away. I was bouncing pressure off the walls. My own hair was now out there and I was maneuvering it: at a distance of 8 feet I was still in control of it. And it served as armor against the spider, as an entrapment.

So actually your piece grew out of your immediate concerns, and Terry's and Vito's work had little effect on you.

None whatsoever. I just had a good feeling about that situation and it was a place where I could do the work.

Compared to the other pieces, Vito, yours seemed very simply structured, partly because you walked in the same circular orbit for an hour, and your attention was fixed on the second hand of the clock. What exactly did this activity involve?

When Terry asked me to do a piece and showed me the space, I was immediately attracted by my space, because it had two protruding walls on either side and formed an alcove distinct from the others. And I felt that it called for a private, self-enclosed activity. But in the context of a public performance it was also part of the whole space. So I decided literally to follow the movement of the clock for one hour. This time-marking activity would be private, but Dennis and Terry were also enclosed within that time.

As far as you were concerned, the shared element between the three of you was the time.

Yes. My privacy consisted of this concentration on the clock, but since the time was universally shared, I was also related to the general time experience. What interested me was that I could be in a period of time which the others would accidentally share, but which I was going to define. What I wanted to do was to enclose myself within a circle. In fact, my physical self, my body, was tracing the perimeter of

movements, they did make an important difference to my private concentration. While I was following the regular motion of the clock, I was very conscious of these arbitrary breathing sounds on either side of me. The breathing was pushing and pulling against my mechanical movements. At first I was focussing on interior things, then I became increasingly conscious of the exterior—my shadow on the wall, the canvas under my feet. I was being surrounded and attacked, or at least invaded by the space around me.

wonder what relation any of you felt to the audience.   I didn't take the audience into account at all. I was really into a ritual which defined the boundaries of my piece. I've never thought about how my work is being received. It's not so much a dismissal as part of the structure of my work.   **I wasn't aware of the spectators at all, because I had practically hypnotised myself beforehand. When I stopped, I didn't even know what stage Dennis and Vito had reached.**

  My immediate concern was how to react to that space. I was always conscious that it was a public piece.

  That seems to be a particular concern of yours. Although you were completely absorbed in your activity, I sensed that you were the most aware of the audience.

  I guess that relates to a lot of my work, the idea of doing something private, self-enclosed, within a public space. When I finished things seemed really lopsided. My aim had been to go along with the clock movement, to almost become that clock. So when I stopped, I was incredibly disoriented, although I had been conscious all the while that other people were present. I didn't think of it at the time, but the audience could focus on any number of points during the performances, one of which was a process of concentration. What happens when their attention is drawn to it? Are they dragged into the circle, or do they always remain on the periphery?

  One person I spoke to about my piece told me that the audience's sympathy was primarily with the spider until it was in close proximity to me. That occurred twice. There was one beautiful point when the spider was fairly near and I blew some looped tumbleweed toward it. Eventually it reached the spider which became entangled in it. But at that point the spider retaliated and carried it off. That just blew my mind.

  What did you feel about the whole thing afterwards?   **The most beautiful aspect of it for me was that three friends could work together.**   I can dig that.   *I think that was an important part of it too. So many programs are involved with what's going to happen, what kind of hierarchy is going to be set up. I felt none of that this time.*   There was no elitism: that's one reason why it was so good. It may or may not occur again. If anything of what we're doing is getting toward something worthwhile, it's that kind of situation.

Photography by Shunk-Kender

Vito Acconci
TERRY LIKE A FOX *(1974 – In His Own Words Stolen / Borrowed By Me)*

CANDLE–FORK–SPOON–BOWL OF WATER–PIECE OF CLOTH–

Putting candle in water & then on piece of cloth: candle devours all oxygen & draws water up & flame goes out, then trying to light candle again when it's wet [...]

Late at night by myself a lot, inventing new situations with the same objects, making a program for children out of them [...]

Everything Foxy watches is bad for him – tension, 15-second cut [...]

I shoot them really close-up, to focus on all the minute events [...]

An attitude of contemplation, of wonderment, of relating to something real, without having to take sides [...]

No make-believe involved, no stylization, no assumption that a child's vision is different from an adult's [...]

CANDLE(CAN)–FORK(FOR)–SPOON(SON/ON)–BOWL (BOW)OF(O)WATER(WAT)–PIECE(PIE)OF(O)CLOTH(LOT)–

Video is a tool, camera on a tripod 3½ feet away, I zoom all the way in to get it in focus, then zoom it back out, put the objects down so I can see how the new situation is set up, then I zoom all the way out or all the way in [...]

Like all the different shapes the candle can assume – fork/candle, candle/water, water/bowl – shown on 2 monitors at once, with 2 monitors all the objects are in use all at once, candle & fork on 1 monitor while spoon & bowl are on the other [...]

No, there doesn't need to be a narrative [...]

Shortest is 1 minute, longest is 17, nothing for sale [...]

Doing things & showing them to Foxy, he really gets into them, he likes watching them & he likes doing them [...]

Setting up situations, using the same objects over & over – candle/fork/spoon/bowl-of-water piece-of-cloth – like putting candle in water & then putting bottle over it, candle devours all oxygen & draws water up so flame goes out, & trying to light candle again when it's wet [...]

After a few months I'd done so many I should make a program for children out of them [...]

Borrowed a Sony port-a-pak & did them all in a week & a half [...]

CANDLE(AND/AN/A)–FORK(OR)–SPOON(SO/NO)–BOWL (OW/LOW)OF(O)WATER(WET/TAR)–PIECE(PI)OF(O)CLOTH(LO)–

He loves to watch, it's horrifying, everything he watches is bad for him, well, it homogenizes him, it takes away his ability to have an actual dialogue with something rather than having passive responses [...]

He can talk well, as well as I can, but his drawings tell me a lot more, you can see exactly what his mood is, what he's feeling, but even those are starting to get stylized [...]

But nobody does anything for children, everybody does something for money [...]

My tapes are meant to give them something else to focus on, something they don't know about & that isn't exploiting them, that doesn't have a consumer message, & maybe the tapes would want them to try out something new [...]

Tension helps kids watch TV, they're so used to watching the 15-second cut, it's too hard to watch something too long, they were going crazy having to leave the camera still [...]

Because they're objects I know, I get off on situations & objects that have their own substance & reality, but it's not an interest in these objects that the tapes convey, it's more an attitude [...]

Amazing things are happening now, that's why I shoot them really close up, to focus in on all the minute events, but besides that there's a kind of attitude in those tapes [...]

Attitude of contemplation, of wonderment, without having to take sides [...]

CANDLE(LED)–FORK(O)–SPOON(POO/SOON)–BOWL(LOW) OF(O)WATER(ATE/TEAR/WAR/RAW)–PIECE(PIC)OF(O)CLOTH(HO/TO/HOT/LOT)–

A child is basically just a small person, the idea that things have to be scaled down to appeal to kids is repression, to keep kids down. When anyone does things for kids, they go into phony artificial childlike worlds of make-believe. Kids don't want that till it's too late, then they want it because that's all they usually get; that's the limit of their world [...]

But I don't feel I had to reduce my art to make these tapes [...]

Video's not a religion, it's a tool [...]

All these videotapes were made in my studio, San Francisco, March '74, between midnight & sunrise, objects on a big table, 4x8-foot door on saw-horses, camera on a tripod 3½ feet away & a studio portrait-light with a 1500-watt light-bulb. Then I'd figure out what light was needed & zoom all the way in to get it in focus, then zoom it all the way back out, then I'd take the objects off the table, put little crumbs down to mark their positions, turn camera on & put objects down so you could see how the situation was set up, & while I was doing that I would zoom all the way out or all the way in [...]

They exposed phenomena & their worlds, like all the different shapes the candle can assume, all the kinds of things you can do to it, things that happen to it. Like with the flame, you can skin the flame, take away all its color & make it invisible with a fork. There were constant variations on those objects together, fork & candle, or candle & water, or water & bowl [...]

With 2 monitors all the objects are used at once, candle & fork on 1 monitor & spoon & bowl on the other, the pieces are all different lengths, the shortest is a minute & the longest 17 [...]

Well, I haven't sold anything, that's not why I show, why I make art [...]

2015

Tom Marioni

Terry Fox and I were drinking buddies in San Francisco back in 1969. In addition to being an artist, I was curator at the art center in the nearby town of Richmond. That year, I organized an exhibition called *The Return of Abstract Expressionism* about process art, conceptual art, anti-form sculpture, etc. I invited Terry to be in that show. The show was not about action paintings, but about actions and materials. Terry Fox contributed a piece of plastic blowing outside in the wind. In 1970, he had a one-man show, *Levitation*, at the Richmond Art Center. Later that year I founded the Museum of Conceptual Art (MOCA) in San Francisco. I called the first show *Sound Sculpture As* and in it Terry made an action with a bowl of water. He hit this bowl against the floor and produced a sound like "bong." Maybe it was the first Sound Art show anywhere.

Terry and I influenced each other during his time in San Francisco. We were both influenced by Joseph Beuys, me in my social art (*The Act of Drinking Beer with Friends is the Highest Form of Art*), and Terry in his use of organic materials. My first meeting with Joseph Beuys took place in 1973 during the Edinburgh Festival, where I participated with my band, the MOCA Ensemble, in the St. Mary's Cathedral. During this Festival Richard Demarco organized a show of artists, including Joseph Beuys, who was the most original European postwar artist. An additional meeting with Beuys happened in 1974 in Belgrade, where I was invited with [the performance] *A Sculpture in 2/3 Time* in the Student Cultural Center. At MOCA, I displayed Beuys' 1973 *12-hour-video-lecture* that he gave in Edinburgh. (A year later the first exhibition of Beuys' work, curated by René Block, took place in New York.) He talked about socialism, the Green Party (he was one of the founders), and that everyone could be an artist.

After 1973, I gave Terry a room in MOCA to use as a studio, and he participated frequently in group shows there until he moved to New York in 1978. I also organized screenings with videotapes from our artist's friends in MOCA. It took place once a week. We displayed the videotapes on a monitor. What we called "action" during this time and what is known as "sculpture-based performance art" today was based on the manipulation of material in the presence of witnesses, and not on the manipulation of emotions, like in theater. During the performance, the artist is the author, not the actor, while in theater the storytelling is the idea, not the material. The performance tape represents real time, unlike theater that represents an artificial time.

I think it is also important to make a difference between artistic photography and documentation. There is often confusion about this. So I emphasized that my publication *Vision#5* (1975) was called "Artists' Photographs." These publications were exhibitions in themselves and the works were mostly designed for the books and didn't exist otherwise. *Vision#5* was combined with an exhibition at Crown Press. I invited and asked each artist to send me a photograph not of an artwork but as an artwork. This should highlight that photography could be an artwork and is only present in the photograph. It also includes photographs by Terry Fox: *My Hands as a Fine Porcelain* and *Who Shall Harm Me?*

Terry Fox, *All Night Sculptures, Memento Mori,*
Terry Fox, Installation (outside), MOCA, San Francisco, 1973

In 1975, I did a performance with Terry Fox that was called *Duologue* at CARP in
Los Angeles. We played a kind of "machine music" that we constructed in our studios
previously. Terry Fox had a bowl full of sand, which he touched with a violin bow.
The sand formed structures from the energy of sound that he created. I worked with my
drum brushes and our both sounds changed thereby the forms of the sand. Terry Fox
was inspired by the museum of natural science in San Francisco that displayed
the concept of Ernst Chladni who invented a technique to show the various modes
of vibration of a rigid surface. Chladni considered streaking a bow over a piece of metal
whose surface was slightly covered with sand. The plate was stroked to the point
of resonance when the vibration causes the sand to move and concentrate along
the nodal lines where the surface is still, outlining the nodal lines. The patterns formed
by these lines are what are now called Chladni figures. (Terry Fox used this experience
from this performances for his videotape *Lunedi*, which he produced together
with Bill Viola at Art/Tapes/22 in Florence, also in 1975.)

He moved the following year to Berlin. I visited him several times when I was
in Europe, usually when we were in performance festivals together.

2015

Paul Kos
Some Ramblings (As I Remember Him)

FISH
FOX
KOS

DeSAISSET MUSEUM & ART GALLERY, UNIVERSITY OF SANTA CLARA,
FEB. 2 - 28, 1971 reception & event feb.2, 7:30·10

Exhibition catalogue, 1971

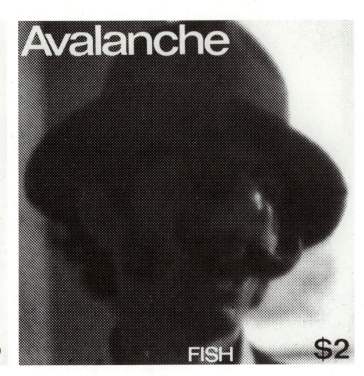

Avalanche

FISH $2

I met Terry Fox in 1970 when we were two of the three chosen artists for the Richmond Sculpture Annual. In the huge exhibition space there were three documents. One was Jim McCready's photo of St. Mary's Church burning, Terry Fox's was directions to his studio in San Francisco where a viewer could see his kinetic wind sculpture and my blank check piece called *Quid Pro Quo*. LA artist, Larry Bell, was the juror. Tom Marioni was the curator. The exhibition caused great turmoil because no actual sculptural objects were accepted. Terry, Tom and I became lifelong friends.

In 1971, we three animals;
    Fish (Tom Marioni's pseudonym),
    Fox,
    Kos (means small blackbird in Slovenian)
presented a show at the de Saisset Gallery at the University of Santa Clara. Fish showed an elegant room-size lithographic print, Fox fell asleep under a waist-high canvas with two fish, flour and flashlights and Kos showed the residue of a 90-minute weight exchange from artist to target using a shotgun.
    Terry Fox was a courier, a carrier pigeon, bringing news from Europe to the Bay Area.

Conceptual work was in its infancy and the three of us were more challenged by events in arte povera than in the NYC semantic/word-based scene. In the 70's, Terry and his wife Marsha spent time in France, Italy and Germany and Terry even collaborated with Joseph Beuys for *Isolation Unit,* a performance recorded on a 45 rpm record where Terry plays steel pipes trying to break panes of glass with sound alone while Beuys spits pomegranate seeds into a tin cup as his recently deceased mouse revolves on a turntable.
    Sound became Terry's forte. He composed pieces for installations that range the gambit of sites, instruments, harmony and dissonance.
    – In an amphitheater on top of Mount Tamalpais Terry strung a wire across the conductors pit, and with a bow played it to the same note as the engine of a small Cessna plane that he hired to fly over the site. If the plane accelerated, Terry retuned the wire, if the plane dove the site, Terry bowed the wire to sound likewise.
    – In his studio on Rose Street in San Francisco, he cut a manhole-sized opening into the wooden floor of his two-story space and situated viewers/listeners on the bottom floor, while he on the floor above bowed and plucked wires strung across the hole. Imagine yourself inside a guitar. The audience was in the belly, the sound box of the instrument.

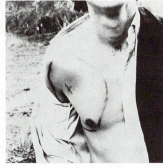

BEFORE · AFTER

George Bolling, video curator at the de Saisset Gallery, taped Terry's performances in a Shunk-Kender/Beuys manner, that is to say, in a sympathetic vibration between performer and documentor. Color, contrast, texture and timing became elements that were unique to these video pieces. *Children's Tapes*, *Turgescent Sex*, *Virtual Volumes*, and *Clutch* are examples.

Terry made two memorable pieces that utilized the specifics and confines of their medium.

The first, titled *Breath* was a Super 8mm film (Kodak made this film in 3-minute cartridges). There was a film festival showing, I believe at the San Francisco Art Institute, and artists' Super 8mm films were projected. Terry's opened with a shot of himself drawing in a very, very deep breath, many if not most of the viewing audience did the same. Everyone holding their breath trying to beat the 3-minute clock determined by the Super 8mm film cartridge, making a mirror of Terry's actions. His eyes and veins on his forehead bulged, gasps were heard in the audience of some people giving up. Terry continued and finally exhaled in a burst of air. No one in the auditorium made it to the 3-minute end-of-film mark.

The second piece was sculptural, perhaps untitled. On the concrete basement floor of the Reese Palley Gallery in the Frank Lloyd Wright Building on Maiden Lane in San Francisco in 1970, Terry poured a bucket of water, which found a natural hollow in the floor. The water reflected the gallery lighting. Prior to this intervention, no one had ever noticed that the floor was not level and the water called attention to this otherwise insignificant architectural detail creating an unexpected aesthetic and possibly spiritual experience.

My wife, Isabelle Sorrell, and I, often when speaking about Terry Fox, claim that he is one of the few artists who can make art from nothing; someone for whom being an artist was a condition not a career.

Since I had been working with ice since 1969, Terry sent me these two riddles in his unique handwriting:

– A prisoner was found in his jail cell who had hung himself with his belt slung over a ceiling pipe, but there was no stool on which to stand, only a large puddle below his dangling feet. How did he do it?

– A man was found stabbed to death in another cell, but no weapon could be found. How did it happen?

Answers: (Terry wrote these upside down)

A block of ice

An icicle

2015

Al Wong

The first time I met Terry was in the early 1970's at the screening of my work
in my studio. After that, I found that his studio was only 2 blocks away from mine in
San Francisco. We both used abandoned buildings for studios with thousands of
square feet available to us. It was free and great. So we started hanging out together
and helping each other with our work. He helped me make a soundtrack for
one of my films titled *Same Difference*. I have always helped him with videotaping
or photographing his work. But besides that, he always felt that what he was
doing with the piano wires was sculpture. Sculpture in the sense that when he
attached the wires to the main beam of any given building (whether it was a museum
or an abandoned building) it would activate the whole structure through the
vibration of the wires.

One time, he was in an empty building lot, so he was able to go underneath
the sidewalk of that empty lot and was underneath a metal elevator door that was part
of the sidewalk. He attached the piano wire to the elevator door and attached
the other end to a large, heavy metal desk that was abandoned there. Then he started
striking the wire with a chopstick, making a vibrating sound out to the empty lot.
But above the metal elevator door, pedestrians were walking over it and would change
the tension of the wire because the door would go up and down, and therefore, it
would automatically change the tone of the vibration. I don't know if other people ever
saw the piece, as it seemed I was the only one that day. It was just wonderful.

One other time, we ran into each other in New York and he invited me to
his apartment in the Bowery. As I walked up the stairs, I heard these loud vibrations.
I knocked on
the door and Terry opened it and I saw these piano wires stretching from the
front window all the way to the kitchen cabinets. He would pluck on the wire to get
the vibration started and would go back and open and close the cabinet doors
in the kitchen which would change the tone of the vibration. Again, it was so magical.
I think only his brother Larry and I saw that piece.

I don't know, Terry and I were like two abandoned kids wandering through
abandoned buildings making artwork together. It was really fun. I miss him so.

2015

The Museum of Modern Art

11 West 53 Street, New York, N.Y. 10019 Tel. 956-6100 Cable: Modernart

June 6 – 6 pm
AL WONG – *Shadow & Chair*

Film Installation – Medium – Film, Chair, Luminous Paint

For Other Works
Contact: S.F.A.I.
     AL WONG – Film Department
     800 Chestnut Street
     San Francisco, CA 94133
     (415) 771-7020, 431-1299

Interview by Tanya Zimbardo
with Al Wong

Al Wong recalls that he first met Terry Fox in the early 1970s at a screening held in his studio in San Francisco's South of Market district, located a couple blocks away from Fox's studio. They spent a lot of time observing one another's working process, as well as socializing together with their girlfriends, artists Dorothy Reid and Ursula Schneider. The four friends participated in the 1976 group exhibition *Exchange: DFW/SFO* at the San Francisco Museum of Modern Art (SFMOMA). The presentation included Wong's experimental film *Same Difference* (1975, 16mm, color, sound, 17 min.) featuring a soundtrack by Fox, as well as Fox's offsite performance *Timbre* (1976), recorded on video by Wong. He assisted with the documentation of other performances including *Blind Forces* (1980) in the basement of SFMOMA.

TANYA ZIMBARDO

You received a grant in 1975 from the American Film Institute in association with the NEA to create *Twin Peaks*. How did the concept for the film develop?

AL WONG

It developed from making *Same Difference* (1975), filming my kitchen window over an entire year. I believe it was shown at SFMOMA [*Exchange: DFW/SFO*, 1976]. I had one person, Ursula Schneider, sitting there in a particular position so that while the sky and seasons are constantly changing, she appears to hardly be moving. We got so good at it that when I said it was time to shoot she was able to just hop right up to the table and fit right in, perfectly. She was so kind to help me with this. I had the camera literally gaffer-taped onto the floor so it wouldn't move. We had to walk around it every time we went in the kitchen. I had to be very careful changing each roll of film. Terry Fox made the soundtrack by looking out my kitchen window and drawing his violin bow over the edge of a large bowl that he had found on Market Street. It was beautiful.
Same Difference made me really look at what was out there. I could see Twin Peaks through that window and wanted to get closer. It is a truly magical place. I'm sure you've seen the fog rolling down Twin Peaks like a volcano erupting. I slowly gathered material and started to see all the natural elements – the sky, the earth, the water in the distance. It was then obvious that I had to get the sound of the ocean. One of my favorite places is Baker Beach, so the soundtrack was recorded there. It has this wonderful, deep breathing that keeps changing. If you've meditated, you notice that your breathing changes, and if you try to make it consistent, you may be forcing it.

[...]

T.Z.   The absence of any ambient or driving noise, and only the sound of the breaking waves, also reminded me of focusing on one's own breathing rhythm or pulsating blood during silence. We're directly observing the environment from within the moving vehicle, but I felt this sort of detachment and an auditory sensation that my attention was simultaneously turning inward. You've also mentioned the role of repetition and the unique feature of the figure-eight Twin Peaks Boulevard.

A.W.   Yes. It is like life. We go through this pattern all the time. It is a form of infinity – waking up, brushing our teeth, getting on the trolley. The infinity loop road representing this continuous pattern of life. There are certain sequences in the film where it appears that the parts of the road aren't meeting and it isn't a single road anymore. The road is shifting. Life is like that. It shifts and it makes you feel off-balance at times. You have trouble, and then you try to slip back in. And your breathing is still going.

[...]

T.Z.   You also used the yearlong parameter for your installation *Sunlight* (1979). Could you describe that work? Did anyone experience it with you?

A.W.   The building at Minna Street and Fourth was from the Redevelopment Agency and had been a newspaper printing place and a dentist's office. I pretty much blocked out everything from the windows and left a small opening where a mirror could be placed. That mirror would shoot a beam of light. For instance, a funnel would be turning around with a pie pan underneath it with magnets and frankincense. The magnets would help move the funnel in a gyration form. The incense created shapes when the light hit it. The funnel had small holes I had drilled in it. The first beam that comes in, where the funnel is, there was another mirror that shoots back to almost where the mirror in the window is that is capturing the first light from the sun. It was tilted, and another beam would shoot up to the ceiling. And then there was a fish-eye mirror that would open up or flare the light. With the smoke, it created a dome shape within that space. I was really pleased by that. I didn't know what it was going to do.
Terry Fox would come over. We spent hours watching it. He was only a block away, and we would go back and forth looking at each other's work. We did some interesting things just walking back and forth. Down from where the museum is now, there was a hotel that was abandoned because of a huge fire. Terry and I got in by climbing through a window from the roof of MOCA (Museum of Conceptual Art). It was almost like a museum of how people had lived there.

[...]

2013

Source: Tanya Zimbardo, "Sunlight and Shadows: In Conversation with Al Wong," San Francisco Museum of Modern Art's Open Space, http://openspace.sfmoma. org/2013/05/al-wong/, accessed September 30, 2015

Terry Fox, *Children's Tapes*, 1974, video stills

Interview by Angela Lammert
with Wulf Herzogenrath

ANGELA LAMMERT

When did you first come into contact with Terry Fox's work?

WULF HERZOGENRATH

It was at the beginning of the 1970s, at the Museum Folkwang in Essen, where I was given the task of looking into the new medium of video. No one back then knew what to do with it or what video could become. Actually, there was only Gerry Schum, and those videos were solely concerned with land art and conceptual art. The films were stylistically very calm – you could say boring – documentations of art actions. At that time, in 1971, we still didn't know there was a completely different form of video being made in the US, like that by Nam June Paik. In 1973 I discovered a very lively video scene in New York: Nam June Paik with all of his wit and electronic games, and of course Terry Fox. Although Fox was also conceptual, he had a hidden and sometimes witty humor. This humor made clear that it was about something else than simply performing conceptual art actions, such as the ones we know from Jochen Gerz's *Rufen bis zur Erschöpfung* (1972). It was somehow different in Terry Fox's case. His most well-known videos, *Children's Tapes* (1974), were really funny. They are minimal, but always witty and you are always waiting to see what is going to happen with this little experimental setup. It was not about an exacting realization of a concept, by which it was clear after 20 seconds how the next 10 minutes were going to pan out; instead he kept the viewer's attention. We assembled a large collection of 110 videos for the first video art exhibition, *Projekt '74*. Terry Fox's *Children's Tapes* were particularly popular with the public, who were learning about video art for the first time. At *documenta 6* in Kassel in 1977, four international curators and I selected 50 videos, including – one can truly say – "of course" Terry Fox's *Children's Tapes*. They are classics, like Paik's *Global Groove* (1973) or Peter Campus' early tapes. That was my introduction to Terry Fox.

Whenever I heard something about him it always caught my interest, although it was difficult to find out much, so it was good to finally meet him in person. Fox was a droll and modest personality. He was very modest, but he had an intensity and clarity of mind that was just marvelous. That was what made it possible for him to convince Joseph Beuys to do a performance with him. And that also caught my attention as a curator. Wow, if those two do something together! Though, I do have to say, if you weren't there yourself, it remained difficult to find out what Terry Fox had actually done. You could only take note of the few photographs and reports, because there was no work in the classic sense that exclaimed: "and this is how it looks, and this is a sculpture and that was an installation." Fox was increasingly doing installations at unusual locations, beyond the white cube of the art associations and museums – in abandoned churches, factories, and apartments. He filled these uncommon spaces with sound, most of the time using specially coated wires. At the time sound was rarely

283

Klaus vom Bruch, *Terry Fox*, 1984

Terry Fox, *Suono Interno*, Chiesa Santa Lucia, Bologna, 1979,
photo: Enzo Pezzi

associated with art. It was already hard enough for video
and performance. His further reduction to an action
with sound – those floating, dissipating, minimal sound
spaces impressed me, and the others who were there.
He didn't present his performance on video. If you hadn't
been there, this of course made it all the more difficult
to know what Terry Fox actually did as an artist.
For example, he was permitted to perform in a church in
Bologna, but he did not allow people to enter the building.
He stretched piano strings across the interior of the
church and made a wonderful work out of it. People could
only see in through a small peephole. The sound, however,
was audible outside the church, so people heard this
unusual sound, but couldn't see anything. The wires were
stretched from right next to the peephole that was visible
on the outside, where the people stood, off to a point
in the distance, and the sound traveled through the wooden
door to the outside. It was similar to Marcel Duchamp's
mysterious, concealed, yet visible work in Philadelphia,
which exists, but at the same time is only visible through
a peephole. Such an homage naturally interests me.
What does an artist who is even more reductive than
Duchamp do?

A.L.   Did you ever experience such a performance?

W.H.   Not the one in Italy, but there were many reports. What I did
experience were his performances in Cologne, in particular
at Elisabeth Jappe's Moltkerei Werkstatt.

A.L.   In 1973, in conjunction with a symposium at MoMA, you
spoke about the great difference between video and film and
between theater and film. Do you still see things the same
today, or has something in the processes changed, which is
now also different in art?

W.H. I always start with the artist, not with some theory or even just with the material or media-based existence. On a technical level, everything that Gerry Shum produced with the land art artists and *Identification* was film, but he intended television to be the playback device for the viewer. I was always more interested in asking: "What does the artist intend with this content and how should it be viewed?" And these theoretical discussions, whether about grain or pixels, has little to do with the content-based or visual work, much like a discussion about painting with oil or watercolors. The information is important for the objective art historical description, but the viewer is interested in what is supposed to be expressed in the first place. The few things that were shown in New York at the Castelli Gallery, by Bruce Nauman or Peter Campus and Vito Acconci, were the first videotapes to be accepted as art. On the other hand, experimental film, by, for example, Birgit and Wilhelm Hein, did not actually succeed within the art scene, because it was thought of as film, and experimental film was considered to be another context. The Gerry Schum productions (also made on film) were purchased as videotapes by a few collectors and museums. Sales and rentals (such as those through the exceptional Neuer Berliner Kunstverein video library) scarcely happened in Europe. Terry Fox became known through his performances, live appearances, and sound works, but very little through his videos. The Ileana Sonnabend Gallery in New York showed his work in the 1970s, but it has been largely forgotten. In Europe it would have been almost unthinkable; even the great Konrad Fischer, who began exhibiting Bruce Nauman in the 1970s, seldom showed performance artists. Neither an Acconci performance took place, nor one by Terry Fox.

A.L. Castelli also gave Bruce Nauman a Portapak camera. Nauman then transferred what he had recorded on Super 8 mm film to videotape.

W.H. A performance on video could be played back immediately. With film, it took a week to find out what, if anything, was on it. Video's capability to check the results live was of course an important aspect, which, theoretically, had already existed at the end of the 1960s. But there was hardly an artist, Terry Fox included, who had the necessary financial means available to them.

A.L. The first showing of *Children's Tapes* took place at the Everson Museum in Syracuse in 1974, on two screens, which was unusual for Terry Fox. At the opening of the exhibition *40 Jahre: Fluxus und die Folgen* in Wiesbaden, which Terry Fox attended, René Block projected Fox's *Children's Tapes* using a large-scale video beam. Fox didn't react negatively, but was rather positively surprised, because he hadn't had such technical means at the time he made them.

W.H. I don't think he was concerned with the video image on a monitor or screen, but rather with playing with the images. That's why he certainly never objected. He was interested in the graphic quality and wit of these images, and *Der Lauf der Dinge* (1987) by Fischli & Weiss is naturally even wittier when projected large-scale. The intimacy as anti-television is of course also appealing and was certainly meant as such. It is neither thriller nor Hollywood; that is why it is also right to show Terry Fox's videos on a television. But I can well imagine that Fox would have accepted the large-scale projections that are standard today.

A.L. I found it very funny that the artists threatened to pull out when they first realized they were not going to be paid at the Venice Biennale in 1984.

W.H. That story is wonderfully documented in Klaus von Bruch's photographs. The artists were told by the Biennale staff in Venice who had invited them to come: "Yes, sure, we will reimburse your expenses." But nothing of the sort happened. So the artists must have announced some sort of strike, whereby they were going to remove their works from the exhibition before the opening. Minds were changed and these stacks of lira notes were passed out to all of them. Terry Fox placed the bills in his jacket breast pocket, like an elegant pocket handkerchief, and Klaus von Bruch photographed him pulling out this big bundle of cash.

A.L. How does an art historian get involved with video art, and how did your connection with David Ross come about?

W.H. At the beginning of 1971, Paul Vogt from the Museum Folkwang in Essen was the only German museum director to respond positively to the electronics industry's offer of a free video studio. No German museum wanted such a thing in 1970. I did my doctorate on the Bauhaus ("Art and Technology: A New Unity" was the slogan in 1923) and, at 26, I was the youngest member of a team of curators. The message at the time was: "Go for it, young man, and find out how it is done." There was a video studio and a technician. We initially made educational films, but quickly realized that we needed specialists for that. What else could be done with the medium? That's why I went to Gerry Schum and we had the first conversations. I was appointed at the Kölnischer Kunstverein in 1972, so I continued my efforts to advance video art in Cologne, instead of in Essen.
The focus immediately turned to preparations for an enormous exhibition, *Projekt '74*, which was intended to be kind of a counter-*documenta* in Cologne. While considering all the new things we might show, I suggested: "Then let's do video." Given that I was already in contact with David Ross, we showed a portion of his selection of US videos for the first time in Germany, and added works by German and European artists, as well as pieces by three artists from the Lijnbaan Centrum in Rotterdam, who produced new material for the space of the Kölnischer Kunstverein during the three-month-long *Projekt '74* exhibition. A video catalogue was also assembled, which, although it did not sell a single copy, managed to be preserved in my archive at the Akademie der Künste in Berlin, where it can now be viewed and shared – 41 years later! And Terry Fox also took part in that exhibition.

2015

The conversation took place on May 27, 2015, at the Akademie der Künste in Berlin.
Translated from the German by James Bell

Bill Viola

An exhibition on Terry Fox will serve to present and reveal perhaps for the first time the full scope of Terry's early explorations of ritual and his use of symbols. His work has a profound connection to the spiritual that is evidenced in his multimedia performances and actions in the 1960s and early 1970s; he explored the inner dimensions of everything that he worked with.

I had the privilege of assisting Terry while I was technical director at Art/tapes/22 in Florence, the production studio that Maria Gloria Bicocchi ran for several years exclusively for artists. Terry completed a work titled *Lunedi*, 1975, a beautiful sound and image piece that he created by rubbing a violin bow on a large metal disc covered with sand. The sound waves created complex patterns of the sand on the metal disc that form and re-form, creating a mesmerizing visual and sonic experience. His style and technique was so unique in these explorations. It is important that the best masters of such works be located and preserved during the research process.

2014

Terry Fox, *The Rake's Progress*, 1971, video stills

Steve Seid

The Suspension of (Dis)Belief: Thoughts about Terry Fox's Video Work
The Rake's Progress

In the collection of the Pacific Film Archive in Berkeley resides a group of Terry Fox videotapes cumulatively titled *The Rake's Progress*,[1] though the art historical reference[2] seems elusive at best when considering this particular triad of ½-inch open-reel tapes. Be that as it may, these master tapes, further identified as Session #1, #2, and #3, give us a poignant glimpse of not just Fox's artistic practice, but of his complicated relationship to electronic media.

The videotapes were executed in Tom Marioni's Museum of Conceptual Art[3] on May 13, 1971. As the first videotape begins, preparation for a performance is already underway, with Fox conferring with his longtime collaborator and cameraman, George Bolling; Fox's twin brother, Larry, nearby; and de Saisset Museum curator Lydia Modi-Vitale observing the process generally off-camera.

In the staging area are three key elements: a free-standing pane of glass, a large mirror, and a Sony video camera on a tripod. Fox faces the pane, his back to the mirror, with the camera capturing him through the glass. Having marked exactly what area of the pane is the video camera's frame limit, Fox, represented really by his hand darting in and out of the image, begins rubbing grease[4] from a small tube onto the glass. He continues slowly until the entire video frame is obscured by a layer of smudged goop.[5] In black-and-white video, this extemporized field painting has an ethereal, cloudlike appearance with a faint outline of the camera on its tripod vaguely visible[6] in reflection.

This is no documentary capture of a performance such as Bolling had often achieved, a time-based trace for future examination; nor does it display the shifting camera positions that we might see, for instance, in Fox's *Turgescent Sex* from the same year, a stunning visual elevation of the actual action. The initial configuration of glass/mirror/camera contains
a deliberate complication that subtly activates what Rosalind Krauss called "the aesthetics of narcissism," an aesthetic where "self-encapsulation" and "mirroring" are the raw materials of the medium.[7] The use of the mirror creates an uncanny doubling effect, not only

faintly foregrounding the camera itself, but layering the final image with Fox's hand mirrored front and back. Bolling's camera peers into the space of Fox's action to witness an electronic doppelganger dogging his gestures. Self-reflectivity meets self-reflexivity.

This recorded action is only the first component of *The Rake's Progress*, the second being a medium-size television set, its screen coated with the identical grease. Fox stands before the TV and as the earlier videotape is played back, slowly removes the grease from the screen with a small rag. The TV screen is simultaneously revealed and obscured as his time-shifted video double performs its contrary task.[8]

As a performance, *The Rake's Progress* is a whirl of unstable temporal relationships, identity collisions, and electronic loopings as only the video medium can provide.[9] The notion of "live," an action transpiring before us, is challenged by the immediacy of a video image that in tandem mimics and mocks Fox's real-world action. Feedback that states which video is essentially consuming itself might come to mind, but here Fox has enacted the doubled metaphor of feedback, not the thing itself. With the temporalities of "inside" and "outside," the TV set negated through their reversal, Fox is, finally, suspended inside a performative loop in which the "Rake" makes no "progress."

1976

1   The full title, taken from the videotape packaging, is *The Rake's Progress: In the Service of Art*.
2   William Hogarth's *A Rake's Progress* is a collection of eight paintings, completed from 1732–33, depicting the accelerating decline of a dissolute young man as he plunges first into debauchery, then destitution, and finally into the halls of Bedlam.
3   MOCA was then located at 86 Third Street in downtown San Francisco.
4   Perhaps this grease is a sly reference to Joseph Beuys, with whom Fox had performed *Isolation Unit* in November 1970.
5   Earlier, in 1970, Vito Acconci made the work *Openings*, in which the camera closely frames his stomach. Acconci slowly and painfully pulls out all the hair surrounding his navel until the frame shows only his denuded paunch. This might be the opposite of Fox's grease application – a subtractive rather than additive action.
6   It should be noted that George Bolling does not stand behind the camera. The video deck is in record mode, with the tripod-mounted camera gazing upon the scene.
7   Rosalind Krauss, "Video: The Aesthetics of Narcissism," *October*, 1, Spring 1976, pp. 50–64, reprinted in *New Artists Video*, Gregory Battcock (ed.), New York, E.P. Dutton, 1978, pp. 43–64.
8   One might ask what twinning means to a twin.
9   Other important works addressing this same kind of medium-specific mirroring would soon follow. See Joan Jonas's *Vertical Roll* (1972), Peter Campus' *Three Transitions* (1973), and Richard Serra's *Boomerang* (1974).

ny Fox   Ⓖ⒮   George Bolling

"Turgescent Sex" 40:00   documentation of
a performance

elements: cloth bandage
          cigarette
          match
          fish
          rope
          bowl of water
          bar of soap

          despair

sit crosslegged surrounded by elements /
wash hands / wash fish bound by rope in many
~~knots~~ knots / blindfold with bandage / mark eyes
on blindfold with blood from fish / release the
fish from bondage / form a nest with the ~~bandage~~ bindings /
wrap the fish with the bandage / cover the fish with
smoke .

George Bolling, Note, c. 1971, source: de Saisset Museum, Santa Clara University

Interview by Tom Kennedy with George Bolling: Invisible is the Medium

Documentation of Untitled (The Trip). George Bolling, Mel Henderson, Paul Kos, Bonnie Sherk (from left to right), photo: Larry Fox

TOM KENNEDY
When did you begin working with video?

GEORGE BOLLING
My involvement in video began in 1969 when a friend bought a Portapak. My first year was spent becoming familiar with the medium. My experience prior to that time had been in photography and film, and video is very different from film. There were no functional half-inch editing machines available. Without editing, it was virtually impossible to manipulate the tape after it was shot. It required then that any shooting be completely choreographed from beginning to end prior to shooting. However, most of my taping opportunities were of artists working in their studios and it was impossible to know what would happen from moment to moment. In doing these documentaries, I developed a sense of dealing with the moment, choreographing the shooting in a flow with the situation at hand. There was concern for image, but the fundamental concern was time, became time. This is very different from film, which is conceived shot by shot, image by image, with time becoming a result of the equation of the image. With video, I found that the objective was to relate the moment first, and the image had to be in tune with that fact (the moment) of the situation.

T.K. How was documentation different from documentary?

G.B. Fundamentally, in documentation you know beforehand pretty much what's going to happen and about how long it will happen. This provides an opportunity to plan in advance a choreography for the shooting. That doesn't mean that you plan each step and each second of the shooting. It means that you can consider the gestures in the performance, their value, and thereby the appropriate recording point. Most importantly, you can judge the pacing of the event, which is necessary for insuring that the transition from point to point is of proper duration to each point at the right time. This is very different from a documentary where you don't know what happens next, which incidentally makes documentary a very valuable learning situation.

T.K. But in documentary, couldn't you simply ask the artist what he's going to do in the studio, and wouldn't that be the same as knowing in advance what the performance is to be?

G.B. Not really, for in documentary, the tape is all yours. It's not the finished sculpture or painting which the artist can keep and sell later. In performance documentation, the videotape becomes the piece to a much greater extent because it is the only physical representation of the performance. As a result, there is a great responsibility to render the performance accurately. It you misrepresent the artist in a documentary, the damage is far less because there is the finished painting or sculpture to counter any misrepresentation – which is not the case in documentation. I had heard rumors before meeting them that performance artists did not want their pieces documented because to you had to be there. Certainly film is no substitution for the real thing because film has its own synthetic time sense. Time is very central to performance. As a video artist I was intrigued by the possibility of documenting performance, because I saw time as the central issue of video. Admittedly, video is no substitution for the real thing, but it does render time with less distortion than film. The challenge then was to render the performance in video with as little interference as possible; the manipulation of the camera had to be invisible.

1976

Source: Interview from *La Mamelle*, vol. 1 (3), Winter 1976, video issue, republished by Tanya Zimbardo, "Georg Bolling: Invisible is the Medium," San Francisco Museum of Modern Art's Open Space, http://openspace.sfmoma.org/2013/03/george-bolling, accessed September 30, 2015

Interview by Dena Beard with Marilyn Bogerd

DENA BEARD

What do you think compelled Terry's generosity, his kindness, and that frankness as well?

MARILYN BOGERD

It's about his being with you, one hundred percent, listening to you without judging, and sharing his side of the story, his experiences. I had personal circumstances in my childhood that made me phobic of death, and I almost died. It was interesting to talk with Terry because he had died for a few minutes while in the hospital, when he had cancer.

D.B.   When he was seventeen?

M.B.   When he was 27 at UCSF (University of California Hospital). His brother put his hand on his arm and asked him to come back and he did. He always laughed and said: "Marilyn, death is not scary, life is!" And then he would tell me many stories of friends and artists that he knew who had serious confrontations with death; some had terminal illnesses. He'd talk about what they did about it and shared his own experiences in the hospital. That was his way of being kind and caring.
Terry also talked about Joseph Beuys, Robert Frank and Chris Burden's kindness as some sort of superior kindness. Or he would talk about Nam June Paik's concentration – seeing him at 3 o'clock in the morning in a subway in NYC where they were the only 2 people on the train and Paik never looked around. He was deeply in his thoughts, completely focused.

D.B.   It's interesting that you equate that generosity, his generosity of spirit with a kind of concentration and a type of concentration that is particularly artistic. And he found that in Beuys, Frank, Burden and Paik […]

M.B.   When Terry found out that he had cancer, about three months left to live and no health insurance, he donated himself to UCSF, a teaching hospital. He stayed there 6 months, had the largest graft ever done to his chest, the radiation entirely burned his sternum, and he had to lay still for weeks at the time. Nowadays in hospitals you get a television right in your face, often a roommate with all their relatives and people coming in and out at any hours. But it wasn't like that back then, almost 45 years ago.
And to be told one day that you were cured!
He dealt with the isolation, the pain, the fear as an artist.

D.B.   You've told me before about these long talks that you and Terry would have throughout the night. Did he ever talk about his work or his process?

M.B.   Yes, of course. Especially when he came back from performing in Europe.

D.B   So you had a funny story about how you met Terry.

M.B.   Yes, I met Terry at a Halloween party in 1974. I was an art student and came from Belgium, wearing a simple man's plaster mask.
Here Terry comes to the party – wearing a stocking over his head […]

D.B.   Like a women's nylon stocking?

M.B.   Yes, like one of these bank robbers. He was laughing and went around spooking everybody. [both laugh]

[…]

M.B.   One other story I wanted to tell you is about Georg, Georg Decristel, a very close friend of Terry's, who became my friend too. Georg was a wonderful person, poet and artist, who was born and lived in Innsbruck. They often traveled and performed together as they did at the Berkeley Art Museum in 1978.
Georg played the Jew's harp and had a large collection of them that he shared with people he met. It was an ongoing conversation with everyone who played with him.
On one evening, at a crowded party, everyone greeted Terry and talked with him since he had moved to New York City and many of his friends hadn't seen him for a while. Terry was staying with me, in San Francisco, for a few days. We came back that evening from a performance, and half way through the party Georg and I sat against the wall at each opposite side of the room. We both played the Jew's harp, back and forth, back and forth. It went on for a long time. When the party ended, Terry joined us and told us that he had heard our entire Jew's harp conversations. Despite so many people talking to him and the loud music, he followed the whole conversation.
It's just an example of Terry's amazing awareness of his environment, and of the people around him. Terry could see the inner person. He never judged people by their looks. As a result, he could form relationships with many different types of people in all sorts of different milieux.

2015

Terry Fox, Untitled, Site, San Francisco, 1977

Renny Pritikin
Alternative Art Spaces in San Francisco

In the mid-1970s San Francisco was an unusually rich stew of artistic ferment.
In particular were the projects of the first generation of conceptual artists, including
Bonnie Sherk, Howard Fried, Jim Pomeroy, Paul Kos, Lynn Hershman, Doug Hall,
David Ireland, Tom Marioni, Jock Reynolds, and many others, including of course
Terry Fox, all defining an alternative form of the movement that mixed in various
elements of performance and body-centered activity, humor, and politics.
At the same time they and their students (my generation) were starting an amazing
network of alternative spaces that supported installation, performance, video and
experimental poetry and music. These organizations – such as New Langton
Arts, (where I worked), La Mamelle, Southern Exposure, SF Camerawork, Site/Cite/
Sight, Galeria de la Raza, and many others – emphasized a participatory
democracy, building installations founded and run by and for artists, cutting out
the role of curators, collectors and other arts professionals. Artists were paid, ran
the organizations, and had primary control of everything. Finally, there was
an unusual fluency between composers of new music and sculptors making sound
installations that opened up all kinds of possibilities, culminating in the historic
New Music America festivals that combined visual art and experimental music and
performance.

    This is the environment in which Terry Fox emerged.

2015

Marilyn Bogerd
Site, Cite, Sight

Site, Cite, Sight Inc. was established in 1976 to support work by artists without
regard to its commercial potential.

    Each artist determined the structure of his/her work, the use of the space,
time, materials and public access to his/her work.

    This non-profit organization was funded by the National Endowment
for the Arts. The artists had the same budget and received the same honorarium.

    During the first 3½ years, the founders curated 32 artists/shows. Then,
each of these artists were asked to select a new artist to exhibit or perform at Site.
For the catalogue, each artist had the choice to write their own description of
their work.

    In April 1982, Site lost its lease at 585 Mission Street and was forced to close.

2015

Marion Gray, Terry Fox and Georg Decristel, University Art Museum, Berkeley, 1978

Interview by Terri Cohn with Terry Fox

TERRY FOX
I have a problem with the word "conceptual."

TERRI COHN
That's a good place to start, because my first question is, when did you become a conceptual artist, and why did you become one?

T.F.   I didn't even hear the word "conceptual" until much later. It may have been when Tom Marioni opened the Museum of Conceptual Art.

T.C.   So how did you identify yourself? As a sculptor?

T.F.   Yes. But I was a painter first. I started seriously painting in 1962. I lived in Rome then. I went there to go to the painting school, but they went on strike and closed so I couldn't. But I stayed there for a year and painted.

[...]

T.C.   Being a painter is very expensive.

T.F.   Yes. And paper was extremely cheap then. So I just bought ink and paper and started making drawings. From my painting experience, which was very conventional, I needed a subject, so I tried to reproduce the Paris walls.

[...]

T.F.   In 1968, the last paintings I was doing were on plexiglass sheets. They were painted black, totally spray painted black on the back. Then I scratched different colors into the paint with a hypodermic needle. They almost couldn't be seen. You had to get down on your hands and knees and really follow them. I think that was the beginning, for me, of a performance sort of idea. At the same time, I had gone to New York, and I found the whole collection of Fluxus books, so I knew all about Fluxus and their activities. When I went to Reese Palley Gallery and talked to Carol Lindsley who ran the gallery then, I told her all about Fluxus, and I think that's why she accepted me!

[...]

In Amsterdam, I had reconnected with Bill Wiley, and I started a dust exchange with him. I would send dust from a certain metro in Paris, and he would send me dust, and we would write letters to each other also, saying where we got the dust. I took dust from the Louvre, and all kinds of very interesting places in Paris, and he would take dust from places like the San Francisco Museum of Art, or the San Francisco Art Institute, and then the dust I sent him from the Louvre, he would put back in the place where he took the dust, and I would take the dust that he sent and put it in the Louvre.

[...]

T.C.   People today would probably be very paranoid because you were introducing spores from one continent to another. But that's about now, and when you were doing your dust exchange people didn't worry about anything like that.

T.F.   No. It was before anthrax. In 1967, I had also brought with me two paintings on glass, I think they were about 1.5 × 1.5 ft., and as an event, I went to Cologne and was in a film screening. While I was there, I deposited these paintings at the Gallery Zwirner, which was the best gallery in Cologne. I don't know what Zwirner did with them. He's not there anymore.

T.C.   He didn't show them?

T.F.   He wasn't there when I went there. So I just left the paintings. They were signed on the back, but I don't know what happened to them. Maybe he sold them. Who knows?

Marion Gray, Terry Fox and Nina Wise, *Yellow Duck and Tonka Beans*, 1978

[...]

T.F. It was for me. Tom was already the curator at the Richmond Art Center. When he invited me in 1969 to be in *The Return of Abstract Expressionism*, I again used flying sheets. Some were outside being moved by the wind, and some were inside.
The next thing Tom did was a sort of radical idea. He had hired Larry Bell to visit a lot of artists and look at their work, and pick out three. Then he invited us to a show in Richmond in the *Sculpture Annual* that they had every year. That was 1970. That's when I did my *Levitation* piece.

T.C. Do you want to talk about it a bit?

T.F. Sure. At that time I had Hodgkin's Disease, and I had just gone through an operation. I really wanted to get rid of it, and I really did want to levitate. I was given the big major gallery, and I covered the floor with white paper so the walls, the ceiling, and the floor were all white. It was already kind of like ... floating.

T.C. Sort of like a hospital room?

T.F. Yes. I lived on Capp Street near Army in San Francisco, and they were just building the freeway there. We rented a truck and took a ton and a half of dirt from there to Richmond, and then I laid the dirt down in a square that was twice my body height on this paper floor. I had polyethylene tubes, and I had some of my blood taken out and I filled a tube with blood and made a circle, like you always see in Leonardo's drawings. Then I lay on the earth in the circle, but I fasted for three days and nights first, to really empty myself. I had four long polyethylene tubes that were much longer than the one full of blood. One was full of milk, and one was full of urine, one blood, and the fourth water. I held two in each hand, and I lay there by myself for six hours trying to levitate. The door was locked, so it wasn't a performance that people could see – nobody was allowed in the room. I really felt like I levitated, because I lost all the sensation in my body. I wanted to leave the Hodgkin's behind, and that was a way of doing it.

T.C.   Did you eventually get rid of the disease?

T.F.   Yes.

T.C.   So maybe that helped?

T.F.   Yes.

T.C.   It sounds like an amazing experience.

T.F.   What I was trying to do was to energize that space in such a way that when people came in after I was gone, they could feel the energy. That was the sculptural idea behind the whole thing.

T.C.   Did the installation stay up for a period of time?

T.F.   No! But Tom can tell you that story. He got fired because of that.

        [...]

T.F.   In 1971, there was a show there called *Fish, Fox, Kos,* which included Paul Kos, Tom (his pseudonym was Allan Fish), and me. That was another kind of strange experience for me. Again, I did a long fast, and didn't sleep beforehand.

T.C.   There seems to be a pattern here, that you spent periods of time either not sleeping or not eating prior to an event.

T.F.   Yes. This was both. It was still in my mind a way of cleansing my body, of cleansing all this disease out. So I bought two live fish in Chinatown, big bass. I used cords and tied one to my tongue and one to my penis. Then I sat up until they died, which was REALLY a long time. I thought it would be like twenty minutes, but it was at least two hours. I thought they'd be dead and then suddenly I'd see the tail flip a little bit and I could feel the vibrations really strongly through the cords. With that, and passing whatever I had to them I hoped they could take it and die with it.
        I had covered the floor in the museum with a white tarp. About three feet off of the floor I made a roofing of white tarp over the whole space and I brought the sheets. I retied the fish, and just lay down and then I immediately went to sleep. There was an opening and people could look through the door, but not come in the space. So they saw me sleeping with these fish tied to me.

        [...]

        There was a show in Dusseldorf, *Prospect '71: Projections,* and it included one of my favorite artists, Joseph Beuys. They paid for my trip to go there, but my main purpose was to meet Beuys. I also wanted to do a performance somewhere. So I went to the Art Academy and I met him. He was really wonderful. His wife and children were gone, so he drove me to his house and made dinner and we talked. He said I could do my performance in the basement of the Art Academy. He arranged to have the poster made; it was really nice. Then he talked to me about a week before, and asked if he could do the performance with me. It was totally incredible for me!
        The reason he wanted to do the performance with me was, he had a mouse that lived under his bed and this mouse had just died. I know, the story doesn't sound believable at all, but it's true. Anyway, this mouse had died, and Beuys wanted to do a kind of funeral for it. When he asked if he could do it, of course I was thrilled. So both of our names were on the announcement card and poster for *Isolation Unit.* They were put up on the walls all around in Dusseldorf. He had just made his Block Edition *Felt Suit* and he wore it for the first time to this performance. He had a reel-to-reel tape recorder and he gave the mouse a ride on the reels as it was going. We recorded the whole thing. I had long iron pipes that I banged together, because I was already as interested in sound as in performance; I was changing a little bit, always including sound in my work. I had a window with six panes in the corner and I tried to break the glass with the vibrations from the pipes. When I felt like it was almost breaking, I'd smash the glass with the pipes. I had a candle in the middle of the space with a light bulb hanging right next to it, so you couldn't see the light from the candle except very close up.

T.C.   Because the light bulb would block the candlelight out?

T.F.   Yes, that's right. Then with the two smallest pipes – they were maybe a foot long [...] at the end of the performance I sat and tried to bend the candle flame with their vibrations. That did work. Beuys walked around holding his hand open, showing the dead mouse to the public, who were behind a rope at the entrance. They couldn't come into the room. It was a real dirty room. It was a former coal bin in the bottom of the academy.

T.C.   It sounds like quite a contrast to all the pristine white spaces you usually work in.

T.F.   It was exactly the opposite. After doing that, I changed my interest in the kinds of spaces I wanted to work in too. I didn't even think about that until you mentioned the white spaces.

T.C.   What kind of spaces did you decide to work in after that?

T.F.   Oh, interesting spaces! That performance helped me a lot.

2005

(abridged)
The interview is published in full in SFAQ, vol. 2, issue 2, Fall 2015

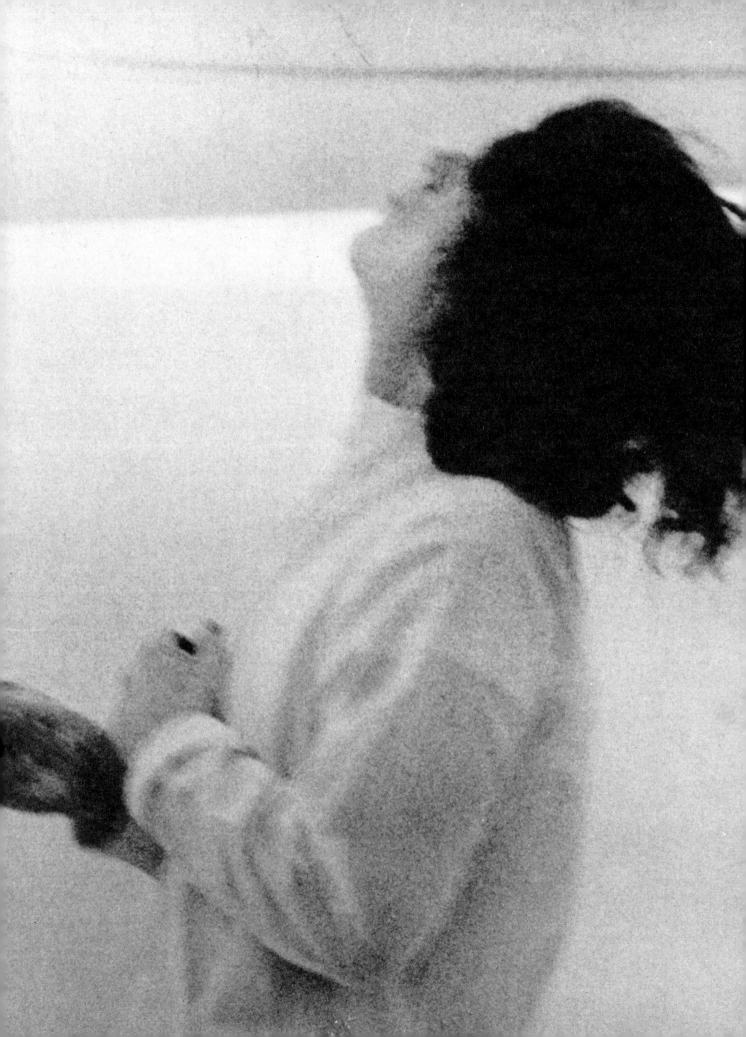

Übersetzung
Dokumente, Statements

Die Dokumentation vereint bislang unpublizierte Archivdokumente aus dem Estate of Terry Fox, Köln, dem Berkeley Art Museum and Pacific Film Archive (BAM/PFA), de Saisset Museum Santa Clara University, dem Archiv der Akademie der Künste, Berlin, Wulf-Herzogenrath-Archiv, sowie eigens für diese Publikation verfasste Statements und Interviews mit Künstlerfreunden und Zeitgenossen von Terry Fox, die ich in den USA befragen konnte. Sie wurden durch Texte aus Zeitschriften wie *Avalanche, Arts Magazine* oder *View* ergänzt.

Angela Lammert

Skulptur wird immer erweitert, neue Elemente werden hinzugefügt. […] Heute, dreißig Jahre später, arbeite ich immer noch mit dem Aspekt der Neudefinition von Skulptur, aber in einer äußerst persönlichen Weise. Ich möchte eher ein sympathisches Ohr oder Auge erreichen als ein breites Publikum […] Der Prozess, eine Skulptur zu machen, schließt das Denken und Handeln auf der Seite des Betrachters ein, um das Werk zu vollenden.

Terry Fox, *1999*

Quelle: Schmidt 2000, S. 200

Seite 244

Eva Schmidt
Zu Künstlerstatements

„Was ist im Einzelnen passiert?" „Wie hängt dieses mit jenem zusammen?" „Was sind die Beweggründe?" Der Künstler antwortet, indem er erzählt, was passiert ist, wobei alle Informationen zunächst einmal gleich wichtig sind: der konkrete Umgang mit Materialien, die Struktur des Ablaufs, Anekdoten am Rande, die Reaktionen des Publikums, existentielle Erfahrungen, Ansichten über Kunst und Performance im Allgemeinen. Diese Hierarchielosigkeit kann nur aus der Perspektive des Künstlers gewährleistet werden. Jede nachfolgende Rezeption und Interpretation wird diese Gleichwertigkeit zerstören und eine Form und Struktur herausdestillieren. Mit der Erzählung in den Interviews verwandt sind eine Reihe kurzer Kommentare. […] In ihnen ist der Sprechende explizit anwesend.

Die Erzählung, der Kommentar des Künstlers, sie sind auch deshalb so wichtig, weil die Performance bekanntermaßen nicht so leicht musealisierbar ist. Sie hat einmal stattgefunden, und die Erinnerung an sie kann – neben Aufzeichnung durch Fotografie und Video – durch die Erzählung in das Archiv eingehen, das in Zukunft als Teil des Museums gerade für die seit den 1960er Jahren entwickelten, nicht ausstellbaren Kunstformen zunehmend wichtiger werden wird. Das Erzählen wird in diesem Buch [*Ocular Language*, Köln 2000] vom Schreiben begleitet: Aus dem Geschriebenen hat sich der Sprechende zurückgezogen. Das Rätsel, das kondensierte, manifestartige Statement sind Konstruktion und Poesie. Besonders ist hier zu erwähnen der große Text *Blood Line*, der einen ungerichteten Wahrnehmungsvorgang beschreibt, ohne konventionelle Syntax, ohne Interpunktion. Unklar ist, wer aus welcher Perspektive spricht, eher gibt es gar kein Subjekt. Der Text tendiert zur Aufzählung, er akzeptiert die Zusammenhanglosigkeit. Er ist mit einer Reihe von Arbeiten verwandt, die auf Untersuchungen von Begriffen, Zeichen und Piktogrammen basieren. Die Serie *Catch Phrases*, die Fox in diesem Buch beschreibt, ist dafür ein weiteres Beispiel: Textmaterial wird in Zeichnungen, Rauminstallationen und skulpturalen Gebilden weiterverarbeitet. Die Buchstaben verlieren die konventionelle Gerichtetheit auf der Buchseite. Die Rechts-Linksorientierung und die Linearität der untereinandergesetzten Zeilen werden aufgegeben zugunsten einer labyrinthischen Komplexität. Diese meist dreidimensionale Verwendung von Schrift und Text kann hier nur angedeutet werden, über sie wird in einigen Interviews gesprochen.

Quelle: Schmidt 2000, S. iv–v

Seite 246 ff.

Elemental Gestures:
Terry Fox

Die Kommentare zu den Fotos sind Zitate aus einem Interview mit dem Künstler. Fotografien von Barry Klinger: Abdruck mit Genehmigung des Museum of Conceptual Art, San Francisco.

1. Terry Fox, *Free Flying Polyethylene Sheet*, Strand im Golden Gate Park, August 1969.

Ich hielt eine 2,75 × 3,65 Meter große Folie aus Polyäthylen in den Wind. Als sie anfing, sich in der Luft aufzubauschen, ließ ich los. Sie bewegte sich vertikal wie eine Flamme den Strand entlang.

2. Terry Fox, *Defoliation Piece*, University Art Museum, Berkeley, März 1970.

Dies war meine erste politische Arbeit. Ich wollte die Blüten auf eine sehr präzise Weise zerstören. Wenn ich ein perfektes Rechteck in die Mitte brannte, würde es aussehen, als ob sie jemand absichtlich zerstört hätte. Die Blüten waren chinesischer Jasmin, der fünf Jahre vorher gepflanzt worden war und nach zwei Jahren blühte. Es war auch ein theatralisches Stück. Jeder sieht gern Feuer. Es prasselte wunderschön laut. Aber auf einmal begriffen die Leute, was los war – die Landschaft wurde beschädigt, Blüten wurden verbrannt. Plötzlich waren alle still. Eine Frau weinte 20 Minuten lang.

3. Terry Fox, *Air Pivot*, Pine Street, San Francisco, Juni 1969.

Ich befestigte eine Polyäthylen-Folie an einer Achse, die sich frei drehen konnte, so dass das Material auf die Veränderungen der Windrichtung reagierte. Die Folie drehte sich um 360 Grad im Kreis. Diese Fotografien zeigen Ausschnitte einer vollständigen Drehung vor einer Standkamera.

4. Terry Fox, *Liquid Smoke*, Third Street, San Francisco, April 1970.

Flüssigrauch an eine Mauer zu werfen, war eigentlich eine anarchistische Gebärde wie der Wurf eines Molotowcocktails. Aber so war es in Wirklichkeit überhaupt nicht. Sobald die Glasphiole am Zement platzte, wurde es ein ästhetisches Ereignis. Im Kontakt mit der Luft fing die Flüssigkeit an

zu rauchen, bis sie völlig verdampft war. Es war so unerwartet und anders als die Vorstellungen, die man sich vorher von der Sache gemacht hatte, dass es zu Kunst wurde. Man würde sich nie eine rauchende Zementmauer ausmalen, und es war spektakulär zu sehen, wie es dazu kam.

5. Terry Fox, *A Sketch for Impacted Lead*, San Francisco, April 1970.

Ich wollte eine Arbeit mit Blei machen, bei der physikalische Kräfte wirken, und ich hatte vor, Gewehrkugeln zu nehmen. Wenn eine Kugel durch den Gewehrlauf schießt, wird sie mit unglaublichem Tempo geschleudert und bewegt sich schneller vorwärts als der Schall. Beim Aufprall verändert das Blei seine Form, einfach durch die bloße Kraft dieser Energie. Ich hoffe, es gelingt mir bei dieser Aktion in der Reese Palley Gallery, die Kugeln eng nebeneinander in horizontaler Linie zu schießen, so dass sie möglichst ein schmales, zerbrechliches Band aus Blei bilden.

6. Terry Fox, *What Do Blind Men Dream?*, 20001 Union Street, San Francisco, April 1969.

Dies war die zweite Aktion in der Reihe Public Theater. Ich hatte eine wunderschöne blinde Dame entdeckt und bat sie, von 17.30 Uhr bis Einbruch der Dunkelheit an einer Straßenecke von San Francisco in der Nähe einer riesigen Baugrube zu singen. Es wurden Einladungen verschickt und eine Menge Leute kamen. Wir machten eine Aufnahme von dieser Arbeit, die ich immer noch habe.

7. Terry Fox, *Push Piece*, Minna Street, San Francisco, April 1970.

Als wir den Umzug von Toms Atelier machten, fiel mir eine Ziegelmauer in einer Gasse auf. Ich ging hin und begann, sie abzutasten. Dann begann ich zu drücken. Während ich das tat, fühlte ich, was diese Mauer war, welche materielle Festigkeit sie hatte. Ich glaube nicht, dass ich jetzt ausdrücken könnte, was das für mich bedeutete.

Willoughby Sharp

Einige Tage vor der Eröffnung der Ausstellung „The Eighties" am 16. März im University Art Museum von Berkeley hatte Terry Fox im Mediterranian Café in der Telegraph Avenue eine kleine Menge Schießpulver in einen Glasaschenbecher gefüllt und angezündet. Die Explosion, mit der er sich eine Verbrennung dritten Grades an der rechten Hand zuzog, hätte fast eine seiner Arbeiten sein können, die mit ihren heftigen physikalischen und chemischen Umwandlungen oft ein charakteristisches Element von Gefahr einbeziehen. Zum Glück hielt dieser Unfall Fox nicht davon ab, sein *Defoliation Piece* durchzuführen, für das er in einem Beet mit seltenem chinesischem Jasmin genau vor dem Museumseingang ein großes Rechteck abbrannte.

Nachdem ich mir die Ausstellung aktueller Arbeiten vieler wichtiger Künstler der Bay Area drei Mal angesehen hatte, fand ich, dass dieses skulpturale Projekt der visionärste Beitrag in dieser zukunftweisenden Ausstellung war. Die Ideen vieler Arbeiten von Fox sind auf seine unmittelbare Wahrnehmung und eine gesteigerte Sensibilität für alltägliche Begebenheiten zurückzuführen. Seine Beschäftigung mit dem Thema Wasser geht auf eine konkrete zufällige Wahrnehmung im März 1968 zurück. An einem trüben Tag ging er eine hügelige Straße im algerischen Teil von Paris entlang, hinter ihm floss ein Wasserlauf „wie ein langsam treibender flüssiger Spiegel". Dieser Eindruck regte ihn zu einer Reihe skulpturaler Experimente mit Wasser an, die sowohl in Innenräumen als auch im Freien stattfanden. Unter den frühen Arbeiten mit Wasser war ein Behälter, der mit schwarzem Rohöl und Wasser gefüllt war, die mit einer Heizspule warmgehalten wurden, was unsichtbar für Austausch sorgte. Ein Holzbalken mit fünf konkaven Vertiefungen, die mit Wasser gefüllt waren, in denen ein kleiner vibrierender Ventilator Wellen erzeugte. Tiefe Traktorspuren, die mit Wasser gefüllt waren. Zwei Plastikfolien, die mit winzigen Tröpfchen besprengt waren und die Reflexionsfähigkeit von Wasser ergründeten.

Diese Arbeiten, und auch die auf dieser Seite abgebildeten Arbeiten mit Luftströmen, verdeutlichen das übergeordnete Thema der Dynamik von physikalischen Prozessen und der elementaren Kräfte im Urzustand. Fox' erklärte Einstellung zu Gegenständen ist unzweideutig: „Mein Leben lang habe ich Gegenstände mit Furcht betrachtet ..., aber jeder Gegenstand, ob eine Zigarette oder ein Stein, erschien mir immer schön, wenn ich nur ihn anschaute." Daher mag Fox' teilweise unorthodoxes Vorgehen bei der Auswahl seines künstlerischen Materials kommen. Ein anderer von Fox benannter Faktor ist die entscheidende Rolle, die seine aktive Teilnahme an den Pariser Protesten im Mai 1968 in seinem Leben spielte. Zwischen der Ästhetik von schwankenden Kopfsteinpflasterstrukturen, die er einmal aufbaute, und den Pflastersteinen, die er auf die französische Polizei warf, zieht er eine enge Parallele: In beiden sah er kinetische Systeme, wenngleich er sich im Letzteren als Künstler des Motivs der Gewalt bediente. Dieser gedankliche Schritt führte dazu, dass Fox die letzten Reste der Atelierbildhauerei abstreifte und Aktionen im echten Leben plante. Seine erste skulpturale Aktion nach seiner Rückkehr nach Amerika bestand darin, dass er in den Straßen von New York und San Francisco Feuerhydranten öffnete. Diese Arbeit war ein Vorläufer für sein Public Theater, zu dem er beispielsweise eine Einladung zu einer Versammlung an einer besonders gefährlichen Straßenkreuzung an der Fillmore Ecke McAllister Street verschickte, oder auch *What Do Blind Men Dream?*. Die aktuelleren Arbeiten sind vom theaterähnlichen Charakter der Straßenaktionen, bei denen Aspekte des gesellschaftlichen Lebens sichtbar werden, zu einer Kunst übergegangen, die sich aus menschlichen Gesten entwickelt. *Liquid Smoke* und *Impacted Lead* verwenden einfache körperliche Gebärden: Werfen und Ziehen und die darauffolgenden physikalischen Veränderungen: Eine Flüssigkeit wird gasförmig, ein Feststoff zerfällt. In beiden Arbeiten stellt sich für Fox das ästhetische Erlebnis ein, nachdem er eine elementare Geste ausgeführt hat. Aber die Theaternähe der Arbeit besteht in anderer Hinsicht fort, da der Künstler die Situation als Handelnder bestimmt, selbst wenn er versucht, „seinen eigenen Willen so wenig wie möglich einwirken zu lassen".

Fox' Hauptanliegen ist die Wechselwirkung zwischen Substanzen und Energie in unterschiedlichen Aggregatzuständen, für das Hinterfragen formaler Fragestellungen hat er wenig Sinn. Bei der Wahl seiner künstlerischen Mittel, ob flüssig, amorph oder nicht materiell, schließt er einen steuernden Einfluss auf die finale Gestalt seiner Stücke aus. „Mir wird erst bewusst, wie ein Stück aussieht, wenn ich die Fotografien sehe." Fox arbeitet eng mit einem Freund zusammen, dem Fotografen Barry Klinger. Die hier abgebildete (nicht vollständige) Fotoserie, zeigt einzigartige Kunstwerke aus eigenem Recht. Das Foto dient nicht mehr vorrangig dem Zweck, über Fakten zu informieren, obwohl es ästhetische Informationen vermittelt. Es ist kein „Andenken" an das Kunstwerk. In vielerlei bedeutsamer Hinsicht übernehmen diese Fotografien die Rolle der Skulptur.

1970

Quelle: *Arts Magazine*, New York, Mai 1970, S. 48–51

Aus dem Englischen übersetzt von Anne Pitz

Seite 250

Videointerview von Jeanette Willison

TERRY FOX

Ich war ungefähr zehn Jahre lang Maler, und das Malen war für mich unbefriedigend, weil ich nicht erreichte, dass die Leute meine Bilder betrachteten, und ich nie irgendein Feedback bekam und weil ich mich in der Malerei nicht wirklich gut ausdrücken konnte. Und ich war am Anfang in die Malerei gegangen, weil man eben, um Künstler zu werden, Maler oder Bildhauer wurde.

JEANETTE WILLISON

Das war damals eine Konvention. In welche Richtung der Malerei ging es?

T.F. Ich malte gegenständlich und später, kurz bevor ich die Malerei 1967 aufgab, waren meine Bilder während des letzten Jahres vollkommen schwarz und auf Glas gemalt. Sie hatten sehr glänzende, reflektierende Oberflächen, an die man wirklich ganz nah herangehen musste. Der Betrachter musste auf die Hände und Knie hinuntergehen und nah herangehen und die feinen Linien suchen. Sonst spiegelten sie einfach nur. Aber mein Ziel bei diesen Bildern war es, den Betrachter wirklich einzubeziehen und ihn dazu zu bringen, einige Zeit mit meiner Arbeit zu verbringen. Ich begann dann, mit alltäglichen und flüchtigen Materialien zu arbeiten, Sachen mit Feuer und Folien aus Plastik und Schüsseln mit Wasser oder flach ausgegrabene Rinnen mit Wasser darin, in denen sich Wolken und anderes spiegelten.

J.W. Also, es ging nicht darum, bleibende Kunstwerke zu machen, es ging um eine momentane Empfindung?

T.F. Ich versuchte, mit meiner Kunst sehr viel direkter zu werden, den Leuten sozusagen auf einer unmittelbar spiegelbildlichen Basis zu begegnen. Die Lösung war schließlich, Performances zu machen. Ich fing 1970 an, Performances zu machen. Weil das dieses Dilemma, das ich mit meinen Bildern hatte, löste. Wenn ich eine Performance machte, dauerte es ungefähr eine Stunde oder drei Stunden. Ich lud Leute dazu ein, und sie erlebten, was ich produzierte. Ich konnte ihnen alles unmittelbar übergeben, statt ihnen ein Objekt für ihre Kontemplation vorzustellen, auf die sie sich nicht einlassen würden, eine Kontemplation, auf die sie sich erfahrungsgemäß nicht einließen. Was die Leute von sich hinzutun, ergibt mit dem, was ich gebe, das, was die ganze Performance ausmacht, mitsamt den Gegenständen und allen weiteren Aspekten. Performancekunst ermöglicht es mir, meine Kunst überall zu machen: zum Beispiel auf der Straße oder bei jemandem zu Hause oder in der Bluxome Street oder in einer Galerie oder sonstwo. Und man braucht kein Geld dafür. Man braucht kein Material. Man kann ein Stück aus dem Nichts machen. Der Grund, warum ich Performances mache, ist, dass ich dabei so viel Energie aus mir hole, wie ich kann. Ich hebe sie mir regelrecht auf und lasse sie in ein, zwei Stunden heraus und versuche, diese Energie weiterzugeben. All die physikalischen Aspekte des Geschehens, wie die Kerze und der Klang und all das, sind wie Werkzeuge. Bei anderen Performances sind es andere Gegenstände. Sie alle sind Hilfsmittel, um die Energie freizusetzen und in Bewegung zu halten. Bei Performances werden viele Gegenstände benutzt, und es werden viele Gegenstände während Performances erschaffen. Meist haben diese Gegenstände aber eine unglaubliche Konzentration erfahren, und sie spiegeln das wieder.

[Kurzfilm: *Children's Tapes*]

[Fortsetzung des Interviews:]

T.F. Die Leute gehen an die Kunstakademie und lernen, wie man Kunstobjekte macht, und sie bekommen einen Abschluss, der bescheinigt, dass sie Meisterschüler für die Herstellung dieser Objekte sind. Und man hat ihnen beigebracht, diese Objekte so zu gestalten, dass es für die Abschlussprüfung passt usw. Ich will nicht sagen, jeder, aber sehr viele machen diese Sache einfach weiter und halten das für Kunst, oder sie denken, dass das Kunst sei. Sie denken, wenn sie etwas herstellen, das wie Kunst aussieht, dass es dann Kunst sei.

Alle Welt und die Öffentlichkeit denken im Allgemeinen, dass man ein Kunstwerk besäße, wenn man ein Bild besitzt. Oder dass Malerei große Kunst sei. Dass der Künstler derjenige sei, der die Kunst macht. Aber so ist es überhaupt nicht. Ich meine, Kunst ist das, was das Bild mitteilt, und nicht das Bild selbst.

Performance überspringt diesen Warencharakter der Kommunikation an der Stelle gewissermaßen und funktioniert einfach unmittelbar. Bei Performancekunst erwartet niemand, der Performances gibt, eine große Masse von Menschen zu erreichen. Performancekunst wird für die Leute gemacht, die dabei sind. Manchmal sind es nur zwei Personen.

[Ende ohne Ton, bricht ab]

1975

Quelle: Private collection

Aus dem Englischen übersetzt von Anne Pitz

Terry Fox
Hospital, Notiz für Barney Bailey

BARNEY

1   Die Staffelei: Die Seite der „Beine" mit Nägeln soll zur Wand zeigen. Die beiden Tafeln sollen einen daumenbreiten Abstand voneinander haben. Sie sollen wie auf der Zeichnung mit *einer* Schraube an die Beine geschraubt werden. Die Schrauben sollten so klein wie möglich sein, aber dick genug, um die Tafeln zu tragen. Die Beine sollen wie auf der Zeichnung nach innen geneigt stehen. Die Tafel soll direkt auf den Beinen festgeschraubt werden. Das Ganze soll an die Wand (in die Mitte der sauberen Wand) gelehnt und möglichst vertikal, aber sicher stehen.

[Zeichnung]

2   Die frei stehende Schultafel und der Pfosten im Brotteig sollen wie auf der Zeichnung gegenüber der Staffelei an die Wand gelehnt werden.
3   Du brauchst ein Verlängerungskabel (der runde, schwarze Typ), das die beiden Rekorder am einen Ende versorgen kann und am Boden verlegt bis zur Krankentrage reicht. (7,60 Meter)
4   Krankentrage angelehnt wie aufgezeichnet.
5   Zeichnungen gehängt wie aufgezeichnet.
6   Die Lampenhalterungen sollen so unauffällig wie möglich sein / die schwarzen Blenden entfernen, die kleinen Halterungen verwenden und weiß anmalen, wo nötig.
7   Den Boden nicht wischen (er sollte jedenfalls nicht glänzen).

Diese Dinge werden alle von mir nachjustiert, wenn ich da bin, aber das wird erst in einigen Tagen sein, so dass es großartig wäre, wenn du bis zum 20. alles so einrichten könntest, wie oben beschrieben.

1971

Quelle: Estate of Terry Fox, Köln / Barney Bailey

Aus dem Englischen übersetzt von Anne Pitz

Seite 251

Brief an Willoughby Sharp

Lieber Willoughby,
nur eine kurze Nachricht, damit Du auf dem Laufenden bleibst. Ich arbeite an einer Ausstellung hier in der neuen [Reese] Palley Gallery, die anschließend nach New York und später, glaube ich, nach Paris gehen soll. Es sind viele Sachen dabei, die ich für Performances gemacht habe, sowie einige neue Objekte, die in Aktionen eingesetzt werden, und einige Bänder, Endlosschleifen auf Tonbandkassetten und natürlich einige Performances mit dem ganzen Material. Es wird eine „substantielle" Ausstellung für mich, und es interessiert mich, weil ich so etwas noch nie gemacht habe.

Ich erhielt einen freundlichen Brief von Beuys. Eine politische Angelegenheit an der Akademie[1] scheint ihn zu blockieren, und er klingt etwas beunruhigt. Er schreibt, dass er in diesem Semester über 400 Studenten haben werde und sie grundlegende Strukturreformen an der Akademie fordern, die er natürlich unterstützt.

Ich habe außerdem einen Brief von Günter Brus erhalten, der in Berlin etwas gemeinsam machen möchte. Das werde ich also tun, wenn ich nach Europa fahre. Er ist der Interessanteste der Gruppe für mich.

Ich komme gerade nach drei Wochen aus dem Krankenhaus und brenne vor kreativem Tatendrang. In einigen Wochen schicke ich Dir neue Fotos, die Dich interessieren könnten. Mein Bruder Larry macht jetzt alle Fotos für mich.

Also, Dir und Liza herzliche Grüße und alles Gute
Ich vermisse Euch beide,
   Herzlich,

                    Terry Fox

                    ca. 1971

1   Kunstakademie Düsseldorf, wo Beuys lehrte.

Quelle: Estate of Terry Fox, Köln

Aus dem Englischen übersetzt von Anne Pitz

WILLOUGHBY SHARP
   Man wird deine Arbeit nicht vollständig verstehen, wenn man dir nicht bei der Durchführung zusieht oder wenn man nicht ein Video davon sieht.

TERRY FOX
   Genau. Fotografien sind ungeeignet, aber ein Video könnte zeigen, was passiert ist. In gewisser Weise hat diese Arbeit ein begrenztes Publikum – genau wie Landschaftsarbeiten. Sehr wenige Leute haben Zugang zu den konkreten Orten dieser Kunst. Ebenso wenig hat man direkten Zugang zu meiner Arbeit, wenn man nicht Zeuge einer Performance ist.

                    1971

Quelle: Ich wollte, dass meine Stimmung ihr Aussehen beeinflusst. Interview mit Willoughby Sharp. In: Schmidt 2000, S. 10

Aus dem Englischen übersetzt von Eva Schmidt

Brief an
Lydia Modi-Vitale

Liebe Lydia,   Paris, 19. September

entschuldige, dass ich nicht früher geschrieben habe, aber ich war so beschäftigt mit allem und bin ohnehin ein miserabler Briefschreiber. Kassel war eine grauenhafte Erfahrung – SCHEISS DEUTSCHE! Alle, außer Beuys und ein oder zwei andere – Als ich ankam, machte ich einen Besichtigungstag, die Performances, und als wir abreisen wollten, weigerten sie sich, mir auch nur einen Penny der restlichen 800 $ zu geben, die sie mir schuldeten – so dass mir Beuys schließlich das Geld anbot. Und jetzt sind sie ihm die 800 $ schuldig, die er geltend machen kann.

Jetzt sind wir wieder in Paris, wo ich am 26. September die Ausstellungssaison für [die Galerie] Sonnabend eröffnen werde. Danach werde ich noch eine Saison für die Modern Art Agency in Neapel eröffnen, in der Beuys, Merz, George + Gilbert usw. ausstellen – von beidem fühle ich mich wirklich geehrt und finde es großartig.

Dieser Brief hat gewissermaßen einen geschäftlichen Anlass. Wir haben hier sehr wenig Geld – wir kochen selbst und auf einem Campingkocher usw. und leben von der Sozialhilfeüberweisung aus San Francisco – also, ich will nicht anfangen zu jobben.

Ich habe in Rotterdam das beste Video produziert, das ich je gemacht habe. Es ist ein 25-minütiges 1-Zoll-Video auf Sony System Color. Die Farbigkeit ist absolut unglaublich, wie ein Farbdia, das lange andauert – nur, dass die Farben perfekt sind – Ich habe sämtliche Weißtöne verwendet – weißes Mehl, eine weiße Kerze, eine weiße Emaille-Schüssel, Rauch, eine Flamme, Hände + Gesicht bilden die einzigen anderen Töne, aber es ist fantastisch!! Die Kamera ist fest und ziemlich nah eingestellt, etwa so:

[Skizze mit Beschriftung:]

weißer Hintergrund, weißes Mehl, schwarze Kante, Wasser.

Es beginnt mit der Einstellung, wie ich es hier skizziert habe, nur dass die Kerze nicht angezündet ist. Ein gesprochener flämischer Text: „Das Feuer im Wasser, das Wasser in der Luft, die Luft im Erdreich und das Erdreich im Meer". Dann kommt meine Hand hinzu, zündet die Kerze an. Ich rauche eine Zigarette und fülle die Schüssel mit Rauch, wie Nebel auf dem Wasser, dann wasche ich mir die Hände und fülle die Schüssel mit Seifenschaum, blase Rauch, dann nehme ich Mehl, tunke es ins Wasser und mache aus der Paste einen Rand rund um die Schüssel, um die schwarze Kante abzudecken, dann qualme ich auf die Kerze. Die Szene sieht genau aus wie eine ganz abgelegene Landschaft – Jedenfalls frage ich mich, ob Du dieses Video vielleicht für Santa Clara kaufen möchtest, da Du auch den Beuys-Film gekauft hast – ich könnte Dir eine signierte und nummerierte Kopie für 200 $ schicken, da ich die Videobänder selbst hergestellt habe und das Studio in Rotterdam nicht-kommerziell arbeitet – George wird Dir sagen können, wie viel allein die Leerkassette dieser 1-Zoll-Video-Bänder wert ist – ich frage Dich, weil ich das Geld wirklich brauche und außerdem eine Kopie des Films in S. F. haben möchte – Du könntest frei entscheiden, wann und wo Du das Video verleihen oder zeigen willst – Die Leute in Rotterdam meinten, es könnte im privaten Fernsehen gezeigt werden.

– ? – meinst du, Jim Narithas könnte Interesse haben? – Wenn Du willst, kannst Du es kaufen. Schicke mir eine internationale Überweisung über die Bank of America oder kaufe am besten American Express Anweisungen oder Schecks.

Bitte gib mir in jedem Fall sofort Bescheid. Ich habe das Layout für Joels Veröffentlichung in Düsseldorf gesehen und es sieht toll aus.

Ich werde später einen etwas persönlicheren, mitteilsameren Brief schreiben – hoffe, dieser war nicht zu geschäftlich oder unangenehm – Alles Liebe und viele Grüße an Dich und George
– T.
c/o Sonnabend
12 Rue Mazarine
Paris VI

ca. 1972

Quelle: de Saisset Museum, Santa Clara University

Aus dem Englischen übersetzt von Anne Pitz

Terry Fox
Zu *Yield*, University Art Museum Berkely

Ich schicke acht Fotos von meiner neuesten Arbeit im University Art Museum von Berkeley. Es war eine zweimonatige Ausstellung (4. September – 21. Oktober) in zwei Räumen. Ich lege eine Zeichnung vom Grundriss bei, in dem meine Aktionen eingezeichnet sind. Diese Ausstellung und die Aktionen gehen auf meine Untersuchungen im Labyrinth von Chartres zurück. Ich machte ein Modell des großen Raums in meinem Atelier und fotografierte darin kleine Objekte durch eine Lupe, darunter einen Eckzahn und einen Apfel, ein Gipsmodell des Labyrinths von Chartres, eine Röhre aus Brotteig und eine Phiole mit Blut. Diese Fotografien ließ ich auf 61 x 92 cm vergrößern und positionierte 22 Abzüge dicht nebeneinander ringsum in den kleineren Raum (B). Eine Schultafel mit einer Zeichnung des Vorhangs im größeren Raum lag auf dem Rücken im kleinen Raum. Die auf den Fotografien abgebildeten Objekte befanden sich auf dieser Tafel (A) und stellten einen Bezug zu den Aktionen, die im großen Raum folgen sollten, her. Dies ist der erste Raum, den der Besucher sah, und er diente dazu, ihn zu verlangsamen und ihn seelisch auf die wesentlichen Funktionen im größeren Raum einzustimmen, weil die dort stattfindenden Aktionen sehr langsam und tranceartig und wie im Labyrinth waren. Der Besucher verließ diesen Raum über einen Gang, der an vier 15,25 Meter langen Röhren vorbeiführte, die mit Blut, Urin, Milch und Wasser (C) gefüllt waren. Dort hatte ich in 3,60 Meter Höhe einen Vorhang aus durchscheinendem Musselin (D) aufgehängt, der 12,20 Meter lang war. Ich kleidete den Raum, der durch eine Glaswand (G) abgetrennt war, komplett damit aus. Der Vorhang formte einen Körper mit einer Sackgasse am einen Ende und einem Ausgang über die Glastüren (E) zum Balkon nach draußen (F). Von dort aus konnte der Zuschauer die Aktion in dem abgeschlossenen

Raum (H), der nicht begehbar war, beobachten. In diesem hermetisch abgeriegelten Raum machte ich meine Aktionen zusammen mit meinem Zwillingsbruder Larry Fox, der alles fotografierte.

Die Aktion dauerte drei Tage: vier Stunden am ersten, zwei Stunden am zweiten und drei Stunden am letzten Tag. Es gab keine Unterbrechungen, und jede Aktion ging da weiter, wo die vorherige aufgehört hatte. Die erste fand bei Tageslicht statt und die beiden nachfolgenden von Sonnenuntergang bis in die Nacht unter Zuhilfenahme eines Scheinwerfers.

Am ersten Tag formte ich mit Linien aus Mehl einen Brustkorb auf dem Boden und machte dann mit meinen Händen eine Rinne. Diese Rinne füllte ich anschließend tropfenweise mit Wasser, das ich mit dem Mund aus einer Metallschale entnahm. Mit dieser Methode machte ich alle Linien aus Mehlpaste. Danach wurde das übrige Mehl weggeblasen.

Am zweiten Tag zog ich eine Linie (Wirbelsäule) vom Brustkorb zum Becken. Hier lag ein 2,45 Meter breiter, quadratischer Spiegel auf dem Boden. Das Becken machte ich mit Mehl auf dem Spiegel, der dieses Bild auf den Vorhang reflektierte. Für das Hüftgelenk nahm ich eine spiegelnde Schale hinzu, in die ich Rauch blies.

Am dritten Tag zog ich eine Linie aus dem Brustbein zu der Metallschale (1), die getrocknetes Mehl enthielt, und blies Rauch. Ich verlängerte diese Linie bis zu der spiegelnden Schale, in der ein Penicillin-Pilz angesetzt war, und blies Rauch. Diese Linie verlängerte ich bis zur Emaille-Schale am Fenster. Darin formte ich einen Brotlaib und lehnte einen Löffel an die Schale. Ich brachte den Brotteig zum Aufgehen, indem ich eine wärmende Schale darüberhielt. Das Brot ging auf und hob den Löffel an.

1973

Quelle: http://www.artperformance.org/article-yield-terry-fox-1973-115448140.html, zuletzt am 30.9.2015

Aus dem Englischen übersetzt von Anne Pitz

Seite 261

Terry Fox
[Zu *Yield*]

Am 1. Juni 1973 füllte ich eine 1-Liter-Glasflasche mit Blut. Sie wurde gut zugekorkt und Flaschenhals und Korken wurden mit mehreren Schichten Isolierband abgedichtet. Gleichzeitig füllte ich einen Teil eines 2,45 m langen Eisenrohrs mit Blut. Für beide Enden hatte ich Pfropfen aus Holz geschnitzt. Diese Pfropfen klopfte ich in das Rohr und versiegelte sie mit Panzerklebeband. Da ich ein Objekt mit einer beweglichen, balancierenden Mitte machen wollte, hatte ich das Rohr nicht ganz gefüllt, so dass das Blut von einem Ende zum anderen laufen konnte, wenn man das Rohr kippen ließ oder in der Mitte aufhängte.

Am 7. Juni hängte ich das Rohr an der Decke meines Ateliers mit einer Schnur so auf, dass es waagerecht in 1,50 m Höhe über dem Fußboden hing. Dafür band ich die Schnur an zwei Punkten des Rohrs wie ein umgekehrtes Y fest und befestigte das andere Ende am Deckenbalken. Das Rohr hatte die Tendenz, sich immer wieder langsam zu drehen, wobei sich die Schnur verdrillte und entdrillte.

Am 9. Juni kamen Dorothy und ich spät abends nach Hause, nachdem wir seit dem Morgen weg gewesen waren. Der Gestank aus dem Atelier bis ins Treppenhaus war ekelhaft und haute uns fast um. Ein Ende des Rohrs war undicht geworden und die Tropfen hatten, während das Rohr sich drehte, einen perfekten Kreis aus geronnenem, getrocknetem Blut mit 2,45 m Durchmesser gebildet. Ich dichtete das leckende Ende des Rohrs mit mehr als einer halben Rolle Isolierband ab und legte das Rohr im Atelier auf den Boden.

Am 3. Juli entdeckte ich, dass sich eine 15 cm breite Blutlache unter dem tropfenden Ende des Rohrs gebildet hatte. Diesmal nahm ich eine ganze Rolle weißes Klebeband, um das Leck zu reparieren, aber nach wenigen Minuten fing das Blut wieder an durchzunässen. Ich klebte mehrere Schichten Panzerklebeband über das Leck, bis es nicht mehr

durchsickerte. Dann nahm ich die Flasche mit Blut aufs Dach, um sie zu öffnen und eine kleine gläserne Phiole mit Blut zu füllen. Als ich den Korken aus der Flasche ziehen wollte, schoss er mir wie ein Sektkorken aus der Hand, und in der Flasche entwickelte sich zähfließend dichter, ätzender gelber Rauch. Es war ekelerregend, aber irgendwann war er verflogen, und ich füllte die Phiole aus der Flasche ab und verschloss sie wieder.

Am 4. Juli entdeckten wir nach dem Aufwachen wieder eine neue scheußliche Blutpfütze unter dem Rohr. Diesmal dichtete Dorothy das Leck mit sehr vielen Lagen medizinischer Gipsbinden gründlich ab. Im September ließ ich das Eisenrohr in den unteren Saum eines Vorhangs einnähen, der für meine Eröffnung im Berkeley Museum angefertigt worden war. Die Flasche mit dem Blut wurde in den Bereich hinter dem Vorhang gestellt, der nicht-öffentlich war. Als am nächsten Morgen die Brandschutzprüfer kamen und den Vorhang untersuchten, hoben sie den Saum und warfen dabei die Flasche mit dem Blut um. Sie fiel auf den Betonboden, explodierte, und das Blut spritzte großflächig auf den Vorhang und den Boden dahinter. Das ganze Museum roch nach Blut.

Beim Abbau der Ausstellung wurde das Rohr aus dem Saum gezogen, und man sah, dass es geleckt und Flecke am Vorhang hinterlassen hatte. Da es offensichtlich aufgehört hatte zu lecken, nahm ich das Rohr mit heim und legte es auf das Dach meines Ateliers. Seit ich es im September 1975 wieder innen aufbewahre, hat es nicht geleckt, und das Blut darin ist immer noch flüssig, obwohl ich nie ein Antigerinnungsmittel hinzugefügt habe.

ca. 1975

Quelle: Estate of Terry Fox, Köln

Aus dem Englischen übersetzt von Anne Pitz

Terry Fox
Children's Videotapes

Interview von Willoughby Sharp und Liza Bear

Die *Children's Videotapes* von Terry Fox wurden zum ersten Mal im Everson Museum in Syracuse vorn 25. Mai bis zum 25. Juni 1974 gezeigt. Nach der Eröffnung der Ausstellung verbrachte Fox einige Wochen in New York. Willoughby Sharp und Liza Bear unterhielten sich mit ihm am 29. Mai und am 5. Juni.

LIZA BEAR
Wie kamst du auf die Idee, Videobänder für Kinder zu machen?

TERRY FOX
Ich habe Dinge gemacht, die ich meinem Sohn Foxy zeigte, und er war von ihnen fasziniert, er mochte sie gerne sehen und liebte es, sie nachzumachen.

L.B. Was für Dinge?

T.F. Ich baute Situationen auf, immer wieder mit den gleichen Gegenständen, eine Kerze, eine Gabel, ein Löffel, eine Schale Wasser und ein Stück Stoff. Wenn man die Kerze in das Wasser stellt und eine Flasche über sie, dann verbraucht die Kerze den ganzen Sauerstoff, zieht das Wasser hoch, und die Flamme erlischt. Und dann geht es darum, die nasse Kerze wieder anzuzünden. Ich machte so etwas oft allein spät in der Nacht – ich erfand neue Situationen immer mit den gleichen Gegenständen. Und nach einigen Monaten hatte ich so viele, dass ich auf die Idee kam, ein Programm für Kinder daraus zu machen. Seit einigen Jahren dachte ich daran, Filme für Kinder zu machen, weil ich mir Foxy vorstellte und die Einflüsse, denen er ausgesetzt ist. Ich lieh mir eine Sony *Port-a-Pak* und machte alle Filme in anderthalb Wochen.

WILLOUGHBY SHARP
Wie alt ist Foxy?

T.F. Fünf. Er geht in den Kindergarten und sein Input ist einfach verdorben, was das Fernsehen angeht. Wir haben keinen Fernseher, aber wenn er drei Tage in der Woche bei mir ist, kann er manchmal dem Mädchen von unten den Fernseher abschwatzen.

W.S. Er geht hinunter und fragt?

T.F. (lacht) Ja. Er liebt das Fernsehen. Aber es ist erschreckend. Alles was er sieht, ist schlecht für ihn.

W.S Wie korrumpiert das Fernsehen sein Sehen?

T.F. Das Fernsehen homogenisiert. Es nimmt ihm die Fähigkeit, einen wirklichen Dialog mit etwas zu haben, eher gestattet es nur passive Reaktionen. Obgleich er wirklich gut sprechen kann, er spricht so gut wie ich, erzählen seine Zeichnungen viel mehr. Man kann genau sehen, wie seine Stimmung ist, seine Gefühle. Aber auch diese werden schon stilisiert, dabei ist er erst im Kindergarten.

W.S. Du hast also gewissermaßen die Videobänder für ihn gemacht?

T.F. Ja, für ihn und seine Gruppe. Es gibt jetzt überall eine Videoausrüstung, jede Schule oder soziale Einrichtung hat eine, auch Foxys Kindergarten. Aber keiner macht etwas für Kinder. Alle machen nur etwas für Geld. Und es ist nicht nur das Geld der Kinder, das sie stehlen, sie stehlen auch alles andere. Meine Videobänder sollen ihnen etwas geben, worauf sie sich konzentrieren können, etwas, was sie nicht kennen und sie nicht ausbeutet, etwas, das keine Konsumbotschaft hat. Und vielleicht möchten sie etwas von dem, was ihnen gezeigt wird, ausprobieren.

W.S. Es scheint viel Dramatik in den Videosequenzen zu stecken, weil wirklich etwas passiert, es gibt Spannung.

T.F. Ja, die Spannung hilft den Kindern, hinzuschauen. Sie sind so an den 15-Sekunden-Schnitt gewöhnt und an Sachen, die toll aussehen, aber deren Inhalt gleich null oder negativ ist, dass es wirklich schwer ist, sie dazu zu bewegen, sich etwas Langsameres anzuschauen. Oder Studiotechniker damit zu beauftragen. Ich zeigte zwei von den Filmen auf KQED in San Francisco, den einen mit der Fliege und der Schale, den ich zuhause gemacht habe, und dann einen anderen, den ich im Studio in Farbe gemacht habe, und diese Techniker waren einfach schrecklich. Sie konnten es nicht aushalten, die Kamera drei Minuten stillzuhalten.

W.S. Warum hast du diese Gegenstände gewählt?

T.F. Es sind Gegenstände, mit denen ich vertraut bin. Mich interessieren sehr bestimmte Situationen und Gegenstände, die ihre eigene Substanz und ihre eigene Realität haben. Aber die Filme vermitteln nicht so sehr ein Interesse an bestimmten Gegenständen, sondern eher eine Haltung …

L.B. Aber ich mochte dem, was passierte, wirklich gerne zuschauen.

T.F. Ja, es passieren erstaunliche Dinge. Deshalb gibt es diese Nahaufnahmen, damit man sich auf all diese winzigen Ereignisse konzentrieren kann. Aber darüber hinaus gibt es eine Art von Haltung, die vermittelt wird.

L.B. Was für eine Haltung?

T.F. Die Haltung der Kontemplation, … des Staunens, der Beziehung zu etwas Realem … ohne Partei zu ergreifen.

L.B. Das stimmt, es gibt keine Scheinwelt, keine Stilisierung. Es wird nicht behauptet, dass die Wahrnehmung eines Kindes anders ist als die eines Erwachsenen.

T.F. Na ja, die kindliche Sichtweise ist eher eine Sichtweise, die der Erwachsene dem Kind auferlegt hat. Ein Kind ist im Grunde genommen eine kleine Person. Die Idee, dass die Dinge verkleinert werden müssten, um Kinder anzusprechen, ist eine Form der Unterdrückung, um sie klein zu halten. Wenn jemand irgendetwas für Kinder tut, dann gleiten sie in diese falsche künstliche kindliche Scheinwelt ab. Aber ich glaube nicht, dass Kinder das wirklich wollen, bis zu einem bestimmten Punkt. Dann wollen sie es, weil es das ist, was sie auch bekommen, das ist die Grenze ihrer Welt … Aber ich hatte nicht den Eindruck, dass ich meine Kunst verkleinern musste, als ich diese Bänder aufnahm.

W.S. Was ist dein Verhältnis zu Video?

T.F. Ich sehe es nicht als eine Religion oder was auch immer an. Es ist ein Werkzeug.

W.S. Aber das ist vielleicht so, weil du mit verschiedenen Medien arbeitest und keine Videoausrüstung hast.

T.F. Ja, klar. Wenn ich eine Videokamera hätte, wer weiß, was passieren würde. Ich kann gar nicht abwarten, bis ich eine habe. Zum einen würde ich sehr viel lockerer in der Kameraführung werden. Als ich diese Bänder machte, hatte ich vorher noch nie eine Videoausrüstung benutzt, sodass ich wirklich nicht locker war.

W.S. Wie hast du die Aufnahmen inszeniert?

T.F. Alle Bänder sind in meinem Atelier in San Francisco im März dieses Jahres zwischen Mitternacht und Sonnenaufgang aufgenommen worden. Ich hatte die Gegenstände auf einem großen Tisch, einer Tür, 1,20 × 3,20 Meter groß, auf Böcken, genau in den Positionen, in denen ich sie haben wollte, und die Kamera stand auf dem Stativ, das 1,50 Meter entfernt war. Es gab einen Scheinwerfer mit einer 1500-Watt-Glühbirne. Dann bestimmte ich, welche Art von Beleuchtung benötigt wurde für das, was geschehen sollte, und fuhr mit der Kamera heran, um die Schärfe einzustellen, und dann wieder zurück. Dann nahm ich die Gegenstände vom Tisch, machte kleine Zeichen, um ihre Positionen zu markieren, schaltete die Kamera ein und stellte die Dinge an ihren Platz, sodass man sehen konnte, wie die Situation aufgebaut war.

Dabei zoomte ich die Dinge entweder ganz nah heran oder in die entfernteste Position.

W.S. Und deiner Meinung nach braucht es zu keinem Zeitpunkt eine Erläuterung zu geben?

T.F. Nein, eine Erläuterung war nicht nötig.

W.S. Die Bänder sind also Demonstrationen von Phänomenen.

T.F. Phänomene und ihre Welten. Denken wir an eine Kerze, die all die verschiedenen Formen annehmen kann, an all die Sachen, die man mit ihr anstellen kann, die mit ihr passieren können. Oder die Flamme: man kann sie formen, ihre Farbe wegnehmen, sie mit einer Gabel unsichtbar machen. Es gibt ständig Variationen in den Zusammenstellungen der Gegenstände – die Gabel und die Kerze, oder die Kerze und das Wasser, oder das Wasser und die Schale …

W.S. Deine Ausstellung im Everson Museum besteht nur aus diesen Videofilmen?

T.F. Ja. Sie werden dort gezeigt, weil es ein städtisches Museum ist, das Museumsbesuche für die Schulkinder von Syracuse organisiert. Dafür hatte ich alles, was ich aufgenommen hatte, von ungefähr zweieinhalb Stunden auf zwei einstündige Bänder gekürzt.

W.S. Sie werden auf zwei Monitoren gleichzeitig gezeigt?

T.F. Ja. Auf zwei Monitoren sind alle Gegenstände auf einmal in Gebrauch, wie beispielsweise die Kerze und die Gabel auf einem Monitor, während der Löffel und die Schale auf dem anderen zu sehen sind. Die Stücke haben verschiedene Längen, das kürzeste ist eine Minute lang und das längste siebzehn Minuten.

W.S. Wie reagierten die Kinder, als du die Bänder in San Francisco zeigtest?

T.F. Ich zeigte sie in einem Kindergarten und sie mochten sie; ich zeigte sie den Söhnen von Marioni und sie wollten einige von ihnen noch einmal sehen. Alle waren erst kurz vor der Everson-Ausstellung wirklich fertig.

W.S. Möchtest du sie jemals in einer Galeriesituation zeigen?

T.F. Nein.

W.S. Und sie sind auch nicht speziell gemacht worden, um sie zu verkaufen? Du bedienst keinen Markt mit diesen Bändern.

T.F. Nein. In meinem ganzen Leben habe ich vier Zeichnungen verkauft und eine Skulptur gegen einen Satz falscher Zähne getauscht, als ich bei Lucio Amelio ausstellte (lacht).

W.S. Es ist ziemlich bemerkenswert, dass du so wenig verkauft hast. Dabei hast du in vielen wichtigen Galerien in New York und in Europa ausgestellt.

T.F. Ja, ich hatte nichts zu verkaufen. Ich stellte bei Sonnabend in Paris aus, da gab es nichts Verkäufliches. Bei Lucio auch nicht. Das ist nicht der Grund, warum ich ausstelle, warum ich Kunst mache.

1974

Quelle: Schmidt 2000, S. 62–68 (Auszug)

Aus dem Englischen übersetzt von Eva Schmidt

Seite 264

Terry Fox
Zu den Videos

1 *Turgescent Sex* Es handelt sich um eine Performance vor der Videokamera, die verschickt werden kann wie ein Brief. Auf diesem Video wasche ich mir die Hände/wasche den Fisch, der mit der Schnur mit vielen Knoten umwickelt ist/verbinde mir die Augen mit der Binde/befreie den Fisch aus der Binde/bedecke das Nest mit Rauch. Der Ton ist der fließende Verkehr vor meiner Haustür, die Beleuchtung ist das Sonnenlicht auf meinem Fußboden. Unveröffentlicht, 1971 aufgezeichnet von George Bolling in meinem Atelier in San Francisco mit einer Sony Portapak.
Schwarzweiß, 40 Minuten

2 *Clutch* Ein Video über Trennung. Ich liege mit dem Gesicht nach unten in meinem Atelier auf dem Fußboden, die Augen geschlossen. Meine Fingerspitzen liegen am Rand eines Flecks aus Sonnenlicht, das durch mein Oberlicht einfällt. Ich folge seinem Weg über den Fußboden anhand der Wärme, die ich mit den Fingern spüre, bis er außer Reichweite ist. Der Ton ist das Geräusch einer hängenden Plattennadel, die sich schließlich abnutzt und hochgeht. 1971, Kamera: George Bolling mit einer Sony Portapak.
Schwarzweiß, 50 Minuten

3 *Children's Tapes:* Eine Auswahl enthält elf der 34 Videofilme, die ich für Kinder gemacht habe. Diese Filme verwenden fünf Elemente (einen Löffel, eine Gabel, eine Kerze, eine Schüssel und Wasser) in immer neuen Formen der Interaktion. Diese Filme wurden als Teil meiner Übersetzung der 34 Pfade des Labyrinths von Chartres konzipiert. Unveröffentlicht. Der Ton sind die natürlichen Geräusche der Handlungen, die Beleuchtung ein 1000-Watt-Strahler. 1974 aufgenommen und performt von mir mit einer Sony Portapak in meinem Atelier in San Francisco.
Schwarzweiß, 30 Minuten

4 *Two Turns* wurde aufgenommen, nachdem ich das Bild des Labyrinths von Chartres in die Vidicon-Bildaufnahmeröhre meiner Portapak-Kamera gebrannt hatte. *Two Turns* sind zwei Gänge. Der erste Gang führt von meinem Atelier auf die Straße und zurück in mein Atelier, wo Sonnenstrahlen durch ein auf Glas gemaltes Labyrinth fallen, das ich für das Einbrennen in die Vidicon-Röhre verwendet hatte. Der Kreis des Labyrinths wird sichtbar durch Rauchkringel in den Sonnenstrahlen. Der zweite Gang auf die Straße und wieder zurück findet nachts bei Regen statt. Die Kamera kommt auf einer Schüssel, die in meinem Atelier auf dem Fußboden steht, zur Ruhe. In ihr sammeln sich Regentropfen, die von den Deckenbalken tropfen, und bilden auf der Oberfläche konzentrische Kreise. Handgeführte Kamera, natürliches Licht und Ton. 1975.
Schwarzweiß, 42 Minuten

5 *Timbre* Ein Film über eine fünfstündige Performance für zwei Instrumente, die am 13. März 1976 auf dem Mount Tamalpais in Nordkalifornien stattfand: Eine Cessna 170, ein einmotoriges Flugzeug, und ein selbstgemachtes Instrument aus Klaviersaiten, das auf das durch den Wald bis zum Ort der Performance durchdringende Brummen und auf den Auftakt der Performance selbst eingestimmt wurde. 1976.
Schwarzweiß, 30 Minuten

1976

Quelle: *Anna Canepa Video Distributions Inc. Represents the Following Artists: Eleanor Antin, Terry Fox, Taka Iimura, Allan Kaprow, Les Levine, Dennis Oppenheim, Roger Welch.* Vertriebsbroschüre, New York 1976, S. 6–7

Aus dem Englischen übersetzt von Anne Pitz

Seite 266

Brief an Marinus Boezem

Lieber M. B.,

es tut mir furchtbar leid, Dir dies so spät zu schicken. Als ich nach San Francisco zurückkam, hatte ich gleich sehr viel zu erledigen, aber jetzt bin ich | frei | und das Material ebenso. | da |
Ich schicke Dir die Zeichnung, die ich aus einem Buch habe, das ich zur Herstellung meines Stempels vom Labyrinth benutzte, da ich glaube, dass die gedruckte Abbildung als Vorlage für den Steinmetz oder für eine Vergrößerung präziser sein wird. Ich schicke Dir dies auf schnellstem Weg, und morgen werde ich weitere Informationen für die Presse usw. schicken.
Ich glaube, wir waren uns über die Größe und die Steinsorte einig, so dass Ihr sofort mit dem Zuschneiden anfangen könnt. Ich hoffe, es ist noch möglich, den einfühlsamen Menschen mit der Metallstange ausfindig zu machen, damit der genaue Ort, an dem der Stein im PODIO [del Mondo per l'Arte] aufgestellt wird, bestimmt werden kann. Ich würde außerdem gerne, wenn möglich, einen Hohlraum unter dem Stein haben, so dass er RESONANT ist, wenn man dagegenschlägt oder mit den Knöcheln dagegenklopft. Dies könnte wie folgt gemacht werden, aber vielleicht kennst Du eine bessere Methode.

[Zeichnung, Pfeil:]

WENDEN

[handschriftlich in Versalien:]

EIN LEERER HOHLRAUM DIREKT UNTER DEM SYMBOL DES LABYRINTHS, JEDOCH NICHT SO BREIT WIE DIE STEINE, VIELLEICHT MIT STEINWÄNDEN + -BODEN ODER IN EINER ANDEREN AUSFÜHRUNG, DIE DU DIR VORSTELLEN KANNST. BEI DEM OBJEKT MUSS DER STEIN MIT DEM LABYRINTH OBENAUF LIEGEN, DAMIT ES DURCH DEN LEEREN RAUM DARUNTER KLINGEN KANN. ICH FREUE MICH SEHR AUF DIESES PROJEKT + HABE SEHR VIELEN LEUTEN DAVON ERZÄHLT!! ICH HOFFE, DU HAST MEINE LABYRINTH-AUSSTELLUNG BEIDE APPEL SEHEN KÖNNEN, DENN SIE ZEIGT MEINE SICHT DES LABYRINTHS BESSER, ALS ICH SIE BESCHREIBEN KÖNNTE!

Ich hoffe, in Middleberg [Middelburg] läuft alles gut und Du und Deine Familie seid wohlauf, und ich möchte Dir nochmals für Deine Unterstützung und Gastfreundschaft danken. Es ist schön, wieder in San Francisco zu sein, aber ich freue mich schon auf meine Rückkehr nach Europa im kommenden Frühling. Wenn Du Material in irgendeiner Form von mir brauchst, schreibe mir bitte, dann werde ich es sofort schicken.
Beste Grüße,
Herzlich,

Terry Fox
16 Rose Street
San Francisco 94102

ca. 1978

Quelle: Akademie der Künste, Berlin, Wulf-Herzogenrath-Archiv, Nr. 122

Aus dem Englischen übersetzt von Anne Pitz

Seite 267

TERRY FOX

Ich bin immer noch daran interessiert, Videobänder zu machen. Ich plane ein langes Projekt, das ich auf Video aufnehmen will. Aber Video ist der Malerei ähnlich, es gibt die gleichen Einschränkungen. Wenn du eine Performance machst, die du aufnehmen willst, weißt du, dass das längste Band, das man bekommen kann, eine Stunde lang ist. Deshalb wird die Performance eine Stunde dauern. Und das ist wirklich dumm. Man hat all diese Restriktionen durch die Ausrüstung. Man hat die Technologie und sieht, was man damit tun kann. Aber man kann nichts tun, was der Recorder nicht tun kann.

1979

Quelle: Es ist der Versuch einer neuen Kommunikation. Interview mit Robin White. In: Schmidt 2000, S. 90

Aus dem Englischen übersetzt von Eva Schmidt

Seite 269

Interview von M. A. Greenstein mit Terry Fox

M. A. GREENSTEIN

Artaud sagt:, „Theater bietet die Gelegenheit, den physischen Raum zu füllen." John Cage sagte: „Man ist immer von Theater umgeben, und die Kunst erleichtert einem bloß die Erkenntnis, dass dies der Fall ist." Der Essay im Katalog der Otis [Gallery] erwähnt den Einfluss, den Artaud und Cage auf Ihre Arbeit hatten, und die Arbeit in der Otis-Ausstellung scheint tatsächlich daran anzuknüpfen.

TERRY FOX

Ja, das tut sie. Artaud beeinflusste mich Ende der 1960er und Anfang der 1970er Jahre auf jeden Fall sehr, aber nicht John Cage. Am Anfang interessierte ich mich stärker für Theater, was damals eine direkte Folge meiner Eindrücke von Paris und vom Straßentheater war, das ich sah, als ich dort lebte. Und da wechselte ich dann von der Malerei zum Theater. Als ich nach San Francisco zurückkehrte, versuchte ich, Straßentheater zu machen, und ich begann sogar [Jerzy] Grotowski zu lesen.

[...]

M.A.G. Der Otis-Katalog erwähnt, dass Sie sich für sein [Artauds] Theater der Grausamkeit interessierten, aber aus meiner Sicht gibt es bei den Fox-Arbeiten eine andere Seite, die Artauds nicht-literarischem oder rituellem Theatermodell näher steht, also einem Theater, das mit Grausamkeit an sich nichts zu tun hat.

T.F. Tatsächlich interessierten mich nicht alle Aspekte bei Artaud. Ich interessierte mich für die transformativen Eigenschaften des Theaters. Wie Sie sagten, ging es mir um die Vorstellung der Transformation eines Ortes durch eine Handlung, und besonders dann, wenn der Ort der Körper ist, diesen Körper durch die Handlung umzuwandeln. Oder wie Artaud schreibt, das Körperinnere nach außen in einen Handlungsraum zu holen – und darum, welche Wirkungen das sowohl auf den physischen Raum als auch auf den Körper hat.

[...]

T.F. Das Labyrinth von Chartres wurde im Jahr 1290 erbaut, und ich finde, dass es wirklich eine Theaterform ist. Unter anderem faszinierte mich daran, dass es ein Gegenstand und zugleich eigentlich kein

Gegenstand ist. Und es muss bespielt werden. Es ist tatsächlich eine Art Bühne mit im Fußboden eingelassenen Regieanweisungen, denen man nachgeht. Also was ist es? Es ist kein Objekt, es ist keine Skulptur. Es ist eine Metapher. Aber es ähnelt auch einer Einteilung, einer Spur für Bewegungen. Was passiert, wenn man diese Bewegungen ausführt, was für eine Art Transformation vollzieht sich dann? Man geht die Bewegungsschritte durch, und ich glaube, dass es Umwandlungsschritte sind. Ich finde, dass es sehr wichtig ist, da durchzugehen, bevor man irgendetwas anderes in dieser Kathedrale macht.

Ich hörte 1972 mit einer bestimmten Art von Performance auf. Und gleichzeitig, als ich damit aufhörte, entdeckte ich das Labyrinth. Und diese Entdeckung war ein Spurwechsel, weil es eine Art Spur *ist*. Es ist eine Bühne, auf der alle Bewegungsrichtungen vorgegeben sind. Als ich anfing, mich innerhalb dieses Labyrinths zu bewegen, veränderte sich meine Arbeit. Die Arbeit wurde immer hermetischer, immer weniger öffentlich. Aber ich habe nach wie vor eine starke Neigung dazu, etwas live vor Publikum zu machen. Ich bin nur zu Klang übergegangen.

[...]

M.A.G. Ich finde, es ergibt Sinn, dass Sie sich aus der Beschäftigung mit Artaud und Transformation für akustischen Klang entschieden. Akustischer Klang ist im Grunde sehr ortsabhängig.

T.F. Ja. Wie jetzt diese Klaviersaiten – die Klaviersaiten selbst erzeugen keinen Klang. Die Wände des Raums erzeugen den Klang. Wenn eine Saite gespielt wird, wandelt sie einerseits den physischen Raum um, aber andererseits ist es der Raum selbst, der den Klang erzeugt. Auf diese Weise wird der Raum zum Instrument.

M.A.G. Und trotzdem stellt man sich die Objekte nicht so vor, dass sie sich selbst umwandeln, richtig?

T.F. Nein, nein, das ist gut. Es stimmt. Aber auch das hier [er zeigt auf *Vortex* auf dem Fußboden in der Nähe]: Eigentlich ist es eine Skulptur aus Stahl. Aber es ist auch ein Instrument. Und andere Personen können es spielen. Jeder kann es spielen.

[...]

M.A.G. Also worum geht es?

T.F. Für mich ist ein Kriterium, ob es funktioniert oder nicht funktioniert. Aber ich weiß nicht, was es bedeutet, wenn es funktioniert. Mir fallen einige Situationen ein, die wirklich nicht zu fassen waren, denn ich weiß vorher nie, welches Ergebnis herauskommt. Aber wenn es funktioniert,

öffnet mich diese Erfahrung. Sie öffnet mich dem Zuhören. Das hat gewissermaßen mit Cage zu tun. Und wenn es anderen auch so geht, ist es eine Form der Kommunikation. Für mich ist es wichtig, dass es Kommunikation ist und nicht nur Unterhaltung. Es *ist* wirklich ein Austausch. Es geht darum wahrzunehmen, was den Klang erzeugt. Wie wird der Klang hergestellt? Und wie nimmt man den Klang wahr? Warum klingt es so? Was passiert gerade? Warum ist es interessant zuzuhören oder auch nicht? Jeder Mensch kann überall hingehen, und jeder Mensch kann danach spielen oder auch vorher.

[...]

1994

Quelle: *Artweek*, 17. Februar 1994, Jg. 25, Nr. 4, S. 15

Aus dem Englischen übersetzt von Anne Pitz

Interview von Willoughby Sharp mit Terry Fox, Vito Acconci und Dennis Oppenheim

[...]

WILLOUGHBY SHARP

Terry, wie kam es dazu, dass ihr, Dennis, Vito und du, gleichzeitig während deiner Einzelausstellung bei Reese Palley Performances gemacht habt?

TERRY FOX

Mir wurde für die Dauer eines Monats eine Ausstellung angeboten, aber eigentlich wollte ich nur eines wirklich machen, ein Ereignis. Ich fragte Dennis und Vito, weil sie Freunde waren, aber auch weil ich der Ansicht war, dass es absurd war, uns der gleichen Kunstkategorie zuzuordnen: *Body Works*.

W.S. Warum?

T.F. Obwohl wir alle mit unserem Körper arbeiten, ist unsere Beziehung zu Raum, Zeit und Material sehr verschieden. Ich dachte, wenn wir zusammen auftreten würden, ohne dass wir uns vorher gegenseitig darüber

informierten, was wir tun würden, dann würden die Unterschiede und Ähnlichkeiten zwischen uns deutlich hervortreten. Und das passierte natürlich. Während der Performance sah ich die anderen nicht, aber ich erfuhr über sie hinterher, und sie waren offensichtlich sehr verschieden. Dennoch gab es einige gemeinsame Themen, die eine Art Zusammenhang herstellten. Zum Beispiel stellte es sich heraus, dass Dennis den Klang einer verstärkten Atmung benutzte. Ich benutzte ein Tonband von meiner Atmung während des Schlafes, das ich die Nacht zuvor aufgenommen hatte, und ich verstärkte ebenfalls meine Atmung während der Veranstaltung. [...] Dennis [korrigierte] das Ungleichgewicht des Raumes, indem er die Videoausrüstung an seinem Ende platzierte, sodass das Areal, das wir absteckten, ein U formte. Es war wie ein rundes Theater, dessen Form durch das Publikum vollendet wurde.

[...]

T.F. Sowohl Dennis als auch Vito hatten eine sehr genaue Beziehung zu ihren Räumen. Die Struktur ihrer Arbeiten beinhaltete eine grundlegende Wiederholung, die einen gewissen gleichmäßigen Zusammenhang herstellte. Meine Arbeit aber bestand aus einer Reihe diskontinuierlicher Handlungen, sie wechselten alle paar Minuten. Als ich auf Dennis' Atmen aufmerksam wurde, fühlte ich, dass ich mit ihnen arbeiten und auf das Ganze eingehen sollte, was die Qualität des Klanges und die Stimmung anging, damit das Publikum auf die ganze Situation reagieren konnte.

[...]

W.S. Warum wähltest du eine Tarantel?

DENNIS OPPENHEIM

Ich verwendete die Spinne als einen Aggressor, als eine sich bewegende Kraft, die davon überzeugt oder abgehalten werden konnte, in eine bestimmte Richtung zu gehen. Sie konnte angelockt oder zurückgestoßen werden. Die Tarantel war dazu gut geeignet, weil sie weder zu groß noch zu klein war, sie war haarig und relativ langsam.

[...]

VITO ACCONCI

Meine Privatheit bestand aus der Konzentration auf die Uhr, aber weil die Zeit universell ist, war ich auch mit der allgemeinen Zeiterfahrung verbunden. Mich interessierte, dass ich mich in einem Zeitabschnitt befand, den die anderen zufällig teilten, den ich aber definieren konnte. Ich wollte mich in einen Kreis einschließen. Tatsächlich zeichnete mein physisches Selbst, mein Körper den Umkreis dieser Einschließung,

sodass ich meinen Körper gerade nicht einschloss. Aber mein Körper und meine physische Präsenz schlossen meine mentale Präsenz ein, die sich auf die Uhr konzentrierte. Was mich beeindruckte: Indem ich den Kreis machte, schloss ich einen Gedankenprozess ein, nämlich die Konzentration auf eine Uhr. [...] Etwas anderes Interessantes war, wie ich auf die anderen Arbeiten reagierte. Obwohl sie nicht meine sichtbaren Bewegungen beeinflussten, stellten sie einen wichtigen Unterschied zu meiner privaten Konzentration dar. Während ich der regelmäßigen Bewegung der Uhr folgte, waren mir die willkürlichen Atemgeräusche neben mir sehr bewusst. Das Atmen zog und zerrte an meinen mechanischen Bewegungen. Zuerst konzentrierte ich mich auf innere Dinge, dann wurde mir das Äußere immer stärker bewusst – mein Schatten an der Wand, die Leinwand unter meinen Füßen. Ich wurde umgeben und attackiert, oder zumindest beeinflusst von dem Raum um mich herum.

1971

Quelle: Schmidt 2000, S. 44–50

Aus dem Englischen übersetzt von Eva Schmidt

Vito Acconci

TERRY WIE EIN FOX/FUCHS (1974 – *In seinen eigenen Worten, gestohlen/geborgt von mir*)

KERZE–GABEL–LÖFFEL–WASSERSCHÜSSEL–STOFFSTÜCK–

Kerze ins Wasser stellen & dann auf Stoffstück: Kerze verzehrt gesamten Sauerstoff & zieht das Wasser nach oben & Flamme geht aus; dann versuchen Kerze erneut anzuzünden, wenn sie nass ist [...]

Spät abends viel allein, neue Situationen mit denselben Gegenständen erfinden, ein Programm für Kinder daraus machen [...]

Alles was Foxy anschaut ist schlecht für ihn – Spannung, 15-Sekunden-Schnitt [...]

Ich nehme sie wirklich von ganz Nahem auf, um mich auf all die winzigen Ereignisse zu konzentrieren [...]

Eine Haltung der Kontemplation, der Verwunderung, des Sich-auf-etwas-Reales-Beziehens, ohne Partei ergreifen zu müssen [...]

Kein Schein involviert, keine Stilisierung, keine Annahme, dass die Sicht eines Kindes sich von der eines Erwachsenen unterscheidet [...]

CANDLE(CAN)–FORK(FOR)–SPOON(SON/ON)–BOWL (BOW)OF(O) WATER(WAT)–PIECE(PIE)OF(O)CLOTH(LOT)–

Video ist ein Werkzeug, Kamera auf einem Stativ 3½ Fuß entfernt, ich zoome ganz nah heran, um sie scharfzustellen, dann zoome ich wieder zurück, lege die Gegenstände hin um sehen zu können, wie die neue Situation beschaffen ist, dann zoome ich ganz weit weg oder ganz nah heran [...]

Wie all die unterschiedlichen Gestalten, die die Kerze annehmen kann – Gabel/Kerze, Kerze/Wasser, Wasser/Schüssel – auf 2 Monitoren zugleich gezeigt, bei 2 Monitoren sind alle Gegenstände gleichzeitig im Gebrauch, Kerze & Gabel auf 1 Monitor während Löffel & Schüssel auf dem anderen sind [...]

Nein, es bedarf keines Narrativs [...]

Das kürzeste dauert 1 Minute, das längste 17, nichts zu verkaufen [...]

Dinge machen & sie Foxy zeigen, er lässt sich wirklich auf sie ein, er betrachtet sie gern & er macht sie gern [...]

Situationen arrangieren, dieselben Gegenstände wieder & wieder verwenden – Kerze/Gabel/Löffel/Wasserschüssel/Stoffstück wie Kerze ins Wasser stellen & dann Flasche darüber stellen, Kerze verzehrt den gesamten Sauerstoff & zieht Wasser nach oben, so dass die Flamme ausgeht, & versuchen Kerze wieder anzuzünden, wenn sie nass ist [...]

Nach ein paar Monaten hatte ich so viele gemacht, dass ich ein Programm für Kinder daraus machen sollte [...]

Borgte mir eine Sony port-a-pak & habe sie alle in eineinhalb Wochen gemacht [...]

CANDLE(AND/AN/A)–FORK(OR)–SPOON(SO/NO)–BOWL (OW/LOW)OF(O) WATER(WET/TAR)–PIECE(PI)OF(O)CLOTH(LO)–

Er beobachtet so gern, es ist entsetzlich, alles, was er beobachtet, ist schlecht für ihn, nun, es homogenisiert ihn, es nimmt ihm seine Fähigkeit, ein echtes Zwiegespräch mit etwas zu führen statt passive Antworten zu empfangen [...]

Er kann gut sprechen, genauso gut wie ich, aber seine Zeichnungen sagen mir viel mehr. Man kann genau sehen, in welcher Stimmung er sich befindet, was er fühlt, aber selbst das beginnt stilisiert zu werden [...]

Aber niemand macht etwas für Kinder, jeder macht etwas für Geld [...]

Meine Videos sollen ihnen etwas anderes geben, auf das sie sich konzentrieren können, etwas, von dem sie nichts wissen & das sie nicht ausbeutet, das keine Botschaft für Konsumenten enthält, vielleicht würden die Videos in ihnen den Wunsch wecken, etwas Neues auszuprobieren Spannung hilft Kindern beim Fernsehen. Sie sind so sehr daran gewöhnt, den 15-Sekunden-Schnitt zu sehen. Es ist zu schwierig, etwas zu lange anzuschauen, sie drehten durch, als sie die Kamera in Ruhe lassen sollten [...]

Weil es Gegenstände sind, die ich kenne, kriege ich einen Kick von Situationen & Gegenständen, die ihre eigene Substanz & Wirklichkeit haben, doch es ist nicht ein Interesse an diesen Gegenständen, das die Videos vermitteln, sondern eher eine Haltung [...]

Verblüffende Dinge geschehen jetzt, deshalb nehme ich von ganz Nahem auf, um mich auf all die winzigen Ereignisse zu konzentrieren, aber abgesehen davon, gibt es eine Art Haltung in diesen Videos [...]

Haltung der Kontemplation, Haltung der Verwunderung, ohne Partei ergreifen zu müssen [...]

> *CANDLE(LED)–FORK(O)–SPOON(POO/ SOON)–BOWL(LOW) OF(O)WATER(ATE/ TEAR/WAR/RAW)–PIECE(PIC)OF(O) CLOTH(HO/TO/HOT/LOT)–*

Ein Kind ist im Grunde einfach nur eine kleine Person. Die Idee, dass Dinge verkleinert werden müssen, damit sie Kindern gefallen, ist Unterdrückung, um Kinder unter Kontrolle zu halten. Wenn Leute etwas für Kinder machen, dann begeben sie sich in verlogene künstliche kindliche Scheinwelten. Kinder wollen das nicht, bis es zu spät ist, dann wollen sie es, weil es alles ist, was sie normalerweise kriegen, das ist die Grenze ihrer Welt [...]

> *Aber ich habe nicht das Gefühl, meine Kunst reduzieren zu müssen, um diese Videos zu machen [...]*
> *Video ist keine Religion, sondern ein Werkzeug [...]*
> *Alle diese Videos entstanden in meinem Atelier, San Francisco, März 74, zwischen Mitternacht & Sonnenaufgang, Gegenstände auf einem großen Tisch, 4x8-Fuß-Tür auf Sägeböcken, Kamera auf einem Stativ 3½ Fuß entfernt & ein Studio-Porträt-Licht mit einer 1500-Watt-Glühbirne, dann fand ich heraus, welches Licht ich benötigte & zoomte ganz nah heran, damit es scharf wurde, dann wieder ganz weit weg zurückzoomen, dann nahm ich die Gegenstände vom Tisch, legte kleine Krumen darauf, um ihre Position zu markieren, stellte Kamera an & legte Gegenstände hin, damit man sehen konnte, wie die Situation arrangiert war, & während ich dies tat, zoomte ich ganz weit weg oder ganz nahe heran [...]*

Die ausgestellten Phänomene & ihre Welten, wie all die verschiedenen Gestalten, die die Kerze annehmen kann, all die Sachen, die man damit machen kann, Dinge, die ihr widerfahren. Wie mit der Flamme, man kann die Flamme häuten, ihre ganze Farbe entfernen & sie mit einer Gabel unsichtbar machen.

Es gab ständige Variationen über diese Gegenstände zusammen, Gabel & Kerze, oder Kerze & Wasser, oder Wasser & Schüssel [...]

Mit 2 Monitoren werden alle Gegenstände auf einmal genutzt, Kerze & Gabel auf 1 Monitor & Löffel & Schüssel auf dem anderen. Die Werke sind alle unterschiedlich lang, das kürzeste dauert eine Minute & das längste 17 [...]
> *Nun, ich habe nichts verkauft, das ist nicht der Grund, warum ich ausstelle, warum ich Kunst mache [...]*

> *2015*

Aus dem Englischen übersetzt von
Nikolaus G. Schneider

Seite 276

Tom Marioni

Terry Fox und ich waren Zechkumpane, damals 1969 in San Francisco. Außer Künstler war ich auch Kurator am Kunstcenter im nahegelegenen Richmond. In diesem Jahr organisierte ich eine Ausstellung mit dem Titel „The Return of Abstract Expressionism" über prozessuale Kunst, Konzeptkunst, Anti-Form-Skulptur usw. Ich lud Terry ein, an dieser Schau teilzunehmen. Es ging darin nicht um Action Paintings, sondern um Aktionen und Materialien. Terry Fox steuerte ein Stück Plastik bei, das draußen im Wind flatterte. 1970 hatte er mit „Levitation" eine Einzelausstellung im Richmond Art Center. Später im selben Jahr gründete ich das Museum of Conceptual Art (MOCA) in San Francisco. Ich nannte die erste Ausstellung „Sound Sculpture As", und Terry machte darin eine Aktion mit einer Schale Wasser. Er schlug diese Schale auf den Boden und erzeugte ein Geräusch, das wie „Bong" klang. Möglicherweise war das die erste Klangkunst-Ausstellung überhaupt.

Terry und ich beeinflussten einander während seiner Zeit in San Francisco. Wir beide waren von Joseph Beuys beeinflusst, ich in meiner sozialen Kunst (*The Act of Drinking Beer with Friends is the Highest Form of Art*) und Terry bei seinem Einsatz organischer Materialien. Meine erste Begegnung mit Beuys fand 1973 während des Edinburgh Festivals statt, an dem ich mit meiner Band, dem MOCA Ensemble, in der St. Mary's Cathedral teilnahm. Während dieses Festivals organisierte Richard Demarco eine Ausstellung mit Künstlern, darunter Joseph Beuys, der der originellste europäische Künstler der Nachkriegszeit war. Zu einem weiteren Treffen mit Beuys kam es 1974 in Belgrad, wohin mich das dortige Studentenkulturzentrum mit *A Sculpture in 2/3 Time* eingeladen hatte. Im MOCA zeigte ich Beuys' *12-hour-video-lecture*, den er in Edinburgh hielt. (Ein Jahr später fand die erste von René Block kuratierte Ausstellung von Beuys in New York statt.) Er sprach über den Sozialismus, die Grünen (er war eines der Gründungsmitglieder der Partei) und darüber, dass jeder ein Künstler sein könne.

Nach 1973 gab ich Terry einen Raum im MOCA, den er als Atelier nutzen konnte, und er nahm häufig an Gruppenausstellungen teil, bevor er 1978 nach New York zog. Außerdem organisierte ich im MOCA einmal pro Woche Vorführungen von Videos unserer Künstlerfreunde. Wir zeigten sie auf einem Monitor. Was wir damals Aktion nannten und was heute als skulpturbasierte Performancekunst bezeichnet wird, beruhte auf der Manipulation von Materialien in Gegenwart von Zeugen und nicht auf der Manipulation von Emotionen wie im Theater. Während der Performance ist der Künstler der Autor, nicht der Schauspieler, während im Theater das Geschichtenerzählen die Idee ist, nicht das Material, das Video der Performance die Echtzeit darstellt, im Gegensatz zum Theater, das eine künstliche Zeit darstellt.

Ich glaube auch, dass es wichtig ist, einen Unterschied zwischen künstlerischer und Dokumentarfotografie zu machen. Da geht häufig Einiges durcheinander. Daher legte ich großen Wert darauf, dass meine Publikation *Vision#5* (1975) „Artists' Photographs" genannt wurde. Diese Publikationen waren bereits für sich genommen Ausstellungen, und die Werke wurden vor allem für die Bücher gestaltet und existierten im Übrigen nicht. *Vision#5* ging mit einer Ausstellung bei Crown Press einher. Ich lud jeden Künstler ein bzw. bat sie darum, mir eine Fotografie nicht eines Kunstwerks,

sondern als ein Kunstwerk zu schicken. Dadurch sollte hervorgehoben werden, dass Fotografie Kunst sein kann und nur in der Aufnahme selbst gegenwärtig ist. Das Buch enthält auch Fotos von Terry Fox, nämlich *My Hands as Fine Porcelain* und *Who Shall Harm Me?*

1975 machte ich mit Terry Fox im CARP in Los Angeles eine Performance namens *Duologue*. Wir spielten eine Art „Maschinenmusik", die wir vorher in unseren Studios ausgeheckt hatten. Terry Fox hatte eine Schüssel voller Sand, die er mit einem Violinbogen berührte. Aufgrund der Energie des von ihm erzeugten Klanges bildete der Sand Strukturen. Ich arbeitete mit meinen Trommelbürsten, und der von uns beiden erzeugte Klang veränderte die Form des Sandes. Terry Fox ließ sich vom Naturkundemuseum in San Francisco inspirieren, das das Konzept Ernst Chladnis präsentierte, der eine Technik erfunden hatte, mittels derer sich die verschiedenen Schwingungsformen einer starren Oberfläche veranschaulichen lassen. Chladni hatte die Idee, mit einem Bogen über den Rand einer Metallplatte zu streichen, deren Oberfläche mit einer dünnen Sandschicht bedeckt war. Die Platte wurde so lange gestrichen, bis ein Widerhall entstand, durch den der Sand in Schwingung versetzt wurde und sich um die Knotenlinien, wo die Oberfläche unbewegt bleibt, ansammelt und diese Linien so zur Geltung bringt. Die von diesen Linien gebildeten Muster werden heute als Chladni'sche Klangfiguren bezeichnet. (Terry Fox nutzte die Erfahrung aus dieser Performance für sein Videotape *Lunedì*, das er, ebenfalls 1975, zusammen mit Bill Viola bei Art/tapes/22 in Florenz produzierte.)

Im darauffolgenden Jahr zog er nach Berlin. Ich besuchte ihn mehrmals, wenn ich in Europa war, normalerweise, wenn wir beide an Performance-Festivals teilnahmen.

2015

Aus dem Englischen übersetzt von Nikolaus G. Schneider

Seite 278

Paul Kos

Etwas Geschwafel (Wie ich ihn in Erinnerung habe)

Ich lernte Terry Fox 1970 kennen, als wir zwei der drei für das Richmond Sculpture Annual ausgewählten Künstler waren. In dem großen Ausstellungsraum befanden sich drei Dokumente. Eines davon war Jim McCreadys Foto der brennenden Kirche St. Mary's. Terry Fox' Dokumente bestanden aus Wegbeschreibungen zu seinem Atelier in San Francisco, wo Betrachter seine kinetische Windskulptur und meinen Blankoscheck mit dem Titel *Quid Pro Quo* sehen konnten. Der aus LA stammende Künstler Larry Bell war der Juror. Tom Marioni war der Kurator. Die Ausstellung sorgte für erhebliches Aufsehen, da keine tatsächlichen skulpturalen Objekte akzeptiert wurden. Terry, Tom und ich wurden lebenslange Freunde.

1971, wir drei Tiere:
Fish (Tom Marionis Pseudoname),
Fox,
Kos (bedeutet auf Slowenisch kleine Amsel)
präsentierten eine Ausstellung in der de Saisset Gallery der University of Santa Clara. Fish zeigte eine elegante raumgroße Lithografie, Fox schlief unter einem hüfthohen Bild mit zwei Fischen, Mehl und Taschenlampen ein, und Kos zeigte die Reste eines neunzigminütigen *weight exchange* zwischen Künstler und Zielscheibe, wobei er sich einer Flinte bediente.

Terry Fox war ein Kurier, eine Brieftaube, die Neuigkeiten aus Europa in die Bay Area brachte.

Die Konzeptkunst steckte noch in den Kinderschuhen, und wir drei fühlten uns mehr von dem herausgefordert, was in der Arte povera geschah, als von der auf der Semantik oder Wörtern beruhenden New Yorker Szene. In den 1970er Jahren verbrachten Terry und seine Frau Marsha einen Teil

ihrer Zeit in Frankreich, Italien und Deutschland, und Terry arbeitete bei *Isolation Unit* sogar mit Joseph Beuys zusammen. In dieser auf einer 45rpm-Schallplatte aufgenommenen Performance versucht Terry allein durch den Klang, den er dadurch erzeugt, dass er auf Stahlröhren spielt, Glasscheiben zu zerbrechen, und Beuys spuckt Granatapfelsamen in eine Blechtasse, während seine unlängst verstorbene Maus auf einem Plattenteller kreist.

Klang wurde Terrys starke Seite. Er komponierte Stücke für Installationen, die die ganze Bandbreite von Orten, Instrumenten, Harmonie und Dissonanz umfassen.

– In einem Amphitheater auf dem Gipfel des Mount Tamalpais spannte Terry einen Draht über den Orchestergraben und spielte darauf einen Ton, der dem des Motors einer kleinen Cessna entsprach, die er mietete, um damit über diesen Ort zu fliegen. Wenn das Flugzeug schneller wurde, stimmte Terry den Draht neu, und wenn es zu einem Sturzflug ansetzte, strich Terry den Draht so, dass er entsprechend klang.

– In seinem Atelier in der Rose Street in San Francisco schnitt er eine gullylochgroße Öffnung in den Holzboden seines zweigeschossigen Raumes und platzierte Betrachter/Zuhörer im unteren Stockwerk, während er im oberen Stockwerk über Drähte, die er über das Loch gespannt hatte, strich und an ihnen zupfte, so als wenn man sich im Inneren einer Gitarre befände. Das Publikum befand sich im Bauch, im Klangkörper des Instruments.

George Bolling, Videokurator an der de Saisset Gallery nahm Terrys Performances in einer Shunk-Kender/Beuys-Manier auf, sprich in einem sich wechselseitig beflügelnden Einverständnis zwischen Darsteller und Dokumentarist. Farbe, Kontrast, Textur und Timing wurden zu einzigartigen Elementen dieser Videoarbeiten. *Children's Tapes*, *Turgescent Sex*, *Virtual Volumes* und *Clutch* sind Beispiele hierfür.

Terry schuf zwei denkwürdige Werke, bei denen er sich der spezifischen Merkmale und Grenzen ihres Mediums bediente.

Das erste mit dem Titel *Breath* war ein Super-8mm-Film (Kodak produzierte diesen Film als 3-Minuten-Kassetten). Es gab eine Vorführung auf einem Filmfestival, ich glaube im San Francisco Art Institute, und es wurden Super-8mm-Filme von Künstlern gezeigt. Terrys begann mit einer Einstellung, in der er ganz tief Atem holt, und ein Großteil des Publikums tat dasselbe. Alle hielten den Atem an, versuchten, die von der Super-8mm-Film-Kassette vorgegebene 3-Minuten-Grenze zu erreichen, und stellten ein

Spiegelbild von Terrys Aktionen dar. Seine Augen und Stirnadern traten hervor, im Publikum war ein vereinzeltes Keuchen von Leuten zu hören, die aufgaben. Terry machte weiter und stieß schließlich einen heftigen Luftstoß aus. Niemand im Publikum schaffte es, bis zum Ende des dreiminütigen Films durchzuhalten.

Das zweite Werk war skulpturaler Art und vielleicht unbetitelt. Auf dem Betonboden der Reese Palley Gallery im Frank Lloyd Wright Building in der Maiden Lane in San Francisco leerte Terry 1970 einen Eimer Wasser aus, der einen natürlichen Hohlraum im Boden fand. Im Wasser spiegelten sich die Lichter der Galerie. Vor dieser Intervention hatte nie irgendwer bemerkt, dass der Boden uneben war, und das Wasser lenkte die Aufmerksamkeit auf dieses im Übrigen unbedeutende architektonische Detail und schuf eine unerwartete ästhetische und möglicherweise spirituelle Erfahrung.

Wenn meine Frau Isabelle Sorrell und ich über Terry Fox sprechen, kommen wir häufig zu dem Schluss, dass er einer der wenigen Künstler ist, die Kunst aus nichts machen können, jemand, für den das Künstlersein eine Bedingung, kein Karriere war.

Da ich seit 1969 mit Eis gearbeitet hatte, schickte mir Terry diese beiden Rätsel in seiner unverwechselbaren Handschrift:

– Ein Gefangener wurde tot in seiner Zelle aufgefunden. Er hatte sich mit seinem Gürtel an einem Rohr an der Decke erhängt, doch es gab keinen Hocker, auf dem er gestanden haben könnte, sondern nur eine große Pfütze unter seinen herabbaumelnden Füßen. Wie hat er sich erhängt?

– In einer anderen Zelle fand man einen Mann, der erstochen worden war, aber keine Waffe. Wie kam es dazu?

Antworten: (Terry schrieb sie auf den Kopf gestellt)

Ein Eisblock

Ein Eiszapfen

2015

Aus dem Englischen übersetzt von
Nikolaus G. Schneider

Seite 280

Al Wong

Ich traf Terry zum ersten Mal in den frühen 1970er Jahren, als ich in meinem Atelier Filme meines Werks zeigte. Danach stellte ich fest, dass sein Atelier nur zwei Blocks von meinem eigenen in San Francisco entfernt war. Wir beide hatten verlassene Gebäude als Ateliers mit vielen Tausend Quadratfuß an Material. Es war gratis und großartig. Wir fingen also an, miteinander rumzuhängen und uns gegenseitig bei unserer Arbeit zu helfen. Er half mir bei der Produktion des Soundtracks für einen meiner Filme mit dem Titel *Same Difference*. Und ich half ihm immer bei den Videoaufnahmen oder dem Fotografieren seiner Werke. Doch abgesehen davon, hatte er immer das Gefühl, dass das, was er mit den Klaviersaiten machte, Skulptur war. Skulptur in dem Sinne, dass er, wenn er die Drähte am Hauptträger irgendeines Bauwerks, sei es ein Museum oder ein aufgegebenes Gebäude, befestigte, die gesamte Konstruktion durch die Schwingung der Drähte aktivierte. Einmal war er auf einem leeren Baugrundstück, wo er sich unter den Gehweg dieses leeren Geländes begeben konnte und sich unter einer metallenen Fahrstuhltür befand, die Teil des Gehwegs war. Er befestigte die Klaviersaite an der Fahrstuhltür und das andere Ende an einem großen, schweren Metallschreibtisch, der dort abgestellt worden war. Dann begann er mit einem Essstäbchen auf den Draht zu hauen, so dass auf dem leeren Grundstück das Geräusch der Schwingungen zu hören war. Doch über der Tür des metallenen Fahrstuhls liefen Fußgänger, die die Spannung des Drahtes änderten, weil die Tür rauf und runter ging und daher automatisch den Ton der Schwingung änderte. Ich weiß nicht, ob irgendjemand anderes das Werk gesehen hat, da ich an diesem Tag offenbar der Einzige war. Es war einfach wunderbar. Ein anderes Mal begegneten wir uns in New York und er lud mich in seine Wohnung in der Bowery ein. Als ich die Treppe raufging, hörte ich diese lauten Schwingungen. Ich klopfte an der Tür, Terry öffnete, und ich sah die Klaviersaiten, die über die gesamte Länge vom Vorderfenster bis zu den Küchenschränken gespannt waren. Er zupfte an den Drähten, um sie in Schwingung zu versetzen, und ging dann zurück, um die Schranktüren in der Küche zu öffnen und zu schließen, was den Ton der Schwingung veränderte. Nochmals: Es war zauberhaft. Ich glaube, nur sein Bruder Larry und ich haben das Werk gesehen.

Ich weiß nicht: Terry und ich waren wie zwei verlassene Kinder, die durch verlassene Gebäude liefen und zusammen Kunst machten. Das hat wirklich Spaß gemacht. Ich vermisse ihn so.

2015

Aus dem Englischen übersetzt von
Nikolaus G. Schneider

Interview von Tanya Zimbardo mit Al Wong

Al Wong erinnert sich, Terry erstmals in den frühen 1970er Jahren bei einer Filmvorführung in seinem Atelier im Bezirk South of Market in San Francisco kennengelernt zu haben. Sie verbrachten viel Zeit damit, den Arbeitsprozess des jeweils anderen zu beobachten und mit ihren Freundinnen, den Künstlerinnen Dorothy Reid und Ursula Schneider, unter die Leute zu gehen. 1976 nahmen die vier Freunde an der Gruppenausstellung „Exchange: DFW/SFO" im San Francisco Museum of Modern Art (SFMOMA) teil. Bei dieser Präsentation wurde auch Wongs Experimentalfilm *Same Difference* (1975, 16mm, Farbe, Ton, 17 Min.) gezeigt, dessen Soundtrack von Fox stammte, sowie Fox' externe Performance *Timbre* (1976), die von Wong auf Video aufgezeichnet wurde. Wong beteiligte sich auch an der Dokumentation anderer Performances, darunter *Blind Forces* (1980) im Keller des SFMOMA.

TANYA ZIMBARDO

1975 hast du ein Stipendium des American Film Institute in Verbindung mit dem NEA [National Endowment for the Arts] erhalten, um *Twin Peaks* zu produzieren. Wie entwickelte sich das Konzept für den Film?

AL WONG

Es entwickelte sich aus *Same Difference* (1975), einem Werk, bei dem ich ein Jahr lang mein Küchenfenster gefilmt habe. Ich glaube, das wurde im SFMOMA gezeigt [„Exchange: DFW/SFO", 1976]. Dabei saß eine Person, Ursula Schneider, in einer bestimmten Position da, so dass sie sich kaum zu bewegen scheint, während sich der Himmel und die Jahreszeiten ständig verändern. Wir wurden so gut darin, dass sie jedes Mal, wenn ich sagte, es sei Zeit für den Dreh, einfach nur aufspringen und zu dem Tisch rübergehen musste und gleich perfekt ins Bild passte. Es war sehr nett von ihr, dass sie mir dabei geholfen hat. Ich hatte die Kamera mit Gafferband am Boden festgeklebt, damit sie nicht verrutschte. Jedes Mal, wenn wir in die Küche gingen, mussten wir um sie herumlaufen. Beim Austauschen der einzelnen Filmrollen musste ich immer extrem sorgfältig sein. Terry Fox machte den Soundtrack, indem

er aus dem Küchenfenster blickte und seinen Violinbogen über den Rand einer großen Schüssel zog, die er in der Market Street gefunden hatte. Es war schön. *Same Difference* brachte mich dazu, mir wirklich anzusehen, was es dort draußen gab. Durch das Fenster konnte ich die Twin Peaks sehen und wollte näher an sie heran. Es ist ein wirklich zauberhafter Ort. Sicher hast du mal gesehen, wie der Nebel an den Twin Peaks runterlief wie bei einem Vulkanausbruch. Ich habe langsam das Material gesammelt und begonnen, die ganzen natürlichen Elemente zu sehen: den Himmel, die Erde, das Wasser in der Ferne. Es war dann offenkundig, dass ich das Geräusch des Meeres einfangen musste. Einer meiner Lieblingsorte ist Baker Beach, so wurde der Soundtrack dort aufgezeichnet. Er hat dieses wunderbare tiefe Atmen, das sich ständig ändert. Wenn du mal meditiert hast, dann fällt dir auf, dass sich dein Atem ändert, und wenn du versuchst, gleichmäßig zu atmen, dann zwingst du dich möglicherweise dazu.

[...]

T.Z. Das Fehlen irgendwelcher Umwelt- oder Fahrgeräusche und dass man nur den Klang der Wellen hört, die sich brechen, hat mich auch daran erinnert, wie man sich in der Stille ganz auf den eigenen Atemrhythmus oder das Pulsieren des Blutes konzentriert. Wir betrachten die Umgebung direkt aus dem Inneren des fahrenden Wagens, aber ich empfand diese Distanziertheit und ein akustisches Gefühl, dass meine Aufmerksamkeit sich zugleich nach innen wandte. Du hast auch die Rolle der Wiederholung und das einzigartige Kennzeichen des Twin-Peaks-Boulevard mit der Achterschleife erwähnt.

A.W. Ja, es ist wie das Leben. Wir durchlaufen dieses Muster die ganze Zeit. Es ist eine Form der Unendlichkeit – Aufwachen, Zähneputzen, in die Straßenbahn steigen. Die Unendlichkeits-Straßenschleife repräsentiert dieses kontinuierliche Muster des Lebens. Es gibt bestimmte Sequenzen in dem Film, wo es den Anschein hat, als würden Teile der Straße nicht mehr zusammentreffen und als wäre es nicht mehr ein- und dieselbe Straße. Die Straße verschiebt sich. So ist das Leben. Es verschiebt sich und gibt dir gelegentlich das Gefühl, das Gleichgewicht verloren zu haben. Du hast Schwierigkeiten, und dann versuchst du, wieder in die Spur zu kommen. Und du atmest weiter.

[...]

T.Z. Du hast auch den Jahres-Parameter für deine Installation *Sunlight* (1979)

verwendet. Könntest du dieses Werk beschreiben? Hat irgendwer es mit dir zusammen erlebt?

A.W. Das Gebäude an der Ecke Minna und Fourth Street stammte von der Redevelopment Agency [Entwicklungs- oder Sanierungsagentur] und war zuvor eine Zeitungsdruckerei und eine Zahnarztpraxis gewesen. Ich habe so gut wie alle Fenster abgedunkelt und lediglich eine kleine Öffnung übriggelassen, in die man einen Spiegel stellen konnte. Von diesem Spiegel ging ein Lichtstrahl aus. Dort drehte sich etwa ein Trichter mit einer flachrandigen Pastetenform, darunter Magneten und Weihrauch. Die Magneten versetzten den Trichter in eine kreisende Bewegung. Wenn Licht auf ihn fiel, bildete der Weihrauch bestimmte Formen. In dem Trichter waren kleine Löcher, die ich dort hineingebohrt hatte. Der erste Strahl, der dort einfällt, wo der Trichter ist, trifft auf einen anderen Spiegel, der fast auf die Stelle zurückreflektiert, wo sich der Spiegel im Fenster befindet, der die ersten Sonnenstrahlen erfasst. Dieser war gekippt und ein anderer Strahl fiel auf die Decke. Und dann gab es noch einen Fischaugenspiegel, der das Licht öffnete oder aufflackern ließ. Mit dem Rauch erzeugte er in diesem Raum eine Kuppelform. Das hat mir wirklich gefallen. Ich wusste nicht, was damit passieren würde.

Terry Fox kam rüber. Wir verbrachten mehrere Stunden damit, es zu betrachten. Er wohnte nur einen Block entfernt, und wir besuchten uns ständig gegenseitig und sahen uns unsere Arbeiten an. Durch diese gegenseitigen Besuche entstanden einige interessante Sachen. Da unten, wo heute das Museum ist, gab es ein Hotel, das wegen eines großen Brandes aufgegeben worden war. Terry und ich stiegen vom Dach des MOCA (Museum of Contemporary Art) aus durch ein Fenster ein. Das war fast ein Museum, in dem es darum ging, wie Menschen dort gelebt hatten.

[...]

2013

Quelle: Tanya Zimbardo, Sunlight and Shadows: In Conversation with Al Wong. San Francisco Museum of Modern Art's Open Pace, http://openspace.sfmoma.org/2013/05/al-wong/, zuletzt am 30.9.2015

Aus dem Englischen übersetzt von Nikolaus G. Schneider

Interview von Angela Lammert mit Wulf Herzogenrath

ANGELA LAMMERT

Wann sind Sie mit der Arbeit von Terry Fox in Kontakt gekommen?

WULF HERZOGENRATH

Das war Anfang der 1970er Jahre, als ich mich im Museum Folkwang Essen um das neue Medium Video kümmern sollte. Kein Mensch wusste damals, was zu machen ist und was Video sein könnte. Eigentlich gab es nur Gerry Schum, und da war Video nur bezogen auf Land Art / Concept Art. Es waren stilistisch sehr ruhige, wenn man so will, langweilige Dokumentationen von Aktionen. Dass es ganz andere Formen von Video in Amerika gab, wie die von Nam June Paik, war uns zu diesem Zeitpunkt 1971 noch nicht bekannt. 1973 traf ich in New York auf eine ganz lebendige Videoszene: Nam June Paik mit seinem ganzen Witz und elektronischen Spielen und eben auch Terry Fox. Fox war zwar auch konzeptuell, aber mit einem untergründigen und manchmal witzigen Humor. Dieser Humor machte deutlich, dass es um etwas ganz anderes ging, als um reine Ausführung von konzeptuellen Aktionen, wie wir sie etwa von Jochen Gerz' *Rufen bis zur Erschöpfung* (1972) kennen. Das war bei Terry Fox irgendwie anders. Seine berühmtesten Videobänder *Children's Tapes* (1974) waren wirklich komisch. Sie sind minimal, aber sie haben immer einen Witz und man wartet darauf, was mit dieser kleinen Versuchsanordnung jetzt passiert. Es ging nicht um die stringente Durchführung eines Konzepts, bei dem oft nach 20 Sekunden klar war, wie die nächsten 10 Minuten ausgehen, sondern man blieb immer gespannt. Wir haben in der ersten Videokunstausstellung, „Projekt '74", eine große Videotape-Sammlung von 110 Videobändern zusammengestellt. Terry Fox' *Children's Tapes* waren besonders beliebt bei den Besuchern, die erstmals Videokunst kennenlernen konnten. Auch auf der documenta 6 in Kassel 1977 habe ich mit den vier internationalen Kuratoren 50 Videobänder ausgewählt, dazu gehörten – man kann wohl sagen „selbstverständlich" – auch Terry Fox' *Children's Tapes*. Sie sind ein ähnlicher Klassiker wie Paiks *Global Groove* (1973) oder Peter Campus' frühe Bänder. Das war mein Einstieg bei Terry Fox.

Ich war natürlich immer wieder interessiert, wenn ich etwas von ihm hörte. Man konnte nur schwer etwas erfahren, deshalb war es gut, ihn persönlich zu treffen. Fox war eine skurrile und bescheidene Persönlichkeit. Er machte überhaupt nichts von sich her, hatte aber eine Intensität und eine Klarheit im Kopf – einfach bewundernswert. Damit hat er Joseph Beuys überzeugen können, eine Performance gemeinsam zu machen. Dafür interessiert man sich dann als Kurator. Donnerwetter, wenn die beiden da gemeinsam etwas machen. Obwohl man sagen muss, wenn man nicht selbst dabei war, blieb es schwer zu erfahren, was Terry Fox da eigentlich gemacht hat. Man konnte nur Fotografien und Berichte zur Kenntnis nehmen, weil es im klassischen Sinne ein Werk – „und so sieht das aus und das ist die Skulptur und das war die Installation" – nicht gab. Fox hat immer stärker an besonderen Orten außerhalb der White Cubes der Kunstvereine und Museen, das heißt in verlassenen Kirchen, Fabriken und Wohnungen, Installationen gemacht. Er hat diese besonderen Räume mit zumeist speziell bestrichenen Drahtsaiten zum Klingen gebracht. Klang gehörte damals noch weniger zur Kunst. Selbst Video und Performance hatten es schon schwer. Diese nochmalige Reduktion auf die Aktion mit dem Klang, diese schwebenden, sich auflösenden, minimal klingenden Räume beeindruckten mich wie auch andere, die dabei waren. Er präsentierte seine Performance nicht im Video. Wenn man also nicht dabei war, machte es das natürlich noch schwieriger zu wissen, was denn Terry Fox als Künstler macht.

So durfte er eine Kirche in Bologna bespielen, aber er hatte die Auflage, keinen Menschen in das Innere der Kirche zu lassen. Er spannte Klaviersaiten im Kirchenraum und hat daraus ein wunderbares Stück gemacht. Man durfte nur durch so ein kleines Loch hineinsehen. Der Klang aber ging nach draußen und man hörte Eigentümliches, konnte aber nichts sehen. In der verschlossenen Kirche entstand etwas: Genau von dem außen sichtbaren Loch, vor dem man stand, gingen die Stränge sozusagen in die Entfernung zu einem Punkt, und der Klang ging durch die Holztür nach draußen. So wie bei Marcel Duchamp mit dem mysteriös verborgen-sichtbaren Werk in Philadelphia, was da ist und gleichzeitig nur durch ein Loch gesehen werden kann. Eine solche Hommage interessierte mich natürlich schon. Was macht ein Künstler, der noch mehr reduziert als ein Duchamp?

A.L. Haben Sie das jemals selbst erleben können?

W.H. Ich habe es in Italien nicht erlebt, aber es wurde natürlich erzählt. Was ich erlebt habe, waren seine Kölner Auftritte insbesondere in der Moltkerei von Elisabeth Jappe.

A.L. Sie haben 1973 im Zusammenhang mit einem Symposium im MoMA von dem großen Unterschied zwischen Video und Film und zwischen Theater und Film gesprochen. Würden Sie das heute noch genauso sehen oder hat sich da in den Prozessen etwas verändert, die auch in der Kunst anders geworden sind?

W.H. Ich gehe immer vom Künstler aus, nicht von irgendeiner Theorie oder gar nur von der materiellen oder medialen Existenz. Technisch war alles Film, was Gerry Schum mit den Künstlern für Land Art und *Identification* realisierte, aber gemeint war der Fernseher als Abspielgerät für die Betrachter. Mir ist immer wichtiger gewesen: „Was will der Künstler mit dem Inhalt und wo will er, dass das abgespielt wird?" Und diese theoretische Diskussion, ob nun Körnung oder Pixel, hat mit der inhaltlichen, bildlichen Arbeit nicht viel zu tun, genauso wie bei der Diskussion um Ölmalerei oder Aquarellmalerei. Das ist für die objektive kunsthistorische Beschreibung wichtig, aber für den Betrachter geht es darum, was damit überhaupt gesagt werden will. Die paar Dinge, die bei der Galerie Castelli in New York liefen, von Bruce Nauman oder Peter Campus und Vito Acconci, waren die ersten Videotapes, die im Kunstbereich aufgenommen wurden. Während der Experimentalfilm etwa von Birgit und Wilhelm Hein eigentlich nicht in der Kunstszene reüssierte, weil man es eben für Film hielt und Experimentalfilm in einem anderen Kontext gesehen wurde. Die Gerry-Schum-Produktionen (eben gemacht auf Film) wurden als Videobänder von wenigen Sammlern und Museen gekauft. Verkäufe und Ausleihe (wie die großartige Videothek des NBK in Berlin!) fanden in Europa kaum statt. Terry Fox wurde durch seine Performances und die Klang- und Live-Auftritte bekannt, kaum durch seine Videos. Die Galerie Ileana Sonnabend in New York hat ihn in den 1970er Jahren gezeigt, das ist nahezu vergessen. In Europa war das fast undenkbar, auch der große Konrad Fischer, der Bruce Nauman seit 1970 ausstellte, hat Performancekünstler selten gezeigt. Ein Acconci fand nicht statt, ein Terry Fox fand da auch nicht statt.

A.L. Castelli hat auch Bruce Nauman die Portapak-Kamera gegeben. Nauman hat dann selbst das, was er zunächst auf Super 8-Film gedreht hatte, auf Videotapes übertragen.

W.H. Im Video konnte man die Performance sofort kontrollieren. Beim Film wartete man eine Woche, ob irgendetwas richtig drauf war oder nicht. Diese bei Video mögliche Live-Kontrolle war natürlich ein wichtiger Aspekt, der theoretisch schon Ende der 1960er Jahre existierte. Aber kaum ein Künstler, auch nicht Terry Fox, hatte die finanziellen Möglichkeiten dafür.

A.L. *Children's Tapes* waren erstmals 1974 im Everson Museum in Syracuse auf zwei Monitoren zu sehen, was untypisch für Terry Fox war. René Block hat dann 2002 bei der Ausstellungseröffnung „40 Jahre: Fluxus und die Folgen" in Wiesbaden, bei der Terry Fox selbst anwesend war, *Children's Tapes* mit Videobeam groß projiziert. Fox reagierte nicht ablehnend, sondern eher positiv überrascht, weil er die technischen Möglichkeiten bei der Realisierung der Videos noch gar nicht hatte.

W.H. Ich meine, ihm ging es nicht um das Videobild auf dem Monitor, sondern um das Spiel mit den Bildern. Deshalb hat er sicherlich nie etwas dagegen gehabt. Ihm ging es um die Bildhaftigkeit und um den Witz in diesen Bildern, und natürlich ist *Der Lauf der Dinge* (1987) von Fischli & Weiss gerade, wenn die Bilder groß projiziert werden, noch witziger. Das Intime als Anti-Fernsehen ist natürlich auch schön und ist sicher auch gemeint. Es ist weder Thriller noch Hollywood, deshalb ist es auch richtig, die Videos von Terry Fox auf dem Fernseher zu spielen. Aber ich kann mir gut vorstellen, dass Fox die heute selbstverständliche Form der großen Projektion akzeptiert hätte.

A.L. Ich fand es sehr witzig, dass die Künstler mit dem Ausstieg drohten, als sie bei der Biennale in Venedig 1984 zunächst nicht bezahlt werden sollten.

W.H. Das ist eine Geschichte, die auf Fotos von Klaus vom Bruch wunderbar dokumentiert ist. Die Künstler hörten von den Biennale-Verantwortlichen in Venedig, die sie eingeladen hatten: „Jaja, wir zahlen euch Eure Unkosten." Aber es passierte nichts. Und dann müssen die Künstler eine Art kleinen Streik angekündigt haben, dass sie die Werke vor der Eröffnung aus der Ausstellung wieder zurückziehen würden. Darauf hat man sich besonnen und jedem diese Packen von Lirescheinen *cash* überreicht. Terry Fox hat die Geldscheine wie ein vornehmes Einstecktuch in die Tasche seines Jacketts getan und Klaus vom Bruch hat ihn fotografiert, wie sich dieses ganze Bündel Geldscheine da herausbog.

A.L. Wie kommt ein Kunsthistoriker zur Videokunst und wie kam es zu Ihrer Verbindung mit David Ross?

W.H. Anfang 1971 hatte Paul Vogt vom Museum Folkwang Essen als einziger deutscher Museumsdirektor auf das Angebot der Elektronikindustrie, ein Videostudio geschenkt zu bekommen, positiv reagiert. Kein deutsches Museum wollte 1970 so etwas haben. Ich hatte über Bauhaus promoviert – Kunst und Technik eine neue Einheit, war 1923 der Slogan! – und war der Jüngste mit 26 Jahren im Team der Kuratoren. Da hieß es: „Mal ran, junger Mann, und gucken Sie mal, was man damit macht." Es gab ein Videostudio und einen Techniker. Wir machten zunächst pädagogische Filme, merkten aber schnell, dass dafür Fachleute gebraucht würden. Was konnte man sonst damit anfangen? Darum bin ich zu Gerry Schum gegangen und habe erste Gespräche geführt. Da ich im Herbst 1972 an den Kölnischen Kunstverein berufen wurde, habe ich mich dann nicht mehr in Essen, sondern in Köln auch weiterhin für die Videokunst engagiert.

Es ging sofort um die Vorbereitung einer riesigen Ausstellung „Projekt '74", die so eine Art Gegen-documenta in Köln sein sollte. Auf die Frage, was wir alles Neues zeigen können, schlug ich vor: „Dann lass uns doch Video machen." Da ich mit David Ross bekannt war, haben wir für „Projekt '74" einen Teil seiner Auswahl von US-Videos erstmals in Deutschland gezeigt und deutsche und europäische Künstler dazu genommen, aber auch von den drei Künstlern des Lijnbaan Centrums Rotterdam in den Räumen des Kölnischen Kunstvereins während der drei Monate der Ausstellung „Projekt '74" neu produzieren lassen – und einen Video-Katalog erstellt, der damals zwar nicht ein einziges Mal verkauft wurde, aber heute in meinem Archiv in der Akademie der Künste in Berlin gerettet wurde, wieder sichtbar und vermittelbar ist – nach 41 Jahren! Und da war Terry Fox auch in der Ausstellung dabei.

2015

Das Gespräch wurde am 27. Mai 2015 in der Akademie der Künste, Berlin, geführt.

Seite 286

Bill Viola

Eine Ausstellung über Terry Fox wird möglicherweise zum ersten Mal das ganze Ausmaß von Terrys frühen Erkundungen von Ritualen und seines Gebrauchs von Symbolen präsentieren und offenlegen. Sein Werk steht in einem profunden Zusammenhang mit dem Spirituellen, das in seinen multimedialen Performances und Aktionen in den 1960er und frühen 1970er Jahren zutage tritt. Er erkundete die inneren Dimensionen von allem, womit er arbeitete. Ich hatte das Privileg, Terry zu assistieren, während ich technischer Direktor bei Art/tapes/22 in Florenz war, dem Produktionsstudio, das Maria Gloria Bicocchi mehrere Jahre lang ausschließlich für Künstler betrieb. Terry stellte ein Werk mit dem Titel *Lunedi*, 1975, fertig, eine schöne Ton/Bild-Arbeit, bei der er mit einem Violinbogen über eine große mit Sand bedeckte Metallscheibe strich. Die Klangwellen erzeugten in dem Sand auf der Metallscheibe komplexe Muster, die eine faszinierende visuelle und akustische Erfahrung gestalteten und umgestalteten. Sein Stil und seine Technik bei diesen Erkundungen waren einzigartig. Es ist wichtig, dass man während des Forschungsprozesses die besten Meister solcher Werke ausfindig macht und an ihnen festhält.

2014

Aus dem Englischen übersetzt von Nikolaus G. Schneider

Steve Seid

Die Aufhebung der (Un-)Gläubigkeit:

Einige Gedanken über Terry Fox' Videoarbeit *The Rake's Progress*

In der Sammlung des Pacific Film Archive befindet sich eine Gruppe von Videobändern von Terry Fox, die unter dem Sammeltitel *The Rake's Progress*[1] zusammengefasst sind, obgleich der kunsthistorische Verweis[2] nur schwer nachvollziehbar ist, wenn man diese spezifische Trias von ½-Zoll-Spulentonbändern betrachtet. Doch sei dem wie ihm wolle, diese Master Tapes, die außerdem als Session #1, #2 und #3 ausgewiesen werden, vermitteln nicht nur einen erhellenden Einblick in Fox' künstlerische Praxis, sondern auch in seine komplizierte Beziehung zu elektronischen Medien.
Die Videobänder wurden am 13. Mai 1971 in Tom Marionis Museum of Conceptual Art[3] realisiert. Zu Beginn des ersten Videos sind die Vorbereitungen für eine Performance zu sehen: Fox berät sich mit seinem langjährigen Mitarbeiter und Kameramann, George Bolling, in der Nähe befindet sich Fox' Zwillingsbruder Larry und außerdem, normalerweise nicht vor der Kamera, Lydia Modi-Vitale, die Kuratorin des de Saisset Museums, die das Geschehen beobachtet. Im Aufführungsbereich gibt es drei wesentliche Elemente: eine freistehende Glasscheibe, einen großen Spiegel und eine Sony-Videokamera auf einem Stativ. Mit dem Rücken zum Spiegel ist Fox der Scheibe zugewandt, während die Kamera ihn durch das Glas filmt. Fox, der genau markiert hat, welcher Bereich der Scheibe von der Videokamera erfasst wird, tritt eigentlich dadurch in Erscheinung, dass seine Hand in das Bild hinein- und aus ihm heraushuscht, und beginnt, Fett[4] aus einer kleinen Tube auf das Glas zu schmieren. Damit macht er langsam weiter, bis das gesamte Videobild von einer verschmierten Schmutzschicht überzogen ist.[5] In dem Schwarzweiß-Video gewinnt dieses improvisierte *Field-Painting* ein ätherisches, wolkenartiges Erscheinungsbild, und im Spiegelbild kann man andeutungsweise eine schwache Umrisslinie der Kamera auf ihrem Stativ erkennen.[6] Es handelt sich hierbei nicht um die Dokumentaraufnahme einer Performance, wie sie Bolling häufig gemacht hatte, keine zeitbasierte Spur für eine zukünftige Untersuchung, und ebensowenig werden die sich verändernden Kamerapositionen präsentiert, die wir beispielsweise in Fox' *Turgescent Sex* aus demselben Jahr sehen können, eine verblüffende visuelle Überhöhung der tatsächlichen Aktion. Die ursprüngliche Konfiguration aus Glas/Spiegel/Kamera enthält eine bewusste Verkomplizierung, die auf subtile Weise das aktiviert, was Rosalind Krauss als „die Ästhetik des Narzissmus" bezeichnet hat, eine Ästhetik, bei der die „Selbsteinkapselung" und das „Spiegeln" die Rohmaterialien des Mediums sind.[7] Der Einsatz des Spiegels erzeugt einen unheimlichen Verdoppelungseffekt, der nicht nur die Kamera selbst dezent in den Vordergrund rückt, sondern über das finale Bild die vorder- und rückseitig gespiegelte Hand von Fox legt. Bollings Kamera späht in den Raum von Fox' Aktion, um Zeuge eines elektronischen Doppelgängers zu werden, der seine Gesten genau verfolgt. Selbstreflexivität trifft auf Selbstreflexivität. Diese aufgezeichnete Aktion ist nur die erste Komponente von *The Rake's Progress*; die zweite ist ein mittelgroßes Fernsehgerät, dessen Bildschirm mit demselben Fett überzogen ist. Fox steht vor dem Fernseher und entfernt das Fett langsam mit einem kleinen Lappen, während das frühere Videoband langsam abgespielt wird. Der Fernsehbildschirm wird zugleich offengelegt und verunklart, da der in der Zeit verschobene Videodoppelgänger des Künstlers seine gegenteilige Aufgabe durchführt.[8]
Als Performance ist *The Rake's Progress* ein Strudel instabiler zeitlicher Beziehungen, Identitätskollisionen und elektronischer Loops, wie sie nur im Medium Video möglich sind.[9] Der Begriff „Live", der Umstand, dass sich hier eine Handlung vor uns abspielt, wird durch die Unmittelbarkeit eines Videobildes herausgefordert, das Fox' in der realen Welt stattfindende Handlung sowohl nachahmt als auch verspottet. Man mag dabei an die Rückkopplung denken, jenen Zustand, in dem sich Video im Wesentlichen konsumiert, doch hier hat Fox die verdoppelte Metapher von Rückkopplung in Szene gesetzt, nicht die Sache selbst. Dadurch dass die Zeitebenen von „innerhalb" und „außerhalb" des Fernsehers durch ihre Umkehrung aufgehoben werden, ist Fox schließlich in einem performativen Loop „aufgehoben", in dem der „Wüstling" (Rake) keine Fortschritte (Progress) mehr macht.

2015

Aus dem Englischen übersetzt von Nikolaus G. Schneider

1   Der vollständige Titel auf der Video-Verpackung lautet *The Rake's Progress: In the Service of Art*.
2   William Hogarth' *A Rake's Progress* ist eine 1732–33 entstandene Sammlung von acht Gemälden, die den rasanten sozialen Niedergang eines liederlichen jungen Mannes schildert, der zunächst ein ausschweifendes Leben führt, dann völlig verarmt und schließlich im Irrenhaus Bedlam landet.
3   Das MOCA befand sich damals in der 86 Third Street im Zentrum von San Francisco.
4   Möglicherweise ist das Fett eine verstohlene Anspielung auf Joseph Beuys, mit dem Fox im November 1970 die Performance *Isolation Unit* aufgeführt hatte.
5   Zu einem früheren Zeitpunkt, 1970, machte Vito Acconci die Arbeit *Openings*, bei der die Kamera den Bauch des Künstlers in Nahaufnahme zeigt. Langsam und schmerzvoll reißt Acconci sämtliche Haare um seinen Nabel herum aus, bis im Bild nur noch sein entblößter Bauch zu sehen ist. Dies dürfte das Gegenteil von Fox' Fettauftrag sein, eine subtraktive statt einer additiven Handlung.
6   Man beachte, dass George Bolling nicht hinter der Kamera steht. Das Videodeck befindet sich im Aufzeichnungsmodus, und die auf dem Stativ montierte Kamera ist auf die Szene gerichtet.
7   Rosalind Krauss, Video: The Aesthetics of Narcissism. In: *October*, 1 (Frühjahr 1976), S. 50–64, Wiederabdruck in: Gregory Battcock (Hg.), *New Artists Video*, New York 1978, S. 43–64
8   Man könnte sich fragen, was Zwillingsbildung (*twinning*) für einen Zwilling bedeutet.
9   Weitere wichtige Werke, die dieselbe Art medienspezifische Spiegelung thematisieren, sollten bald folgen. Siehe Joan Jonas' *Vertical Roll* (1972), Peter Campus' *Three Transitions* (1973) und Richard Serras *Boomerang* (1974).

[George Bolling]
Terry Fox

„Turgescent Sex" 40:00 [Minuten]

Dokumentation
einer Performance

Bestandteile: Textilverband
Zigarette
Streichholz
Fisch
Schnur
Schale mit Wasser
Stück Seife
Verzweiflung

Sitze im Schneidersitz mit den Gegenständen
um mich herum / wasche mir die Hände /
wasche den Fisch, der mit der Schnur mit
vielen Knoten gefesselt ist / verbinde die
Augen mit dem Verband / markiere mit dem
Blut des Fisches die Augen auf der Augenbinde / löse den Fisch aus den Fesseln /
forme mit den Schnüren ein Nest / wickle
den Fisch in den Verband / hülle den Fisch
in Rauch.

ca. 1971

Quelle: de Saisset Museum, Santa Clara University

Aus dem Englischen übersetzt von Anne Pitz

Interview von
Tom Kennedy mit
George Bolling:
Unsichtbar
ist das Medium

TOM KENNEDY

Wann hast du angefangen, mit Video
zu arbeiten?

GEORGE BOLLING

[...] Meine Auseinandersetzung mit Video
begann 1969, als ein Freund eine Portapak-
Kamera kaufte. Das erste Jahr brachte ich
damit zu, mich mit dem Medium vertraut zu
machen. Meine Erfahrungen hatte ich
davor mit Fotografie und Film gemacht, und
Video unterscheidet sich sehr stark von Film.
Es gab damals keine funktionstüchtigen
½-Zoll-Schneidemaschinen, ohne die
es praktisch unmöglich war, das Band nach
der Aufnahme zu bearbeiten. Man musste
daher jede Aufnahme vorab vom Anfang bis
zum Ende durchchoreografieren. Doch
die meisten Aufnahmegelegenheiten hatte
ich bei Künstlern, die in ihren Ateliers
arbeiteten, und man konnte unmöglich
wissen, was von einem Moment zum
nächsten geschehen würde. Bei der Herstellung dieser Dokumentarfilme entwickelte
ich ein Gespür für den Augenblick und
choreografierte die Aufnahme im Einklang
mit der jeweils gegebenen Situation. Es gab

ein Interesse am Bild, doch das Hauptinteresse galt der Zeit, wurde die Zeit. Das
ist ein großer Unterschied zum Film, der
Einstellung für Einstellung, Bild für Bild
konzipiert wird und bei dem die Zeit zum
Ergebnis der Gleichung der Bilder wird. Bei
Video habe ich festgestellt, dass das Ziel
darin bestand, zuerst den Moment zu erzählen, und das Bild musste im Einklang mit
dieser Tatsache (dem Moment) der Situation
stehen. [...]

T.K. Inwiefern unterschied sich eine Dokumentation von einem Dokumentarfilm?

G.B. Grundsätzlich weiß man bei der Dokumentation bereits im Vorhinein ziemlich
genau, was geschehen und wie lange es
dauern wird. Das bietet eine Gelegenheit,
bereits im Vorfeld eine Choreografie für die
Aufnahme zu planen. Das bedeutet aber
nicht, dass man jeden Schritt und jede
Sekunde der Aufnahme plant, sondern es
bedeutet, dass man die Gesten in der
Performance, ihren Wert, in Betracht ziehen
kann und damit auch den angemessenen
Aufnahmepunkt. Am wichtigsten aber
ist, dass man die Abfolge des Ereignisses
beurteilen kann, was erforderlich ist, um
sicherzustellen, dass der Übergang von einem
Punkt zum nächsten die richtige Dauer hat
und jeweils im richtigen Moment erfolgt.
Das ist ein großer Unterschied zu einem
Dokumentarfilm, bei dem man nicht weiß,
was als Nächstes geschieht, weshalb man
bei der Arbeit an einem Dokumentarfilm
eine Menge lernen kann.

T.K. Aber könnte man den Künstler bei
einem Dokumentarfilm nicht einfach fragen,
was er im Atelier machen wird, und wäre
es nicht dasselbe, wenn man bereits im
Voraus weiß, wie die Performance aussehen
wird?

G.B. Eigentlich nicht, denn bei einem
Dokumentarfilm gehört das Video ganz dir.
Es ist nicht die fertige Skulptur oder das
fertige Gemälde, die der Künstler behalten
und später verkaufen kann. Bei der Dokumentation einer Performance wird das Video
in wesentlich größerem Maße das Werk,
weil es die einzige physische Darstellung
der Performance ist. Deshalb hat man eine
große Verantwortung, die Performance
auf zutreffende Weise wiederzugeben. Wenn
man den Künstler in einem Dokumentarfilm
falsch darstellt, ist der Schaden wesentlich
geringer, denn es gibt ja das fertige Bild
oder die fertige Skulptur, mit der sich jeder
falschen Darstellung begegnen lässt, was
bei einer Dokumentation nicht der Fall ist.
Bevor ich Performancekünstler kennenlernte, hatte ich Gerüchte gehört, sie wollten
nicht, dass man ihre Werke dokumentiert,

weil man dabei sein müsse. Sicherlich ist Film kein Ersatz für die eigentliche Sache, denn Film hat sein eigenes synthetisches Zeitgefühl. Zeit ist von ziemlich zentraler Bedeutung für Performance. Als Video-künstler faszinierte mich die Möglichkeit, Performance zu dokumentieren, da ich Zeit als den zentralen Punkt von Video begriff. Zugegebenermaßen ist Video kein Ersatz für die eigentliche Sache, aber es gibt die Zeit weniger verzerrt wieder als der Film. Die Herausforderung bestand also darin, die Performance in Video mit möglichst geringer Beeinträchtigung wiederzugeben; die Mani-pulation der Kamera musste unsichtbar sein. [...]

1976

Quelle: Interview aus: *La Mamelle*, Bd. 1 (3), Winter 1976, Videoausgabe, wiederveröffentlicht von Tanya Zimbardo: „George Bolling: Invisible is the Medium", San Francisco Museum of Modern Art's Open Space, http://openspace.sfmoma.org/2013/03/george-bolling, zuletzt am 30.9.2015

Aus dem Englischen übersetzt von Nikolaus G. Schneider

Seite 290

Interview von Dena Beard mit Marilyn Bogerd

DENA BEARD

Was, meinst du, waren die Gründe für Terrys Großzügigkeit, seine Freundlichkeit, aber auch diese Offenheit?

MARILYN BOGERD

Es hat etwas mit seinem Bei-dir-Sein zu tun, 100%, seinem Dir-Zuhören, ohne zu urteilen, und dem Umstand, dass er dich an seiner Sicht der Dinge, seinen Erfahrun-gen teilhaben ließ. Ich hatte persönliche Erlebnisse in meiner Kindheit, aufgrund derer ich mich vor dem Tod fürchtete und beinah gestorben wäre. Es war interes-sant, mit Terry zu sprechen, denn er war einige Minuten lang tot, als er mit Krebs im Krankenhaus lag.
D.B. Als er siebzehn war?
M.B. Als er mit 27 im UCSF (University of California Hospital) war. Sein Bruder legte ihm seine Hand auf den Arm und forderte ihn auf, zurückzukommen – und das tat er. Er lachte immer und sagte: „Marilyn, nicht der Tod ist furchterregend, sondern das Leben!" Und dann erzählte er mir viele Geschichten von Freunden und Künstlern, die dem Tod begegnet waren; einige von ihnen hatten eine tödliche Krankheit. Er sprach darüber, wie sie damit umgingen, und berichtete von seinen eigenen Erleb-nissen im Krankenhaus. Das war seine Art, freundlich und einfühlsam zu sein. Terry sprach auch über die Freundlichkeit von Joseph Beuys, Robert Frank und Chris Burden als eine Art übergeordnete Freundlichkeit. Oder er erzählte von Nam June Paiks Konzentration, wie er ihn um 3 Uhr morgens in der U-Bahn in New York City gesehen habe, wo sie die beiden einzigen Fahrgäste waren und Paik sich kein einziges Mal umsah. Er war völlig in seine Gedanken versunken, vollkommen fokussiert.

D.B. Es ist interessant, dass du diese Großzügigkeit, seine geistige Großzügigkeit, mit einer Art Konzentration und einem Typus von Konzentration gleichsetzt, der spezifisch künstlerisch ist. Und er fand das in Beuys, Frank und Burden und Paik [...].
M.B. Als Terry erfuhr, dass er Krebs hatte, nur noch drei Monate zu leben und keine Krankenversicherung hatte, spendete er seinen Körper dem UCSF, einem Lehr-krankenhaus. Er blieb dort 6 Monate, hatte dort die größte Transplantation, die jemals an seiner Brust vorgenommen wurde. Durch die Bestrahlung wurde sein gesamtes Brustbein verbrannt, und er musste dort mehrere Wochen lang still liegen. Heute hängen sie einem im Krankenhaus gleich einen Fernseher vors Gesicht, und häufig gibt es einen Zimmergenossen und dann die ganzen Verwandten und Leute, die rund um die Uhr rein- und rausgehen. Aber so war das damals, vor fast 45 Jahren, noch nicht. Und dann eines Tages gesagt bekommen, man sei geheilt!
Als Künstler hat er sich mit der Isolation, dem Schmerz, der Furcht auseinandergesetzt.
D.B. Du hast mir schon früher von diesen langen Gesprächen erzählt, die du und Terry nächtelang geführt haben. Hat er dabei jemals über seine Arbeit oder seine Vor-gehensweise gesprochen?
M.B. Ja, natürlich. Vor allem nachdem er mit seinen Performances in Europa aufgetreten war.
D.B. Du hast eine lustige Geschichte, wie du Terry kennengelernt hast.
M.B. Ja, ich lernte Terry 1974 auf einer Halloweenparty kennen. Ich war Kunst-student, kam aus Belgien und trug die Gips-maske eines Biedermanns. Da erschien Terry auf der Party – mit einer Strumpfhose über dem Kopf [...].
D.B. So einer Damen-Nylonstrumpfhose?
M.B. Ja, wie so ein Bankräuber. Er lachte und lief rum und jagte allen einen Schrecken ein. [Beide lachen]
[...]
M.B. Eine weitere Geschichte, die ich dir erzählen wollte, handelt von Georg, Georg Decristel, einem ganz engen Freund von Terry, der auch mein Freund wurde. Georg war ein wunderbarer Mensch, Dichter und Künstler, der in Innsbruck geboren wurde und lebte. Häufig verreisten sie zusammen und traten zusammen auf, etwa im Berkeley Art Museum 1978.
Georg spielte Maultrommel und hatte eine große Sammlung davon, die er mit Leuten teilte, die er traf. Es war ein laufendes Gespräch mit jedermann, der mit ihm spielte. Eines Abends auf einer vollen Party

begrüßten alle Terry und sprachen mit ihm, da er nach New York City gezogen war und viele seiner Freunde ihn eine ganze Weile nicht gesehen hatten. Terry wohnte damals einige Tage bei mir in San Francisco. Wir kamen an diesem Abend von einer Performance und etwa in der Mitte der Party saßen Georg und ich an entgegengesetzten Seiten des Raumes an der Wand. Wir beide spielten die Maultrommel, hin und her, hin und her. Das ging lange Zeit so. Als die Party zu Ende ging, kam Terry zu uns und sagte, er habe unsere ganzen Maultrommel-Gespräche gehört. Trotz der vielen Leute, die mit ihm sprachen, und trotz der lauten Musik hatte er das ganze Gespräch verfolgt. Das ist nur ein Beispiel für Terrys verblüffende Wahrnehmung seiner Umwelt und der Menschen um ihn herum. Terry konnte den inneren Menschen sehen. Er beurteilte Menschen nie nach ihrem Aussehen. Daher konnte er mit vielen unterschiedlichen Menschen in allen möglichen Milieus Beziehungen aufbauen.

2015

Aus dem Englischen übersetzt von
Nikolaus G. Schneider

Renny Pritikin

Alternative Kunsträume in San Francisco

Mitte der 1970er Jahre war San Fancisco eine ungewöhnlich fruchtbare Brutstätte künstlerischer Entwicklungen. Insbesondere die Projekte der ersten Generation der Konzeptualisten, darunter Bonni Sherk, Howard Fried, Jim Pomeroy, Paul Kos, Lynn Hershman, Doug Hall, David Ireland, Tom Marioni, Jock Reynolds und viele andere, darunter natürlich Terry Fox, definierten allesamt eine alternative Form der Bewegung, die diverse Elemente von Performance und körperzentrierten Aktivitäten, Humor und Politik miteinander vermengten. Gleichzeitig riefen sie und ihre Studenten (meine Generation) ein verblüffendes Netzwerk alternativer Räume ins Leben, das Installation, Performance, Video und experimentelle Poesie und Musik unterstützte. Diese Organisationen, etwa New Langton Arts (wo ich arbeitete), La Mamelle, Southern Exposure, SF Camerawork, Site/Cite/Sight, Galeria de la Raza und viele andere, betonten eine partizipatorische Demokratie; sie bauten Installationen, die von und für Künstler gegründet und von ihnen betreut wurden, prägten die Rolle von Kuratoren, Sammlern und anderen Profis im Kunstbetrieb. Künstler wurden bezahlt, leiteten die Organisationen und übten die Hauptkontrolle über alles aus. Schließlich gab es ungewöhnlich fließende Übergänge zwischen Komponisten neuer Musik und Bildhauern, die Klanginstallationen machten, was allerlei Möglichkeiten eröffnete, die in den inzwischen historischen New-Music-America-Festivals gipfelten, die bildende Kunst und experimentelle Musik und Performance miteinander verbanden. Das ist das Umfeld, aus dem Terry Fox hervorging.

2015

Aus dem Englischen übersetzt von
Nikolaus G. Schneider

Marilyn Bogerd

Site, Cite, Sight

Site, Cite, Sight Inc. wurde 1976 gegründet, um die Arbeit von Künstlern unabhängig von ihrem kommerziellen Potenzial zu unterstützen.

Jeder Künstler / Jede Künstlerin bestimmte die Struktur seines/ihres Werks, die Verwendung des Raums, der Zeit, der Materialien sowie des öffentlichen Zugangs zu seinem/ihrem Werk.

Diese gemeinnützige Organisation wurde vom National Endowment for the Arts gefördert. Die Künstler verfügten alle über dasselbe Budget und erhielten dasselbe Honorar.

Während der ersten 3½ Jahre kuratierten die Gründer 32 Künstler/Ausstellungen. Anschließend wurde jeder dieser Künstler gebeten, einen neuen Künstler auszuwählen, der bei Site ausstellen oder eine Performance machen sollte. Im Katalog konnte jeder Künstler seine eigene Werkbeschreibung verfassen.

Im April 1982 wurde Site der Mietvertrag für die 585 Mission Street gekündigt, und es musste daher schließen.

2015

Aus dem Englischen übersetzt von
Nikolaus G. Schneider

Interview von Terri Cohn mit Terry Fox

TERRY FOX

Ich habe ein Problem mit dem Wort „konzeptuell".

TERRI COHN

Das ist ein guter Einstieg, denn meine erste Frage ist, wann du ein Konzeptkünstler wurdest und warum?

T.F. Ich habe das Wort „konzeptuell" überhaupt erst sehr viel später gehört. Das war wahrscheinlich, als Tom Marioni das Museum of Conceptual Art eröffnete.

T.C. Als was hast du dich dann bezeichnet? Als Bildhauer?

T.F. Ja. Aber zuerst war ich Maler. Ich fing 1962 an, ernsthaft zu malen. Damals lebte ich in Rom. Ich war dorthin gezogen, um Malerei zu studieren. Aber da die Schule bestreikt und geschlossen wurde, konnte ich das nicht. Doch ich blieb ein Jahr lang dort und malte. [...]

T.C. Maler zu sein, ist sehr kostspielig.

T.F. Ja. Und Papier war damals extrem preiswert. Deshalb kaufte ich einfach Tusche und Papier und fing an zu zeichnen. Von der Malerei her brauchte ich ganz traditionell ein Thema und fing deshalb an, die Pariser Mauern abzubilden. [...]

T.F. Im Jahr 1968 habe ich die letzten Bilder, die ich machte, auf Plexiglasscheiben gemalt. Sie waren schwarz bemalt, ganz und gar schwarz übersprayt. Dann kratzte ich mit einer hypodermischen Nadel einige andere Farben in die Farbschicht. Sie waren beinahe nicht zu sehen. Man musste auf Hände und Knie heruntergehen und sie wirklich suchen. Das war, glaube ich, für mich der Anfang einer Idee in Richtung Performance. In dieser Phase fuhr ich nach New York und entdeckte die ganzen Fluxus-Bücher, und so erfuhr ich alles über Fluxus und die Aktionen der Bewegung. Als ich zur Reese Palley Gallery ging und mit Carol Lindsley sprach, die die Galerie damals führte, erzählte ich ihr alles über Fluxus, und ich glaube, dass sie mich deshalb akzeptierte! [...] In Amsterdam hatte ich wieder Kontakt mit Bill Wiley aufgenommen, und ich machte eine Staub-Tausch-Aktion mit ihm. Ich schickte ihm Staub von einer bestimmten Pariser Metro, und er schickte mir Staub, und dazu schrieben wir uns gegenseitig in Briefen, wo wir den Staub herhatten. Ich nahm Staub aus dem Louvre und von allem möglichen interessanten Orten in Paris, und er nahm Staub von Orten wie dem San Francisco Museum of Art oder dem San Francisco Art Institute. Und den Staub vom Louvre, den ich ihm geschickt hatte, legte er dann wieder an die Stelle, wo er Staub entnommen hatte, und ich nahm den Staub, den er geschickt hatte, und legte ihn in den Louvre. [...]

T.C. Man würde jetzt wahrscheinlich ziemlich paranoid reagieren, weil ihr Sporen von einem Kontinent in den anderen eingeführt habt. Aber das ist heute anders als damals. Als ihr eure Staub-Tausch-Aktionen gemacht habt, machte man sich keine Sorgen über solche Dinge.

T.F. Nein. Das war vor Anthrax. 1967 habe ich auch zwei Bilder auf Glas mitgenommen, die, glaube ich, ungefähr 45 × 45 cm groß waren. Es war ein Event, ich fuhr nach Köln, und ein Film zeigte das. Während meines Aufenthalts dort deponierte ich diese Bilder in der Galerie Zwirner, der besten Galerie in Köln. Ich weiß nicht, was Zwirner mit ihnen gemacht hat. Er ist nicht mehr dort.

T.C. Hat er sie nicht ausgestellt?

T.F. Er war nicht da, als ich dort war. Also ließ ich die Bilder einfach stehen. Sie waren auf der Rückseite signiert, aber ich weiß nicht, was aus ihnen geworden ist. Vielleicht hat er sie verkauft. Wer weiß? [...]

T.F. [...] Tom war bereits der Kurator des Richmond Art Center. Als er mir 1969 anbot, bei „The Return of Abstract Expressionism" mitzumachen, verwendete ich wieder fliegende Folien. Einige waren außen und wurden vom Wind bewegt, andere waren innen.

Die nächste Sache, die Tom kuratierte, war eigentlich eine radikale Idee. Er hatte Larry Bell beauftragt, viele Künstler zu besuchen und ihre Arbeiten anzusehen und drei auszuwählen. Er lud uns ein, uns an der „Sculpture Annual", die das Richmond jährlich machte, zu beteiligen. Das war im Jahr 1970, und ich machte mein *Levitation*-Stück.

T.C. Willst du mehr davon erzählen?

T.F. Gern. Damals hatte ich die Hodgkin'sche Krankheit und gerade eine Operation überstanden. Ich wollte sie unbedingt loswerden, und ich wollte wirklich schweben. Ich bekam den großen Hauptraum und deckte den Boden mit weißem Papier ab, so dass die Wände, die Decke und der Boden komplett weiß waren. Es war schon fast wie ... schweben.

T.C. Eigentlich wie ein Krankenhauszimmer?

T.F. Ja. Ich wohnte in der Capp Street in der Nähe der Army Street in San Francisco, und dort wurde gerade eine Schnellstraße gebaut. Wir mieteten einen Lastwagen und holten anderthalb Tonnen Erde von dort ins Richmond und legten die Erde auf dem Papier in einem Quadrat aus, das meiner doppelten Körperlänge entsprach. Ich hatte Polyäthylen-Schläuche und hatte mir etwas Blut abgenommen. Damit füllte ich einen Schlauch und machte einen Kreis, wie man ihn immer auf Leonardo-Zeichnungen sieht. Dann legte ich mich auf die Erde in den Kreis, aber vorher fastete ich drei Tage und Nächte, um wirklich leer zu sein. Ich hatte vier lange Polyäthylen-Schläuche, die viel länger waren als der eine, mit Blut gefüllte. Einer war mit Milch gefüllt und einer war mit Urin gefüllt, einer mit Blut und ein vierter mit Wasser. Ich hielt in jeder Hand zwei Stück und legte mich dort sechs Stunden lang allein hin und versuchte zu schweben. Die Tür war abgeschlossen, denn es war keine Performance für Zuschauer – niemand wurde in den Raum gelassen. Ich hatte wirklich das Gefühl zu schweben, weil ich jedes Gefühl für meinen Körper verloren hatte. Ich wollte die Hodgkin'sche Krankheit hinter mir lassen, und das war ein Weg, es zu erreichen.

T.C. Bist du die Krankheit schließlich losgeworden?

T.F. Ja.

T.C. Dann hat das offenbar geholfen?

T.F. Ja.

T.C. Das hört sich an wie ein Wunder.

T.F. Mein Ziel war es, den Raum so aufzuladen, dass die Leute, die hereinkamen, nachdem ich gegangen war, die Spannung spüren könnten. Das war die skulpturale Idee, die der ganzen Sache zugrunde lag.

T.C. Blieb die Installation für einen längeren Zeitraum stehen?

T.F. Nein! Aber Tom kann dir diese Geschichte erzählen. Er wurde deshalb gefeuert. [...]

T.F. Im Jahr 1971 gab es eine Ausstellung mit dem Titel „Fish, Fox, Kos", die Paul Kos, Tom (sein Pseudonym war Allan Fish) und ich machten. Das war eine weitere seltsame Erfahrung für mich. Wieder hatte ich lange gefastet und vorher nicht geschlafen.

T.C. Da scheint sich ein Muster herauszubilden, dass du in der Zeit vor einer Veranstaltung entweder nicht geschlafen oder nicht gegessen hast.

T.F. Ja. Diesmal war es beides. Ich war immer noch damit beschäftigt, wie ich meinen Körper reinigen und diese ganze Krankheit austreiben könnte. Also kaufte ich zwei lebende Fische in Chinatown, große Barsche. Ich nahm Schnüre und band einen an meine Zunge und einen an meinen Penis. Dann blieb ich sitzen und wartete, bis sie starben,

was *wirklich* lange dauerte. Ich dachte, es würde ungefähr 20 Minuten dauern, aber es waren mindestens zwei Stunden. Wenn ich meinte, sie wären tot, sah ich plötzlich ein kleines Schwanzzucken und konnte die Schwingungen wirklich deutlich über die Schnüre spüren. Dadurch und während ich alles, was ich hatte, an sie übergab, hoffte ich, dass sie es in den Tod mitnehmen könnten.

Ich hatte den Fußboden im Museum mit weißer Plane abgedeckt. Ungefähr 90 Zentimeter über dem Boden spannte ich ein Dach aus weißer Plane über den ganzen Bereich und holte die Laken. Ich band die Fische wieder fest, legte mich einfach hin und schlief sofort ein. Es gab eine Öffnung, so dass mich die Leute durch die Tür sehen, den Raum aber nicht betreten konnten.

Sie sahen dann, dass ich schlief und die Fische an mir befestigt waren. [...]

Da war die Ausstellung „Prospect '71: Projections" in Düsseldorf, und einer meiner Lieblingskünstler, Joseph Beuys, war dabei. Sie bezahlten mir die Reise dorthin, aber mein Hauptziel war, Beuys zu treffen. Ich wollte außerdem irgendwo eine Performance machen. Deshalb ging ich in die Akademie und besuchte ihn. Er war wirklich wunderbar. Seine Frau und seine Kinder waren nicht da, so fuhren wir zu ihm nach Hause, machten Abendessen und unterhielten uns. Er sagte, ich könnte meine Performance im Keller der Kunstakademie machen. Er kümmerte sich darum, dass das Plakat gemacht wurde. Es war wirklich schön. Dann sprach er mich etwa eine Woche vorher an und fragte, ob er die Performance mit mir machen könne. Das konnte ich gar nicht fassen!

Der Grund, warum er die Performance mit mir machen wollte, war, dass er eine Maus hatte, die unter seinem Bett gelebt hatte, und diese Maus war gerade gestorben. Ich weiß, dass diese Geschichte völlig unglaubwürdig klingt, aber sie ist wahr. Jedenfalls war diese Maus gestorben, und Beuys wollte eine Art Bestattung machen. Als er fragte, ob er das machen könne, war ich natürlich begeistert. Also waren unsere beiden Namen auf der Einladungskarte und dem Plakat zu *Isolation Unit*. Sie hingen in Düsseldorf an allen Wänden. Er hatte gerade seinen *Filzanzug*, Edition Block, gemacht und trug ihn das erste Mal für diese Performance. Er hatte ein Spulentonbandgerät und ließ die Maus auf der laufenden Spule kreisen. Wir zeichneten die ganze Sache auf. Ich hatte lange Eisenrohre, die ich aneinanderschlug, weil ich mich da schon in gleichem Maße für

Klang interessierte wie für Performance. Ich war dabei, mich zu verändern, und arbeitete jetzt immer mit Klang. Ich hatte ein Fenster mit sechs Glasscheiben in die Ecke gestellt und versuchte, das Glas durch die Klangschwingungen der Röhren zu brechen. Als ich das Gefühl hatte, sie wären kurz davor zu brechen, zertrümmerte ich das Glas mit den Rohren. Ich hatte eine Kerze in die Mitte des Raumes gestellt, und direkt daneben hing eine Glühbirne. Man konnte das Licht der Kerze nicht unterscheiden, außer wenn man sehr nah heranging.

T.C. Weil die Glühbirne das Kerzenlicht nicht durchließ?

T.F. Ja, richtig. Dann saß ich am Schluss der Performance mit den zwei kürzesten Rohren, die vielleicht 30 Zentimeter lang waren, und versuchte, die Kerzenflamme mit ihren Klangschwingungen zu biegen. Das funktionierte. Beuys lief herum und hielt die tote Maus in der offenen Hand, die er dem Publikum, das hinter einem Seil am Eingang stand, zeigte. Sie konnten den Raum nicht betreten. Der Raum war wirklich schmutzig. Es war der ehemalige Kohlenkeller unter der Akademie.

T.C. Das hört sich nach einem starken Kontrast zu all den makellos weißen Räumen an, in denen du sonst arbeitest.

T.F. Er war genau das Gegenteil. Nachdem ich das gemacht hatte, veränderte sich auch mein Interesse bezüglich der Räume, in denen ich arbeiten wollte. Ich habe darüber noch nie nachgedacht, bevor du die weißen Räume erwähnt hast.

T.C. In welchen Räumen wolltest du von da an arbeiten?

T.F. Oh, in interessanten Räumen! Diese Performance hat mir sehr geholfen.

2005

(gekürzt) Das Gespräch ist ungekürzt veröffentlicht in: *SFAQ*, Bd. 2, Nr. 2, Herbst 2015.

Aus dem Englischen übersetzt von Anne Pitz

List of Exhibited Works by Terry Fox

1967

Terry Fox, Untitled, 1967
Ink on paper
77.47 × 58.74 cm
San Francisco Museum of Modern Art
Gift of Joy E. Feinberg, Berkeley
ill. p. 240

1968

Terry Fox, *Amsterdam, July 19, 1968, from 11:00 AM to Noon*, 1968
Photograph of a collage (series of 36 b/w photographs by Terry Fox)
22.2 × 25.1 cm
Estate of Terry Fox, Cologne

Terry Fox, *Amsterdam, July 19, 1968, from 11:00 AM to Noon*, 1968
Photograph of a collage / detail (9 of 36 b/w photographs by Terry Fox)
22.2 × 25.1 cm
Details: Colin McRae, Berkeley
Estate of Terry Fox, Cologne

1969

Terry Fox, *What Do Blind Men Dream?*, 1969
8 b/w photographs, exhibition copies
15 × 22 cm each
Photographs: Barry Klinger
Published in *Arts Magazine*, May 1970
Estate of Terry Fox, Cologne
ill. p. 119

1970

Terry Fox, *Tonguings*, 1970
Video, 21 min, b/w, sound
Camera: Terry Fox, sound: Terry Fox
Produced by Terry Fox for the traveling video exhibition *Body Works* that Willoughby Sharp organized for several locations and venues, New York, 1970
Electronic Arts Intermix, New York
ills. pp. 9, 74

Isolation Unit, performance by Terry Fox and Joseph Beuys in the cellar of the Kunstakademie Düsseldorf, 1970
22 b/w photographs, vintage prints
32.2 × 41.0 cm each
Photographs: Ute Klophaus
Estate of Terry Fox, Cologne
ills. pp. 77, 78, 79, 80, 81

Isolation Unit, performance by Terry Fox and Joseph Beuys in the cellar of the Kunstakademie Düsseldorf, 1970
Vinyl record
Estate of Terry Fox, Cologne

Terry Fox, *Defoliation*, 1970
4 b/w photographs, exhibition copies
20.2 × 25.4 cm
Photographs: Barry Klinger
Performance during the opening of the exhibition *The Eighties* at the University Art Museum, Berkeley. Terry Fox burned rare jasmine blossoms using fuel gel, which had an effect that seemed like napalm.

Estate of Terry Fox, Cologne
ills. pp. 102, 103

Invitation card for the solo exhibition by Terry Fox at the Richmond Art Center, 1970
Postcard / print on paper
29.8 × 39.4 cm
Estate of Terry Fox, Cologne

Terry Fox, *Virtual Volume* (*Smoke Exhalation*), 1970
5 b/w photographs, exhibition copies
17.0 × 22.8 cm each
Photographs: Barry Klinger
During a solo exhibition at Reese Palley Gallery, San Francisco, Terry Fox performed some situations without an audience. They were documented with photographs. One was published on the back cover of *Avalanche*, Winter 1971.
Estate of Terry Fox, Cologne
ills. pp. 110, 111

Terry Fox, *Virtual Volume*, 1970
3 b/w photographs, exhibition copies
21.1 × 26.3 cm each
Photographs: Barry Klinger
During a solo exhibition at Reese Palley Gallery, San Francisco, Terry Fox performed some situations without an audience. They were documented with photographs.
Estate of Terry Fox, Cologne
ills. pp. 108, 109, cover

Terry Fox, *Open Hands*, 1970
3 b/w photographs, exhibition copies
21.0 × 26.2 cm each
Photographs: Barry Klinger
During a solo exhibition at Reese Palley Gallery, San Francisco, Terry Fox performed some situations without an audience. They were documented with photographs. Published in *Avalanche*, Winter 1971.
Estate of Terry Fox, Cologne

Terry Fox, *Liquid Smoke*, 1970
8 b/w photographs, exhibition copies
14.4 × 21.0 cm each
Photographs: Barry Klinger
Street event, Third Street, San Francisco, 1970
Published in *Arts Magazine*, May 1970
Estate of Terry Fox, Cologne

1971

Terry Fox, Untitled (*4 Match Pieces*), 1970–71
Wooden matches and glue on fiberboard (four sheets)
35.56 × 27.94 cm each
Photographs: Ben Blackwell
Private collection
ills. pp. 112, 113

Terry Fox, *Turgescent Sex*, 1971
Video, 40 min, b/w, sound
Camera: George Bolling, San Francisco
Produced by Terry Fox in 1971 at his studio in San Francisco without an audience. First shown in 1971 at the exhibition *Prospect 71: Projections* in Düsseldorf. Then in 1972 during the exhibition *Pont* performed at the Galerie

Sonnabend in Paris under the title *Turgescent Sex*. Performed for a second time in modified form in a public performance in 1972, in the context of the installation *L'Unita* in modified form, at Lucio Amelio's gallery Moderna Art Agency in Naples. Each performance included a different concept of space.
Ludwig Forum für Internationale Kunst, Videoarchiv, Aachen

Terry Fox, Stills from Terry Fox's video *Turgescent Sex*, 1971
Contact sheet, 36 b/w photographs, vintage print
27.7 × 35.5 cm
Ross Family Collection
ill. p. 76

Poster of the exhibition *Hospital* by Terry Fox at Reese Palley Gallery, New York, 1971
Print on paper
20.4 × 17.2 cm
See note no. 3
Estate of Terry Fox, Cologne
ill. p. 114

Terry Fox, Untitled (*Hospital Piece*), 1971
Fiberboard, gauze and tape
28.0 × 17.8 cm
Photograph: Ben Blackwell
Barney Bailey, Berkeley

Barney Bailey, *Terry Fox's studio*, c. 1971
b/w photograph, gelatin silver print
20.32 × 25.40 cm
Private collection

Terry Fox, *The Rake's Progress* (*Rubbing Window Pane*), 1971
Video, 30 min, b/w, sound
Camera: George Bolling, San Francisco
Produced by Terry Fox for the 11th São Paulo Biennale in 1971. Shown in the exhibition *San Francisco Performance – 1972* at Newport Harbor Art Museum in 1972. Taped at Terry Fox's studio in San Francisco.
Berkeley Art Museum and Pacific Film Archive
ills. pp. 75, 286

Terry Fox, *Clutch*, 1971
Video, 50 min, b/w, sound
Camera: George Bolling, San Francisco
Produced by Terry Fox in 1971, based on a non-public performance.
De Saisset Museum, Santa Clara University
ill. p. 209

Terry Fox, *Pisces*, 1971
5 b/w photographs, exhibition copies
21.0 × 25.7 cm each
Photographs: Joel Glassman
Performance in two different, but sequential parts at two locations. The first part at the Museum of Contemporary Art, San Francisco, the second part at de Saisset Museum, Santa Clara University. Ritual element: two fishes.
Estate of Terry Fox, Cologne
ills. pp. 104, 105, 106, 107

Terry Fox, *10 Recipes*, 1971
Typewritten index cards
12.7 × 20.3 cm each
Galerie Löhrl, Mönchengladbach

Terry Fox, *Hefe* (Performance for Ute Klophaus), 1971
30 b/w photographs, vintage prints
c. 20 × 30 cm each
Photographs: Ute Klophaus
Performance by Terry Fox for Ute Klophaus without an audience
Estate of Terry Fox, Cologne
ills. pp. 83, 84, 85, 86, 87

Environmental Surfaces, Three Simultaneous Situational Enclosures, performance by Vito Acconci, Terry Fox and Dennis Oppenheim, Reese Palley Gallery, New York, 1971
6 b/w photographs
20.4 × 25.3 cm
Photographs: Peter Moore
Estate of Terry Fox, Cologne
ills. pp. 96, 97, 99

Environmental Surfaces, Three Simultaneous Situational Enclosures, performance by Vito Acconci, Terry Fox and Dennis Oppenheim, Reese Palley Gallery, New York, January 16, 1971
7 of 26 original b/w photographs, exhibition copies, reprinted
20.4 × 25.3 cm each
Photographs: Harry Shunk and Janos Kender
Published in *Avalanche*, Winter 1971
Getty Research Institute, Getty Center, Los Angeles
ills. pp. 98, 100, 101, 118

1972

Terry Fox, *A.A.*
Book with photographs, photocopies, typed / taped entries, and notes, 1971–72
36.20 × 28.58 × 3.18 cm
Purchase, by exchange, through gifts of Albert M. Bender, A. A. Ehresmann, William L. Gerstle, and Mr. and Mrs. Christopher L. Palombi
San Francisco Museum of Modern Art
ills. pp. 16, 17, 22, 242, 243, 245

Terry Fox, *Pont*, Galerie Sonnabend, Paris, 1972
11 b/w photographs, vintage prints
16.1 × 23.3 cm each
Photographs: Sarkis, b/w print by Colin McRae, Berkeley, from color slides by Richard Reisman, San Francisco
Refers to the studio performance without an audience, performed by Terry Fox at his studio in San Francisco in 1971. Shown again in 1972 during the exhibition *Pont* performed at the Galerie Sonnabend in Paris under the title *Turgescent Sex*. Performed for a second time in a public performance in 1972, in the context of the installation *L'Unita* in modified form, at Lucio Amelio's gallery Moderna Art

Agency in Naples. Each performance included a different concept of space.
See note no. 5
Estate of Terry Fox, Cologne
ills. pp. 92, 93, 94, 95

Terry Fox, *L'Unita*, 1972
16 b/w photographs, vintage prints
c. 31 × 20.8 cm each
Photographs: Bruno de Monaco
Refers to the studio performance without an audience, performed by Terry Fox in 1971 at his studio in San Francisco. Shown again in 1972 during the exhibition *Pont* performed at the Galerie Sonnabend in Paris under the title *Turgescent Sex*.
Performed for a second time in a public performance in 1972, in the context of the installation *L'Unita* in modified form, at Lucio Amelio's gallery Moderna Art Agency in Naples. Each performance included a different concept of space.
Estate of Terry Fox, Cologne
ills. pp. 88, 89, 90, 91

Terry Fox, *L'Unita*, 1972
Mixed media / collage
55 × 55 cm
De Vleeshal, Middelburg, Netherlands
ill. p. 18

Terry Fox, *Wind, water, vuur, aarde*, 1972
Video, 24 min 34 sec, color, sound
Camera: Rotterdam Arts Foundation
NIMk (Netherlands Media Art Institute, Amsterdam) / LIMA (Lijnbaancentrum, Amsterdam)
ills. p. 156

Terry Fox, *Hoc est corals meum*, 1972
Drawing on handmade paper with ink, water, rope and blood
83 × 76 cm
De Vleeshal, Middelburg, Netherlands
ill. p. 116

Terry Fox, *Action for a Tower Room*, 1972
2 b/w photographs, exhibition copies
19.2 × 24.8 cm
Photograph: James Pennuto, San Francisco; sound performance for *documenta 5*, Kassel
Estate of Terry Fox, Cologne
ill. p. 49

1973

Terry Fox, *Incision*, 1973
Video, 15 min, b/w, sound
Camera: Terry Fox, sound: Terry Fox and Tom Marioni, San Francisco
Produced by Terry Fox in 1973 for the traveling exhibition *Circuit*, curated by David Ross, shown in Los Angeles and at Kölnischer Kunstverein (curator: Wulf Herzogenrath)
Estate of Terry Fox, Cologne
ill. p. 204

Terry Fox, Untitled, 1973
10 b/w photographs, vintage prints
c. 17 × 24.2 cm each
Photographs: Terry Fox
Highly enlarged stills taken from *Incision*, produced by Terry Fox in 1973, during his solo exhibition at the University Art Museum, Berkeley. See notes no. 6–8 and exhibition/installation views
Estate of Terry Fox, Cologne
ills. pp. 151, 152, 153

Terry Fox, *Yield*, 1973
30 b/w photographs, vintage prints
28.4 × 35.6 cm each
Photographs: Larry Fox
Performance in a space, not accessible to the public, during Terry Fox's solo exhibition at the University Art Museum in Berkeley. The performance could be seen through a large front window and as a shadow on a curtain defining the space.
See notes no. 6–8
Estate of Terry Fox, Cologne
ills. pp. 143, 144, 145, 146, 147, 149

Terry Fox, *Yield*, 1973
28 b/w photographs, vintage prints
20.3 × 25.4 cm
Photographs: Larry Fox
Performance in a space, not accessible to the public, during Terry Fox's solo exhibition at the University Art Museum in Berkeley. The performance could be seen through a large front window and as a shadow on a curtain defining the space.
See notes no. 6–8
Marilyn Bogerd, San Francisco
ills. pp. 144, 146, 148, 259

Terry Fox, *Cell*, 1973
b/w photograph, 4 parts
17 × 23.5 cm each
Photographs: Terry Fox
Staatliche Museen zu Berlin, Nationalgalerie, Sammlung Marzona
ill. p. 277

Terry Fox, *The Burning of the Labyrinth into the Vidicon Tube*, 1973
b/w photograph, 3 parts
52.5 × 72.5 × 2.5 cm, each; 17 × 23.5 cm
Photographs: Terry Fox
Staatliche Museen zu Berlin, Nationalgalerie, Sammlung Marzona

Terry Fox, *The Labyrinth Scored for the Purrs of 11 Different Cats*, 1973
Score, pigment ink liner on music paper
66 × 36 × 3.5 cm
Estate of Terry Fox, Cologne
ills. pp. 238, 239

Terry Fox, *The Labyrinth at Chartres Scored for Cat Purrs*, c. 1973
Article / print on paper
26.7 × 21.6 cm
Marilyn Bogerd, San Francisco

Terry Fox, *Immersion*, 1973
3 b/w photographs, exhibition copies
23.9 × 17.7 cm each
Photographs: Thys Schouten
Estate of Terry Fox, Cologne
ills. pp. 140, 141, 142

1974

Terry Fox, *Children's Tapes*, 1974
Video, 30 min, b/w, sound
Camera: Terry Fox, San Francisco
Produced by Terry Fox in 1974 for the traveling exhibition *Circuit*, 1973, curated by David Ross, shown in Los Angeles and at the Kölnischer Kunstverein (curator: Wulf Herzogenrath)
See notes no. 9–11
Estate of Terry Fox, Cologne
ills. pp. 44, 138, 283

1975

Interview with Terry Fox by Jeanette Willison, 1975
Part of *11 Video Interviews, San Francisco*, Museum of Contemporary Art, San Francisco, 1975
(A series of eleven videotaped interviews, sponsored by the Museum of Conceptual Art, San Francisco, exhibited in MOCA, 1975. Each artist was interviewed for ½ hour. Participants included: Kevin Costello, Bonnie Sherk, Stephen Laub, Richard Alpert, Linda Montana, Jim Melchert, Irv Tepper, Terry Fox, Tom Marioni, Howard Fried)
Private collection
ill. p. 250

Terry Fox, *Lunedi*, 1975
Video, 21 min, color, sound
Camera: Bill Viola
Produced by Maria Gloria Bicocchi in 1975, Art/tapes/22, Florence.
The performance took place without an audience.
NIMk (Netherlands Media Art Institute, Amsterdam) / LIMA (Lijnbaancentrum, Amsterdam)
ills. pp. 124, 139

Terry Fox, *Two Turns*, 1975
Video, 30 min, b/w, sound
Camera: Terry Fox
Produced by Terry Fox in 1975 for the exhibition *Terry Fox: The Children's Tapes and Other Works* at Long Beach Museum of Art, curated by David Ross, 1975
Getty Research Institute, Getty Center, Los Angeles
ills. pp. 42, 210, 211, 256

Terry Fox, *The Beginning of the "Dream of the Eyetooth in the Labyrinth,"* 1975
Vintage photograph
18 × 13 cm
Photograph: Terry Fox
Estate of Terry Fox, Cologne
ill. p. 52

1976

Terry Fox, *Lunar Rambles*, 1976
Video, one of five videos, each 30 min, color, sound
Camera: Michael Shamberg
Produced by Terry Fox in 1976, together with The Kitchen, New York. Performances on the streets of New York, sound made by a violin bow against a metal bowl.
Estate of Terry Fox, Cologne

Terry Fox, *A Metaphor*, 1976
Wooden stools, magazine text, string, paper, and ink
142.24 × 42.55 cm
San Francisco Museum of Modern Art, purchased with the aid of funds from the National Endowment for the Arts, the Soap Box Derby Fund and the New Future Fund Drive
ill. p. 213

1977

Terry Fox, *The Labyrinth Scored for the Purrs of Different 11 Cats*, 1977
Audio Installation (4 channel version by Terry Fox and Peter Simon)
70 min.
Estate of Terry Fox, Cologne

Terry Fox, *Pendulum Spit Bite*, 1977
Aquatint etching on paper
101.4 × 124.3 cm
Produced at Crown Point Press, San Francisco
Estate of Terry Fox, Cologne
ill. p. 157

Terry Fox, *Transference*, 1977
Text: typewritten paper
28 × 21.5 cm
Drawings: pencil on packing paper
90 × 126 cm
Object: iron
87 × 87 cm
mumok | museum moderner kunst stiftung ludwig wien
ills. pp. 214, 215, 216, 217

1978

Terry Fox, *Erossore*, New York, 1978
2 photographs, exhibition copies
20.5 × 25.3 cm and 20 × 25.3 cm
Photographs: Larry Fox
The first action with piano strings in a public space
Estate of Terry Fox, Cologne
ill. p. 268

Marion Gray, Terry Fox and Georg Decristel, *Strolling Performance*, University Art Museum, Berkeley, California, 1978
Gelatin silver print, 1978, archival pigment print, 2015
60.9 × 50.8 cm
Courtesy of the artist
ill. p. 293

Marion Gray, Terry Fox and Nina Wise, *Yellow Duck and Tonka Beans*, San Francisco Museum of Modern Art, San Francisco, California, 1978
Gelatin silver print, 1978, archival pigment print, 2015
50.8 × 60.9 cm
Courtesy of the artist
ill. p. 294

1979

Terry Fox, *Holes and Entrances*, 1979
Video, 30 min, b/w, sound
Camera: Terry Fox
Produced by Terry Fox in 1979
Estate of Terry Fox, Cologne
ills. pp. 206, 207

Terry Fox, *Slide on the River Inn*, 1979
Poster
60 × 41.5 cm
Galerie Krinzinger, Vienna
ill. p. 2

Terry Fox, Untitled (three drawings used during the performance *Declination* at the Dany Keller Galerie, Munich), 1979
Pencil on paper
110 × 80 cm each
Courtesy of the Dany Keller Galerie

Terry Fox, Untitled (sketch for the performance *Declination* at the Dany Keller Galerie, Munich), 1979
Pencil on paper
44 × 76 cm
Courtesy of the Dany Keller Galerie

Terry Fox, Untitled (sketch for the performance *Declination* at the Dany Keller Galerie, Munich), 1979
Collage, pencil on paper
44.5 × 66.2 cm
Courtesy of the Dany Keller Galerie

Terry Fox, *Declination*, 1979
6 b/w photographs
18.1 × 23.9 cm
Photographs: Roland Fischer
Documentation of the performance *Declination* at the Dany Keller Galerie, Munich, 1979
Courtesy of the Dany Keller Galerie
ill. p. 236

1980

Terry Fox, *Flour Dumpling*, 1980
Video, 5 × 30 min, color, sound
Camera: Ohio State University Crew, Dayton, Ohio
Produced by the Ohio State University in 1980: Live video action of a performance by Terry Fox at Ohio State University without an audience.
Includes: Live broadcast of a television show, taped recordings of the type-generator that projected scripts on the monitor in real-time, plus the recordings of two studio cameras.
Shown again at Arsenal Berlin in 1980, organized by DAAD Berlin, Freunde der Deutschen Kinemathek e.V., Anthology Film Archives, New York
Ludwig Forum für Internationale Kunst, Videoarchiv, Aachen
ills. pp. 184, 185

1981

Terry Fox, *Quattro Stagioni*, 1981
Box with 33 original photos by Enzo Pezzi, Terry Fox: 1 wire object, 1 drawing, 1 audio cassette, 1 flyleaf
6 × 44 cm
Galerie Löhrl, Mönchengladbach

Terry Fox, *Sound Score from the Berlin Wall*, 1981
Pencil and red felt-tip pen on brownish vellum paper
69.7 × 89.6 cm
Staatliche Museen zu Berlin, Kupferstichkabinett
ill. p. 229

Terry Fox, *Berlin Wall*, 1981
Pencil and felt-tip pen on packing paper
42.5 × 30.5 cm
Private collection Stephan Oehmen, Hilden

1982

Terry Fox, Drawing for *Berlin Wall Scored for Sound*, c. 1981–82
Pencil on paper
Signed "Berlin 1981"
30.9 × 22.7 cm
Estate of Terry Fox, Cologne
ill. p. 231

Terry Fox, Sketches for *Berlin Wall Scored for Sound*, Berlin Wall transferred to lines, c. 1981–82
Pencil on paper, (5 parts, collection of loose sheets)
West: 25.4 × 11.2 cm
North: 20.8 × 8.3 cm
East: 30.4 × 10.2 cm
South: 59.9 × 11.5 cm
Dividing wall: 59.9 × 14.2 cm
Estate of Terry Fox, Cologne
ills. pp. 232, 233

Terry Fox, *Berlin Wall Scored for Sound*, 1982
Pencil and felt-tip pen on paper
102 × 73 cm
Private collection

Terry Fox, Map of Berlin with the outline of the Berlin Wall, back side: drawing for *Berlin Wall Scored for Sound*, c. 1982
Pigment ink liner on paper
43.5 × 52 cm
Estate of Terry Fox, Cologne

Terry Fox, *Der Holzfäller*, 1982
Mixed media on paper, wood, nails, yarn
148.5 × 100 cm
Galerie Krinzinger, Vienna

1984

Terry Fox, *Catch Phrases*, 1981–84
Steel, felt-tip pen, pencil on paper, mounted on wooden board
151 × 100 cm
See note no. 14
Staatliche Museen zu Berlin, Nationalgalerie, gift of Wolfram and Martina Gärtner

Terry Fox, *Catch Phrases*, 1981–84
Steel, felt-tip pen, pencil on paper, mounted on wooden board
177 × 100 cm
See note no. 14
Staatliche Museen zu Berlin, Nationalgalerie, gift of Wolfram and Martina Gärtner
ill. p. 188

Klaus vom Bruch, *Terry Fox mit 1 Million Lire (1+2)*, 1984/2015
Color photograph, printed on HP photo paper, framed
40 × 50 cm
Photograph: Klaus vom Bruch
For the 1984 41st Biennale, Venice
Klaus vom Bruch, Berlin
ill. p. 284

1985

Terry Fox, *Children's Drawings*, 1985
Ink, pencil, felt-tip pen on paper, 32 sheets
55 × 53.5 cm each
Museum Folkwang, Essen
ills. p. 182, 183

Terry Fox, *Hobo Signs*, 1985
Book, pencil and felt-tip pen on paper
25.3 × 17.7 cm
ill. p. 191

Terry Fox, *Two Children, Four Men and Three Women Passed This Way*, 1985
Graphite and felt-tipped pen drawing in red, with typewritten text on handmade cardboard
25.6 × 18 cm
Staatliche Museen zu Berlin, Nationalgalerie, 2013, gift of Wolfram and Martina Gärtner

1986

Terry Fox, *Instrument zur Erkennung von Erdbeben* (Instrument for Recognizing an Earthquake), 1986
Plaster, lead, iron, cord
100 × 26 cm
Galerie Löhrl, Mönchengladbach

Terry Fox, *Dal cielo del fuoco* (for *Joseph Beuys*), 1986
Scratched mirror
87 × 83.3 cm
See note no. 13
Kunstmuseum Bern
ill. p. 129

Terry Fox, Sketch for *Dal cielo del fuoco* (for *Joseph Beuys*), 1986
Pencil and felt-tip pen on Fabriano
76 × 76 cm
See note no. 13
Kunstmuseum Bern
ill. p. 174

Terry Fox, Sketch for *Dal cielo del fuoco* (for *Joseph Beuys*), n.d.
Pencil and collage on paper
51 × 50.3 cm
See note no. 13
Kunstmuseum Bern
ill. p. 175

Terry Fox, Sketch for *Dal cielo del fuoco* (for *Joseph Beuys*), n.d.
Watercolor and India ink
76 × 42.3 cm
See note no. 13
Kunstmuseum Bern

1987

Terry Fox, *Dal cielo del fuoco* (for *Joseph Beuys*), 1987
Pencil, India ink
39 × 35 cm
See note no. 13
Anne Lühn, Emsbühren

Terry Fox, *Instruments to be Played by the Movement of the Earth*, 1987
28 photographs, exhibition prints
c. 30 × 45 cm
Photographs: Ben Blackwell
Documentation during an exhibition of Terry Fox's work at the Capp Street Project, 65 Capp Street, San Francisco
Capp Street Project Archive at California College of the Arts Libraries, San Francisco, California
ills. pp. 154–155

Terry Fox, *Instrument to be Played by the Movement of the Earth*, 1987
Steel wok, metal, welded steel and grain
140 × 122 cm
Object for an exhibition of Terry Fox's work at the Capp Street Project, 65 Capp Street, San Francisco
Private collection, Oakland

Terry Fox, *Ricochet*, 1987
Video, c. 47 min (documentation)
Camera: Elisabeth Jappe
Documentation of the performance *Ricochet* by Terry Fox for *documenta 8*, Kassel
Estate of Terry Fox, Cologne

Terry Fox, *Ricochet*, 1987
4 drawings
pencil, pen, watercolor on paper
71 × 52 cm each
Estate of Terry Fox, Cologne

Terry Fox, *Untitled*, 1987
Pen and ink on paper
29.7 × 21 cm
Edition Block GmbH, Berlin

Terry Fox, *Untitled*, 1987
Postcard to Arnold Dreyblatt
9 × 13 cm
Arnold Dreyblatt Collection
ill. p. 21

1988

Terry Fox, Material used for the LP sleeve, c. 1988
Paste up materials
Cover 30.5 × 40 cm
Private collection, Panhuysen

1989

Terry Fox, *Sheets of Slate*, from *TEXTUM (Web)*, 1989
Graphite, watercolor, India ink, collage on cardboard
30.2 × 18.5 cm
Von der Heydt-Museum, Wuppertal
ill. p. 193

Terry Fox, Sheet from *TEXTUM (Web)*, 1989
Graphite, watercolor, India ink, collage on cardboard
See note no. 12
28.9 × 20 cm
Von der Heydt-Museum, Wuppertal

Terry Fox, *TEXTUM (Web)*, 1989
Typewritten text, graphite, India ink
29.5 × 21 cm
See note no. 12
Galerie Löhrl, Mönchengladbach

Terry Fox, *The Eye is Not the Only Glass that Burns the Mind*, 1989
Mirror, ink on paper
38.5 × 59 cm
Private collection
ill. p. 177

Terry Fox, Untitled (*The Alphabet of Flowers*), 1989
Pen on paper
29.7 × 21 cm
Edition Block GmbH, Berlin

Terry Fox, Untitled, 1989
Pen on paper
29.7 × 21.0 cm
Edition Block GmbH, Berlin

1990

Terry Fox, *Cynosure*, 1990
Oil paint, wood, lead, India ink on paper
35.5 × 149 cm
See note no. 12
Kunstmuseum Bern
ill. p. 131

Terry Fox, *Ovum Anguinum*, 1990
Wood, oil paint, India ink on paper
240 × 210 cm
See note no. 12
Von der Heydt-Museum, Wuppertal
ill. p. 168

Terry Fox, *Model*, 1990
Wood, wire, nails, collage
22.0 × 8.5 cm
Private collection

1991

Terry Fox, *Schema Nr. 1*, 1991
Drawing and installation, paper,
gouache, pencil and ink
106 × 343 cm
Museum Ludwig, Cologne
ill. p. 196

Terry Fox, *Envelope*, 1991
Wood, lead, oil paint, acrylic
90.5 × 41.5 cm
See note no. 14
Museum Ludwig, Cologne
ills. pp. 165, 166

Terry Fox, *Mock up*, 1991
Drawing and installation, pencil, wood,
paper
179.7 × 99 cm
Museum Ludwig, Cologne
ill. p. 167

Terry Fox, *Self-Government*, 1991
Drawing, collage, copper, lead, cord
30 × 30 cm
Galerie Löhrl, Mönchengladbach

Terry Fox, Untitled, 1991
Pen on paper
29.7 × 21.0 cm
Edition Block GmbH, Berlin

1992

Terry Fox, *Corpora Cavernosa,* 1992
Video, 20 min, color, sound (doc)
Directed by: Marita Loosen
Camera: Klaus Sturm
Part of a video documentation, during
the project *Amphion – Sound Installa-
tions in Cologne and Potsdam* with
Terry Fox, Toine Horvers, Rolf Julius,
Annebarbe Kau, Christina Kubisch,
Hans Peter Kuhn
Estate of Terry Fox, Cologne

Terry Fox, *Footnotes*, 1992
Text collages made of 33 strips, 3 parts
112 × 164 cm
Estate of Terry Fox, Cologne

1993

Terry Fox, *Rib Cage*, 1993
Paper, cardboard, pencil, felt-tip pen,
framed behind glass
56 × 68 cm
See note no. 13
Private collection
ill. p. 115

Terry Fox, *Gin the Sea*, 1993
Collage, paper, cardboard, pencil,
colored pencil
70 × 100 cm
Galerie Löhrl, Mönchengladbach
ills. pp. 172, 173

Terry Fox, *Le décapité parlant*, 1993
Spiral with cardboard
40 × 40 cm
Galerie Löhrl, Mönchengladbach
ill. p. 169

1995

Terry Fox, *Chappe Railway*, 1995
Collage, watercolor, India ink, pencil
Four parts:
70 × 15 cm
10 × 15 cm
Galerie Löhrl, Mönchengladbach

1996

Terry Fox, *The School of Velocity, 1996*
Video, 54 sec, color, sound (doc)
Directed by: Sabine Groschup
Part of a documentation for the festival
*Sonambiente – Festival für Hören
und Sehen*, 1996, Akademie der Künste,
Berlin
Courtesy Sabine Groschup & Akademie
der Künste, Berlin

1997

Terry Fox, *Blood*, 1997
Test tube with blood, wire and pencil
on cardboard in a wooden box
41.8 × 74.8 cm
Kunstmuseum Bern
ill. p. 132

Terry Fox, *Salt*, 1997
Sea salt and copper pipe in a wooden
box
41.8 × 74.9 cm
Kunstmuseum Bern
ill. p. 133

Terry Fox, *Vesica*, 1997
Mixed media on paper in a wooden box
37.7 × 70.7 cm
Kunstmuseum Bern

2000

Terry Fox, *Cone of Silence*, 2000
ceramics (edition, 2 of 11)
40.6 × 40.6 cm each
Estate of Terry Fox, Cologne

2002

Terry Fox, *Sumer is icumen in*, 2002
Cherry pits and pencil on cardboard
88.7 × 88.7 cm
Ursula Block – Broken Music Archive
ill. p. 237

2005

Terry Fox, *Enigma*, 2005
Stamp print on cardboard, tuning fork
Total height: 108 cm
Galerie Löhrl, Mönchengladbach

2006

Terry Fox, *Labyrinth of the Inner Ear*,
2006
Pencil and typewriter on paper
29.7 × 21 cm
Private collection, Vienna/Hattorf
am Harz
ill. p. 225

Terry Fox, *Labyrinth of the Inner Ear,*
2006
Stereo audio installation
70 min.
Estate of Terry Fox, Cologne

Terry Fox, *Shadow Drawings: Balanced,
Vaporous, Deserted, Temporal, Thinning,
Fugitive, Extended*, 2006
Pencil on paper
48 × 34 cm each
Estate of Terry Fox, Cologne
ills. pp. 218, 219, 220, 221

2007

Barbara Klemm, *Terry Fox*, Cologne,
2007
2 b/w photographs
30.6 × 40.3 cm
Photographs: Barbara Klemm
Barbara Klemm's photographs originated in the context of a series of
portraits by sound-art-pioneers, for use
in the planned cinematic essay "A View
Of Ears" by Sabine Groschup and Georg
Weckwerth
Courtesy Barbara Klemm and Sabine
Groschup & Georg Weckwerth
ill. p. 303

2015

Terry Fox, *Berlino,* 1988/2015
Audio Installation (8 channel version)
Spatial realization and interpretation
by Arnold Dreyblatt, in collaboration
with Gregorio García Karman and
the Studio für Elektroakustische Musik
at the Akademie der Künste, Berlin
19 min.
Estate of Terry Fox, Cologne

Terry Fox, *Quatrain*, n.d.
Diverse materials mounted on canvas
100 × 100 cm
Staatliche Museen zu Berlin,
Nationalgalerie, 2011, gift of Wolfram
and Martina Gärtner

Notes

Terry Fox, Notebook, 1970
Typewritten text and pigment ink liner
on paper, 9 parts
32.3 × 22.8 cm (cover)
27.8 × 21.5 cm (pages)
Estate of Terry Fox, Cologne
Note no. 1

Terry Fox, Letter to Willoughby Sharp,
c. 1971
Facsimile
21× 15.5 cm
Estate of Terry Fox, Cologne
ill. p. 251
Note no. 2

Terry Fox, Sketch for the exhibition
Hospital, Reese Palley Gallery, 1971
Pigment ink liner on paper
23.4 × 37.4 cm
Estate of Terry Fox, Cologne
ills. pp. 58, 251
Note no. 3

Installation view of the exhibition
Hospital by Terry Fox, Reese Palley
Gallery, New York, 1970
Exhibition copy on baryta paper
20.6 × 25.2 cm
Photograph: Schopplein Studio,
San Francisco
Estate of Terry Fox, Cologne
ill. p. 59
Note no. 4

Terry Fox, Sketch for *Pont*, Galerie
Sonnabend, Paris, 1972
Printed flyer of the exhibition
20.8 × 29.5 cm
Refers to the studio performance with-
out an audience, performed by Terry Fox
at his studio in San Francisco in 1971.
Shown again in 1972 during the exhibi-
tion *Pont* performed at the Galerie
Sonnabend in Paris under the title
Turgescent Sex. Also performed in 1972
at the gallery Moderna Art Agency,
Naples, in front of an audience. Each
performance included a different
concept of space.
Estate of Terry Fox, Cologne
ill. p. 121
Note no. 5

Terry Fox, Notebook "Berkeley
Drawings", c. 1973
Pigment ink liner on paper, 36 parts
(collection of loose sheets)
33 × 24.5 cm (cover)
30.5 × 22.9 cm (page 1)
28 × 21.6 cm (pages)
Estate of Terry Fox, Cologne
ills. pp. 55, 56
Note no. 6

Terry Fox, Description of the exhibition
at the Berkeley Art Museum, 1973
Typewritten text on paper
26.6 × 18.3 cm
Estate of Terry Fox, Cologne
ill. p. 260
Note no. 7

Installation views of the exhibition at
the Berkeley Art Museum, 1973
4 b/w photographs, vintage prints
1 b/w photograph (performance space
Yield)

20.3 × 25.5 cm
Photograph: Colin McRae
Estate of Terry Fox, Cologne
ill. p. 59
Note no. 8

Terry Fox, Loose leaf collection,
"*Children's Tapes* – notes with
stills from video," c. 1974
Typewritten text, pigment ink liner
on paper, photocollage
28.0 × 21.5 cm
Estate of Terry Fox, Cologne
ills. pp. 12, 61
Note no. 9

Terry Fox, Notebook "Video Originals –
Children's Tapes," c. 1974
Pigment ink liner on paper, 15-part
bound notebook
25.4 × 40.3 cm
Estate of Terry Fox, Cologne
Note no. 10

Terry Fox, Sketch for *Children's Tapes*,
c. 1974
Pigment ink liner on paper
27.9 × 21.5 cm
Estate of Terry Fox, Cologne
ill. p. 65
Note no. 11

Terry Fox, Notebook "TEXTUM (Web),"
n.d.
Pigment ink liner on graph paper,
24-part bound notebook
29.7 × 21.3 cm (cover)
29.7 × 21 cm (pages)
Estate of Terry Fox, Cologne
Note no. 12

Terry Fox, Notebook "Beuys Mirror,
Bern," n.d.
Mixed media on graph paper, 12-part
bound notebook
29.8 × 21 cm
Estate of Terry Fox, Cologne
ills. pp. 160, 170, 171
Note no. 13

Terry Fox, "Red Notebook," n.d.
Pigment ink liner, 44-part bound
notebook
21.5 × 15.5 cm
Estate of Terry Fox, Cologne
ills. pp. 180, 181
Note no. 14

Terry Fox, Notebook "c/c/c," n.d.
Pencil and pigment ink liner, 17-part
bound notebook
29.6 × 21 cm
Estate of Terry Fox, Cologne
ills. pp. 162, 163, 164
Note no. 15

Terry Fox, Notebook, n.d.
Stamp print, pigment ink liner, 2-part
bound notebook
27.9 × 21.7 cm
Estate of Terry Fox, Cologne
ills. pp. 234, 235
Note no. 16

Terry Fox, *Alphabet-Signet*, n.d.
Pencil on paper
27.9 × 21.7 cm
Estate of Terry Fox, Cologne
ill. p. 179
Note no. 17
Terry Fox, *Human figure*, n.d.

Pencil on paper
27.9 × 21.7 cm
Estate of Terry Fox, Cologne
ill. p. 178
Note no. 18

Terry Fox, Sketch for the labyrinth *A
Triptych of Crosses ...*, n.d.
Mixed media
27.9 × 21.7 cm
Estate of Terry Fox, Cologne
ill. p. 203
Note no. 19

Terry Fox, Drawing on a print with a
seated human figure, n.d.
Mixed media
12.5 × 10 cm
Estate of Terry Fox, Cologne
Note no. 20

Magazines
Books
Posters

Catalogue of the exhibition by Terry Fox
in the Reese Palley Gallery, New York,
1970
Estate of Terry Fox, Cologne

Catalogue *Free*, accompanying the
exhibition *The Eighties* at the University
Art Museum, Berkeley, 1970
Photographer: Neil Houston
Published by the University Art
Museum, Berkeley, 1970
Private collection, Berlin

One record, one print and one
description accompanying *Isolation
Unit* at Kunstakademie Düsseldorf, 1970
Record: vinyl, 45 rpm
17.7 × 18 cm
Pipes: Terry Fox
Seeds: Joseph Beuys
Private collection, Berlin

Arts Magazine, May 1970
Estate of Terry Fox, Cologne
ills. pp. 246, 247, 248, 249

Avalanche, Fall 1970
Avalanche, Winter 1971
Estate of Terry Fox, Cologne
ills. pp. 252–255, 262, 263, 270–273

Avalanche, Fall 1972
Faksimile
Private collection Hubertus Butin,
Berlin

Catalogue *Prospect '71 – Projection*,
accompanying the exhibition *Prospect
'71 – Projection* at Städtische Kunsthalle
Düsseldorf, 1971
Art Press Verlag, Düsseldorf,
Private collection Hubertus Butin,
Berlin

Invitational card for *Fish Fox Kos*,
de Saisset Museum & Art Gallery,
University of Santa Clara, California,
1971
Private collection, Berlin
ill. p. 278

Catalogue of the exhibition *Fish Fox
Kos*, de Saisset Museum & Art Gallery,
University of Santa Clara, 1971
Private collection, Berlin

Announcement card for the 12th Annual
St. Jude Invitational Catalogue, 1972
Printed for the 12th Annual St. Jude
Competition Video Tape International,
de Saisset Art Gallery, University of
Santa Clara, California
Private collection, Berlin

3 images by Paul Kos ("shoot")
accompanying *Fish Fox Kos*, de Saisset
Museum & Art Gallery, University of
Santa Clara, California, 1971
Private collection, Berlin
ill. p. 278

2 pages of an invitational card by
Tom Marioni ("Avalanche Fish $ 2")
printed for *Fish Fox Kos*, de Saisset
Museum & Art Gallery, University of
Santa Clara, California, 1971
Private collection, Berlin
ill. p. 276

Posters of the exhibition *Twelfth Annual
October St. Jude Invitational. Videotapes*,
de Saisset Art Gallery & Museum,
University of Santa Clara, 1972
Private collection, Berlin

Interfunktionen 9, Cologne, 1972–73
Catalogue includes a poster
of Sigmar Polke
Verlag Heubach, Cologne
Private collection Hubertus Butin,
Berlin

San Francisco Chronicle: article on
Terry Fox's work at the exhibition
Site, Cite, Sight, March 24, 1977
Marilyn Bogerd, San Francisco
ill. p. 291

La Mamelle: portrait photograph of
Terry Fox, 1977
Revue
Marilyn Bogerd, San Francisco

San Francisco Chronicle: front page
article with photograph of Terry Fox,
1978
Estate of Terry Fox, Cologne

View, 1979
Estate of Terry Fox, Cologne
ill. p. 267

Poster for the exhibition *Furkart*, 1992
Artists: Vito Acconci, Aan Anüll,
Terry Atkinson, Andreas Christen,
John Nixon, Ria Pacquée, Hermann
de Vries, etc.
Estate of Terry Fox, Cologne

Catalogue for the exhibition *Insite –
Five Conceptual Artists from the
Bay Area: Terry Fox, Howard Fried,
David Ireland, Paul Kos, Tom Marioni*,
1990
Estate of Terry Fox, Cologne

Akupunktur-Ohr-Modell, n.d.
Estate of Terry Fox, Cologne

The set of Terry Fox's works shown
at the various exhibition venues are
largely identical.

Terry Fox

Kurzbiografie

1943
geboren in Seattle, Washington

1962–1963
Accademia di Belle Arti, Rom
(Studium der Malerei)

1963–1967
San Francisco und Amsterdam

1967–1968
Paris, Straßenaktionen, prozessuale
Skulpturen

Seit 1969
San Francisco, Arbeiten
im Kontext von Konzeptkunst

1971–1978
Environments, Performances,
Videos, Skulpturen und Zeichnungen
bezogen auf das Bodenlabyrinth
der Kathedrale von Chartres, erste
Sound-Performances mit Klaviersaiten

1981–1982
Aufenthalt in Neapel

1982–1983
Berliner Künstlerprogramm
des Deutschen Akademischen
Austauschdienstes (DAAD),
Berlin (Stipendium)

Seit 1984
Arbeiten im Bereich von Zeichnung,
Skulptur, Klanginstallation, oftmals in
Kombination mit Sprache: Texte,
Wortspiele, Rätsel, Rebus-Objekte

1987–1995
Liège

Seit 1996
überwiegend in Köln

2008
gestorben in Köln

Short Biography

1943
Born in Seattle, Washington

1962–1963
Accademia di Belle Arti, Rome
(studied painting)

1963–1967
San Francisco and Amsterdam

1967–1968
Paris: street actions, process-
oriented sculpture

As of 1969
San Francisco: works in the context
of conceptual art

1971–1978
Environments, performances, videos,
sculptures and drawings related to
the labyrinth in the floor of Chartres
Cathedral; first sound performances
with piano stings

1981–1982
Stayed in Naples

1982–1983
Artists-in-Berlin Program of the German
Academic Exchange Service (DAAD),
Berlin (fellowship)

As of 1984
Works that included drawings,
sculpture, sound installations, often
in combination with language:
texts, puns, riddles, rebus objects

1987–1995
Liège

As of 1996
Lived and worked predominantly
in Cologne

2008
Died in Cologne

Barbara Klemm, *Terry Fox*, Cologne, 2007, courtesy Barbara Klemm and Sabine Groschup & Georg Weckwerth

Solo Exhibitions (Selection)

1970
· Reese Palley Gallery, San Francisco (catalogue)
· Museum of Conceptual Art, San Francisco
· Richmond Art Center, Richmond

1971
· *Hospital*, Reese Palley Gallery, San Francisco
· Reese Palley Gallery, New York

1972
· Galerie Ileana Sonnabend, Paris
· Lucio Amelio, Naples

1973
· University Art Museum, Berkeley (catalogue)

1974
· Everson Museum, Syracuse, New York

1975
· Long Beach Museum of Art, Long Beach, California
· Galleria Schema, Florence

1976
· The Kitchen, New York

1977
· De Appel, Amsterdam
· Site, San Francisco
· Galerie Krinzinger, Innsbruck
· The Kitchen, New York

1978
· San Francisco Art Institute, San Francisco
· Podio Del Mondo Per L'Arte, Middelburg (permanent installation)

1979
· Galerie Dany Keller, Munich

1980
· Museum of Modern Art, New York (special projects)

1982
· *Linkage*, Kunstmuseum, Lucerne, Switzerland (LP Record, catalogue insert)
· *Metaphorical Instruments*, Museum Folkwang, Essen, DAAD Galerie, Berlin (catalogue)

1983
· Galerie Nächst St. Stephan, Vienna

1984
· Ronald Feldman Gallery, New York

1985
· *Catch Phrases*, Kunstraum, Munich (book)

1986
· Galerie Löhrl, Mönchengladbach

1987
· University Art Museum, Berkeley
· Capp Street Project, San Francisco

1988
· *Ultima Multis*, Gesellschaft für Aktuelle Kunst, Bremen

1989
· Het Appolohuis, Eindhoven (LP Record, Book, Audio Cassette)

1990
· Galerie L'A, Liège
· Syndikat-Halle, Bonn

1992
· *Echo and Narcissus*, Gallery Paule Anglim, San Francisco

1992–94
· *Terry Fox: Articulations (Labyrinth/ Text Works)*, 1992: Goldie Paley; Gallery at Moore College of Art and Design, Philadelphia, 1993: University Art Museum, Berkeley, 1994: Otis Gallery, Otis School of Art and Design, Los Angeles, Santa Monica Museum of Art, Santa Monica (catalogue)

1995
· *bloodline*, Galerie Löhrl, Mönchengladbach (catalogue)

1997
· *Vesica Pisces*, Galerie Francesca Pia, Bern
· *Three Times Three Times Three*, Galerie Barbara Claassen-Schmal, Bremen
· *Elementary Parallelism*, Gesellschaft für Aktuelle Kunst, Bremen

1998
· *Ataraxia*, Stadtgalerie Saarbrücken (catalogue with CD Disc)

2000
· *Sidereal Time*, Gallery Paule Anglim, San Francisco
· *Au default du silence*, Galerie Lara Vincy, Paris
· *Raison d'etre*, maly.Service Kulturell Edition, Cologne

2001
· *Cornered and Articulated*, Galerie Löhrl, Mönchengladbach
· *A Cloud Ladder*, text and sound installation at the Singuhr – hörgalerie in parochial, Berlin
· *Sumer is icumen in*, Gelbe Musik, Berlin

2002
· *Vocale Vocale*, e/static, Turin

2003
· *(RE/DE) CONSTRUCTIONS & c.*, Kunsthalle Fridericianum Kassel (catalogue)

2004
· *The Cats Remixed*, Sound installation, Chapel/Foundation Serralves, Porto

2007
· *Illuminations*, Gallery Ronald Feldman, New York

2008
· *Acousticks*, 8-Channel Sound Installation, TONSPUR 23 / quartier 21, MQ Vienna

2009
· *A Tribute to Terry Fox*, commemoration ceremony, Hamburger Bahnhof – Museum für Gegenwart, Berlin
· *34 turns*, installation, Großer Wasserspeicher Berlin, Singuhr e.V., Berlin (Realisation: Marita Loosen-Fox and Carsten Seiffarth)

2011
· *Locus Solus*, Barkenhoff, Heinrich-Vogeler-Museum, Worpswede (catalogue)

2015
· *Terry Fox: The Labyrinth Scored for 11 Different Cats*, Atelier Nord ANX, Oslo

Group Exhibitions (Selection)

1969
· *The Return of Abstract Expressionism*, Richmond Art Center, Richmond

1970
· *The Eighties*, University Art Museum, Berkeley (catalogue)
· *Body Works*, traveling video exhibition organized by Willoughby Sharp
· *Fish Fox Kos*, de Saisset Museum, Santa Clara, California (catalogue)

1971
· *Project: Pier 18*, Museum of Modern Art, New York
· *Prospect 71*, Kunsthalle, Düsseldorf (catalogue)

1972
· *documenta 5*, Kassel (catalogue)
· *Notes and Scores for Sound*, Mills College, Oakland

1973
· *Video International*, Everson Museum, Syracuse, New York
· *Circuit*, simultaneous video exhibition, Everson Museum Syracuse, Kölnischer Kunstverein, Cologne, et al.
· *All Night Sculptures*, MOCA, San Francisco

1974
· *Record as Artwork*, Galerie Francois Lambert, Milan traveling exhibition (catalogue)

1975
· Biennial of Contemporary American Art, Whitney Museum of American Art, New York (catalogue)
· *Video Art U.S.A.*, São Paulo Museum

1976
· *Video Art: A Survey*, San Francisco Museum of Modern Art, San Francisco (catalogue)

1977
· *Whitney Biennial*, Whitney Museum of American Art, New York (catalogue)
· *documenta 6*, Kassel (catalogue)

1978
· International Performance Festival, Galerie Nächst St. Stephan, Vienna
· *Video Selection*, Venice Biennale Archives, Venice

1979
· *Sound*, Los Angeles Institute of Contemporary Art, Los Angeles
· *Space, Time, Sound*, San Francisco Museum of Modern Art, San Francisco

1980
· Video Wochen Essen, Folkwang Museum, Essen

1981
· *Performance*, Künstlerhaus Bethanien, Berlin

1983
· *Holland Festival*, Amsterdam
· *Site Strategies*, Oakland Museum

1984
· Venice Biennale, Venice (catalogue)

1985
· Paris Biennale, Paris
· *Biennale des Friedens*, Kunsthaus und Kunstverein, Hamburg (catalogue)

1987
· *Berlin Art 1961–1987*, Museum of Modern Art, New York
· *Echo Festival*, Het Apollohuis, Eindhoven
· *Ricochet, documenta 8*, Kassel (catalogue)

1988
· *Die Gleichzeitigkeit des Anderen*, Kunstmuseum, Bern (catalogue)

1989
· *Ressource Kunst*, Künstlerhaus Bethanien, Berlin (catalogue)
· *Art in the Anchorage 89*, Brooklyn Bridge, New York

1990
· Sydney Biennale, Sydney (catalogue)
· *Furkart 1990*, Furkapass
· *Animalia*, Haus am Waldsee, Berlin (catalogue)
· *Art Conceptual / Formes Conceptuelles*, Galerie 1990–2000, Paris

1991
· *Buchstäblich: Bild und Wort in der Kunst heute*, Von der Heydt-Museum, Wuppertal and Kunsthalle Barmen (catalogue)
· *Living Dangerously*, Astrophysikalisches Observatorium, Potsdam

1992
· *Amphion – Sound Installations*, Cologne and Potsdam (catalogue)
· *Block's Collection*, Statens Museum for Kunst, Copenhagen (catalogue)

1994
· *Die Stillen*, Skulpturenmuseum Glaskasten, Marl, Germany

1995
· *A table of simple sounds*, Kleinodieen, Maastricht

1996
· *Withdrawing*, Ronald Feldman Fine Arts Gallery, New York
· *sonambiente. festival für hören und sehen. internationale klangkunst im rahmen der 300-jahrfeier der Akademie der Künste Berlin*, Berlin (catalogue)

- *John Cage, Terry Fox, Gudrun Wasser-mann*, Pfalzgalerie, Kaiserslautern (catalogue)

2000
- *The American Century, Part II: 1950–2000*, Whitney Museum of American Art, New York (catalogue)

2002
- *First Decade: Video from the EAI Archives*, Museum of Modern Art, Department of Film and Video, New York
- *Litanies of Interference*, Inventionen, Berliner Festival Neuer Musik, Berlin
- *40 Jahre: Fluxus und die Folgen*, Kunstsommer Wiesbaden (catalogue)
- *Berner Himmelsleiter*, Soundfestival EMIT TIME, Bern

2005
- *50 Jahre/Years documenta, 1955–2005*, Kunsthalle Fridericianum, Kassel
- *Solid Concept V* (with David Ireland, Paul Kos, Tom Marioni, Alan Scarritt), Gallery Paule Anglim, San Francisco
- *Vinyl. Schallplatten und Cover von Künstlern*, Neues Museum Weserburg Bremen, Barcelona, Porto
- *After the Act*, The (Re)Presentation of Performance Art, Museum Moderner Kunst Stiftung Ludwig Wien (catalogue)

2006
- *sonambiente. klang kunst sound art*, Akademie der Künste, Berlin (catalogue)

2007
- *Evidence of Movement*, Getty Museum, Los Angeles
- *Japan and the West*, Kunstmuseum Wolfsburg (catalogue)

2008
- *California Video*, J. Paul Getty Museum, Los Angeles (catalogue)
- *Art/tapes/22*, University Art Museum, Long Beach
- *Looking For Mushrooms. Beat Poets, Hippies, Funk, Minimal Art San Francisco 1955–1968*, Museum Ludwig, Cologne (catalogue)

2010
- *Through Labyrinths*, Centre de Cultura Contemporània de Barcelona and Centre Cultural Bancaja, Valencia (catalogue)
- *Resurrectine*, Ronald Feldman Fine Arts, New York
- *Radical Light – Alternative Film & Video in the San Francisco Bay Area, 1945–2000*, University of California, BAM/PFA, San Francisco (catalogue)

2011
- *Under the Big Black Sun: California Art 1974–1981*, The Museum of Contemporary Art, Los Angeles (catalogue)

2012
- *Locus Solus. Impressions of Raymond Roussel*, Museo Nacional Centro de Arte Reina Sofia, Madrid (catalogue)

2012–13
- *State of Mind: New California Art circa 1970*, 2012, Orange County Museum of Art, New Port Beach, University of California, Berkeley Museum of Art, San Francisco, Morris and Helen Belkin Art Gallery, Vancouver, BC Canada, Site Santa Fe, The Bronx Museum of the Arts, New York, Smart Museum of Art, The University of Chicago (catalogue)

2013
- Galerie Krinzinger, Vienna (with lecture by Lisa Steib)
- Art Basel, Galerie Löhrl
- Armory Show, New York, Ronald Feldman Gallery

2014
- *INPUT /OUTPUT – Schnittpunkt Worpswede*, Künstlerhäuser Worpswede
- *Performance Art Week / RITUAL BODY - POLITICAL BODY*, Palazzo Mora, Venice

Performances

1967
- *Dust Exchange*, (with William T. Wiley), Europe/California
- *Art Deposit*, Galerie Rudolf Zwirner, Cologne
- *Fish Vault*, Sarphatikade, Amsterdam

1968
- *Public Theater: Billingsgate Market*, London
- *Public Theater: Simultaneous Theater*, Anna Halprin Studio, San Francisco, Central Station, Cologne

1969
- *Public Theater: What Do Blind Men Dream?*, Union Street, San Francisco

1970
- *Wall Push*, MOCA, San Francisco
- *Liquid Smoke*, Third Street, San Francisco
- *Defoliation*, University Art Museum, Berkeley
- *Opening Hand*, Reese Palley Gallery, San Francisco
- *Corner Push*, Reese Palley Gallery, San Francisco
- *Asbestos Tracking*, Reese Palley Gallery, San Francisco
- *Virtual Volume*, MOCA, San Francisco
- *Sound: Bowl, Water, Shovel*, MOCA, San Francisco
- *Cellar*, Reese Palley Gallery, New York
- *Levitation*, Richmond Art Center, Richmond
- *Soluble Fish*, under the Pont Neuf, Paris
- *Isolation Unit* (with Joseph Beuys), Kunstakademie, Düsseldorf

1971
- *Environmental Surfaces*, (with Vito Acconci and Dennis Oppenheim), Reese Palley Gallery, New York
- *Pisces*, MOCA, San Francisco/ de Saisset Museum, Santa Clara
- *Zyklus* (by Tomas Schmit), MOCA, San Francisco

- *Hefe*, (for Ute Klophaus), 43 Martingerstrasse, Mönchengladbach
- *Clutch*, Artists' Studio, 16 Rose Street, San Francisco
- *Turgescent Sex*, Artists' Studio, San Francisco, 1972
- *Action in a Tower Room*, documenta, Kassel
- *Pont*, Galerie Sonnabend, Paris
- *L'Unita*, Lucio Amelio, Naples

1973
- *Yield*, University Art Museum, Berkeley

1974
- *Bowing*, MOCA, San Francisco
- *Halation*, 63 Bluxome Street, San Francisco

1975
- *Capillary Action*, Galleria Schema, Florence
- *Duologue* (with Tom Marioni), C.A.R.P., Los Angeles

1976
- *Lunar Rambles*, 5 Days Streets of New York City, The Kitchen, New York
- *52 Steps Through 11 Pairs of Strings*, Artists' Studio, San Francisco
- *Timbre*, Amphitheater, Mount Tamalpais, California

1977
- *Culvert*, Clark Fork River, Missoula, Montana
- *Immersion*, De Appel, Amsterdam
- *T.B.Y.D.* (with Nina Wise), Museum of Modern Art, San Francisco

1978
- *Strolling Performances* (with Georg Decristel), Galleria Pellegrino, Bologna
- *Flagellating Doppler* (with Georg DeCristel), University Art Museum, Berkeley
- *Mystification of Moving Away* (with Georg Decristel), Museum of Contemporary Art, Chicago

1979
- *Eversion*, Galerie Löhrl, Mönchengladbach
- *Erossore* (with Romaine Perin), King and West Housten, New York
- *Wenia Ring*, Galerie Nächst St. Stephan, Vienna
- *Suono con Tensione*, Sala Polivalente, Ferrara
- *Suno Interno*, Chiesa Santa Lucia, Bologna
- *Declination*, Galerie Dany Keller, Munich
- *Radiation*, Museum Folkwang, Essen

1980
- *A Candle for A. W.*, Kunstmuseum, Bern

1981
- *A Table of Simple Sounds* (with Georg Decristel), Künstlerhaus Bethanien, Berlin

1982
- *Left Sided Sleepers Dream*, Opera House, Graz

1984
- *White Bread* (with Alan Scarritt), Pillsbury Gold Medal Building, Minneapolis

1986
- *Eversion*, Galerie Löhrl, Mönchengladbach
- *Reso/Nator*, Provinciaal Museum, Hasselt, Belgium
- *Tiefland* (with Henning Christensen and Bjor Norgaard), Teatro Olympico, Rome
- *Opening Oysters* (with Marino Vismara), La Scala, Rome

1987
- *Ricochet*, documenta 8, Kassel
- *Pyrofilo*, Commune, Di Forinine
- *Rallentando*, Victoria Theater, San Francisco
- *Vaccilando*, Molkerei Werkstatt, Cologne

1988
- *The Eye is Not the Only Glass that Burns the Mind*, Kunstmuseum Bern
- *Tisch Konzert*, Villa Oppenhem, Berlin
- *P.D.* (with Rolf Julius), Hochschule für Bildende Kunst, Hamburg

1989
- *Resonators* (with Yoshi Wada), The Anchorage, Brooklyn, New York

1990
- *Arrectus Auribus* (with Yoshi Wada), Cell Block Theater, Sydney
- *Locus Harmonium*, Furkapass
- *Lesung*, Syndikat-Halte, Bonn

1991
- *Cynosure*, Von der Heydt-Museum, Wuppertal
- *Le Charriot D'Arthur* (with Claudine Denis), Molkerei Werkstatt, Cologne

1992
- *Corpora Cavernosa*, Cologne
- *Sette Selle* (with Claudine Denis), Selle di Borgo Valsugana
- *Ventre Affamé n'a pas d'Oreilles* (with Claudine Denis), Kunstraum Fuhrwerkswaage, Cologne

1998
- *Zona* (with Marita Loosen), Galerie Metronom, Barcelona
- *Mystification of Moving Away*, Stadtgalerie Saarbrücken

2003
- *Hachinoco*, (with Junko Wada, Akio Suzuki, Rolf Julius, Felix Hess), Haus der Kulturen der Welt, Berlin
- *Berliner Straße* (with Junko Wada), Berlin
- *Phases*, Kunsthalle Fridericianum Kassel

2004
- *Ohne Strom* (with Ralf Peters), three performances for piano wire and voice, Cologne

2006
- Caixias, Museu de Arte Contempora-nea de Serralves, Porto
- Lecture, Performance *Shut Speech*, Hochschule für Künste, Bremen

Authors

Kathleen Bühler, Bern, studied art history, philosophy and film studies. She earned a doctorate at the University of Zurich about the experimental films of Carolee Schneemann and works as a curator in the Department for Contemporary Art at the Kunstmuseum Bern. She has organized many exhibitions, among others with Tracey Emin (2009), Thomas Hirschhorn (2011) and Bill Viola (2014).

Nikola Doll, Berlin, works as a curator and has organized numerous exhibitions, including *Signes des Temps – Œuvres d'art visionnaire* (2014), *WeltWissen. 300 Jahre Wissenschaften in Berlin* (2009–10) and *Kunst und Propaganda im Streit der Nationen 1930–1945* (2007). She conceived the exhibition *Wissen Gestalten* (Giving Form to Knowledge), which will be shown at the Martin-Gropius-Bau, Berlin from September 2016 until January 2017.

Arnold Dreyblatt, Berlin, born in New York, is an American media artist and composer known for his installations, public artworks and performances. He has been based in Berlin, Germany since 1984. In 2007, Dreyblatt was elected a member of the Visual Arts Section at the Akademie der Künste, Berlin. He is currently professor of Media Art at the Muthesius Academy of Fine Arts and Design in Kiel, Germany.

Beate Eickhoff, Wuppertal, has worked as a curator at the Von der Heydt-Museum in Wuppertal since 2004. She earned a doctorate in art criticism at the Bergische Universität Wuppertal in the 1950s. She also taught at the Bergische Universität Wuppertal from 2002–08.

Angela Lammert, Berlin, is head of special interdisciplinary projects in the Visual Arts Section at the Akademie der Künste, Berlin and associate professor at the Institute of Art and Visual History, Humboldt University zu Berlin. She has organized numerous exhibitions and published widely on the arts of the 19th to the 21st centuries.

Constance Lewallen, San Francisco, is adjunct curator at the University of California, Berkeley Art Museum and Pacific Film Archive, where she has curated many influential exhibitions, including *Everything Matters:*

Paul Kos, A Retrospective (2003), *Ant Farm, 1968–1978* (2004), *A Rose Has No Teeth: Bruce Nauman in the 1960s* (2007), and *State of Mind: New California Art circa 1970* (2011).

David A. Ross, New York, is the founder and chair of the MFA program in Art Practice at the School of Visual Arts in New York City. In 1971 he became world's first curator of Video Art at the Everson Museum in Syracuse, NY. Other positions of note include: deputy director of the Long Beach Museum of Art, associate director for Collections and Programs at the Berkeley Art Museum, director of the Whitney Museum of American Art throughout the 1990s; director of the San Francisco Museum of Modern Art, cofounder of the Artist Pension Trust (APT).

Lisa Steib, Baden-Baden / Leipzig, is currently writing a dissertation about Terry Fox. She was research associate at the Braunschweig University of Art (HBK) from 2008–10. Since 2014 she has been working on a catalogue raisonné on all of Terry Fox's works funded by the Stiftung Kunstfonds Bonn.

Documents, Statements

Vito Acconci, New York, is a designer, landscape architect, performance and installation artist. He earned a BA with a major in literature from Holy Cross College in Worcester, Massachusetts, in 1962 and a MFA in writing at the University of Iowa in Iowa City. Acconci has taught at numerous institutions, among them the School of the Art Institute of Chicago, School of Visual Arts in New York. Acconci has participated in numerous exhibitions. Retrospectives of his work have been organized by the Stedelijk Museum, Amsterdam (1978) and the Museum of Contemporary Art in Chicago (1980).

Barney Bailey started his career as an artist, worked at the Reese Palley Gallery in San Francisco in 1970 and became the exhibitions designer at the UC Berkeley Art Museum and Pacific Film Archive (BAM/PFA) in 1972. Bailey's studio in San Francisco was in the same building as Terry Fox's at 16 Rose Street, where they first met.

Liza Béar is a New York-based filmmaker, writer, photographer, and media activist who makes both individual and collaborative works. Béar cofounded two early independent art magazines: *Avalanche* and *Bomb*. Since 1968 she has lived and worked in New York City.

Dena Beard, Oakland, California, worked as assistant curator at UC Berkeley Art Museum and Pacific Film Archive (BAM/PFA) until 2014. During her time at BAM/PFA she worked on over 50 projects, among others with Barry McGee and Apichatpong Weerasethakul. She has been working as executive director at "The Lab," San Francisco – a center for the performing and visual arts – since 2014.

Marinus Lambertus van den Boezem is a Dutch artist. He is known for his radical view of art and his works in public space. Together with Wim T. Schippers, Ger van Elk and Jan Dibbets, Boezem is seen as one of the main representatives of conceptual art and *arte povera* in the Netherlands in the late 1960s. His works can be found in museum collections that include MoMA, New York, Stedelijk Museum, Amsterdam, Museum Boijmans van Beuningen, Rotterdam, Museum Kröller-Müller, Otterlo and many other public art collections.

Marilyn Bogerd, San Francisco. In 1976, she was the cofounder with Alan Scarritt of the artist's space "Site, Sight, Cite, Inc." in San Francisco. Bogerd is currently the SF Lighthouse photographer at Enchanted Hills Camp for the Blind where she teaches photography to visually-impaired teenagers.

George Bolling (1946–2009) was curator of the de Saisset Art Gallery and Museum at the University of Santa Clara, California during the 1960s. He is known for his filming and recording of art performances by Paul Kos and Terry Fox, among others.

Terri Cohn, San Francisco, is a writer, curator, and art historian. She was a contributing editor to *Artweek* magazine for twenty years, and has contributed to books, exhibition catalogues and numerous journals. She currently works as an independent curator in addition to her position on the faculty of the Interdisciplinary Studies Department at the San Francisco Art Institute.

M. A. Greenstein, Pasadena, California, teaches at the Art Center College of Design, Pasadena. She is an internationally recognized arts and an science researcher, design thinker and innovator of applied neuroscience culture and products.

Wulf Herzogenrath, Berlin, is an art historian and curator. He is known for his outstanding knowledge about early video art and video installation. From 1973–89, Herzogenrath

directed the Kölnischer Kunstverein in Cologne, and from 1989–94 he worked as a head curator at the Nationalgalerie in Berlin, where he helped develop the concept for the future museum of contemporary art, Hamburger Bahnhof – Museum für Gegenwart. He was director of the Kunsthalle Bremen from 1994–2011, where, among other exhibitions, he curated a retrospective on the work of the video art pioneer Nam June Paik in 1999. Herzogenrath has been a member of the Akademie der Künste, Berlin since 2006 and the Section for Visual Arts has been under his direction since 2012.

Paul Kos, San Francisco/Sierras, is one of the pioneers of Bay Area conceptual art. His works are in the collections at the Guggenheim and MoMA, New York, the San Francisco Museum of Art, San Diego Museum of Art, and the Stedelijk Museum, Amsterdam. He started the earliest conceptual art class in the United States in 1970 at the University of Santa Clara and, beginning in 1978, he taught performance/video for the next 30 years at the San Francisco Art Institute.

Tom Marioni, San Francisco, studied painting and sculpture at the Art Academy of Cincinnati from 1955–59. From 1968–71, he was curator at the Richmond Art Center, and from 1970–84 the founding director of the Museum of Conceptual Art. In the 1970s he organized such exhibitions as: *Sound Sculpture As*, *Body Works* and *All Night Sculptures*. He was founding editor and designer of *VISION* magazine, published by Crown Point Press from 1975–81.

Lydia Modi-Vitale, San Francisco (1917–2010), studied at the Art Students League in New York. She was the first director of the Triton Museum of Art in Santa Clara and was the first director of the de Saisset Museum of Art at the University of Santa Clara.

Renny Pritikin is chief curator of San Francisco's Contemporary Jewish Museum. From 2004–12, he was director of the Richard L. Nelson Gallery and the Fine Arts Collection at the University of California, Davis. In addition to the California College of the Arts, he has taught art administration and professional skills training for artists at California State University, San Francisco and Golden Gate University.

Eva Schmidt, Siegen, has been the director of the Museum of Contemporary Art, Siegen since 2004. She studied art theory and history, media theory and philosophy at the universities of Osnabrück, Heidelberg and Hamburg. She earned a doctorate in 1989 with her dissertation "Zwischen Kino, Museum und Landschaft – Erfahrung und Fiktion bei Robert Smithson."

Bernd Schulz, Berlin, studied the natural sciences at the Albert-Ludwigs-Universität Freiburg and worked as a journalist in the fields of culture and science (as manager of the Departments for Culture and Science at Radio Saarland). In 1984, he founded the Stadtgalerie Saarbrücken, which he also directed until 2002. He is an honorary professor of Art and Science at the Saarland College of Fine Arts in Saarbrücken and a member of the Terry Fox Association e.V.

Steve Seid, San Francisco, was formerly a film and video curator at the Pacific Film Archive, at the University of California, Berkeley. Seid has taught video aesthetics and history courses at the University of California, Berkeley, San Francisco State University, the California College of Arts, and the San Francisco Art Institute. He co-curated the first museum retrospective of *Ant Farm*, and his exhibition *Radical Light*, a fifty year history of moving image art from the San Francisco Bay Area, appeared in 2010 as both a co-edited book (UCPress) and a film/video.

Willoughby Sharp (1936–2008) was an internationally known artist, independent curator, independent publisher, gallerist, teacher, author, and telecom activist. Since 1969, Sharp has had more than 20 solo exhibitions at museums and art galleries, including: Brown University, the University Art Museum, Berkeley and The Museum of Conceptual Art (MOCA), San Francisco.

Dennis Oppenheim (1938 –2011) was an American conceptual artist, performance artist, earth artist, sculptor and photographer. Coming out of the conceptual art movement, Oppenheim's early work was associated both with performance/body art and the early earthworks/land art movement. In 1968, Oppenheim became friends with Vito Acconci and began producing body art. He received fellowships from the Guggenheim Foundation and the National Endowment for the Arts. He was included in both the Venice Biennale and the Johannesburg Biennale in 1997.

Kathrin Röggla studied German literature and journalism in Salzburg and Berlin. In Salzburg she staged plays and performance events before turning her focus to writing.

She has been writing radio plays (including collaboration with the Internet radio collective convextv) since 1998, and plays for the theater since 2001. She has received numerous awards, including the Bruno Kreisky Award for the Political Book (2004), the Solothurn Literature Award and the International Art Award of Salzburg (2005). A member of the Literature Section of the Akademie der Künste, Berlin since 2012, she was elected as its vice president in 2015.

Bill Viola, Long Beach, is a contemporary video artist. He works with electronic, sound, and image technology in new media. In 1973, Viola graduated from Syracuse University with a Bachelor of Fine Arts. During the 1970s he lived in Florence, Italy, where he worked as technical director on productions for Art/tapes/22, one of the first video art studios in Europe (where he met Terry Fox). Viola's video art works have been shown in exhibitions worldwide since the early 1970s, including *Bill Viola: Installations and Videotapes*, MoMA, New York (1987), at the Whitney Museum of American (1997) and at the J. Paul Getty Museum, Los Angeles (2003). He was inducted into the American Academy of Arts and Sciences in 2000.

Robin White was one of the founders of Printed Matter, Inc. in New York and she conducted and published interviews with John Cage, Vito Acconci, Tom Marioni, Terry Fox and many other artists for the *View Interview Series* of Crown Point Press in the early 1980s.

Al Wong, San Francisco. Primarily known as a filmmaker, the artist taught at the San Francisco Art Institute from 1975–2003. His work has been the subject of solo presentations, among others, at the San Francisco Museum of Modern Art, MoMA, New York, Whitney Museum of American Art, Collective for Living Cinema, the New Museum, Millenium, New York, Mini Galeria, Zurich and the Nexus Foundation for Today's Art.

Tanya Zimbardo is a San Francisco-based curator. She founded "Open Space" in 2012. Her research and writing is primarily centered on conceptual art and experimental media in California in the 1970s and 1980s. As the assistant curator of media arts at the San Francisco Museum of Modern Art, she has curated select film and video screenings and co-organized the past two SECA Art Award exhibitions and overview *Fifty Years of Bay Area Art: The SECA Awards*, among other exhibitions.

Im Einzelnen danken wir / We would like to thank the following individuals

Vito Acconci, New York
Paule Anglim (†),
    Ed Gilbert, Shannon Trimble,
    Gilbert Anglim Gallery, San Francisco
Barney Bailey, Berkeley
Dena Beard, The Lab, San Francisco
Ingrid Beirer, Carsten Seiffarth,
    Terry Fox Association e.V.
Malu Beltram, Oakland
Neal Benezra, Rachel Federman,
    Gary Garrels, Sriba Kwadjovie,
    Alison Spangler, Peggy Tran-Le,
    Thomas Yarker, Tanya Zimbardo,
    San Francisco Museum of Modern Art
    (SFMOMA), San Francisco
Ariane Beyn, Julia Gerlach, Bettina Klein,
    Berliner Künstlerprogramm, Deutscher
    Akademischer Austauschdienst (DAAD) /
    Artists-in-Berlin Program of the German
    Academic Exchange Service, Berlin
Tobia Bezzola, Marcel Schumacher,
    Folkwang Museum Essen
René Block, Edition Block GmbH, Berlin
Ursula Block, Gelbe Musik, Berlin
Marilyn Bogerd, San Francisco
Monika Branicka, Egidio Marzona,
    Archiv Marzona, Berlin
Klaus vom Bruch, Berlin
Matthias Bruhn,
    Hermann-Helmholtz-Zentrum für Kultur-
    technik „Das Technische Bild",
    Institut für Kunst- und Bildgeschichte,
    Humboldt-Universität zu Berlin
Tobias Burg,
    Von der Heydt-Museum, Wuppertal
Hubertus Butin, Berlin
Diana Cohn,
    Yerba Buena Center for the Arts,
    San Francisco
Terri Cohn, San Francisco
Jacqueline Cijsouw, Roos Gortzak,
    De Vleeshal, Middelburg
Kaj Duncan David, Berlin
Edith Dekyndt, Tournai, Berlin
Jenny Dirksen, Ludwigforum für
    internationale Kunst, Videoarchiv, Aachen
Yilmaz Dziewior, Barbara Engelbach,
    Museum Ludwig, Köln/Cologne
Mary T. Faria, Oakland
Ronald Feldman, Peggy Kaplan,
    Feldman Gallery, New York
Fanni Fetzer, Kunstmuseum Luzern
Nancy Frank-Radin, Oakland
Howard Fried, Berkeley

Thomas W. Gaehtgens, Glenn Philips,
    Martha Alfaro, Irene Lotspeich-Philips,
    Tracey Schuster, The Getty Research
    Institute, Art Video Archive, Los Angeles
Marion Gray, San Francisco
Jeff Gunderson, San Francisco Art Institute
Stephanie Hanor,
    Mills College Art Museum, Oakland
Matthias Haldemann, Kunsthaus Zug
Ann Hatch, San Francisco
Wulf Herzogenrath, Berlin
Jörg Hiller, Berlin
Neele Hülcker, Berlin
Anthony Huberman, Nina Wexelblatt,
    Wattis Institute for Contemporary Arts,
    San Francisco
Elisabeth Jappe, Köln/Cologne
Nina Julius, Berlin
Dany Keller, Dany Keller Galerie, Eichelhardt
Gunnar Kettler, Andrea Schmidt,
    Druckverlag Kettler, Dortmund
Udo Kittelmann, Eugen Blume,
    Gabriele Knapstein, Nationalgalerie im
    Hamburger Bahnhof – Museum für
    Gegenwart – Berlin, Staatliche Museen,
    Preußischer Kulturbesitz
Barbara Klemm, Frankfurt am Main
Paul Kos, San Francisco
Jiří Kovanda, Prag/Prague
Karola Kraus, Naoko Kaltschmidt,
    mumok, museum moderner Kunst
    stiftung ludwig wien/Vienna
Johannes Kreidler, Berlin
Ursula Krinzinger, Lisa Pehnelt,
    Galerie Krinzinger, Wien/Vienna
Chistina Kubisch, Hoppegarten
Ofri Lapid, Berlin
Siegfried Langbehn, Simone Hahn,
    Hauptstadtkulturfonds, Berlin
Youcef und/and Nacery Laribi, San José
Dirk Lebahn, Berlin
Christian, Christa und / and Dietmar Löhrl,
    Galerie Löhrl, Mönchengladbach
Chip Lord,
    University of California, Santa Cruz
Annemarie Lühn, Emsbüren
Elmar Lutz, Köln/Cologne
Paul McCarthy, Los Angeles
Karl McCool,
    Electronic Arts Intermix (EAI), New York
Hesse McGraw, San Francisco Art Institute
Tom Marioni, San Francisco
Ron Meyers, Los Angeles
Stephan Oehmen, Hilden
Amy Plumb Oppenheim, New York
Hélène Panhuysen, Eindhoven

Phuong Phan, Berlin
Renny Pritikin, Contemporary Jewish
    Museum, San Francisco
Annett Reckert, Städtische Galerie
    Delmenhorst
Stephanie Reuter,
    Rudolf Augstein Stiftung, Hamburg
Alan Scarritt, San Francisco
Brenda Richardson, Seattle
Lawrence Rinder, Lucinda Barnes,
    Stephanie Canizzo, Nancy Goldman,
    Mona Nagai, Steve Seid,
    Berkeley Art Museum and Pacific Film
    Archive (BAM/PFA), Berkeley
Jennine Scarboro,
    Capp Street Project Archive, California
    College of the Arts, Meyer Library,
    Oakland
Andreas Schalhorn,
    Kupferstichkabinett, Staatliche Museen
    zu Berlin, Preußischer Kulturbesitz
Rebecca Schapp, Stephanie Battle,
    de Saisset Museum at Santa Clara
    University, Santa Clara
Ottavio Schipper, Rio de Janeiro
Eva Schmidt,
    Museum für Gegenwartskunst, Siegen
Petra Schmidt Dreyblatt, Berlin
Peter Simon, Köln/Cologne
Andrew Smith,
    Harvard University, Cambridge
Bernd Schulz, Berlin
Karin Seinsoth,
    Galerie Hauser & Wirth, Zürich
Charles Shere, San Francisco
Daniela Stöppel,
    Kunstraum München/Munich
Manos Tsangaris, Köln/Cologne
Bill Viola, Kira Perov,
    Bill Viola Studio, Long Beach
Jan St. Werner, Berlin
Georg Weckwerth, Sabine Groschup,
    Wien/Vienna
Bernd J. Wieczorek, Corinna Hadeler,
    Gesellschaft der Freunde der Akademie
    der Künste/Society of Friends of the
    Academy of Arts, Berlin
Al Wong, San Francisco
Theus Zwakhals, LIMA, Amsterdam
Dorothea und/and Rudolf Zwirner, Berlin.

Zitatnachweis / Quotation References

Die Zitate und Übersetzungen entnahmen wir der Publikation / The original quotations and their translations have been taken from the following publication:
Eva Schmidt (Hg./ed.), *Terry Fox. Ocular Language. 30 Jahre Reden und Schreiben über Kunst. 30 Years of Speaking and Writing about Art.* Gesellschaft für Aktuelle Kunst Bremen, Köln/Cologne, 2000, fortan/hereafter Schmidt 2000
Wir danken dem Salon-Verlag, Köln, und der Herausgeberin und Übersetzerin Eva Schmidt für ihre freundliche Genehmigung. / We are grateful both to the Salon-Verlag, Cologne, and to the editor and translator Eva Schmidt for their kind permission to reprint them here.

S. / p. 72
Schmidt 2000, S. 28 / p. 29 (zuerst / first published in: *Avalanche,* New York, Winter 1971, pp. 70–81)

S. / p. 73
Schmidt 2000, S. 74, 76 / p. 75 (zuerst / first published in: *View,* vol. II, June 1979, No. 3)

S. / pp. 136–137
Schmidt 2000, S. 66 / p. 67 (zuerst / first published in: *Avalanche,* New York, December 1974, pp. 32–33)

S. / p. 159
Schmidt 2000, S. 196 / p. 199

S. / p. 199
Schmidt 2000, S. 96 / p. 95 (zuerst / first published in: *View,* vol. II, June 1979, no. 3)

S. / p. 223
Schmidt 2000, S. 74, 92 / pp. 75, 93 (zuerst / first published in: *View,* vol. II, June 1979, no. 3)

Impressum / Imprint

Dieser Katalog erscheint anlässlich der Ausstellung
This catalogue is published for the exhibition

Elemental Gestures – Terry Fox

Eine Kooperation von / A cooperation of the

Akademie der Künste, Berlin
BAM – Musée des Beaux-Arts, Mons
Von der Heydt-Museum, Wuppertal
Kunstmuseum Bern

6. November 2015 – 10. Januar 2016
November 6, 2015 – January 10, 2016

Akademie der Künste
Hanseatenweg 10, 10557 Berlin-Tiergarten
Deutschland / Germany

5. März 2016 – 12. Juni 2016
March 5 – June 12, 2016

BAM – Musée des Beaux-Arts, Mons
Rue Neuve 8, 7000 Mons
Belgien / Belgium

2. Oktober 2016 – 26. Februar 2017
October 2, 2016 – February 26, 2017

Von der Heydt-Museum, Wuppertal
Turmhof 8, 12103 Wuppertal
Deutschland / Germany

3. März 2017 – 4. Juni 2017
March 3 – June 4, 2017

Kunstmuseum Bern
Hodlerstraße 8–12, 3000 Bern 7
Schweiz / Switzerland

Ausstellung / Exhibition

AKADEMIE DER KÜNSTE

Akademie der Künste, Berlin

Kuratoren / Curators
Arnold Dreyblatt, Angela Lammert

Projektleitung / Project Managment
Angela Lammert

Ausstellungsassistenz / Exhibition Assistance
Pamina Gerhardt, Yvonne Reiners

Mitarbeit / Assistance
Bettina Friedli Faber

Ausstellungsgestaltung / Exhibition Design
Simone Schmaus

**Ausstellungsrealisierung / Implementation of
the Exhibition Design**
Antje Mollenhauer, Jörg Scheil,
Isabel Schlenther, Simone Schmaus,
Mount Berlin

**Medientechnik und Licht / Media Services
and Lighting**
Kathy Lieber, Frank Kwiatkowski,
Wolfgang Hinkeldey, János Kachelmann,
Uwe Ziegenhagen, Anja Gerlach,
Nadine Doberschütz, visionb
Kunstservice UG: Bert Günther,
Björn Matzen

Ausstellungsgrafik / Exhibition Graphics
Heimann und Schwantes, Berlin

Registrar, Leihverkehr / Registrar, Loans
Stefan Kaltenbach

Restauratoren / Conservators
Dirk Schönbohm, Rüdiger Tertel

**Presse- und Öffentlichkeitsarbeit / Press and
Public Relations**
Brigitte Heilmann, Marianne König,
Mareike Wenzlau und/and
ARTPRESS – Ute Weingarten, Alexandra
Saheb

**Vermittlungsprogramm KUNSTWELTEN /
ART WORLDS Education program**
Marion Neumann, Martina Krafczyk

BAM – Musée des Beaux-Arts, Mons

Kuratorin / Curator
Nikola Doll

Mit Unterstützung folgender Personen und Institutionen / Supported by
Elio Di Rupo, Bourgmestre de la Ville de Mons & Ministre d'État
Rudy Demotte, Ministre-Président de la Fédération Wallonie-Bruxelles
Joëlle Milquet, Ministre de la Culture et de la Fédération Wallonie-Bruxelles

Organisationskomitee / Organization Committee
Le Pôle muséal de la Ville de Mons
Xavier Roland, Responsable du Service Pôle muséal
Murielle Laurent, adjointe du Responsable du Service Pôle muséal

Gesamtkoordination / General Coordination
Alice Cantigniau, chargé de mission du Pôle muséal de la Ville de Mons

Kommunikation / Communications
Géraldine Simonet, chargée de communication des expositions du Pôle muséal, assistée de Marie Bertouil

Medientechnik und Licht / Media Services and Lighting
Joanna Karcher, régisseur général des expositions et l'équipe de la régie du Pôle Muséal

Museumspädagogik / Museum Education
Joëlle Laurant et l'équipe des animateurs du Dynamusée
Laurence Herman, médiatrice culturelle du Pôle muséal

Bewachung / Security
Alexandre Mbo, responsable sécurité du Pôle Muséal et l'équipe du Service interne du gardiennage

Partnerschaft / Partnership
Virginie Parijs, chef de projet Partenariat du Pôle muséal

Verwaltung / Administration
Kathleen Lecocq, assistante administrative cellule expositions Pôle muséal
Service de gestion financière
Service des Marchés Publics

Von der Heydt-Museum, Wuppertal

Direktor / Director
Gerhard Finckh

Kurator / Curator
Beate Eickhoff

Registrar / Registrar
Brigitte Müller

Restauratorische Betreuung / Conservator
Andreas Iglhaut

Grafik und Buchbinderei / Graphic Design and Printing
Sylvia Stascheit-Wermert, Stefanie Wachmann

Presse- und Öffentlichkeitsarbeit / Press and Public Relations
Marion Meyer

Museumspädagogik / Museum Education
Julia Dürbeck, Karoline Bürger

Technik / Technical Services
Ulrich Schultz, Meinhard Mach

Verwaltung und Service / Administration and Service
Nicole Schey, Eva Djokic, Yvonne Henatzki

Kunstmuseum Bern

Direktor / Director
Matthias Frehner

Kuratorin / Curator
Kathleen Bühler

Kuratorische Assistenz / Curatorial Assistant
Sarah Merten

Restaurierung / Conservators
Nathalie Bäschlin, Katja Friese, Katharina Sautter

Leihverkehr / Registrars, Loans
Jessica Skolovski, Franziska Vassella

Ausstellungsaufbau / Installation of the Exhibition
René Wochner (Leitung/Head), Mike Carol, Raphael Frey, Andres Meschter, Roman Studer, Wilfried von Gunten, Martin Schnidrig, Daniel Stettler, Volker Thies, Markus Ingold, Simon Stalder

Kunstvermittlung / Educational Services
Magdalena Schindler, Beat Schüpbach, Anina Büschlen

Öffentlichkeitsarbeit / Public Relations
Michèle Thüring (Leitung/Head), Magali Cirasa, Nadja Imhof, David Oester, Séverine Spillmann, Marie Louise Suter

Katalog / Catalogue

Herausgeber / Editors
Arnold Dreyblatt, Angela Lammert

im Auftrag von / on behalf of the
Akademie der Künste, Berlin,
Musée de Beaux-Arts, Mons,
Von der Heydt-Museum Wuppertal
Kunstmuseum Bern

**Redaktion / Editorial Staff,
Publications Department**
Julia Bernhard, Barbara Voigt

Koordination / Coordination
Bettina Friedli Faber

Bildredaktion / Image Editing
Bettina Friedli Faber, Yvonne Reiners

Lektorat / Editing
Julia Bernhard, Barbara Voigt,
Wendy Wallis, Martine Passelaigue

Mitarbeit / Assistance
Sabine Hagen, Ellen Mey, Fatih Tarhan
(Praktikant / Intern)

Übersetzungen / Translations
James Bell, Andrew Boreham,
Allison Brown, Denis-Armand Canal,
Mitch Cohen, Émile Notéris,
Martine Passelaigue, Anne Pitz,
Bernard Rival, Dominique Rival,
Nikolaus G. Schneider, Wendy Wallis

Biografien / Biographies
Yvonne Reiners

Gestaltung / Design
Heimann und Schwantes, Berlin

Umschlagabbildung / Cover Illustration
Terry Fox, *Virtual Volume,* 1970,
photos: Barry Klinger

Gesamtherstellung / Production
Druckerei Kettler, Bönen

© The Estate of Terry Fox, Köln / Cologne
© VG Bild-Kunst, Bonn 2015, für die
Werke von / for the works by Vito Acconci,
Joseph Beuys, Klaus vom Bruch,
Roland Fischer, Sarkis
© 2015, Akademie der Künste, Berlin,
Künstler, Fotografen, Autoren / artists,
photographers, authors
© 2015, Verlag Kettler, Dortmund

Erschienen im / Published by
Verlag Kettler, Dortmund
www.verlag-kettler.de

**Englisch-deutsche Ausgabe /
English-German edition**
ISBN 978-3-86206-515-8

**Englisch-französische Ausgabe /
English-French edition**
ISBN 978-3-86206-524-0

Gefördert durch / Supported by

Die Akademie der Künste wird gefördert von
der Beauftragten der Bundesregierung für Kultur
und Medien. / The Akademie der Künste is
funded by the Federal Government Comissioner
for Culture and the Media.

www.adk.de